ENVIRONMENT, HUMAN RIGHTS AND INTERNATIONAL TRADE

Environment, Human Rights and International Trade

Edited by

FRANCESCO FRANCIONI

• HART •
PUBLISHING

OXFORD – PORTLAND OREGON

2001

Hart Publishing
Oxford and Portland, Oregon

Published in North America (US and Canada) by
Hart Publishing c/o
International Specialized Book Services
5804 NE Hassalo Street
Portland, Oregon
97213-3644
USA

Distributed in the Netherlands, Belgium and Luxembourg by
Intersentia, Churchillaan 108
B2900 Schoten
Antwerpen
Belgium

Hart Publishing is a specialist legal publisher based in Oxford, England.
To order further copies of this book or to request a list of other publications please write to:

Hart Publishing, Salter's Boatyard, Folly Bridge,
Abingdon Road, Oxford OX1 4LB
Telephone: +44 (0)1865 245533 or Fax: +44 (0)1865 794882
e-mail: mail@hartpub.co.uk
WEBSITE: http//www.hartpub.co.uk

British Library Cataloguing in Publication Data
Data Available
ISBN 1–84113–217–9 (hardback)

Typeset by Hope Services (Abingdon) Ltd.
Printed and bound in Great Britain on acid-free paper by
Biddles Ltd, www.biddles.co.uk

Foreword

This book builds on a research project initiated at the University of Siena and carried out in conjunction with the University of Milan between 1998 and 2000. The original aim of the project was to address the interaction between trade liberalisation and international regimes for the protection of non-commercial public interests. The specific focus of this volume is environment and human rights. This does not exclude the possibility that trade may collide with other public interests. On the contrary, the management of the global trade regime increasingly requires the accommodation of values such as public morality, national security, or the protection of cultural heritage. The reason for concentrating on environment and human rights is due to the fact that in the past ten years these two values have provided by far the most important source of challenge to the justice and legitimacy of the present international trade regime. On the one hand the compulsory and binding adjudicatory mechanism in the WTO is viewed with distrust by those who question the right of an economic organisation to trump democratically approved national policies in the field of ecological welfare and human rights. On the other hand, the question arises as to what are the limits of free trade when we face novel dilemmas such as the commercialisation of genetically modified organisms, market access for products resulting from serious violations of human rights, or trade restraints in the name of intellectual property rights even if the products covered are essential to the life and health of large segments of the population.

This book does not intend to provide definitive answers to these questions. Rather, it aims at developing an analytical approach to the international trade regime based on the contextual interpretation of treaty provisions and customary international law in view of accommodating competing values that the international community has clearly deemed to be worth pursuing: trade liberalisation, on the one hand, and environmental protection and human rights, on the other. It is to be hoped that the interpretative method suggested for the two above areas may prove relevant also for other areas of conflict between free trade and fundamental public policies.

Several institutions and persons have helped to achieve this project. The Italian Ministry for University and Scientific Research and the Italian Council for Research provided financial support for the project. The University of Siena funded the organisation of a discussion workshop at the Certosa di Pontignano, Siena, in April 2000. Colleagues at the University of Oxford and the University of Texas joined their colleagues from the University of Siena, Genova, Parma, and UNCTAD to form a well integrated international team. It was a great pleasure to co-ordinate their labour. To all of them I offer my sincere thanks.

Francesco Francioni
Siena
April 2001

Contents

List of Contributors ix
Table of Cases xi
Table of Legislation xv
Table of Abbreviations xxvii

1 Environment, Human Rights and the Limits of Free Trade 1
FRANCESCO FRANCIONI

2 International Trade in Living Modified Organisms 27
THOMAS J. SCHOENBAUM

3 International Trade in Genetically Modified Organisms and Multilateral Negotiations: a New Dilemma for Developing Countries 39
SIMONETTA ZARRILLI

4 Biosafety and Intellectual Property Rights: Balancing Trade and Environment Security—The Jurisprudence of the European Patent Office as a Paradigm of an International Public Policy Issue 87
RICCARDO PAVONI

5 The Impact of International Trade Law on Environmental Law and Process 105
ANDREA BIANCHI

6 The Necessity Principle as an Instrument to Balance Trade and the Protection of the Environment 135
MASSIMILIANO MONTINI

7 Technology Transfer and the Protection of the Environment 157
FRANCESCO MUNARI

8 A Perspective on Trade and Labour Rights 179
CHRISTOPHER MCCRUDDEN and ANNE DAVIES

9 Human Rights Sanctions and the World Trade Organisation 199
SARAH H. CLEVELAND

10 Which Intellectual Property Rights are Trade-Related? 263
MICHAEL SPENCE

11 International Trade and Child Labour Standards 287
FEDERICO LENZERINI

12 The Interplay Between Trade and the Environment Within the NAFTA Framework 313
PATRICIA ISELA HANSEN

Index 325

List of Contributors

Andrea Bianchi Associate Professor of International Law, Faculty of Law, University of Parma; Professorial Lecturer in International Law, The John Hopkins University School of Advanced International Studies, Bologna Centre; Visiting Professor, Catholic University, Milan.

Sarah H. Cleveland AB 1987, Brown University; M St 1989, Oxford University; JD 1992, Yale Law School; Professor, University of Texas School of Law.

Anne C. L. Davies Fellow, All Souls College, Oxford University; Visiting Scholar, University of Michigan Law School.

Francesco Francioni Juris Dr. (Florence); LL.M (Harvard); Chair of International Law (Siena); Visiting Professor, Oxford University; Fellow, Lincoln College, Oxford.

Patricia Isela Hansen Professor, University of Texas School of Law; AB 1982, Harvard University; MPA 1997, Woodrow Wilson School of Public & International Affairs, Princeton University; JD 1987, Yale Law School.

Federico Lenzerini Juris Dr., University of Siena; Ph D Candidate.

Christopher McCrudden Professor of Human Rights Law, Oxford University; Fellow, Lincoln College, Oxford; Visiting Professor, University of Michigan Law School.

Massimiliano Montini Juris Dr. (Siena); LL.M (University College, London); Researcher, University of Siena.

Francesco Munari Professor of International Law and European Community Law, Faculty of Political Science, University of Genoa, Italy.

Riccardo Pavoni Juris Dr. (Siena); MJur (Oxford); Researcher, University of Siena.

Thomas J. Schoenbaum BA, St Joseph's College; DESS, Universitee catholique de Louvrain; JD, University of Michigan; Ph D, University of Cambridge.

Michael Spence Fellow, St Catherines College, Oxford.

Simonetta Zarrilli Juris Dr. (Siena), LL.M (Bruges) Staff member of the Trade Negotiations and Commercial Diplomacy Branch, Division on International Trade and Commodities, UNCTAD Secretariat. Member of the Italian Bar.

Table of Cases

GATT Panel

Argentina—*Measures Affecting Imports of Footwear, Textiles, Apparel and Other Items*, 22 April 1998 239
Australia—*Measures Affecting the Importation of Salmon*, 6 November 1998 ....11, 31, 32, 94, 124
EC—*Measures Affecting Meat and Meat Products (Hormones)*, 13 February 1998 ....17, 30, 35, 36, 66, 91, 94, 96, 123, 124, 125, 152, 254, 316
EC—*Measures Affecting Asbestos and Asbestos-containing Products*, 18 September 2000 13
India—*Patent Protection for Pharmaceutical and Agricultural Chemical* Products, 19 December 1997 265
Japan—*Customs Duties, Taxes and Labeling Practices on Imported Wines and Alcoholic Beverages*, 10 November 1987 227
Japan—*Trade in Semi-conductors*, 4 May 1988 9
Japan—*Taxes on Alcoholic Beverages*, 4 October 1996 9
Japan—*Measures Affecting Agricultural Products*, 22 February 1999 ....11, 31, 67
Japan—*Measures Affecting Agricultural Products (Varietals)*, 19 March 1999 ....94, 95, 113, 123, 124
Thailand—*Restrictions on Importation of and Internal Taxes on Cigarettes*, 7 November 1990 ....10, 240
US—*Imports of Certain Automotive Spring Assemblies*, 26 May 1983 12
US Restrictions on Imports of Tuna, (1991) 30 ILM 1594 ....116, 117, 118, 121 145, 146, 148, 194, 227, 228, 235, 240
US Restrictions on Imports of Tuna, (1994) ILM 839 ....7, 14, 24, 106, 114, 116, 117, 118, 145, 146, 148, 167, 194, 235, 243, 244, 301, 303, 304
US—*Taxes on Automobiles*, 29 September 1994 ....10, 302, 304
US Standards for Reformulated and Conventional Gasoline, 29 September 1996 (Panel), 20 May 1996 (Appellate Body) ..12, 16, 63, 90, 97 119, 142, 146, 147, 149, 151, 153, 240, 242, 243, 245, 246, 249, 302, 304

US Import Prohibition of Certain Shrimp and Shrimp Products, 15 May 1998 ....5, 7, 14, 23, 63, 71, 90, 102, 112, 114, 115, 117, 118, 120, 121, 129, 134, 143, 147, 149, 150, 153, 170, 193, 236, 237, 238, 240, 242, 243, 244, 246, 247, 249, 253, 256 , 258, 259, 303
US—*s. 110(3) of the US Copyright Act*, 15 June 2000 ....259, 279
US—*Taxes on Petroleum and Certain Imported Substances* 10, 304

Permanent Court of International Justice

Oscar Chinn [1934] PCIJ, A/B 63 113 137

International Court of Justice

Barcelona Traction, Light and Power Co. Ltd (Belgium v. Spain) [1970] ICJ Rep. 3 ....205, 209, 294, 295
Case concerning the Application of the Convention on the Prevention of the Crime of Genocide (Bosnia and Herzegovina v. *Yugoslovakia (Serbia and Montenegro))* [1993] ICJ Rep. 325 205
Corfu Channel Case [1949] ICJ Rep. 244 21
Gabcikova-Nagymares [1997] ICJ Rep. 7 140
Legal Consequences for States of the Continued Presence of South Africa in Namibia (South West Africa) [1971] ICJ Rep. 16 ....121, 205, 238
Military and Paramilitary Activities (Nicaragua v. *US)* [1986] ICJ Rep. 14 ....209, 231
South West Africa (Ethiopia and Liberia v. *South Africa)* [1966] ICJ Rep. 6 206
US Diplomatic and Consular Staff in Tehran (US v. *Iran)* [1980] ICJ Rep., 3 ....210, 294

The Human Rights Committee

Monguya Mbenge v. *Zaire*, 16/1977 310
Solórzano de Pena v. *Venezuela*, 156/1983 310

Inter-American Court of Human Rights

Velasquez Rodriguez, 29 July 1988 310

US–Canada FTA Binational Panel

In the Matter of Canada's Landing Requirements for Pacific Coast Salmon and Herring, 16 October 1989 ....24, 97, 119, 148, 149

European Court of Human Rights

Bozano v. *France* (1987) 9 EHRR 927 310

Guerra et al. v. *Italy* (1998) 26 EHRR 357 101
Loizidou v. *Turkey*, (1995) 23 EHRR 513 101
Lopez Ostra v. *Spain*, Series A No. 303-C 101
X and Y v. *Netherlands*, Series A (1985) 310

European Court of Justice

Case 302/86, Commission v. *Denmark* [1988] ECR 4607 ....25, 97, 120

European Patent Office

Greenpeace UK v. *Plant Genetic Systems NV (PGS 1)*, 15 December 1992 ....91, 94, 96, 98, 99
Greenpeace Ltd v. *Plant Genetic Systems NV (PGS II)* [1995] OJ EPO 545....................91, 93, 94, 96, 98, 99
Novartis AG (In re) [1998] OJ EPO 511....................99, 102
Onco-Mouse/Harvard I [1989] OJ EPO 451 ....91, 96, 98, 100
Onco-Mouse/Harvard II [1990] OJ EPO 476 ....91, 96, 98, 100
Onco-Mouse/Harvard III [1992] OJ EPO 588 ....91, 96, 98, 100

United Kingdom

al-Adsani v. *Kuwait* (1994) 107 ILR 1536 (CA)....................209

United States

Board of Trustees v. *Mayor of Baltimore* 562 A 2d 720 (Md. 1989)....................223
Bruce Pickett et al. v. *Monsanto Co.* (US DC, DC) 28
Crosby v. *National Foreign Trade Council*, 120 S Ct. 2288 (2000) 223
Dames v. *Moore and Regan* 453 US 654 (1981) 221
Demjanjuk v. *Petrovsky* 776 F 2d 571 (6 Cir. 1983)....................210
Earth Island Institute v. *Christopher* 913 F Supp. 539 (Ct. Intl. Trade, 1995)....................117
Filártiga v. *Peña-Irala* 630 F 2d 876 (2 Cir. 1980) 210, 294
Kadic v. *Karadzic* 70 F 3d 232 (2 Cir. 1995)....................205
Princz v. *Federal Republic of Germany* 26 F 3d 1166 (DC Cir. 1994)....................209
Siderman de Blake v. *Republic of Argentina* 965 F 2d 699 ....209, 210
State Street Bank and Trust Co. v. *Signature Financial Group Inc.* 149 F 3d 1368 (1 Cir. 1998)....................264
US v. *Smith* 18 US (5 Wheat.) 153, 5 L Ed., 57 (1820)....................210

Table of Legislation

1. INTERNATIONAL

Additional Convention between Great Britain and Portugal for the Prevention of the Slave Trade 1817
  Arts. III, IV 200
African Charter on Human and People's Rights....................204
  Art. 3 293
African Charter on the Rights and Welfare of the Child 1990
  Art. 27 293
    29....................293
Agreement Establishing the International Trade Organisation
  Art. 7 287
Agreement on Import Licensing Procedures
  Art. 7.3 113
Agreement on the Reduction of Dolphin Mortality in the East Pacific Ocean 1992....................114
Agreement on Sanitary and Phytosanitary Standards 1994 (SPS Agreement), 1994 ILM 1140..................16–17, 29, 30, 32, 33, 37, 39, 57, 61, 62, 65, 68, 70, 75, 82, 83, 84, 94, 95, 113, 115–116, 122, 123, 125, 150, 151, 152, 153, 154, 155, 235, 255, 314
  Art. 2....................29, 31
    (2) 16, 31, 65, 66, 95, 123
    (3) 66
    (4) 29
    3 29
    (1) 29
    (2)....................29, 95
    (3)....................30, 31
    5....................29, 31
    (1-3) 30
    (1-6) 66
    (1) 31, 66, 95
    (2) 66
    (4) 30
    (5)....................30, 124, 125
    (6)....................30, 32, 124
    (7) 30, 65, 66, 67, 84, 86, 91, 152

Annex 37
Annex A(5) 95
Agreement on Technical Barriers to Trade 1994,
1994 ILM 81 ....16–17, 39, 57, 63, 65, 67, 68, 69,
70, 71, 75, 82, 83, 84, 113, 122, 123, 125, 127, 150, 151, 155
Art. 2 113
(2) 63, 151
(4) 122
(9) 113
(11) 113
5 113
(1) 123
(6) 113
(8) 113
6 123
10 113
American Convention on Human Rights 204
Art. 6(2) 292
61 293
Bamako Convention on the Ban on the Import into Africa and the
Control of Transboundary Movement and Management of
Hazardous Wastes within Africa 1991 79
Basel Convention on the Control of Transboundary Movement of
Hazardous Waste 1989, 1989 ILM 649......................8, 21, 114, 133, 211, 318
Art. 10 159
Prot. 21
Cartagena Protocol on Biosafety 2000 ....21, 29, 32-34, 37, 40, 41, 57,
60, 61, 62, 63, 64, 76, 79, 83, 84, 115, 255
Preamble 36, 61
Art. 1 61
3 ....57, 60
5 33
6 33
7 33
(2) 60
8 33
9 33
10 ....32, 33, 61
11 ....33, 35, 61, 255
(8) 35, 36
15 33
16 33
17 34
18 ....33, 34, 35

20 ....32, 35
25 34
27 34
Arts. 28-31 34
33-35....................34
Art. 34 37
37 34
Convention for the Abolition of Import and Export
Restrictions 1927 301
Convention on Biological Diversity 37, 41, 44, 57, 58, 64,
79, 83, 88, 115, 172, 176
3rd Preambular para. 91
Art. 8 88
10 88
15....................172
16 ....88, 159
(3) 170
(5)....................88, 102, 170
19....................115
(3) 87
20....................173
27 37
Montreal Protocol 87, 115
Convention to Combat Desertification in Those Countries Experiencing
Serious Drought and/or Desertification Particularly in
Africa 1994, 1994 ILM 1328 15
Convention on the Prevention and Punishment of the Crime
of Genocide 1948, 78 UNTS 277....................204, 212, 247
Art. I....................212
III....................213
IV 209
V....................212
IX 212
Convention on the Prior Informed Consent (PIC) Procedure
for Certain Hazardous Chemicals and Pesticides in
International Trade....................167
Convention on the Rights of the Child 1989,
28 ILM 1448 ....204 , 207, 208, 247
Art. 19 ....208, 294
32....................290, 294
34....................293, 294
39....................294
Convention for the Suppression of the Traffic in Persons and of the
Exploitation of the Prostitution of Others 1949, 96 UNTS 271....................293

Convention on Trade in Endangered Species (CITES) 1973 .....8, 15, 23, 79, 114 133, 211, 315
Annex 1 ....117, 119
Dispute Settlement Understanding........258
Art. 3.2 303
12(1)........259
13........258
17(6)........119
23........129
Energy Charter Treaty 1994, (1995) 34 ILM, 360
Art. 19 159
Prot. on Energy Efficiency and Related Environmental Aspects 159
European Convention on Human Rights204
Art. 4(1) 293
(2) 292
Prot. 3 204
European Convention on the Protection of the Marine Environment of the Baltic Sea Area 1992 79–80
European Convention for the Protection of the Marine Environment of the North East Atlantic 1992 79
European Convention for the Protection and Use of Transboundary Watercourses and Lakes 199279 Forced Labour Convention 1930 238
Framework Convention on Climate Change
Art. 4(5) 159
Kyoto Prot., Art. 10........174
12........174
General Act for the Repression of the African Slave Trade 1890
Arts. VII, IX, LXII........200
General Agreement on Tariffs and Services (GATS)........287
Art. I........131
XIV 131
General Agreement on Tariffs and Trade (GATT) 1947..........4, 5, 29, 238, 301
General Agreement on Tariffs and Trade (GATT) 1994,
53 UNTS 194 ....4, 10, 12, 13, 14, 16, 17, 18, 22, 23, 24, 25, 65, 106, 113, 116, 117, 118, 120, 121, 134, 136, 141, 169, 187, 194, 195, 201, 202, 203, 212, 217, 219, 226, 235, 237, 251, 252, 256, 258, 261, 287, 294, 298, 301, 308, 312
Preamble para. 1 180
Part II 203
III 203
IV 203
V 203
Art. I........8, 11, 141, 225, 227, 228, 243, 289

II 8, 9
III 8, 9, 10, 11, 12, 13, 16, 17, 70,
125, 141, 225, 227, 228, 243, 289, 314
VI 298–299
IX 133
X 120
XI 8, 9, 11, 13, 63, 70, 113, 117,
141, 225, 227, 228, 243, 289, 314
XIX 299–300
XX ....4 , 8, 9, 11, 12, 13, 14, 15, 16, 17, 18, 19, 20, 23, 24, 25,
29, 39, 63, 68, 70, 71, 72, 83, 84, 86, 90, 99, 112, 115, 116,
117, 118, 119, 120, 121 , 131, 133, 134, 136, 141, 142,
143, 144, 145, 146, 147, 148, 149, 150, 151, 153, 154, 155,
167, 187, 193, 225, 226, 230, 231, 233, 234, 235, 236, 237, 238,
239, 240, 241, 242, 243, 244, 246, 249, 250, 251, 252, 253,
255, 257, 259, 295, 300–305, 306
XXI ....2, 203, 225, 226, 229, 230 , 231,
232, 233, 250 , 251, 253, 257, 259
XXIII 305
Geneva Convention Relative to the Protection of Civilian Persons in
Time of War 1949, 75 UNTS 287 ....204, 205, 212
Art. 40 292
51 292
146..212
Hague Convention for the Protection of Cultural Property in
the Event of Armed Conflicts 1954
Prot. 3
Havana Charter for an International Trade Organisation 287, 301
Helsinki Convention on the Protection and Use of Transboundary
Watercourses and International Lakes 1992, (1992) 31 ILM 1312 159
Inter-American Convention for the Protection and Conservation of
Sea Turtles 1996 304
International Convention on the Elimination of All Forms of Racial
Discrimination, 1966, 660 UNTS 195 204
International Covenant on Civil and Political
Rights 1966 (ICCPR), 999 UNTS 171 ....6, 204, 208, 209, 247, 259, 307
Art. 2 211
8 208
(1) 292
(3) 292
22 208
24 294
26 208
27 281

International Covenant on Economic, Social and
Cultural Rights 1966 (ICESCR), 993 UNTS, 3 ....6, 204, 207, 208, 307
Art. 7(a)(1) 208
8 208
International Covenant on the Elimination of All Forms of Racial
Discrimination 1965, 660 UNTS 1956
Art. 2.1(d) 294
International Covenant on the Suppression and Punishment of the Crime
of Apartheid 1973, 1015 UNTS 2436
Art. IV 211
V 211
International Convention on the Suppression and Punishment of the
Crime of Apartheid
Art. 2(e) 292
Lomé IV Convention 1990, 1990 ILM 783
Art. 366a 296
Montreal Protocol on Substances that Deplete the Ozone Layer 1987............79
Montreal Protocol on Substances that Deplete the Ozone Layer 1990
1990 ILM 537 ....8, 114, 133, 211, 315
Art. 10A 159
North American Agreement on Environmental Cooperation (NAAEC)
1992, 32 ILM 1480 ....108, 321, 323
North American Agreement on Labour Cooperation 1993,
(1993) 32 ILM 1499 ....191, 297
North American Free Trade Association
(NAFTA) Agreement 108, 133, 191, 201,
217, 224, 297 Ch.12
Chap. 11 ....317, 318, 319, 320, 321, 324
B..316
20 322
Art. 14 322
104..133
1114..316, 317
1135(1)b..317
2011(1)..315
2018..315
2021..314
Paris Convention for the Protection of Industrial Property 1883, 828
UNTS 107
Art. 5(2) 170
Race Discrimination Convention..259
Rotterdam Convention of Prior Informed Consent for Certain Hazardous
Chemicals and Pesticides in International Trade 1998 21
Slavery Convention 1926..238, 292

Art. 1.1 .... 293, 308
5 292
Supplementary Convention on the Abolition of Slavery, the Slave Trade and Institutions and Practices Similar to Slavery 1956, 266 UNTS 3 .... 207, 211, 292
Art. 1 211
a 308
(d) 293, 309
7a 308
Treaty of Vienna
Annex XV 200
TRIPS 44, 65, 72, 73, 88, 93, 99, 101, 160, 164, 170, 171, 172, 176, 252, 263, 264, 265, 267, 268, 269, 270, 271, 274, 280, 285, 287
Preamble 263
Art. 2(7) 263
3 88
4 88
7 .... 264, 265, 266–274, 276, 279, 281, 285
27(1) 88, 170
(2) 89, 90, 92, 170
(3) 72, 170
31 170
39 272
66(2) 279
UN Charter 211
Art. 2(7) 208
39 247
41 247
51 231
55(c) 307
56 211
103 307
UN Convention on the Elimination of All Forms of Discrimination against Women 1979 (CEDAW) 6, 207, 208, 247
Art. 6 293
11 208
UN Convention on the Law of the Sea (UNCLOS) Art. 202 158
UN Convention against Torture and Other Cruel, Inhuman and Degrading Treatment or Punishment 1984, (1985) 23 ILM 1027 .... 6, 204, 212
Art. 2(1) 212
4 213
Additional Prot. 1977 212

UN Framework Convention on Climate Change 1992, 1992 ILM 849 15
UNESCO Convention on the Prevention and Suppression of Illicit Trade in Cultural Objects 1970, 823 UNTS 231 3
UNIDROIT Convention on the Return of Stolen and Illegally Exported Cultural Objects 1995, 1995 ILM 1322...........3
Universal Declaration of Human Rights, 1948...........204, 208, 259, 296, 307
Art. 4...........208, 293
20...........208
Arts. 22-25...........180
22-27...........5
Art. 23(2)...........208
(4)...........208
Vienna Convention for the Protection of the Ozone Layer 1985...........79
Art. 4.2...........158
Vienna Convention on the Law of Treaties 1969, 1155 UNTS 331...........122
Art. 30...........23, 36
(3)...........212
31(3)...........36, 99, 100, 102, 226, 306
41...........23
53...........205, 226, 294, 309
60(3)(b)...........297
(5)...........209
64...........205, 309
WTO Agreement 1994, 1994 ILM, 1144...........1, 40, 82, 83, 90, 126 128, 287, 298
Art. XIII...........305–306
31...........23
1927 Convention...........18

2. INTERNATIONAL LABOUR ORGANISATION (in numerical order)

ILO Constitution
Art. 26...........248
Child Labour Convention 1973...........207
Fundamental Conventions 2000...........207
White Lead Painting Convention (No. 13) 1921
Art. 3...........291
Medical Examination of Young Persons (Sea) Convention (No. 16) 1921...........291
Convention (No. 29) concerning Forced Labour 1930...........292, 297
Art. 1(1)...........212
2...........292
26...........212

Medical Examination of Young Persons (Industry) Convention
(No. 77) 1946 291
Medical Examination of Young Persons (Non-industrial Occupations)
Convention (No. 78) 1946..291
Night Work of Young Persons (Non-industrial Occupations) Convention
(No. 79) 1946 291
Night Work of Young Persons (Industry) Convention (Revised)
(No. 90) 1948 291
Convention No. 105 on the Abolition of Forced Labour...................207, 211, 247, 292, 297
Art. 2 212
Radiation Protection Convention (No. 115) 1960
Art. 6 291
7 291
Maximum Weight Convention (No. 127) 1967
Art. 1 291
7 291
Benzene Convention (No. 136) 1971
Art. 11 291
Minimum Age Convention (No. 138) 1973290, 291
Art. 1 290
2 290
3 290
7 290
Occupational Safety and Health (Dock Work) Convention
(No. 152) 1979 Art. 38 291
Convention (No. 182) concerning the Prohibition and
Immediate Action for the Elimination of the Worst Forms
of Child Labour..6, 11, 192, 207, 214, 291, 292, 300
Art. 3 ....291, 292, 293
4 291

3. EUROPEAN COMMUNITIES

EC Treaty

Art. 2 109
6 109
28 (ex 30) 25
Maastricht Treaty 1992..80
Treaty of Amsterdam 1997 191
Treaty on European Union 1997 191

Art. 2 191
6 306
11 306
Arts. 125-130 191
136-145 191
European Patent Convention 101
Art. 52(2)(c) 264
53 .... 92, 93, 94, 96, 99, 101
EC Directives:
Biotechnology 93, 99
90/219 [1990] OJ L117/1 47
90/220 [1990] OJ L117/15 .... 40, 47, 48, 50
97/35 [1997] OJ L169/73 .... 48, 50
98/44 [1998] OJ L213/13 92
EC Regulations:
3254/91 [1991] OJ L308/1 15
880/92 [1992] OJ L99/1 126
1836/93 [1993] OJ L168/1 126
3281/94 [1994] OJ L348/1 296
3281/94 as amended [1997] OJ L348/1 189
1256/96 296
2271/96 [1996] OJ L309/ 217
258/97 [1997] OJ L43/1 .... 49, 50
722/97 [1997] OJ L108/97 174
1139/98 [1998] OJ L159/4 69
49/2000 [2000] OJ L6/13 50

4. NATIONAL LEGISLATION

Australia
Crimes (Child Sex Tourism) Amendment Act 1994 19

Austria
Amendment #54 CPC 19

Canada
Foreign Extraterritorial Measures Act incorporating the Amendments Countering the US Helms-Burton Act 1996, (1997) 36 ILM 111 217

Colombia
Law 99 80

Costa Rica
Law 7788 80

Italy

Law No. 269 of 3 August 1998 19

Mexico

Act to Protect Trade and Investment from Foreign Norms that
Contravene International Law 1996, (1997) 36 ILM 133 217
General Health Law....................56

New Zealand

Hazardous Substances and New Organisms Act 1996 55

United States

Constitution
Art. 1 241
s.8....................267
Act to Amend the Bretton Woods Agreement Act,
92 Stat. 1051 (1978) 199
Alien Tort Act, 28 USC § 1350....................189
Andean Trade Preference Act, 19 USS 3202 (2000) 220
Arms Export Control Act....................214
Caribbean Basin Economic Recovery Act, 1
9 USC § 2702 (1994)....................220, 297
Civil Rights Act 1991
Title VII....................187
Clean Air Act 16, 80
Clean Water Act 80
Copyright Act....................259
Cuban Democracy Act 1992, 22 USC §6001-6010....................217, 222
Endangered Species Act 80
Export Administration Act 1979,
50 USCA 2401-2420 (1994) 221, 231
Federal Food, Drug and Cosmetic Act.................... 27, 80
Federal Insecticide, Fungicide and Rodenticide Act....................27
Foreign Operations, Export Financing, and Related Programs
Appropriations Act 1997 ....256, 297
Foreign Sovereign Immunity Act 209
Generalised System of Preferences....................7
Helms-Burton Act 1996 (Cuban Liberty and Democratic
Solidarity (LIBERTAD) Act) 216-217, 222, 223, 230
International Emergency Economic Powers Act 1994,
50 USC § 1701 et seq....................221, 231
Marine Mammal Protection Act 1972....................145
National Emergencies Act 1994, 50 USC § 1601....................221
National Environmental Policy Act 80

Oil Pollution Act 80
Omnibus Consolidated Appropriations Act 1997 297
Omnibus Trade and Competitiveness Act 1988,
19 USC § 2411 ....7, 216, 297
Pub. L 101-162 117
Pub. L 105-206 219
Tariff Act 1930 ....187, 214, 297
1997 Amendment 297
Trade Act 1974 ....187, 189, 216, 279
Jackson-Vanik Amendment 219
Trade and Development Act 2000, Pub. L 106-200 ....214, 220
Trading with the Enemy Act 221
Uruguay Round Agreements Act 202
19 USC § 2462 (2000) 220

Table of Abbreviations

AIA	Advance Informed Agreement
ANZFA	Australia-New Zealand Food Authority
BSP	Cartagena Protocol on Biosafety
CBA	cost-benefit analysis
CBD	Convention on Biological Diversity
CITES	Convention on Trade in Endangered Species 1973
CDM	Clean Development Mechanism
CEDAW	Convention on the Elimination of All Forms of Discrimination Against Women
COPS	Cost Per Unit Service
CSD	Commission on Sustainable Development
CTE	WTO Committee on Trade and Environment
DPG	domestically prohibited good
ECHR	European Convention on Human Rights
EPC	European Patent Convention
EPO	European Patent Office
EST	environmentally sound technology
FAO	Food and agriculture Organization
FCCC	Framework Convention on Climate Change
FDA	US Food and Drug Administration
FDI	foreign direct investment
FFP-LMO	Food, feed and process living modified organism
GATS	General Agreement on Trade in Services
GATT	General Agreement on Tariffs and Trade
GM	genetically modified
GMO	genetically modified organism
GSP	Generalized System of Preferences
ICCPR	International Covenant on Civil and Political Rights
ICESCR	International Covenant on Economic, Social and Cultural Rights
ICSID	International Centre for the Settlement of International Disputes
ILC	International Law Commission
ILO	International Labor Organization
IMF	International Monetary Fund
ITL	international trade law
IPR	intellectual property right
LMO	living modified organism
MEA	Multilateral Environmental Agreement
MFN	most favoured nation

NAAEC	North American Agreement on Environmental Cooperation
NAALC	North American Agreement on Labor Cooperation
NAFTA	North American Free Trade Agreement
NGO	non-governmental organization
NT	national treatment
OECD	Organisation for Economic Co-operation and Development
PIC	prior informed consent
PPM	Process/production methods
SPS	Sanitary and Phytosanitary Agreement
TBT	Technical Barriers to Trade Agreement
TNC	transnational corporation
TREMs	Trade Related Environmental Measures
TRIPS	Trade-Related Aspects of Intellectual Property Rights Agreement
UNCED	United Nations Conference on Environment and Development
UNCLOS	United Nations Convention on the Law of the Sea
UNCTAD	United Nations Conference on Trade and Development
UNEP	United Nations Environmental Program
UPOV	International Union for the Protection of New Varieties of Plants
WHO	World Health Organization
WTO	World Trade Organization
WTO-DSU	WTO Dispute Settlement Understanding

1

Environment, Human Rights and the Limits of Free Trade

FRANCESCO FRANCIONI

I. INTRODUCTION

AFTER THE COMPLETION of the Uruguay round and the adoption in 1994 of the agreement establishing of the World Trade Organisation (WTO),[1] the role of international trade in the context of the international legal order has changed radically. Once the preserve of a restricted circle of experts and lawyers, international trade law has now become a subject of widespread interest, cutting across traditional boundaries of specialised disciplines and even affecting spheres of non-trade interests. One consequence of this spillover effect of trade liberalisation is the increasing concern with the legitimacy of the process through which decisions within the WTO are made, especially when such decisions affect public policy goals already governed by domestic law.[2] Several difficult questions have emerged in this context. What right does the WTO have to trump legitimate (in the sense of democratically approved) national policies in the name of free trade? Whom can we trust when we face novel dilemmas, such as the commercialisation of genetically modified organisms? Where is the truth more likely to be found when we hear the discordant voices of scientists, politicians, and the business community? These are some of the complex questions that lie at the origin of the Seattle revolt and the lingering discontent with the global trade agenda.

While the discontent largely relates to the *process* and the perception of a lack of recognition of democratic legitimacy in the WTO rule-making deliberation, the conflicts are rooted in the increasing *substantive impact* that international commitments to trade liberalisation generate on traditional

[1] The texts of WTO and of related agreements are reprinted in (1994) *ILM* 1144. For introductory treatment of the global trading system, see Società Italiana di Diritto Internazionale (SIDI), *Diritto e organizzazione del commercio internazionale dopo la creazione della Organizzazione Mondiale del Commercio* (Napoli, 1998); Jackson, *The World Trading System: Law and Policy of International Economic Relations* (2nd edn. Cambridge Ma., 1997). For an economic analysis of the legal approach to WTO and international trade, see Trebilcock and Howse, *The Regulation of International trade* (2nd edn., London/New York, 1999).

[2] See Kingsbury, "The Tuna-Dolphin Controversy, the World Trade Organisation, and the Liberal Project to Reconceptualise International Law", in (1995) *Yrbk Intl Env L* 16.

spheres of domestic regulation and national public policy. The pervasive effects of international trade law in these spheres erode the ability of national authorities and their civil societies to maintain control over traditional non-economic values such as the environment, human health and social standards. In a democratic society, conflicts of this nature should be mediated by the ordinary electoral process which leads to the constitution of legislative and administrative bodies empowered with the capacity to make the necessary policy decisions.[3] In international law, there is not yet a global civil society. Even if one were to accept that such a global civil society is rapidly emerging from the global web of electronic communication, it would still lack the structure and the formal processes to channel its decisions to the approved international institutions. Such institutions exist only in limited areas. They are controlled, with few exceptions (ILO, IUCN), by representatives of the respective national governments and the role of NGOs, although very important, largely depends on cooperation with government representatives in such institutions. In contemporary international law, states remain the main actors, and in the field of international trade, states are indeed the actors of last resort in so far as remedies before the WTO dispute settlement body are open only to states and other governmental organisations and not to private entities.[4]

Thus, in the absence of a world government capable of functioning as global arbiter in resolving conflicts between trade and non-commercial interests, states must inevitably address such conflicts on the basis of principles and methods which are typical of the decentralised structure of international law. These methods include international cooperation for appropriate standard-setting, diplomatic negotiation and binding adjudication, and as a last resort, unilateral State action.

In this chapter, I shall examine the role and limits of unilateral trade measures as an instrument to protect legitimate non-commercial values. The focus of this chapter, as well as of this whole volume, is on environmental values and human rights. This does not imply by any means that free trade may not collide with other interests. Suffice it to mention the obvious example of national security,[5] or the less obvious but nonetheless important example of cultural heritage,

[3] In regional economic integration regimes, such as the European Union, institutional mechanisms exist to ensure harmonisation of national law and, when necessary, such regimes permit that free movement of goods may be limited in order to prevent trade from damaging other legitimate public interests sometimes referred to as "mandatory requirements".

[4] In spite of the far-reaching innovations introduced by the Uruguay Round with the comprehensive agreement on dispute settlement—including compulsory and binding adjudication and review procedure before a permanent organ, the Appellate Body—the system remains open only to states. In this regard, it stands in sharp contrast to the settlement of investment disputes under the 1965 World Bank Convention establishing ICSID which is open also to private parties involved in investment disputes with host Governments. For a good and comprehensive treatment of dispute settlement under WTO, see Ligustro, *Le controversie tra Stati nel diritto del commercio internazionale: dal GATT all'OMC* (Padova, 1996).

[5] See Art. XXI GATT, *55 UNTS* 194, Art. XXI.

where the tension between the reasons for free trade and those of national conservation underlie the various international regimes for the protection of cultural objects.[6] The choice to limit our analysis to the environment and human rights is due to: (1) the fact that the overwhelming majority of relevant international practice and disputes in the past ten years is concentrated in the area of environmental protection;[7] (2) the emerging claim that certain human rights, such as the rights of workers to be free from violent suppression and the right of children not to be abused by certain extreme forms of child labour and certain minimum labour standards, must not be subservient to the principle of free trade;[8] and (3) the conviction that the analytical approach applicable to the two above areas is also relevant to other areas of trade-related conflicts involving public interests different from the environment or human rights.

The following analysis is presented in four parts. The first provides a very brief historical survey of the evolution of international environmental law and human rights law in relation to trade. The second part focuses on the problem of the admissibility of unilateral import restrictions based on environmental or human rights concerns. The third section addresses the issue of export restrictions in relation to trade in substances or technologies that present a high degree of risk for the environment or human life and health. Lastly, the fourth part provides a list of basic principles and criteria which, in our view, should be followed to resolve disputes involving the conflict of trade norms with norms and policies protecting the environment and human rights.

[6] See, in particular, the 1970 UNESCO Convention on the prevention and suppression of illicit trade in cultural objects, 823 UNTS 231, the 1995 UNIDROIT Convention on the return of stolen and illegally exported cultural objects, [1995] *ILM* 1322, and the Protocol to the 1954 Hague Convention for the Protection of Cultural Property in the Event of Armed Conflicts, http://www.unesco.org/culture/laws/hague/html_eng/page8.htm. For a trade-oriented view on the subject see Merryman, "Two Ways of Thinking about Cultural Property", [1996] *Am J Intl L* 831. For a view more inclined to reconcile trade with cultural conservation, see Francioni, "Le commerce illicite d'objets d'art et son controle", *Revue du Marché Unique Européen,* 1998, 69.

[7] See *infra* Part IV. Legal literature on the subject of trade and the environment is so abundant that we can only refer to a selected list of titles: Jackson, "World Trade Rules and Environmental Policies: Congruence or Conflict? 11 (1992), *Washington and Lee Law Review* 1226; Petersmann, "Trade Policy, Environmental Policy and the GATT. Why Trade Rules and Environmental Rules Should be Mutually Consistent", *Aussenwirtschaft*, 1991, 197; Shoenbaum, "Free International Trade and Protection of the Environment: Irreconcilable Conflicts?", (1992) *Am J Intl L* 700; Brown-Weiss, "Environment and Trade as Partners in Sustainable Development: a Commentary", *ibid.* at 728; Cameron, Demaret and Geradin, *Trade and the Environment: the Search for Balance* (London, 1994); Tarasofsky, "Ensuring Compatibility between Multilateral Environmental Agreements and GATT/WTO", (1996) *Yrbk Intl Env L* 52; Munari, "La libertà degli scambi internazionali e la tutela dell'ambiente", *Riv Dir Intern,* 1994, 389; Francioni, "La tutela dell'ambiente e la disciplina del commercio internazionale", in SIDI, *supra* n. 1, p. 147; Sands, "Sustainable Development: Treaty, Custom, and the Cross-fertilization of International Law", in Boyle and Freestone (eds), *International Law and Sustainable Development* (1999), p. 39 *et seq.*

[8] See Lenzerini, *infra* Chapter 11; McCrudden and Davies, *infra* Chapter 8.

II. THE RELATIONSHIP OF FREE TRADE TO THE ENVIRONMENT AND HUMAN RIGHTS

To understand the interrelationship between free trade, on the one hand, and the environment and human rights on the other, it is useful to put into the proper historical perspective the origin and the development of the respective branches of international law. International environmental law, as a coherent body of norms, has developed only recently. Treaties and customs in this area are largely the product of the emerging awareness in the early 1970s that certain types of environmental degradation resulting from industrialisation and prevailing models of consumption must be dealt with by means of international cooperation and standard-setting. The starting point of this process was the Stockholm Declaration adopted in 1972 at the close of the first United Nations conference on the human environment.[9] This Conference gave birth to the United Nations Environmental Programme (UNEP) and set in motion wide-ranging environmental diplomacy that in the following years produced a great variety of multilateral agreements ranging from marine pollution, protection of the atmosphere, and conservation of species, to hazardous waste and many other types of environmental risks. Twenty years later, the Rio Conference on Environment and Development[10] tried to conjugate the protection of environmental quality with the imperative of economic growth and gave rise to a new generation of multilateral treaties dealing with global environmental problems such as climate change and the depletion of biodiversity.

In 1944, almost fifty years before the Rio summit, the states that were to form the United Nations convened at the Bretton Woods Conference and laid down the ground rules for the post-war neoliberal order of which GATT was to become a central component. The text of the GATT agreement, adopted in 1947, did not contain a specific reference to the protection of the environment. On the contrary, the preamble of GATT 1947 sets as its primary objective the "*full use* of the resources of the world", a concept that seems far removed from the contemporary notion of rational use of resources and sustainable development. However, the legislative history of GATT reveals that nature conservation concerns had been an important item in the discussion[11] and that such concerns eventually played a role in the drafting of Article XX exceptions concerning life/health protection and the conservation of exhaustible resources. With the adoption in 1994 of the agreement establishing the World Trade

[9] Stockholm Declaration of the UN Conference on the Human Environment (1972) *ILM* 1416.

[10] Rio Declaration on Environment and Development (1992) *ILM* 874.

[11] See UN Doc. E/PC/T/34, p. 43. For a detailed analysis of GATT negotiations supporting this view, see Charnovitz, "Exploring the Environmental Exceptions in the GATT", (1991) *Journal of World Trade* 37. For a more restrictive view of environmental concerns in the GATT, see Shrybman, "International Trade and the Environment: an Environmental Assessment of the General Agreement on Tariffs and Trade" (1990) *Ecologist* 33.

Organisation, although the text of GATT 1947 was left unchanged in its lack of a specific linkage with the environment, an explicit note in the preamble makes reference to the principle of sustainable development and to the need to consider that principle in the making of trade.[12] Whether or not this is sufficient to achieve the goal of "greening the GATT"[13] remains doubtful. However, at a minimum, this reference must be taken to indicate that the GATT interpretation and application of the correct analytical approach, requires weighing environmental values in making and implementing trade policy.[14] Therefore, although international environmental law has developed separately and later in time as compared to trade law, today the two branches, rather than remaining segregated, must converge toward the common objective of sustainable development.

If we look at the development of human rights in the context of trade liberalisation, the picture is reversed. The movement toward the adoption of international human rights standards, predates the effort to establish a global system of free trade. As early as 1919, with the constitution of the International Labour Organisation, social and economic rights began to develop within the unique tripartite institutional structure of the ILO made up of governments, with both labour and business representatives jointly participating in the negotiating and deliberative process. Notwithstanding the demise of the League of Nations, the ILO, together with the international court, managed to survive the Second World War. Its legacy proved to be relevant in the early formulation of the instruments designed to set up and govern the institutions of the United Nations. This was particularly true with regard to the infusion of labour and social standards in the preparatory work for the International Monetary Fund and the World Bank,[15] and more explicitly in the Havana Charter, which recognised the link between trade and the respect for labour standards. It is true that the Havana Charter never came into force, and that the ambitious project of the International Trade Organisation only produced the GATT, an agreement that does not contain any explicit link between trade and human rights. Nonetheless, just after the adoption of GATT, the United Nations adopted the Universal Declaration of Human Rights in 1948, which contains an important catalogue of social and economic rights (see Articles 22–27) of direct relevance for the ordering of the international trading system.[16]

[12] The preamble to the WTO agreement reads as follows: "allowing for the optimal use of the world's resources *in accordance with the objective of sustainable development*, seeking both to *protect and preserve the environment* and to enhance the means for doing so in a manner consistent with their respective needs and concerns at different levels of economic development" (emphasis added).

[13] The expression is used by Esty, *Greening the Gatt* (Washington DC, 1994).

[14] For a jurisprudential application of this approach, see the *Shrimps/Turtles* case discussed *infra* in *Part IV*.

[15] For a full treatment of these aspects, see Charnowitz, "The Influence of International Labour Standards on the World Trading Regime: a Historical Overview", (1987) *International Labour Review* 565; McCrudden and Davies, *infra* Chapter 8.

[16] Universal Declaration of Human Rights, UN, GA Res.217A (III); UN Doc. A/810 (1948), Arts 22–27.

After 1948, the development of human rights standards and their effective implementation in international and national law has been a constant concern of the international community. Despite the cold war, the two UN Covenants on civil and political rights and on social and economic rights were adopted in 1966, entering into force ten years later.[17] Many ad hoc treaties protecting specific human rights have been adopted prohibiting, inter alia, arbitrary discrimination,[18] torture,[19] and the abuse of children. Regional human rights system, such as the European, the African and the American systems have developed at the substantive and institutional level, thus contributing to the consolidation of the idea that, at least with regard to the most basic rights, states are bound to respect and ensure their respect as a matter of international customary law.[20]

More recently, international attention has focused on the specific issue of enhancing compliance with certain minimum social and labour standards as part of the universally accepted human rights norms. A watershed in this respect was the 1998 ILO Declaration on Fundamental Principles and Rights at Work.[21] The Declaration lays down a catalogue of core principles which include: the right to collective bargaining; and the prohibition of forced labour, of gender discrimination and of exploitative child labour.[22] In as much as these core principles tend to form the content of international obligations, their adoption in domestic law may result in denial of market access for countries responsible for egregious violations. Such denial can be seen as instrumental in inducing compliance with recognised international standards and not protectionist or discriminatory in nature. Its legal justification stems from the necessity of stopping an illicit international practice. It is not based on competitiveness considerations. This approach would facilitate the convergence between trade policy and human rights values in a manner similar to that which we have indicated with regard to environmental values. Unfortunately, this idea is still problematic within the WTO, and other chapters in this book will discuss the nature and the

[17] 1966 Covenant on Civil and Political Rights, 999 *UNTS* 171; 1966 Covenant on Social, Economic and Cultural Rights, 993 UNTS 3.

[18] 1965 International Convention on the Elimination of All Forms of Racial Discrimination, 660 *UNTS* 195; 1973 International Convention on the Suppression and Punishment of the Crime of Apartheid, 1015 *UNTS* 243; 1979 UN Convention on the Elimination of All Forms of Discrimination Against Women, UN, GA Res. 34/180, UN Doc. A/34/46.

[19] 1984 Convention Against Torture and Other Cruel, Inhuman and Degrading Treatment or Punishment, UN, GA Res. 39/46, UN Doc. A/39/51.

[20] On the link between human rights treaties and customary international law, see Francioni, "An International Bill of Rights: Why It Matters, How It can be Used", (1997) *Texas Int'l L.J.* For an analysis of the different ways in which international human rights are applied by domestic courts, see Conforti and Francioni (eds), *Enforcing International Human Rights in Domestic Courts* (London/The Hague/Boston, 1997).

[21] ILO, Declaration on Fundamental Principles and Rights at Work, 1998, International Labour Conference, 86th Session, see http://www.ilo.org/public/english/standards/relm/ilc/ilc86/com-dtxt.htm. Further on the general context in which this instrument was adopted, see McCrudden and Davies, *infra* Chapter 8.

[22] The issue of exploitative child labour has been subsequently developed by the 1999 Worst Form of Child Labour Convention (No. 182), available in the ILO Internet site (http://ilolex.ilo.ch:1567/scripts/conv.de.pl?C182).

extent of the resistance against this convergence and the possible strategies to be pursued within the WTO.[23] For the purpose of this chapter it is sufficient to recognise that it is exactly from this resistance that the current tendency toward unilateralism arises. I shall thus turn to examining the role and limits of unilateral trade measures as instruments to protect environmental or human rights values.

III. UNILATERAL MEASURES AFFECTING IMPORTS

Unilateral import restrictions or trade incentives for the purpose of protecting environmental or human rights standards are an increasingly common feature of state practice. Especially in the USA, action at the administrative level is permitted against countries which have been found to engage in practices "that constitute a persistent pattern of conduct denying internationally recognised workers rights".[24] Such action is promoted by NGOs which can claim *locus standi* in domestic courts to force government to adopt trade sanctions.[25] Similarly, in Europe, common commercial policy regulations permit the adoption of trade-related measures to ensure protection of animals, the administration of advantages and penalties to foreign countries within the Generalised System of Preferences and similar measures inspired by nature protection or the promotion of human rights standards.[26]

From a policy point of view, unilateral action of this kind presents one clear advantage: it is responsive to the domestic constituency's demands for effective protection of certain shared values and does not require lengthy negotiations with other countries in order to agree upon common environmental or human rights standards. It can also serve as a means to pressure non-cooperating states into some international regulatory scheme once the unilateral measures have proven to be effective. At the same time, this practice presents some serious

[23] See (with reference to child labour) Lenzerini, *infra* Chapter 11; McCrudden and Davies, *infra* Chapter 8.

[24] See Omnibus Trade and Competitiveness Act 1988, Pub. L. 100–418, 102 Stat. 1107 (1988,1101(b)(14)); Trade incentives in the USA are included in the Generalised System of Preferences (GSP), 19 U.S.C. § 2461 (1994). See, in general, Cleveland, *infra* Chapter 9.

[25] Some of the major disputes brought before the GATT WTO Dispute Settlement were triggered by judicial actions by NGOs in US courts to force the administration to adopt mandatory sanctions. The notorious *Tuna/Dolphin* dispute (*United States—Restrictions on Imports of Tuna*, Report of the Panel, June 1994, (1994) *ILM* 839) as well as the recent *Shrimps/Turtle* case (*US Import Prohibition of Certain Shrimp and Shrimp Products*, Appellate Body Report, WT/DS58/AB/R, (1999) *ILM* 118) fall into this category.

[26] In 1995 the EU amended its GSP programme in order to condition its application to comply with core labour rights and to terminate its application in relation to countries that permit any form of slave labour. For detailed analysis, see Brandtner and Rosas, "Trade Preferences and Human Rights", in Alston (ed.), *The European Union and Human Rights* (Oxford, 1999), p. 699; Dufour, *Les droits des travailleurs et les accords commerciaux* (Sherbrooke, 1998), especially p. 60; Lenzerini, *infra* Chapter 11; Riedel and Will, "Human Rights Clauses in External Agreements of EC", in Alston, *The EU and Human Rights* (Oxford, 1999), p. 723.

drawbacks. For example, affected trading countries do not normally have the opportunity to make their voice heard in the decision-making process; furthermore, the measures may be totally ineffective, or even counter-productive, in terms of improving the target state's environmental or human rights record.

From a legal point of view, there is nothing in customary international law nor in treaty law relating to the environment or to human rights that would require ruling out the use of unilateral measures in principle. On the contrary, one can argue that trade restriction as a means of enhancing nature protection dates back to the early 1970s when the Convention on Trade in Endangered Species (CITES 1973) was adopted in apparent accordance with Article XX of GATT.[27] It was soon followed by a series of similar treaties among which the most significant are the 1987 Montreal Protocol on the ozone layer[28] and the 1989 Basel Convention on hazardous waste.[29] In favour of unilateral trade measures, one can argue also that, once a state has undertaken a treaty commitment to protect certain environmental or human rights standards, there is a duty to implement those standards effectively by adopting appropriate national legislative and administrative measures. However, under GATT/WTO law such unilateral action may constitute a breach per se of specific trade liberalisation commitments, or may become illegal through the arbitrary or protectionist manner in which they are applied. In the following analysis, I will examine the way in which the GATT/WTO bodies have addressed this issue, and I will try to highlight how, starting from an initial attitude of obtuse closure to the consideration of non-commercial values, such as life, health and the conservation of exhaustible resources, the more recent practice has remarkably evolved toward an attitude that tends to weigh such values carefully against the need to comply with GATT/WTO free trade rules.

Articles I, II, III, XI and XX GATT

One of the objectives of GATT/WTO is to reduce to a minimum the macro-economic measures that prohibit or restrict access to national markets of products and services imported from other contracting parties (or "members" under WTO terminology). This objective is pursued, insofar as goods are concerned, through a series of provisions, the most important of which are Articles I, II, III, and XI of the General Agreement. As is well known, Article I concerns the "external" parity and non-discriminatory treatment that every member must reserve to products imported from other members (the most favoured nation

[27] See *infra* n. 83.

[28] Montreal Protocol on Substances that Deplete the Ozone Layer (amended in London, 1990), (1990) *ILM* 537.

[29] 1989 Basel Convention on the Control of Transboundary Movements of Hazardous Waste, (1989) *ILM* 649.

clause).[30] Article II introduces the obligation to limit and progressively reduce customs tariffs.[31] This is an obligation of conduct, not of result. Article III fixes the concept of "internal" parity consisting in the obligation not to discriminate between imported products and "like" domestic products (national treatment).[32] Article XI establishes the general obligation to eliminate non-tariff restrictions and prohibitions on trade.[33] All of these rules are subject to the general exceptions under Article XX.[34]

How much room for discretion is left to individual states to adopt unilateral decisions restricting imports based on environmental or human rights conditions? Trade lawyers and the practice of GATT/WTO have answered this question by departing from the basic distinction between "product requirements", which relate to the physical characteristics of the products and "process or production methods PPM" which concern the manner in which those products have been made in the exporting country. In the following analysis I will try to demonstrate that, although this distinction has been followed in GATT/WTO case law, its application as an inflexible rule is neither mandated in point of law by the relevant treaty norms, nor is it responsive, as a matter of policy, to the reality that some of the most pressing environmental and human rights concerns stem from process and production methods.

Import restrictions based on product requirements

The practice developed by GATT/WTO Panels in the implementation of the above-mentioned Articles (namely, I, II, III, and XI) demonstrates that states retain a considerable degree of discretion in the determination of environmental, safety and health standards applicable to imported products. The only binding requirement imposed by GATT, beyond the Article XI prohibition of quantitative restrictions, including voluntary restrictions (*Japanese Semi-Conductors* case),[35] pertain to: (1) the obligation of non-discrimination between like products imported from different countries (Article I); and (2) the obligation of non-discrimination between imported products and like domestic products (Article III). A rigorous implementation of the latter obligation can be found in the *Italian Agricultural Machinery* case[36] and in the *Japan-Alcoholic Beverages* case.[37] Under GATT case law, a state is free to exclude from its own national market motor vehicles that do not conform to national emission

[30] Art. I GATT, *supra* n. 5.
[31] Art. II GATT, *supra* n. 5.
[32] Art. III GATT, *supra* n. 5.
[33] Art. XI GATT, *supra* n. 5.
[34] Art. XX GATT, *supra* n. 5.
[35] *Japan—Trade in Semi-Conductors*, Panel Report, 4 May 1988, 35th Supp. BISD 116, 1989.
[36] *Italian Agricultural Machinery case,* Report, 23 October 1958, 7th Supp. BISD 60, 1959.
[37] *Japan—Taxes on Alcoholic Beverages*, Report of the Appellate Body, 4 October 1996, WT/DS 8/R, WT/DS 10R, WT/DS 11/R, AB—1996.

standards or machinery that does not meet safety standards provided that such standards apply also to goods produced nationally or originating from third states. This principle was applied in the 1994 Panel Report on *US Taxes on Automobiles*.[38] Similarly, the test of non-discrimination was applied in the case of *Thailand's Restrictions on Importation of Cigarettes*[39] where the Panel upheld the USA claim that Thailand had violated GATT by refusing to authorise an import licence for foreign cigarettes based on health concerns, but without adopting analogous restrictive measures on domestically produced cigarettes.

Similarly, GATT's recognition of the principle of sovereignty of individual states in determining their own environmental policy allows imported products to be subjected to eco-taxes in order to incorporate the environmental costs of the product related to its use or its disposal, provided that the tax measure is non-discriminatory. This principle was affirmed in the case concerning *US Taxes on Petroleum and Certain Imported Substances 1987*.[40] The Report on this case concerning the US tax on imported chemical substances, widens the admissibility of eco-taxes to a border adjustment duty corresponding to the domestic tax levied on the national production of like chemicals for the purpose of financing domestic environmental programmes. In that case, the EC had challenged the US duty on the ground that the "Polluter Pays Principle" (PPP), recognised by the EC law and by OECD resolutions, would justify only a tax on the polluting activities related to *the production of those substances in the territory of the USA*. In rejecting this argument, the Panel held that the US tax conformed with Article III GATT to the extent that it was equivalent to like national products, independently of its purpose. The Panel asserted in this regard that:

> "the tax adjustment rules of the General Agreement distinguish between taxes on products and taxes not directly levied on products; they do not distinguish between taxes with different policy purposes. Whether a sale tax is levied on a product for general revenue purposes or to encourage the rational use of environmental resources is therefore not relevant for the determination of the eligibility of a tax for border adjustment".[41]

This statement leaves the importing state free to make use of eco-taxes to internalise environmental costs arising not only from polluting industries and production processes within its territory, but also from the use, consumption, distribution and disposal of similar substances produced elsewhere. This approach is in line with the national legislation of the most advanced industrial states which tend to regulate the environmental impact of products "from cradle to grave".

[38] *United States—Taxes on Automobiles*, Report of the Panel, 29 September 1994, DS31/R.

[39] *Thailand—Restriction on Importation of and Internal Taxes on Cigarettes*, 37th Supp. *BISD* 200, 1990.

[40] *US—Taxes on Petroleum and Certain Imported Substances*, 34th Supp. *BISD* 136, 1987.

[41] See para. 5.2.4.

The logic of the internalisation of environmental costs also entails the freedom of a state to exempt national products destined for export from eco-taxes in order to eliminate the risk of doubling the tax burden (state of origin and state of import).

Above and beyond the ample room left by Articles I, III, and XI GATT, a state can also adopt *discriminatory* import restrictions when one of the general exceptions of Article XX apply. Exceptions under paragraphs (b) and (g)[42] are directly relevant for the adoption of trade-related environmental measures, insofar as they contemplate respectively, the protection of life and health, and the conservation of exhaustible resources.

As far as human rights are concerned, no specific exception is provided in Article XX and no specific jurisprudence has developed so far in the practice of the WTO dispute settlement mechanism. However, as we shall see *infra* some basis can be found for the adoption of trade-related human rights measures in the prison labour exception of paragraph (e)[43] in cases where such prison labour is connected to situations of practical workers enslavement, political persecution and human rights abuses.[44] Similarly, the "public morals" exceptions under paragraph (a) can sustain a human rights exception in regard to some objectionable products such as child pornography and, perhaps, also in relation to the products of the worst form of child labour and exploitation.[45] Although apparently different, these two hypotheses have more in common than meets the eye. I shall return to them in the following section concerning restrictions based on process and production methods.

There is a substantial body of "case law" concerning the interpretation of Article XX and, with the exception of three recent reports applying the Sanitary and Phytosanitary Agreement (SPS),[46] all the pronouncements concerning the

[42] Article XX GATT, *supra* n. 5, provides that: "Subject to the requirement that such measures are not applied in a manner which would constitute a means of arbitrary or unjustifiable discrimination between countries where the same conditions prevail, or a disguised restriction on international trade, nothing in this Agreement shall be construed to prevent the adoption or enforcement by any contracting party of measures: . . . (b) necessary to protect human, animal or plant life; . . . (g) relating to the conservation of exhaustible natural resources if such measures are made effective in conjunction with domestic production or consumption".

[43] See *supra* n. 42. Article XX(e) GATT includes the exception "relating to the products of prison labour".

[44] See Charnovitz, "Fair Labor Standards and International Trade" (1986) *Journal of World Trade Law* 61, at 68; "Promoting World Labor Rules", (1994) *Journal of Commerce*, 19 April 8A; Diller and Levy, "Child Labour, Trade and Investment: Toward the Harmonisation of International Law", (1997) *Am J Intl L* 663, at 684; Leary, "Workers' Rights and International Trade: the Social Clause (GATT, ILO, NAFTA, U.S. Laws)", in Bhagwati and Hudec (eds), *Fair Trade and Harmonization,* vol.2*: Legal Analysis* (Cambridge/London, 1996), p. 177, at p. 204; Lenzerini, *infra*, Chapter 11.

[45] See the forms of child labour listed in Art. 3(b) (use, procuring or offering of a child: for prostitution; for the production of pornography; or for pornographic performances) and (c) (use and procuring or offering of a child for illicit activities, in particular for the production and trafficking of drugs) of the 1999 ILO Convention No. 182, *supra* n. 22.

[46] These cases are the well known *Hormones* case, decided by the Appellate Body, 16 January 1998, WT/DS27/AB/R; *Australia—Measures Affecting the Importation of Salmon*, Report of the Appellate Body, 6 November 1998, WT/DS18/AB/R; and *Japan—Measures Affecting Agricultural Products*, 22 February 1999, WT/DS76/AB/R.

compatibility of environmental measures with GATT/WTO are concentrated on that article. This case law is remarkable for two reasons. First, it shows a healthy tendency to open up the general categories of Article XX exceptions to accommodate national public policies pursuing non-commercial interests, even if such interests are not localised in the territory of the acting state (air quality, migratory species). Secondly, since 1996, a trade-restrictive measure found permissible under one of the exceptions in Article XX must also meet the test of the preambular paragraph of Article XX. This "chapeau" requires that measures justified by their nature and content under Article XX must be applied in such a manner so as to avoid "arbitrary or unjustifiable" discrimination or a "disguised" restriction on international trade.[47] Of course, what constitutes "arbitrary", "unjustified" discrimination or "disguised" protectionism may be difficult to determine in light of the increasing tension between free trade and domestic policy goals. Recent Panel and Appellate Body practice has increasingly tried to clarify these negative conditions. For example, the question of discrimination in the implementation of measures otherwise justified under Article XX came up in the case concerning the *US Standards for Reformulated and Conventional Gasoline* (1996).[48] The technical regulations adopted by the United States Environmental Protection Agency (USEPA), to reduce atmospheric pollution by fixing qualitative standards for imported gasoline and like products of national origin, were found by the Panel to be incompatible with Article III, paragraph 4 of GATT.[49] The Appellate Body's report reversed this part of the opinion. In a two-step analysis, it first found that the US environmental measures fell under the "exhaustible natural resources" (clean air) exception of Article XX(g), and, secondly reviewed the manner in which the measures were applied under the arbitrary/unjustifiable discrimination test of the preambular paragraph. Ultimately, the Appellate Body concluded that the US measures did not satisfy the second test, but in doing so, it made clear that "the *chapeau* by its express terms addresses, not so much the questioned measure or its specific contents as such, but rather the manner in which the measure is applied" (citing a similar interpretation provided by the 1983 Panel Report on *US—Imports of Certain Automotive Spring Assemblies*, p. 22).[50]

This is a sound approach. On the one hand, it provides that a unilateral measure restricting imports may be justified on its face if it fits one of the broad categories of exception contemplated by Article XX, which directly covers environmental concerns and indirectly relates to human rights. On the other hand, it provides a closer scrutiny of the disputed measure with regard to the

[47] See *supra* n. 42.

[48] *US Standards for Reformulated and Conventional Gasoline*, Appellate Body Report, 20 May 1996, (1996) *ILM* 603.

[49] *US Standards for Reformulated and Conventional Gasoline*, Panel Report, 29 January 1996, (1996) *ILM* 274.

[50] *US—Imports of Certain Automotive Spring Assemblies*, Panel Report, 26 May 1983, 30th Supp. BISD 107, 1983.

manner in which it is implemented, thereby introducing a review of the exercise of administrative discretion of a type that can be found in domestic administrative law. Such review, being based on the notions of "arbitrary" or "unjustifiable" discrimination, can provide an effective substantive check against protectionist or arbitrary measures even if they are presented under the seductive garb of environmentally motivated restrictions. At the same time, the test of "unjustifiability" entails some kind of balancing of the free trade objective pursued by GATT with the competing public interests protected by Article XX. If balancing is the proper method, then the principle of proportionality must also be employed. Proportionality requires that the implementation of the disputed measure does not exceed what is reasonably necessary to satisfy the non-commercial value covered by the Article XX exception. I shall return to the principle of proportionality in Part V of this chapter.

With regard to import restrictions based on human rights considerations, the margin of discretion left to individual States under Article XX is less clear. In a recent report,[51] a WTO Panel has found that national measures banning the import of asbestos products could be justified by reason of health considerations under Article XX(b) of GATT. Besides this provision which relates to the right to life and health, human rights considerations may find indirect support in the already mentioned Article XX(e) provision relating to product of prison labour and Article XX(a) relating to "public morals". These exceptions, however, would apply to the processes and methods by which the products are made, i.e., in a manner that involves unacceptable human rights abuses in the producing country, and are to be discussed in the following section.

Import restrictions based on process/production methods (PPM)

A widely held view among GATT commentators is that contrary to product requirements, processes through which products are made are not contemplated by the GATT rules Article III and XI, as they refer only to "products" and "like products". Besides the strict textual interpretation arguments, supporters of this view also rely on the policy argument commonly referred to as the "slippery slope": once you open the door to PPM restrictions it would be very difficult, if not impossible, to set a limit to the virtually unlimited variety of potential objections that states might unilaterally raise against the way in which products are made in the exporting countries. This raises the spectre of systemic protectionism and of the arbitrary imposition of one country's national policies on another country's sphere of domestic jurisdiction. These are legitimate concerns. But the real issue is whether such legitimate concerns can be accommodated *only* by shutting the door to PPM consideration and whether as a matter of positive law, GATT/WTO mandates such an exclusive approach.

[51] *European Communities—Measures Affecting Asbestos and Asbestos Containing Products*, 18 September 2000, WT/DS 135/R.

GATT/WTO practice in the area of nature protection

The answer to this question has been inconsistent in the practice of GATT/WTO. In the first major case involving trade and the environment, the by now notorious Mexico/USA *Tuna/Dolphins* dispute,[52] the Panel rejected the USA's claim to a right to protect living resources beyond national jurisdiction. The Panel asserted that the production method (fishing with unsafe nets and techniques) was irrelevant in assessing the quality of the product (tuna) and unreasonably read a territorial limitation into the Article XX(b) and (g) exceptions. When the same dispute was adjudicated three years later, this time involving the USA and the EC, the Panel reached the same conclusion as to the illegality of the USA's measures under GATT, but admitted the possibility of a GATT party adopting unilateral trade measures for the protection of the general environment when these measures are consistent with international standards including norms on the exercise of jurisdiction. In the more recent *Shrimp/Turtle* dispute,[53] the WTO Appellate Body has further repositioned itself. In this case the question was whether the USA could impose a ban on imports of shrimps from countries that did not ensure the adoption by their fishing industry of technology capable of avoiding the incidental killing of sea turtles (the so-called Turtle Exclusion Device). Further changing the interpretation of Article XX, the Appellate Body opened more room for unilateral measures by ruling that:

> "it is not necessary to assume that requiring from exporting countries compliance with, or adopting certain policies (although covered in principle by one or other of the exceptions) prescribed by the importing country, renders a measure a priori incapable of justification under Article XX. Such an interpretation renders most, if not all, of the specific exceptions of Art. XX, inutile, a result abhorrent to the principles we are bound to apply".[54]

Under this ruling it was recognized that import restrictions adopted for the protection of one of the legitimate interests listed in Article XX may go as far as to require an extraterritorial application of environmental standards (as in the specific case the adoption of turtle-safe fishing technology) as a means to induce foreign countries to cooperate in the conservation of common resources. Ultimately, the Appellate Body found that the manner in which the US measures were *applied* constituted arbitrary or unjustifiable discrimination between countries where the same conditions prevailed, in breach of the Article XX Preamble. However, the ruling marks major progress as compared to the *Tuna/Dolphin* case in that it explicitly recognises that in principle there is no legal basis for the argument that if a country sets forth a given public policy requiring compliance with it by domestic and foreign exporting producers, such

[52] (1991) *ILM* 1594.
[53] See *supra* n. 25.
[54] *Appellate Body Report*, supra n. 25, para. 121.

unilateral requirement is per se inconsistent with Article XX. This is an important recognition that, in the long run, is bound to undermine the superficial distinction between product requirement and PPMs because the language of the Article XX exceptions is general enough to permit the adoption of protective policies that address noxious PPMs rather than product characteristics.

This more expansive interpretation of Article XX is consistent with the evolving structure of international environmental law that more and more tends to address the problem of environmental degradation by attacking processes and production methods rather than products. Consider for example: the Climate Change Convention,[55] which aims at cutting emissions of greenhouse gases; the Convention on Desertification,[56] which aims at combating irresponsible agricultural practices; and the emerging prohibition of large driftnet fishing, that causes severe and lasting damage to the marine environment. From a policy point of view, this development of international law is indispensable for a number of reasons. First, it is now universally recognised that certain PPMs may have global environmental effects as in the industrial use of halons and clorofluorocarbons with regard to the ozone. Secondly, PPM can cause a transboundary "spill-over" in terms of air or water pollution with injurious consequences for other countries and peoples. Thirdly, they can indirectly harm human, animal or plant health by introducing into the food chain harmful substances used or released in the production cycle and capable of long-term harm, even if not immediately detectable in the product (issue of genetically modified organisms and products). Fourthly, the PPM may entail the abhorrent destruction of valuable endangered species or natural resources, as in the case of ivory, whales products and other products of species protected under CITES.[57] Finally, the targeting of PPM may be the only effective tool to deter exploitation of natural resources through reckless methods such as the destruction of rain forests to expand cattle ranching or to clear cut for timber in an unsustainable manner, not to mention the use of inhumane methods of fur trapping (for example, the capture of animals by leg-hold traps which inspired EC Regulation 3254/91 prohibiting the importation of furs and hides and manufactured goods derived from animals captured in countries where such a method of capture is practised).[58]

[55] 1992 UN Framework Convention on Climate Change (1992) *ILM* 849.

[56] 1994 Convention to Combat Desertification in Those Countries Experiencing Serious Drought and/or Desertification, Particularly in Africa (1994) *ILM* 1328.

[57] 1973 Convention on International Trade in Endangered Species of Wild Fauna and Flora (CITES) (1973) *ILM* 1085.

[58] Council Regulation 3254/91/EC 4 November 1991 prohibiting the use of leghold traps in the Community and introducing into the Community pelts and manufactured goods of certain wild animals species originating in countries which catch them by means of leghold traps or trapping methods which do not meet international humane trapping standards, OJ 1991 L308 1.

The Agreement on Technical Barriers to Trade (TBT) and on Sanitary and Phytosanitary Measures (SPM)

Further support for an inclusionary approach to PPMs in the interpretation of Article XX exceptions comes from the adoption in the WTO of the two additional agreements on Technical Barriers to Trade[59] and on Sanitary and Phytosanitary measures.[60] Contrary to the view expressed in the early case law on trade and the environment, these agreements do not imply a GATT exclusion of trade restrictions based on processes rather than product requirements. On the contrary, the TBT agreement expressly provides (Article 2.2) that:

> "technical regulations shall not be more trade-restrictive than necessary to fulfil a legitimate objective . . . inter alia: national security requirements; the prevention of deceptive practices; protection of human health or safety; animal or plant life or health; or the environment. In assessing such risks, relevant elements of considerations are, inter alia: available scientific and technical information, *related processing technology* or intended end-uses of products" (emphasis added).[61]

This Article recognises that: (1) the environment may be a "legitimate objective" in the adoption of trade restrictive regulations; and (2) that in assessing the risk posed by products, related processing technology may be a relevant factor. Another innovative feature of this article is also the introduction of the principle of proportionality ("not . . . more restrictive than necessary") which opens the way for a careful balancing of trade policy with environmental policy in the implementation of Article XX. So far, the way in which processing technology and the proportionality tests may be used under the TBT agreement remains uncertain. In the already mentioned case of *US Standards for Reformulated and Conventional Gasoline*,[62] the plaintiffs, Venezuela and Brazil, had invoked Article 2.2 of the TBT agreement to dispute the legality of the US law concerning the chemical processing requirements for imported gasoline under the Clean Air Act.[63] However, a decision by the Panel and Appellate Body on this point was preempted by the finding that the US regulations were in violation of Article III.4 of the General Agreement and that they were not justified under the preamble of Article XX.

As far as the SPS agreement is concerned, it is true that its text does not contain any specific reference to process technology. At the same time, it is also true that nothing in the text excludes that the manner in which products are made may give rise to legitimate concerns and possible exceptions under Article XX. Indeed, the SPS agreement is meant to provide guidance in the interpretation and implementation of Article XX especially from the point of view of the pro-

[59] Agreement on Technical Barriers to Trade (TBT) (1994) *ILM* 81.

[60] Agreement on Sanitary and Phytosanitary Standards (SPS), Final Act Embodying the Results of the Uruguay Round of the Multilateral Trade Negotiations (1994) *ILM* 1140, Annex 1A(4).

[61] See *supra* n. 59, Art. 2.2.

[62] See *supra* n. 48.

[63] Clean Air Act, 42 U.S.C. s. 7401 *et seq.*; as amended in 1990, Pub. L. 101–594.

cedural obligations concerning appropriate risk assessment and proper scientific experimentation. Therefore it is unavoidable that review under the SPS agreement will extend to process and production methods. The first case brought before the Dispute Settlement Body under the SPS agreement, the 1998 *Hormones* case,[64] focused on a non-discriminatory ban on the non-therapeutic administration of hormones in the *process* of cattle raising industry, which confirms this conclusion.

PPM and the protection of human rights

Import restrictions based on human rights considerations are, by definition, almost always based on the manner in which the products are made. As mentioned in the first part of this chapter, import restrictions of this kind may be related to extreme forms of child labour;[65] forced suppression of workers rights, services or products relating to prostitution; sex or racial discrimination in violation of international standards. Unlike the environment and nature protection exceptions examined in the previous sections, the extent to which fundamental human rights policies may be infused into the trade system has not yet formed the object of adjudication by GATT/WTO.

If we leave aside the clear exception of Article XX(e), concerning the products of prison labour, the way in which production processes entailing human rights violations may be a factor in legitimising import restriction can be identified at two distinct levels. The first one is through the use of Article III paragraph 4 which allows every WTO member to set non-discriminatory rules for the sale, distribution and use of products within its own territory.[66] The second is through the general exceptions of Article XX.[67]

As is evident from our analysis on trade-related environmental measures, the early GATT jurisprudence based on the notion of "like products" would leave very little margin of appreciation for national authorities to restrict the importation of products on the ground of objectionable human rights practices in the making of those products. However, the analysis of this jurisprudence with regard to the environment has shown the fallacy of the rigid product/process distinction and the absence of clear language in the GATT that prohibits PPM trade measures. Therefore, the correct approach, in our view, is to establish first whether certain human rights policies are required by international law, and then to determine whether the importing state has exercised its regulatory autonomy in a manner consistent with Article III; that is, in a-non-discriminatory or protectionist manner. In fact, there is no compelling reason, based on the text of GATT or on logic, that would compel a state to consider that the tennis shoes

[64] See *European Communities—Measures Affecting Meat and Meat Products (Hormones)*, Report of the Appellate Body, 13 February 1998, WT/DS 26, DS48/AB/R.

[65] On the issue of child labour see Lenzerini, *infra* Chapter 11.

[66] Art. III GATT, *supra* n. 5, at para. 4.

[67] See, in particular, para. II.2.

manufactured under slave labour conditions and those manufactured according to practices that conform to minimum humanitarian standards are "like products". It is the public policy of the regulating state that dictates the limit and extent of the "likeness" of products and not their naively presumed physical characteristics. The only plausible reason to oppose such approach is the understandable concern with possible abuses connected with the adoption of idiosyncratic or arbitrary policies capable of impairing the functioning of the trade system. However, if we shift to such a policy argument, the question is not so much *whether* production practices may be relevant in point of law to the adoption of trade-restrictive measures. Rather the question is *how* we can effectively control the exercise of member states' right to resort to process-based trade measures so as to prevent abuses incompatible with GATT/WTO obligations. This task can be facilitated by the proper application of the *chapeau* of Article XX and by the adoption of a set of criteria that will form the object of Part V of this chapter.

The second level at which certain violations of human rights may be assumed as a relevant factor in the justification of trade restrictions is the use of the general exceptions in Article XX. The prison labour exception has already been mentioned as an explicit source of justification. This may be an exception motivated more by unfair competition concerns than by human rights considerations. However, if competitiveness was the original *rationale* for the exception, such an exception should, *a fortiori*, cover situations where the depriving of liberty engenders the serious violations of workers' rights. So, an evolutive interpretation of this clause should allow the adoption of import restrictions on products made by workers that have been subject to conditions of unacceptable confinement and personal coercion, such that it amounts to slavery or servitude. Past practice favours this analogy[68] and the current development of international standards by ILO can clarify the limits of this analogy and prevent possible abuses for protectionist purposes.[69]

Another general exception in Article XX, which may be relevant to the adoption of trade-related human rights measures is paragraph (a) concerning the protection of "public morals". Obviously, the concept of "public morals" may vary from country to country and its inherent relativity entails that national authorities enjoy a wide margin of appreciation with regard to its application in the respective national societies. "Public morals" may require the exclusion of nudity pictures from lawful commerce that in another society are deemed to be a work of art. It may lead to the exclusion of alcoholic beverages on grounds of stern religious principles that are totally alien to other cultures. This relative concept of "public morals", in so far as it reflects national beliefs and values that are likely to be extraneous to other societies, may be applied only territorially

[68] See the US position in the instrument of the adhesion to the 1927 Convention for the abolition of import and export restrictions according to which prison labour was to include "goods the product of forced and slave labor however employed": Lenzerini, *infra* Chapter 11.

[69] The necessity to limit the recourse to unilateral measures has been pointed out also by the ILO Declaration on Fundamental Principles and Rights at Work, *supra* n. 21, at No. 5.

and may not affect production processes that take place abroad. But next to this relative concept of "public morals" there is an "international public morals" concept that has emerged from the evolution of mandatory norms for the protection of human rights.[70] These norms concern the prohibition of: slavery; the extreme forms of child labour; and the prohibition of gross and systematic violations of human rights including workers' rights. With regard to these fundamental human rights, one can speak of a form of international public morality capable of adding an international dimension to the clause of Article XX(a). In this sense, the general exception of Article XX(a) is susceptible of extraterritorial application to reach practices and production methods that constitute a breach of basic care of universal human rights. This interpretation is also consistent with the object and purpose of the "public morals" exception. To appreciate this, we may think of a situation in which a country prohibits audio-visuals and film products depicting scenes of child pornography and paedophilia. Nobody can reasonably expect objections to import restrictions on such materials, which indeed, any decent country would prohibit, freedom of expression and of commerce notwithstanding. Does this mean that we are only protecting "public morals" in the consuming country? Or are we *especially* protecting children in the producing country from becoming the raw material of abhorrent forms of corruption and exploitation? Are we not really restricting trade in the generalised conviction that such sordid exploitation of children must be fought with a common commitment to prevent it all over the world? The recent legislative initiatives in many developed countries to prohibit the organisation of tourism involving sexual exploitation of minors abroad,[71] which in principle are trade restrictive in the area of services, prove that the morality concerns focus on the practices rather than on the products.

Even if we were to concede that the hypothetical import restrictions on pornographic material was *primarily* intended to protect "public morals" in the consumer country, could we not circumvent the public moral obstacle by limiting the distribution of the pornographic materials to restricted private clubs where the perverted consumer would not need the protection of "public morals"? Further, if we believe that child pornography is really bad, is it not then unreasonable and discriminating against unfortunate children in foreign countries to construe "public morals" in a way so as to render irrelevant the practices to which they are subjected in the country of origin and only protect those who may be exposed (willingly) to the final product of their immoral exploitation? The incongruence of such a product-oriented approach is evident.

[70] In this sense see Viviani, *Coordinamento tra valori fondamentali internazionali e statali: la tutela dei diritti dell'uomo e la clausola di ordine pubblico"*, in *Riv.Dir.Int.Priv.Proc.*, 1999, 847.

[71] See, inter alia, Crimes (Child Sex Tourism) Amendment Act 1994 (Australia), s. 50AD; Amendment #54 CPC (Austria); Law 3 August 1998, No. 269, art. 10 (Italy). For a comprehensive survey see ECPAT, *1996—1997, Commercial Sexual Exploitation of Children* (Bangkok, 1997); O'Brain, "The International Legal Framework and Current National Legislative and Enforcement Responses", paper for the 1996 Stockholm World Congress Against Commercial Sexual Exploitation of Children, at http://www.childhub.ch/webpub/csechome.

A more satisfactory approach is to link the idea of "public morals" to the international standards of morality and human dignity and make those standards an integral part of the logical process by which Article XX exceptions are applied.

IV. EXPORT RESTRICTIONS FOR THE PROTECTION OF THE ENVIRONMENT AND HUMAN RIGHTS

The considerations developed in the preceding section may also apply, *mutatis mutandis*, to restrictions on exports which are adopted by a state to prevent the transfer abroad of substances or services that entail a serious risk of harm for the environment or human rights values. On the side of exports, however, the dialectic between free trade and environmental or human values takes a different character in view of the different political and moral context in which export restrictions are to be placed.

Apart from export restriction motivated by security or political considerations, export restrictions for the protection of the environment may be justified under Article XX(g), the "exhaustible resources" exception, in order to prevent, for example, the depletion of endangered species or the destruction of rain forests.[72] By the same token, Article XX will permit export restrictions on products that are deemed to be offensive to "public morals", on cultural objects that constitute part of the national treasures as well as on substances or technologies that are banned or severely restricted because of the serious hazard involved in their use. As long as the export restrictions are enforced in a manner so as to avoid arbitrary discrimination and disguised protectionism,[73] every country has the right to impose them.

The more interesting question, however, is whether there is a duty in certain circumstances to prohibit the export of substances or technologies when their export is likely to cause a high degree of risk for the environment or for human rights. In the abstract world of sovereign and equal states, each state endowed with the capacity autonomously to take control of the risk posed by the presence in its territory of hazardous substances or technologies, the above question would make little sense. Every state should be considered to be free to determine its own preventive measures in relation to the developmental, environmental and social policies that it deems appropriate. In the real world, however, the great disparity in the level of economic and technological development among states entails a different capacity of risk awareness and risk assessment as well as a different capacity in reactive and systematic monitoring of the use of hazardous products or technologies. It goes without saying that such inequality is magnified when on the export side we have a highly industrialised country and on the import side there is a less developed country.

[72] See *supra* n. 42.

[73] See Article XX *chapeau*, *supra* n. 42.

One may choose intentionally to ignore such disparity. The cost of it may be an increasing number of accidents, such as Bhopal,[74] or of international scandals such as those that have involved the traffic in ultra-hazardous waste or serious contamination in foreign countries (Kolko, Mitsubishi etc.). Besides, intentional ignorance of the problem in the name of the paramount value of free trade may be counter-productive in the sense that it may exacerbate disputes surrounding new technologies, such as those raging over genetically modified organisms and products.

A better approach is to address the problem on the basis of the notion of minimum standards of due diligence that every state must adopt in order to prevent damage to the environment, life, and health in foreign importing countries. The standard of due diligence may be construed in light of customary international law, taking into consideration the *Trail Smelter*[75] and the *Corfu Channel*[76] cases, as well as Principle 21 and 2 of the Stockholm[77] and Rio[78] Declarations, respectively. Such a standard may be more precisely identified in light of treaty commitments or of specific instruments of soft law that have been adopted at a multilateral level. Several examples exist of such multilateral instruments in the field of environmental protection. One is the 1989 Basel Convention,[79] which aims at protecting import countries against the hazard of unregulated traffic in hazardous waste by a regime of informed consent, sound disposal requirement and, most recently, of liability for harm.[80] Another example is the UNEP Guidelines on Banned or Severely Restricted Chemicals[81] and the Rotterdam Convention on Prior Informed Consent for Certain Hazardous Chemicals and Pesticides in International Trade, adopted in 1998.[82] Finally, a most recent example, which is the subject of another chapter in this book, is provided by the February 2000 Biosafety Protocol[83] adopted by the conference of the Parties to the Biodiversity Convention in order to meet some of the concerns arising from the export of genetically modified organisms.

The evolution of international safety standards through customary law, international treaties and soft law indicates that the goals of free trade must be

[74] For a comprehensive survey of the Bhopal case see Morehouse and Subramaniam, *The Bhopal Tragedy: What Really Happened and What It Means for American Workers and Communities at Risk* (Council of International and Public Affairs, 1986), p. 1; Zilioli, "Il caso Bhopal e il controllo sulle attività pericolose svolte da società multinazionali", in *Rivista Giuridica dell'Ambiente*, 1987, 199.

[75] *Trail Smelter* case, 3 *RIAA*, 1905.

[76] *Corfu Channel* case [1949] ICJ Reports 244.

[77] See *supra* n. 9.

[78] See *supra* n. 10.

[79] See *supra* n. 29.

[80] See the 1999 Protocol to the Basel Convention, at http://www.unep.ch/basel/COP5/docs/prot-e.pdf.

[81] 1987 UNEP Governing Council Decision on London Guidelines for the Exchange of Informations on Chemicals in International Trade, Doc. UNEP/PIC/WG.2/2, at 9.

[82] 1998 Rotterdam Convention on the Prior Informed Consent Procedure for Certain Hazardous Chemicals and Pesticides in International Trade, Doc. UNEP/FAO/PIC/CONF/2.

[83] 2000 Cartagena Protocol on Biosafety, at http://www.biodiv.org/biosafe/BIOSAFETY-PROTOCOL.htm. See Shoenbaum, *infra* Chapter 2.

reconciled with the duty to prevent serious damage to the environment and health of individuals in foreign countries and in the general environment. Striving for such reconciliation is not only part of the responsibility to prevent environmental damage but also an aspect of the general obligation to respect and ensure respect for fundamental human rights. In an open and non-discriminatory trade system, as the WTO aspires to be, there should be no excuse for practising intentional discrimination between different human beings based solely on economic gain and on the location of the people exposed to risk. When preparing and implementing regulatory schemes applicable to substances posing a high risk for life and the environment, the value of life and health of the people affected in the importing country must be taken into consideration as well. Conscious discrimination, consisting in exempting exports from safeguards required for banned or strictly controlled substances, and from the prior informed consent of the importing country does not conform to the obligation to prevent harm to the environment or health and life of the people beyond the limits of national jurisdiction.

V. PRINCIPLES FOR DISPUTE SETTLEMENT

In the preceding analysis, I have tried to indicate the latitude of discretion left to individual states in the adoption of trade-related measures for environmental or human rights ends. Such analysis supports the conclusion that, without sacrificing the principles and the objectives of GATT/WTO, ample room is left for the pursuit of public policies aimed at nature conservation and the protection of human values. Now, I will try to propose a set of operational principles that, consistent with the law of treaties, should be applied to settle the increasing number of disputes arising in this area of international law and practice.

The principle of "presumption of conformity"

This principle, as we all know, plays an important role in the application of international law by municipal courts. It should also be applied to create a presumption of compatibility of GATT/WTO rules with earlier treaties concerning the protection of the environment and of human rights to which the parties to a dispute are bound. As the WTO was established in 1994 and went into effect in 1995, this criterion would apply to the overwhelming majority of multilateral treaties applicable to the environment and human rights. In this regard, we must note that the contracting parties to WTO are, for the most part, also contracting parties to the relevant environmental and human rights treaties. Furthermore, at no time during the Uruguay Round negotiations were reservation made as to the compatibility of WTO rules with existing environmental and human rights treaties. On the contrary, it appears that trade restriction contained in some nature conservation treaties, such as CITES and the Montreal Protocol on the ozone, were expressly considered to be GATT compatible.[84] Thus, this is persuasive evidence that the members of WTO consider the obligations under WTO to be compatible with the obligations undertaken pursuant to prior environmental and human rights treaties. In this situation it is clear that Article 41 of the Vienna Convention[85] does not operate to infer or presume a modification through successive agreements among the WTO members of earlier environmental or human rights agreements to which all or some of them are parties. At the same time, one should be cautious in applying Article 30 of the Vienna Convention[86] since, in the present context, it is not correct to postulate a relationship of incompatibility between trade obligations, on the one hand, and environmental and human rights obligations on the other. On the contrary, the preamble of the agreement establishing the WTO recognises that trade and economic endeavour must be conducted in a way so as to allow "optimal use of the world resources in accordance with the objective of sustainable development, seeking both to project and preserve the enviironment".[87]

The principle of evolutive interpretation

This principle entails that, in construing GATT/WTO provisions, account must be taken of the evolving body of international norms. Article 31[88] encapsulates this principle in its paragraph 3(c) which states: "[t]here shall be taken into account, together with the context . . . any relevant rule of international law applicable in the relations between the parties". There is no doubt that among the rules of international law applicable between the WTO parties there are rules concerning the protection of the environment and of human rights, two areas among the most developed in international law today in relation to which an overarching duty of international cooperation is widely accepted. The Appellate Body of the WTO, in the 1998 decision concerning the US ban on the import of shrimp,[89] has upheld the principle of evolutive interpretation of GATT law by recognising that the notion of exhaustible resources under Article XX(g) must be interpreted not in light of the original intent of the GATT Parties, but in light of present realities and of the emerging necessity to cooperate in the enforcement of conservation of endangered species. Likewise, as we

[84] For CITES see the letter from G. Patterson (GATT) to F. G. Nichols (IUCN) cited in Wold, "The Convention on International Trade in Endangered Species of Wild Flora and Fauna", in Houseman et al. (eds), *The Use of Trade Measures in Select Multilateral Agreements* (1995), p. 165; for the Montreal Protocol see Lang, in Wolfrum (ed.), Enforcing Environmental Standards: Economic Mechanisms as Viable Means? (Berlin, 1995), p. 265.

[85] See the 1969 Vienna Convention on the Law of Treaties, 1155 *UNTS* 331, Art. 41.

[86] *Ibid.*, Art. 30.

[87] See *supra* n. 12.

[88] *Ibid.*, Art. 31.

[89] See *supra* n. 25.

have pointed out *supra*, a principle of dynamic interpretation could help identify the content of the general provision of "public morals" at Article XX(a). The interpretation of this provision, rather than referring to the meaning of "public morals" at the time of the adoption of the GATT in 1947, should take into account the evolution of universal human rights,[90] in the period from 1948 to the present, and their constitutive role as an element of international public morality.

The concept of "necessity"

This concept surfaces in various provisions of GATT, notably Article XX paragraphs (a) and (b), concerning "public morals" and the protection of life and health. However, no definition is provided for such a concept nor can any conclusive indication be found in the context of the GATT agreement as to what must be considered "necessary" to protect such values. Unfortunately, the practice of GATT has evolved around a misconceived idea of necessity as proof, to be given by the state invoking an Article XX exception, that no alternative measures were available which would have been less restrictive of trade (*Canadian Salmon, Tuna /Dolphins).*[91] Such approach does not rest on any textual or logical basis. On the contrary, it seems to distort the ordinary meaning of the terms used in Article XX. The language is clear and when it permits the adoption of measures "necessary to protect human, animal or plant life or health" or "public morals" it must mean what it says: that states must first establish that protection of the above value is required or indispensable and that the measures adopted are the means to the end of ensuring such protection. To transform the concept of necessity into an incremental cost/benefit analysis test to establish whether the disputed measures have the least impact on trade among an infinite variety of measures that could have been adopted, is to do violence to the plain meaning of Article XX. The correct interpretation of this article, and one that avoids arbitrary or protectionist uses of its exceptions, is to construe the concept of necessity in an impartial and objective manner by referring to international standards, when such standards exist in the relevant areas of nature protection and "public morals". When no international standards exists, the case for the necessity of protective measures must rest on available science and adequate risk assessment, as provided for in the SPS agreement discussed *supra*, or on a good faith determination of the appropriate levels of protection pursuant to legitimate public policies of the importing state.

[90] See *supra*, text and n. 69.

[91] See *Canadian Herring and Salmon*, Report of the Panel, 35th Supp. 98 BISD; *United States—Restrictions on Imports of Tuna*, *supra* n. 25.

The "proportionality" principle

Once ascertained that a given protective measure is "necessary" pursuant to the above test, the proportionality principle may play an important additional role in assessing the legitimacy of trade restrictions under the GATT/WTO system. The proportionality test focuses on the balance between the cost imposed on trade by a national measure and the benefits that such measure is intended to ensure in terms of environmental or human rights protection. This test requires a sophisticated dispute settlement mechanism capable of evaluating, with an ample margin of discretion, whether the means exceed the goals and whether the same goal of protecting one of the values covered by Article XX exceptions could be achieved by less trade-restrictive measures. There is no reason to think that the WTO dispute settlement organs, the Panels and the Appellate Body, are not in a position to administer this test. As a matter of fact they have already applied this test in various cases (see *supra*) although in the wrong way, i.e. in place of the necessity test rather than in addition to it. A good model for the application of the proportionality test is provided by the European Court of Justice. In the well known *Danish Bottles* case,[92] the Court held that the Danish measures imposing a ban on plastic and metal containers for beverages was legitimate because it was necessary to pursue one of public interest objectives (environmental protection) capable of trumping the free commerce clause of Article 28 (ex 30) of the EC Treaty. Nevertheless, the Court struck down the part of the Danish law that required a cumbersome system of governmental licences to authorise the form and quality of the glass containers. Such licensing system was considered excessively burdensome for the foreign producers when compared to the declared need of protecting the environment from disposable metal and plastic containers.

VI. CONCLUSION

The establishment of the WTO represents an important step toward the realisation of the age- old objective of freeing human beings from governmental constraints on their economic freedom. The removal of barriers to trade and the implementation of a global trading system based on the principles of non-discrimination and non-protectionist treatment of national products are the indispensable means to achieve such economic freedom. In accepting and supporting the WTO, the great majority of the states that compose the international community have clearly indicated that they consider freedom of trade as a positive value of international law and, indeed, an essential condition for the economic progress and material well-being of all peoples. In this sense, the

[92] Case 302/86, *Commission* v. *Denmark* [1988] ECR 4607.

creation of the WTO is also a contribution to the liberal ideas of individual liberty and political democracy which historically have flourished whenever and wherever civil society has struggled for economic freedom and for the removal of public interventions in favour of privileges and special interests.[93] Nevertheless, at a time when humanity is reaching unprecedented levels of economic well-being, which still coexist with the abject poverty and environmental and social degradation of many nations, it may be helpful for international lawyers to reflect on what is the ultimate goal of economic freedom. There seems to be no dispute that the fundamental goals are wealth maximisation, growth and material progress of peoples. The underlying idea in this chapter is that economic freedom is also a means for the moral and civil progress of the national and international society. The analysis of the relevant international norms hopefully has demonstrated that material progress predicated by the contemporary trade agenda can be pursued without sacrificing the moral and civil progress represented by the advancement of human dignity and the protection of the environment that supports our existence.

[93] For an illuminating essay on the origins of the liberal thought and on the relationship between economic freedom and political liberty, see R. Vivarelli, "Libertà politica e libertà economica", in A. Cardini and F. Pulitini (eds), *Cattolicesimo e liberalismo* (Rubbettino Editore, 2000), p. 23 *et seq*.

2

International Trade in Living Modified Organisms

THOMAS J. SCHOENBAUM*

I. INTRODUCTION

NEW TECHNOLOGIES BRING new problems as well as benefits. New technologies also involve unknown dangers and fears. So it is with biotechnology and living modified organisms (LMOs).

Living modified organisms, also called genetically modified organisms (or GMOs), are living organisms that contain novel combinations of genetic material as a result of the application of biotechnology. Thus far the principle introduction of LMOs has been in agriculture. Dozens of agricultural biotechnology products are on the market and more are on the way.[1] Over thirty varieties of biotech crops have been approved for sale in the USA, and US and Canadian farmers planted 81 million acres of bio-engineered seed in 1999, which accounted for 47 per cent of the US soybean harvest and 37 per cent of the US corn crop.[2] Virtually every processed food sold in the USA today contains LMOs of some kind.[3]

Of course, the manipulation of genetic traits of agricultural plants is not new. Natural selection and breeding techniques have long been used to develop favourable plant varieties. What is new is that through genetic bio-engineering desirable traits can now be directly implanted from genes derived from totally different varieties of living organisms.

* This chapter was presented originally at a conference, "Trade, the Environment, and Human Rights", at the University of Siena, Italy, 8–10 April 2000.

1 See "To Plant or not to Plant," *The Economist*, 15 January 2000, p. 30.

2 Source: Biotechnology Industry Association, Washington D.C. as reported by *USA Today*, 13 January 2000, p. 1.

3 "Sticky Labels", *The Economist*, 1 May 1999., pp. 75–6. In the USA, three governmental agencies regulate the introduction of genetically-modified plants and foods: the US Department of Agriculture has responsibility for protecting plants and US agriculture under the Federal Plant Pest Act, 7 U.S.C. §§ 150aa–190jj; the Food and Drug Administration regulates novel foods under the Federal Food, Drug, and Cosmetic Act, 21 U.S.C. §§ 301–395; and the US Environmental Protection Agency regulates genetic techniques to develop plants that produce their own pesticides under the Federal Insecticide, Fungicide, and Rodenticide Act, 7 U.S.C. §§ 136–136y.

So far the purpose of most genetic alterations has been to enhance traits useful in the production or marketing of foods. Examples are tolerance of weed-killing herbicides, resistance to insects, improvement in taste, colour and lengthened shelf-life. However, a new generation of LMOs could provide medical or nutritional benefits to consumers, such as foods with less saturated fat and more vitamin and nutritional value. LMOs could also benefit the environment by allowing greater production per acre, freeing rural lands for parks, natural areas and green space, and reducing the need for environmentally destructive pesticides and chemical fertilizers. Thus, we may be at the dawn of an agricultural revolution that will benefit society.

Nevertheless, controversy over LMOs is increasing. Criticism began in Europe, where food safety was an important issue because of several unrelated incidents, such as bovine spongiform encephalopathy ("mad cow disease") that resulted in an EU ban on imports of beef from Britain and the chicken-dioxin problem in Belgium in 1999. Recently, unease over LMOs has spread to the USA and other countries.

Critics make several points: first, although there is no scientific evidence of any danger to consumers of genetically modified foods, some urge caution and demand that GM foods be labelled or marketed separately. Secondly, environmental groups argue LMOs may pose a danger for the environment if LMO plants invade native ecosystems; cross-pollinate with native plants; or prove toxic to native species of animals, birds or butterflies. Again, there is little evidence of this apart from a study on monarch butterflies[4] and a flawed British study over the effects of GM potatoes on experimental animals.[5] Thirdly, critics argue that widespread LMO technology in agriculture will benefit a few large multinational companies and allow them to establish a global cartel to the detriment of the world's consumers and farmers. An antitrust suit has already been filed on this ground in the USA.[6] In developing countries critics argue that using GM seeds will disrupt traditional farming practices and raise costs to farmers.[7] Thus the issue of LMOs raises serious health, environmental, economic and social issues, but the nature and extent of these problems are ill-defined.[8]

[4] An entomological study indicated that monarch butterfly caterpillars could be killed by pollen from GM corn crops planted in the vicinity of the milkweed plants on which the caterpillars feed. This conclusion was debated at a Monarch Butterfly Research Symposium hosted by the US Environmental Protection Agency in Chicago, 2 November 1999. Peer reviewers minimized the problem, but research is continuing on possible "sub-lethal" effects on caterpillars, (1999) 22 *Int'l Envt. Rptr.* (BNA) 822 ("Current Developments", 10 November).

[5] A study carried out in the United Kingdom which concluded that GM potatoes have negative impacts on the health of rats was criticised by scientists as "half-baked" and "hopelessly confused" because of procedural flaws: *The Economist*, 16 October 1999, p. 85.

[6] The case is *Bruce Pickett et al.* v. *Monsanto Co.*, Case No. 1: 99CVO3337 (Antitrust), United States District Court for the District of Columbia.

[7] Susan Boensch Meyer, "Genetically Modified Organisms" (1998) *YB Colo. J. Int'l Envt. L. & Pol'y* 102, 111.

[8] For perhaps the most comprehensive review to date of the issues and problems as well as recommendations for future research, see *Genetically Modified Pest-Protected Plants: Science and Regulation* (US National Academy of Sciences, 2000).

While LMOs obviously pose a great many legal and political issues, the focus of this chapter is on the regulation of LMOs in international trade. Two international agreements now regulate LMO/GMOs. The first, the Agreement on the Application of Sanitary and Phytosanitary measures (SPS Agreement)[9] which was negotiated at the World Trade Organisation (WTO) at the conclusion of the Uruguay Round in 1994, covers measures restricting international trade in LMOs for the purpose of protecting human, animal and plant health and safety. The second, the Cartagena Protocol on Biosafety[10] of 29 January 2000, is a broader agreement that governs the transboundary movement of most bio-engineered products. The two international regimes overlap to some extent, and this sows the seeds of future problems.[11]

II. AGREEMENT ON THE APPLICATION OF SANITARY AND PHYTOSANITARY MEASURES

The SPS Agreement is based on a provision of the 1947 General Agreement on Tariffs and Trade (GATT),[12] which contains a "general exception" for measures to protect human, plant, or animal health and safety.[13] Article 2 of the SPS Agreement sets out two relevant "basic rights and obligations":

> "2. Members shall ensure that any sanitary and phytosanitary measure is applied only to the extent necessary to protect human, animal or plant life or health, is based on scientific principles and is not maintained without sufficient scientific evidence, except as provided for in paragraph 7 of Article 5.
>
> 3. Members shall ensure that their sanitary and phytosanitary measures do not arbitrarily or unjustifiably discriminate between Members where identical or similar conditions prevail, including between their own territory and that of other Members. Sanitary and phytosanitary measures shall not be applied in a manner which would constitute a disguised restriction on international trade".

Article 3 of the SPS Agreement sets out a further obligation on WTO members to engage in a process to *harmonise* their phytosanitary measures "on as wide a basis as possible", in conformance with or based upon international standards.[14] However, higher-level national standards may be employed "if there is a scientific justification or as a consequence of the level of . . . protection a Member determines to be appropriate in accordance with . . . Article 5 [of the Agreement]". Article 5, in turn, requires that members undertake a "risk

[9] Legal Texts of the Uruguay Round (WTO, 1994) 69.

[10] Conference of the Parties to the Convention on Biological Diversity, First Extraordinary Meeting, Montreal, 24–28 January 2000, Draft Final Text.

[11] This was duly predicted by John H. Barton, "Biotechnology, the Environment, and International Agricultural Trade", (1996) 9 *Geo. Int'l Envt'l L. Rev.* 95, 112–15.

[12] 30 October 1947, TIAS No. 1700, 55 *UNTS* 188. As a result of the Uruguay Round of trade negotiations, this was repromulgated as "GATT 1994": Legal Texts, *supra* n. 11 at 481.

[13] Art. XX(b) GATT. This is specifically referred to by Art. 2.4 of the SPS Agreement.

[14] Art. 3.1 and 3.2 SPS.

assessment", taking "into account economic factors", when adopting national standards.[15] Members must also minimise "negative trade effects"[16] and avoid "arbitrary or unjustifiable" discrimination and "disguised restrictions on international trade".[17] Measures also cannot be more trade restrictive than required to achieve their objectives.[18]

In cases where scientific evidence is insufficient, provisional restrictions may be adopted, but the information needed for a more objective assessment of risk must be obtained "within a reasonable period of time".[19]

These provisions were first interpreted in the WTO decision on *Hormones*.[20] In ruling against the EU import ban on hormone-fed beef, the WTO Appellate Body made a number of points:

(1) In a case where a WTO member seeks to enforce an SPS measure that differs from international norms, it has the burden of justifying such a measure after a complaining member has made a prima facie case of violation of a provision of the SPS Agreement.[21]

(2) A WTO panel is entitled to review a national measure on the basis of an "objective assessment of the facts of the case and the applicability of and conformity with the relevant agreements".[22]

(3) It is "less that clear" that the precautionary principle is a principle of general or customary international law, and this cannot, in any case, override the provisions of the SPS Agreement.[23]

(4) Where a WTO member exercises its right under Article 3.3 of the SPS Agreement to set its own level of SPS protection, it must have "sufficient scientific evidence" gathered as a result of a "risk assessment" required under SPS Article 5.[24]

The key interpretative problem in the *Hormones* case involved Article 3.3, which ambiguously provides as follows:

> "Members may introduce or maintain sanitary or phytosanitary measures which result in a higher level of sanitary or phytosanitary protection than would be achieved by measures based on the relevant international standards, guidelines or recommendations, if there is a scientific justification, or as a consequence of the level of sanitary or phytosanitary protection a Member determines to be appropriate in accordance with the relevant provisions of paragraphs 1 through 8 of Article 5. Notwithstanding

[15] Art. 5.1–5.3 SPS.

[16] Art. 5.4 SPS.

[17] Art. 5.5 SPS.

[18] Art. 5.6 SPS.

[19] Art. 5.7 SPS.

[20] European Communities, *Measures Concerning Meat and Meat Products*, WTO Doc. WT/DS 26/AB/R and WT/DS48/AB/R (World Trade Organisation Appellate Body, 16 January 1998) ("*Hormones*").

[21] *Ibid.* para. 109.

[22] *Ibid.* paras 118–19.

[23] *Ibid.* paras 123–5.

[24] *Ibid.* para. 177.

the above, all measures which result in a level of sanitary or phytosanitary protection different from that which would be achieved by measures based on international standards, guidelines or recommendations shall not be inconsistent with any other provision of this Agreement".

The EC argued that the "or" clause allows national standards for which there is simply "a scientific justification" that satisfies Article 2.2 without a risk assessment meeting the standards of Article 5.[25] The Appellate Body rejected this argument, citing the "notwithstanding" clause to mean that all higher protection measures must meet the standards of Article 5.[26] This effectively transforms the "or" in Article 3.3 into an "and".

In a subsequent decision under the SPS Agreement, the WTO Appellate Body clarified some of the key concepts of Article 5. The occasion was review of an import prohibition taken by Australia on fresh, chilled, and frozen salmon.[27] The Appellate Body ruled that the import measures in question did not comply with Article 5 and, by implication, with the standards of Article 2 of the SPS Agreement.

In particular, the Appellate Body addressed three important points. First, it developed the standards for risk assessment under Article 5.1:

"[W]e consider that, in this case, a risk assessment within the meaning of Article 5.1 must:

(1) *identify* the diseases whose entry, establishment or spread a Member wants to prevent within its territory, as well as the potential biological and economic consequence associated with the entry, establishment or spread of these diseases;

(2) *evaluate the likelihood* of entry, establishment or spread of these diseases according to the SPS measures which might be applied".

The Appellate Body faulted Australia for failing to meet the standard for a risk assessment, specifically by inadequately assessing the biological and economic consequences of potential diseases as well as inadequately evaluating the effectiveness of the import measures in reducing these risks.[28]

Secondly, the import measures undertaken by Australia were held to be arbitrary, unjustifiable, and disguised restrictions on international trade in violation of Article 5.5 because the import bans were levied only against ocean-caught Pacific salmon, while other imported fish not banned carried similar risks of diseases.[29]

[25] *Ibid.* para. 174.

[26] *Ibid.* paras 175–6.

[27] *Australia—Measures Affecting Importation of Salmon*, WTO Doc. WT/DS18/AB/R (World Trade Organisation Appellate Body, 6 November 1998). A similar case was decided by a WTO Dispute Settlement Panel, which ruled that Japan violated Art. 2.2 and 5.6 of the SPS Agreement by maintaining phytosanitary measures without sufficient scientific evidence and failing to ensure that they were not more trade restrictive than necessary. Japan also breached its duty of transparency under para. 1 of Annex B and Art. 7 of the SPS Agreement: *Japan—Measures Affecting Agricultural Products*, WTO Doc. WT/DS76/R (World Trade Organisation Panel Report, 27 October 1998).

[28] *Australia—Measures Affecting Importation of Salmon*, *supra* n. 29, paras 128–38.

[29] *Ibid.* paras 141–78.

Thirdly, the Appellate Body set out its interpretation of Article 5.6 of the SPS Agreement:

> "194. We agree with the Panel that Article 5.6 and, in particular, the footnote to this provision, clearly provides a three-pronged test to establish a violation of Article 5.6. As already noted, the three elements of this test under Article 5.6 are that there is an SPS measure which:
> (1) is reasonably available taking into account technical and economic feasibility;
> (2) achieves the Member's appropriate level of sanitary or phytosanitary protection; and
> (3) is significantly less restrictive to trade than the SPS measure contested".

The Appellate Body found that it was not in a position to evaluate whether there was another measure that achieves the same level of sanitary protection.[30] However, the import ban could not be maintained in the face of an inadequate risk assessment and the arbitrary and unjustifiable discrimination involved.

III. THE CARTAGENA BIOSAFETY PROTOCOL

The Cartagena Biosafety Protocol (BSP) effectively covers ground already addressed by the WTO in the SPS Agreement. However, it attempts a reconciliation with this Agreement by stating that rights and obligations under other international agreements are preserved.[31] However, the Protocol is not to be subordinated to the SPS Agreement.[32] This will make it difficult to resolve the inevitable conflicts between the two agreements.

Importantly, the Biosafety Protocol sets up a Clearing-House, which is intended to be a means of sharing information on all aspects of international information on biotechnology.[33] This will include information on national laws and regulations, international agreements, importation decisions, and risk assessments or environmental reviews. This Clearing-House will be an important institution that will allow harmonisation of risk assessment and management techniques and will be a source of transparency to dispel myths about the dangers of GM products.

The Biosafety Protocol divides LMOs into two groups for the purpose of international regulatory action. First, the transboundary movements of living modified organisms (LMOs) are subject to an "Advance Informed Agreement" procedure under which the transboundary movement may proceed only after advance written consent by the competent national authority of the putative importing state.[34] The Advance Informed Agreement procedure (AIA proce-

[30] *Australia—Measures Affecting Importation of Salmon*, *supra* n. 29, para. 211.
[31] Biosafety Protocol, Preamble.
[32] *Ibid.*
[33] Art. 20 BSP.
[34] Art. 10 BSP.

dure) involves several steps: (1) notification by the party of export;[35] (2) acknowledgement of receipt of notification by the party of import;[36] (3) a decision procedure;[37] and (4) possible review of decisions in the light of new scientific information. Decisions regarding importation must be made using scientifically sound risk assessment procedures and recognized risk assessment techniques.[38] Importantly, however, lack of scientific certainty due to insufficient scientific evidence can be resolved in favour of banning importation.[39] Risk management techniques also may be used by the importing state.[40]

There are several exceptions to the AIA procedure: (1) pharmaceuticals;[41] (2) transit LMOs;[42] (3) contained-use LMOs;[43] and (4) LMOs "intended for direct use as food, feed, or for processing".[44] In addition, the Conference of the Parties may exempt other LMOs from the AIA Procedure.[45]

LMOs intended for direct use as food, feed, or for processing are subject to a less rigorous regulatory regime. This is appropriate because most such LMOs also are subject to the WTO's SPS Agreement. Food, feed and process LMOs (FFP-LMOs) are not subject to the AIA Procedure, but a party may make a decision to ban or limit imports of FFP-LMOs under its "domestic regulatory framework" as long as it is "consistent with the objective of the [Biosafety] Protocol".[46]

Obviously, this opens the door to import regulation, subject to the international discipline of the WTO's SPS Agreement. Thus, it should not be difficult to harmonize the BSP with the SPS Agreement except for one important point. The BSP explicitly adopts the precautionary principle for the regulation of FFP-LMOs, allowing import regulation even in the face of "lack of scientific certainty due to insufficient scientific information".[47] This undoubtedly will result in future conflict with the SPS Agreement, which allows the precautionary principle only for preliminary regulatory decisions.[48]

The BSP also breaks new ground compared with the SPS Agreement in subjecting LMOs to international standards regarding transport, packaging, and labeling.[49] FFP-LMOs, in particular, are subject to labelling and identification in three respects: (1) that they "may contain" LMOs, (2) that they are not

[35] Art. 8 BSP.
[36] Art. 9 BSP.
[37] Art. 10 BSP.
[38] Art. 15 BSP.
[39] Art. 10.6 BSP.
[40] Art. 16 BSP.
[41] Art. 5 BSP.
[42] Art. 6 BSP.
[43] *Ibid.*
[44] Art. 7.1–7.2 BSP.
[45] Art. 7.4 BSP.
[46] Art. 11 BSP.
[47] Art. 11.8 BSP.
[48] See discussion accompanying nn. 53–6 *infra*.
[49] Art. 18 BSP.

intended for intentional introduction into the environment, and (3) that they specify a contact for further information.[50]

The BSP also envisages the development of a standard international labelling system. LMOs intended for introduction into the environment are subject to a different labelling regime that identifies them as LMOs, specifies their identity and relevant traits, requirements for safe handling, storage, transport and use, a contact point for further information, the name of the exporter, and a declaration of compliance with regulatory requirements.

Additional provisions of the BSP require notification of any international transboundary movement of an LMO[51] and prevention of illegal transboundary movements.[52] The Secretariat and Conference of the Parties, and the financial mechanism of the Convention on Biological Diversity also serve the BSP.[53] Provision is made for monitoring, reporting, and the assessment and review of compliance.[54] The important matter of liability and redress for damages is left for future consideration, but the parties "shall endeavor to complete this process within four years".[55] The BSP will enter into force ninety days after the fiftieth ratification is received.[56]

IV. EVALUATION AND SYNTHESIS

Can these two agreements be reconciled? Who will decide the inevitable conflicts and disputes? Are these two international regimes reasonable and workable? The best way of reconciling and synthesising the two agreements is to read them together as setting up two distinctly different procedures for regulation in international trade.

On the one hand are LMOs intended for direct use as food, feed, or for processing. These are largely exempt from the BSP and are left to the discipline of the SPS Agreement. As such FFP-LMOs can be sold in international trade without advance informed agreement, and any restrictions on trade will have to meet all the requirements of the SPS Agreement, most importantly scientific justification as the result of a risk assessment. Trade restrictions also cannot involve arbitrary or unjustifiable distinctions or a disguised restriction on international trade.

On the other hand, the transboundary movement of non-FFP-LMOs (with minor exceptions), in particular those intended for introduction into the environment, are subject to a much stricter international regulatory regime, the Advance Informed Agreement procedure of the BSP. This ensures that inter-

[50] Art. 18(b) BSP.
[51] Art. 17 BSP.
[52] Art. 25 BSP.
[53] Arts 28–31 BSP.
[54] Arts 33–35 BSP.
[55] Art. 27 BSP.
[56] Art. 37 BSP.

national trade in such LMOs will not take place absent the written consent of the country of import. This AIA procedure requires a risk assessment under the BSP, but the precautionary principle applies.

FFP-LMOs are not subject to the risk assessment requirements of the BSP or the AIA Procedures. Nevertheless, FFP-LMOs must meet BSP standards in three key respects. First, information concerning regulatory matters and risk assessments must be transmitted to the Biosafety Clearing House.[57] This is a needed reform that should not pose any problems. Secondly, FFP-LMOs must comply with the BSP provisions on handling, transport, packaging and identification.[58] Most notably this involves development of an international labelling regime.[59] Again, this should not pose any problems. The development of international labelling requirements is much preferable to having to comply with a large variety of national labelling requirements. Moreover, the weak "may contain" labelling requirement will not necessitate the segregation of GMO foods; GMOs can continue to be combined with non-GMO foods as is now the case.

The third and by far most important point the BSP adds to regulation of FFP-LMOs under the SPS Agreement is the language of BSP Article 11.8 which states as follows:

> "8. Lack of scientific certainty due to insufficient relevant scientific information and knowledge regarding the extent of the potential adverse effects of a living modified organism on the conservation and sustainable use of biological diversity in the Party of import, taking also into account risks to human health, shall not prevent that Party from taking a decision, as appropriate, with regard to the import of that living modified organism intended for direct use as food or feed, or for processing in order to avoid or minimize such potential adverse effects".

This provision is a statement of the precautionary principle as a method of dealing with scientific uncertainty.[60] Under the BSP, it is fully applicable to national trade restrictions involving FFP-LMOs. *In effect, therefore, Article 11.8 injects the precautionary principle into the SPS Agreement.* This effectively reverses the finding of the WTO Appellate Body in the *Hormones* case that the precautionary principle is not yet customary international law capable of overriding the specific provisions of the SPS Agreement.

The key question is, therefore, although the *Hormones* case itself will be unaffected by the BSP, since hormone-fed beef is not an LMO, will an import ban of a GM food be upheld without sufficient scientific evidence as required by the

[57] Arts 11 and 20 BSP.

[58] Art. 18 BSP.

[59] Art. 18.2(a) BSP.

[60] The "precautionary principle" appears in a number of international documents and agreements, but has never been definitively codified, and scholars differ in the content and whether it is an emerging norm of international law. A version of the precautionary principle was adopted as Principle 15 of the Rio Declaration on Environment and Development, a non-binding declaration adopted in 1992. See Edith Brown Weiss, Stephen C. McCaffrey, Daniel B. McGraw, Paul C. Szasz and Robert E. Lutz, *International Environmental Law and Policy* (1998), pp. 127–35.

Appellate Body in the *Hormones* case? The answer to this question depends on several factors.

First, does Article 11.8 extend the precautionary principle to human health? The wording is clumsy: "adverse effects of a living modified organism on the conservation and sustainable use of biological diversity in the party of import, taking into account risks to human health". Clearly this applies the precautionary principle to biological diversity, but it is less direct regarding human health concerns. Yet it would be extraordinary to interpret Article 11.8 as protecting only animal and plant health and welfare. Surely the phrase "taking into account" is intended to allow the precautionary principle to be applied to human health as well.

Secondly, what is the relationship between the two treaties? This is addressed in the Preamble to the BSP as follows:

> "*Emphasizing* that this Protocol shall not be interpreted as implying a change in the rights and obligations of a Party under any existing international agreements.
>
> *Understanding* that the above recital is not intended to subordinate this Protocol to other international agreements".

These two statements appear to cancel one another out to some degree. The matter may be resolved with reference to the Vienna Convention on the Law of Treaties.[61] Article 30 on the application of successive treaties relating to the same subject matter,[62] would not seem to apply in the light of the Preamble, which clearly intends both Agreements to be regarded on the same level; neither is intended to be superior to the other. Thus, the applicable rule of interpretation would be Article 31.3 of the Vienna Convention, which provides that "There shall be taken into account, together with the context, any subsequent agreement between the parties regarding the interpretation of the treaty or the application of its provisions".

The application of this rule of interpretation would appear to mean that the statement of the precautionary principle in Article 11.8 BSP is intended to supplement the risk assessment requirements of the SPS Agreement. This interpretation is the only one that gives maximum effect to both the BSP and SPS Agreements so that neither cancels out the other. This interpretation, however, has a great impact: it potentially reverses the Appellate Body's reasoning in the *Hormones* case. Specifically, it would seem to allow import restrictions on GM food in the face of insufficient scientific evidence as long as a risk assessment was carried out using available scientific evidence and areas of scientific uncertainty were identified and addressed.

[61] U.N. Doc. A/Conf. 39/27 (1969), (1969) 8 *ILM* 679. Done in Vienna on 23 May 1969, entered into force on 27 January 1980.

[62] Article 30 reads as follows in relevant part: "2. When a treaty specifies that it is subject to, or that it is not to be considered as incompatible with, an earlier or later treaty, the provisions of that other treaty will prevail. 3. When all parties to the earlier treaty are parties also to the later treaty but the earlier treaty is not terminated or suspended in operation under article 59, the earlier treaty applies only to the extent that its provisions are compatible with those of the later treaty".

Another point of interpretation arising out of the overlap of the two agreements has to do with the fact that, literally speaking, LMOs in international trade are now subject to a dual barrier approach. This is because the SPS Agreement defines SPS measures broadly to include all legal requirements and procedures applied to protect human, animal or plant life and health.[63] This would include measures passed to implement the AIA procedure of the BSP with respect to LMOs. Thus, it could be argued that trade restrictions represented by the AIA procedures are also subject to the SPS Agreement, which has stricter risk assessment standards. However, this would be clearly duplicative and could not have been intended by the drafters of the BSP despite the Preamble savings-clause language.

Still another point of conflict between the BSP and SPS Agreements will come to the fore when mandatory labelling for GM foods is developed. This is permissible under the "may contain" standard agreed in the BSP. However, mandatory labels as a food safety measure would be subject to the "scientific principles" and "sufficient scientific evidence" standards of the SPS Agreement.[64]

Who will decide these questions and other interpretative disputes over the two agreements? The BSP has no dispute settlement provision but refers to the mechanisms of the Convention on Biological Diversity (BD).[65] Under Article 27 of the CBD, dispute settlement is largely optional.[66] Thus, disputes over these two regimes is likely to be resolved through the WTO dispute settlement mechanism.

V. CONCLUSION

The international regimes agreed upon to regulate trade in living modified organisms are in many respects a reasonable compromise to solve difficult issues

[63] See the definition in Annex A of the SPS Agreement.

[64] SPS Agreement, Annex A, Definition 1. See the discussion in Sara Pardo Quintillan, "Free Trade, Public Health Protection and Consumer Information in the European and WTO Context", (1999) 33 *J. World Trade* 147, 171–2, and 190–1.

[65] Art. 34 BSP.

[66] Art. 27 CBD provides as follows:

"1. In the event of a dispute between Contracting Parties concerning the interpretation or application of this Convention, the parties concerned shall seek solution by negotiation.
2. If the parties concerned cannot reach agreement by negotiation, they may jointly seek the good offices of, or request mediation by, a third party.
3. When ratifying, accepting, approving or acceding to this Convention, or at any time thereafter, a State or regional economic integration organization may declare in writing to the Depositary that for a dispute not resolved in accordance with paragraph 1 or paragraph 2 above, it accepts one or both of the following means of dispute settlement as compulsory:
(a) arbitration in accordance with the procedure laid down in Part 1 of Annex II;
(b) submission of the dispute to the International Court of Justice.
4. If the parties to the dispute have not, in accordance with paragraph 3 above, accepted the same or any procedure, the dispute shall be submitted to conciliation in accordance with Part 2 of Annex II unless the parties otherwise agree.
5. The provisions of this Article shall apply with respect to any protocol except as otherwise provided in the protocol concerned.

and to resolve a key conflict in the trade and environment debate. Although there is to date no credible scientific evidence that LMOs pose a danger either to human health or the environment,[67] there is profound political and public concern in many quarters. The key legal issue in this debate is the extent to which the precautionary principle should be applied. Unfortunately, the BSP and SPS Agreements contradict each other on this point. This will lead to future conflicts. Hopefully, these questions can be worked out in the future.

[67] See the Report of the US Academy of Sciences, *supra* n. 8, at 6.

3

International Trade in Genetically Modified Organisms and Multilateral Negotiations: A New Dilemma for Developing Countries

SIMONETTA ZARRILLI*

I. PROLOGUE

IN ORDER TO be able to export their products, developing countries increasingly have to be able to prove that they comply with the standards and regulations of the importing countries. Standards and regulations are aimed at ensuring, inter alia, that domestically produced and imported products are safe, of good quality and have as little a detrimental effect on the environment as possible. For quite a long time developing countries' main concern in this field has been that their trade partners could use, for protectionist purposes, measures intended to protect health, safety and the environment, or to ensure high product quality. Because of this, developing countries have tried to be vigilant regarding the imposition of unnecessarily strict regulations, and have opposed modifications of the Agreement on Technical Barriers to Trade (TBT) and the Agreement on the Application of Sanitary and Phytosanitary Measures (SPS). They have also opposed modifications of Article XX of the General Agreement on Tariffs and Trade (GATT), which deals with general exceptions to GATT obligations. These modifications were proposed by several developed countries to better accommodate non-trade concerns in the multilateral trading system, especially those related to environmental protection.

However, the situation seems to have become more complex lately. Developing country preoccupations related to market access are still very much present; but these countries are now facing a new challenge related to trade in products whose safety and possible environmental impacts are currently not

* The author is especially grateful to Gabrielle Marceau and Matthew Stilwell for their many comments, especially on the legal aspects of the chapter. Thanks also go to K. Bergholm, S. Briceño, A. Cosbey, M. Gibbs, B. Gosovic, R. Kaukab, C. Pierce, F. Pythoud, P. Roffe, R. Sanchez, H. Torres and J. VanGrasstek for the comments and information provided. Any errors are the author's alone. This chapter is up-to-date as of 30 June 2000.

well known, namely genetically modified organisms (GMOs) and products derived from them. A GMO is an organism in which the genetic material has been altered in a way that does not occur naturally by mating and/or natural recombination.[1] Most developing countries have not yet passed legislation in this field and believe that their limited scientific capacities, their recurrent problems with checking products at the border, and their restricted ability to make their own assessment of the risks and benefits involved do not allow them to manage properly the challenges that GMOs pose. They have therefore called for the establishment of international rules in this field. Once it is in force, the Cartagena Protocol on Biosafety, which represents the multilaterally agreed response to these and other non-trade-related concerns, will provide the legal framework for conducting international trade in GMOs, at least among parties to it, although its relationship with the multilateral trade disciplines set out in the World Trade Organisation (WTO) agreements is unclear. The Protocol gives quite substantial discretionary power to importing countries with regard to the goods they are willing to import. The trade framework established by it is therefore rather different from the one that developing countries have traditionally supported within the WTO.

Thus, there are two sets of challenges facing developing countries. The first is to reconcile the preoccupations related to market access with those related to the need to protect human and animal health and the environment from potentially harmful products which could be introduced through international trade. The second is that WTO members may reach the conclusion that a decision about modifying the multilateral trade rules to accommodate better environment- and health-related concerns cannot be delayed any longer. This could happen because of the magnitude of concerns related to biotechnology, a certain lack of clarity in the Cartagena Protocol and the already existing divergent interpretations of it, and countries' unwillingness to leave the solution of conflicts in this area in the hands of the WTO Panels and Appellate Body.

There are at least four (not mutually exclusive) forums within the WTO where issues related to trade in biotechnology products could be addressed or have already been addressed, directly or indirectly: the Committee on Sanitary and Phytosanitary Measures, the Committee on Technical Barriers to Trade, the Committee on Trade and Environment, the Committee on Agriculture (negotiations on agriculture started in March 2000, in accordance with Article 20 of the Agreement on Agriculture), and, if a new round of multilateral negotiations is launched, possibly an ad hoc working group established within the WTO. However, the way in which international trade in GMOs is going to be regulated is likely to have an impact extending beyond the specific sector. If the WTO system, for instance, allows in the future a more flexible interpretation of the precautionary principle in order to respond to the health and environmental

[1] This definition is included in EC Directive 90/220, *infra* n. 15.

concerns related to trade in GMOs, the same flexible interpretation will probably apply in other fields, such as trade in conventional agricultural products. If, because of the economic interests involved, an effort is made to clarify the relationship between the trade rules in the Cartagena Protocol and those emerging from specific WTO agreements, the same approach is likely to apply to other multilateral agreements containing trade rules. Each negotiating forum has different characteristics, and discussions may reach different results according to where they are held.

Discussions on GMOs are also taking place in multilateral forums other than the WTO, such as the Convention on Biological Diversity, the Codex Alimentarius Commission and the Food and Agriculture Organization (FAO). These forums offer some considerable advantages as compared with the WTO: they are specialised and have technical expertise in the issue at stake; and they are forums where developing countries' concerns are usually heard sympathetically. Nevertheless, decisions taken there may be challenged in the WTO if a WTO Member believes that the decisions taken in other forums are affecting its market access rights.

Developing countries may wish to ready themselves to become active participants in the debate that may start on these issues, so as to ensure that their multifaceted concerns are taken into account and their weaknesses are recognised and addressed.

II. BIOTECHNOLOGY: RISKS AND OPPORTUNITIES

Biotechnology is a revolutionary technology.[2] It offers humanity the power to change the characteristics of living organisms by transferring the genetic information from one organism, across species boundaries, into another organism. These solutions continue the tradition of selection and improvement of cultivated crops and livestock developed over the centuries. However, biotechnology identifies desirable traits more quickly and accurately than conventional plant and livestock breeding and allows gene transfers impossible with traditional breeding. The use of biotechnology in sectors such as agriculture and medicine has produced a growing number of genetically modified organisms and products derived from them. Changing the characteristics of organisms may provide benefits to society, including new drugs and enhanced plant varieties and food. However, biotechnology does not come without risks and uncertainty. Its potential effects on the environment, human health and food security are being actively debated at the national and international levels. Countries' positions depend on many factors, such as their policy awareness, the level of

[2] The Convention on Biological Diversity defines biotechnology as "any technological application that uses biological systems, living organisms, or derivatives thereof, to make or modify products or processes for specific use". The biotechnology industry provides products for human health care, industrial processing, environmental bioremediation, and food and agriculture.

risk they are willing to accept, their capacity to carry out risk assessments in the sector and implement adequate legislation, their perception of the benefits they could gain from biotechnology, and the investments they have already made in the sector.[3] However, there is a sharp contrast at present between the widespread international acceptance of biotechnology's benefits in pharmaceuticals and industrial products, and the widespread concerns about its possible dangers in agricultural and food production.

At present, the perceived benefits of genetically modified crops are better weed and insect control, higher productivity and more flexible crop management. These benefits accrue primarily to farmers and agribusiness, who can obtain higher yields and lower costs. The broader and long-term benefits, however, would be more sustainable agriculture and better food security that would benefit everybody, and especially the developing countries. For instance, breeding for drought tolerance could greatly benefit tropical crops, which are often grown in harsh environments and in poor soils. Increasing the amount of food produced per hectare could be a way to feed the world's growing population, without diverting land from other purposes such as forestry, animal grazing or conservation. Scientists have recently created a strain of genetically altered rice to combat vitamin A deficiency, the world's leading cause of blindness and a malaise that affects as many as 250 million children. Economic development experts describe the vitamin A rice as a breakthrough in efforts to improve the health of millions of poor people, most of them in Asia.[4] The impact of biotechnology on food production, post-harvest losses and the nutritional value of food could improve the livelihoods of millions of people.

The biotechnology industry reports that among the transgenic products on the market in which beneficial product traits have already been included are the following: GM crops that are protected against insect damage and reduce pesticide use[5] (these are already used in corn, cotton and potatoes, and will be used in the future in sunflower, soybeans, canola, wheat and tomatoes); herbicide-tolerant crops that allow farmers to apply a specific herbicide to control weeds without harm to the crop (these are already used in soybeans, cotton, corn, canola and rice, and will be used in the future in wheat and sugar beet); disease-resistant crops that are armed against destructive viral plant diseases with a plant equivalent of a vaccine (sweet potatoes, cassava, rice, corn, squash, papaya and, in the future, tomatoes and bananas); high-performance cooking oils that create healthier products (sunflowers, peanuts and soybeans); delayed-ripening fruits and vegetables that have superior flavour, colour and texture, are

[3] Whereas public funding for agricultural research has stagnated or declined, the biotechnology industry has continued to invest heavily in agricultural research because of the considerable advances made in the area and the strengthening of intellectual property rights for biological material.

[4] See "Generically Altered Rice: A Tool Against Blindness", *International Herald Tribune*, 15–16 January 2000.

[5] The modification involves taking genes from a soil bacterium, called *Bacillus thuringiensis*, and making them part of the plants themselves. The GM plants are toxic only to specific pests.

firmer for shipping and stay fresh longer (tomatoes, and in the future raspberries, strawberries, cherries, tomatoes, bananas and pineapples); nutritionally enhanced foods that offer increased levels of nutrients, vitamins and other healthful phytochemicals (protein-enhanced sweet potatoes and rice, high-vitamin-A canola oil, and increased-antioxidant fruits and vegetables).[6] A shift is occurring from the current generation of "agronomic" traits to the next generation of "quality" traits, which are aimed at improved and specialized nutritional food and feed products.

However, a number of risks are associated with biotechnology.[7]

(1) *Biodiversity protection:* Genetically modified plants may transfer genetic material and associated traits to conventional varieties, developing more aggressive weeds, threatening ecosystems and harming biological diversity. Biodiversity may also be lost, as a result of the displacement of conventional cultivars by a small number of genetically modified cultivars. A number of developing countries could be particularly affected since they are home to a large share of the world's biodiversity.

(2) *Food security*: Genetically modified crops may fail to deal with unexpectedly altered climatic conditions. Biotechnology may change the nature, structure and ownership of food production systems. At present, real food security problems are caused, more than by food shortages, by inequity, poverty and concentration of food production. Biotechnology is likely to further consolidate control in the hands of a few large firms. The "terminator technologies", which employ germination control as an intellectual property protection tool requiring farmers to buy new seed every season, have been mainly developed to help transnational agrochemical firms increase their monopoly over seed production and recoup their investment in R&D.

(3) *Ethical and religious concerns:* Biotechnology allows scientists to move genetic material across species boundaries and allows, for example, animal genes to be placed in plants. This may raise ethical and religious concerns. The patenting of some aspects of human life and the possibility of human cloning give rise to major preoccupations.

(4) *Human and animal life or health:* Genetic modification may change the toxicity, allergenicity or nutritional value of food, and alter antibiotic resistance.

(5) *Economic considerations*: Private sector research in agricultural biotechnology has dramatically increased, driven in part by the possibility of profits supported by intellectual property rights. Moreover, private sector industry has become very centralised. What was once an industry in which small seed

[6] See Biotechnology Industry Organisation, "Transgenic Products on the Market", *Guide to Biotechnology*, (website: http://www.bio.org/food&ag/transgenic_products.html).

[7] See M.T. Stilwell, "Implications for Developing Countries of Proposals to Consider Trade in Genetically Modified Organisms at the WTO", Center for International Environmental Law, Geneva, 1999.

breeders played a major role has now become a global oligopoly dominated by about five leading transnational corporations. A large number of patents have been issued in the sector. If the results of plant research continue to be patented, there is a risk that they may become too expensive for poor farmers, especially in developing countries. Moreover, the private sector invests in areas where there are hopes of a financial return; as a consequence, private science may focus on crops and innovations that are of interest to rich markets and ignore those of interest to poor countries.

(6) *Equity considerations*: Private enterprises and research institutes could gain unremunerated control of the genes of plants native to a number of developing countries, use them to produce superior varieties, and then sell the new varieties back to developing countries at high prices. While the concept of "benefit sharing" is included in the Convention on Biological Diversity, it is not addressed in the WTO Agreement on Trade-Related Aspects of Intellectual Property Rights (the TRIPS Agreement).

In order to evaluate the risks related to biotechnology, a distinction has been suggested between technology-inherent risks and technology-transcending risks.[8] Technology-inherent risks are those associated with threats to human health and the environment. They could be addressed and minimised by instituting state-of-the-art risk management that takes local ecological conditions into account. Proper risk assessment should be carried out. This would allow governments, communities and business to make informed decisions about the risks and benefits inherent in using a particular technology to solve a specific problem. Legislation should be developed to ensure the safe production, transfer, handling, use and disposal of GMOs and their products.

Technology-transcending risks emanate from the political and social context in which a technology is used. The global economy and the country-specific political and social circumstances play a key role in making biotechnology a risk (e.g. increasing the poverty gap within and between societies, loss of biodiversity, negative impact on the ecosystems) or a benefit for local populations (e.g. improved food security, reduced malnutrition).

The above classification of risks, however, may not always prove appropriate for accurately dividing up the ultimate impacts of complex causal chains. For example, the impact of GMOs on biodiversity would fall into both the technology-inherent and the technology-transcending risks. Risks to biodiversity may be caused directly by the modified organisms (through, for instance, the involuntary transfer of genetic material to conventional species) or indirectly (by, for example, interaction with other events, such as changes in agricultural practices or market structure). Similarly, food security may be threatened by "inherent" risks, such as the failure of modified crops to deal with unexpectedly altered

[8] See K.M. Leisinger, "Disentangling Risk Issues", in G.J. Persley (ed.), *Biotechnology for Developing-Country Agriculture: Problems and Opportunities, A 2020 Vision for Food, Agriculture, and the Environment* (International Food Policy Research Institute, 1999).

climate conditions, and by "transcending risks", such as oligopoly control of food supply by a few agrochemical and seed companies. The "inherent" and "transcending" risks cut across all areas. It seems difficult, therefore, to divide them clearly and use risk assessment for the former and other techniques for the latter.

III. THE MARKET FOR GMOS

The global area planted with transgenic crops was 1.7 million hectares in 1996, 11 million hectares in 1997 and 27.8 million hectares in 1998; it reached 39.9 million hectares in 1999, with a twenty-fold increase between 1996 and 1999. Adoption rates for transgenic crops have so far been unprecedented and are the highest for any new technology by agricultural industry standards.[9]

In 1999, almost 99 per cent of the global area planted with genetically modified crops was accounted for by three countries: the USA (28.7 million hectares, representing 72 per cent of the global area), Argentina (6.7 million hectares, equivalent to 17 per cent of the global area) and Canada (4 million hectares, representing 10 per cent of the global area). The remaining 1 per cent was accounted for by China, Australia and South Africa. Production started in Mexico, Spain, France, Portugal, Romania and Ukraine. China's transgenic crop area increase was the largest relative change in 1999, increasing from less than 0.1 million hectares of insect-resistant cotton in 1998 to approximately 0.3 million hectares in 1999, equivalent to 1 per cent of the global share.

As in 1998, the largest increase in transgenic crops in 1999 occurred in the USA, where there was a 8.2 million hectares increase, followed by Argentina with a 2.4 million hectares increase and Canada with a 1.2 million hectares increase.

The seven genetically modified crops grown commercially in 1999 were soybean (54 per cent of the global transgenic crop area), corn/maize (28 per cent of the global transgenic crop area), cotton (9 per cent), canola/rapeseed (9 per cent), potato, squash and papaya.

The global market for transgenic crops products grew rapidly during the period from 1995 to 1999. Global sales of transgenic crops were estimated at US$ 75 million in 1995. In 1999, they reached an estimated US$ 2.2 billion (a thirty-fold increase). The global market for transgenic crops is projected to reach approximately US$ 3 billion in 2000, US$ 8 billion in 2005 and US$ 25 billion in 2010.

However, a proliferation of initiatives at the national and international levels aimed at banning or putting under strict control planting of GMOs and trading in GMOs and GM products, mounting public resistance, refusal by a growing number of food manufacturers and grocery chains to use and sell transgenic

[9] This section is based on: C. James, *Preview. Global Review of Commercialized Transgenic Crops: 1999* (International Service for the Acquisition of Agri-biotech Applications, ISAAA Briefs, No. 12, 1999).

products,[10] and an increasing number of questions about liability are causing an inversion of the industry's growth trend in several countries. Stock prices for agricultural biotech companies are falling and exports of transgenic crops are tumbling. American exports of soybeans to the European Union (EU) plummeted from 11 million tons in 1998 to 6 million tons in 1999, while American corn shipped to Europe dropped from 2 million tons in 1998 to 137,000 tons in 1999, with a combined loss of nearly US$ 1 billion in sales for US agriculture.[11] US exports to Europe could be further affected once legislation is passed in the European Union regarding mandatory labelling of animal feed. The Worldwatch Institute and the American Corn Growers Association estimate that GM planting could be reduced by 25 per cent in 2000 as compared with the previous year, since farmers have serious doubts about whether they will be able to sell genetically modified crops. The seed companies and the American Soybean Association dispute this, arguing that plantings in 2000 are likely to be similar to those in 1999. Although reliable data to evaluate these forecasts will become available only by mid-year,[12] there is a small but significant amount of evidence that public resistance to the use of bio-engineered foods is affecting US farmers' planting decisions. According to the April 2000 report of the United States Agricultural Statistics Board, US farmers appear to be reducing plantings of modified corn—from 33 per cent in 1999 to 25 per cent in 2000. Data are less dramatic for modified cotton and soybeans, but there are some indications that, especially for soybeans, farmer's demand for modified seeds may be stagnating, or falling slightly.[13] On the other hand, China has begun a huge push to commercialize genetically modified crops, with around half of its fields expected to be planted with GM rice, tomatoes, sweet peppers, potatoes and cotton in five to ten years. The reasons for this move are reduced pesticide and herbicide requirements and bumper yields from GM crops. Half of the genetically modified seeds used in China have been developed by local scientists: in 2000 China allocated more than US$ 350 million for research into applying biotechnology to agriculture.[14]

[10] An increasing number of producers and retailers have decided not to produce and stock products with GM ingredients—or which cannot be certified as GM-free—in response to mounting concern among consumers. Frito-Lay, the world's largest producer of snack foods, recently announced that it would stop buying genetically modified corn and soybeans. It is following similar moves by a number of other food companies, including Gerber and H.J. Heinz baby foods, the British chains Iceland and Sainsbury's, Japan's Asahi Breweries, and the supermarket chains Tesco (United Kingdom) and Migros (Switzerland). Nestlé, the world's biggest food company, has stopped buying any grain from genetically altered seed for its European operations. Fast-food chains such as McDonald's and Burger King have declared their intention to stop using GM ingredients. See "International: GMO Politics", *Oxford Analytica Brief*, 13 March 2000, p. 3, and "Vade Retro OGM", *L'Expansion*, 2–15 March 2000, No. 616.

[11] See Halweil B., "Portrait of an Industry in Trouble", *Worldwatch News Brief*, 17 February 2000 (Internet website: http://www.worldwatch.org/alerts/000217.html).

[12] See *Oxford Analytica Brief supra* n. 10.

[13] See Washington Trade Reports, Vol. VIII, No. 7, 11 April 2000.

[14] See "China Sows Seeds of GM Crop Expansion", *The Times*, 29 February 2000; "Differences Widen on Use of Modified Foods", *Financial Times*, 29 February 2000; and "Genetic Engineering: Modified Crops Take Root in China", *BBC World Update*, 7 June 2000.

IV. THE PRESENT REGULATORY FRAMEWORK: SELECTED COUNTRIES

The EC/EU

At the beginning of the 1990s the European Community introduced an approval system for the deliberate (non-accidental) release into the environment of GMOs ("live GMOs") for experimental purposes or as commercial products, with the aim of ensuring a high and uniform level of protection of health and the environment throughout the Community and the efficient functioning of the internal market.[15] This "horizontal" legislation is based on a process-oriented approach, which pays special attention to genetic modification.[16]

Any person wishing to undertake the deliberate release of a GMO for research and development purposes must submit a notification to the competent authorities of the country within whose territory the release is to take place. The notification must include a full risk assessment and details of appropriate safety and emergency response measures. The notifier may proceed with the release only when he/she has obtained consent. Since the Directive came into force, over 1,600 such notifications have been received for over sixty species of plants.[17] In the case of applications for placing on the market products containing or consisting of GMOs additional data, including instructions and conditions for use, are required. Consent is given by the competent authorities of the country concerned, but on behalf of all member states, on the basis of a rather long and complex procedure where, in the event of conflict among member states, the final decision has to be taken by the Commission.[18] The following GM varieties have so far been approved for placing on the market under Directive 90/220/EEC: three insect-resistant maizes, one herbicide-tolerant maize, one herbicide-resistant soya bean,

[15] Council Directive 90/220/EEC, 23 April 1990, OJ 1990 L117/15.

[16] The other part of the horizontal legislation consists of a Directive on the contained use of genetically modified micro-organisms which focuses on the manufacturing process of GMMs (Council Directive 90/219/EEC, 23 April 1990, OJ 1990 L117/1).

[17] For further details see the website http://food.jrc.it/gmo/ maintained by the European Commission.

[18] If the country concerned decides to consent to a proposed release, the dossier is forwarded to the other member countries through the Commission. They can present reasoned objections. If no objections are presented, the competent authority of the country where the authorisation procedure was initiated gives its consent, enabling the product to be placed on the market. If objections are presented, the competent authorities of the member states have to try to reach an agreement. If they do not succeed within sixty days, the Commission has to submit a draft of the proposed measures to a committee composed of the representatives of the member states. The Commission can suggest that the GMO should or should not be authorised, but so far the Commission has always been in favour of authorising the deliberate release. If the committee does not agree with the Commission's draft measure or does not give its opinion, the proposed measures are submitted to the Council. Council decisions can be taken with a qualified majority, but if the Council does not reach consensus within three months, it is up to the Commission to take the final decision. For an analysis of Directive 90/220, see Douma W.Th. and Matthee M., "Towards New EC Rules on the Release of Genetically Modified Organisms", *Review of European Community & International Environmental Law* (1999) 8 Issue 2, 152.

one herbicide-resistant swede-rape, one herbicide-resistant tobacco, one herbicide-tolerant chicory; and three varieties of flowers (carnations). However, since June 1999 a de facto moratorium has been in place on GMO approvals as a response to a chorus of demands across Europe for a ban, or at least some restrictions, on planting genetically modified crops and on importing GM commodities and foods. On the basis of Article 16 of the Directive—which allows a member state provisionally to restrict or prohibit the use and sale of an approved product if it has justifiable reasons for considering that the product constitutes a risk to human health or the environment—Austria, Luxembourg, Germany, France and Greece have banned or restricted the use of GM crop varieties.

Originally, Directive 90/220/EEC made virtually no provision with regard to labelling. Following a 1997 amendment,[19] however, the EC Commission has made labelling mandatory when a product consists of or contains GMOs. For products consisting of a mixture of GMOs and organisms not genetically modified, the possible presence of GMOs must be indicated.

On February 1998 the Commission submitted to the Council a proposal for a Directive amending Directive 90/220/EEC. After the European Parliament had given its opinion, the Commission submitted a new version of its proposal to the Council on March 1999. In December 1999 the Council adopted its common position for a revised Directive.[20] The main innovations of the new Directive are that consent to placing GMOs on the market is limited to a fixed period (renewable), and that a system of compulsory monitoring after GMOs have been placed on the market has been introduced in order to trace and identify any direct or indirect, immediate, delayed or unforeseen effects on human health or the environment. The Directive makes reference to the precautionary principle and to the need to respect ethical principles; it includes public information and consultation. It provides for a common methodology to assess the risks associated with the release of GMOs and a mechanism allowing their release to be modified, suspended or terminated where new information becomes available on the risks of such release. The new text makes it clear that products containing and/or consisting of GMOs covered by the Directive cannot be imported into the EU if they do not comply with its provisions.

The European Parliament approved a number of amendments to the revised text of the Directive on 12 April 2000. There is a call for environmental risk assessment to be strengthened and for the Directive to be further amended and clarified in the light of the Biosafety Protocol. An amendment was also adopted that would require the prior consent of third countries that are importing GMOs. The year 2005 was set as a definitive date for phasing out the use of GMOs that are resistant to antibiotics. The European Commission hopes that this new legal instrument will increase consumers' confidence in the regulatory system. Although the Directive contains rigorous approval and monitoring rules for GMOs, biotech-

[19] Commission Directive 97/35/EC, 18 June 1997, OJ 1997 L169/73.

[20] EC Council, Common Position (EC) No. 12/2000, adopted by the Council on 9 December 1999, OJ 2000 C64/1.

nology companies are supporting it in the hope that it will help to end the *de facto moratorium* on registration of new modified products in the EU.

In addition to "horizontal" legislation, the EC has adopted a number of "vertical" Directives and Regulations. This "vertical" legislation is product-oriented, and deals with specific aspects or products resulting from genetic modification. The introduction of the vertical legislation has altered the hitherto purely process-oriented nature of EC legislation on GMOs.

Legislation related to novel foods and novel food ingredients is part of the "vertical" regulatory approach.[21] It stipulates that, in order to protect public health, guarantee the proper functioning of the internal market and create conditions of fair competition, it is necessary to ensure that novel foods and novel food ingredients[22] are subject to a single safety assessment through a Community procedure before they are placed on the EU market. Companies wishing to market a novel food in the EU are required to submit an application to the competent authority in the member state where they intend to market their product first. A copy of the application should be sent to the EC Commission. For food and food ingredients containing GMOs, a specific environmental risk assessment has to be provided. The competent authority completes an initial safety assessment and forwards it to the Commission. The Commission then copies this assessment to other member states for their comments. If the initial assessment is favourable and no objections are raised by other member states, the product can be marketed. The competent authority may ask for more data or research at any time during this assessment. The competent authorities in other member states may also choose to raise objections or concerns. If objections are raised, or if the initial member state considers that an additional assessment is required, the application will be referred to the EC Standing Committee for Foodstuffs for final agreement, with the EC Scientific Committee for Food being consulted as necessary. If no agreement is reached there, the matter will be referred to the Council of Ministers. The Regulation allows member states to suspend or restrict temporarily the trade in and use of a novel food and food ingredient in their territories if a country, on the basis of new information or the reassessment of existing information, has grounds for considering that the novel food or ingredient endangers human health or the environment (Article 12).

The Novel Foods Regulation incorporates specific labelling rules for products developed through biotechnology. It provides for mandatory labelling and requires that consumers be informed of differences between a new product and existing equivalent products.[23]

[21] Regulation (EC) 258/97, 27 January 1997, OJ 1997 L043/1.

[22] Under the Regulation, novel foods and food ingredients are those which have not yet been used for human consumption to a significant degree within the Community, in particular those containing or derived from GMOs.

[23] The label has to provide the final consumers with information on (a) any characteristic of food property which renders a novel food or food ingredient no longer equivalent to an existing food or

The procedure for authorising the placing on the market of novel foods is expected to be clarified and made more transparent. The European Commission is likely to adopt by the end of 2000 an implementing regulation to clarify the procedures laid down in the Novel Foods Regulation. It will also present a proposal to improve this Regulation in accordance with the revised Directive for the deliberate release of GMOs into the environment. Furthermore, the labelling provisions will be completed and harmonized.[24]

On 21 October 1999, legislation to further strengthen GM labelling was agreed.[25] In the new rules,[26] which came into force on 10 April 2000, labelling requirements have been extended to include foodstuffs and food ingredients containing additives and flavourings that have been genetically modified or have been produced from genetically modified organisms. Regulation 49/2000 allows a *de minimis* labelling threshold of one per cent (of each ingredient individually considered) for the accidental content of genetically modified material in non-GM products. The aim of the threshold is to solve the problem faced by operators who have tried to avoid GMOs but who, owing to accidental contamination, still find themselves with a low percentage of modified material in their products.

In conclusion, products authorised under the Novel Foods Regulation which either contain or comprise GMOs (e.g. a plant, part of a plant or the processed plant where there is still genetic material present, such as a sweet corn which can be eaten directly or a genetically modified tomato) must be labelled. Products derived from GMOs and authorised under the Novel Foods Regulation must be labelled if they are no longer equivalent to an existing foodstuff or food ingredient (e.g. oil from a GM maize or a tomato paste, where the processing refines the product so that DNA is no longer present). Non-GM foods adventitiously contaminated must be labelled when contamination, at the level of the ingredient, is greater than 1 per cent.

In January 2000, the Commission presented a proposal for a Directive that will include a requirement for animal feeds to be labelled.[27] The Directive will amend previous legislation on the marketing of compound feeding stuffs aimed,

food ingredient; (b) the presence in the novel food or food ingredient of material which is not present in an existing equivalent foodstuff and which may have implications for the health of certain sections of the population; (c) the presence in the novel food or food ingredient of material which is not present in an existing equivalent foodstuff and which gives rise to ethical concerns; and (d) the presence of an organism genetically modified by techniques of genetic modification, the non-exhaustive list of which is laid down in Directive 90/220/EEC (Article 8).

[24] See Communication by the European Communities, *White Paper on Food Security*, COM(1999) 719 final, 12 January 2000.

[25] See European Commission, Press Release, "Commission proposes de minimis threshold and labelling rules for GMOs", Brussels, 22 October 1999. website: http://europa.eu.int/comm/dg03/press/1999/IP99783.htm.

[26] Regulation (EC) 50/2000, 10 January 2000, OJ 2000 L006/15, and Commission Regulation (EC) 49/2000 of 10 January 2000, OJ 2000 L006/13.

[27] Commission of the European Communities, Proposal for a European Parliament and Council Directive amending Directive 79/373/EEC on the marketing of compound feeding stuffs, COM(1999) 744 final, 2000/0015 (COD), 7 January 2000.

as regards labelling, at ensuring that stock farmers are informed of the composition and use of feeding stuffs. In the aftermath of the BSE (bovine spongiform encephalopathy) crisis and the events in 1999 relating to oils and additives contaminated by dioxin, the EC member states have expressed their dissatisfaction with the existing labelling provisions and stressed the importance of detailed qualitative and quantitative information on the labels of compound feeding stuffs. The Commission's proposal imposes a compulsory declaration of all the food materials, as well as their amount in the compound feeding stuffs, listed on a label or in the accompanying document. Member states are also looking at the need for labelling of the presence or absence in animal feed of material derived from GM material.

Since there are currently no specific regulations in the EU covering "GM-free" labelling, some EU member states, such as the United Kingdom, are pressing for the development of a comprehensive discipline at a European level on "GM-free" labelling.[28]

European consumers are increasingly showing an interest in "organic" products—whose market is growing exponentially—as a reaction to the multiple scandals where food safety has been at stake, but also as a way to protect themselves against involuntary consumption of genetically modified food, and to protect the environment. In the European Union, it is reported that 100,000 farmers and food processors are producing organic food. There are 2.5 million hectares under organic cultivation. While this amount represents less than two per cent of the global cultivated area, it has tripled in the last four years.[29]

Japan

Following European moves on GMOs, the Japanese Government recently introduced mandatory labelling requirements for final products containing GMOs in response to consumers' concerns. A committee in charge of developing rules for labelling was established in 1997 under the auspices of the Ministry of Agriculture, Forestry and Fishery (MAFF). The public was encouraged to comment on the draft legislation and the committee received more than 10,000 submissions. The labelling system will apply to a variety of food products, most of them included in the Japanese traditional diet, which contain genetically modified ingredients, such as modified corn, soybeans, potatoes and rapeseeds. Labelling standards were issued in April 2000 and compliance with them is likely to become mandatory by April 2001. The labelling system is supposed to give information to consumers to allow them to make an informed choice.

[28] See "Genetic Modifications Issues (GM): GM Food Labelling" (website of the United Kingdom Cabinet Office Genetic Modification (GM) Issues, http://www.gm-info.gov.uk/1999/gmfoodlabel.htm).

[29] See "Europe Sees Potential in Organic Foods", Reuters, 9 March 2000 and "L'euphorie de l'agriculture verte", *Le Figaro*, 2 April 2000.

Where the presence of genetically modified inputs is not proved, but the producers cannot exclude that some GM materials have been used, this has to be indicated on the label. A voluntary "GM-free" labelling system has already been implemented.

The MAFF started inspections of imported GM products at major ports in the autumn of 1999. There are currently twenty-two GMOs which are officially recognized as "safety-proven". The inspections are carried out to ensure the safety of the "safety-proven" GM products and to separate them from non-approved GM products. Inspected products may be denied entry if it is found that they are not on the GMO approved list.

On 20 January 2000, the MAFF circulated the official definition of organic farm products and organic processed foods made from agricultural products in order to stop the proliferation of "organic" labels based on producers' own definitions. GM products are among the products that cannot be labelled "organic". The new system will enter into effect on 1 October 2000.[30]

USA

Biotech crops have been sold in the US since 1996 and are already planted on millions of acres. They account for about a half of the nation's soybeans and cotton, a third of all corn, and smaller proportions of canola, potatoes and squash. The Government has approved some 50 varieties of genetically modified crops. Genetically modified soybeans and corn can be found in hundreds of processed foods.

On 3 May 2000 the Clinton administration released a plan that would increase federal oversight of genetically modified foods and make details of that oversight more available to the public in an effort to increase consumer confidence in GM foods. In particular, the new proposal is the result of an effort by the Food and Drug Administration (FDA), which is a part of the Department of Health and Human Services, to solicit the public's views on its policies for handling GM foods. In response to its call for comments and hearings in October 1999, the FDA heard testimony from several hundred interested parties and received more than 30,000 written comments. These comments came from pharmaceutical and biotechnology companies, seed companies, agricultural groups, food producers and processors, marketers, consumer groups, environmentalists, and others.[31]

Under the proposal, biotech companies would have to notify the FDA four months before marketing a new genetically modified food, providing the agency

[30] See *MAFF Update*, No. 345, 4 February 2000, website: http://www.maff.go.jp/mud/345.html.

[31] The paragraphs related to the 3 May 2000 proposal are based on "U.S. to Add Oversight on Biotech Food", *Washington Post* online, 3 May 2000, website: www.washingtonpost.com/wp-dyn/articles/A56999–2000May2.html, and on information provided by the team of Washington Trade Reports.

and the public with the research results that affirm the new food's safety. Until now, the process has been voluntary. Moreover, the FDA intends to create a regulatory mechanism by which foods could for the first time be voluntarily labelled as either genetically modified or free of gene-altered ingredients.

One of the significant developments in the proposal is the greater involvement in the regulatory process of the Agricultural Department (USDA) and the Environment Protection Agency (EPA). The USDA would become directly involved in validating new scientific tests aimed at detecting the presence of gene-altered ingredients. The EPA would conduct a six-month review of its environmental regulations dealing with testing, monitoring and approving the use of genetically engineered crops.

The growing consumer resistance to GM food has apparently changed the food and agriculture industries' views about government regulation. Whereas industry groups have previously resisted attempts to introduce new regulatory procedures, they now seem to believe that a stronger, clearer government approach may reassure the consumer that the products are independently deemed to be safe. The biotech industry, which in the past has strongly opposed labelling because it could stigmatise or could imply the superiority of foods not containing GM ingredients over genetically engineered foods, is now more willing to accept labelling as a necessary instrument to combat consumer scepticism. The industry may decide to couple its support for voluntary labels with greater efforts to make consumers aware of the benefits of GM foods. The Biotechnology Industry Organisation, for instance, has begun a major television and print media advertising campaign extolling the benefits of biotechnology in food and medicine.

On 2 May 2000, thirteen State Governors[32] announced that they would begin a campaign to improve the public image of genetically modified foods by informing consumers about the science of genetically modified foods. They declared that they were going to do so because of the economic challenges for farmers and of the need to enhance the value of crops so that farming would yield good profits. Also, they stressed that their initiative was related to environmental concerns concerning the quality of water and air resulting from heavy reliance on herbicides and fertilisers.[33]

In contrast to the food industry's positive reaction, the proposal by the Clinton administration has not elicited an enthusiastic reaction from consumer groups, which have charged that the plan falls short of what consumers need, especially in the field of mandatory labelling of GM foods.

Interested parties will have opportunities to submit written comments on the proposal and hearings are likely to be held until the end of 2000. Because of the complexity of the issues and the large number of comments expected, the FDA

[32] The States in question are Delaware, Idaho, Illinois, Indiana, Iowa, Michigan, Missouri, Nebraska, Nevada, North Carolina, North Dakota, Washington and Wisconsin.

[33] See "13 Governors Will Promote Genetically Altered Foods", *St. Louis Post-Dispatch*, 3 May 2000.

will most likely have to adjust the proposal before it is ready to move to the final-rule stage. The process is expected to be long and to continue after the end of the Clinton administration (20 January 2001).

A bill requiring the labelling of all foods that contain a genetically modified entity was introduced to the United States Congress in November 1999 (Kucinich bill, H.R.3377). As of 15 April 2000, the bill had fifty-one co-sponsors. However, the prospects of its moving forward in Congress before the end of the 106th Congress (on about 8 October 2000) are quite remote. Even though a total of fifty-one co-sponsors is a respectable number, no one on the co-sponsor list is close to the US agriculture industry. Secondly, like all bills, H.R.3377 has to be "referred" to one or more committees of jurisdiction. In this case, those two committees are the House Agriculture Committee and the House Commerce Committee. Currently, neither committee has plans to take up the GMO issue in general, let alone the Kucinich measure in particular. In the committees' views the issue is so new and undeveloped that Congress should not be eager to rush in to legislate. On March 2000 Mr Kucinich introduced additional legislation (H.R. 3883), directing the FDA to overhaul its procedures for reviewing the safety of genetically engineered foods. In the Senate, Senator Barbara Boxer (Democrat, California) introduced her GMO food-labelling bill on 22 February 2000 (S.2080). She has attracted no co-sponsors so far. There is great reluctance to start legislating on GMO issues in the Senate, for the same reasons as in the House of Representatives.

In conclusion, there does not appear to be any eagerness in Congress to take up GMO legislation in the year 2000. The Congress is definitely interested, but it has not been able to resolve many of the issues yet. In those circumstances, it is reluctant to act, even though farmers are requesting a definitive direction from government. The issue is regarded as being of paramount importance in the USA.[34]

On 8 March 2000, the FDA released its proposed final rule for "organic" foods. The proposal marks the Government's second attempt to define "organic" food after the first such effort failed amid controversy two years ago. After months of review of more than 2,000 comments received in response to its earlier proposal, the FDA appears to be adopting a rather strict standard. Any food labelled "organic" would have to have been produced without the use of many fertiliser types, including processed sewage sludge, could not be irradiated for pest control, and could not have been developed using genetic modifications of any sort. There is a growing assumption in the USA that organic agricultural products may be commanding a higher price than conventionally produced goods. By contrast, bio-engineered products may be selling at a discount, compared with conventional agricultural products, despite possible higher costs associated with segregating, storing, transporting and labelling modified crops.[35]

[34] Information provided by the team of *Washington Trade Reports*.

[35] See *Washington Trade Reports*, Vol. VIII, No. 7, 11 April 2000.

Other countries' initiatives

The Australia-New Zealand Food Authority (ANZFA) has developed standards for genetically modified foods which came into effect on 13 May 1999. They require a pre-market safety assessment to be carried out by ANZFA before such foods can be sold. They also require labelling of foods which are substantially different from their conventional counterparts. Recently the Australian and New Zealand Health Ministers agreed that the labelling requirements should be extended to all GM foods for the purpose of consumer information. A draft standard and a draft protocol intended to provide guidance on the practical implementation of the new labelling system have been released for public comment. The Ministers expect to finalise the details of the extension of the system by July 2000.[36]

In New Zealand, the field tests and release of GMOs take place under the 1996 Hazardous Substances and New Organisms Act. The Environmental Risk Management Authority decides on the development, production, import and release of GMOs in the country. Risk management decisions are made on the basis of scientific evidence and take account of environmental, health, social and economic considerations, as well as of the multilateral commitments entered into by New Zealand.[37]

In Canada, the Canadian Council of Grocery Distributors, representing about 80 per cent of Canadian food industry retailers, agreed in September 1999 to develop a voluntary GM food labelling regime in partnership with the Canadian General Standards Board and a variety of stakeholders from industry, environmental groups, consumer groups and academia. The label will indicate whether a specific food has been produced through genetic modification. The committee established for this purpose is developing general principles and models for voluntary declarations, procedures required to verify the truthfulness of these declarations, principles of a certification mechanism, and definitions that are clear and concise. A draft standard is expected to be completed before the end of 2000. This initiative is largely in response to consumer demand for more information on GM foods. The Canadian Government is supporting this approach and considers it to be consistent with its international trade obligations.[38]

In Switzerland, approval of a bill presented by the Federal Council in January 2000, which would authorise the voluntary release of GMOs into the environment under certain conditions, seems to be going to face obstacles, since a broad

[36] The OECD and UNIDO have jointly developed a database on regulatory developments in the field of biotechnology. The information can be accessed through the following websites: www.binas.unido.org/binas (for UNIDO member countries) and www.oecd.org/ehs/country.htm (for OECD member countries).

[37] Information provided by the Ministry of Agriculture and Forestry of New Zealand.

[38] See WTO, Communication from Canada. The Development of a Voluntary Standard for the Labelling of Foods Derived from Biotechnology, G/TBT/W/134, 23 May 2000.

alliance including the Farmers' Association, environmental groups and consumer associations is opposing it and proposing a ten-year moratorium on the release of GMO into the environment. According to the Farmers' Association, there are two reasons for not planting modified seeds in Switzerland: consumers are against them; and it is the transnational companies, not the farmers, that are currently benefiting from biotechnology. [39]

In 1994, Thailand's legislation on plant quarantine was expanded to cover GMOs. Since then, the release into the environment and the import of genetically modified seeds and crops have been subject to a strict approval system. The Thai authorities have so far approved only the release into the environment of GMOs for experimental purposes. Imports of GM soya and maize, however, have been derestricted and do not need to go through the approval process. In response to consumers' concern, the Thai Food and Drug Administration is considering imposing a labelling system for all products using GMOs, starting in 2001. Discussions are being held about whether the system should be mandatory or voluntary and about how much GMO content in a product should warrant labelling. A precondition for the implementation of the proposed labelling system will obviously be to equip the authorities concerned with the technology needed for testing GM products.[40]

The Republic of Korea passed legislation in March 2000 regarding mandatory labelling of genetically modified soybeans, corn and soybean sprouts. It will enter into force in 2001.[41]

In Sri Lanka, the National Food Advisory Committee is considering the possibility of imposing a ban on the import of GMOs and GM foods, as it lacks precise information about the long-term effects of these new products. The list of foods that may be banned is being studied, while the Sri Lankan authorities are also considering other less trade-restrictive options.[42]

In March 2000, the Mexican Senate unanimously approved a reform of the General Health Law so that transgenic foods, whether produced nationally or outside Mexico, carry a label that identifies them as such and specifies the type of genetic modification which has taken place. The bill must still be approved by the Mexican Chamber of Deputies.[43]

V. THE MULTILATERAL SOLUTIONS

At present, international trade in GMOs has to take place according to the rules agreed by WTO Members at the end of the Uruguay Round, in particular those

[39] See "Le projet du Conseil fédéral sur les OGM court à la défaite" and " S'adapter au marché? Les paysans prennent au mot les partisans du génie génétique", *Le Temps*, 28 April 2000.

[40] Information provided by the National Science and Technology Development Agency of Thailand.

[41] WTO, G/TBT/Notif.00/49, 1 February 2000.

[42] See "Sri Lanka: Government Bans Genetically Engineered Foods", *South-North Development Monitor*, 14 April 2000, and information provided by Sri Lanka's Permanent Mission in Geneva.

[43] See "Trade: Mexico Senate Approves Transgenic Product Labelling", *SUNS*, 4 April 2000.

spelt out in the SPS and TBT Agreements and in GATT 1994. However, disciplines regarding trade in GMOs are also emerging from specific multilateral agreements being negotiated outside the purely trade context, such as the recently agreed Cartagena Protocol on Biosafety, or may be developed in the future by ad hoc groups, such as the proposed WTO Working Party on Biotechnology. Intergovernmental organisations that have specific expertise in the field are carrying out technical work in key areas, such as the risk analysis of food derived from biotechnology or the methodology to identify food derived from biotechnology. Other organisations are providing a forum for discussion to respond to the interests and concerns of their member countries. The rules included in different legal instruments and the conclusions reached in different forums may not be fully consistent with each other and may give rise to conflicts between GMO-exporting countries and potential importers.

The Cartagena Protocol on Biosafety

The Cartagena Protocol on Biosafety,[44] which was negotiated under the auspices of the Convention on Biological Diversity (Rio de Janeiro, 1992), was adopted on 29 January 2000 after four years of negotiations. It will enter into force ninety days after the fiftieth instrument of ratification is received. The Protocol was opened for signature at the Fifth Meeting of the Conference of the Parties to the Convention on Biological Diversity (Nairobi, 15–26 May 2000) and sixty-four countries, plus the European Community, signed it. It will be available for signature for one year, beginning 5 June 2000.

The Protocol provides rules for the safe transfer, handling, use and disposal of "living modified organisms" (LMOs). Its aim is to address the threats posed by LMOs to biological diversity, also taking into account risks to human health. The use of the term "living modified organism" instead of "genetically modified organism" was supported by some delegations that felt that it was a more precise definition. The USA, on the other hand, strongly supported the use of the term "living modified organism" to stress that the use of genetic engineering resulted in products which were no more risky than those obtained through other means of modifying living entities. Living modified organisms are defined by the Protocol as "any living organism that possesses a novel combination of genetic material obtained through the use of modern biotechnology" (Article 3(g)).

The proposal for provisions in the field of the safe transfer, handling and use of LMOs within the Convention on Biological Diversity (CBD) came first from an expert group that was established during the negotiations on the CBD. However, there was neither time nor a wholehearted willingness to develop

[44] In general, the term "biosafety" describes a set of measures used to assess and manage any risk associated with GMOs.

such provisions and include them into the Convention, and it was therefore agreed that specific provisions on biosafety would be negotiated at a later stage and included in a protocol. Malaysia and Ethiopia, on behalf of the African Group, were the most vocal advocates of the idea of developing a Protocol on Biosafety, and were supported by most developing countries, the Nordic countries and environmental groups.[45]

During the long and complex negotiations on the Protocol, five main negotiating groups emerged. The *Like-Minded Group* consisted of the large majority of developing countries (with the exception of the developing countries members of the Miami Group and the Compromise Group). The emphasis of developing countries was on their lack of capacity to assess and manage the hazards that GMOs may pose to biodiversity and to human health. They made it clear that, given the lack of a regulatory framework for biosafety in most developing countries, they risked becoming the testing grounds for release of GMOs produced in the developed countries. Thus, they called for internationally mandated information-sharing obligations to be put in place for all kinds of LMOs. The Like-Minded Group therefore supported a wide coverage by the Protocol, a strong formulation and implementation of the precautionary principle, the inclusion of the requirement that those exporting LMOs should provide information to allow importing countries the possibility of informed consent, a comprehensive identification and documentation of LMOs shipments, and the possibility of taking into account human health and socio-economic considerations in decision-making. The *Miami Group* included the main exporters of genetically modified seeds and crops, and the principal holders of the related technology: Argentina, Australia, Canada, Chile, the USA and Uruguay. Although Argentina, Chile and Uruguay were producers and exporters of GM seeds and crops, they were not in a position to develop new GMOs. The main aims of the group were to narrow the scope of the Protocol by keeping genetically modified commodities out of it, to limit the possibility of referring to the precautionary principle and socio-economic considerations in decision-making, and to apply the strict system of Advance Informed Agreement (AIA) only to LMOs intended for introduction into the environment. The *European Union (EU)* negotiators, who were facing food-safety scandals at home and were under scrutiny and pressure from consumers' organisations and environmental groups with serious concerns about GMOs' safety, strove for a strong protocol which would include risks to human health, cover genetically modified commodities, include strong language on the precautionary principle, and make reference to the principle of non-discrimination between domestically produced and

[45] The paragraphs on the negotiating history of the Biosafety Protocol draw on A. Gupta, "Framing 'Biosafety' in an International Context", ENRP Discussion Paper E–99–10 (Kennedy School of Government, Harvard University, 1999); and A. Cosbey and S. Burgiel, "The Cartagena Protocol on Biosafety: An Analysis of Results", IISD Briefing Note, International Institute for Sustainable Development, 1999.

imported items. Moreover, the EU was in the process of developing and implementing legislation in this field and was therefore striving for the conclusion of a multilateral instrument under which its existing legislation could be accommodated. The *Compromise Group* included Japan, Mexico, the Republic of Korea, Singapore, Switzerland and New Zealand. Although the group had a common position on the inclusion of the precautionary principle and on wide coverage by the Protocol, its main aim was to bridge the major differences between the other groups. In fact, it played a key role in building the final consensus on the text of the Protocol. The *Central and Eastern European bloc of countries (CEE)* had a position in between that of the EU and the Like-Minded Group. Its main aim during the negotiations was to contribute to a text that would be practical and applicable. Two non-state coalitions had a strong presence during the negotiations: the Global Industry Coalition, consisting of over 2,200 agricultural, food and pharmaceutical firms, which had a position almost identical to that of the Miami Group; and an international coalition of consumer safety and green groups, which supported the Like-Minded Group's perspective.

One of the central points of contention during the negotiations was whether, in the presence of significant scientific uncertainty, the precautionary approach would represent an appropriate basis on which to take decisions. The Miami Group and industry called for all decisions under the Protocol to be based on science, on the assumption that the potential risks posed by LMOs were already well known. According to them, science would be the only objective and standardisable basis for the decision-making process as regards biosafety. To rely on the precautionary principle, on the contrary, would open the Protocol to abuses and trade protectionism. Moreover, the Miami Group argued that the precautionary approach was inconsistent with WTO rules, in particular with those spelt out in the SPS Agreement.

The EU, the Like-Minded Group, and consumer and green groups, on the other hand, argued that while scientific input remained essential in the field of biosafety, risks posed by LMOs were still not fully understood and could be potentially irreversible. Therefore, the possibility of taking a precautionary approach was seen as crucial for the decision-making regime under the Protocol. They wanted flexibility in decision-making and regarded it as paramount to the predictability that would result from an approach mainly based on "sound science".

The final text of the Protocol, which is obviously a "compromise text", includes elements from the different negotiating groups; it seems, however, to go more in the direction of the EU's and the Like-Minded Group's approach. It reflects the complexity of the issues discussed and the effort to translate environmental and trade requirements into international binding obligations.

One of the main features of the Protocol is the system of Advance Informed Agreement. The AIA covers seeds for planting, live fish for release, microorganisms for bioremediation, and other LMOs which are "intentionally introduced" into the environment.[46] It provides that the exporter must provide, through notification, detailed information on the product exported to the competent national authority of the country of import in advance of the first shipment. Information must include the modification introduced, the technique used and the resulting characteristics of the LMO, the regulatory status of the LMO in the country of export (e.g. whether it is prohibited, subject to other restrictions, or has been approved for general release), and the contact details of the importer and the exporter. The notification has to be accompanied by a risk assessment report. Within ninety days of notification, the importing country has to inform the notifier either that it will have to wait for written consent, or that it can proceed to export. If the importing country indicates that written consent will have to be awaited, it has 270 days from the date of notification to decide whether to approve the import (adding conditions as appropriate), prohibit it, request additional information or extend the deadline for response. This decision has to be notified also to the Biosafety Clearing-House (based on the Internet).[47] Failure by the importing country to communicate its decision does not imply consent. Countries of import must give reasons of their decisions, except for unconditional approval. Decisions must be based on available scientific evidence and on risk assessment; however, importing countries can invoke the precautionary principle provisions. The country of export must bear the financial responsibility for risk assessment if the country of import so requires.

LMOs intended for release into the environment must be accompanied by documentation that identifies them as LMOs, specifies the relevant traits/characteristics, provides information on safe handling, storage, transport and use, and specifies the name and address of the importer and the exporter. A declaration that the movement is in conformity with the requirements of the Protocol is also needed. In the future, the Conference of the Parties to the Protocol will consider the need for and modalities of developing standards with regard to identification, handling, packaging and transport practices.

The AIA system, however, covers only a small percentage of traded LMOs, since LMOs for direct use as food or feed or for processing are subject to a different and less strict notification procedure. Four types of LMOs are also excluded from the AIA system, namely most pharmaceuticals for humans, LMOs in transit, LMOs destined for "contained use",[48] and LMOs which have been declared safe by a meeting of the Parties to the Biosafety Protocol. Consumer products derived from LMOs are not covered by the Protocol.

[46] According to Article 7.2 of the Protocol, LMOs for intentional introduction into the environment are all LMOs other than those intended for direct use as food or feed, or for processing.

[47] Alternative ways will have to be found to make information available to those countries which do not yet have full access to the Internet.

[48] According to Article 3(b) of the Protocol, " 'contained use' means any operation, undertaken within a facility, installation or other physical structure, which involves living modified organisms that are controlled by specific measures that effectively limit their contact with, and their impact on, the external environment".

For LMOs for direct use as food or feed or for processing (i.e. commodities, identified as FFP-LMOs in the Protocol), imports are based on an advanced information procedure and take place according to domestic legislation. Importers have to announce their decision regarding domestic use of FFP-LMOs to the Biosafety Clearing-House. Decisions should be based on a risk assessment. Developing countries and countries with economies in transition may indicate their need for financial and technical assistance and capacity building with respect to FFP-LMOs . Although the Protocol spells out two different procedures depending on the final use of the LMOs (for voluntary introduction into the environment, or for food, feed or processing), it is actually rather difficult to separate them into two categories, considering that it may happen that grains imported as food or feed or for processing are used as seeds, being significantly less expensive than proper seeds.

Shipments of commodities for food, feed or processing containing LMOs will have to carry documentation specifying the possible presence of LMOs and indicate that the products are not intended for intentional introduction into the environment. The details of this procedure remain to be worked out, and are supposed to be settled within two years after the Protocol enters into force. The "soft" rules agreed upon were welcomed by the Miami Group, which had argued that strict requirements on documentation and identification would imply segregation of crops and be unfeasible. On the other hand, the fact that some countries have passed legislation on mandatory labelling for GMOs and GM crops is already imposing segregation. The category of FFP-LMOs includes the large majority of traded LMOs, such as modified corn, soya, wheat, rapeseeds, tomatoes and cotton.

The Protocol permits the countries of import to take a precautionary approach; this means that lack of scientific certainty due to insufficient information on the potential negative effects of LMOs on biodiversity, taking also into account risks for human health, will not prevent the receiving country from taking decisions regarding shipments of LMOs. This principle applies to LMOs for intentional introduction into the environment, as well as to those for direct use as food or feed or for processing. The precautionary approach is one of the main features of the Protocol and reference is made to it in the Preamble, in Article 1 ("Objective"), and in Articles 10 and 11. It allows importing countries to ban imports because of lack of scientific certainty. The ban may last until the importing country decides that it has arrived at scientific certainty about the effects of the products on biodiversity and human health. However, since the importing country is not obliged to seek the information necessary for reaching scientific certainty, a trade-restrictive measure may be in force without time limits. By contrast, the SPS Agreement allows countries provisionally to adopt sanitary or phytosanitary measures when relevant scientific evidence is insufficient, but obliges them to seek the additional information necessary for a more objective assessment of risk and to review the SPS measure within a reasonable period of time.

For LMOs for intentional introduction into the environment, the Protocol allows the exporting country to request the importing country to review a decision it has taken when a change in circumstances has occurred that may influence the outcome of the risk assessment upon which the decision was based, or additional relevant scientific or technical information has become available. The importing country must respond to such a request in writing within ninety days and set out the reasons for its decision. This provision therefore gives the exporter the right to request the importer to review its decision in the light of new information; however, the importer retains the flexibility to confirm its previous decision, but it has to justify so doing. This discipline echoes the need for review contained in the SPS Agreement when precautionary measures are used, although there are some basic differences: in the case of the SPS Agreement, the country implementing the measure is obliged to seek additional information[49] and review the SPS measure within a reasonable period of time. In the case of the Protocol, the country implementing a restrictive measure is obliged only to consider the request made by the exporter, analyse the new circumstances or the new scientific or technical information brought to its attention and give a justified reply within ninety days. Moreover, this rule does not apply to LMOs for direct use as food or feed or for processing.

It seems that there are already some rather divergent interpretations of the Protocol. According to a US press release, Mr Loy, Secretary of State for Global Affairs, said that "the agreement emphasises that regulatory decisions must be based on science". In a Fact Sheet published by the United States Department of State on 16 February 2000, it is stated that "The language [on the precautionary approach] acknowledges the role that precaution may serve during decision-making. However, the language does not replace science-based decision-making, nor does it authorise decisions contrary to a country's WTO obligations".[50] In a meeting held in March 2000 in Geneva immediately after the first 2000 meeting of the WTO Committee on Trade and Environment (CTE), representatives of the USA declared that according to their interpretation the Protocol is subordinated to the WTO Agreements. On the other hand, Ms Wallstrom, the EU Environment Commissioner, said at the conclusion of the negotiations that "the Protocol in general . . . and the inclusion of the precautionary principle in particular . . . represented a victory for consumers".

The Preamble of the Biosafety Protocol states that it shall not be interpreted as implying a change in the rights and obligations of the parties under existing international agreements and that this recital is not intended to subordinate the Protocol to other international agreements. These provisions may prove not to be very helpful if a conflict arises between countries with divergent interests in

[49] It is interesting to note that under the SPS Agreement a country can base its measures on the risk assessments carried out by other countries or by international organisations, and may seek additional information from other member countries or from the industry.

[50] See United States Department of State, Office of the Spokesman, Fact Sheet, "The Cartagena Protocol on Biosafety", EUR312 02/16/00.

the area of biotechnology. Disputes may occur between parties to the Protocol, for instance on the interpretation of the role that the precautionary approach can play in decision-making, or between parties and non-parties.

Usually, countries which are parties to a multilateral agreement are supposed to solve their possible conflicts within the framework of the agreement they have signed and ratified. However, in the case of the Biosafety Protocol, if a party believes that in a specific circumstance its interests are better protected by WTO rules, it may invoke those rules, arguing that the Protocol clearly states that it shall not be interpreted as implying a change in the rights and obligations of the parties under existing international agreements. A possible conflict between parties may therefore be settled under the WTO dispute settlement mechanism. It flows from Article 23 of the Dispute Settlement Understanding that any WTO Member can initiate a case in the WTO if it considers that its market access rights have been violated. The United States Department of Agriculture, for example, observed that "The Protocol preserves countries' rights under other international agreements, including the WTO. . . The Protocol does not undermine an exporting country's right to challenge, under the WTO, an unwarranted decision of an importing country not to accept a bio-engineered product".[51] The issue then is which WTO violation would be alleged by the exporting country and which defence is admissible. If the justification of the trade-restrictive measure is not safety, the SPS Agreement is not applicable and not violated. The exporting country could therefore claim violation of Article XI of GATT or Article 2.2 of the TBT Agreement, and the importing country could justify its trade-restrictive measure by using the exceptions of Article XX of GATT, particularly paragraphs (b) and (g). On the other hand, a country which has an interest in solving a dispute according to the discipline laid down in the Biosafety Protocol may invoke the fact that the Protocol represents *lex specialis,* which has priority over *lex generalis* (WTO agreements). It may also refer to the principle that later in time prevails. Finally, it could ask for its WTO obligations to be interpreted in the light of the Protocol. If a dispute occurs between a party and a non-party to the Protocol, the case will most likely be brought to the attention of the WTO Dispute Settlement Body. It will be up to the panels and, possibly, the Appellate Body to decide how much legal weight they wish to give to the provisions of the Protocol. Even though the Appellate Body stated in two disputes[52] that the WTO legal system does not operate in

[51] See US Department of Agriculture, Foreign Agricultural Service Fact Sheet, "International Protocol on Biosafety: What it Means for Agriculture", February 2000 (website: *http://www.usia.gov/topical/ global/ biosafe/00021402.htm).*

[52] In the *Gasoline* case (*United States—Standards for Reformulated and Conventional Gasoline*, Appellate Body Report, 20 May 1996, WT/DS2/9) the Appellate Body cited Art. 3.2 of the Dispute Settlement Understanding, which requires Panels and the Appellate Body to use "customary rules of interpretation" to interpret the provisions of the WTO Agreements. The Appellate Body linked the WTO legal system to the rest of international legal order and imposed on Panels and WTO Members the obligation to interpret the WTO Agreements in accordance with customary rules of interpretation of public international law. In the *Shrimp* case (*United States—Import Prohibition of Certain Shrimp and Shrimp Products*, Appellate Body Report, 12 October 1998, WT/DS58/AB/R),

"clinical isolation" from existing rules of public international law, it would be difficult to predict which principles and rules would apply to a specific dispute.

The issue of the consistency between the trade rules included in multilateral agreements and WTO rights and obligations, and the position on non-parties to a multilateral agreement which may be affected by the trade rules agreed by the parties to a multilateral agreement has been discussed for several years in various international forums, without any conclusive result. Even though the trade provisions of a multilateral agreement have not yet been challenged before a dispute settlement panel, it may be argued that the Biosafety Protocol is different from other multilateral agreements and that there is a more concrete risk that its WTO compatibility may be challenged. This is because the economic interests involved in international trade in GMOs are huge; public opinion is still very much divided on whether biotechnology is a risk or an opportunity; the main player, the USA, on one hand has actively participated in the negotiations of the Protocol as member of the Miami Group, but, on the other hand, is not a party to the CBD Convention; and the Protocol is already being interpreted in divergent ways.

The US Trade Representative has raised the possibility that the USA may consider a possible dispute settlement case in the WTO against the EU for its failure to approve biotechnology varieties of corn. In a related development, the USA is seeking to unblock corn exports to the EU, which were halted because of its moratorium on approving new biotechnology varieties, with a new proposal whereby US laboratories would be certified to conduct certain tests. These would ensure that US shipments would not contain any unapproved varieties of genetically modified corn. The proposal requires that pre-shipment tests in the USA not be duplicated by subsequent tests in the EU, thus freeing exporters from the risk that their shipments would be blocked at the port of entry. The proposal is apparently viewed by the European authorities as a positive sign of cooperation on a contentious issue, although it is too early for the EU to approve the plan. On the other hand, industry sources in the USA said that the proposal, even if it were to meet with EU approval, would be problematic, because of the degree to which it would require segregation of unapproved varieties of GM corn from approved GM varieties and from conventional corn.[53]

the Appellate Body made reference to various international conventions to interpret the term "natural resources". Therefore, non-WTO treaties, practices, customs and general principles of law may be relevant in the interpretation of WTO provisions and can become quite influential in defining the parameters and the content of WTO obligations. For a detailed discussion on this topic see G. Marceau, "A Call for Coherence in International Law: Praises for the Prohibition Against 'Clinical Isolation' in WTO Dispute Settlement", *Journal of World Trade* (October 1999) 87.

[53] See "Barshefsky Hints at Considering Possible Biotech Case Against EU", *Inside US Trade*, Vol. 18, No. 24, 16 June 2000.

WTO Agreements which have implications for international trade in GMOs

Four WTO Agreements appear to have special relevance for international trade in GMOs: the Agreement on the Application of Sanitary and Phytosanitary Measures (SPS), the Agreement on Technical Barriers to Trade (TBT), the Agreement on Trade-Related Aspects of Intellectual Property Rights (TRIPS), and the General Agreement on Tariffs and Trade 1994 (GATT).

The main goal of the SPS Agreement is to prevent domestic SPS measures from having unnecessary negative effects on international trade and being misused for protectionist purposes. The Agreement covers measures adopted by countries to protect human or animal life from food-borne risks; human health from animal or plant-carried diseases; and animal and plants from pests and diseases. Therefore, the specific aims of SPS measures are to ensure food safety and to prevent the spread of diseases among animals and plants. Although the WTO SPS Committee has not so far been requested to address issues related to trade in GMOs, it can be argued that measures aimed at regulating such a trade could reasonably come within the scope of the Agreement. This is because measures related to GMOs may have the goal of protecting "human or animal life from food-borne risks" or protecting "plants from pests and diseases" (in view of the lack of scientific certainty about the impact of GMOs on the environment, avoiding the transfer of genetic material and associated traits from engineered varieties to conventional varieties could be regarded as similar to protecting plants from pests and diseases). In other words, measures related to GMOs may fall within the spirit, if not the letter, of the SPS Agreement. There is, however, no consensus on this assumption.

Article 2.2 of the SPS Agreement states that "Members shall ensure that any sanitary or phytosanitary measure is applied only to the extent necessary to protect human, animal or plant life or health, is based on scientific principles and is not maintained without sufficient scientific evidence, except as provided for in paragraph 7 of Article 5". The Agreement permits the adoption of SPS measures on a provisional basis as a precautionary step in cases where there is an immediate risk of the spread of disease but where the scientific evidence is insufficient. However, "Members shall seek to obtain the additional information necessary to a more objective assessment of risk and review the sanitary or phytosanitary measure accordingly within a reasonable period of time" (Article 5.7, second sentence). Countries must establish SPS measures on the basis of an appropriate assessment of the actual risks involved. The procedures and decisions used by a country in assessing the risk to food safety or animal or plant health must be made available to other countries upon request.

The Agreement, then, maintains the sovereign right of any government to provide the level of health protection it deems appropriate; however, it expects countries, inter alia, to base their SPS measures on scientific evidence and on an appropriate risk assessment.

In the well-known *Hormone* case,[54] related to a ban imposed by the EU on bovine meat and meat products from cattle treated with growth hormones, the role of the precautionary principle in the framework of the SPS Agreement was addressed.

The EU invoked the precautionary principle[55] in support of its claim that its measures were based on a risk assessment. Its basic submission was that the precautionary principle was or had become a "general customary rule of international law" or at least a "general principle of law". Referring more specifically to Article 5.1 and 5.2 of the SPS Agreement, the EU reached the conclusion that since applying the precautionary principle meant that it was not necessary for all scientists around the world to agree on the possibility and magnitude of the risk, or for all or most of the WTO Members to perceive and evaluate the risk in the same way, its measures (an import ban) were precautionary in nature and satisfied the requirements of Article 2.2 and 2.3 of the Agreement, as well as the requirements of paragraphs 1 to 6 of Article 5. According to the USA, on the other hand, the precautionary principle did not represent customary international law: it was more an approach than a principle. For Canada, the precautionary approach or concept was "an emerging principle of law", but had not yet been incorporated into the corpus of public international law. The Panels concluded that the precautionary principle had not been written into the SPS Agreement as a ground for justifying SPS measures that were otherwise inconsistent with the obligations of members set out in particular provisions of the Agreement and that it did not by itself, and without a clear textual directive to that effect, relieve a panel of the duty of applying the normal (i.e. customary international law) principles of treaty interpretation in reading the provisions of the SPS Agreement. The Appellate Body[56] stated that it was unnecessary, and probably imprudent, for it to take a position on the important but abstract question of the status of the precautionary principle in international law. However, it appeared important to note some aspects of the relationship of the precautionary principle with the SPS Agreement. The Appellate Body upheld the Panels' conclusions that the precautionary principle would not override the explicit wording of Article 5.1 and 5.2 and stressed that it had been incorporated into Article 5.7 of the SPS Agreement, but this provision did not exhaust the relevance of the precautionary principle for SPS.

In the *Hormone* case the Panels and the Appellate Body did not have a chance to interpret directly Article 5.7 of the SPS Agreement, because the EU had not invoked it to justify the measures in dispute. However, Article 5.7 of that

[54] *EC—Measures Concerning Meat and Meat Products (Hormones)*, Complaint by the United States, WT/DS26/R, 18 August 1997; Complaint by Canada, WT/DS48/R, 18 August 1997.

[55] The formulation of the precautionary principle contained in Principle 15 of the Rio Declaration of 1992 is the following: "Where there are threats of serious or irreversible damage, lack of full scientific certainty shall not be used as a reason for postponing cost-effective measures to prevent environmental degradation".

[56] WT/DS26/AB/R, WT/DS48/AB/R, 16 January 1998.

Agreement was explicitly addressed in the *Japan Varietals* case.[57] The case was about a complaint by the USA relating to the requirement imposed by Japan for testing and confirming the efficacy of the quarantine treatment for each variety of certain agricultural products. In support of its varietal testing requirement, Japan invoked Article 5.7. According to the Appellate Body, Article 5.7 sets out four cumulative requirements that must be met for adopting and maintaining provisional SPS measures. A country may provisionally adopt an SPS measure if this measure is: (1) imposed in respect of a situation where relevant scientific information is insufficient; and (2) adopted on the basis of available pertinent information. Such a measure may not be maintained unless the country that adopted it: (i) seeks to obtain the additional information necessary for a more objective assessment of risk; and (ii) reviews the measure accordingly within a reasonable period of time.

It seems, therefore, that the WTO jurisprudence is proposing a rather narrow interpretation of Article 5.7 of the SPS Agreement: by stressing the need for countries to comply with four specific requirements in order to be able to invoke the right to adopt and maintain provisional measures, and by stating that the precautionary principle would not override the need for countries to base their SPS measures on a risk assessment—and, in general, by avoiding the expression of any view on the status of the precautionary principle in public international law. However, the Appellate Body also stated that Article 5.7 did not exhaust the precautionary principle for SPS. It seems that the central role of scientific evidence and risk assessment as the necessary bases for taking and maintaining SPS measures is reconfirmed. While the precautionary principle may be invoked to justify time-limited measures, it does not represent a long-term alternative to risk assessment and scientific evidence.

Labelling requirements related to food, nutrition claims and concerns, quality and packaging regulations are normally subject to the TBT Agreement. While SPS measures may be imposed only to the extent necessary to protect human, animal or plant health from food-borne risks or from pests or diseases, governments may introduce TBT regulations when necessary to meet a number of legitimate objectives, including the prevention of deceptive practices, the protection of human health or safety, animal or plant life or health, or the environment. Both the SPS and TBT Agreements encourage the use of international standards. However, under the SPS Agreement the only reasons accepted for not using such standards for food safety and animal/plant health protection are scientific arguments resulting from an assessment of the potential health risks. In contrast, under the TBT Agreement governments may decide that international standards are not appropriate for other reasons, including fundamental technological problems or geographical factors.[58] It seems, therefore, that the TBT

[57] *Japan—Measures Affecting Agricultural Products*, WT/DS76/R, 27 October 1998, and WT/DS76/AB/R, 22 February 1999.

[58] See WTO, "Understanding the WTO Agreement on Sanitary and Phytosanitary (SPS) Measures", May 1998 (Internet website: http://www.WTO.org/wto/goods/spsund.htm).

Agreement places less emphasis than the SPS Agreement on the need to justify measures on the basis of scientific considerations. However, technical regulations should not be more trade-restrictive than is necessary to fulfil a legitimate objective, taking account of the risks that non-fulfilment would create. The requirement that measures not be more trade-restrictive than necessary, and the linked "proportionality test" in respect of the restrictive trade impact of a measure and the risks that non-fulfilment of the stated objectives would create, seem to be relevant in the framework of international trade in GMOs. At the same time, if the stated objective of a measure is the protection of human health or safety, animal or plant life or health, or the environment, the application of the proportionality test would seem to be particularly problematic, considering that there are at present very divergent views on the magnitude of the risk that GMOs might create. On the other hand, some argue that there is no proportionality test included in the TBT Agreement and the issue is only whether the measure chosen is not unnecessarily trade-restrictive, considering the level of protection that a country has chosen. In that case, a country could implement strict technical regulations regarding GMOs, even though the regulations might have a considerable trade-restrictive impact, on condition that they were not more trade-restrictive than necessary.

It has not yet been determined whether an import ban applying to GMOs or GM products could be regarded as a technical regulation falling under the TBT Agreement. Similarly, it is not clear whether the general exceptions of Article XX of GATT could be invoked to justify measures otherwise inconsistent with the TBT Agreement.

Another relevant aspect of the TBT Agreement is the concept of "like products". If GMOs and GM products are considered "like products" in relation to conventional products, there are no grounds for applying any special treatment to them.

It seems that there are two important issues to consider. The first one is whether "like products" are determined by a "substantial equivalence" test. Under such a test, a genetically engineered food that sufficiently resembles a conventional food product in outward characteristics would be considered substantially equivalent to the conventional product, and the two products would therefore be regarded as equally safe and should be treated in the same way. "Substantial equivalence" has been promoted within the framework of the activities of the Codex Alimentarius Commission by a group of GMO-exporting countries. However, the EU and many developing countries have not supported the use of the substantial equivalence test, considering it unscientific and too narrow. They have taken the position that GM and non-GM products are physically dissimilar. This physical difference arises because, as a result of modification to develop different characteristics, GM-products contain DNA and/or proteins that their conventional counterparts do not contain. That being the case, a national labelling scheme that requires only GM products to be labelled could not be found to contravene the TBT Agreement's non-discrimination requirements that prohibit WTO Members from distinguishing among like products. Genetic modification could be regarded as a "product-related process and production methods" (product-related PPMs). The TBT Agreement allows countries to distinguish products on the basis of PPMs that are reflected in the final product characteristics. This interpretation of TBT rules, however, could be threatened if the substantial equivalence test is adopted by the Codex Alimentarius Commission as an international standard. A second issue that may be worth addressing, if "like products" is not determined by a "substantial equivalence" test, is which other test could be used.[59]

The issue of "like products" within the framework of international trade in GMOs has already been brought to the attention of the TBT Committee. The starting point for the discussions was the complaints made by a number of GMO-exporting countries about EC Regulation 1139/98,[60] which prescribes specific labelling requirements for food and food ingredients produced from genetically modified soya beans or genetically modified maize. In the EU's view, food and food ingredients containing DNA or proteins resulting from genetic modification are not equivalent to their conventional counterparts and consequently have to be subject to labelling requirements with a view to providing relevant information to consumers. In the exporting countries' view, the EC Regulation would negatively affect trade and set an unfortunate example for future regulation of food and agricultural products. The basis of the exporting countries' position was that food or food ingredients developed through genetic engineering or modification did not differ as a class in composition, quality or safety from products produced by other methods of breeding. Moreover, they believed that excessive labelling tended to confuse, rather than inform, consumers.[61]

The issue of labelling of GMOs and GM crops remains open within the WTO. Because it relates to concepts which are complex and controversial, such as the definition of "like" products, it is unlikely to be solved by the TBT Committee. Provisions on information to be included in the accompanying documentation of GMOs and genetically modified commodities have been included in the Biosafety Protocol. However, the problem of the consistency of these provisions with those of the TBT Agreement has not been addressed.

A number of notifications concerning agricultural and food products derived from modern biotechnology were made under the TBT and SPS Agreements, utilising the transparency provisions included in both Agreements. A total of

[59] See Stilwell, *supra* n. 7.

[60] Regulation (EC) 1139/98, 26 May 1998, OJ 1998 L159/4.

[61] WTO, Committee on Technical Barriers to Trade, *Communication from the European Community, Reply by the European Commission to the comments by the United States and Canada on Notification 97.766*, G/TBT/W/78, 27 August 1998; and WTO, Committee on Technical Barriers to Trade, *Communication from the United States, European Council Regulation No. 1139/98—Compulsory Indication of the Labelling of Certain Foodstuffs from Genetically Modified Organisms*, G/TBT/W/94, 16 October 1998. The TBT Committee discussed this topic in the meetings held on 15 September 1998, 11 June 1999 and 1 October 1999.

forty-eight notifications were made between 1 January 1995 and 10 June 2000 (which include a revision and some identical measures notified by more than one country and/or under both Agreements). The notifications were made by a number of developed countries (the USA, Japan, Canada, New Zealand, Australia, Switzerland, the EU, Norway, Germany and the Netherlands), some developing countries (Mexico, Colombia, the Republic of Korea and Malaysia), and by a country in transition (the Czech Republic).[62] Increasingly, members are undertaking efforts to implement national rules for products derived from biotechnology: eleven notifications have already been submitted in 2000, compared with four in 1995. It is interesting to note that the EU has notified its draft regulations under the TBT Agreement, invoking labelling-related issues in respect of their objective and rationale. The USA has notified its draft regulations under the SPS Agreement.

If uncertainties exist about the scope for applying the SPS and TBT Agreements to international trade in GMOs, the multilateral rules that undoubtedly apply to it are Articles III, XI, and XX of GATT.

The national treatment principle, which is incorporated into Article III, implies non-discrimination between domestic and imported goods. Translating this principle into the GMO context implies that the importing country is not allowed to apply to foreign products measures more onerous than those applied to like domestic products. In the context of Article III as well, the determination of what constitutes "like products" is a crucial issue since the national treatment obligations apply only if two products are "like".

The general elimination of quantitative restrictions is embodied in Article XI, which provides that no prohibitions or restrictions other than duties, taxes or charges shall be instituted or maintained on the importation or exportation of any product.

The obligations of Articles III and XI can be derogated from by using the exceptions set out in Article XX. The provisions of the latter which are of special relevance for trade in GMOs are as follows:

> "General Exceptions
>
> Subject to the requirement that such measures are not applied in a manner which would constitute a means of arbitrarily or unjustifiable discrimination between countries where the same conditions prevail, or a disguised restriction on international trade, nothing in this Agreement shall be construed to prevent the adoption or enforcement by any contracting party of measures:
>
> . . .
>
> (b) necessary to protect human, animal or plant life or health;
>
> . . .
>
> (g) relating to the conservation of exhaustible resources if such measures are made effective in conjunction with restrictions on domestic production or consumption.
>
> . . .

[62] WTO, Committee on Sanitary and Phytosanitary Measures, *Submission by the United States—National Regulatory Measures Related to Trade in Agricultural and Food Products Modified by Modern Biotechnology*, G/SPS/GEN/186, 21 June 2000.

Article XX gives countries the legal means to balance their trade obligations with important non-trade objectives, such as health protection or the preservation of the environment, which form part of their overall national policies. In the *Shrimp* case[63] the Appellate Body, referring to the introductory text of Article XX, stated that:

> "[W]e consider that it embodies the recognition on the part of WTO Members of the need to maintain a balance of rights and obligations between the right of a Member to invoke one or another of the exceptions of Article XX, specified in paragraphs (a) to (j), on the one hand, and the substantive rights of the other Members under the GATT 1994, on the other hand. . . A balance must be struck between the right of a Member to invoke an exception under Article XX and the duty of that same Member to respect the treaty rights of the other Members".[64]

According to the Appellate Body, the purpose of the introductory text of Article XX is "generally the prevention of the abuse of the exceptions of Article XX".[65]

A country which bans imports of GMOs or GM products may be infringing its trade obligations; it can, however, invoke a number of provisions to justify its trade-restrictive measure. It may invoke the SPS Agreement. In this case, it has to prove that the measure is necessary to protect human, animal or plant life or health, is based on scientific principles and is not maintained without sufficient scientific evidence. If the measure is applied on a provisional basis, it must seek to obtain the additional information necessary for a more objective assessment of risk and review the measure accordingly within a reasonable period of time. There are some difficulties at present in invoking the SPS Agreement to justify a trade-restrictive measure in respect of GMOs. GMO-related measures come within the spirit but not the letter of the Agreement. There is no scientific evidence that clearly identifies the level of risk that GMOs create for human, animal or plant life or health. If a measure is taken on the basis of the precautionary principle, it has to be reviewed within a reasonable time frame. A second option is to justify a GM trade-restrictive measure under the TBT Agreement. Some difficulties also arise in this case. First of all, it is unclear whether an import ban can be regarded as a technical regulation. Secondly, it is unclear whether GMOs can be considered different from conventional products or whether they are "like products". Even though several considerations lead to the conclusion that genetically modified products and conventional products are dissimilar, no consensus has been reached on this issue. The third option is to invoke Article XX of GATT. In this case, the country implementing the trade-restrictive measure has to prove not only that its measure is consistent with the specific exception invoked (paragraphs (b) or (g)), but also that it complies

[63] Appellate Body Report on *United States—Import Prohibition of Certain Shrimp and Shrimp Products*, 12 October 1998, WT/DS58/AB/R.

[64] *Ibid.* at para. 156.

[65] *Ibid.* at para. 150.

with the requirements of the introductory text of Article XX, i.e. that it does not constitute unjustifiable or arbitrary discrimination between countries where the same conditions prevail and does not constitute a disguised restriction on international trade.

Strengthened protection of intellectual property rights may make investment by the biotechnology industry more profitable.[66] The TRIPS Agreement, then, may be seen as promoting the adoption of GMOs in the food system. Related to the issue of biotechnology applied to agricultural and food products is the issue of obtaining patents on live plants or animals, including biotechnological inventions and plant varieties. Concerns are being expressed in both developed and developing countries about the economic, social, environmental and ethical impacts of life patenting. Moreover, many developing country governments are concerned that the control of the nature and distribution of new life forms by transnational corporations may affect their countries' development prospects and food security. Life patenting raises concerns about consumer rights, biodiversity conservation, environmental protection, sustainability of agriculture, indigenous rights, scientific and academic freedom, and, ultimately, the economic development of many developing countries dependent on new technologies. An additional concern is the degree to which patent holders and licensees will be responsible and liable for any adverse consequences of the application of biotechnology for the environment and human well-being.

Currently, the TRIPS Agreement does not require that countries grant patents for plants and animals; however, they have to provide for the protection of plant varieties either by patents or by an effective *sui generis* system,[67] or by a mixture of both (Article 27.3(b)). The revision of Article 27.3(b) is part of the "built-in agenda" agreed at the conclusion of the Uruguay Round. In accordance with that agenda, the WTO Council for TRIPS started the revision of Article 27.3(b) in 1999; however, owing to lack of consensus among members, the revision is still going on in 2000. Most developed countries see it as a review of implementation, while most developing countries see it as a review of the provisions themselves which could lead to a revision of the text.

While most developed countries consider that the model provided by the UPOV[68] system of Plant Breeders' Rights is the most appropriate *sui generis* system to afford protection to plant varieties, developing countries wish to retain flexibility in implementing legislation in this field. The UPOV system produces a fairly strong intellectual property rights (IPRs) regime for plant varieties

[66] The analysis of IPRs is based on G. Tansey, "Trade, Intellectual Property, Food and Biodiversity", Discussion Paper (Quaker Peace & Service, London, February 1999).

[67] A *sui generis* system of protection is an alternative, unique form of intellectual property protection, designed to fit a country's particular context and needs. In the case of plant varieties, it means that countries can make their own rules to protect new plant varieties with some form of intellectual property rights (IPRs), provided that such protection is effective. The Agreement does not define the elements of an effective system.

[68] Union Internationale pour la Protection des Obtentions Végétales (International Union for the Protection of New Varieties of Plants).

mainly geared to industrial breeding, which may not suit all countries. It promotes commercially bred varieties for industrial agricultural systems in which farmers have to pay royalties on such seed and the seed sector becomes an investment opportunity for the chemical and biotechnology industries. The alternative is for countries, especially those characterised by subsistence farming, to develop their own solutions with special legislation protecting plant varieties appropriate to their situation. For instance, developing countries could establish non-monopoly rights that allow different property rights to coexist, in recognition of the fact that a variety of actors participate in plant variety management and that they may have claims to the same innovations or knowledge. It should be noted that traditionally there has been no legal protection of plant varieties at the domestic or international levels. Patents and plant breeders' rights were progressively granted to give the private sector the incentive to enter the seed industry. These developments were until recently confined mainly to developed countries. Hardly any developing country had protection of plant variety included in its national legislation before the implementation of the TRIPS Agreement.[69]

Considering that patenting is linked to the development and introduction of GM plants, it can be argued that a country needs first to establish appropriate biosafety rules and control systems before considering the implementation of patent regimes that could encourage the development and release of these plants.

The Third WTO Ministerial Conference and its preparatory process

Most developing countries went to the Third Ministerial Conference of the World Trade Organisation (Seattle, 30 November–3 December 1999) with the idea that, in the field of biotechnology, the status quo would most likely be the best option. They opposed the view that environmental considerations should permeate the whole trade debate and remained hostile to the position that environmental concerns should be given greater weight within the WTO framework.[70] Also, they felt that by keeping the GMOs issue out of the negotiations and by avoiding the setting up of new multilateral rules in this field, they would have the time to develop regulatory frameworks to address the issue.

[69] See Ph. Cullet, *Protecting Rights in Plant Varieties* (Center for International Development at Harvard University, 1999), website: http://www.cid.harvard.edu/cidbiotech/comments/comments56.htm.

[70] See, for example, WTO, *Submission from India, General Council—Preparations for the 1999 Ministerial Conference—Discussion on Paragraph 9a(iii) of the Geneva Ministerial Declaration*, WT/GC/W/151, 8 March 1999: "The trade and environment interface issue is a complex one and in our assessment the existing WTO provisions are more than adequate to deal with genuine and bona fide environmental concerns. The real solution for the problem, if any, lies with international institutions dealing with multilateral environmental agreements".

GMO-exporting countries were hoping that some decisions would be taken at the Seattle Conference that would facilitate their future exports of GMOs and GM crops. In particular, they intended to tackle the problem of national GMO approvals (having in mind the very slow approval process in the EU and the de facto moratorium), reconfirm that scientific evidence should be the basis of any measure meant to protect human and animal health and the environment, characterize GM products and conventional products as "like products", and, eventually, launch the idea that a new set of rules should be developed to deal with trade in GMOs.

In particular, there were two sets of issues related to GMOs that different countries wished to tackle. The holders of the technology to produce GMOs wanted the WTO system to produce new disciplines on GMOs which would limit the regulatory capacity of countries in this field. A condition for reaching this goal was to ensure that a decision would be taken at the multilateral level in favour of a speedy and reliable system of approval of new GMOs in all countries. For those countries that were producers and exporters of GMOs, but not holders of the relevant technology, the main concern was to safeguard existing market access opportunities. While the first group of countries was in favour of including the issue of international trade in GMOs in the negotiations on agriculture, the latter was against this option, being concerned that this would move the focus of the negotiations from market access to biotechnology. As a compromise solution, some countries put forward proposals related to biotechnology and international trade during the preparatory process of the Seattle Conference.

The USA asked for the WTO "to address disciplines to ensure trade in biotechnology products is based on transparent, predictable and timely processes".[71] Through this proposal, the USA tried to achieve several goals: to ensure rapid exports of biotechnology products by limiting the time frame for the importing countries to take a decision about imports (timely processes); to allow GMO-exporting countries to provide inputs into the decision-making process of other countries at an early stage and therefore to be able to influence the policy development of other nations, in particular that of countries lacking scientific and technical capacity (transparent processes); and to consider GM products "like products" in relation to conventional products on the basis of a "substantial equivalence" test (predictable processes).

Canada suggested that there be established "a Working Party on biotechnology in the WTO with a fact finding mandate to consider adequacy and effectiveness of existing rules as well as the capacity of WTO Members to implement these rules effectively. One year after its establishment, the WP would report on its findings to the Steering Body (to be established at Seattle) and provide any

[71] WTO, *Communication from the United States—Preparations for the 1999 Ministerial Conference—Negotiations on Agriculture—Measures Affecting Trade in Agricultural Biotechnology Products*, WT/GC/W/288, 4 August 1999.

conclusions it considered appropriate".[72] Canada's wish, therefore, was to discuss biotechnology and international trade not only in the context of agriculture. Moreover, Canada wanted to maintain flexibility about the use of the findings of the Working Party, i.e. the establishment of the Working Party would not automatically imply that biotechnology would be included in the negotiations on agriculture.

Japan suggested that the WTO "establish an appropriate forum to address new issues, including GMOs. Such a forum would hold discussions from a broad perspective in order to analyse the current situation of GMOs, to examine the issues which need to be addressed, and to consider their relationship with existing WTO Agreements". This could be "a sub-group of an independent negotiating group on agriculture to identify topics on food-related matters of GMOs". Such a group should inter alia consider whether the relevant WTO Agreements, such as SPS, TBT and TRIPS, are capable of responding to GMO-related matters; what is the current situation of members with regard to their evaluation of the safety of GMOs and the labelling of food containing GMOs; and what would be the appropriate way for the WTO to deal with the contents and outcomes of discussions in other international forums.[73]

Under pressure from the promoters and from other GMO-exporting countries, these proposals were incorporated into the Draft Ministerial Declaration of 19 October 1999 in two parts. Paragraph 71, under the heading "Other elements of work programme", reads: "We agree to establish a Working Party on Biotechnology. The Working Party shall have a fact-finding mandate to consider the adequacy and effectiveness of existing rules as well as the capacity of WTO members to implement these rules. It is appropriate for this Group to deliberate within an X period of time".

Under the heading "Negotiations mandated at Marrakesh. Agriculture", Paragraph 29 (vi) refers to "Improvements in the rules and disciplines as appropriate, including with respect to . . . disciplines to ensure that trade in products of agricultural biotechnology is based on transparent, predictable and timely processes".

In Seattle, there was an initial discussion on these proposals. The USA confirmed that its aim was not to give the WTO the role of assessing the scientific basis of members' decisions on whether or not to allow certain products in their markets, but rather to give it a role with respect to the process by which countries approve bio-engineered agricultural products. The European Commission attempted to bridge its differences with the USA in this field by endorsing the creation of a working group in biotechnology, on condition that such a group would have a fact-finding rather than a negotiating mandate and would be part

[72] WTO, *Communication from Canada—Preparations for the 1999 Ministerial Conference—Proposal for Establishment of a Working Party on Biotechnology in WTO*, WT/GC/W/359, 12 October 1999.

[73] WTO, *Communication from Japan—Preparations for the 1999 Ministerial Conference—Proposal of Japan on Genetically Modified Organisms (GMOs)*, WT/GC/W/365, 12 October 1999.

of a comprehensive package on environment-related issues. Also, it reconfirmed that it would not relinquish its rights to ban agricultural and food products on safety grounds. However, the Commission lacked the specific mandate to make this concession and the EU environment and trade ministers reversed its positions and opposed discussion on biotechnology in the WTO. There may have been several reasons for this position: the fear that the creation of a WTO working group would jeopardise the successful conclusion of the negotiations on the Biosafety Protocol; the conviction that the WTO was not the most adequate forum for developing a multilateral approach to biotechnology issues; and the fear that if a specific mandate were given to the WTO, trade considerations would have precedence over environmental concerns. After the EU ministers opposed the Commission's initial position, the Commission declared that it would accept a working group on biotechnology only if all countries pledged to work in good faith to conclude the biosafety talks and agreed a broad negotiating agenda in the WTO which would include environmental and consumer issues.

Following the failure of the Seattle Conference, the future status of the proposals submitted during the preparatory process has not been clarified. However, whatever the decision that is taken about their legal status, they reflect countries' concerns which did not have a chance to be addressed during the ministerial conference, but which are still present. In the specific area of biotechnology and GMOs, the launching of the new negotiations on agriculture in March 2000 has provided a forum where these issues could be discussed; some GMO-producing and exporting countries have already proposed that this topic be included in the negotiations. It is very doubtful, however, whether this forum will prove to be the most appropriate place for holding discussions on biotechnology-related issues. It will probably be very difficult for developing countries to obtain positive overall results from the negotiations on agriculture if the issue of biotechnology looms too large and attracts too much attention from delegations. The successful conclusion of the Biosafety Protocol will most probably have an impact on the positions that countries held during the Seattle preparatory process and at the Conference itself.

The initiatives taken by the Codex Alimentarius Commission and the Food and Agriculture Organisation

The Codex Alimentarius Commission established in June 1999 an Ad Hoc Intergovernmental Task Force on Foods Derived from Biotechnology to develop standards, guidelines or recommendations, as appropriate, for foods derived from biotechnologies or traits introduced into foods by biotechnological methods. The expectation of the global community is that the Task Force will reach an agreement on the modalities of the safety assessment of food derived from biotechnology within a period of four years. The Task Force held its first session from 14 to 17 March 2000. During the meeting, many delegations and observer organisations identified safety and nutrition assessment of foods derived from biotechnology as the main priority area of work.[74]

The Task Force decided that it would proceed with the elaboration of two major texts: (1) a set of broad general principles for risk analysis of foods derived from biotechnology, including science-based decision-making, pre-market assessment, post-market monitoring and transparency; and (2) specific guidance on the risk assessment of foods derived from biotechnology, including matters such as food safety and nutrition, substantial equivalence, non-intentional effects and potential long-term health effects. A Working Group chaired by Japan was charged with the task of elaborating those texts.

In addition, the Task Force agreed that a list of available analytical methods, including those for the detection or identification of foods or food ingredients derived from biotechnology, should be prepared, and that it should indicate the performance criteria of each method and the status of its validation. A Working Group chaired by Germany is in charge of compiling the list.

The Codex Committee on Food Labelling is considering the adoption of an international standard for GMO labelling.

In 1996, the Food and Agriculture Organisation (FAO) and the World Health Organisation (WHO) held an Expert Consultation and recommended that developing countries be provided with assistance and education regarding approaches to the safety assessment of foods and food components produced by genetic modification. At the first meeting of the Task Force, FAO and WHO reaffirmed their support for technical assistance to developing countries.

FAO published a statement on the occasion of the first meeting of the Task Force.[75] It stressed that genetic engineering provides powerful tools for the sustainable development of agriculture, forestry and fisheries and can be of significant help in meeting the food needs of a growing and increasingly urbanised population. In the case of GMOs, however, FAO called for a science-based evaluation that would objectively determine the benefits and risks of each individual GMO and address the legitimate concerns regarding the biosafety of each product and process prior to its release. FAO noted that investment in biotechnological research tends to be concentrated in the private sector and oriented towards agriculture in higher-income countries where there is purchasing power for its products. In view of the potential contribution of biotechnologies for increasing food supply and overcoming food insecurity and vulnerability, FAO called for efforts to be made to ensure that developing countries in general, and resource-poor farmers in particular, benefit more from biotechnological

[74] Joint FAO/WHO Food Standard Programme, *Report of the First Session of the Codex Ad Hoc Intergovernmental Task Force on Foods Derived from Biotechnology* (Chiba, Japan, 14–17 March 2000, ALINOR 01/34). The report will be considered by the 24th Session of the Codex Alimentarius Commission (Geneva, 2–7 July 2001).

[75] See "FAO Stresses Potential of Biotechnology but Calls for Caution", FAO Press Release 00/17.

research while continuing to have access to a diversity of sources of genetic material. FAO proposed that this need be addressed through increased public funding and dialogue between the public and private sectors.

On 28 June 2000, the Director-General of FAO acknowledged in an interview that conventional crops could feed the 800 million hungry people in the world if only they were fairly distributed across the developing world. He predicted, however, that a shortage of land available for cultivation would make it impossible to feed a global population expected to peak at 9 billion people without recourse to genetically engineered plants and animals. In addition, he stressed that there is a need to take all necessary precautions to protect human health and the environment. He said he believed that consensus on GM food standards could be achieved, despite a division of opinion. The FAO, he added, is setting up a special "ethics committee", with input from philosophers and religious representatives, to investigate human factors related to GM agriculture.[76]

In July 1999, the Codex Alimentarius Commission approved international guidelines for the production, processing, labelling and marketing of organically produced food. The guidelines define the nature of organic food production and will prevent claims that could mislead consumers about the quality of a product or the way it is produced. The final objective is to provide the consumer with a choice while giving assurances that organic agricultural standards have been met.[77]

The initiatives taken by the OECD

Biotechnology, genetically modified crops and other aspects of food safety have rapidly become issues of major interest to the member countries of the Organisation for Economic Co-operation and Development (OECD). OECD has a number of projects related to biosafety, such as the Working Group for the Harmonization of Regulatory Oversight in Biotechnology, the Working Party on Biotechnology, and the Task Force for the Safety of Novel Foods and Feeds. Currently, it is preparing a response to a request received from the G8 Heads of State and Government in June 1999 for a study to be undertaken on "the implications of biotechnology and other aspects of food safety".[78] OECD has

[76] See "World Needs GM Crops, Says UN Food Chief", *Financial Times,* 28 June 2000.

[77] See "The Codex Alimentarius Commission Approves Guidelines for Organic Food and Sets Up Taskforces on Standards for Foods Derived from Biotechnology, Animal Feeding and Fruit Juices", FAO Press Release 99/41.

[78] "Biotechnology offers great opportunities but also represents significant challenges and has given rise to public debate on its implications. Ministers stressed the importance of safeguarding human health and the environment while enabling people to enjoy the benefits that flow from advances in biotechnology. Scientific research is essential to the process. The OECD should continue to examine the various dimensions of this issue, including in the discussion at the forthcoming CSTP (Committee on Science and Technology Policy) ministerial meeting and in other fora": Communiqué of the OECD Council meeting at Ministerial level, May 1999, para. 9. "Because trade is increasingly global, the consequences of developments in biotechnology must be dealt with at the

planned five elements in response to the G8: a report on the safety assessment of novel foods; a report on related environmental issues; a compendium describing national and international food safety systems; the results of an OECD consultation with non-governmental organisations held on 20 November 1999; and the results of the OECD Conference on "GM and Food Safety: Facts, Uncertainties and Assessment" (Edinburgh, 28 February–1 March 2000).[79]

VI. THE PRECAUTIONARY PRINCIPLE

The precautionary principle started to appear in multilateral agreements in the mid-1980s. Reference was made to it in the 1985 Vienna Convention for the Protection of the Ozone Layer and the 1987 Montreal Protocol on Substances that Deplete the Ozone Layer. The text of the 1973 Convention on International Trade in Endangered Species of Wild Fauna and Flora (CITES) did not explicitly invoke the principle, however, the Conference of the Parties explicitly endorsed it in 1994. The use of the principle increased further in the 1990s, when the United Nations Conference on Environment and Development (UNCED) significantly enlarged the consensus on it. Principle 15 of the Rio Declaration was adopted.[80] In addition, UNCED delegates invoked the principle in the United Nations Framework Convention on Climate Change, in the Convention on Biological Diversity and in Agenda 21. As already mentioned, the precautionary principle is one of the central features of the Cartagena Protocol.[81]

By 1990, the precautionary principle was also appearing in regional declarations and treaties. The 1991 Bamako Convention on the Ban of the Import into Africa and the Control of Transboundary Movement and Management of Hazardous Wastes within Africa calls for the implementation of the precautionary principle. In Europe, the principle was included in the 1992 Convention for the Protection of the Marine Environment of the North-East Atlantic, in the 1992 Convention on the Protection and Use of Transboundary Watercourses and Lakes, and in the 1992 Convention on the Protection of the Marine

national and international levels in all the appropriate fora. We are committed to a science-based, rules-based approach to addressing these issues": Communiqué of the G8 Heads of State and Government meeting, Cologne, June 1999, para. 11.

[79] See Inter-Agency Network for Safety in Biotechnology (IANB), *Safety in Biotechnology—IANB Newsletter*, No. 1, 19 April 2000, and *OECD Work on Biotechnology and Other Aspects of Food Safety*, Note by the Secretary-General, C(99)148/REV4, 15 November 1999.

[80] In the Rio Declaration's formulation, the principle has several elements. The threshold for triggering the principle is that there are identifiable threats of serious or irreversible damage. Where such threats exist, governments are free to take preventive cost-effective measures. Governments may also refuse to take such measures, but not on the ground that there is a lack of scientific certainty. Other than reference to cost-effective measures, Principle 15 places no conditions or restrictions on the preventive measures a government chooses.

[81] For a recent analysis of the precautionary principle in international trade, see H. Ward, *Science and Precaution in the Trading System* (Royal Institute of International Affairs and the International Institute for Sustainable Development, 1999).

Environment of the Baltic Sea Area. The precautionary principle was written into the Maastricht Treaty in 1992 as the basis for EU action on the environment.

Since 1992, the precautionary principle has also been reflected in the domestic legislation and case law of an increasing number of countries. According to most commentators, it originated in the municipal environmental policy of the Federal Republic of Germany, where it materialised in the concepts that environmental hazards must be avoided before they occur, and that governmental authorities can order measures or act themselves, even in the face of uncertainty. In Colombia, Law No. 99 (approved in 1993) incorporates the precautionary principle as fundamental to the country's environmental policy. In 1988, Costa Rica passed Law No. 7788 to conserve biodiversity, to foster the sustainable use of natural resources and to distribute in an equitable fashion the benefits and costs derived from biodiversity. The precautionary criterion is one of the criteria for implementing the law. In Australia the precautionary principle has been incorporated into nearly all recent federal environmental policies and strategies. In addition, Australia's judiciary has recognised the principle in a number of environmental cases. Canada has adopted the precautionary approach in legislation and intergovernmental agreements and it has appeared in Canadian case law. Several of Canada's provinces have adopted the precautionary principle in their environmental legislation. The precautionary approach is reflected, at least implicitly, in numerous domestic environmental laws in the USA, including the Endangered Species Act, the National Environmental Policy Act, the Clean Air Act, the Federal Food, Drug and Cosmetic Act, the Clean Water Act and the Oil Pollution Act. The USA, however, has consistently maintained that the precautionary approach is not a rule of customary law; thus, although it arguably adopts a precautionary approach in several environmental laws, it does not do so out of a sense of international obligation.

In the *Vellore Citizens Welfare Forum* v. *Union of India and others*, the Indian Supreme Court adopted the precautionary principle in addressing pollution caused by tanneries and concluded that it was an essential element of sustainable development. Also, the Court found that the precautionary principle was part of the law of India, at least in part because the rules of customary international law, presumably including the precautionary principle, are deemed to be incorporated into domestic law if they are not contrary to domestic law. In *Shehla Zia* v. *WAPDA*, the Pakistani Supreme Court reviewed the challenge by a citizens'group to the proposed construction of an electric grid station. On the basis of the precautionary principle as expressed in international law and the Pakistan Constitution, the Court prohibited construction of the grid station until further studies could clarify its potential impact.[82]

[82] The analysis of the precautionary principle in regional and national legislation and in case law is based on M.T. Stilwell, "The Precautionary Principle in International and Domestic Law" (mimeo, 2000).

On 2 February 2000, the European Commission adopted a Communication[83] on the use of the precautionary principle as a complement to the Biosafety Protocol and the White Paper on Food Security. The stated objectives of the Communication are to inform all interested parties about how the Commission intends to apply the principle; establish guidelines for its application; provide input to the ongoing debate on this issue both at EU and international level; build a common understanding of how to assess, appraise, manage and communicate risks that science is not yet able to evaluate fully; and avoid unwarranted recourse to the precautionary principle as a disguised form of protectionism.

According to the Communication, the Commission considers that the precautionary principle has a scope far wider than the environmental field and also covers the protection of human, animal and plant health. It provides a basis for action when science is unable to give a clear answer, but when there are reasonable grounds for concern that potential hazards may affect the environment or human, animal or plant health in a way inconsistent with the high level of protection chosen by the EU. Decision-makers need to be aware of the degree of uncertainty surrounding the results of the evaluation of the available scientific information; however, determining what is an acceptable level of risk is, in the Commission's view, an eminently political responsibility. Measures based on the precautionary principle should be, inter alia, proportional to the chosen level of protection; non-discriminatory in their application; consistent with similar measures already taken; based on the examination of the potential benefits and costs of action or lack of action; subject to review, in the light of new scientific data; and capable of assigning responsibility for producing the scientific evidence necessary for a more comprehensive risk assessment. The Commission makes it clear that examining costs and benefits of action and lack of action is not simply an economic cost-benefit analysis: it includes non-economic considerations, such as the efficacy of possible options and their acceptability to the public. In the conduct of such an examination, the protection of health takes precedence over economic considerations.

The Environment Commissioner, who presented the White Paper on Food Security at a plenary session of the European Parliament, admitted that the use of the precautionary principle by the EU could trigger further trade friction with the USA, but said that disputes could be worked out.[84]

During the Seattle preparatory process, the EU addressed the issue of the precautionary principle and suggested that WTO members focus on, inter alia, "reviewing if a clarification of the relationship between multilateral trade rules and core environmental principles, notably the precautionary principle, is needed". It added that "it is necessary to ensure the right balance between

[83] Commission of the European Communities, *Communication from the Commission on the Precautionary Principle*, Brussels, 2 February 2000, COM(2000) 1 final.

[84] See "EC's Precautionary Principle Seeks Proportionate, Unbiased Risk Analysis", (2000) 17 *International Trade Reporter* (2 February 2000) No. 6.

prompt, proportional action, where justified, and the avoidance of unjustified precaution, bearing in mind that the basic concept of the precautionary principle is already present in the WTO in several key provisions, such as the SPS and TBT Agreements".[85]

The reference in multilateral, regional and national legal texts to the precautionary principle does not make it less controversial in the context of international trade: although the precautionary principle has been included in a number of crucial legal instruments dealing with the environment, its status within the framework of the international trading system is still unclear.

The WTO SPS Committee discussed the precautionary principle at its first meeting in 2000 (15–16 March), when the EU introduced its Communication on the principle. Both the developed and the developing countries that participated in the debate voiced their concerns about the Communication and stressed that the SPS Agreement already contained rules for dealing with cases where emergency measures were needed but related scientific evidence was not fully available. They stated that a broad application of the precautionary principle in international trade would lead to a situation of unpredictability in relation to market access, which would jeopardise the results of the Uruguay Round. Moreover, the implementation of precautionary measures without a strict time frame would encourage inefficiency and slow down scientific research. Countries that expressed themselves in the SPS Committee against a broad interpretation of the precautionary principle include those that had taken up a position against it during the Biosafety Protocol negotiations, as well as some of those that were in favour of it within the Biosafety Protocol framework.

VII. CONCLUSIONS

As *exporters*, developing countries have traditionally been concerned that developed countries would use measures for health, environment or consumer protection as tools to protect their domestic industry with a consequent risk for developing country market access opportunities.

As *importers*, developing countries are facing a different risk in the biotechnology field—that of importing and utilising products which may prove to be harmful for human health or the environment. The limited capacity of most developing countries to check products at the border and make their own assessment of the risks and benefits involved, and the lack of domestic legislation in this field, make their concern serious.

If, as *exporters*, developing countries have pleaded against any modification of the existing multilateral trade rules that would allow more flexibility to use trade-restrictive measures for the protection of human or animal life and health

[85] WTO, *Communication from the European Communities, Preparations for the 1999 Ministerial Conference—EC Approach to Trade and Environment in the New WTO Round*, WT/GC/W/194, 1 June 1999.

or the environment, as potential *importers* of GMOs, most developing countries have requested the flexibility to decide whether to accept or refuse products whose effects on health and the environment are not yet fully known.

In practical terms, these different preoccupations have been reflected in the fact that developing countries have requested TBT and SPS measures to be based, as far as possible, on international standards and scientific evidence, have supported a narrow interpretation of the precautionary principle within the WTO Agreements, and rejected developed country proposals for modifying Article XX of GATT. On the other hand, most developing countries have taken a strong position in favour of flexibility in decision-making within the Biosafety Protocol and have struggled to make the precautionary approach one of the key features of the Protocol.

These conflicting positions are not a sign of a lack of understanding of the issues at stake, but show how difficult it is for countries—especially countries with scarce financial and technical resources and competing needs—to take an unequivocal position in an international trade scenario which is becoming increasingly complex.

Biotechnology may be an area where developing countries do not have a particular interest in negotiating further, especially within the WTO, since in any negotiations they would be likely to face several risks. Introducing GMOs into the WTO may bring the trade and environment communities into conflict and allow the GMO-exporting countries to develop new disciplines which could undermine the Biosafety Protocol. On the other hand, it may allow some countries to develop new rules on the precautionary principle that extend far beyond the GM products that developing countries are concerned about, thus undermining their market access for conventional products.

There are forums outside the WTO where GMO-related issues have been addressed and could be addressed further, such as the CBD/Biosafety Protocol or the FAO. Scientific, legal and tactical considerations would justify choosing to hold discussions on GMOs there. Countries are represented in these forums by delegates with specific expertise in the sector. The Biosafety Protocol is targeted at GMOs, whereas WTO Agreements, such as the TBT and SPS Agreements, apply across the board. Developing countries are usually more able to make their voice heard in the CBD or FAO context than in the WTO. Discussions held in these forums can be very productive, but the conclusions reached may be challenged on the basis of their WTO consistency.

There are also several forums within the WTO where issues related to trade in biotechnology products and, more specifically, GMOs could be addressed or have already been addressed, directly or indirectly. Each forum has its own characteristics and discussions may have different results according to where they take place. The SPS and TBT Committees are technical committees with a rather well defined mandate and relatively little room for trade-offs, even though the TBT Agreement is at present going through its second triennial review. The Committee on Trade and Environment is a forum where non-trade concerns are given special attention. The Committee on Agriculture, where agricultural negotiations are ongoing, is the forum that offers at present the widest margin of manoeuvre and the broadest opportunities for trade-offs. However, it may also be a risky forum for developing countries. GMO-producing and exporting countries may exchange concessions in the field of biotechnology for concessions in other fields, such as export subsidies, and this could lead to a situation which would go against developing country interests in the sector. Moreover, too great a focus on biotechnology would divert attention from the issues that are of most relevance to developing countries, namely tariff reductions and dismantling of subsidies, and jeopardise the global outcomes of the negotiations. Furthermore, it could be argued that trade in GMOs is an horizontal issue that has implications extending beyond agriculture and that the Committee on Agriculture is therefore not the most appropriate forum in which to discuss it. An ad hoc working group within the WTO could contribute to enhancing the understanding of the issue; however, working groups have often been the first step towards the negotiation of new trade rules.

If the question of international trade in GMOs and products derived from them is brought to the WTO, two possible scenarios could be envisaged.

Scenario 1

Since some powerful trading partners strongly support changes in the WTO system in order better to accommodate their non-trade-related concerns, and in view of the pressure put on the system by very vocal consumer and environmental groups, the multilateral trading system may become more flexible by allowing countries to make use of restrictive trade measures to protect their markets from products which may have detrimental effects on human, animal or plant life and health or on the environment. Negotiations may therefore start in the WTO to modify Article XX of GATT and, possibly, Article 5.7 of the SPS Agreement.

A wholesale change to the SPS Agreement and to Article XX of GATT affecting not only trade in GMOs but also trade in non-GM crops and food products would be a risky option for developing countries since it could jeopardise their existing market access opportunities. On the other hand, it would be unnecessary for them when seeking to protect domestic health and safety in the field of GMOs, since they could use the Biosafety Protocol for that purpose.

Nevertheless, if trade rules are changed in the way described above, the developing country attitude could be that technical and financial assistance should be provided to them to ensure that they will be able to comply with the new and stricter requirements which will be likely to be implemented by the importing countries. Full implementation by developed countries of the provisions on technical cooperation and special and differential treatment contained in the SPS and TBT Agreements should be encouraged. The market access opportunities of developing countries should be preserved and the balance of rights and obligations emerging from the Uruguay Round should not be changed. This option may be risky: strict requirements will be implemented, but technical and financial cooperation may not follow, as the experience with best endeavour clauses has shown. However, developing countries have also to keep in mind that retailers and consumers may refuse products which do not comply with strict standards; therefore, enhanced capacities to produce quality and safe products are, in the long run, the most promising alternative.

This option implies building up knowledge, skills and capabilities in developing countries. Strengthening domestic capacities in this domain would have positive spillover effects, as it would also help developing countries, *as importers*, to identify reliably the kind of products they wish to allow into their markets. From a position where, owing to the lack of capacity to assess the potential risks and benefits related to genetically modified products, they are sceptical about importing and using them, they could move to a position where, on the basis of increased scientific capacities and of their own assessment of the potential risks and benefits involved, they would block the entry of those products that are actually or potentially detrimental to domestic health and safety, taking into account local conditions, while letting in those products which may prove to be beneficial for addressing serious domestic problems, such as food security, public health or environmental protection. In other words, strengthening developing country ability to deal with scientific issues in the agricultural field would improve their capacities as *exporters* as well as *importers,* and, in the future, as *producers*. Developing countries may benefit from biotechnology if they are able to deal with it and participate in its development.

Scenario 2

Legal uncertainty is already affecting international trade flows in GMOs and products derived from them, and the economic interests of GMO-exporting countries, primarily the USA and Canada, are being affected. Transnational corporations which have made significant investments in biotechnology are already putting pressure on their governments to ensure that the multilateral trading system includes as few limitations as possible on the transborder movement of biotechnology products. As a result of the pressure exerted by key trading partners and by manufacturers' lobbies, the existing Uruguay Round Agreements remain unchanged.

The attitude of the developing countries could be that the present trade scenario presents difficulties for them, since they have to cope with new phenomena, such as biotechnology, and they lack the expertise to do so. Therefore, they need technical and financial cooperation to build policy and technical capacities in the new fields. An international fund, sponsored by public and private contributions and run under the auspices of the CBD secretariat, the FAO or the

Codex Alimentarius Commission, could be set up to finance technical training in biotechnology applied to agriculture and make it possible for developing countries to assess the risk and benefits of biotechnology products. On the basis of such an assessment, they would decide which products to import or which seed to sow, and, eventually, which technology to develop to address their own agricultural and food security problems. The FAO/WHO offer to provide support to developing countries in the safety assessment of foods and food components produced by genetic modification could be a starting point. Technical cooperation offered by those developing countries that have already acquired some expertise in the field of biotechnology to the other developing countries that are still in the process of familiarising themselves with this new phenomenon would also be an important contribution towards capacity building.

The status quo option is less risky than the first one from a trade point of view (in order to be able to implement WTO-consistent trade-restrictive measures to pursue health- or environment-related objectives, countries will have to comply with the strict requirements of Article XX of GATT and Article 5.7 of the SPS Agreement). However, it may be more risky from the point of view of domestic health and environmental protection, if the competent international organisations and the developed countries do not provide the cooperation requested. The Biosafety Protocol, however, contains specific provisions related to technical cooperation and these should also be utilised.

If the status quo prevails, the chances of having numerous trade disputes brought to the WTO dispute settlement system are quite high. This is because the issue of the relationship between the trade rules included in specific multilateral agreements and WTO rights and obligations has not yet been solved. The WTO Panels and the Appellate Body will provide solutions on a case-by-case basis. Developing countries face some difficulties in this field: to be party to a dispute settlement case is time-consuming and very costly, especially if they have to rely on foreign lawyers. Moreover, if a specific dispute is solved in a certain way, it does not mean that a similar case will be settled on exactly the same terms. Therefore, it is necessary to be constantly vigilant about the evolution of WTO jurisprudence. These are additional considerations to be taken into account.

4

Biosafety and Intellectual Property Rights: Balancing Trade and Environmental Security—The Jurisprudence of the European Patent Office as a Paradigm of an International Public Policy Issue

RICCARDO PAVONI

I. INTRODUCTION

THE GRANT OF intellectual property protection for genetically modified organisms (GMOs) has been accompanied by wide controversy on the extent to which such organisms may adversely affect biological diversity.[1] A new concept, that of *biosafety*, has been forged to denote the paramount importance which the international community attaches to the "safe transfer, handling and use of any living modified organism resulting from biotechnology that may have adverse effect on the conservation and sustainable use of biological diversity".[2]

The controversy has important consequences, not only for the international rules governing trade in goods, but also for the aspects of intellectual property rights (IPRs) which may run counter to the protection of the global environment.[3] Insofar as international conventions are concerned, it is well known

[1] R. Acharya, "Patenting of Biotechnology: GATT and the Erosion of the World's Biodiversity", (1991) 6 *Journal of World Trade* 71 80–5; J. Rissler and M.G. Mellon, *The Ecological Risks of Engineered Crops*, (Cambridge (MA), 1996); R.A. Steinbrecher, "From Green to Gene Revolution: The Environmental Risks of Genetically Engineered Crops", (1996) *The Ecologist* 273; J. Rifkin, *The Biotech Century* (Washington D.C., 1998), pp. 121–87.

[2] Cf. Art. 19(3) of the Convention on Biological Diversity, which mandates the Contracting Parties to conclude a Protocol on Biosafety. Following a very complex negotiating process such Protocol was finally adopted in Montreal on 29 January 2000: text in (2000) *ILM* 1027. On the issue of compatibility between the Biosafety Protocol and the rules provided for in the Agreement on the Application of Sanitary and Phytosanitary Measures, see Schoenbaum, *supra* Chapter 2.

[3] G. Winter, "Patent Law Policy in Biotechnology", (1992) *Journal of Environmental Law* 167; D. Alexander, "Some Themes in Intellectual Property and the Environment", (1993) *RECIEL* 113;

that the Convention on Biological Diversity (CBD) and the Agreement on Trade-Related Aspects of Intellectual Property Rights (TRIPs)[4] raise complex issues of mutual consistency.[5]

States parties to the CBD, "recognising that patents and other intellectual property rights may have an influence on the implementation of th[e] convention", have undertaken the obligation to cooperate "subject to national legislation and international law in order to ensure that such rights *are supportive of and do not run counter* to its objectives".[6] Conversely, the TRIPs Agreement stipulates that in principle "patents shall be available for any inventions . . . in all fields of technology, provided they are new, involve an inventive step and are capable of industrial application".[7]

Legal literature has mainly dealt with the issue of technology transfer, which is strongly advocated by the CBD and potentially hindered by a comprehensive granting of IPRs for technologies,[8] or on the opportunity to widen the category of IPRs so as to include indigenous people's knowledge, practices and innovations relevant to the conservation of biodiversity and with a view to opposing the phenomenon known as *biopiracy*.[9]

I. Walden, "Intellectual Property Rights and Biodiversity", in C. Redgwell and M. Bowman (eds), *International Law and the Conservation of Biological Diversity* (London, 1995), p. 171; R. McNally and P. Wheale, "Biopatenting and Biodiversity: Comparative Advantages in the New Global Order", (1996) *The Ecologist* 222.

[4] The text of the two treaties is reproduced, respectively, in (1992) *ILM* 818, and in (1994) *Int. Review of Industrial Property and Copyright Law* 209.

[5] J. Straus, "The Rio Biodiversity Convention and Intellectual Property", (1993) *Int. Review of Industrial Property and Copyright Law* 602; R.G. Tarasofski, "The Relationship Between the TRIPs Agreement and the Convention on Biological Diversity: Towards a Pragmatic Approach", (1997) *RECIEL* 148; G. Dutfield, *Can the TRIPS Agreement Protect Biological and Cultural Diversity?* (Nairobi, 1997); S. Prakash, "Towards a Synergy between Biodiversity and Intellectual Property Rights", (1999) *Journal of World Intellectual Property* 821.

[6] Art. 16(5) CBD, emphasis added.

[7] Art. 27(1) TRIPs.

[8] Cf. Art. 16 CBD; Tarasofski, *supra* n. 5, p. 150 (addressing problems of consistency between agreements on technology transfer and the fundamental clauses of national treatment and most-favoured-nation of Arts. 3 and 4 TRIPs); M.D. Coughlin Jr., "Using the Merck-INBio Agreement to Clarify the Convention on Biological Diversity", (1993) *Columbia JTL* 337; F. Munari, "Il rapporto tra liberalizzazione del commercio internazionale e tutela dell'ambiente con particolare riguardo agli aspetti relativi alla proprietà intellettuale e agli investimenti", in *Diritto e organizzazione del commercio internazionale dopo la creazione della Organizzazione Mondiale del Commercio* (Proceedings of the symposium of the *Società Italiana di Diritto Internazionale*, Milano, 5–7 June 1997) (Napoli, 1998), p. 181. For further issues relating to technology transfer, see Spence, *infra* Chapter 10 and Munari, *infra* Chapter 7.

[9] Arts. 8(j) and 10(c) CBD. Cf. C.D. Stone, "What To Do about Biodiversity: Property Rights, Public Goods, and the Earth's Biological Riches", (1995) *Southern California Law Review* 577. "Biopiracy" consists in the appropriation of genetic resources discovered in the Southern hemisphere (where they are principally located), or of indigenous' practices, by multinationals of the industrialized world. Such multinationals will then develop commercial products starting from those resources, obtain patent protection and eventually market them. The communities responsible for safeguarding the resources all over the centuries will usually not receive any rewards. The recognition of property rights on genetic resources, as well as traditional practices and knowledge, may contribute to halt this dangerous trend. Cf. e.g. V. Shiva, *Biopiracy: The Plunder of Nature and Knowledge* (Boston, 1997); A. Pottage, "The Inscription of Life in Law: Genes, Patents, and Bio-Politics", (1998) *MLR* 740.

My enquiry will instead be focused on the lawfulness of the grant of patents for biotechnology products and processes whose exploitation may adversely and irreversibly affect the preservation of biological diversity. Patent protection may represent a formidable incentive for the development and marketing of such potentially harmful products and processes. Of course, this will not be the right place to give a detailed account of the controversial debate concerning the environmental risks associated with the release of GMOs, especially transgenic plants and animals. It will suffice to recall that the most commonly known biotechnology applications might cause:

(a) the extinction of harmless species of microrganisms and insects;
(b) an increased utilisation of chemical products, such as herbicides;
(c) the development of new strains of super-weeds or super-insects, having an absolute tolerance to chemical products;
(d) an uncontrollable propagation into the wild leading to the inevitable supplantation of local species (so-called "genetic pollution");
(e) severe problems to human and animal health, due to toxic or allergic reactions, or to the development of antibiotics resistance.[10]

In this respect, the conflict between IPRs and environmental protection appears more tangible than the sometimes speculative issues of WTO law versus IPR-free technology transfer, or versus recognition of indigenous rights, which after all appear more apt to pragmatic solution than legal analysis.[11] Still, many problems remain open: first, to what extent is it legitimate to challenge patent protection for inventions posing a threat to the environment? Secondly, what is the legal basis available for the denial of patents on GMOs? Thirdly, what role is played by scientific uncertainty (concerning the environmental impact of GMOs) in patent litigation? Fourthly, what is the impact on such litigation of the cost-benefit analysis (CBA) often advocated by trade dispute settlement bodies?

After addressing these issues, I will highlight the relevant international rules and principles which should guide the regulatory efforts currently being undertaken at international and regional levels to devise a coherent legal framework for trade in biotechnology.

II. THE JURISPRUDENCE OF THE EUROPEAN PATENT OFFICE AS A PARADIGM OF TRADE/ENVIRONMENT DISPUTES

Whilst no judicial decisions have been taken at WTO level specifically dealing with the environmental exception to patentability provided for in Article 27(2)

[10] For more detail, see the works cited *supra* n. 1.

[11] Cf. Tarasofski, *supra* n. 5.

TRIPs,[12] a particularly interesting jurisprudence has emerged within the European patent system.

Such jurisprudence may thus be viewed as paradigmatic with respect to the problem of consistency between the protection of IPRs and environmental security, a problem which otherwise possesses a global dimension. Furthermore, there exist several similarities between the core issues arising in such cases and some of those tackled by GATT/WTO adjudicative bodies in trade/environment litigation. It is then worth contrasting the judicial methods and criteria developed in the two systems in order to assess whether trade dispute settlement bodies are developing a set of common rules applicable to the solution of disputes involving environmental concerns.[13]

International environmental law as a foreign body in patent litigation

It has been often pointed out that the approach of adjudicative bodies within the multilateral trading system towards the integration of international environmental law into the body of law applicable to disputes involving environmental and health concerns has been unduly restrictive.[14] At the same time, I am aware that the 1994 reform of that system has brought a new line of jurisprudence which, in accordance with the reference to the objective of sustainable development included in the preamble of the Agreement Establishing the World Trade Organisation and with that to the customary norms of interpretation in Article 3(2) of the Dispute Settlement Understanding, has increasingly endeavoured to interpret WTO provisions in the light of (non-WTO) rules of international law.[15] However, whether such jurisprudence will eventually determine a mean-

[12] Art. 27(2) TRIPs reads: "Members may exclude from patentability inventions, the prevention within their territory of the commercial exploitation of which is necessary to protect 'ordre public' or morality, including to protect human, animal or plant life or health or to *avoid serious prejudice to the environment*" (emphasis added).

[13] Throughout this article, the reference to disputes involving *environmental* concerns must be broadly understood to include also those cases where protection of human, animal and plant life or *health* was at stake.

[14] See e.g. P.J. Kuyper, "The Law of GATT as a Special Field of International Law", (1994) *Netherlands Yearbook of Int. Law* 227.

[15] The turning point of such jurisprudence is commonly considered the *dictum* of the Appellate Body in the *Gasoline* case whereby it was recognised that the WTO Agreements are "not to be read in clinical isolation from public international law": *United States—Standards for Reformulated and Conventional Gasoline*, Report of the Appellate Body adopted on 20 May 1996, WT/DS2/AB/R, p. 17, reproduced in (1996) *ILM* 603. In this respect, however, the landmark case is certainly *United States—Import Prohibition of Certain Shrimp and Shrimp Products*, Report of the Appellate Body adopted on 6 November 1998, WT/DS58/AB/R, reproduced in (1999) *ILM* 121. Here, the Appellate Body stated that the reference to the objective of sustainable development in the preamble of the WTO Agreement "must add colour, texture and shading to [the] interpretation of the agreements annexed to the *WTO Agreement*": para. 153. Accordingly, the meaning of the expression "exhaustible natural resources" in Art. XX(g) GATT was deduced from a number of environmental agreements, see paras. 129–31. For further discussion and analysis see the excellent work by G. Marceau, "A Call for Coherence in International Law—Praises for the Prohibition Against 'Clinical Isolation' in WTO Dispute Settlement", (1999) 5 *Journal of World Trade* 87.

ingful and coherent consideration of environmental issues within the WTO dispute settlement mechanism is at least questionable.

For present purposes, it is interesting to note that similar problems affect the European patent adjudication system. In practice, in its decisions rejecting claims based on the environmental risks of biotechnological inventions,[16] the European Patent Office (EPO) has never undertaken the slightest effort to consider and evaluate principles and legal instruments of international environmental law. Given that the major environmental threat posed by GMOs corresponds to the depletion and decline of biological diversity, one would at least expect an early mention of the most relevant provisions of the UN Framework Convention of 1992, which solemnly proclaims the conservation of biodiversity as "a common concern of humankind".[17]

On the other hand, the *precautionary principle* certainly represents the legal rule more appropriately connected with the lawfulness of commercial transactions over biotechnology products. The state of widespread scientific disagreement about the environmental adverse impact of these products would in fact appear to be apt for a solution consistent with the principle's call for measures to minimise or avoid such scientifically uncertain risks.[18] Unfortunately, the EPO has disregarded the principle in a way similar to what has been done by WTO bodies. More importantly, it has endorsed conceptions which are completely at variance even with the timid recognition of the principle which has occurred at WTO level.[19]

In the first phase of the *Onco-Mouse* proceedings, the environmental risks associated with the claimed subject-matter (a mouse which had been genetically engineered so as to develop cancer) were no bar to patentability, because patent law was not deemed to be "the right legislative tool"[20] for providing a solution to the problem of biosafety. The reasons for this laconic remark were eventually

[16] The pertinent decisions are *Onco-Mouse/Harvard I*, OJ EPO 1989, 451; *Onco-Mouse/Harvard II*, OJ EPO 1990, 476; *Onco-Mouse/Harvard III*, OJ EPO 1992, 588; *Greenpeace UK* v. *Plant Genetic Systems N.V. (PGS I)*, decision of 15 December 1992, reproduced in (1993) *Int. Review of Industrial Property and Copyright Law* 618; *Greenpeace Ltd.* v. *Plant Genetic Systems N.V. (PGS II)*, OJ EPO 1995, 545.

[17] Third preambular paragraph, CBD. Note that all states parties to the European Patent Convention have now ratified the CBD.

[18] Cf. e.g. Principle 15 of the Rio Declaration on Environment and Development, reproduced in (1992) *ILM* 874.

[19] *European Communities—Measures Affecting Meat and Meat Products (Hormones)*, Report of the Appellate Body, adopted on 13 February 1998, WT/DS48/R/CAN and WT/DS48/AB/R, para. 124, where the Body found that "the precautionary principle indeed finds reflection in Article 5.7 of the *SPS Agreement*". On the interaction between the adjudicatory standards and methods used by the EPO and the precautionary principle, cf. *infra* Part III.

[20] *Onco-Mouse/Harvard I*, *supra* n. 16, para. 10.3 (for further aspects of the case, see *infra*). Consider also the following statements: "If the legislator is of the opinion that certain technical knowledge should be used under limited conditions only, it is up to him to enact appropriate legislation"; "[t]he regulation of the handling of dangerous material is not the task of the European Patent Office but is rather the business of specialised governmental authorities": *Onco-Mouse/Harvard III*, *supra* n. 16, respectively para. 3 and para. 4(iv); furthermore, "[t]he assessment of risks and the consequent regulation of the exploitation of the invention are a matter for other bodies to consider; they are outside the scope of the EPO", *PGS I*, *supra* n. 16, para. 3.16. Cf. also *PGS II*, *supra* n. 16, paras. 18.2, 18.3, 18.7.

clarified by the EPO organs: patents should be regarded as *neutral instruments*, as they only allow owners to prevent third parties from using and marketing the invention. Conversely, the right to exploit the invention itself is not unconditional, as long as it depends on the legal constraints placed upon it by international and domestic regulation. In other words, there would exist a division of labour between patent offices and legislative authorities, whereby the former should rule on the fulfilment of the technical criteria for patentability and the latter assess the environmental risks stemming from inventions (whether patented or not) and consistently decide whether to authorise their marketing ("technical conception of patentability" or "inherent rights approach").[21]

This idea of patent law as a self-contained system, immune from environmental and any other public policy concerns, is opposed by those authors who regard IPRs adjudicative systems as "social and moral filter[s]" or as "servant[s] of public policy".[22] The dispute, far from being a merely theoretical one, carries important consequences: the acceptance of the technical conception of patentability, in fact, suggests that the conferment of patents on environmentally harmful technologies is in no way capable of jeopardising environmental security. Such a public policy goal would legitimately be achieved only through the enactment of biosafety legislation, which may prohibit the exploitation of "dangerous" inventions.

My point here is that the argument according to which patents are not instruments of public policy implies that it is not possible to enforce principles and rules of environmental law in patent adjudicative proceedings, the precautionary principle being the most relevant one.

In my opinion, there are no legal grounds which can warrant such an argument. It simply reflects (political) preconceptions widely shared by the patent community and aimed at insulating patent law from the pursuit of conflicting public policies. At the same time, it runs counter to any substantial interpretations of Article 53(a) of the European Patent Convention (EPC) which stipulates, as far as material, that patents shall not be granted for "inventions the publication or exploitation of which would be contrary to 'ordre public' or morality", and to the parallel provisions of international and regional instruments concerning patent protection.[23]

However, the idea of a self-contained system cannot be approved, not only because Article 53(a) risks otherwise becoming a dead letter, but also for prag-

[21] See Alexander, *supra* n. 3, p. 113; D. Beyleveld and R. Brownsword, *Mice, Morality and Patents* (London, 1993), pp. 33–46.

[22] Cf. respectively A.J. Wells, "Patenting New Life Forms: An Ecological Perspective", (1994) *EIPR* 111, 112–13, and Alexander, *supra* n. 3, p. 113.

[23] See *supra* n. 12 for the text of Art. 27(2) TRIPs. Similarly, Art. 6(1) of Directive 98/44/EC (European Parliament and Council Directive of 6 July 1998 on the Legal Protection of Biotechnological Inventions, OJ 1998 L213/13) provides that inventions shall be unpatentable where their commercial exploitation would be contrary to *public policy* or morality. It is however regrettable that the Community legislature did not include an explicit environmental exception in the non-exhaustive list of unpatentable inventions in Art. 6(2).

matic reasons: a patent is not a neutral instrument and technological innovation is not a "good" in itself.[24] On the contrary, the act of granting corresponds to a public reward for a contribution to scientific progress and consequently to the well-being of humankind: thus, inventions which create threats of irreversible damage to the global environment do not fulfil this basic requirement. Moreover, the same idea was (although cautiously) rejected by the EPO itself, when it admitted that "patent offices are placed at the *crossroads between science and public policy*" and are thus qualified to make value judgments about a given technology.[25]

The technical conception of patentability represents a powerful tool which reinforces the tendency to ignore principles and rules of environmental law in trade disputes settlement. In addition, it constitutes the first factor which discloses a strong preference on the part of the patents adjudicative bodies for the trade values which are intrinsically linked to intellectual property protection and, consistently, their substantial disregard for environmental concerns.

Non-scientifically proven environmental risks constitute no bar to patentability

My argument is that the issue of biosafety should legitimately and appropriately be considered at the level of patent litigation. Accordingly, adjudicative bodies would simply deny patent protection to environmentally-harmful inventions, or revoke patents if it eventually emerges that their subject matter adversely affects environmental security.

There is no question of legal base for such decisions: for example, in the European patent system (and the same holds true for TRIPs and the EC Biotechnology Directive) the 'ordre public' clause of Article 53(a) is available. This general exception "encompasses the protection of the environment", and consequently "inventions the exploitation of which is likely to . . . seriously prejudice the environment are to be excluded from patentability".[26]

However, these decisions raise the controversial issue of the role which scientific principles and evidence legitimately play in the determination that an ecological threat posed by an invention precludes its patentability, bearing in mind that the impact GMOs will have on the environment, especially on a long-term basis, is currently and inevitably uncertain. In fact, lack of scientific certainty constitutes, at least prima facie, the *determining factor* for the EPO's refusal to uphold the claims based on the environmental risks of biotechnology inventions.

[24] Cf. P. Drahos, "Biotechnology Patents, Markets and Morality", (1999) *EIPR* 441, 449: "no regulatory system connected with technology can remain aloof from moral debate and the responsibility of control".

[25] *PGS II, supra* n. 16, para. 18.3. (emphasis added). Cf. also para. IX(c) of the Summary of Facts and Submissions.

[26] *PGS II, ibid.*, para. 5.

In this respect, the *Plant Genetic Systems* case is paradigmatic.[27] The case involved the granting of a patent for a herbicide-resistant plant and genetic material therefrom, which was twice challenged on the grounds of serious and irreversible damage which the release of the plant would produce on the environment and, more specifically, on biodiversity. The Opposition Division of the Office (which, together with the Board of Appeal, is the body competent to review the granting of European patents) first emphasised the impossibility of determining with *certainty* the extent of the ecological threat posed by the invention, as well as the widespread scientific disagreement on the issue, and then stated: "[s]cientific expertise thus does not provide a sufficient basis to conclude that the risks associated with the genetic engineering of plants preclude any application of this technology".[28]

Although the Board of Appeal was more cautious in its approach to scientific uncertainty, its reasoning prompted the same outcome: first, it found that the test of the *likelihood to seriously prejudice the environment* (representing, as outlined above, the environmental exception to patentability) is only satisfied when "the threat to the environment [is] *sufficiently substantiated* at the time the decision to revoke the patent is taken",[29] and secondly, it held that the requirement of "sufficient substantiality" was not met by the documentary evidence submitted by the appellants, as such evidence was *not scientifically accurate*. In other words, the documents did not provide sufficient scientific evidence, because they merely referred to "*possible, not yet conclusively-documented hazards*".[30] At the end of the day, the decision was taken not to revoke the patent on the basis of Article 53(a): in fact, scientific expertise did not allow the conclusion that the invention was environmentally harmful.

It is natural to draw a parallel between the *PGS* case and the disputes decided at WTO level on the basis of the Agreement on the Application of Sanitary and Phytosanitary Measures (SPS Agreement)[31] which, as is well known, places a heavy reliance on the role of scientific evidence as a watershed between lawful and unlawful regulations adopted by WTO members to protect human, animal and plant life or health.

I believe that the outcome of such disputes (every national measure was found to violate the SPS Agreement) demonstrates that there exists a strong presumption of inconsistency with the WTO regime against trade-restrictive environ-

[27] *PGS I* and *PGS II, supra* n. 16.

[28] *PGS I*, *ibid.*, para. 3.13.

[29] *PGS II*, *supra* n. 16, para. 18.5 (emphasis added).

[30] *PGS II*, *ibid.*, para. 18.7 (emphasis added).

[31] GATT Secretariat, *The Results of the Uruguay Round of Multilateral Trade Negotiations: The Legal Texts* (1994), p. 69. The relevant decisions are *European Communities—Measures Affecting Meat and Meat Products (Hormones)*, Reports of the Panels and Appellate Body adopted on 13 February 1998, WT/DS26/R/USA and WT/DS26/AB/R, and WT/DS48/R/CAN and WT/DS48/ AB/R; *Australia—Measures Affecting the Importation of Salmon*, Reports of the Panel and Appellate Body adopted on 6 November 1998, WT/DS18/R and WT/DS18/AB/R; *Japan—Measures Affecting Agricultural Products (Varietals)*, Reports of the Panel and Appellate Body adopted on 19 March 1999, WT/DS76/R and WT/DS76/AB/R.

mental regulations which are not firmly grounded upon a *high degree of scientific certainty* when such measures are not based on generally recognised international standards. Of course, this should not be the case: the SPS Agreement only prevents members, who are sovereign to select the level of sanitary and phytosanitary protection they deem to be appropriate within their territory,[32] adopting measures without *sufficient scientific evidence*.[33] Sufficient evidence simply means, as outlined by the Appellate Body in the *Varietals* case, evidence "of a quantity, extent, or scope adequate to a certain purpose or object".[34] There are no predetermined quantitative thresholds which need to be respected.

Now, in the same disputes WTO adjudicative bodies invariably held that the measures at stake were unlawful since they were not based on risk assessment.[35] They were at pains to demonstrate procedural and substantial flaws in the evidence produced by the defendants, while the latter insisted that they had indeed conducted such assessment and that the real problem were the discrepancies between the different scientific analysis and opinions.

It thus seems legitimate to maintain that both WTO and EPO adjudicative organs overestimate the role which scientific evidence may legitimately play in trade/environment disputes, namely that of a rational device which helps the decision-maker to distinguish between speculative or theoretical risks and well-founded, though not conclusively demonstrated ones.[36] In this respect, the only reasonable normative standard which should be taken into account by trade dispute settlement bodies in reconciling conflicting trade and environmental values is the *scientific plausibility* of ecological threats.[37] Such standard should prima facie legitimate trade-restrictive environmental measures, a notion which can be extended beyond its original domain to encompass decisions to deny patent protection for environmentally harmful inventions.

The reference to the prima facie value of scientifically plausible evidence inevitably touches upon another thorny issue in trade/environment disputes, i.e. that of the allocation of the *burden of proof*. Given the emphasis which both WTO and EPO adjudicative organs put on the scientific nature of evidence, it is not surprising that they have devised comparably strict rules concerning the discharge of the burden by parties who support trade restrictions due to scientifically uncertain environmental risks.

32 Annex A(5) SPS.

33 Cf. Arts. 2(2) and 3(2) SPS.

34 *Japan—Varietals*, Appellate Body Report, *supra* n. 31, para. 73.

35 As required by Art. 5(1) SPS. Cf. M.M. Slotboom, "The *Hormones* Case: An Increased Risk of Illegality of Sanitary and Phytosanitary Measures", (1999) *Common Market Law Review* 471, 484: "[t]he conceptual distinction between a scientific justification and a risk assessment seems . . . to be non-existent in practice".

36 See especially, V.R. Walker, "Keeping the WTO from Becoming the 'World Trans-science Organisation': Scientific Uncertainty, Science Policy, and Factfinding in the Growth Hormones Dispute", (1998) *Cornell ILJ* 251, 304–5.

37 *Ibid.*, 262–3 and 279–85. Another commentator similarly refers to a "minimum level of scientific rationality": D.A. Wirth, "The Role of Science in the Uruguay Round and NAFTA Trade Disciplines", (1994) *Cornell ILJ* 817, 855–6.

In short, while at WTO level a claimant need only establish a *prima facie* case of inconsistency[38] (e.g. that the contested measure was adopted without sufficient scientific evidence) with the defendant having to counter it (e.g. by demonstrating that the measure is indeed scientifically sound), in the European patent system the rules governing the burden of proof are blatantly dispositive of the result.

In fact, claims based on the environmental adverse impact of inventions are normally presented in opposition and appeal proceedings where, as a rule, the burden of proof lies with the opponent or appellant. This means, as we know, that the latter need to "sufficiently substantiate" the alleged ecological risks arising from the invention. In practical terms, such requirement is only fulfiled when the probability of occurrence of the risks is demonstrated by more or less *incontrovertible* scientific data: a long list of scientific reports and commentaries, which Greenpeace produced during the *PGS* proceedings with a view to illustrating the *possibility* of occurrence of destructive events, did not meet the "sufficient substantiation" test.

It is then worth investigating whether the EPO, as well as trade dispute settlement bodies in general, makes use of judicial methods and reasoning more subtle than those based on the scientific approach.

Patentability is only precluded when environmental risks outweigh the socio-economic benefits of the invention

In the *Onco-Mouse* case, the EPO Board of Appeal instructed the Examining Division to decide over the patentability of the claimed transgenic animal by taking into account Article 53(a)—the *ordre public* and morality exception—through "a careful weighing up of the suffering of animals and possible risks to the environment, on the one hand, and the invention's usefulness to mankind on the other".[39] Eventually, such balancing exercise was resolved in favour of patentability: according to the Examining Division, in fact, the interest of mankind in identifying new, more effective remedies for cancer (the objective pursued with the invention) uncontestably outweighed environmental (and moral) concerns.[40]

The performance of a *cost-benefit analysis* (CBA)[41] is not an unknown approach in the trade/environment arena. Indeed, there are good reasons to

[38] Which was defined in the *Hormones* case, Report of the Appellate Body, *supra* n. 31, para. 104, as a case "which, in the absence of effective refutation by the defending party, requires a panel, as a matter of law, to rule in favor of the complaining party presenting the *prima facie* case".

[39] *Onco-Mouse/Harvard II*, *supra* n. 16, para. 5.

[40] *Onco-Mouse/Harvard III*, *supra* n. 16, para. 4(v). An opposition to the granting of the patent is currently lying with the EPO Opposition Division.

[41] Leaving aside the technicalities of economic theory, throughout this work CBA will simply refer to the comparative assessment of benefits and costs likely to arise from measures and decisions having an adverse impact on international trade.

consider CBA as one of the key judicial standards used by dispute settlement bodies to deal with trade restrictions aimed at the protection of the environment.

CBA may take place (and has actually taken place) in two distinct ways: through an *explicit* balancing, or in the guise of a *hidden* balancing. Examples of the former are not numerous: there exist a few decisions taken in the GATT/WTO context which are heavily influenced by an explicit balancing of the economic, social and environmental consequences of the measure at stake,[42] and, as outlined above, *Onco-Mouse* is the European patent system's landmark case in this respect.

However, the device which "trade courts" favour by far is that consisting of a hidden CBA. In the GATT/WTO dispute settlement system,[43] the liberal interpretation which often affects the well-known *necessity, least-trade restrictiveness and proportionality* tests discloses a departure from genuine legal discourse in the decision-making process and the consequent introduction of *political* arguments. Such arguments more or less frankly refer to the prejudice which international trade would suffer if a particular measure were endorsed.[44] In other words, these tests turn out to be *trade-off devices* helping adjudicative bodies to choose the extent to which trade and conflicting values are to be implemented.[45] Divergent opinions, however, exist with respect to the desirability of CBA in trade/environment disputes[46] and much necessarily depends on the real nature of the CBA which is performed in the specific circumstances of the case. Is such adjudicative standard a fair and equitable one?

[42] Cf. *In the Matter of Canada's Landing Requirement for Pacific Coast Salmon and Herring*, United States-Canada Free Trade Agreement Binational Panel Review, Panel No. CDA–89–1807–01, 16 October 1989, paras. 7.04–7.11 (LEXIS, Intlaw library, USCFTA file). Moreover, in the *Gasoline* case, *supra* n. 15, para. IV, p. 28, the discriminatory nature of the measure at stake was partly due to the US omission "to count the costs for foreign refiners that would result from the imposition of statutory baselines". For a critical reading of the case, see R.G. Tarasofski and F. Weiss, (1997) 8 *Yearbook of Int. Environmental Law* 591. (ironically concluding that, since no explanation is given why regulators have a legal obligation to take foreign costs into account nor how this should be done, "[i]s this to be interpreted as a novel WTO requirement that governments must weigh the regulatory impact of their measures on foreigners, for instance, of a ban on elephant ivory or a pesticide residue restriction[?]", *ibid.*, 593. In addition, at the EU level, the CBA test has determined, more or less explicitly, the outcome of a number of cases, such as the landmark *Danish Bottles* case, where the measure was found to be inconsistent with Art. 28 (ex Art. 30) EC Treaty because the environmental benefits deriving therefrom were considered marginal when compared with the costs for intraCommunity trade: Case 302/86, *Commission* v. *Denmark*, [1988] ECR 4619, paras. 20–1.

[43] The same considerations largely apply to the EU and US adjudicative bodies: cf. J.P. Trachtman, "Trade and . . . Problems, Cost-Benefit Analysis and Subsidiarity", (1998) *EJIL* 32.

[44] Cf. e.g. F. Francioni, "La tutela dell'ambiente e la disciplina del commercio internazionale", in *Diritto e organizzazione del commercio internazionale dopo la creazione dell'Organizzazione Mondiale del Commercio*, *supra* n. 8, p. 147, 162.

[45] Trachtman, *supra* n. 43, 33.

[46] For instance, cf. Montini, *infra* Chapter 6; *ibid.*, "The Nature and Function of the Necessity and Proportionality Principles in the Trade and Environment Context", (1997) *RECIEL* 121, 129 (holding that the performance of a balancing exercise is the correct and desirable standard to deal with the concept of "necessity" in the trade/environment context); J.J. Barcelò III, "Product Standards to Protect the Local Environment—The GATT and the Uruguay Round Sanitary and Phytosanitary Agreement", (1994) *Cornell ILJ* 755, 774 (pointing at CBA as "the greatest threat to a [GATT] member's freedom to pursue its own level of environmental protection").

If one looks at the EPO jurisprudence concerning the environmental risks of biotechnology inventions, the answer is inevitably in the negative. After the *Onco-Mouse* ruling outlined above, in the *PGS* case the EPO expressly declined to perform a CBA, as the claimants did not sufficiently demonstrate the scientific foundations of the alleged ecological threat.[47] In other words, a CBA could not be performed given the lack of one of the reference terms necessary to the balancing exercise (namely, the environmental costs). However, I am convinced that a CBA-type of reasoning, although in the *hidden* modality, affected the outcome of the case.

First, certain assertions of the EPO organs are patently tantamount to *political* arguments: thus, according to the Opposition Division, objections to the patentability of transgenic organisms "must also be seen in the light of the fact that several member states of the EPC subsidise plant molecular biology research", and "[i]t must therefore be asked whether the EPO *could reasonably declare immoral the results of research financially supported by some of its member States*".[48] Here, the disregard for environmental risks is clearly prompted by an arbitrary weighing up of the relevance of economic interests linked to intellectual property protection.

Secondly, and more importantly, the argument that environmental costs are speculative and cannot therefore constitute a proper balancing term is ill-founded. The reasons for this are necessarily connected with the role legitimately played by scientific evidence in trade/environment disputes.[49] In any event, the EPO itself acknowledges that the real problem is not the existence of risks, but the "inability to prove the *extent* of the risks". Indeed, the destructive events highlighted by the claimants "may occur to some extent".[50] Why does the EPO refrain from weighing up scientifically plausible risks, then? And why are the possibly catastrophic damages resulting from the occurrence of risks not taken into account? Simply because the Office is aware that the decision to give precedence to trade values in the field of plant biotechnology through an explicit balancing would appear patently biased and arbitrary. As a matter of fact, the existence of actual benefits brought to mankind by plant biotechnology is notably a matter of considerable controversy.

In this context, the Office astutely makes use of misleading characterisations of the threshold of risk[51] needed to meet the test of the *likelihood to seriously*

[47] *PGS I, supra* n. 16, para. 3.16; *PGS II, supra* n. 16, para. 18.8.

[48] *PGS I, supra* n. 16, para. 3.8 (emphasis added). By the same token, cf. *Onco-Mouse III, supra* n. 16, para. 3: "[t]he development of new technologies is normally afflicted with new risks . . . The experience has . . . shown that these risks should not generally lead to a negative attitude vis-à-vis new technologies but rather to a careful weighing up of risks on the one hand and the positive aspects on the other".

[49] As described *supra* text accompanying notes 36 and 37.

[50] Cf. respectively, *PGS I, supra* n. 16, para. 3.13 (emphasis added); *PGS II, supra* n. 16, para. 18.6.

[51] In particular, the Board of Appeal seems to attach the same meaning to its frequent references to *potential risks, possible, not yet conclusively-documented hazards, potential effects, hazards that are not easily quantified*, and the like: cf. *PGS II, ibid.*, paras. 18.6–18.7.

prejudice the environment and thus preclude patentability. In addition, this test corresponds to commonly-used formulas in international environmental law whose inherent flexibility favours arbitrary interpretations and makes it "difficult to assess whether . . . a determination that a threshold is or is not crossed is a *purely scientific affair or involves some consideration of costs*".[52] The *hidden balancing* performed by the EPO is thus revealed by arguments whose political nature is easy to detect and by trade-off devices shaped in the form of ambiguous references to risk levels and thresholds.

At this juncture, I have set out all elements for concluding that CBA is not an appropriate and equitable judicial standard for addressing the conflict between trade and environmental values, for the following complementary reasons:

(a) the standard is not expressly contemplated in the environmental exceptions to trade rules, such as Article 53(a) EPC and Article XX GATT;
(b) CBA ensures an almost unfettered discretion to adjudicative bodies in the determination of the prevailing interest. It is therefore a device used by such bodies to convey political arguments into the decision-making process to the detriment of effective environmental protection;
(c) CBA, especially in the "hidden" modality, is essentially exempted from legal scrutiny and undermines the basic requirement of transparency of judicial decisions, as aptly illustrated by the *PGS* case.

III. *ORDRE PUBLIC* AND THE EMERGING INTERNATIONAL PUBLIC POLICY

The most natural solution to the inadequate treatment which the issue of biosafety has so far received from the adjudicative bodies of the European patent system would be a careful and unbiased consideration of pertinent legal principles and norms of international law.

In this respect, an aspect of the recent *Novartis* case[53] is particularly telling. Here, the Board of Appeal ruled on the significance of Article 31(3)(b)(c) of the Vienna Convention on the Law of Treaties for the interpretation of the EPC. Such provisions stipulate that treaties need to be interpreted in the light of subsequent practice and "any relevant rules of international law applicable in the relations between the parties" (so-called "evolutive interpretation"). The Board succeeded in reconciling the rules on plant patentability provided for in the EPC, the TRIPS Agreement and the EC Biotechnology Directive, respectively.

However, what is worth pointing out is, first, that the EPO tendency to overlook international law norms[54] is manifestly contradicted by the application of Article 31(3) of the Vienna Convention in the *Novartis* case. Secondly, and more

[52] A. Nollkaemper, "'What You Risk Reveals What You Value', and Other Dilemmas Encountered in the Legal Assaults on Risks", in D. Freestone and E. Hey (eds.), *The Precautionary Principle and International Law* (The Hague, 1996), p. 73, 82 (emphasis added).

[53] *In re Novartis AG*, OJ EPO 1998, 511.

[54] Cf. *supra* Part II.

importantly, the use of the same rule could be tantamount to opening a Pandora's box which conveys inter alia principles and rules of international environmental law into the dispute settlement process.[55] Obviously, the precautionary principle should constitute the first candidate to be selected and taken into account,[56] but I doubt that, by itself, it would determine a different, more environmentally-friendly approach on the part of the adjudicative bodies. This scepticism does not primarily arise from the alleged non-justiciability of the principle, but again from the relevant function which *balancing tests* play with respect to the enforcement of environmental law. In fact, it is widely accepted that the performance of some kind of CBA is a condition which needs to be fulfiled before taking decisions based on the precautionary principle. For instance, an author has asserted that one of the cases which indisputably triggers the application of the principle is "where the benefit to be derived from a particular activity is completely out of proportion to the negative impact which that activity may have on the environment".[57] A specular reasoning was followed by the EPO when it decided to grant a patent for the Onco-Mouse.[58]

If we want to foster a coherent and viable consideration of environmental concerns in trade dispute settlement fora, an alternative approach is then necessary. International law is rapidly evolving in the area of environmental security and celebrated legal doctrines, such as *jus cogens* and *obligations erga omnes*, are increasingly advocated as including the basic norms aimed at the preservation of global environmental resources (climate, ozone layer, biodiversity).

A major problem, however, continues to be that of the enforcement of environmental principles and standards within adjudicative systems, such as the WTO and the EPO, based upon rules which inevitably reflect and pursue trade interests. How viable are the legal basis available therein for the safeguarding of fundamental environmental values?

[55] Interestingly enough, in legal literature there seems to be an increasing recognition of the relevance of Art. 31(3)(c) of the Vienna Convention as a key provision for adjudicating trade and environment disputes: see Francioni, *supra* Chapter 1, Part IV; *ibid.*, *supra* n. 44, p. 161; see further Marceau, *supra* n. 15, p. 120–130 (also for illuminating references to the *travaux préparatoires* of the Vienna Convention).

[56] Cf. *supra* text accompanying notes 18 and 19.

[57] A. Kiss, "The Rights and Interests of Future Generations and the Precautionary Principle", in *The Precautionary Principle and International Law*, *supra* n. 52, p. 19, 27. In a similar vein, Nollkaemper, *supra* n. 52, 87, points out that "the principle is embedded in broader regimes allowing for a balancing of risks and benefits" (cf. *ibid.*, p. 88–93); cf. also J. Cameron and J. Abouchar, "The Status of the Precautionary Principle in International Law", *idem*, p. 29, 44–5; T. Scovazzi, "Sul principio precauzionale nel diritto internazionale dell'ambiente", (1992) *Rivista di diritto internazionale*, 699, 700. Last but not least, in its recently adopted Communication on the Precautionary Principle, 2 February 2000, COM(2000) 1 final, pp. 19–20, the European Commission holds that the examination of the benefits and costs of action and lack of action constitutes one of the general principles of application of the precautionary principle. Even though the Commission specifies that "requirements linked to the protection of public health should undoubtedly be given greater weight than economic considerations" (at p. 20), it is predicted that this aspect of the document will attract considerable criticism.

[58] Cf. *supra* text accompanying note 40.

As we know, both the TRIPs Agreement and the EPC contemplate an "*ordre public*" exception to patentability which the EPO ruled to include the protection of the environment, absent any explicit reference to this aim in Article 53(a) of the Convention. Such ruling bears important consequences: the notion of "*ordre public*", far from being a volatile one, is conceptually rich. For example, it may be invoked as an argument in favour of those authors[59] who endeavour to establish a link between the European patent adjudicative process and the European system for the protection of human rights, and accordingly hold that the European Court of Human Rights represents the ultimate judge of the legality of European patents. Such view necessarily implies that the judicial review of the grant of patents should also be based upon the core of essential and peremptory rights and obligations enshrined in the European Convention on Human Rights (ECHR) and often described as establishing a *European ordre public*.[60]

It goes beyond my intention to account for the many conceptual and practical difficulties which confront such a position. I would here simply point out that the ECHR system is not a reliable basis for comprehensive and coherent environmental protection: in fact, the latter is only pursued indirectly, i.e. if and when it is demonstrated that an environmentally harmful conduct or activity infringes one of the substantive rights expressly guaranteed.[61]

Alternatively and preferably, the concept of "ordre public" relates to *a core of fundamental public policy values* pursued by the international community as a whole,[62] and encompassing, not only fundamental human rights and socio-economic standards, but also the protection of global environmental resources that constitute a *common concern of humankind*.[63]

[59] Cf. Beyleveld and Brownsword, *supra* n. 21, pp. 68–70, 89–90.

[60] See the Court's ruling in *Loizidou v. Turkey* (preliminary objections), Ser. A, Vol. 310, paras. 75, 93. In legal literature, cf. F. Sudre, "Existe t-il un ordre public européen?", in P. Tavernier (ed.), *Quelle Europe pour les droits de l'homme?* (Bruxelles, 1996), p. 39; J.A. Frowein, "The European Convention on Human Rights as the Public Order of Europe", (1990–I/2) *Collected Courses of the Academy of European Law*, 267. For a critical view, F. Francioni, "Customary International Law and the European Convention on Human Rights", (1999) *Italian Yearbook of Int. Law* 11.

[61] See *Lòpez Ostra* v. *Spain*, Ser. A, Vol. 303-C; *Guerra et al.* v. *Italy*, reproduced in (1999) *Journal of Environmental Law* 157, with a comment by C. Miller.

[62] A tentative, non-exhaustive list of such fundamental values may be found in Art. 19 of the ILC's 1996 Draft Articles on State Responsibility, according to which international crimes result from serious breaches of fundamental norms relating to the maintenance of international peace and security, the right of self-determination of peoples, the protection of human beings, and *the safeguarding and preservation of the human environment*.

[63] Note that the notion of a *common concern of humankind* is conceptually proximate to that of an international public policy: cf. A. Kiss, "The Common Concern of Mankind", (1997) *Environmental Policy and Law* 244: "[t]he protection of fundamental values is generally recognized as a common concern of the community", and "[a]s a consequence, legal orders are articulated around the common concern (*intérêt général*)". Moreover, the reference to fundamental international rules and principles in connection with "ordre public" clauses is not unknown in legal doctrine: indeed, it is advocated by several authors with respect to the corresponding exception of private international law systems: cf. in the Italian literature, P. Benvenuti, *Comunità statale, comunità internazionale e ordine pubblico* (Milano, 1977), and G. Barile, "Ordine pubblico (dir. intern. priv.)", *Enciclopedia del diritto*, Vol. XXX (Milano, 1980), p. 1106, 1110–13.

The preceding analysis advocates a careful reconsideration of the significance of those rules which expressly or implicitly address the conflict between intellectual property regimes and environmental security: thus, the obligation to make sure that the former are supportive of and do not run counter to the latter (Article 16(5) CBD) necessarily requires judicial bodies and legislatures to give precedence to biosafety concerns over trade values which are fostered by patents on potentially devastating inventions. In turn, the basic objectives which are pursued by states through the CBD should represent an authoritative guidance for the future interpretation of the "*ordre public*" exception to patentability, in accordance with the criterion prescribed by Article 31(3)(c) of the Vienna Convention on the Law of Treaties and applied by the EPO, although for a different purpose, in the *Novartis* case.

IV. CONCLUSION

Adjudicative bodies within systems aimed at the protection of trade values frequently resort to similar legal concepts and decision-making standards. Such concepts and standards result in an unsatisfactory consideration of environmental concerns.

One important reason thereof relates to an overstated reliance on the value of scientific evidence, as long as scientifically uncertain environmental threats are unduly rejected as ill-founded. In the presence of environmental risks which are inevitably uncertain, such as those posed by transgenic organisms and products, adjudicative bodies should thus refer to the different standard of their *scientific plausibility*.

On the other hand, a *cost-benefit analysis* type of reasoning is increasingly gaining support[64] as a rational device to balance trade and environmental values. It is deeply rooted in judicial reasoning and legislative activity, but this should not detract from the fact that, especially in its more genuinely political connotation, it has to be condemned for the potentially unfettered discretion it leaves to adjudicative bodies in the performance of the balancing exercise.

However, the idea of an *international public policy* is embedded in the "*ordre public*" exception to patentability and provides a viable link with international obligations having an *erga omnes* character and a *jus cogens* status. It remains

[64] A balancing approach consisting of a weighing up between the members' market access rights and the right of members to adopt measures for the protection of the environment was expressly endorsed by the Appellate Body of the WTO in the *Shrimp* case, *supra* n. 15, paras. 156, 159. A similar trend, however, can also be identified outside the context of the world trading system: for example, the Food and Agriculture Organisation recently released a Statement on Biotechnology (see www.fao.org/biotech/state.htm), which "supports a science-based evaluation system that would objectively determine the *benefits and risks* of each individual GMO" and accordingly points out that "[t]he possible effects on biodiversity, the environment and food safety need to be evaluated, *and the extent to which the benefits of the product or process outweigh its risks* assessed" (emphasis added). Cf. also *supra* n. 57 the position of the EC Commission as outlined in its Communication on the Precautionary Principle.

to be seen whether adjudicative organs will be finally ready to acknowledge the concept as a justiciable one and thus defer to such a set of peremptory norms and fundamental values. If so, the assertion that the EPO, as well as other adjudicative bodies, is at the crossroads between science, *public policy* and trade will no longer be on paper only, but be firmly established in practice.

5

The Impact of International Trade Law on Environmental Law and Process

ANDREA BIANCHI

I. INTRODUCTION

THE MANY INTERRELATIONS between trade and environment have been the object of an immense amount of writing.[1] The issue of how environmental protection and the liberalisation of international trade could be reconciled came dramatically to the fore in the early 1990s. Ever since it has become an essential ingredient of any scholarly discourse on globalisation and sustainable development. In fact, the prominent role of the trade and environment debate in the international legal and political agenda is hardly surprising. The close link established between growth, liberalisation of trade and environmental protection by the notion of sustainable development, one of the most popular, albeit rather undefined, catchwords in contemporary international politics, rendered the clash between such distinct values almost inevitable.[2] While this sense of inevitability could have been partly averted, had the international community

[1] It is impossible to detail the vast literature on the subject. Among others see the contributions by Francioni "La tutela dell'ambiente e la disciplina del commercio internazionale" with comments by Munari, in Societa' Italiana di Diritto Internazionale, *Diritto e organizzazione del commercio internazionale dopo la creazione della Organizzazione mondiale del commercio* (1998), at 147; Steinberg, "Trade-Environment Negotiations in the EU, NAFTA and WTO: Regional Trajectories of Rule Development", (1997) 1991 *American J. Int'l L.* 231; Schoenbaum, "International Trade and Protection of the Environment: the Continuing Search for Reconciliation", *ibid.* at 268; Esty, *Greening the GATT. Trade, Environment and the Future* (1994); Kingsbury, "Environment and Trade: the GATT-WTO Regime in the International Legal System", in Boyle (ed.), *Environmental Regulation and Economic Growth* (1994) p. 189; Cameron, Demaret and Geradin, *Trade and the Environment: the Search for Balance* (London, 1994); Anderson and Blackhurst, *The Greening of World Trade Issues* (London, 1992); Schoenbaum, "Free International Trade and Protection of the Environment: Irreconcilable Conflict?", (1992) 86 *American J. Int'l l.* 700; Patterson, "GATT and the Environment. Rules Change to Minimize Adverse Trade and Environmental Effects", (1992) 26 *Journal of World Trade* 99; Sorsa, "GATT and the Environment", (1992) 15 *The World Economy* 115; Petersmann, "Trade Policy, Environmental Policy and the GATT. Why Trade Rules and Environmental Rules Should be Mutually Consistent", (1991) 46 *Aussenwirtschaft* 197.

[2] See Malanczuk, "Sustainable Development: Some Critical Thoughts in the Light of the Rio Conference", in Ginther, Denters and De Waart, *Sustainable Development and Good Governance* (1995), p. 23; Lang (ed.), *Sustainable Development and International Law* (1995); Sands, "International Law in the Field of Sustainable Development", (1994) 65 *British Yearbook of Int'l L.* 303.

decided not to link indissolubly the two issues,[3] the practical problem of how to coordinate national and international environmental law and policies with the law of international trade is going to remain topical for quite some time. To eschew the current fashion of addressing the range of viable options to reconcile trade and environment is no easy task.[4] Different analytical perspectives exist, however, which may help evaluate, independently of the debate on sustainable development, what impact the new law of international trade has already had on environmental law and process. The analysis is best made having regard to the recent developments which have occurred in the past decade. Starting from the *Tuna/Dolphin* seminal case on trade and environment in the context of GATT, through the establishment of the WTO, the international regulation of trade has brought about several changes in environmental law and process. This impact needs to be carefully scrutinised, as it may contribute to understanding to what extent the current regulatory framework for international trade can accommodate environmental concerns, short of institutional reforms by treaty amendment, which might be difficult to achieve in the short term.

The opportunity of linking directly environmental issues to the regulation of international trade is a policy choice that one can take as a *datum* for the purpose of this analysis. At present, any international negotiation of environmentally-related regimes, likely to affect transnational economic transactions even in the slightest manner, is coerced by the complex web of obligations regulating international trade. International trade-related negotiations, in turn, advance trudgingly through the muds of international politics, increasingly burdened with environmental and public health concerns. The recent involvement of large sectors of transnational civil society through the medium of NGOs and interest groups and the ensuing ideological confrontation between conflicting interests render the debate almost intractable at times. Clearly, this is a social process which lies at the interface of law, economics and politics. The legal dimension of it, however, cannot be underestimated as it affects both decision-making processes and substantive outcomes. Leaving aside certain specific aspects, which are the object of ad hoc studies in this book,[5] the rather limited goal of this chapter is to provide, drawing from some selected areas, a few examples of how the law of international trade has affected or is likely to affect in the near future the making of environmental law at international, regional and national level. If, generally, any speculation of this kind never can be a neutral exercise, as different inferences can be drawn from the very same instances of state

[3] See Brown-Weiss, "Environment and Trade as Partners in Sustainable Development: a Commentary", (1992) 86 *Amer. J. Int'l L.* 728.

[4] Brack, "Reconciling the GATT and Multilateral Environmental Agreements with Trade Provisions: the Latest Debate", (1997) 6 *RECIEL* 105; Tarasofsky "Ensuring Compatibility Between Multilateral Environmental Agreements and GATT/WTO", (1996) 7 *Yearbook of Int'l Env'l L.* 52; Cameron and Robinson, "The Use of Trade Provisions in International Environmental Agreements and their Compatibility with GATT", (1991) 2 *Yearbook Int'l Env'l L.* 3.

[5] In particular, see Schoenbaum, *supra* Chapter 2, Pavoni, *supra* Chapter 4, Montini, *infra* Chapter 6 and Munari, *infra* Chapter 7.

practice, the proposed evaluation implies an even higher degree of subjectivity. All the more so when one realises that the scale of priorities between the different and often conflicting components of the concept of sustainable development is far from clear.

II. SPURRING THE CREATION OF NEW INSTITUTIONAL ARRANGEMENTS

Among the first and most obvious consequences of the linking of trade liberalisation and environmental protection is the creation of ad hoc institutions and less formal arrangements to provide a forum for discussion and standard-setting. The panoply of technical bodies, working groups and ad hoc organs in international organisations is hardly amenable to any coherent categorisation scheme. Despite their different nature and tasks, however, all such bodies can be deemed to have originated from the need to accommodate liberalisation of trade and environmental protection concerns. The creation of the Committee on Trade and Environment (CTE) within the framework of the World Trade Organisation (WTO) is possibly the best illustration of this trend.[6] As is known, the CTE was entrusted with the specific task of recommending appropriate rules to improve the interaction between trade and environment with a view to promoting sustainable development. The wide array of issues addressed by the CTE include the interrelationship between the multilateral trade system, on the one hand, and Multilateral Environmental Agreements (MEAs) and/or national environmental policies and national trade measures enacted for environmental purposes on the other. Moreover, the CTE is intended to tackle the problems of the export of domestically prohibited goods, the effect of environmental measures on market access, the issue of transparency of national environmental measures, the compatibility of national standards and technical regulation with the international trading regime as well as the relation between the dispute settlement provisions of the WTO and the other dispute settlement mechanisms provided by MEAs. It is somewhat disappointing to realize that the CTE has achieved very little progress on the above issues. The report submitted by the Committee to the 1996 Ministerial Conference held in Singapore does little more than summarise the lengthy and relatively unproductive debates within the Committee.[7] Despite the renewal of its mandate at the Singapore Conference,[8] the CTE has continued to act mainly as a discussion forum, where the lack of consensus among the parties on the most relevant issues has so far prevented the adoption of concrete recommendations.

The Commission on Sustainable Development (CSD) can be deemed to have originated from the perception of the close link between trade and environment issues, particularly as a result of UNCED and the adoption of Agenda 21, the

[6] See the GATT Ministerial Declaration of 14 April 1994, reproduced in (1994) 32 *ILM* 1267.

[7] See CTE Report, WTO Doc. WT/CTE/1 of 12 November 1996.

[8] See para. 16 of the Singapore Ministerial Declaration, reproduced in (1997) 36 *ILM* 218.

implementation of which the CSD is supposed to supervise. In particular, Chapter II of Agenda 21 expressly devoted to "International Cooperation to Accelerate Sustainable Development in Developing Countries and Related Domestic Policies" has provided the basis for the CSD to address the issue of trade and environment during its first sessions. A number of documents have been submitted to the CSD and the item will be taken up again officially at the eighth session of the CSD scheduled for this year.[9] The Commission, which according to its mandate, must ensure the effective follow-up of UNCED, enhance international cooperation and rationalise the intergovernmental decision-making capacity for the integration of environment and development, discharges a number of functions which are relevant to the trade and environment debate. Besides monitoring the progress on the implementation of Agenda 21 and the integration of environmental and developmental considerations in national and international policy-making, it also receives and considers information concerning the implementation of environmental agreements, as provided by the relevant Conference of the Parties (COPs). Information-gathering occurs with the contribution of State and non-State actors which makes the Commission a privileged observatory for the global partnership for sustainable development that UNCED meant to establish.[10]

The North American Agreement on Environmental Cooperation (NAAEC) can also be seen as an institutional development prompted by the need to accommodate trade and environment concerns.[11] As a side agreement to the North American Free Trade Agreement (NAFTA), the NAAEC set up an institutional framework in which environmental measures likely to have an effect on freedom of trade can be addressed. It suffices to mention the power of the Council to make recommendations on the "greater compatibility of environmental technical regulations, standards and conformity assessment procedures", which does in fact amount to a general power of harmonising environmental standards. Particularly worth noting is the potentially considerable involvement of NGOs in submitting claims and triggering the dispute settlement procedure, thus contributing to monitoring and enforcing NAAEC substantive obligations.[12] At the regional level, other developments have occurred. Following the inclusion, after the Treaty of Amsterdam amendments, of sustainable development and the principle of integration of environmental protection in all other EU policies in the general principles of EC law, respectively at Articles 2 and 6 of the EC Treaty, the EU has set up a Consultative

[9] See the Report prepared by the UNCTAD Secretariat on *Trade and Environment: Concrete Progress Achieved and Some Outstanding Issues*, submitted to the fifth session of the CSD (1997); and the Report of the Secretary General on *Trade, Environment and Sustainable Development*, UN Doc. E/CN.17/1996/8, submitted to the fourth session of the CSD (1996).

[10] *Ibid.*

[11] North American Agreement on Environmental Cooperation, September 1992, reproduced in (1993) 32 *Int'l Legal Materials* 1480.

[12] On the content, institutional machinery and early practice of enforcement of the NAAEC see Trebilcock and Howse, *The Regulation of International Trade* (2nd edn., 1999), at p. 434.

Forum on the Environment and Sustainable Development.[13] While it is to be presumed that the more technical legal issues will continue to be handled by the EU institutions, the Forum's consultative functions will probably be discharged by addressing the issues of general policy inherent in the stated commitment to foster sustainable development.[14]

Also within the framework of the OECD, several interesting developments have taken place.[15] A Joint Working Party on Trade and Environment[16] was set up in 1991 to address such questions as trade aspects of sustainable product policies, methodologies for environment and trade assessments, the use of trade measures in several Multilateral Environmental Agreements, the environmental effects of trade liberalisation in various sectors, and Procedural Guidelines on Trade and Environment, including transparency and consultation.[17] In particular, the 1993 Guidelines on Trade and Environment have provided member states with guidance on how to integrate trade and environmental policies, with a view to enhancing transparency and ensuring constant consultation with the civil society. Although the guidelines are mainly concerned with setting decision-making standards, they also emphasise the need for international cooperation both in environmental law-making and dispute settlement. Most recently a study has been produced which provides a critical overview of current methodologies for the assessment of the environmental effects of trade liberalisation agreements.[18] While giving an important interdisciplinary scientific contribution, the OECD has also contributed to a deeper understanding of the practical interface between trade and environment. So have other agencies such as the United Nations Environment Programme (UNEP), which in cooperation with the WTO and the United Nations Conference on Trade and Development (UNCTAD) has organized meetings and workshops for policy-makers and experts and produced monographs series, background materials and reports. UNEP cooperates closely also with such NGOs as the IUCN (the World Conservation Union) with which a formal agreement was signed in 1995.[19] UNCTAD is also very active to promote the integration of trade, environment

[13] See Commission Decision of 24 February 1997 (97/150/EC in OJ 1997 L58/48) on the setting up of a European Consultative Forum on the environment and sustainable development, successor to the General Consultative Forum on the Environment established by Commission Decision 93/701/EC in OJ 1993 L328/53. The Forum is one of the three informal consultative bodies created under the Fifth Action Programme of the Community on environmental protection. According to Art. 1.2 of the 1997 Commission Decision, the Forum is to consist of figures from the sectors of manufacture, the business world, regional and local authorities, professional associations, unions and environmental protection and consumer organisations.

[14] It is of note that in 1996 the European Commission had submitted a *Communication on Trade and Environment* to the Council and the European Parliament (COM(96) 54 final of 28 February 1996).

[15] See, generally, Youngman and Andrew, *Trade and Environment in the OECD* (1997).

[16] Previously named Joint Session of Trade and Environment Experts.

[17] See OECD Council, *Report on Trade and Environment*, OECD Doc. C/MIN(99)14 (1999).

[18] OECD, *Assessing the Environmental Effects of Trade Liberalisation Agreements* (1990).

[19] See (1995) 3 *Biannual Bulletin of Environmental Law* (July) at 3.

and development. To this effect, it received a clear mandate from Agenda 21, which has recently been renewed by the General Assembly of the United Nations. Besides undertaking analytical studies and building consensus among member states on the positive interaction between environment and trade in a development perspective, UNCTAD assists developing countries in several ways including ad hoc projects with the financial support of developed countries and the practical involvement of business groups and other professional associations.[20]

Several inferences can be drawn even from the sketchy overview of the institutional developments prompted by the linkage between trade and environment issues. First, the proliferation of institutional arrangements has mainly occurred within the established framework of existing international organisations. Most of the relevant activities consist of background studies, standard-setting, consensus-building and, occasionally, highly specialised projects in specific areas. Overall, this has contributed to enhancing the transparency of the debate and has helped to engage large sectors of civil society with a view to establishing an ever growing public support for the "greening" of international trade law. While this may be regarded as a transnational social process of a much broader scope, its legal dimension lies in the attempt to lay the groundwork for the development or further consolidation of legal rules and for the emergence of interpretative criteria which can be of guidance in the implementation of already existing rules and principles. The increasing role of private actors in this process, while not yet sufficiently developed to undermine the state-centred monopoly of formal international decision-making processes, attests to the blurring of the public/private distinction in international trade and environmental law, which can be seen as yet another element of novelty brought about by the intermingling of the different interests at stake in the trade and environment debate.

III. THE STRENGTHENING OF COMMUNICATION PROCESSES AMONG INTERNATIONAL BODIES

Increased coordination in information-gathering and sharing among international bodies has led to a proliferation of studies and background materials for the purpose of disseminating knowledge and helping decision-makers to address properly policy and legal issues. What may appear as a relatively

[20] See e.g. the "Reconciliation of Environmental and Trade Policies" project, funded by the government of the Netherlands and implemented jointly by UNCTAD, the International Trade Center (ITC), the International Rubber Study Group (IRSG) and the German Association for Technical Co-operation (GTZ). The purpose of the project is that of encouraging the use of economic instruments for internalizing environmental costs and benefits in prices of commodities and their products and promoting the export of environmentally preferable products of developing countries.

uninteresting process from the legal point of view, is in fact an indispensable tool given the complexities and technicalities of international economic law. In a recent initiative of the CTE, the Secretariats of major MEAs were invited at an information session to provide the CTE members with an update on trade-related developments in environmental fora. MEAs Secretariats submitted presentations and background papers which helped the CTE members focus on the linkages between the multilateral environment and trade agendas. The papers submitted by MEAs Secretariats vary remarkably from one another. While some state in considerable detail the nature, content, scope of application and rationale of those trade-related measures which may raise issues of compatibility with international trade law (ITL),[21] others simply refer to the need to develop trade measures to enhance the effectiveness of the regime they are meant to administer.[22] Finally, the CTE monitors legal developments which may lead to the adoption of treaties or soft law instruments which might have a bearing on the current regulatory framework of international trade.[23] Such advance notices, early information and technical clarifications about legal regulation of environmental issues give the CTE the opportunity of discharging its function of providing a forum for states to address informally legal and policy issues with a view to building the consensus necessary for the adoption of concrete measures to ensure the smooth integration of trade and environmental concerns.

In this context, of particular interest is the debate within the CTE on the linkage between the provisions of the multilateral trade system and the use of trade measures for environmental purposes, including those pursuant to MEAs.[24] While some countries, including India and Brazil, characterised the need to accommodate trade measures taken under MEAs within the WTO as a "non-issue", as MEAs regimes seem to be working effectively without undue interferences from the WTO, other countries proposed different approaches. Switzerland maintained that, regardless of actual conflict, it would be desirable to adopt a general interpretative "coherence clause", rather than amending

[21] See, *Communication from the Secretariat for the Vienna Convention and the Montreal Protocol, UNEP* WTO Doc. WT/CTE/W/115, 25 June 1999 (99–2630); *Communication from the Secretariat of the Convention on International Trade in Endangered Species (CITES)* WTO Doc. WT/CTE/W/119, 25 June 1999 (99–2642); *Communication from the Secretariat of the Convention on Biological Diversity on the Draft Protocol on Biosafety*, WTO Doc. WT/CTE/W/117, 28 June 1999 (99–2446).

[22] See, *Communication from the Commission for the Conservation of Atlantic Marine Living Resources,* WTO Doc. WT/CTE/W/113, 28 May 1999 (99–2165).

[23] See for instance the recent note prepared by the CTE Secretariat on *Recent Developments in Multilateral Environmental Agreements (MEAs)*, WTO Doc. WT/CTE/W/128, 29 November 1999 (99–5134), covering the works of the recent sessions of the Intergovernmental Negotiating Committee for the adoption of a Convention on the Prior Informed Consent (PIC) Procedure for Certain Hazardous Chemicals and Pesticides in International Trade, and reporting also on the negotiation process for the conclusion of a Draft Internationally Legally Binding Instrument for Implementing International Action on Certain Persistent Organic Pollutants (POPs).

[24] The stances taken by governments as illustrated in the text are reported in *Trade and Environment Bulletin* No. 29, 2. (WT/CTE/4) (99–0000), 12 October 1999.

Article XX of GATT. The EU welcomed the Appellate Body's Report on the *Shrimp/Turtle* case to the extent it allows measures not merely enacted on domestic policy considerations, but rather aimed at multilateral cooperation. The USA and Australia advocated an approach based on cooperation between trade and environment officials and on policy coordination, whereas New Zealand proposed the adoption of "savings clauses" to provide the necessary coordination between the two categories of treaties. The range of options envisaged by governments within the CTE goes well beyond the solutions proposed by scholarly works and attests to the usefulness of debating such crucial issues against the background of the materials and information provided by other international bodies.

The legal significance of the strengthening of communication processes should not be underestimated.[25] One of the main hurdles in conceiving of a balanced and mutually supportive relation between MEAs and the world trading system has long been the scant attention paid to the issue of coordination of relevant treaty commitments. Negotiators are often unaware of possible areas of conflict with other international treaty provisions. Sometimes the package-deal negotiation technique adopted in multilateral negotiations prevents states from being too preoccupied with the issue of overlapping with other international norms. Be that as it may, the lack of savings or consistency clauses in international agreements or the relative casuality of their formulation and stated purpose are often cause for legal uncertainty and potentially conducive to disputes. It is of note that to date no trade measure in widely accepted MEAs has been challenged internationally, despite scholarly speculation on possibile areas of conflicting obligations. Indirectly, this reinforces the argument that communication processes among the parties to both MEAs and ITL instruments have remarkably improved over the years. What was not or could not be achieved at the drafting stage by the use of consistency clauses or other similar mechanisms is being attained by information-sharing, policy dialogue and coordination.

IV. ENHANCED TRANSPARENCY OF NATIONAL ENVIRONMENTAL REGULATIONS: NOTIFICATION REQUIREMENTS

The rationale for advocating transparency of national environmental measures lies in the need to make sure that foreign producers and importers are fully aware of the requirements and technical standards which may affect their activities. Adequate advance notice and possibly participation in the setting up of relevant standards should guarantee that technical requirements do not develop into barriers to trade. The issue of transparency has long been in the agenda of

[25] On the legal relevance of transnational communication processes, although in the field of human rights, see Bianchi, "Globalisation of Human Rights: the Role of Non-state Actors", in Teubner (ed.), *Global Law Without a State* (1997) p. 179, at p. 191.

the GATT. Article X.1 requires the parties to publish promptly all requirements, restrictions or prohibitions on imports or exports or affecting their sale or distribution. The general transparency clause of GATT has now been specified in the TBT and SPS Agreements. According to TBT Articles 2.9 and 5.6, members proposing to adopt technical regulations or conformity assessment procedures not based on international standards must give prior notice and opportunity to comment to other members at an early stage when amendments can still be introduced and comments taken into account. Moreover, members must publish final technical regulations and any conformity assessment procedure promptly (Articles 2.11 and 5.8). Inquiry points should be created at which all other members may address their requests for information (Article 10). Substantially similar obligations are laid down in the SPS Agreement.[26] Interestingly, in the recent *Japan-Varietals* case, the Panel determined the applicability of the publication requirements also to non-mandatory government measures "in the event compliance with the measure is necessary to obtain an advantage from the government or, in other words, if sufficient incentives or disincentives exist for that measure to be abided by".[27] Despite this web of obligations, some have wondered whether notification of environmentally related standards or procedures should be the object of stricter requirements.

According to a recently de-restricted document of the CTE, notifications of environment-related measures adopted by states in 1998 mark a remarkable increase as compared to previous years.[28] The national measures in question include those notified pursuant to specific obligations laid down in the multilateral trade agreements. Several notification requirements are set out in the WTO Agreements. As regards measures notified under Articles 2 and 5 of the Agreement on Technical Barriers to Trade (TBT), those expressly justified on environmental protection concerns account for about 15 per cent of the total. Among them, measures concerning eco-taxes; soil, water and air pollution prevention measures; the management of waste, both solid and hazardous, as well as rules for environmental management systems. Many notifications were also made pursuant to Article 7.3 of the Agreement on Import Licensing Procedures.

[26] Annex B to the SPS Agreement lays down relevant transparency obligations. Among other things it provides for the notification of an inquiry point from which relevant information and documentation can be obtained from other members, of the national authority responsible for the notification of SPS measures to other WTO members, as well as notification of proposed modifications to existing SPS or new SPS measures which could affect international trade. For a detailed overview of the SPS transparency provisions and their early practice of enforcement see Roberts, "Preliminary Assessment of the Effects of the WTO Agreement on Sanitary and Phitosanitary Trade Regulations", (1998) 1 *Journal of Int'l Economic L.* 377, at 399.

[27] *Japan-Varietals* case, WTO Doc. WT/DS76/1, Panel Report, para. 8.111. The Appellate Body confirmed that the scope of application of the publication requirement is not limited to laws, decrees or ordinances but also include "other instruments which are applicable generally and are similar in character to the instruments explicitly referred to" (Appellate Body Report, para. 105).

[28] See WTO Doc. WT/CTE/W/118, 28 June 1999 (99–2664): "*Item 4: Provisions of the multilateral trading system with respect to the transparency of trade measures used for environmental purposes and environmental measures and requirements, which have significant trade effects*".

It is interesting to note that most measures concerned the procedural requirements for import licences in accordance with such MEAs as the Basel Convention, the Montreal Protocol and CITES. Apart from notification requirements, such environmental measures as import/export restrictions, government policies and programmes are also regularly mentioned in the Trade Policy Reviews carried out each year by the WTO.

What should be clear from the above remarks is that the steady increase in the notification of environmentally-related trade measures, while generally enhancing the transparency of national environmental policies and standards, is only prompted by the need to comply with the requirements established by ITL. Ultimately, what notification procedures and trade policy reviews aim at is to avoid that national measures related to the environment encroach upon the liberalisation of trade or breach the obligations states have undertaken under the various legal instruments which regulate this process internationally. It must be conceded that this has very little to do with environmental protection concerns and much to do with the effort of eliminating barriers to international trade.

V. INTERNATIONAL TRADE LAW AS A CATALYST FOR THE ADOPTION OF MULTILATERAL ENVIRONMENTAL AGREEMENTS

Restraints imposed by international trade law on the use of unilateral environmental measures by states to protect natural resources beyond the regulating state's jurisdiction may occasionally act as a catalyst for the development of multilateral regimes for the conservation of resources. A good illustration of this process is the *Tuna/Dolphin* dispute. The wish to provide appropriate means of protection for dolphins led to the adoption of the 1992 Agreement on the Reduction of Dolphin Mortality in the Eastern Pacific Ocean.[29] It seems beyond doubt that the consensus required for the Treaty was prompted by the first GATT Panel's findings that commercially restrictive measures unilaterally adopted by states to protect natural resources located outside the jurisdiction of the regulating state are inconsistent with GATT and that the legitimate objective of protecting such resources can be best pursued by international cooperation and agreement. The good enforcement record of the 1992 Treaty gives further strength to the argument and supports the trend, already envisaged in the 1992 Rio Declaration, that unilateral environmental measures should be discouraged to the benefit of multilateral agreements.[30]

Support for international cooperation and agreements was later confirmed by the Appellate Body of the WTO-DSU in relation to the *Shrimp/Turtle* case. The Appellate Body in finding the US regulations on the protection of sea turtles in

[29] (1994) 33 *ILM* 936.

[30] See Principle 12 of the Declaration of the UN Conference on Environment and Development.

breach of the *chapeau* of Article XX stressed that had the USA pursued more effectively with the claimant states an international agreement on the protection of sea turtles, its measures could have been upheld. It is of note that the USA in forwarding to the Dispute Settlement Body its fourth report on the status of implementation of the Recommendations and Rulings in the *Shrimp/Turtle* case, drew attention to the resolution adopted at the end of a Symposium on sea turtle conservation held in Australia in October 1999.[31] The resolution calls for efforts to initiate negotiations among states of the Indian Ocean Region within the first half of the year 2000 with a view to adopting an India-Ocean and South-East Asian Regional Agreement on Conservation of Marine Turtles and their Habitats.[32] Should the agreement materialise it would represent yet another instance of ITL acting as a catalyst for the conclusion of MEAs. All the more so, when one realises that the USA considers the Agreement as part of its more comprehensive effort to implement the DSB recommendations and rulings.

In a different perspective also the recent adoption, after five years of negotiations, of the Cartagena Biosafety Protocol attests to the almost indissoluble link between trade and environmental issues and the difficulty of substituting unilateral action for multilateral cooperation.[33] The Protocol, which applies to the transboundary movement, transit, handling and use of all living modified organisms that may have adverse effects on the conservation and sustainable use of biological diversity, taking into account risks to human health, implements Article 19 of the Biodiversity Convention.[34] It is not unreasonable to speculate, however, that the confrontation between such major negotiating actors as the EU and the USA and the risk of jeopardising the agreement by threatening unilateral action or by allowing the proposed WTO Working Group on biotechnology to take the lead and establish a more trade-centred regime,[35] might have hastened the consensus-building process which led the negotiations to completion last January. As is known, the need to regulate such a complex subject, while at the same time subordinating its application to the SPS agreement, under which the Miami Group wanted to retain the possibility of challenging potential trade restrictions, was a cause of friction during the negotiations.[36] Once again, one could see in the Miami Group's negotiating stance the determination to coerce the environmental issues at stake in the agreement into the established boundaries of ITL. In fact, by incorporating the precautionary principle in the text, the Protocol's consistency with the SPS

[31] See WTO Doc. WT/DS58/15/Add.3, 9 November 1999.

[32] *Ibid.* at 3.

[33] The Biosafety Protocol was adopted by more than 130 countries on 29 January 2000 in Montreal, Canada. The text can be retrieved at the following website: www.biodiv.org/biosafe.

[34] Reproduced in (1992) 31 *ILM* 818, at 830.

[35] See the declarations of the Chairperson of the final Montreal negotiating session, Minister Mayr, reported in 4 *Bridges Between Trade and Sustainable Development* (January-February 2000), at 18.

[36] The Miami Group was formed by the USA, Canada, Australia, Argentina, Chile and Uruguay. Throughout the negotiations the Miami Group, contrary to the EU and the developing countries, supported a more trade-friendly agreement which would not disrupt trade in biotechnologies.

Agreement, which requires scientifically proven evidence of harm, remains to be tested. An additional aura of uncertainty is given by the preamble of the Protocol which, after emphasising that the Protocol "shall not be interpreted as implying a change in the rights and obligations of a Party under any existing international agreement", states that "the above recital is not intended to subordinate this Protocol to other international agreements".

VI. THE SCOPE OF UNILATERAL MEASURES AND ITL: THE CURRENT STATE OF PLAY AFTER THE *SHRIMP/TURTLE* CASE UNDER GATT LAW

By and large the most significant impact that ITL has had on national environmental law processes consists of having limited the scope of national measures enacted by states to protect the environment or natural resources beyond their territorial jurisdiction. Trade restrictive measures can be upheld under the GATT general exceptions provided for in Article XX, even when they violate substantive rules of conduct. As for national environmental measures, otherwise inconsistent with GATT provisions, the Article XX exceptions, particularly (b) and (g), represent the only available grounds on which they can be justified.[37] Regardless of their actual wording, the exceptions have been interpreted differently by GATT Panels and, lately, by WTO Panels and the Appellate Body. It may be worth recalling that after the *Tuna/Dolphin* dispute, the issue of the compatibility of unilateral environmental measures with the multilateral trading system had been constrained within a fairly restrictive interpretation of the scope of application of the Article XX exceptions. Particularly, in the *Tuna/Dolphin I* case the Panel interpreted restrictively, in the light of the *travaux préparatoires*, both Article XX(b) and (g) exceptions holding that they could only be applied territorially.[38] Although in *Tuna/Dolphin II*[39] the Panel took a somewhat different stance on this point, holding that a state can enforce its own normative standards also outside its territorial jurisdiction but only against its own nationals and vessels,[40] both Panels held the US measures not to be amenable within the exceptions of Article XX. The first Panel considered them not to be necessary for the protection of animal life as the goal they intended to pursue should have been addressed

[37] Art. XX reads in the relevant parts: "Subject to the requirement that such measures are not applied in a manner which would constitute a means of arbitrary or unjustifiable discrimination between countries where the same conditions prevail, or a disguised restriction on international trade, nothing in this Agreement shall be construed to prevent the adoption or enforcement by any Member of measures: . . . (b) necessary to protect human, animal or plant life or health; . . . (g) relating to the conservation of exhaustible natural resources if such measures are made effective in conjunction with restrictions on domestic production or consumption".

[38] *United States—Restrictions on Imports of Tuna*, reproduced in (1991) 30 *Int'l Legal Materials* 1594, at 1620.

[39] *United States—Restrictions on Imports of Tuna*, reproduced in (1994) 33 *Int'l Legal Materials* 839.

[40] *Ibid.* at 892 and 896 respectively in relation to Art. XX(g) and (b).

through multilateral negotiations.[41] Along similar lines, the second Panel held them not to be in the purview of Article XX as they were not aimed at environmental goals, but rather attempted to impose the regulating state's environmental policy to foreign countries.[42] Overall, the dispute left one with the sense that purely unilateral measures, outside a multilateral framework of cooperation, are incompatible with GATT and that a state may not unilaterally attempt to coerce the environmental policy of other states. Environmental goals ought to be pursued multilaterally by way of cooperation, unless they are confined to resources located within the regulating state's jurisdiction.

If, in many respects, the *Shrimp/Turtle* case is a refinement of the previous jurisprudence, its contribution to a more reasonable interpretation of the Article XX exceptions is important and its departure from *Tuna/Dolphin* quite marked. The dispute originated from some Asian countries which challenged the legislation that the USA had adopted to protect sea turtles by preventing shrimp fishing techniques which would cause a high mortality rate of sea turtles, an endangered species listed in Annex I of CITES.[43] Section 609 of Pub. L. 101–162 prohibited the import of shrimps harvested with techniques which were prejudicial to the conservation of sea turtles.[44] Access to the US market would be allowed, however, from countries which had a similar regulatory programme for the protection of sea turtles or whose shrimp trawling vessels had "turtle excluder devices" to limit the incidental killing of sea turtles. Following a decision of the US Court of International Trade, however, the legislation was interpreted to require that the import of shrimp products from countries having no regulatory programme such as that of the USA had to be banned.[45]

As in the *Tuna/Dolphin* dispute, the facts showed a violation of Article XI of GATT, which the USA did not dispute. In its report,[46] the Panel held that the US measures were unjustified under the *chapeau* of Article XX and therefore could not be upheld. The reasoning of the Panel is fairly peculiar. First, it held that the US measures were discriminatory as certified countries and un-certified countries were countries in which the same conditions prevail, according to the *chapeau* of Article XX.[47] Next, the Panel found that the discrimination was unjustifiable by resorting to a teleological interpretation of the WTO Agreement. In particular, since the central focus of the WTO Agreement "remains the promotion of economic development through trade" and that GATT is "essentially turned toward liberalisation of access to markets on a

41 *Tuna/Dolphin I*, *supra* n. 38, at 1620.

42 *Tuna/Dolphin II*, *supra* n. 39, at 894.

43 For a detailed account of the factual and legal background see the case note by Shaffer in (1999) 93 *American J. Int'l L.* 507.

44 Pub. L. No. 101–162 § 609 (b), 103 Stat. 1038 (1989).

45 *Earth Island Inst.* v. *Christopher*, 913 F. Supp. 559 (Ct. Int'l Trade 1995).

46 Panel Report, *United States—Import Prohibition of Certain Shrimp and Shrimp Products*, WT/DS58/R (98–1710), 15 May 1998.

47 *Ibid.* para. 7.33.

non-discriminatory basis",[48] measures can be upheld under Article XX only to the extent that they "do not undermine the multilateral trading system".[49] Rather unjustifiably, the Panel backed up its conclusion by saying that the evaluation of whether certain measures can actually undermine the trading system cannot be confined to the contested measures. Regard ought to be given also to the possibility that a proliferation of similar measures could lead to jeopardising the multilateral trading system. Finally, the Panel found support also in *Tuna/Dolphin II* in maintaining that national measures that make access to the importing market conditional on a foreign country's adoption of a similar regulatory programme is not amenable within Article XX.

It is quite interesting to note, that besides the many inaccuracies and, possibly, mistakes included in its report, the Panel deliberately distinguished measures taken pursuant to MEAs, by holding that such measures or any other action undertaken multilaterally might be a way to avoid the disruption of the multilateral trading system.[50] This statement is rather unconvincing as one can easily imagine that the extensive use of trade measures to implement MEAs could equally, or perhaps even more so, disrupt the balance of the world trading system. Surprisingly, the Panel did not draw the obvious conclusion that measures undertaken under MEAs could be an admissible exception amenable within the scope of Article XX. After the Panel's decision in the *Shrimp/Turtle* case the scope for upholding environmental unilateral measures under Article XX seemed even more drastically reduced than under the *Tuna/Dolphin II* case. Recourse to such an indeterminate and all-encompassing interpretative criterion of "threat to the multilateral trading system", which, incidentally, appears nowhere in the text, had the practical effect of rendering Article XX potentially useless.

Fortunately, the Appellate Body has reconsidered most of the controversial aspects of the Panel's decision and eventually reached a more balanced solution.[51] Relying on the *Gasoline* case, the Appellate Body clarified that the *chapeau* of Article XX is not concerned with the nature of the measures, which is considered in the various exceptions listed in the article, but rather with the manner of their application. Making a more proper treatment of interpretative rules, the Appellate Body, while acknowledging that the maintenance of the international trading system is a fundamental objective of GATT as a whole, held that the above principle cannot be used as an interpretative rule for the *chapeau* of Article XX.[52] Relying again on *Gasoline*, the Appellate Body identified as the object and purpose of the *chapeau* that of avoiding abuse of any of the exceptions listed in the article. Therefore, the applicability of the relevant exceptions of Article XX to the facts of the case was a prerequisite for the consideration of the *chapeau*. As a matter of logic the Appellate Body's reasoning is straightforward.

[48] *Ibid.* para. 7.42.

[49] *Ibid.* para. 7.44.

[50] *Ibid.* para. 7.55.

[51] WTO Appellate Body Report, *United States—Import Prohibition of Certain Shrimp and Shrimp Products*, AB–1998–4 WT/DS58/AB/R (98–0000), 12 October 1998, in (1998) 38 *ILM* 121.

[52] *Ibid.* para. 116.

There cannot be any abuse of an exception if the exception is not applicable.[53] In a rather unprecedented procedural move, the Appellate Body, having dismissed the reasoning of the Panel, went on with its own analysis and concentrated on Article XX(g).[54] Stating that the exception has to be interpreted in the light of contemporary standards of international law, particularly "in the light of contemporary concerns of the community of nations about the protection and conservation of the environment",[55] the Appellate Body looked at the fact that sea turtles are included in Annex I of the CITES and therefore can be considered as an "exhaustible natural resource" for the purpose of Article XX(g). Given the migratory character of sea turtles the Appellate Body could avoid any determination on the jurisdictional reach of the exception.[56] The Appellate Body then considered whether the US measures could be qualified as "related to" the conservation of exhaustible natural resources, which had always been interpreted as "primarily aimed at" in past GATT jurisprudence[57] and found that the import ban was reasonably related to the purpose of protecting sea turtles.[58]

The Appellate Body then turned its attention to the *chapeau*, where it sought to locate and mark out a "line of equilibrium", between the exceptions of Article XX and the general obligations of GATT. This balance, in the words of the Appellate Body, "is not fixed and unchanging" and "moves as the kind and the shape of the measures at stake vary and as the facts making up specific cases differ".[59] Applying a balancing test in determining whether the US measures had been applied reasonably,[60] the Court found that the US requirement that all

[53] *Ibid.* para. 120.

[54] *Ibid.* para. 123. Interestingly enough, the Appellate Body did not confine itself to reviewing the legal issues highlighted by the Panel. It made also findings of fact to support its conclusions that the US measures were an arbitrary and unjustifiable discrimination in violation of Article XX. Arguably, this is inconsistent with Article 17.6 of the DSU, according to which "An appeal shall be limited to issues of law covered in the panel report and legal interpretations developed by the panel". A departure from the text of Article 17.6 had already materialised, starting from the *Gasoline* case, where the Appellate Body had reserved the right to address legal issues not covered in the Panel's report (reproduced in (1996) 35 *ILM* 603). On the point, generally, see Appleton, *Shrimp/Turtle: Untangling the Nets*, (1999) 2 *Journal of Int'l Economic L.* 477, at 478.

[55] Appellate Body Report, para. 129.

[56] *Ibid.* para. 133.

[57] See, among others, the *Canada Herring* case, cited in para. 6.39 of the *Gasoline* Panel Report ((1996) 35 *ILM* 274 at 299), and the Appellate Body Report in the *Gasoline* case at III.B ((1996) 35 *ILM* 603 at 618). For criticism of this interpretative approach see Schoenbaum, *International Trade and Protection of the Environment: the Continuing Search for Reconciliation*, *supra* n. 1, pp. 278–9.

[58] As regards the third prong of Art. XX(g) the Appellate Body was satisfied that the measures were made effective in conjunction with restrictions on the domestic harvesting of shrimps. The Appellate Body did not address the applicability of Art. XX (b), thus failing to answer the question of whether the US measures were necessary to protect animal life. It would have been interesting to see whether the Appellate Body would have used the same type of analysis as regards the "necessity" requirement of Art. XX(b). On the point see Montini, *infra* Chapter 6.

[59] Appellate Body Report, para. 159.

[60] The need to evaluate the reasonableness of the application of the unilateral measures had been highlighted by the Appellate Body in the *Reformulated Gasoline* case (*United States—Reformulated Gasoline*, WT/DS2/AB/R, 20 May 1996 at 22: "the measures falling within the particular exceptions must be applied reasonably, with due regard both to the legal duties of the party claiming the exception and the legal rights of the other parties concerned").

exporting countries essentially adopt the same policy amounted to an unjustifiable "coercive effect" on the foreign countries' policy decisions.[61] Moreover, by noting that the USA had successfully concluded an Inter-American Convention on the Protection and Conservation of Sea Turtles, the Appellate Body concluded that "multilateral procedures are available and feasible" and blamed the USA for not having pursued a similar agreement with the claimant states.[62] Besides considering as discriminatory the application of different phase-in periods to different countries for the introduction and use of Turtles Excluding Devices (TEDs) as well as the transfer of TEDs technology to some states rather than others,[63] the Appellate Body concentrated on the concept of arbitrary discrimination under the *chapeau* and elaborated a due process doctrine in connection with Article XX. In particular, the failure by the USA to set up an administrative procedure in which foreign parties could be heard and possibly challenge the US regulations, the lack of transparency and the unpredictable character of decisions as well as the absence of an appeal or judicial review procedure amounted to a violation of the due process rights enshrined in Article X of the GATT.[64] By contrast one can reasonably presume that the US measures could have been upheld, had they been more carefully drafted, taking into account the different conditions of different countries, had the USA provided foreign governments and traders with the due process rights they are entitled to under GATT, or had the claimant states refused to cooperate in the negotiations of a MEA on sea turtles.

The *Shrimp/Turtle* case should not be interpreted too broadly so as to allow environmental unilateral measures almost unconditionally to qualify for an exception under Article XX, as some would have wished. In this respect, the Appellate Body's reluctance explicitly to accept that Article XX could accommodate a general exception for MEAs is quite telling of its prudent approach. On the other hand, however, the Appellate Body reversed the trade-centred approach that the prior GATT-WTO jurisprudence had seemed to adopt by acknowledging the importance of environmental measures and recommending multilateral ones. Most importantly, it chose to opt for a case-by-case approach in which a balance must be struck between the right of states to avail themselves of the exceptions in Article XX and the obligation incumbent upon them to respect the treaty rights of other members. In so doing, the Appellate Body introduced an element of reasonableness in the test to evaluate the compatibility of national environmental measures which is somewhat reminiscent of the approach used in the regional context of the EU.[65] This change, which had been

[61] Appellate Body Report, para. 161

[62] *Ibid.* paras 166–70.

[63] *Ibid.* para. 173.

[64] *Ibid.* paras 182–3. Art. X.3 of GATT requires states to "administer in a uniform, impartial and reasonable manner" their laws and regulations and imposes an obligation to "maintain . . . judicial, arbitral or administrative tribunals or procedures for the purpose, inter alia, of the prompt review and correction of administrative action".

[65] See Case 302/86, *Commission* v. *Denmark* [1988] ECR 4607.

advocated by scholars since the *Tuna/Dolphin I* case,[66] will have to be tested in future cases. The abandonment of interpretative criteria based on original intent in favour of an evolutionary method of interpretation in the light of the contemporary standards of international law bears witness to the determination of the Appellate Body to discharge its adjudicatory functions in a way which can accommodate values other than trade.[67]

As to what is left for unilateral state action in the field of environmental protection much will depend on the subsequent practice of the WTO dispute settlement organs. Certainly, the Appellate Body paved the way for a more flexible approach to the issue of whether environmental concerns underlying unilateral measures can be accommodated within the GATT. Indeed, this element of flexibility inherent in the balancing test used by the Appellate Body to determine the compatibility of the US measures with Article XX is the most remarkable achievement. Although the EU's belief that the Appellate Body has eventually provided for an indirect exception to accommodate MEAs within Article XX might be too optimistic,[68] undoubtedly the Appellate Body's holding in the *Shrimp/Turtle* case can now provide, at least in principle, a sound basis for upholding the validity of certain environmental measures, be they taken unilaterally or on the basis of a MEA. More troubling is the case of unilateral actions undertaken in the absence of any internationally recognized environmental standards. One can infer from the jurisprudence of the GATT and the WTO that multilateral cooperation should be pursued. But that fails to account for all those cases in which cooperation is refused or unduly postponed by the target state. Should the regulating state be permitted to resort to unilateral measures which are trade-restrictive? The answer ought to be in the affirmative if the measures are amenable within one of the exceptions of Article XX and if their application is not arbitrary or unjustifiable in the light of the balancing test proposed by the Appellate Body in the *Shrimp/Turtle* case. The fact that unilateral action may occasionally spur international cooperation with otherwise recalcitrant states should be an important element in the evaluation of the reasonableness of the measures and therefore of their validity under GATT law. Finally, one cannot rule out that certain unilateral measures can be qualified as countermeasures against a state which has violated international obligations in the area of environmental protection. In this case, the Panel or the Appellate Body should administer the relevant principles and rules of international law to address the issue. The frequent use of international law

66 Koppen, "Free Trade Versus Environment: Catching Tuna Fish and Dolphins in GATT Backwaters", in Morgan, Lorentzen, Leander and Guzzini (eds.), *New Diplomacy in the Post-Cold-War World* (London, 1993), p. 213; Schoenbaum, *Free International Trade and Protection of the Environment: Irreconcilable Conflict*, *supra* n. 1, p. 716.

67 See the interesting reference by the Appellate Body to the *Namibia Advisory Opinion* ([1971] ICJ Reports 31) to anchor its concept of evolutionary, as opposed to static, interpretation with regard to the definition of "exhaustible natural resources".

68 See the submission by the EU at the CTE session of 29–30 June 1999, reported in *Trade and Environment Bulletin* No. 29, at 2 (WT/CTE/4) (99–0000), 12 October 1999.

principles (e.g. recourse to the rules of treaty interpretation laid down in the Vienna Convention) shows that the dispute settlement organs of the WTO are now in the position to act almost as international courts, administering whatever international law question may be incidentally relevant to determine issues under their jurisdiction.

VII. FURTHER LIMITS TO NATIONAL MEASURES UNDER THE SPS AND TBT AGREEMENTS

National policies, programmes and standards can be affected also by the operation of the Agreement on Technical Barriers to Trade (TBT) and the Agreement on Sanitary and Phytosanitary Measures (SPS). The SPS is meant to protect, on the one hand, human or animal life from the risks arising from additives, contaminants, toxins or disease-causing organisms in their food, beverages, feedstuffs and, on the other, animal or plant life from pests, diseases, or disease-causing organisms. The TBT, in turn, is meant to cover all other product standards and related processes and production methods which reflect on the product itself. The TBT applies to mandatory technical regulations and voluntary standards for products. The two agreements are different *ratione materiae* and therefore can be considered as mutually exclusive.[69] Their relevance to our subject lies in their being an additional constraint imposed on states, especially as regards the import of products.

Both agreements are meant to foster the harmonisation of technical rules and the use of international standards. States, however, enjoy a certain measure of discretion on whether or not to follow international standards. Under the TBT, international standards may be refused when they would be "ineffective or inappropriate" for the fulfilment of a legitimate objective such as environmental protection.[70] States may either base their technical regulations on international standards, in which case a rebuttable presumption that they do not create an unnecessary obstacle to trade is established. Or, they may decide to adopt their own standards, in which case a set of procedural and substantial requirements must be met. Procedurally, states must give prior notice and opportunity to comment at an early stage of the procedure to other members of the Agreement and must publish the final regulations or conformity assessment procedures promptly. As already noted enquiry points must be created at which the other members may obtain all relevant information about a state's technical regulations. From the substantive point of view, besides complying with GATT MFN (most favoured nation) and NT (national treatment) clauses, national standards must not be more trade-restrictive than necessary to fulfil a legitimate objective,

[69] See WTO, Committee on Sanitary and Phitosanitary Measures, *The Difference Between SPS and TBT Measures*, Presentation made by the Secretariat at the Special Meeting of the SPS Committee on Transparency Provisions held on 9 November 1999, WTO Doc. G/SPS/GEN/151, 6 December 1999.

[70] Art. 2.4 TBT.

taking into account the risks that non-conformity would create.[71] The TBT Agreement also lays down rules on conformity assessment, including such matters as product testing and inspection and laboratory accreditation, calling on states to harmonise standards or to recognise each other's results of conformity assessment procedures even when they are carried out in a different way.[72] Overall, when states decide to depart from international standards they are subject to several obligations which de facto constrain their freedom to adopt technical regulations. Although under the TBT, unlike the SPS Agreement, for states that want to adopt standards which are more stringent than those provided internationally there is no requirement to base their regulations on scientific evidence, it will be difficult to distinguish between a validly different standard and a trade-restrictive one.

The constraints mentioned above are even stricter for the SPS Agreement, as has become apparent in its early applications. According to the SPS Agreement, which applies to all SPS measures affecting international trade, independently of GATT, whether enacted subsequent or prior to the entry into force of the Agreement, a state which wants to adopt an SPS measure may choose a measure which conforms with an international standard (such as those established by the Codex Alimentarius Commission), thus creating a rebuttable presumption that the measure satisfies the criteria set forth in the SPS Agreement; or it may base its measure on the international standard, adopting some but not all the elements of the international standard; or, it may depart from the international standard, setting for itself the desired level of protection. The Appellate Body in the *Hormones* case recognised the "autonomous right" of Member States to establish a higher level of sanitary protection than that set by international standards.[73] In fact, if the sanitary or phitosanitary measure is only based on an international standard or has been enacted independently of international standards some strict requirements must be met, which undoubtedly limit the theoretical freedom of the state.

First the measure must be based upon "scientific principles" and therefore SPS measures cannot be maintained without "sufficient scientific evidence".[74] This rather undefined standard was specified by the Appellate Body in the *Japan—Varietals* case concerning the Japanese ban on certain US fruit to protect its

[71] Art. 5.1.2 TBT.

[72] Art. 6 TBT.

[73] Appellate Body Report, para. 104.

[74] Art. 2.2 SPS measures can be taken provisionally where "relevant scientific information is insufficient" (Art. 5.7 SPS), provided that they are adopted on the basis of available pertinent information. Such measures cannot be maintained, however, unless the regulating state seeks to obtain the additional information necessary for a more objective assessment of risk and reviews the measures accordingly "within a reasonable period of time" (see *Japan—Varietals*, Appellate Body Report, para. 89). It is interesting to note that the EU never claimed the provisional character of its import ban on hormone-treated beef from the USA, but rather invoked the precautionary principle. The Appellate Body, expressing doubts on the status of the precautionary principle under general international law, held that it could not in any event override the risk assessment requirement imposed by the SPS Agreement (see *Hormones*, Appellate Body Report, paras 123–5)

plants from a pest. The Appellate Body held that the sufficiency requirement implies that there be a rational or objective relationship between the SPS measure and the scientific evidence.[75] This determination must be made on a case-by-case basis, having regard to all relevant circumstances including the characteristics of the national measure as well as the quality and quantity of the scientific evidence. SPS measures must be based also on a risk assessment.[76] In the *Australia—Salmon* case concerning the protection of fish from a number of diseases, the Appellate Body made a distinction between the risk assessment to be carried out in relation to food-borne risks and that for disease or pest risks. In particular, the Appellate Body maintained that while for food-borne risks the risk assessment requires only the evaluation of the potential for adverse effects on human or animal health, in the case of disease or pest risks it "demands an evaluation of the likelihood of entry, establishment or spread of a disease, and of the associated potential biological and economic consequences". It may be worth recalling that in the *Hormones* case both the Panel and the Appellate Body found the EU in violation of the risk assessment requirement using a two-tiered test requiring that the party establishing the SPS measure identifies relevant adverse effects and evaluate the potential of occurrence of such adverse effects.[77]

An additional hurdle in the adoption of national SPS measures consists of the limits to which states are subject as regards the choice of the measure to adopt once the "sufficient scientific evidence" and "risk assessment" requirements have been met. Article 5.6 of the SPS Agreement provides that states "shall ensure that such measures are not more trade-restrictive than required to achieve their appropriate level of sanitary or phitosanitary protection". The requirement was clarified in the *Australia—Salmon* case where the Appellate Body elaborated a test in which three cumulative criteria were identified to assess the consistency of the national measure with the SPS Agreement. In particular, the Appellate Body affirmed the inconsistency of the national measure if an alternative measure exists which is reasonably available taking into account technical and economical feasibility; achieves the member's appropriate level of sanitary or phitosanitary protection and is significantly less restrictive to trade than the SPS measure contested.[78] Of particular interest is also the provision laid down in Article 5.5 SPS concerning the prohibition of "arbitrary or unjustifiable distinctions in the levels [of protection] it [the State] considers to be appropriate in different situations, if such distinctions result in discrimination or a disguised restriction on international trade". This clause has been the object of a varying interpretation by the Appellate Body. In the *Australia—Salmon* case the Appellate Body compared the ban on imports of fresh,

[75] *Japan—Varietals* Appellate Body Report, paras 73 and 84.

[76] The expression "based on" has been interpreted as requiring that "there be a rational relationship between the measure and the risk assessment" (see *Hormones* case, Appellate Body Report, para. 193).

[77] *Ibid.* para. 208.

[78] *Australia—Salmon*, Appellate Body Report, para. 123.

chilled or frozen salmon for human consumption with the different treatment accorded to the imports of ornamental finfish and herring to be used as bait, which present even higher risks of disease introduction, and held that a finding that a national SPS measure is not based on a risk assessment or is based on an insufficient risk assessment provides an indication that the measure in question is not meant to protect human, animal, plant life or health, "but is instead a trade-restrictive measure taken in the guise of an SPS measure, i.e. a 'disguised restriction on international trade' ".[79] By contrast in the *Hormones* case, the Appellate Body, after comparing regulation of the use of hormones for the growth of cattle and the regulation of antimicrobial growth promoters in swine and finding this to amount to an arbitrary or unjustifiable distinction, refused to find a violation of Article 5.5 of the SPS as it could not be inferred from the EU import ban that the measures had been designed to protect the domestic beef producers in the EU rather than protecting people from the risk of cancer. This interpretation impliedly requires evidence of a protectionist intent of the measure, which does not seem to be necessary under Article 5.5.

The above remarks are meant to show how the alleged right of states to determine the levels of environmental and sanitary and phitosanitary protection are severely constrained by ITL, which imposes on them a heavy burden of proof in order to justify their departure from accepted international standards. Since often international standards may result in some sort of lowest common denominator, this may be prejudicial to strict national policies of environmental and health protection. A fair evaluation of the effects of the SPS and TBT Agreements on environmental and health standards is no easy task. On the one hand, it could be argued that once again the compelling force of the free trade doctrine has overridden environmental and health concerns. On the other, one could say that the two Agreements simply specify the principle of non-discrimination contained in Article III of GATT and may effectively counteract the practice of some countries of adopting protectionist measures in the guise of environmental or sanitary or phytosanitary standards. Whether the SPS and TBT Agreements strike a reasonable balance between the two conflicting needs can only be assessed over time.[80] As is often the case, much will depend on how they will be interpreted and applied by the WTO.

VIII. THE HARMONISATION OF ENVIRONMENTAL PRODUCT STANDARDS AND PPMS: REGULATIONS v. MARKET-BASED MECHANISMS

The regulatory philosophy of ITL rests on a fairly restricted number of fundamental principles. Among them, the principle of non-discrimination certainly

[79] *Ibid.* para. 166.

[80] For a preliminary tentative assessment of the effects of the SPS Agreement, see Roberts, "Preliminary Assessment of the Effects of the WTO Agreement on Sanitary and Phitosanitary Trade Regulations", (1998) 1 *Journal of Int'l Economic Law* 377.

stands out. In fact, it would not be too simplistic to hold that to avoid discrimination and to abolish barriers to trade can be seen as the two basic pillars of the whole edifice of ITL. This is why so much emphasis is put on the issue of harmonisation of national standards and technical regulations, including environmental ones. Different national regimes are potentially disruptive to the multilateral trading system, although their uniformity is unattainable and their relative harmonisation incredibly complex. If this holds true for product standards, the harmonisation of PPMs, only partly covered by WTO Agreements, is almost impossible to achieve. The SPS and TBT Agreements, while leaving some room for national diversity, encourage the use, but do not impose the adoption, of international standards. The latter are produced by a variety of organisations of a different nature. As far as SPS measures are concerned international standards are provided by the Codex Alimentarius Commission, the International Office of Epizootics and the numerous organisations operating under the framework of the International Plant Protection Convention. For TBT measures reference is made to the International Standardisation Organisation (ISO), the International Electrotechnical Commission, the Codex Alimentarius, the Food and Agricultural Organisation and the World Methereological Organisation.[81]

Given the difficulty of providing a satisfactory degree of harmonisation by traditional command-and-control legal instruments, lately the tendency of developing self-regulatory, consumer-based, voluntary mechanisms mainly addressed to private economic operators has emerged. This new approach, which relies heavily on private standard-setting and implementation has led to the adoption of private standards, codes of conduct and agreements on environmental law-making and enforcement processes to be implemented by firms generally or enterprises operating in certain sectors.[82] The coupling of such market-based instruments as environmental management and auditing schemes as well as eco-labelling programmes with traditional regulatory instruments aims to foster an integrated approach to the process of harmonisation of environmental standards. The enactment by the EU of Regulation 1836/93 establishing a voluntary system of internal management and auditing systems with a view to improving environmental performances,[83] and Regulation 880/92 on eco-labelling[84] can be regarded as an application of this new trend at the regional level. Although the practice of implementation of the above instruments is not entirely satisfactory, their introduction in the EC legal system has

[81] See also the WTO, *TBT Standards Code Directory*, which contains details of standardising bodies which have notified the acceptance of the TBT Code of Good Practice for the Preparation, Adoption and Application of Standards (Annex 3 to the TBT Agreement). Acceptance of the code is notified to the ISO Central Secretariat in Geneva.

[82] See Roth-Arriaza, "Private Voluntary Standard-Setting, the International Organisation for Standardisation and International Environmental Lawmaking", (1995) *Yearbook of Int'l Env'l L.* 109.

[83] See OJ 1993 L168/1.

[84] See OJ 1992 L99/1.

created a combination of regulatory instruments which may represent a model for analogous developments at the global level.

In fact, the recent work of the ISO confirms this evolutionary trend. The ISO has recently adopted three types of environmental labelling programmes, prepared by the ISO/TC 207/SC 3 environmental labelling sub-committee. The first type is a voluntary, multiple-criteria-based, third party programme that awards a licence which authorises the use of environmental labels on products, indicating the overall environmental preferability of a product within a product category based on life cycle considerations (ISO 14024). The second type consists of a self-declared environmental claim by manufacturers, importers, distributors without any external certification (ISO 14021). Finally, the third programme is a voluntary programme based on life cycle assessment in accordance with the ISO 14040 series, verified by a qualified third party. As a parallel development it is worth noting that the sub-committee ISO/TC/ 207/SC 5 on "Life Cycle Assessment" of the ISO 14040 series has produced a number of documents and standards on principles, goals, scope, inventory analysis, assessment and interpretation of the environmental management of life cycle. The work of the ISO in this domain is particularly useful, given the potentially disruptive effects that life cycle national regulations and environmental labelling schemes may have on the multilateral trading system.[85] Consistently with the trend described above of improving inter-organisational cooperation, the ISO has recently submitted to the CTE, at the invitation of the EU, a document in which the latest achievements are described.[86]

The potentially less trade-restrictive effects of harmonisation by means of market-based instruments, which has spurred their promotion also within the precincts of ITL, is yet to be tested. Developing countries have voiced concerns that eco-labelling schemes might distort international trade by favouring firms from developed countries to the disadvantage of those firms from third world countries which might find it difficult to adjust to the requirements of any such scheme, with the obvious consequence of being penalised by consumers in international markets.[87] The fact that in any event, those eco-labelling schemes related to product characteristics would be subject to the discipline of the TBT Agreement, partly deprives the argument of its persuasive force. Moreover, ISO intends to promote mutual recognition of programmes with equivalent, if not identical, criteria. The real hazards seem to lie elsewhere. In particular, the process of setting and drafting ISO standards remains largely unsatisfactory. The predominance of transnational corporate interests and the heavy weight of

[85] Schoenbaum, *International Trade and Protection of the Environment: the Continuing Search for Reconciliation*, *supra* n. 1, p. 287.

[86] See WTO Doc. WT/CTE/W/114, 31 May 1999. At the time most of the ISO standards described in the text were still being negotiated.

[87] The current effort to promote standardisation, mainly advocated by industrialised states, may confine developing countries to the mere role of "regulation takers" depriving them of their right to fix autonomously their desired level of environmental and health protection: see Atik, "Science and International Regulatory Convergence", (1996–1997) 17 *Northwestern J. Int'l L. and Business* 736.

industrialised states in the negotiating process affect the balance of power in the peculiar negotiating setting of the ISO, where the distinction between public and private actors tends to be blurred, partly undermining the legitimacy of the organisation. Although improvements have been achieved lately in terms of legitimacy-enhancing and representation of more interest groups, additional efforts are required to improve the functioning of the ISO as well as the transparency of its activities. The decision-making process within ISO is also likely to bring about negative effects on the quality and efficacy of environmental standards. The consensus-based nature of the decision-making process and the need to achieve compromises on controversial issues tend to favour lowest common denominator standards. This is often caused by the participation in the decision-making process of powerful states and non-state actors which may have an interest in lowering standards, either by omitting controversial points or by watering down undesired outcomes.

Overall, the quest for harmonisation of product and PPMs standards has favoured the development of market-based instruments which, in principle, could aptly complement traditional legal rules enacted either nationally or internationally. The technical expertise provided by standardisation bodies as well as the participation of non-state actors in their decision-making processes could be considered as additional assets of a new method of law-making. Depending on how widespread the adoption of such standards is in each particular sector and on how efficiently compliance with them can be achieved, the liberalisation of international trade might benefit from the international standardisation, which ITL has so strongly favoured in the past few years. From the perspective of the environment, however, increased harmonisation will not necessarily lead to a constant improvement of environmental protection. While it is true that the introduction of market-based instruments has expanded the range of tools which can be utilised internationally to develop global environmental strategies, current discussions about their use remain primarily geared to the achievement of trade goals. Paradoxically, the main concern at the moment is that international standards may themselves represent those barriers to trade which they had set about to abolish by their harmonising effect.

IX. THE WTO-DSU AND ITS PRACTICE OF ENFORCEMENT VIS-À-VIS OTHER MEAs DISPUTE SETTLEMENT MECHANISMS

Clearly, the relationship between the dispute settlement mechanisms in MEAs and those of the multilateral trading system is part of the broader issue of the relation between MEAs and the WTO Agreements. So far most of the environmentally-related disputes handled by GATT panels and WTO panels and Appellate Body concerned the use of potentially trade-restrictive unilateral measures enacted by states on alleged environmental protection grounds. Short of treaty amendments which may provide a solution to the problem, the capacity of the multilateral trading system dispute settlement organs to handle such disputes has improved remarkably. In particular, reference to international environmental agreements for the purpose of interpreting GATT rules as well as the discretion that panels enjoy in accepting submissions by NGOs or even in requesting experts' advice and expertise, are tools which can aptly be used to enhance the quality of the findings of dispute settlement organs whenever issues related to the environment come into play.[88] The inherent capacity of the system to adjust to the specific needs of environmentally-related cases begs the question of what dispute settlement the parties to a dispute should choose when the object of their controversy is one which may come under the jurisdiction of different dispute settlement mechanisms. In this respect, the CTE had recommended that trade disputes arising under a MEA ought to be addressed within the dispute settlement procedures provided for in the relevant MEA.[89]

Although there is to date no practice on the issue of what would be the appropiate forum for disputes concerning the use of trade measures in MEAs and given the current uncertainty on the general relation between MEAs and the WTO, several points can be made expressing scepticism about the course of action proposed by the CTE. First, Article 23 of the Dispute Settlement Understanding (DSU) establishes an obligation for WTO members to have recourse to the rules and procedures of the DSU, when they seek redress of a violation of obligations or other nullification or impairment of benefits under the agreements covered or an impediment to the attainment of any objective of those agreements. Although exceptions to the jurisdiction of the WTO can be envisaged,[90] Article 23 leaves little doubt as to the primacy of the dispute settlement understanding which is meant to play a fundamental role in the strenghtening of the multilateral system established by the WTO. The quasi-jurisdictional character of dispute settlement under the WTO and the increasing trust states seem to have developed towards its operation render the choice of the WTO forum fairly palatable to states whenever disputes which bear on international trade arise. Indirect access of private operators to the WTO dispute settlement mechanism through the medium of either their national state or a regional organisation provides an additional explanation for the high favour in which the DSU is currently standing as compared to other international law adjudicatory mechanisms.[91]

[88] These issues are discussed at some length in Appleton, *Shrimp/Turtle: Untangling the Nets*, *supra* n. 54 at 478. It is of particular note that in the *Shrimp/Turtle* case the Appellate Body, in reversing the Panel decision, decided that "authority to *seek* information is not properly equated with a *prohibition* on accepting information which has been submitted to it, *whether requested by a panel or not*" (Appellate Body Report, para 108 (emphasis in original text)) and that NGO submissions could be accepted.

[89] *Contra Communication from the Commission to the Council and the European Parliament*, *supra* n. 14, para. 4.5.

[90] Ligustro, *Le controversie tra Stati nel diritto del commercio internazionale: dal GATT all'OMC* (Padova, 1996).

[91] Jackson, *The World Trading System* (2nd edn., 1997), p. 127. illustrating relevant procedures under US law and EC law, particularly Regulation 3286/94.

Ultimately, it should not be forgotten that dispute settlement in most MEAs is hardly ever used. Consistently with the prevailing trends in contemporary international environmental law most treaty regimes are geared to compliance.[92] This entails the use of a number of mechanisms and devices which tend to bypass or complement traditional international responsibility and dispute settlement mechanisms, which in most cases are not meant to produce binding decisions. These instruments include reporting, implementation review mechanisms, economic incentives and, sometimes, the couching of international obligations in private law terms so as to channel liability for violation of treaty commitments on private operators rather than national governments. Although, in principle, also other fora could become occasionally available to adjudicate environmentally-related trade disputes, the WTO-DSU provides the most efficient and reliable forum to address this type of disputes.

X. FUTURE CHALLENGES: TRADE IN SERVICES AND OTHER ITEMS CURRENTLY UNDER CONSIDERATION OF THE CTE

Future challenges loom through the horizon for the multilateral trading system as regards environmental concerns. Particularly, measures in areas not yet fully explored may soon come to the surface as potentially disruptive for the current regulatory framework of international trade. Many such issues are currently under scrutiny within the CTE. Besides the various aspects of the relationship between the Convention on Biological Diversity and the TRIPs Agreement, discussion continues on the sensitive issues of domestically prohibited goods (DPGs). Although several treaties and soft law instruments dealing with the monitoring and control of trade in several DPGs exist, many developing countries still complain about the insufficient information available for the characteristics of certain DPGs as well as their lack of technical capacity to adopt informed decisions about their imports. The CTE has started working more closely on other items including subsidies and non-tariff measures in such sectors as agriculture, fisheries, forestry, textiles and clothing and leather, which pose particular problems. An issue of particular concern is that of subsidies in the fisheries sector. Overfishing, driven by excess capacity and government support, risks leading key fish stocks to collapse, thus causing irreparable environmental damage. A recent submission of New Zealand to the CTE on the benefits of eliminating trade-distorting and environmentally-damaging subsidies in the fisheries sector calls for urgent action to be taken within the WTO and other international fora to halt the granting of such subsidies.[93]

Also, the little explored service sector is likely to represent a challenge in the not too distant future. As an international market for environmental services

[92] For a general overview see Sands, *Principles of International Environmental Law*, vol. I (1995), p. 141; Boyle, *International Law & the Environment* (1992), p. 136.

[93] See WTO Doc. WT/CTE/W/121, 28 June 1999.

seems to develop, independently of governmental involvement, "international trade in these services is growing from previously low levels".[94] Although Article XIV(b) of the General Agreement on Trade in Services (GATS) is a general exception clause modelled upon Article XX (b) of GATT, it is yet unclear how and to what extent national regulation of environmental services may come to clash with the substantive provisions of GATS. However, potential challenges may take unexpected and unpredictable forms. If one takes the example of the Clean Development Mechanism (CDM) projects, under the Kyoto Protocol, to be implemented jointly by developed and developing countries, it is not impossible to speculate that the host country's production of offsets might be qualified as a supply of service (decarbonisation service) in the territory of one member to the service consumer of another member and therefore trigger the applicability of GATS.[95] But also the design and implementation of the CDM project by a developed state's project developer might itself constitute a service supplied to the developing country through the modes of supply provided for in GATS. Under GATS, a host country would be bound to accord MFN treatment and therefore could not freely grant contractual concessions to favour developers of one country. As rightly noted "[j]oint implementation and trade within the CDM may prove to be . . . new forms of trade in services, and they may likewise come to be accepted as such when they are more widely understood and utilized".[96]

XI. CONCLUSION: THE CAPACITY OF THE ITL SYSTEM TO ACCOMMODATE ENVIRONMENTAL CONCERNS: ACHIEVEMENTS AND PROSPECTS

A tentative evaluation of the impact of ITL on environmental law and process on the basis of the above-selected areas may be too ambitious a task. Furthermore, any impact assessment necessarily entails a value-judgement based on preferences and priority setting. Some inferences, however, can be legitimately drawn from recent practice and some speculations can be made on the impact of ITL on environmental law and process. The integration of trade and environmental concerns into the concept of sustainable development has brought about different effects. On the one hand it has somewhat exacerbated the North/South divide by widening the already existing gap between developed and developing countries. The negotiation of international environmental agreements, which even indirectly bear on trade issues, has become increasingly difficult. The pro-environment attitude of developed states is almost invariably taken by developing countries as protectionism in disguise. Developing countries, in turn, insist

[94] WTO, Council for Trade in Services, *Environmental Services*, Background Note Prepared by the Secretariat, WTO Doc. S/C/W/46, 6 July 1998, recently de-restricted.

[95] Art. I, para. 1.2(b) GATS. The point is aptly made in an article by Wiser, "The Clean Development MechanismVersus the World Trade Organisation: Can Free-Market Greenhouse Gas Emissions Abatement Survive Free Trade?", 11 *Georgetown Int'l Env. Law Review* 531 (1999).

[96] Wiser, *ibid.* at 561.

on trade benefits, economic advantages and incentives of all sorts to make environmental concessions.

It would be unfair, however, to draw attention only to the shortcomings of the process, which, undoubtedly, has produced also positive effects. The strenghtening of communication processes and, consequently, of cooperation among different institutional actors is certainly one of them. The increased transparency of the interaction of trade and environmental regulations as well as the higher visibility of the conflicting interests involved has induced the active participation of some sectors of civil society in the debate. This in turn has enhanced the role that NGOs and interest groups play in the shaping of international policy-making. Also the introduction and more frequent use of market-based instruments as opposed to more traditional command and control regulatory techniques can be seen as a positive development in so far as it has broadened the spectrum of policy and legal instruments which can be used to reconcile and foster compliance with both environmental and trade law. By contrast ITL can be deemed to have had a negative impact on environmental law processes by considerably restraining the capacity of states to act unilaterally for the protection of the environment. Such curtailment of the power of states to enact measures which allegedly aim at protecting natural resources outside the regulating state's jurisdiction can be detrimental to environmental protection. After all, the protection of certain areas or resources, in the absence of any international regime, can only be attained by unilateral measures. Moreover, the latter have proved to be strategically important in fostering the development of multilateral cooperation. Despite their apparent freedom, states are also constrained in their choices of setting standards of environmental and health protection nationally, as they have to justify departures from international standards. Furthermore, the tendency to attract environmentally related disputes within the WTO dispute settlement mechanism, inevitably constrains environmental concerns into the web of trade obligations, which for a long time have constituted the preeminent (if not the only) normative terms of reference for GATT and WTO Panels.

There is a great deal of ideology involved in the debate on trade and environment. In particular, the statement that trade liberalisation and economic growth are conducive to a better environmental protection seems more an article of faith than a finding supported by empirical evidence. The uncertainty about the effects of freer trade on the environment has been acknowledged by several institutions. Even a recently published report of the WTO [97] has recognised for the first time that in some specific cases trade can damage the environment, while rejecting the general argument that the constraints put by ITL on national measures can be prejudicial to the environment.[98] The report eventually called

[97] WTO Secretariat, *Trade and Environment*, Special Studies 4 (1999).

[98] The emphasis on either aspect of the report varies depending on each commentator's interest or inclination. The report was hailed by some sectors of the press as evidence that trade helps to increase the level of environmental protection: see *Why Greens Should Love Trade*, *The Economist*, 9 October 1999, p. 17.

for an increasing effort to devise "a new global architecture of environmental cooperation", confining the role of the WTO to addressing "the remaining trade barriers on environmentally-friendly production technologies and environmental services to reduce the cost of investing in clean production technologies and environmental management systems".[99] It may very well be that the critical approach of the report manifests the increasing sense of unease with the idea that the WTO can serve as a forum for environmental policy-making. After all, at times of growing hostility by large sectors of world public opinion towards the broad regulatory powers and trade-centred policies of the organisation, the WTO might find it convenient to drop environmental issues from its agenda or, in any event, to disclaim responsibility for environmental protection concerns.

This development should not be regarded as a negative one. Loosening the tight grip of ITL on environmental law and policy-making might contribute to foster both goals, namely the liberalisation of trade and environmental protection, more effectively in the near future. This is not to say that environmental issues will no longer come to the fore in the context of the WTO, nor to deny that environmental concerns must be accommodated to some extent within the web of international trade law obligations, particularly those stemming from GATT. Scholarly works have highlighted the legal options that are available to accomplish this task, with particular emphasis on MEAs which provide for the use of trade measures. The most obvious solution would be to amend Article XX to the effect of validating existing MEAs and providing the criteria for the approval of future agreements. This partly corresponds to the solution given to the problem in NAFTA.[100] Another option could be to provide a collective interpretation of Article XX under Article IX.2[101] or—as some suggested—add another exception to Article XX modelled upon Article XX(h) which allows trade measures pursuant to obligations in international commodity agreements.[102] A list of factors which should be included in the test for approval of MEAs under the new exception has been proposed and criticised, but certainly this is a way of dealing directly with the problem.[103] Alternatively, each MEA could be the object of a waiver under Article IX.3 of the WTO Treaty. This option has several shortcomings. In the first place the exceptional circumstances which justify the procedure could hardly be proven. Secondly, this procedure would only guarantee ex-post validation and leave states with no clue as to what criteria should be satisfied for the MEA to be compatible with GATT.

[99] WTO Secretariat, *Trade and Environment*, *supra* n. 97, at 59.

[100] See Art. 104.1 NAFTA. While validating existing MEAs such as CITES, the Montreal Protocol and the Basel Convention, this treaty arrangement does not provide a solution for future MEAs.

[101] A collective interpretation by the WTO Ministerial Conference requires a three-fourths majority.

[102] See Hudec, "GATT Legal Restraints on the Use of Trade Measures Against Foreign Environmental Practices", in Bhagwati and Hudec (eds.), *Fair Trade and Harmonization*, vol. 2 (1996), p. 125.

[103] See the discussion on this point in Schoenbaum, *Reconciling Trade and Environmental Protection: the Continuing Search for Reconciliation*, *supra* n. 1, pp. 283–4.

Apart from the legal technicalities of "immunising" MEAs on the basis of the solutions proposed by legal scholars, political difficulties exist which would make amendments or waiver procedures very difficult to accomplish in an organization with over 140 states, still sharply divided on environmental (and other) issues. Moreover, resorting to a formal treaty amendment procedure would have the effect of incorporating environmental concerns other than the existing Article XX exceptions within the Treaty, thus expanding further the power of GATT to deal with environmental issues and, quite regardless of the formulation of the amendment, introducing an element of rigidity which is perhaps unnecessary. What is required to accommodate environmental concerns is flexibility which can be better achieved by interpretative means. The recent Appellate Body's decision in the *Shrimp/Turtle* case indicates the path to follow. By an evolutionary interpretation of GATT rules, in the light of contemporary standards of international environmental law, the Appellate Body paved the way for a balanced approach to the issue. The development of a sort of balancing test to assess the conformity of national measures with the requirements of the *chapeau* of Article XX provides a flexible tool to address environmentally-based trade measures on a case-by-case basis. Policy dialogue and information-sharing among trade and environment officials in such fora as the CTE may also help to ensure the necessary coordination between potentially conflicting legal provisions. While environmental concerns should continue to be taken into account and accommodated within the framework of ITL by interpretative means or by policy principles to secure the constant adjustment of the multilateral trading system to the changing demands of the international community, it would be equally desirable that environmental law and policy-making freed themselves from the shackles of the free trade doctrine.[104]

[104] Some recent instances of international practice can be taken as signs of a move in this direction: see, for example, the adoption of the Biosafety Protocol with the inclusion of the precautionary principle and other environmentally-friendly provisions and the cautious approach on the trade-environment future relation taken by the WTO Report on Trade and Environment. For a contrary interpretation of the recent WTO Report see "Embracing Greenery", *The Economist*, 9 October 1999, p. 103.

6

The Necessity Principle as an Instrument to Balance Trade and the Protection of the Environment

MASSIMILIANO MONTINI

I. HOW TO BALANCE TRADE AND THE PROTECTION OF THE ENVIRONMENT?

THE STORY OF the relationship between the freedom of international trade and the protection of the environment is the story of the continuous search for a balance between two conflicting interests which has not yet found a satisfactory solution.[1]

It is undeniable that an important move towards the progressive reduction of conflict between trade and environment has come in recent years from the conclusion of several Multilateral Environmental Agreements (MEAs), which at best have the double positive effect of tackling more efficiently many of the environmental problems, which often present transboundary or global features, and of reducing the risks of litigation among states, since MEAs are generally presumed to be compatible with the world trading rules and thus tolerated by the WTO.[2]

However, in many circumstances states wish to maintain a certain degree of freedom in setting their environmental protection and health and safety standards, and they wish to maintain the right to determine unilaterally the degree of protection that they consider adequate to protect certain important interests, in the absence of internationally agreed rules or where they consider the existing rules not sufficiently protective.[3]

[1] For a general overview on the major trade and environment issues see for instance J. Cameron, P. Demaret and D. Geradin (eds), *Trade and Environment: the Search for a Balance* (London, 1994); D. Esty, *Greening the GATT: Trade, Environment and the Future* (Washington DC, 1994); E.U. Petersmann, *International and European Law after the Uruguay Round* (London, 1995).

[2] The evolution of the position of GATT/WTO towards the issue of the protection of the environment and the basic preference towards the conclusion of MEAs to address on a multilateral basis the main trade and environment conflicts can be understood comparing three documents: (1) the 1992 GATT Secretariat *Report on Trade and Environment*; (2) the 1994 Singapore Ministerial Decision on Trade and Environment; (3) the 1999 Background Note on "Trade and Environment" in the GATT/WTO prepared by the WTO Secretariat for High Level Symposium on Trade and Environment. See these documents at www.wto.org.

[3] It is interesting to note that all major economic powers around the world share this view. Consider, e.g., the position of the EU in the recent *Hormones* case (discussed *infra*) as compared

How should one assess the compatibility of unilateral measures aiming at the protection of the environment with the world trading rules in the framework of the WTO dispute settlement regime?

If one looks at the text of the GATT Treaty and relevant case law, when assessing the compatibility of unilateral measures aimed at the protection of the environment or public health and safety with the world trading rules, and in particular with the public policy exceptions provided by Article XX GATT, the issue arises as to whether such measures are "necessary" to protect the environment or the other important interests considered by the provisions at stake. What is meant by "necessary" in the trade and environment context and what is and might be the role of the "necessity principle", as a possible balancing tool between these conflicting goals, becomes therefore a relevant question in the search for the appropriate balance between freedom of trade and protection of the environment.

The "*necessity principle*", as developed and applied, albeit not in a completely satisfactory way, in the GATT and WTO context, as an instrument to resolve trade and environment controversies,[4] may be said to derive from the general *concept of necessity*, which has a long-standing tradition in every system of municipal laws, starting from the Roman tradition through the medieval period up to the modern times, and was first recognised as a *general principle of international law* by Grotius in the seventeenth century.[5]

In the present chapter, after a brief introduction on the concept of necessity as a general principle of international law within the meaning of article 38 of the Statute of the International Court of Justice, I will first look at the way the concept of necessity has crystallised in the instrument of the *state of necessity*, as a circumstance precluding wrongfulness for a conduct normally in violation of an international obligation of a state. I will then focus on the analysis of the *necessity principle* as interpreted and applied by GATT and WTO Panels in the trade and environment context, to assess whether its current application in this context may be considered correct and satisfactory, and, since this is not the case, I will conclude with the proposition of a more appropriate method of application of the necessity principle in this field.

with the position of the USA, as summarized by President Clinton when he affirmed that "international trade rules must permit sovereign nations to exercise their right to set protective standards for health , safety and the environment and biodiversity" (Speech given at the celebration for 50 years of GATT, 17 June 1998, published on the website of the WTO (www.wto.org)).

[4] For a comparison on the application of the necessity principle to trade and environment cases in the GATT, US and EC legal regimes see M. Montini, "The Necessity and Proportionality Principles in the Trade and Environment Context", (1997) 6 *Review of European Community and International Environmental Law*.

[5] See Grotius, *De jure belli ac pacis libri tres, in quibus jus naturae et gentium, item juris publici paecipua explicantur* (1625). On the origins of the doctrine of necessity and on its early applications in the field of public international law see B.C. Rodick, *The Doctrine of Necessity in International Law* (New York, 1928); J. Weiden, "Necessity in International Law", in XXIV *Transactions of the Grotius Society* (1938), p. 105.

II. NECESSITY AS A GENERAL PRINCIPLE OF INTERNATIONAL LAW

The concept of necessity has been recognised as a universal concept in law, which is present in most systems of domestic law and has been constantly invoked and applied in many circumstances also in international law. The fundamental role of necessity in law has been correctly defined as follows by Julio Barboza:

> "Necessity plays a role in preventing the occurrence of *summun jus, summa iniuria* in the application of the law in some extreme cases. It provides a very exceptional excuse to avoid the ensuing of legal consequences normally following certain acts".[6]

In the context of international law necessity has been recognised by Dionisio Anzilotti as a "logical limit to the obligatory character of international law" in the following way:

> "The obligatory character of legal norms stops at this point, not because of a supposed wisdom or prudence of the will of States, but because of the imposition of the legal order: only thus must be understood what we once called a logical limit to the obligatory character of international law".[7]

In more laconic and pervasive terms, Judge Dionisio Anzilotti in its Individual Opinion in the *Oscar Chinn* case (1934) affirmed that "Necessity may excuse the non observance of international obligations".[8] In order not to overestimate the scope of necessity in general terms, the words of Judge Anzilotti must be read in the context of the distinction between legal principles and legal rules. Necessity as a general principle of international law falls within the framework of legal principles and not of legal rules, even if, as it will be shown below, it may then also crystallise in prescriptive legal rules.

The distinction between legal principles and legal rules has been aptly explained by Ronald Dworkin:

> "The difference between legal principles and legal rules is a logical distinction. Both sets of standards point to particular decisions about legal obligation in particular circumstances, but they differ in the character of the direction they give. Rules are applicable in all-or-nothing fashion. If the facts a rule stipulates are given, then either the rule is valid, in which case the answer it supplies must be accepted, or it is not, in which case it contributes nothing to the decision".[9]

In the context of public international law, the application of Dworkin's definition of principles and rules can be found in a statement of the Umpire in the *Gentini* case (1903), according to which:

[6] See J. Barboza, "Necessity Revisited in International Law", in *Essays in International Law in Honour of Judge Manfred Lachs* (1984), p. 27.

[7] See D. Anzilotti, *Corso di Diritto Internazionale* (Padova, 1964), p. 148.

[8] *Oscar Chinn* case (1934), PCIJ, A/B 63, p. 113.

[9] See R. Dworkin, *Taking Rights Seriously* (London, 1977), p. 24.

> "A rule . . . is essentially practical and, moreover, binding . . .; there are rules of art as there are rules of government . . . a principle expresses a general truth, which guides our action, serves as a theoretical basis for the various acts of our life, and the application of which to reality produces a given consequence".[10]

On the basis of this statement, the relationship between legal principles and rules and their respective role has been well explained by Bin Cheng in the following way:

> "Since principles express general truth, general principles of law express general juridical truth. They form the theoretical bases of positive rules of law. The latter are the practical formulation of principles and, for reasons of expediency, may vary and depart, to a greater or lesser extent, form the principle from which they spring. The application of the principle to the infinitely varying circumstances of practical life aims at bringing about substantive justice in every case; the application of rules, however, results only in justice according to law, with inescapable risk that in individual cases there may be a departure from subjective justice".[11]

The qualification of *necessity* as a *legal principle* rather than a legal rule explains why necessity can be found in different branches of law and even in different fields of public international law with slightly different features and ways of application and interpretation, while its basic features, its role and its meaning remain substantially unchanged.

As regards public international law in particular, the *concept of necessity* can be correctly qualified as a *general principle of international law*, which per se does not impose any specific duty or obligation upon states, but simply represents a sort of "*safety valve*" of the international legal order "by means of which States can escape the inevitably harmful consequences of trying at all costs to comply with the requirements of rules of law".[12]

Such general principle may be then applied in different sectors and contexts and may crystallise in various prescriptive rules or interpretative instruments, which all resemble its basic features while adapting to different needs and circumstances. At the same time, necessity as it stands, as a general principle of (international) law, may play a role in the framework of the sources of international law, within the meaning of article 38(1)(c) of the Statute of the International Court of Justice (ICJ).[13]

[10] See *Gentini* case (Italy-Venezuela Mixed Claim Commission,1903), in J.H. Ralston and W.T.S. Doyle, *Venezuelan Arbitrations of 1903* (Washington, 1904).

[11] See Bin Cheng, *General Principles of Law as applied by International Courts and Tribunals* (London, 1953), p. 376.

[12] See ILC Commentary to art. 33 (1980) II *Yearbook of the International Law Commission*, Part 2, p. 49, para. 31; see also J. Barboza, *ibid.*, p. 29.

[13] On the role of the General Principles of Law and the General Principles of International Law within the framework of art. 38(1)(c) of Statute of the ICJ see I. Brownlie, *Principles of Public International Law* (5th edn., Oxford, 1998), p. 15.

II. THE STATE OF NECESSITY IN PUBLIC INTERNATIONAL LAW

The most important instrument in which the concept of necessity as a general principle of international law has crystallised in contemporary international law is the instrument of the *state of necessity*, as defined by the International Law Commission (ILC). The instrument of the state of necessity, whose existence in practice in public international law can be traced back to the eighteenth century, has been subject to a detailed and accurate analysis by the ILC in the framework of the preparation of the Draft Articles on the International Responsibility of States, which were adopted on a first reading in 1980.[14] In such a context, the state of necessity has been included by the ILC at article 33 of the Draft Articles among the circumstances precluding wrongfulness.[15]

In its Commentary to article 33, the ILC defined the *state of necessity* as being:

> "the situation of a State whose sole means of safeguarding an essential interest threatened by a grave and imminent peril is to adopt conduct not in conformity with what is required of it by an international obligation to another State".[16]

From this definition of the state of necessity provided by the ILC, it emerges clearly that its basic features are on the one the *grave and imminent peril* by which an essential interest of the state is threatened and on the other the *reactive conduct* adopted by the state to avoid that peril, which is not in conformity with one of its international obligations. Obviously the peril and the reactive conduct must be linked by a strong *causality nexus*. It emerges from the analysis of the ILC that the state of necessity can be invoked to justify a conduct not in conformity with an international law obligation only if it was the only means available to the state to escape the grave and imminent peril.

Inherent in such an approach is the use of some sort of necessity and proportionality tests to judge on the possibility of justifying a national measure under the heading of the state of necessity. Under the *necessity test*, in fact, the state of necessity cannot be invoked by a state to preclude the wrongfulness of a

[14] The text of the Draft Articles on the International Responsibility of States adopted on first reading in 1980, together with the commentary issued by the ILC can be read in (1980) II *Yearbook of the International Law Commission*, Part 2, p. 1.

[15] Article 33 of the Draft Articles (State of necessity) is worded as follows:

> "1. A state of necessity may not be invoked by a State as a ground for precluding the wrongfulness of an act of that State not in conformity with an international obligation of the State unless: (a) the act was the only means of safeguarding an essential interest of the State against a grave and imminent peril; and (b) the act did not seriously impair an essential interest of the State towards which the obligation existed.
> 2. In any case, a state of necessity may not be invoked by a State as a ground for precluding wrongfulness: (a) if the international obligation with which the act of the State is not in conformity arises out of a peremptory norm of general international law; or (b) if the international obligation with which the act of the State is not in conformity is laid down by a treaty which, explicitly or implicitly, excludes the possibility of invoking the state of necessity with respect to that obligation; or (c) if the State in question has contributed to the occurrence of the state of necessity": (1980) II *Yearbook of the International Law Commission*, Part 2, p. 34.

[16] See ILC Commentary to art. 33 (1980) II *Yearbook of the International Law Commission* Part 2, p. 34, para. 1.

conduct contrary to one of its international obligations if the grave and imminent peril could have been escaped by another conduct, even more costly, that could be adopted in compliance with its international obligations. Moreover, under the *proportionality test*, the state of necessity can justify reactive conduct of a state in violation of one of its international obligations only to the extent that the conduct does not exceed what is strictly necessary to achieve the aim sought. A conduct in excess of what is strictly necessary to achieve the objective pursued becomes automatically illegitimate and unjustifiable under the circumstance of the state of necessity.

The state of necessity as a circumstance precluding wrongfulness, in the formulation given by the ILC at article 33 of the Draft Articles, was expressly endorsed by the ICJ in the recent *Gabcikovo—Nagymaros* case (1998), a case concerning a system of dams to be built of the Danube, which opposed Hungary and Slovakia.[17] In the decision rendered on that case:

> "The Court considers, first of all, that the state of necessity is a ground recognized by customary international law for precluding the wrongfulness of an act not in conformity with an international obligation. It observes moreover that such ground for precluding wrongfulness can only be accepted on an exceptional basis. The International Law Commission was of the same opinion when it explained that it had opted for a negative form of words in Article 33 of its Draft 'in order to show, by this formal means also, that the case of invocation of a state of necessity as a justification must be considered as really constituting an exception — and one even more rarely admissible than is the case with the other circumstances precluding wrongfulness'.
>
> Thus, according to the Commission, the state of necessity can only be invoked under certain strictly defined conditions which must be cumulatively satisfied; and the State concerned is not the sole judge of whether those conditions have been met.
>
> In the present case, the following basic conditions set forth in Draft Article 33 are relevant: it must have been occasioned by an 'essential interest' of the State which is the author of the act conflicting with one of its international obligations; that interest must have been threatened by a 'grave and imminent peril'; the act being challenged must have been the 'only means' of safeguarding that interest; that act must not have 'seriously impair[ed] an essential interest' of the State towards which the obligation existed; and the State which is the author of that act must not have 'contributed to the occurrence of the state of necessity'. Those conditions reflect customary international law".[18]

After these general statement on the state of necessity, the Court finally rejected the claim made by Hungary on the facts of the case, since it found that Hungary had contributed with its behaviour to the occurrence of the situation of necessity and could not therefore invoke it as a circumstance precluding

[17] See Report of the ICJ decision on the *Gabcikovo—Nagymaros case* [1997] ICJ Reports p.7. For a comment on the *Gabcikovo—Nagymaros case* see e.g. Owen McIntyre, "Environmental Protection of International Rivers", in (1998) *Journal of Environmental Law* 79; F.N. Bocthway, "The Gabcikovo—Nagymaros case: a Step Forward for Environmental Considerations in the Joint Development of Transboundary Resources", in (1999) *European Environmental Law Review* 76.

[18] See Report of the ICJ, *supra* n. 17, at paras 51–2.

wrongfulness of its conduct contrary to a treaty obligation it had towards Slovakia.

However, the decision of the ICJ is extremely important for at least two reasons. The first one is that the Court for the first time states that the state of necessity as expressed at article 33 of the ILC Project corresponds to customary international law. The second one is that the Court for the first time officially recognises the applicability of the concept of state of necessity to the protection of the environment or the ecological balance of the territory of a state, considered as "essential interests of the State" within the meaning of article 33 of the Draft Articles.[19]

Having examined how the concept of necessity as a general principle of international law has crystallised in the legal tool of the state of necessity, and having verified how it has been concretely applied as a circumstance precluding wrongfulness for the protection of the environment, in the next section I will focus on an analysis of the necessity principle as interpreted and applied in the trade and environment context.

IV. THE NECESSITY PRINCIPLE IN GATT

Introduction

The basic principle upon which GATT is based is the principle of non-discrimination which is enshrined in (1) the "most favoured nation" clause (MFN clause), according to which all tariff concessions accorded to one state must be automatically extended to all other GATT contracting parties (Article I GATT), and (2) the "national treatment" clause (NT clause), on the basis of which imported goods, once they have entered into the national market of a given state, must not be subject to a less favourable treatment than national products (Article III GATT). The two clauses are supplemented by the fundamental provision which prohibits all restrictions on imported products other than tariffs (Article XI GATT). These norms, all together, aim at promoting a freer and fairer trade with the ultimate goal of furthering economic growth through the expansion of international trade.

In such a legal regime, obviously, freedom of trade is the main goal and the main concern. However, this does not mean that international trade must remain unrestricted in all circumstances. The GATT Treaty itself contemplates some circumstances in which trade can be legitimately restricted to afford an adequate protection to important interests of the contracting parties, provided that certain requirements are met. The main reasons which a state can invoke to limit the free flow of international trade are those listed at Article XX of GATT, which is titled "General Exceptions".

[19] See *ibid.* paras 53; see also ILC Commentary to art. 33 (1980) II *Yearbook of the International Law Commission,* Part 2, p. 39, para. 14).

According to Article XX GATT, the burden imposed on trade by unilateral measures taken by a contracting party with the aim of protecting one of the interests listed therein, can be held compatible with the GATT rules provided that "such measures are not applied in a manner which would constitute a means of arbitrary or unjustifiable discrimination between countries where the same conditions prevail, or a disguised restriction on international trade". For the purpose of the present chapter, among the several exceptions contemplated by Article XX which may justify a limitation to the unrestricted flow of international trade, special attention will be devoted to the exceptions contained at:

(1) Article XX(b) which deals with the national measures "necessary to protect human, animal or plant life or health";
(2) Article XX(g) which refers to the national measures "relating to the conservation of exhaustible natural resources, if such measures are made effective in conjunction with restriction on domestic production or consumption".

This is because, since GATT does not include an explicit reference to the "environment" as such, unilaterally taken national measures aiming at environmental protection have been justified either under Article XX(b) or (g).

General remarks on the application of Article XX GATT

With particular reference to the application of the exceptions contained at Article XX for environmental purposes, it has been correctly stated by one commentator that:

> "the 'general exceptions' in Article XX are designed to allow Contracting Parties to give priority to the 'public policies' listed in Article XX over trade liberalisation by authorising trade restrictions necessary for the pursuit of overriding public policy goals, including protection of life, health and environmental resources".[20]

The correct method of application of Article XX GATT for the possible justification of a national measure aiming at the protection of one of the legitimate "public policies" listed therein, has been summarised as follows by the Appellate Body:

> "In order that the justifying protection of Article XX may be extended to it, the measure at issue must not only come under one or another of the particular exceptions—paragraphs (a) to (j)—listed under Article XX; it must also satisfy the requirements imposed by the opening clauses of Article XX. The analysis is, in other words, two-tiered: first, provisional justification by reason of characterisation of the measure under XX paragraphs (a) to (j); second, further appraisal of the same measure under the introductory clauses of Article XX".[21]

[20] See E.U. Petersmann, *supra* n. 1, p. 29.
[21] *Gasoline* case, Report of the Appellate Body, (1996) 35 *ILM* 626.

In the next paragraphs, I will focus on the interpretation and application of the exceptions contained in Article XX(b) and (g). First of all, however, it is worth recalling here that the introductory clause of Article XX, the so-called *chapeau*, as interpreted in the most recent cases decided by the WTO Appellate Body, bears a paramount role, in so far as it constitutes the safeguard clause against any possible abuse or misuse by the contracting parties of the legitimate exceptions listed at Article XX. In other words, according to the definition of the Appellate Body, the *chapeau* "embodies the recognition on the part of the WTO Members of the need to maintain a balance of rights and obligations between the right of a member to invoke one or another of the exceptions of article XX, specified in paragraphs (a) to (j), on the one hand, and the substantive rights of the other members under GATT 1994, on the other hand".[22]

In concrete terms, the two-tiered analysis proposed by the Appellate Body for the correct application of Article XX requires the interpreter first to verify whether a national measure of a contracting party falls within one of exceptions listed at Article XX, paragraphs (a) to (j), that is in other words whether it pursues one of legitimate objectives considered in one of the exceptions, having regard to the nature and design of the given national measure. Secondly, once it is ascertained that the national measure falls within the scope of one of the exceptions and can therefore be "provisionally justified" under Article XX, the interpreter must verify that the national measure at stake is not concretely applied in a manner which constitutes a means of "arbitrary or unjustifiable discrimination between countries where the same conditions prevail" or a "disguised restriction on international trade".

The application of the Article XX(b) exception

As seen *supra*, the exception contained in Article XX(b) of GATT refers to national measures "necessary to protect human, animal or plant life or health".[23] The first case in which the term "necessary" contained in Article XX(b) GATT has been interpreted by a Panel was the *Thai Cigarettes* (1990).[24] The case concerned restrictions on import and export of tobacco and tobacco products applied by Thailand. Thailand sought justification for the unilateral measures under Article XX(b), holding that the measures were taken for health concerns, on the basis that chemicals and other additives contained in foreign, mainly US, cigarettes made them more harmful than Thai cigarettes.

The Panel called on to examine the compatibility of the Thai national measure with the exception contained at Article XX(b) GATT "accepted that smoking constituted a serious risk to human health and that consequently measures

[22] *Shrimps/Turtles* case, Report of the Appellate Body, WT/DS58/AB/R, at 156.

[23] See in particular S. Charnovitz, "Exploring the Environmental Exceptions in GATT Article XX", in (1991) *Journal of World Trade* 5.

[24] *Thai Cigarettes* case, Report of the Panel, BISD 37 S/200–228.

designed to reduce the consumption of cigarettes fall within the scope of Article XX(b)". The Panel also noted that "this provision clearly allowed Contracting Parties to give priority to human health over trade liberalisation; however, for a measure to be covered by article XX(b) it had to be 'necessary' ".

When interpreting the term "necessary" for the purpose of the application of Article XX(b) exception, the Panel took inspiration from the interpretation of the same term "necessary" which had been previously given by another Panel within the context of Article XX(d) GATT, in the *Section 337* case (1989).[25] In the latter case, the Panel when interpreting the term "necessary" had stated that:

> "A contracting Party cannot justify a measure inconsistent with other GATT provisions as 'necessary' in terms of article XX(d) if an alternative measure which it could reasonably be expected to employ and which is not inconsistent with other GATT provisions is available to it. By the same token, in cases where a measure consistent with other GATT provisions is not reasonably available, a contracting party is bound to use, among the measures reasonably available to it, that which entails the least degree of inconsistency with other GATT provisions".[26]

According to such interpretation of the term "necessary" proposed by the Panel in the *Section 337* case, and endorsed by the Panel in the *Thai Cigarettes* case, in the framework of Article XX(b), a national measure can be accepted as being "necessary" within the meaning of Article XX(b) GATT and thus justifiable under that exception only if it appears to have been "indispensable" to achieve the aim sought, in the sense that the measure actually chosen by the contracting party was the only one which it could reasonably adopt in the circumstance at stake. To use the *Thai Cigarettes* Panel's own words:

> "the import restrictions imposed by Thailand could be considered to be 'necessary' in terms of article XX(b) only if there were no alternative measures consistent with the General Agreement, or less inconsistent with, which Thailand could reasonably be expected to employ to achieve its health policy objectives".[27]

The Panel in the *Thai Cigarettes* case seems in fact to propose a two-fold test, to be used by the interpreter to judge the possibility of justifying a national measure aiming at the protection of the environment or human, animal and plant life or health, within the meaning of Article XX(b). On the basis of the proposed two-fold test, the interpreter must verify in the first place that in the material case there was no alternative measure consistent with the GATT provisions which was reasonably available to the contracting party, and that could have been adopted in lieu of the GATT-inconsistent measure the party actually adopted to achieve the legitimate aim sought. Secondly, the interpreter must verify that in the material case there was no other measure reasonably available to the contracting party, which entailed a less degree of inconsistency with the GATT provisions, that the party could have adopted in lieu of the measure actually adopted.

[25] *Section 337* case, Report of the Panel, BISD 36 S/345.
[26] *Section 337* case, Report of the Panel, BISD 36 S/345, at 5.26.
[27] *Thai Cigarettes* case, Report of the Panel, BISD 37 S/200–228, at 75.

In other words, on the basis of the interpretation of the term "necessary", proposed by the Panels in the *Section 337* case and the *Thai Cigarettes* case, necessary would basically mean least/less GATT inconsistent or least/less trade restrictive. According to this interpretation, in fact, a GATT contracting party which adopts a unilateral measure which affects international trade is bound to choose, among the possible measures reasonably available to it, a measure which is consistent with the GATT provisions, or where no GATT-consistent measure is available, the measure which is the least inconsistent with the GATT provisions. In brief, the Panels seem to interpret the term "necessary" as requiring a contracting party to choose among all the measures reasonably available the one which entails the "least degree of inconsistency with other GATT provisions".

On the basis of this line of reasoning, the GATT Panel in the *Thai Cigarettes* case finally found that other measures consistent with the GATT provisions were in fact reasonably available to Thailand to control the quality and quantity of cigarettes smoked, including for instance non-discriminatory labelling regulations or a ban on advertisement, and therefore concluded that the Thai unilateral measures could not be considered "necessary" within the meaning of Article XX(b).

The term "necessary" in the context of Article XX(b) was interpreted and applied again by a GATT Panel in the two *Tuna/Dolphins* cases. *Tuna/Dolphins I* (1991) [28] concerned restrictions adopted by the USA, pursuant to the US Marine Mammal Protection Act 1972, on import of yellowfin tuna and yellowfin tuna products from Mexico. The US authorities justified the restrictions on import on the basis of animal health and life considerations, alleging that the harvesting methods adopted by Mexican fishermen in the Eastern Tropical Pacific Ocean, which included the use of purse-seine nets, resulted in high levels of dolphin mortality. The Panel appointed to judge on that case, when interpreting GATT Article XX(b), effectively recalled the interpretative line which had been proposed by the Panel in the *Thai Cigarette* case. As regards in particular the purpose of Article XX(b), the Panel in the material case made the following interesting statement:

> "article XX(b) was intended to allow contracting Parties to impose trade restrictive measures inconsistent with the General Agreement to pursue overriding public policy goals to the extent that such inconsistencies were unavoidable".[29]

According to the interpretation proposed by the Panel, since the aim of the Article XX(b) exception is to avoid unavoidable restraints to international trade, a GATT contracting party wishing to adopt unilateral measures aimed at affording adequate protection to one of the interests listed in Article XX(b), in order to justify its provisions under the GATT rules, has to prove either that the

[28] *Tuna/Dolphins I*, Report of the Panel, BISD 39 S/155–205, (1991) 30 *ILM* 1594. For a comment see F. Francioni, "Extraterritorial Application of Environmental Law", in K. Meessen (ed.), *Extraterritoriality in Theory and Practice* (The Hague, 1996), p. 112.

[29] *Tuna/Dolphins I*, Report of the Panel, BISD 39 S/155–205, at 5.27.

chosen measures were the only ones reasonable available to it, or where various measures were theoretically available to achieve the aim sought, that it had chosen the measures which entailed the least inconsistencies with the international trade rules and which restricted trade only to the extent that this was really unavoidable.

In practice, then, in *Tuna/Dolphins I*, the Panel found that the US had not demonstrated that other measures consistent with GATT were not available to it to pursue its dolphin protection objectives. Therefore the Panel held that the US import restrictions were not "necessary" and could not be justified under Article XX(b).

The Report of the Panel in *Tuna/Dolphins I* was never adopted by the GATT contracting parties, thus remaining at the level of a "potential" adjudication of the controversy. Moreover, notwithstanding the findings of the Panel against the compatibility of the US national measure with the GATT provisions, the US authorities did not lift the embargo on Mexican Tuna and indeed extended it also to tuna and tuna products imported from intermediary nations. The intermediary nations embargo was therefore challenged jointly by the Netherlands and the EU, in *Tuna/Dolphins II* (1994).[30]

In this second case, the appointed GATT Panel held that in general terms "article XX as a provision for exceptions, should be interpreted narrowly and in a way that preserves the basic objectives and principles of the General Agreement". When analysing in particular the "necessity" of the US measure to protect animal life or health, the Panel confirmed that, in the light of the case law of previous GATT Panels, "necessary" in the context of Article XX(b) should refer to measures taken in circumstances in which no alternative existed for the party taking the unilateral measures.[31]

The Panel, in fact, in its decision in the material case endorsed the interpretation suggested by the EU, according to which necessary meant "indispensable" or "unavoidable", and rebutted the interpretation proposed by the USA, according to which necessary simply meant "needed", and finally concluded that the US embargo could not be justified under the Article XX(b) exception.

The *Gasoline* case (1996)[32] arose from a US regulation which imposed on foreign gasoline refiners wishing to export their products into US territory stricter environmental standards, as compared to those imposed on US national refiners. The Panel, when examining the national measure under Article XX(b), recalled the interpretation of the concept of "necessity" already given by the Panels in the *Section 337* case and in *Thai Cigarettes* case, and with regard to the US measure at stake held that: "If there were consistent or less inconsistent measures reasonably available to the United States, the requirement to demonstrate necessity would not have been met".[33]

[30] *Tuna/Dolphins II*, Report of the Panel, (1994) 33 *ILM* 839.
[31] *Tuna/Dolphins II*, Report of the Panel, at 5.35.
[32] *Gasoline* case, Report of the Panel, (1996) 35 *ILM* 274.
[33] *Gasoline* case, Report of the Panel, at 6.24.

The decision of the Panel, which found the US measure unjustifiable under Article XX, was appealed before the WTO Appellate Body.[34] However, the Appellate Body did not explicitly deal with the Article XX(b) exception and with the interpretation of the term "necessary" contained thereto, but rather decided the case on the basis of Article XX(g) only. However, from an *obiter dictum* of the decision, it appears that the Appellate Body substantially endorsed the line of reasoning previously proposed by the GATT Panels in the cases discussed *supra*, according to which a national measure can be considered necessary within the meaning of Article XX(b) only if in the case at stake there were no alternative measures reasonably available to the state, which could achieve the aim sought with less impact on international trade.[35]

In the most recent "environmental" case involving Article XX, decided in the framework of the WTO Dispute Settlement regime, the *Shrimps/Turtles*,[36] where a US regulation imposed certain fishing technologies to prevent accidental take of sea turtles also on fishing activities occurring outside the jurisdiction of the USA, the US authorities sought justification under both Article XX(b) and (g), but the Panel and the Appellate Body only addressed the issues under the Article XX(g) exception, and did not provide any further contribution to the interpretation and application of the Article XX(b) exception. The case will be therefore dealt with *infra* in discussion of the Article XX(g) exception.

The analysis of the decisions of the Panels dealing with the interpretation and application of the term "necessary" in the context of Article XX(b), reveals that Panels when judging the possibility of justifying a national measure taken by a contracting party under the Article XX(b) exception have constantly applied a sort of *necessity principle*. The basic feature of the necessity principle, as applied by the GATT Panels, lies certainly with the least/less trade restrictiveness test, according to which a unilateral measure adopted by a Contracting Party may be justified under the GATT only if it constituted in the material case the least/less restrictive measure reasonably available to the state to pursue the legitimate objective sought. As a consequence, in all circumstances in which it appeared to the interpreter that other measures with less impact on international trade could have achieved with a comparable degree of efficiency the objective sought by the state, the measure at stake should be considered as unjustifiable under Article XX(b) GATT.

Unfortunately, no decision of the WTO Appellate Body has up to now explicitly dealt with the interpretation and application of the Article XX(b) exception, and no progress has been made in the interpretation of this clause which might be comparable with that observed with regard to Article XX(g), thanks mainly to the decision of the Appellate Body.

[34] *Gasoline* case, Report of the Appellate Body, (1996) 35 *ILM*.

[35] *Gasoline* case, Report of the Appellate Body, at p. 620.

[36] *Shrimps/Turtles* case, Report of the Panel, WT/DS58/R and Report of the Appellate Body, WT/DS58/AB/R.

The application of the Article XX(g) exception

As seen *supra*, the Article XX(g) exception refers to national measures "relating to the conservation of exhaustible natural resources, if such measures are made effective in conjunction with restriction on domestic production or consumption".[37]

The first case in which the issue of the interpretation of Article XX(g) was raised was the *Canadian Herring and Salmon* case (1988).[38] In that case, the USA complained against a Canadian national measure which had made it compulsory for herring and salmon caught in Canadian waters to be processed in Canada before being exported. According to the Canadian authorities, such restriction on export was part of a management scheme of fisheries resources within Canadian waters and therefore was "related to the conservation exhaustible natural resources" within the meaning of Article XX(g). The Panel appointed to settle the controversy proposed the following interpretation of the Article XX(g) exception:

> "The purpose of including article XX(g) in the General Agreement was not to widen the scope for measures serving trade policy purposes but merely to ensure that the commitments under the General Agreement do not hinder the pursuit of policies aimed at the conservation of exhaustible natural resources. The Panel concluded, for these reasons, that, while a trade measure did not have to be necessary or essential to the conservation of an exhaustible natural resource, it had to be primarily aimed at the conservation of an exhaustible natural resource to be considered as 'relating to' conservation within the meaning of article XX(g). The Panel, similarly, considered that . . . a trade measure could . . . only be considered to be made effective 'in conjunction with' production restrictions if it was primarily aimed at rendering effective these restrictions".[39]

Such an interpretation of the term national measures "relating to" the conservation of an exhaustible natural resource as meaning "primarily aimed at" the conservation of an exhaustible natural resource was then endorsed by the Panels in *Tuna/Dolphins I* and *Tuna/Dolphins II*. In the latter case, in particular, the Panel explicitly affirmed the reasoning of the previous Panels "on the understanding that the words 'primarily aimed at' referred not only to the purpose of the measure, but also to its effect on the conservation of the natural resource".[40]

As one can see, in these early cases on the interpretation and application of the Article XX(g) exception, the Panels limit themselves to a superficial and restrictive reading of the text of Article XX(g), which reduces the possible scope of application of the exception by interpreting the term "relating to" the

[37] See *supra* n. 23.

[38] *Canadian Herring and Salmon* case, Report of the Panel, BISD 35 S/98.

[39] *Canadian Herring and Salmon* case, Report of the Panel, BISD 35 S/98, at 6.39.

[40] *Tuna/Dolphins II*, Report of the Panel, at 5.22.

protection of an exhaustible natural resource as "primarily aimed at" such a protection, and by interpreting the term "made effective in conjunction with restrictions on domestic production or consumption" as "primarily aimed at rendering effective these restrictions", having regard at the concrete effect of the protective measures on the natural resource they wish to protect.

In subsequent cases, decided after the creation of the WTO, the interpretation of the Panels Article XX(g) has been supplemented by the more careful analysis of the Appellate Body. For instance, in the *Gasoline case*, the Panel did not substantially depart from the interpretation of the terms "relating to" the protection of an exhaustible natural resource as "primarily aimed at" such a protection, as well as from the interpretation of the term "made effective in conjunction with restrictions on domestic production or consumption" as "primarily aimed at rendering effective these restrictions", which had been consistently adopted proposed by the previous Panels.[41]

Conversely, the Appellate Body, while affirming on the one hand that there was no need to examine any further the issue of the interpretation of the term "relating to" as meaning "primarily aimed at" the conservation of an exhaustible natural resource, since all the parties to the controversy seemed to agree on that line of reasoning first proposed by the Panel in the *Canadian Herring and Salmon* case, on the other hand made an important statement, noting that: "the phrase 'primarily aimed at' is not itself treaty language and was not designed as a simple litmus test for inclusion or exclusion from article XX(g)".[42]

Moreover, and more importantly, the Appellate Body when interpreting the term "made effective in conjunction with restrictions on domestic production or consumption" noted that the clause appears to require not so much that the measures must be "primarily aimed at rendering effective these restrictions", as had been held by the Panel, but rather that "the measures concerned impose restrictions, not just in respect of imported gasoline but also with respect to domestic gasoline". In other words, according to the Appellate Body:

> "the clause ['if made effective in conjunction with restrictions on domestic production or consumption'] is a requirement of *even-handedness* in the imposition of restrictions, in the name of conservation, upon the production or consumption of exhaustible natural resources [and moreover] the clause [is not] intended to establish an empirical 'effects test' for the availability of the article XX(g) exception".[43]

In the following "environmental" case, the *Shrimps/Turtles case* (1998),[44] the issue of the interpretation of the Article XX(g) exception was not explicitly addressed by the Panel, but once again the Appellate Body was to provide interesting interpretative statements.[45] In particular, the Appellate Body when examining the term "relating to" the conservation of an exhaustible natural resource,

[41] *Gasoline* case, Report of the Panel, at 6.35–6.42.
[42] *Gasoline* case, Report of the Appellate Body, (1996) 35 *ILM* 623.
[43] *Gasoline* case, Report of the Appellate Body, (1996) 35 *ILM* at 624–5
[44] *Shrimps/Turtles* case, Report of the Panel, WT/DS58/R.
[45] *Shrimps/Turtles* case, Report of the Appellate Body, WT/DS58/AB/R.

while formally not departing from the "classic" interpretation of the term as referring to measures "primarily aimed at" the conservation of an exhaustible natural resource, in practice better defined how the "relationship between the general structure and design of the measure at stake and the policy goal it purports to serve" should be examined by the interpreter, and finally found that:

> "Focusing on the design of the measure here at stake, it appears to us that [the US measure] is not disproportionately wide in its scope and reach in relation to the policy objective of the protection and conservation of sea turtles species. The means are in principle reasonably related to the ends".[46]

With this statement, the Appellate Body seems to suggest a new test on the basis of which the possibility of justifying a national measure under Article XX(g) would depend not so much on whether the measure at stake is "primarily aimed" at the conservation of an exhaustible natural resource, but rather on the evaluation that the measure is not "disproportionately wide in its scope and reach in relation to the policy objective" or in other words is "reasonably related to the ends".

This new test proposed by the Appellate Body in its decision the *Shrimps/Turtles* case, although not making any reference to the necessity, in my opinion introduces a sort of necessity and proportionality dimension in the evaluation of a national measure under Article XX(g), which could be aptly identified under the heading of the *necessity principle*. In fact, the Appellate Body in its recent decisions seems to propose a progressive departure from the "classic" interpretation which made the possibility of justification of a national measure under the Article XX(g) exception dependent on the proof of the non-availability of other less trade restrictive measures, to a new interpretative line which rather considers whether the national measure is not "disproportionately wide in its scope and reach in relation to the policy objective" and is "reasonably related to the ends".

V. THE NECESSITY PRINCIPLE OUTSIDE GATT

The TBT and SPS Agreements

Outside GATT, the necessity principle, composed of the necessity and proportionality tests, plays an important role in two agreements concluded in the framework of the WTO Multilateral Agreements, namely the *Agreement on Technical Barriers to Trade* (TBT) and the *Agreement on the Application of Sanitary and Phytosanitary Measures* (SPS).

The TBT Agreement encourages countries to use internationally agreed technical standards whenever possible. However, countries are not prevented from

[46] *Shrimps/Turtles* case, Report of the Appellate Body, at 141.

taking unilateral measures necessary to protect human, animal and plant life or health or the environment, and in principle each country has the right to determine the level of protection that it deems more appropriate. The TBT members simply have the following general obligation, pursuant to Article 2.2:

> "Members shall ensure that technical regulations are not prepared, adopted or applied with a view to or with the effect of creating unnecessary obstacles to international trade. For this purpose, technical regulations shall not be more trade restrictive than necessary to fulfil a legitimate objective, taking into account the risk non-fulfilment would create. Such legitimate objectives are, *inter alia*: national security requirements; the prevention of deceptive practices; protection of human health or safety, animal or plant life or health, or the environment. In assessing such risks, relevant elements of consideration are, *inter alia*: available scientific and technical information, related processing technology or intended end-use of products".

As one can see, the TBT Agreement fully embodies the necessity principle, by imposing upon members wishing to adopt their own national technical standards the burden to ensure that they satisfy both the necessity test, in the sense that they fulfil a legitimate objective, such as the protection of the environment, and the proportionality test, in the sense they are not "more trade restrictive than necessary to fulfil a legitimate objective" nor adopted or applied "with a view to or with the effect of creating unnecessary obstacles to trade".

Unfortunately, such highly developed necessity and proportionality tests were never subject to interpretation and application in the framework of the WTO dispute settlement regime. The only case up to now in which the application of the TBT Agreement had been explicitly invoked, namely the *Gasoline* case *supra*, was in fact decided by the Panel and the Appellate Body simply with regard to Article XX GATT, and the issue of its compatibility with the TBT Agreement was never considered.

The SPS Agreement, in general terms, sets a preference for the use of internationally agreed standards, whenever possible. However, the SPS Agreement recognises the right of members to take appropriate measures to protect human, animal and plant life or health, provided that they are based on a risk assessment and conducted on the basis of the available scientific evidence. In any case, members, when determining the appropriate level of sanitary and phytosanitary protection, must "take into account the objective of minimising negative trade effects". More specifically, according to Article 5.6:

> "When establishing or maintaining sanitary and phytosanitary measures to achieve the appropriate level of sanitary and phytosanitary protection, Members shall ensure that such measures are not more trade restrictive than required to achieve their appropriate level of sanitary and phytosanitary protection, taking into account the technical and economic feasibility".

As one can see, the SPS Agreement contains a clear reference to both the necessity and the proportionality tests. The necessity test requires members to determine the appropriate SPS measure on the basis of a risk assessment procedure based on available scientific evidence, while taking into account the objective of minimising negative trade effects. The proportionality test comes into play when members are required to ensure that the measures they choose "are not more trade restrictive than required to achieve their appropriate level of sanitary and phytosanitary protection, taking into account the technical and economic feasibility".

In cases where relevant scientific evidence is not available, SPS members are allowed to adopt provisionally their sanitary and phytosanitary measures based on a sort of "precautionary" risk assessment, provided that once additional information for a more objective risk assessment is obtained, the chosen measures will be reviewed within a reasonable period of time.[47]

This possibility to adopt provisionally precautionary SPS standards, where full scientific evidence is still lacking, has been invoked by the EU to justify its ban on US meat and meat products treated with hormones for growth purposes, which has given rise to the well-known *Hormones* case (1998),[48] decided in the framework of the WTO dispute settlement regime.

For the purpose of the present chapter, I will not deal more extensively with the issues at stake and the final decisions of the Panel and the Appellate Body in the *Hormones* case. It is, in fact, well known that both the Panel and the Appellate Body have finally rejected the EU ban and the EU proposal to interpret the SPS Agreement on the basis of the "precautionary principle", according to which where there is scientific uncertainty, among all the feasible options, a preference should be given to the option which ensures the highest degree of protection for the environment or public health.[49]

I will instead focus on the requirements on the basis of which SPS members may adopt higher standards than the internationally agreed ones, and I will then analyse in particular their relevance in the light of the necessity principle. First of all, unilateral national measures aiming at the protection of human, animal or plant health or life must be based on a "risk assessment" based on available scientific evidence. Secondly, when determining the appropriate level of SPS protection, members should "take into account the objective of minimising negative trade effects". Thirdly, the SPS measures chosen should not be "more trade-restrictive than required, to achieve their appropriate level of SPS protection, taking into account technical and economic feasibility". Fourthly, but only in cases where full scientific certainty does not exist, members may provisionally adopt "precautionary measures" which are to be reviewed as soon as possible.

Analysing the four requirements described above, one can easily see that in order to determine whether a national measure adopted by a SPS member setting

[47] See Article 5.7 SPS.

[48] *Hormones* case, Report of the Panel, WT/DS26/R/USA and WT/DS26/R/CAN; Report of the Appellate Body, WT/DS26-DS48/AB/R.

[49] For a comment on the *Hormones* case see for instance W. Douma and M. Jacobs, "The Beef Hormones Dispute and the Use of National Standards under WTO Law", in (1999) *European Environmental Law Review* 137.

standards higher than the internationally agreed ones can be upheld under the SPS Agreement, the interpreter is in fact called to verify that (1) the national measure is necessary to afford an adequate protection to human, animal or plant health or life and (2) the national measure is not more trade-restrictive than required to achieve the aim sought. This is nothing but an application of the traditional necessity principle, comprised of the necessity and the proportionality tests, which we have already seen in the case law under GATT.

VI. THE NECESSITY PRINCIPLE AS AN INSTRUMENT TO BALANCE TRADE AND PROTECTION OF THE ENVIRONMENT

As it emerges from the above analysis of the most relevant trade and environment controversies, in the case law of the GATT Panels under Article XX GATT, the necessity principle was initially applied with the main focus on the least trade restrictiveness test. This means that the Panels, after having confirmed that the aim sought, namely the protection of human, animal or plant life or health or also the protection of the environment in more general terms, fell within the scope of one of the Article XX exceptions (in practice in this case either Articles XX(b) or (g)), in their analysis of the national measures at stake usually went on to determine whether the measures were "necessary", in the sense of "indispensable" or "unavoidable" to achieve the aim sought, rather than simply "needed". This "restrictive" approach required the state invoking justification for its measures under Article XX GATT to demonstrate that the measures actually chosen were the only possible ones that could be adopted to achieve a certain legitimate aim and that no alternative measures existed which could have achieved the same result with less impact on international trade.

How could a state possibly prove that no alternative existed to the measures he had actually chosen to achieve the legitimate aim sought ? And how could the Panel make the ex post finding that there were other measures in the material case that the state could have been adopted and that would have achieved the same results? It is obvious that in fact the least trade restrictiveness test amounted to a sort of *probatio diabolica*, a requirement that no state could possibly satisfy and in practice had the consequence of rendering incapable of justification under Article XX GATT all national measures ever analysed by a Panel.

In 1995, with the creation of the WTO the dispute settlement mechanism was restructured and the jurisdiction of the GATT Panels was replaced by the more sophisticated two-level regime, based on WTO Panels and the Appellate Body. It is certainly not a coincidence that thanks to the decisions of the Appellate Body the strict and sometimes inaccurate interpretative paths followed by the GATT Panels in the trade and environment cases decided under Article XX have progressively given way to a more detailed and accurate case law.

If one looks for instance at the decisions rendered by the Appellate Body in the *Gasoline* case and even more so in the *Shrimps/Turtles* case, it is easy to see that the interpretation and application of the necessity principle in the trade and environment sphere under GATT has begun to change. In fact, after having confirmed whether the national measures at stake pursue a legitimate objective under Article XX, the Appellate Body now considers not so much whether other alternative measures existed but rather tries to determine whether the measures actually chosen by the state are "reasonably related to the ends" and are "not disproportionately wide in their scope and reach in relation to the policy objective".

As one can see, in the case law of the Appellate Body the least trade restrictiveness test gives way to a sort of reasonableness test, on the basis of which the question whether the measure adopted by a GATT contracting party can be justified under Article XX, notwithstanding its impact on international trade, is to be determined first of all with regard to the relationship of the measure to the legitimate ends sought. The reasonableness test proposed by the Appellate Body could be even better identified under the title of proportionality test, considering that in practice under the proposed test the national measure adopted by a state must be held compatible with the Article XX exceptions if it is not disproportionately wide in its scope and reach in relation to its legitimate policy objective.

In other words, the shift from the least trade restrictiveness test to the reasonableness or proportionality test also means a shift from a judgement on the compatibility of a national measure with article XX exceptions which used as an interpretative instrument the reference to elements external to the measure chosen, such as the availability in the material case of other measures with a potentially equivalent effect for the objective sought but less impact on international trade, to a judgement that is based exclusively on elements internal to the measure adopted by the given state, that is the reasonableness and the proportionality of the measure chosen to the objective sought. The interpreter will now judge a national measure for what it really is and for what negative effects it may effectively pose on international trade, and the decision on whether the measure is justifiable under Article XX will not be based on elements external to the considered measure.

We have seen above that a quite similar line of reasoning has been proposed by the Appellate Body when interpreting the compatibility with the SPS Agreement provisions of a national measure aiming at affording a higher degree of protection to human health than those afforded by internationally agreed standards. On the basis of the decision of the Appellate Body rendered in the *Hormones* case, in fact, it can be observed that the interpretative test proposed by the Appellate Body to determine whether a national standard stricter than the internationally agreed ones can be upheld under the SPS Agreement consists basically in a revised and adapted version of the necessity principle. In this case the necessity principle is composed first by the traditional necessity test, according to which it has to be verified first of all that the measure at stake is necessary to afford an adequate protection to human, animal or plant health or life, and secondly by a kind of proportionality test, on the basis of which it has to be confirmed that the measure at stake is not more trade-restrictive than required to achieve its appropriate level of sanitary and phytosanitary protection.

On the basis of the analysis conducted above, it has been possible to ascertain that in the trade and environment sphere both Article XX GATT and the relevant provisions of the TBT and SPS Agreements call on the Panels and the Appellate Body to verify whether a national measure taken for the protection of the environment or another public policy exceptions is necessary and proportionate to achieve the aim sought and whether it can be justified notwithstanding the burden it imposes on international trade.

Moreover, it has been possible to ascertain that the Panels and the Appellate Body have progressively, albeit not consistently and uniformly, developed and applied a sort of necessity principle as a balancing instrument to judge the compatibility of a national measure aimed at the protection of the environment with the world trading rules. However, in more concrete terms, while not underestimating the efforts made by the Panels and the Appellate Body in their effort to solve the controversies brought before them, it must be finally recognised that up to now they have substantially failed to provide a consistent and satisfactory method of interpretation and application of the necessity principle in the trade and environment context.

It is for this reason that I will conclude the present chapter by suggesting a more appropriate method of application of the necessity principle, which is consistent with the fundamental principle of necessity as a general principle of international law, and which is suitable in my opinion for a consistent and uniform application in the trade and environment context, and not necessarily only in this context, to provide an adequate balance of the conflicting interests at stake.

Under the proposed method of application, the necessity principle in the trade and environment sphere should consist of the necessity and the proportionality tests, each one having the following features:

(1) the *necessity test* should focus on the purpose of a national measure which must pursue a legitimate objective, such as the protection of the environment or of human, animal or plant life or health, and must be necessary, in the sense of being required and apt to achieve such a legitimate objective;
(2) the *proportionality test* should focus on the balance between the burden imposed on trade by a national measure and the potential benefits which may derive from its implementation. In the trade and environment context, in particular, the proportionality test should consist in weighing in absolute terms the expected environmental benefits of the measure against the burden imposed on trade.

7

Technology Transfer and the Protection of the Environment

FRANCESCO MUNARI

I. INTRODUCTION

THERE CAN BE little doubt that a strong relationship exists between protection of the environment and technology, and that, in particular, technology transfer does improve—or affect—the (protection of the) environment.

On the one hand, possession of environmentally sound technology (EST) is capable of substantially reducing, and even nullifying, the harmful effects on the environment normally arising out of human production or consumption activities; on the other hand, use of hazardous technology without adequate safeguards and standards may—and often does—accelerate depletion of the environment and sometimes even cause environmental disasters.

Normally, scholars and international law devote their attention to the first question, which, in fact, has been an issue since the Stockholm Declaration of the United Nations Conference on the Human Environment:[1] Principle 20 of the Stockholm Declaration is clear in stating that "environmental technologies should be made available to developing countries on terms which would encourage their wide dissemination without constituting an economic burden on the developing countries". As we shall see also *infra*, from Stockholm onwards this principle has been restated, reaffirmed and refined: yet it is still controversial how it should actually be given substance and enforced in the North-South relationship.

However, a second issue regarding technology transfer and the environment is worth studying, especially in our context of liberalised trade, where foreign enterprises may establish hazardous production facilities in less "environmental sensitive" (or less developed) countries, avoid transferring EST (or relevant know-how associated therewith), thereby increasing the risk of environmental harm: the recent sad story of the death of the Timis river in Rumania is, from this point of view, the latest of a too long (and apparently never-ending) series of environmental disasters caused by the non-use by foreign firms of those technological safeguards and standards which, at home, they would certainly be compelled to respect.

[1] See (1972) 11 *ILM* 1416.

II. THE GAP BETWEEN GOOD PROPOSITIONS OF INTERNATIONAL LAW REGARDING EST AND THE ACTUAL IMPLEMENTATION OF THESE PROPOSITIONS: DID SOMETHING GO WRONG?

The importance of technology transfer for sustainable development and for environmental protection, especially in the present context of international liberalised trade, is demonstrated by the number of treaties dealing with this matter. The good intentions regarding EST transfer which were embodied in the Stockholm Declaration were soon after followed by other statements of principle in this matter, and sometimes by true—albeit quite general—rules of treaty law: after an implicit referral to technology transfer contained in Article 202 of the United Nations Convention on the Law of the Sea (UNCLOS),[2] the obligation to cooperate "in promoting . . . the development and transfer of technology and knowledge" was made clear in Article 4.2 of the Vienna Convention on the Protection of the Ozone Layer.[3] Soon after, strong impetus to this "obligation" was provided by the Brundtland Report,[4] where promotion of sustainable development was strictly linked to the development and diffusion of new technologies, especially in the agricultural/forests fields, in the use of energy and in pollution control systems. More precisely, the Report acknowledged the fact that technology is a powerful tool for reducing the effects on the environment caused by human activities,[5] and the need was strongly pointed out to carry out the proposals through international exchange of technology, by means of trade in improved equipment, technology transfer agreements, provision of experts and research collaboration.

The ideas in the Report had, in fact, remarkable consequences for international conventions on the protection of the environment (although, as we shall see, these consequences are more apparent than actual): thus, almost all "grand treaties" adopted to try to cope with global environmental problems contain rules which, albeit to different extents, and sometimes subject to conditional requirements, do sponsor technology transfer as a tool for achieving the goals of these treaties.

Suffice it to mention, inter alia (and leaving out the provisions of Agenda 21 or Principles 7 and 9 of the Rio Declaration on Environment and Development):[6]

[2] See (1982) 21 *ILM* 1261, at 1309. For a view on Article 202 UNCLOS see Verhoosel, "Beyond the Unsustainable Rhetoric of Sustainable Development: Transferring Environmentally Sound Technologies", (1998) 11 *Geo. Int'l Envtl. L. Rev.* 49, at 54, distinguishing between obligations to transfer technology for purposes of environmental conservation and technology transfer obligations related to exploitation of (marine) environment. Quite correctly, the author points out that, especially in a state-to-state perspective, the first transfer has been and is still far less problematic than the second one.

[3] See (1987) 26 *ILM* 1516, 1531.

[4] World Commission on Environment and Development *Our Common Future* (Oxford/New York, 1987), especially pp. 87–9.

[5] See *ibid.* pp. 217–19.

[6] See (1992) 31 *ILM* 874. Principle 7 envisages the acknowledgement by developed countries of their special responsibility in pursuing sustainable development in view of the technology and financial

(1) Article 10 of the Basel Convention on the Control of Transboundary Movements of Hazardous Waste of 1989;[7]
(2) Article 10A of the Montreal Protocol on the Ozone Layer;[8]
(3) Article 16 of the Convention on Biological Diversity (CBD);[9]
(4) Article 4.(5) of the Framework Convention on Climate Change (FCCC);[10]
(5) 1992 UNCED Statement of Principles on the management, conservation and sustainable development of all type of forests;[11]
(6) 1992 Helsinki Convention on the Protection and Use of Transboundary Watercourses and International Lakes;[12]
(7) Article 19 of the 1994 Energy Charter Treaty[13] and its Protocol on Energy Efficiency and Related Environmental Aspects.[14]

This said, however, the issue is then to see *how* these principles are actually enforced. The answers here are quite different and, in my view, do not amount to a success story.

In certain cases, such as for the rules on technology transfer envisaged by the Montreal Protocol on the protection of the ozone layer, it seems that some positive results have been achieved. There may be different reasons for this, such as (1) the relatively small number of causes of ozone depletion, and therefore the possibility of "handling" the matter with relatively little effort, (2) the relative simplicity of the solutions technically individuated to solve the problem (the ban on certain products and processes and their replacement with others), and, as a consequence thereof, (3) the relative ease with which the international community could mobilise its forces, take a common position and actually do something for providing less developed countries with the means and the technologies necessary to contribute to the achievement of the Protocol's objectives.[15]

Yet, when we move from the ozone layer scenario to other global environmental emergencies considered by other framework conventions, the outcome

resources they possess. Principle 9 states a duty to co-operate "to strengthen endogenous capacity-building of sustainable development by improving scientific understanding through exchange of . . . technological knowledge, and by enhancing the . . . transfer of technologies, including new and innovative technologies".

[7] See (1989) 28 *ILM* 649, 667–8.

[8] Adjustments to the Montreal Protocol on Substances that Deplete the Ozone Layer, as amended in London, 1990, in (1990) 30 *ILM* 537, 551.

[9] See (1992) 31 *ILM* 818, 829.

[10] See (1992) 31 *ILM* 849, 858. Other rules of analogous content may be also found in two of the 1988 and 1991 Protocols on Long-Range Transboundary Air Pollution Concerning the Control of Emissions of Nitrogen Oxides or their Transboundary Fluxes (respectively Art. 8, in (1989) 28 *ILM* 214, 281 and Art. 4, in (1992) 31 *ILM* 568, 578).

[11] See (1992) 31 *ILM* 881.

[12] See (1992) 31 *ILM* 1312.

[13] See (1995) 34 *ILM* 360, 395.

[14] See in particular Art. 3.2.(e), in (1995) 34 *ILM* 360, 448.

[15] See also Verhoosel, *supra* n. 2, at 65; Alberts, "Technology Transfer and Its Role in International Environmental Law: A Structural Dilemma", (1992) 6 *Harv. J. Law & Tec* 63, at 76, dealing however with other failures in the implementation of technology transfer treaty provisions.

is quite different. Far from seeing a situation under which poor countries are supplied with EST, an opposite and quite unfortunate evolution is being experienced: patents and patent protection is steadily increasing and widening its scope of application to genetic resources, plant varieties, living organisms, even to ideas.[16] The entry into force of the Agreement on Trade-Related Aspects of Intellectual Property Rights (TRIPS)[17] compels WTO members (i.e. some 136 states, among which are very many less developed countries)[18] to enact and widen legislation protecting patents, hence hampering the free flow and circulation of (patented or patentable) technology. Given that patents are largely possessed by transnational corporations (TNCs),[19] and that these (newly developed) patents are almost exclusively owned by them, it can hardly be doubted that at the very least an increase in access costs to technology (including EST) is taking place for those entities needing them.

This phenomenon, in turn, seems difficult to reconcile with the principle of EST transfer arising out of the "grand environmental treaties" referred *supra*. Meanwhile, misallocation of technologies among rich and poor countries steadily grows, and the same can be said for the (overall) costs which are necessary to fill the gap. It is worth stressing that these circumstances are fully known: there is an awareness that a strong inequality in technology possession and availability exists between poor and rich countries, that the existing technological gap is an obstacle to environmental protection, and that the need to pay for the use of technology may be an additional problem in those countries where poverty and balance of payments' problems hamper the acquisition of relevant technology.[20] There is also awareness that, furthermore, proprietary rights do affect circulation and diffusion of technology and can contribute to an increase in inequalities.

Moving from diagnosis into therapy seems an impossible mission. Yet I am inclined to believe that picture is not the result of the willingness of anybody, and in particular of industrialised countries, to disregard the undertakings on technology transfer they have accepted in the environmental scenarios, or, more generally, to escape from the "common but differentiated responsibility" they have taken on under the Multilateral Environmental agreements (MEAs) as well as, in my view, under customary environmental law. Rather, I believe that this failure lies more in the flaws in perception regarding technology—and technology transfer—at international level.

[16] Shulman, "Patent Absurdities", *The Sciences* (Jan-Feb 1999). An Italian translation of the article has appeared in (1999) 6 *Internazionale* (10–16 September), 34.

[17] See (1994) 33 *ILM* 81.

[18] See the list provided by the WTO website (www.wto.org/wto/about/organsn6.htm).

[19] See the data quoted by Verhoosel, *supra* n. 2, at p. 66.

[20] See Munari, "Il rapporto tra liberalizzazione del commercio internazionale e tutela dell'ambiente con particolare riguardo agli aspetti relativi alla proprietà intellettuale e agli investimenti", in Sacerdoti (ed.), *Diritto e organizzazione del commercio internazionale dopo la creazione della organizzazione mondiale del commercio* (Naples 1997), pp. 181, 185.

III. HIGHLIGHTING THE SPECIFIC FEATURES OF TECHNOLOGY TRANSFER IN EVALUATING PROBLEMS AND PERSPECTIVES IN PROMOTING EST AT INTERNATIONAL LEVEL

As summarised *supra*, the evident disparity between statutory principles of international law on EST and their practical enforcement seems to be linked with a general misperception of some key issues which should be clearly identified. The approach still prevailing, or even dominant, considers technology as a "good", which can be theoretically transferred an indefinite number of times, and which, upon transfer, may "magically" change the way underdeveloped people produce goods, consume other goods, or altogether conduct their lives.

Such an approach dates back probably to the debates and tough negotiations between industrialised and less developed countries taking place within UNCTAD at the time of the NIEO almost thirty years ago.[21] Yet, and with few exceptions,[22] the great majority of scholars still discuss the issue of EST under the above perspective.

Therefore, prior to any framework on EST at international level, some key issues should highlighted. Clearly, this is not to say that merely understanding these issues may be able to provide complete answers, let alone solutions, to the many questions affecting the problems of achieving and enhancing EST. However, I believe that it would contribute to ameliorate legally and factually the sad picture we have painted *supra*.

The subjective framework: rules applicable to states v. actual owners and recipients of technology

In the first place, difficulties arise even in shaping the subjective framework of the issues at stake: as international legal scholars, we tend to concentrate our attention on states, or on international organisations; normally, however, technology is possessed by, and technology transfer takes place between, private individuals (or enterprises), whose standing in international law is much more delicate. As a matter of fact, more than 90 per cent of existing EST involve proprietary knowledge, often developed and belonging to TNCs.[23]

Hence, any inquiry on technology transfer must give due consideration to the property rules (on technology), including intellectual property rules, existing

[21] See the Declaration on the Establishment of a New International Economic Order, General Assembly Resolution 3202 (S-VI), 6th Special Session, Agenda Item 7, U.N. Doc. A/RES/3202 (S-VI) (1974); Programme of Action on the Establishment of a New International Economic Order, General Assembly Resolution 3202 (S-VI), 6th Special Session, Agenda Item 7, U.N. Doc. A/RES/3202 (S-VI) (1974); Charter of Economic Rights and Duties of States, General Assembly Resolution 3281 U.N. GAOR, 29th Session, Supp. No. 31, U.N. Doc. A/9631 (1974).

[22] Verhoosel, *supra* n. 2.

[23] See Verhoosel, *supra* n. 2, p. 66.

both in the home state of the owner, and in the host state where technology transfer should take place, and in international treaties dealing with the issue.

What is understood as "technology"?

The definition of technology is, at best, vague, and certainly far from being "user friendly": it is reasonable to consider technology as "the use of scientific knowledge by a given society at a given moment to resolve problems facing its development".[24] And yet, the practical use of this notion to assess *what* should be transferred to *whom*, in order to benefit (or not to harm) the environment, seems to be close to nil. This, in turn, tends to shift the focus from technology to *patented* or *patentable* technology, given the fact that this latter technology seems to be more easily identifiable.

However, such a shift may alter the picture and the possibility we have clearly to address the problems under examination, let alone any further complexity and obstacles to technology transfer in a world where protection of patents is generally shared and accepted, and is sponsored by international conventions which, in fact, may be used as a tool whose effects and purposes are inconsistent with the tenet of technology transfer as a powerful means to protect the environment.[25]

Supply v. demand of technology: technology acquisition as a social process

The analysis of EST transfer is often flawed by the conviction that the problem is to be tackled mainly (or even exclusively) from the supply side; hence, the effort is made to ensure the legitimacy of rules imposing technology transfer from donors (TNCs) to poor recipients residing in less developed countries. Again, this is only partially true: in fact, the demand side is crucial, namely the ability of poor countries to exploit technology upon its transfer, and, prior to that, even to realise that they need technology to improve their status quo. If this paramount aspect is not constantly taken into account, then the risk is very high of opening the path to rhetoric and pointless ideological disputes.

In this perspective, rather than a cause of development, technology stands more as a consequence of it; therefore, "transplants" of pure technology into societies having a low level of development seldom work. In fact, they may cause a waste of resources and discourage "efficient" technology transfer.

[24] Haug, "The International Transfer of Technology: Lessons that East Europe can learn from the Failed Third World Experience", *(1992)* 5 *Harv. J. L.& Tech.* 209, at 221.

[25] From this point of view, I am absolutely sympathetic to the critical view expressed by Spence, *infra* Chapter 10, on the increasing trend to patent goods and enhance intellectual property protection, therefore increasing monopoly rights which are at odds with a liberalised context of trade and distribution of wealth at global level.

Technology transfer provides good results when it accompanies (hence, is a part of) sound (foreign direct) investments.[26] For these investments, however, two conditions precedent are required: a favourable normative environment and adequate economic conditions in the recipient country.

Furthermore, technology is more a "dynamic" than a "static" concept: technology is largely made up of know-how and of constant use of it. Even the transfer of patented technology yields the best result for the recipient person when it may work within an environment which is technically fit for the purpose. This implies the (pre-)existence of knowledge, skills, education and training.

Possession and use of adequate technology cannot be perceived exclusively from the economic standpoint. In fact, transfer of technology has much to do also with social processes. The more development is achieved in standards of living and in the development of the society, the more demand for increasing the technological patrimony of populations is perceived. From this point of view, technology "is not an independent variable in this case, but is very much dependent on social change"[27].

Who are the ultimate beneficiaries of EST?

Very little information exists on who is eventually better off from technology transfer, and whether this assessment is to be made in the short or in the long run. In fact, the idea under which technology transfer implies an allocation of resources from North to South may not be completely persuasive. The idea that industrialised countries should protect (patented or patentable) technology from being exploited without the consent of their (national) owners has much to do with a short-run search for profits, while at the same time neglecting the fact that market failures are huge in this context, and that long-run reasoning is the only feasible way to take sustainable development seriously. With the exception of pressure on the environment arising out of population growth, typical of a developing country, the highest contribution to environmental depletion is made by industrialised countries, and this is true also for global environmental problems. Since environmental degradation associated with human activities is a typical negative externality from the economic point of view, hence a misallocation of resources, when industrialised countries "give" or "pay" anything to developing countries to help environmental protection, they merely re-balance such misallocation, therefore reducing also the distortions of trade patterns arising therefrom.

[26] See Thomas, "Transfer of Technology in the Contemporary International Order", (1999) 22 *Fordham Int'l L.J.* 2096, at 2107.

[27] Brundtland Report, *supra* n. 4, p. 88, quoting M.N. Hasan speaking during WCED at Jakarta, 26 March 1985. Strangely enough, this aspect of technology transfer did not gain the same visibility as other arguments set out in the Report.

In the light of the above, it comes as no surprise that the principle of EST transfer, which has enjoyed a number of restatements and repetitions seldom awarded to other general rules of international law, is still deprived of any substantial enforcement, or at least is enforced in a way which is hugely disappointing with respect to the expectations one has by simply reading the norms embodying it.

By the same token, it is no wonder that (apparently) conflicting norms seem to have precedence, at least from the practical point of view, *vis-à-vis* the above mentioned principle, even if the international consensus on those norms is far less than that underlying the need for EST transfer: reference may be made to some conclusions emerging from an interpretation of TRIPS capable of limiting the free circulation or use of "knowledge" which may have become "patented technology", even if the negative effects of this for sustainable development are crystal-clear.[28]

This is not to say that there is nothing to be done to improve technology transfer aimed at protecting the environment, nor that the special responsibility belonging to industrialised countries in environmental matters should not require them to adopt precise strategies and behaviours to improve EST transfer.

In particular, and with a view to attempting to provide a series of more "practicable" options in lieu of ideological disputes, I shall attempt *infra* to investigate some of the main issues to be highlighted: enhancing the control of the export of hazardous technology; envisaging methodologies to allocate correctly proprietary rights to patentable knowledge or goods, and sponsoring foreign direct investments (FDI) carrying with them substantial EST transfer. Besides these, some other "incidental" matters will also be considered, such as the legitimacy of state measures attacking non-use of patented technology in local markets or of preparing adequate ground for environmentally sound FDI in less developed countries.

In conclusion, and probably not surprisingly, one can clearly affirm that there is no single recipe to deal with EST transfer. Quite the contrary, very many solutions are available to adopt rules and methods to improve the environment through technology transfer, and each of these solutions may be suitable for a particular purpose, without being exclusive of other solutions.

IV. TRANSFER OF HAZARDOUS TECHNOLOGY AND FOREIGN INVESTMENTS IN ENVIRONMENTALLY SENSITIVE SECTORS

Issues to be highlighted

As briefly set out *supra*, the relationship between environmental protection and technology transfer may assume a particular character for those cases in which

[28] For an example, and for further references, see Marden, "The Neem Tree Patent: International Conflict over the Commodification of Life", (1999) 22 *B. C. Int'l & Comp. L. Rev.* 279.

technology is transferred together with industrial activities whose exploitation entails significant risks for the environment.

This transfer of "hazardous" technology may correspond to different scenarios: for instance, the transfer of environmentally destructive productions from stricter to more relaxed environmental legal systems. One may also consider, however, the transfer of activities from an industrialised country to a developing one as a consequence of the prohibition of these activities in the first country, in order to exploit the opportunity of prolonging the life of a product or of a production. Finally, of considerable interest is also the case in which the production is carried out (by the same TNC) both in the industrialised and in the developing world, but the technology used is not the same, given the different environmental standards existing in the countries where this production takes place.

In all these cases, it should be noticed that technology transfer is a side-effect of foreign investment, and the question to be posed rests on the role of the municipal regimes affected by this kind of export transactions. One should, consequently, examine powers and prerogatives of the state whose firms carry out the investment abroad in a way capable of affecting the environment.[29] In particular, the relevant issue is whether or not this state may—or even ought to—impose its firms the environmental standards envisaged in its (home) legislation.

Before trying to find an answer to this question, in my view the following elements should be considered. In the first place, one should remember that developing countries (whose global share as receivers of foreign investments is rather small)[30] encounter difficulties in setting adequate environmental standards. On the one hand, this is not a priority of theirs, due consideration being also taken to the fact that, as we have seen *supra*, environmental protection tends to be a consequence of development; on the other hand, the non-existence of environmental standards is often seen as a way to gain competitive advantage in international trade.[31]

Therefore, any idea under which it should be (exclusively) for the developing countries to care for the environmental standards of foreigners willing to establish production facilities seems in fact, and at least, hypocritical. In other words,

[29] On this topic, see, inter alia, Ashford-Ayers, "Policy Issues for Consideration in Transferring Technology to Developing Countries", (1985) 12 *Ecol. L. Q'ly* 871; Lutz, "The Export of Danger: A View from the Developed World", (1988) 20 *Int'l L. & Pol.* 629.

[30] Significantly, however, foreign direct investments in developing countries are increasing at a higher rate than in developed ones, and this is particularly true for pollution-intensive industries (Fowler, "International Environmental Standards for Transnational Corporations", (1995) 25 *Envtl. L. J.*, at 7 and 16). These data seem contradicted by the WTO Secretariat, *Trade and Environment Report* (14 October 1999) (hereinafter WTO, *T&E Report*) a summary of which is contained in *WTO FOCUS Newsletter* (Sept-Oct. 1999), stressing that migration of industries takes place especially in labour-intensive sectors.

[31] While there is little evidence to prove that differences in environmental regimes have played a significant role in the decision by TNCs to locate an investment, it seems undisputed that environmental performance by firms operating in these countries is weaker, and is almost non-existent for truly local firms.

if the world is interested in coping with this problem, it should be for the industrialised states to take appropriate measures, at least as long as international law does not supply an adequate regime, or as long as harmonised regimes among different states have not been put in place.[32]

Moreover, one should also consider that, in the case of environmental disasters, a complex set of rules has been established for determining the relevant responsibilities of the authors of the disasters, especially when they are private individuals doing business, and especially when these individuals are TNCs operating in a developing countries.[33] Furthermore, when the disaster caused by the TNC is associated with the use (or non-use) of technology, claims are brought against such TNC in its country of origin; additionally, in these cases the idea of considering the need to control this technology by its state of origin comes out quite strongly.

Accordingly, I do not see any reason why we should differentiate between controlling ex post (after an accident has taken place) the technology utilised by TNCs on the part of their national states, and exerting an ex ante jurisdiction to prevent such accidents from taking place. This seems consistent with the special responsibility of the developed countries in managing sustainable development issues, and moreover with the duty of cooperation industrialised countries have *vis-à-vis* their developing counterparts. In fact, if the former have undertaken to allow for EST transfer to the benefit of the latter, it seems difficult to deny that, within this broad statement of principles, there is a need to ensure that TNCs, bound by environmental regimes in their home state, do not infringe such regimes when operating in a foreign country.

From the point of view of the firm affected by this extraterritorial application of their (domestic) environmental law, it should be borne in mind that, in practice, this kind of obligation does not seem to involve significant additional production costs, nor is this "burden" capable of diminishing its overall competitiveness in international trade patterns.[34]

However, the nuances of this principle may vary significantly, together with the powers and duties of the home country.

[32] The need for industrialised states to enforce with extraterritorial effect their legislation towards their firms operating abroad in order to safeguard "global welfare standards" has been a firm conviction of mine for a long time. See Munari, *Il dirito comunitario antitrust nel commercio internazionale* (Padova, 1993).

[33] See Lutz, *supra* n. 29, especially at p. 642 *et seq*.

[34] See also WTO, *T&E Report*, *supra* n. 30: "the competitiveness effects of environmental regulation are minor". For instance, it has been calculated that a sustainable use of forest made with the highest technological standards costs approximately 2 per cent of the capital budget (see *Canada, l'ambiente come risorsa, Il Sole–24 Ore*, 4 August 1999, p. 4). I am not aware of significant differential costs for complying with sound environmental standards in polluting or hazardous industries, let alone any consideration of the "fairness" of the differing use of technology depending on where the production is located. On the other hand, given the fact that, as we shall see *infra*, positive externalities arise out of the utilisation of EST, this policy could be integrated with the funding of FDI carrying out EST transfer, thus helping the firms involved to accept the extraterritorial application of their domestic environmental laws.

Domestically prohibited goods and technology

When the use of the relevant technology is banned by mandatory laws in one country (such as, for example, in the case of the production of some pesticides), a first best solution would be that the TNC be prevented from utilising these technologies abroad.

This approach, however, may have seemed too extreme in the international fora; hence, a less radical (and less satisfactory) solution has been recently found, although its scope of application is not universal: the Convention on the Prior Informed Consent (PIC) Procedure for Certain Hazardous Chemicals and Pesticides in International Trade, which was recently enacted under the auspices of UNEP and FAO.[35] The prior informed consent—prohibiting the export of domestically prohibited goods without the notice and express consent of the competent authorities in the recipient country—is a second best solution, since there is surely no reason why industrialised countries should allow their firms to (massively) pollute abroad, especially when this kind of pollution has been prohibited at home. Furthermore, I am rather sceptical that this "informed consent" coming from the recipient developing state may well be inter alia affected by the "prisoner's dilemma" referred to *supra*; in other words, one may consider it at least doubtful that the recipient country is really spontaneously convinced to import hazardous technology (or the production deriving therefrom) notwithstanding its effects on the environment.

Therefore, I believe that an export ban on domestically prohibited goods or technology still remains the most effective solution, and should be adopted in all cases where the PIC Convention is not (or will not be) applicable. This solution, moreover, is consistent with WTO rules, at least since the second *Tuna-Dolphin* case, where it has been stated that unilateral trade measures adopted by a state to protect the health or safety of persons located outside its territory are consistent with Article XX of GATT.[36] But I would like to go even beyond this: my suggestion is that the export ban should be not only available to industrialised countries, but should become a mandatory requirement under the principles of international environmental law regarding technology transfer referred to *supra*.

Products allowed in the home country subject to the adoption of (technological) precautions and standards

A more articulated answer should be given when dealing with domestically non-prohibited goods or technology, hence for those cases in which the end-product is not per se banned in the home country, but its production is to be carried out

[35] See (1999) 38 *ILM* 1.
[36] *United States—Restrictions on Imports of Tuna*, also in (1994) 33 *ILM* 839.

pursuant to specific technologies, in order to avoid environmental damage. In fact, it would seem desirable also for this case that the TNC be prevented from utilising a "dual" technology between local and home country performance.[37] Such a result could be achieved by imposing extraterritorial effect on home country environmental regulations, in the same way as is suggested for domestically prohibited goods or technology, at least as long as international environmental standards have not been agreed.[38] It is worth noticing that the idea is not to impose these standards all firms active in foreign markets, but only in relation to the operations of the state's own TNCs abroad.

Yet, it is de facto very difficult to have access to relevant information regarding *how* TNCs behave in foreign countries, and therefore to have adequate evidence of hazardous technologies being adopted, or even of actual dumping of obsolete environmental technologies by the TNCs.[39]

Therefore, a simple obligation for these TNCs to employ home standards also in local (foreign) markets might not necessarily be a useful tool for achieving the goal of avoiding the "dual" technology being put in place by TNCs, depending on the place of their performance.

Other pseudo-voluntary means to achieve compliance with home country environmental standards

In order to envisage alternative measures, one should consider the strength of public opinion in the industrialised countries as a powerful means of pressure to compel TNCs to abide by the highest environmental standards, at least for marketing or image reasons. These is also an increasing trend by TNCs to abide spontaneously by private codes of conduct enhancing the overall environmental performance of these firms, irrespective of the existence of mandatory rules in all countries where they operate, since they have perceived that this choice will improve their competitiveness especially in the rich markets of the industrialised countries, where "environmental constraints and values are becoming even more significant than product price".[40]

[37] The extent and magnitude of this phenomenon is still unclear, but there seems no doubt that it exists and is not negligible (Fowler, *supra* n. 30, at 14). It seems also clear that, at least in certain fields, uniform standards should be welcome or even necessary. "Even critics of uniform international standards agree that such standards are appropriate in two areas: first, with respect to product standards and testing procedures; and second, where there are international externalities in the form of transboundary pollution (including global concerns such as ozone depletion and the greenhouse effect) or damage to or loss of biodiversity which is of worldwide value" (Fowler, *supra* n. 30, at 21). In this vein, it is worth mentioning the WTO, *T&E Report*that, *supra* n. 30, maintains that environmental standards should not necessarily be harmonised only when they refer to *local* pollution problems.

[38] This solution is sponsored by Fowler, *supra* n. 30, at 28.

[39] See *U.N. Dept. of Eco. & Social Dev. World Investment Report 1992: Transnational Corporations as Engines of Growth*, 231 U.N. Doc. ST/CTC/130 (1992), in particular at 239.

[40] See also Baram, "Multinational Corporations, Private Codes, and Technology Transfer for Sustainable Development", (1994) 24 *Envtl. L.* 33.

In order to strengthen this trend, it could be worth considering the enactment even of "soft" rules by industrialised states concerning a duty or recommendation of periodical disclosure by TNCs of their environmental performance abroad, with subsequent publication of these data. This would allow for circulation of the information on these topics which is presently lacking, and would probably intensify worldwide compliance with high environmental standards by TNCs.

In addition to this, one could also establish economic incentives to use and transfer EST, as explained further *infra*.

This kind of measures seems more appropriate (and probably more effective and realistic) than the imposing by industrialised countries of TREMs on the export of goods manufactured without using EST, let alone any reasoning regarding (a) the compliance of these Trade Related Environmental Measures (TREMs) with GATT and (b) the possibility that commercialisation of these goods in world markets creates unfair disruptions of trade.[41]

V. LOCAL WORKING REQUIREMENTS AND COMPULSORY LICENSING

The approach of this chapter is focused on the role of industrialised countries in complying with their duty to transfer EST as mandated by international environmental law. It tries to envisages cumulative ways and solutions to move from mere ideological (i.e. rhetorical statements of principle) to actual implementation of this duty.

This is not to say, however, that developing states have no alternatives other than remaining idle when technology transfer does not take place, or when foreign TNCs do not use their technology when operating locally, while doing so in their country of origin or in other developed states, possibly due to higher environmental standards (or for image/marketing reasons) existing in the latter countries.

In my view, developing countries *can* prevent these kinds of abuses by TNCs both through the imposition of so called "local working" requirements (i.e. the obligation to use relevant patented product or process in the country) as a condition precedent to grant the patent, and through a compulsory licensing of the technology which the original patentees have failed to introduce or have failed to use upon its introduction in the local country. In addition to that, a third option

[41] However, under specific circumstances, and the negative GATT jurisprudence notwithstanding, unilateral trade measures for protecting the environment might be also envisaged (see for fuller comments Munari, "La libertà degli scambi internazionali e la tutela dell'ambiente", (1994) *Riv. Dir. Int.* 389, and *supra* n. 20, at p. 203). Yet, their popularity seems (fortunately) decreasing nowadays, considering the high risks of greater environmental damage arising out of (wrongly) decided TREMs: for example, boycotts of tropical timber put in place by buyers in industrialised countries risk increasing—instead of stopping—deforestation. They fail to consider that the main cause of deforestation is agriculture, rather than timber industry; given the fact that in large tropical areas (where forests are) the only economic activities available to the local population are timber and agriculture, if the timber industry suffers drawbacks, then people return to agricultural activities, therefore increasing deforestation (see also Gardino, *La gestione sostenibile delle foreste tropicali*, mimeo, on file with the author).

is available, under which they may exclude altogether patentability for certain products or processes, hence allowing them to circulate freely in the country.

This approach is not generally maintained, especially after the entry into force of TRIPS. While the exclusion of patentability is limited by Article 27.2 and 27.3 of TRIPS to particular inventions only,[42] commentators have argued that the general patent protection afforded by Article 27.1 of TRIPS prevents member states establishing local working requirements and compulsory licences when the patentee "imports" into the country the relevant product which includes the patented technology.[43]

This view, however, does not seem convincing. Much more persuasive are the arguments set out by other scholars,[44] whose conclusions confirm that, for environmental protection reasons, states are still empowered to require local working and oblige patentees to license their technology, albeit against payment of a reasonable fee, this being a possibility also envisaged by TRIPS (in particular, Article 31), as well as the established proscription of the abuse of patent protection envisaged by the Paris Convention of 1883.[45] Furthermore, when dealing with technology covered by the scope of application of CBD, it seems even more difficult to deny the existence of rights for developing states (at any rate, for states owning biogenetic resources) to compel licensing and, quite probably, even to impose local working requirements.[46]

[42] In particular, when this is necessary "to protect ordre public or morality, including to protect human, animal or plant life or health or to avoid serious prejudice to the environment" (Art. 27.2) or when patentable products or processes are "diagnostic, therapeutic and surgical methods for the treatment of human or animals", as well as "plants and animals other than non-biological and microbiological processes, [provided that] Members shall provide for the protection of plant varieties either by patents or by an effective sui generis system or by any combination thereof". While I have emphasised the need to interpret these provisions broadly and with a view to preventing the "*effet utile*" of MEAs from being frustrated (Munari, *supra* note 20, at pp. 186–7), and while other scholars have since long pointed out the need to interpret the WTO Agreements in the light of and consistently with MEAs (Francioni, *supra* Chapter 1), with this approach having—albeit shown itself also in recent case law of the Appellate Body (see *United States—Import Prohibition of Certain Shrimp and Shrimp Products*, 12 October 1998, available on the WTO website, *supra* n. 18), it is unquestionable that the TRIPS Agreement per se strikes a balance for increasing, rather than diminishing, patent protection worldwide.

[43] See among others Doane, "TRIPS and International Intellectual Property Protection in an Age of Advancing Technology", (1994) 9 *Am. U. J. int'l L. & Pol'y* 465 at 479; Oddi, "Natural Rights and a 'Polite Form of Economic Imperialism' " (1996) 29 *Vand. J. Transnat. L.* 415, at 451.

[44] See Halewood, "Regulating Patent Holders: Local Working Requirements and Compulsory Licenses at International Law", (1997) 35 *Osgoode Hall L. J.* 243, at 274, and, with some more caution, McManis, The Interface Between International Intellectual Property and Environmental Protection: Biodiversity and Biotechnology", (1998) 76 *Wash. U. L. Q.* 255, at 266.

[45] See Art. 5.2 of the Paris Convention for the Protection of Industrial Property (20 March 1883), 828 *UNTS* 107, as revised. The fact that the Paris Convention establishes prerequisites prior to allowing compulsory licensing does not clearly alter this conclusion.

[46] Under Art. 16.3 CBD "developing countries, which provide genetic resources are provided access to and transfer of technology which makes use of those resources". Moreover Art. 16.5 adds that "the Contracting Parties, recognising that patents and other intellectual property rights may have an influence on the implementation of this Convention, shall cooperate in this regard subject to national legislation and international law *in order to ensure that such rights are supportive and do not run counter to its objectives*" (emphasis added). See also Halewood, *supra* n. 44, at p. 278.

That said, one is nevertheless obliged to point out that, although they may contribute to implementing the principles regarding EST we have been dealing with in this chapter, these solutions do not seem per se capable of furnishing satisfactory results. Compulsory licensing still needs payment of royalties and is therefore often impracticable for economic reasons. Local working seems preferable: not only is it gratuitous (the patentee himself "transfers" its technology), but has the advantage of bringing with it the transfer of non-patentable technology (such as know-how) and training of local workers, hence multiplying the positive effects of technology transfer.

However, this leaves largely unresolved the critical issue of EST transfer summarised above,[47] namely the lack of technology demand by developing countries, as well as their substantial incapability of making use of it.

IV. THE NEED TO ADDRESS THE ULTIMATE "OWNERSHIP" OF TECHNOLOGY TO ALLOCATE PROPERTY RIGHTS EQUALLY BETWEEN POOR AND RICH COUNTRIES: THE ISSUE OF PATENTING BIOLOGICAL DIVERSITY

One of the most relevant consequences of the successful ending of the Uruguay Round is the enactment of TRIPS, hence of a generalised system of protecting information and technology through patents.

For many environmentalists, TRIPS is seen as one of the enemies of EST transfer: not only are patents largely owned by firms in industrialised countries, but their superior technological skills put them at a competitive advantage *vis-à-vis* (firms of) developing countries in respect of the patentability of new technology. This is particularly true for the newly discovered "biotechnologies": these are patents developed through prospecting activities in the developing countries, using knowledge or genetic resources, which were generally available at no cost to the local population. When these knowledge or resources are patented, then their use by the local population may be restricted.[48] In any event, and above all, TNCs as patent holders exploit these resources and yield substantial revenues therefrom, with no advantages for developing countries, even if they are the actual (and ultimate) source of these patents.[49]

As generally recognised and many times repeated in this chapter already, there is no doubt that misallocation of technology among (owners located respectively in) rich and poor countries is a severe cause of environmental depletion. While it may be open to discussion who is to blame for such a misallocation, one cannot doubt that the further impoverishment in technology of poor countries should be avoided.

[47] See *supra*.

[48] See inter alia McManis, *supra* n. 44, p. 268.

[49] McManis, *supra* n. 44, at pp. 273–4, recalling the case of the commercial exploitation by the US pharmaceutical company Eli Lilly of two cancer-fighting alkaloids from a flower in Madagascar (the rosy periwinkle), earning several hundreds of million US dollars without providing any compensation to "the impoverished and environmentally endangered country of Madagascar".

TRIPS and biotechnology have proven that genetic resources are "commodities" whose commercialisation in international trade does produce revenues and richness. Whether ethically sound or not (and some authors say it is not)[50] this is a fact. The issue, therefore, is to envisage solutions aimed at allowing a more balanced allocation of benefits resulting from the exploitation of these resources.[51] I am convinced that this is possible, and is even provided for in the CBD, which establishes, already in its Article 1, a (necessary) trade-off between access to genetic resources from developing to industrialised countries and access to the technologies arising out of these resources from the latter to the former.[52]

This is confirmed by Article 15 CBD, where the statement of principle is made under which genetic resources belong to the state where they are located, and this state enjoys the (sovereign) right to determine ways of access to them.

In the light of the above, a mechanism must therefore be generalised in order to permit developing countries not to be deprived of the (economic) advantages deriving from their possession of resources which can be transformed into valuable technology. This implies the enactment in such countries of legislation establishing property rights in genetic resources in the state or (even better) public entities entrusted with the role of protecting the environment, hence paving the way for being granted some form of income (to be used for environmental purposes) from exploitation by TNCs or foreign firms of such resources. Alternatively, one may envisage payment of royalties or rents for bio-prospecting activities carried out by TNCs for patenting discoveries arising out of genetic resources, or may consider the possibility of requiring these bio-prospecting activities to incorporate joint ventures with local entities (possibly entrusted with environmental tasks) aimed at permitting these entities to enjoy part of the benefits arising out of bio-prospecting performed in their countries. Examples already exist in this field.[53] Yet, whether this possibility is actually available for developing countries is still under discussion at WTO level.[54] Meanwhile, and probably

[50] See Marden, *supra* n. 28, at p. 284 for further references.

[51] "Most of us developing countries find it difficult to accept the notion that biodiversity should flow freely to industrial countries while the flow of biological products from the industrial countries is patented, expensive and considered the private property of the firms that produce them. This asymmetry reflects the inequality of opportunity and is unjust" (declaration of Mr Mwinyi, President of Tanzania, during the Rio de Janeiro UNCED summit, quoted from Jacoby-Weiss, "Recognizing Property Rights in Traditional Biocultural Contribution", (1997) 16 *Stan. Envtl. L. J.* 74, at 89). See also McManis, *supra* n. 44, at p. 268.

[52] This opinion is shared also, and inter alia, by Halewood, *supra* n. 44; Date, "*Global 'Development' and its Environmental Ramifications*—The Interlinking of Ecologically Sustainable Development and Intellectual Property Rights", (1997) 27 *Golden Gate U. L. Rev.* 631, at pp. 634–49; McManis, *supra* n. 44, at p. 270.

[53] Reference is made in particular to the INBio-Merck Agreement signed in Costa Rica, a biodiversity prospective venture under which the results of researches and commercial exploitation by Merck of bio-genetic resources existing in Costa Rica are shared with a Costa Rican public legal entity, INBio (for further references and for other examples see McManis, *supra* n. 44, at p. 269).

[54] See *WTO Trade and Environmental Bulletin* (press/TE/032, 17 March 2000). See, however, in favour of this approach, the key-note address by Ms. Koch-Weser, Director-General of World Conservation Union at the WTO High Level Symposium on Trade and Environment (Geneva, 15–16 March 1999) (see wto.org/wto/hlms/sumhlenv.htm).

under the effects of well targeted lobbying, some other developing states have enacted legislation which does not protect their genetic resources. Hence, the battle is fierce for a more equal allocation of opportunities and benefits arising out of technology exploitation.

It is clear that means and solutions for allowing developing countries to share these opportunities and benefits should be generalized, with a view to obtaining funds for developing countries to be utilised for the achievement of environmental protection programmes, as stated by Article 20 CBD, where a mutual balance is declared between the duty of developing countries to abide by the commitments stated in the Convention and "the effective implementation by developed country Parties of their commitments . . . related to financial resources and transfer of technology".

In my view, this is to be interpreted as establishing a duty on industrialised countries to assist developing countries in studying and enacting opportune legislation, sponsoring and funding its adoption, and, conversely, helping to oppose any lobbying coming from TNCs aimed at preventing this "balancing" of opportunities from taking place.

VII. TECHNOLOGY TRANSFER AS A "SIDE-EFFECT" OF PUBLIC-SPONSORED FDI

Replacing lack of demand for EST with sponsored supply

As repeatedly pointed out, technology transfer must not necessarily be dealt with in a North-South perspective, where northern countries appear as donors of EST to southern ones, apparently waiting for this transfer to solve their technological gap: the need is to induce and invite developing countries to build up their own technological capabilities by creating and enhancing research and technology infrastructures.

In the present situation, and given (1) the general ownership of technology in the hands of TNCs located in industrialized countries, (2) the worldwide liberalization of investments, (3) the scarcity of "fruitful" demand for technology originated by developing countries, and (4) the fact that most transfers of technology occur as a by-product of FDI,[55] significant results for EST transfer can be achieved through joint projects and ventures sponsored by industrialised countries and implying the establishment of FDI by their home country firms in developing country markets, being FDI characterized by effective EST transfer.

The need is therefore to envisage solutions aimed at enabling the private sector (i.e. the owner of technology) to carry out this transfer, and for the states to create the optimal legislative and administrative environment for this to take place.[56]

Therefore, industrialised countries should comply with their obligation to facilitate or even to cause EST transfer to take place to the benefit of developing

[55] See *supra* n. 26 and related text.

[56] See also Verhoosel, *supra* n. 2, at 66.

countries through the adoption of programmes whereby TNCs locate investments in these latter countries and receive aids or other forms of public support as a compensation for their undertaking to transfer relevant technology (whether patented, patentable or not) as a by-product of the investment.

Examples of this approach of export incentives for EST transfer to developing countries can be already found: some years ago the EU adopted a Regulation providing for subsidies to industries presenting programmes for sustainable development to be implemented in developing countries,[57] and EST transfer was expressly considered as one of the initiatives capable of benefiting the aids provided from by the Regulation in favour of private EC investors.

But also at the international level, movements in this direction seem (albeit slowly) to be appearing: Article 10(c) of the Kyoto Protocol to the FCCC[58] establishes a principle under which "all Parties shall cooperate in the creation of an enabling environment for the private sector", and Article 12 creates a mechanism under which industrialised countries may invest in projects located in developing countries whose aim is to achieve sustainable development and to contribute to the objectives of the Convention, it being agreed that the certified emissions reductions arising out of these investments will be taken into account to calculate the industrialised countries' contribution to compliance with their quantified emission limitation and reduction commitments.[59]

This kind of solutions should be clearly improved and broadened, with a view to channelling EST transfer from private firms to developing countries. In this way, moreover, one of the obstacles to developing countries receiving technology, namely the cost of purchasing it, would be transferred to wealthier pockets, being moreover the owners of the pockets, for several reasons much better able to control whether the EST has been actually transferred.

On the other hand, developing countries should also contribute to this process by means of providing (local) incentives to foreign firms desirous to invest in these countries when such investments include the transfer of EST. This could take place through appropriate tax measures, whose ultimate burden, again, might also (or partially) rest on developed countries as donors, or on international institutions.

More generally, however, one should consider the offer of assistance in screening legislation existing in developing countries with a view to amending it when it runs counter to EST transfer: for instance, in most African states forests are state-owned, and franchise rights to exploit forests are given to private persons for a limited number of years (in the average, five), hence preventing the use of EST for harvesting timber, which normally requires the management of the forest for a cycle of twenty-five to thirty years,[60] and, in fact, therefore inciting

[57] Council Regulation 722 of 22 April 1997, in OJ 1997 L108/97. The Regulation expired on 31 December 1999.

[58] See (1998) 37 *ILM* 22.

[59] See also Verhoosel, *supra* n. 2, at 70.

[60] This is the average interval for permitting replacement and harvesting of trees.

a non-sustainable exploitation of forests.[61] Needless to say, in the face of this kind of legislation, the simple idea of realising technology transfer in this sector and applying the results to the timber industry as generally practised now in non-tropical (and often industrialised) countries would be nonsensical in such states. And yet this technology has proven to be quite fruitful, given the fact that, according to recent data, the extent of forests in developed countries is no longer diminishing, and is actually growing.[62]

"Export incentives" for investments carrying EST and GATT-WTO rules on subsidies

It has been maintained that the granting of monetary benefits associated with FDI realised through EST transfer, and specifically those measures channelling exports to developing countries through the payment of contributions for such transfer by developed countries, might conflict with WTO rules prohibiting, with limited exceptions, export subsidies.[63] In my view, however, this should not be the case: in the first place, states could establish these subsidies according to the mechanisms provided for at WTO level capable of reducing the risk of their illegitimacy (i.e. transparently and through relevant appropriate procedures); secondly, the compliance of these subsidies with ultimate goals stemming from international environmental law as established in several MEAs should impose an interpretation of WTO rules on subsidies consistent with these norms.[64]

In any event, with respect to measures adopted by developing countries to facilitate FDI associated with EST transfer, their legitimacy under international trade law as "non-actionable subsidies" should be secure.[65]

Within this perspective, one further point should be highlighted: in the first place, and from a mere economic point of view, EST transfer typically creates positive externalities, due to the overall advantages arising out of reducing the impact on the environment caused by human activities. In this regard, subsidising this transfer is tantamount to providing a more efficient allocation of resources, which is perfectly in line with the principles of fair and undistorted trade generally welcomed at WTO level.

[61] Even worse, for environmental protection purposes, is another feature of this legislation, namely that the state-owned forests become private property as soon as the forest is destroyed in order to use the land for agricultural purposes. Again, from the point of view of saving forests, these rules are the clearest example of non-sustainability (see Gardino, *supra* n. 41).

[62] Gardino, *supra* n. 41.

[63] Verhoosel, "International Transfer of Environmentally Sound Technology: The New Dimension of an Old Stumbling Block", (1997) 27 *Envtl. Pol'y L.* 470, at 479–80.

[64] This is the approach suggested inter alia by Francioni, *supra* Chapter 1, which I feel is convincing.

[65] See Munari, *supra* n. 20, at p. 189.

VIII. CONCLUSION

I have tried to outline briefly some ideas and proposals on how technology transfer for environmental purposes should be approached, with a view to moving from the old-fashioned (and probably wrong or at least impracticable) perspective under which the developing countries are entitled to receive (environmentally sound) "technology" from developed countries, being technology transfer thought to take place in a state-to-state perspective, and being especially such technology transfer considered as substantially isolated from other transactions and initiatives aimed at enhancing international (economic) cooperation.

In my view, the approach should be that of envisaging possible alternative forms of action, which are in fact manifold and not mutually exclusive.

Starting from the special responsibility of industrialised countries in the international environmental field, and from the difficulties of developing countries to establish, and even to conceive, environmental standards and related legislation, I have first highlighted the necessity of strong enforcement by the former countries of their own environmental legislation *vis-à-vis* their firms and TNCs operating in foreign markets, in particular with respect to "hazardous" technologies and domestically prohibited goods and technologies. In addition, I have suggested the need to put in place legislation aimed at gathering knowledge on technology transfer carried out by TNCs in foreign countries, with a view to disseminating this information to the public and achieveing an (induced) self-compliance by TNCs with the highest possible environmental standards.

In any event, I have argued that, TRIPS notwithstanding, both local working requirements and compulsory licensing should be available for developing countries where TNCs refuse to utilise in these countries technology they have patented there.

In addition, other measures should be put in place to enable developing countries to "fund" or have funded the technology transfer they need for environmental protection purposes: I have sponsored an interpretation of CBD capable of giving these countries some value for the resources used for patenting new (bio)technology, sharing the view of other authors in this respect and following already existing examples of bio-prospecting agreements.

As a further—and much more generally available—instrument for facilitating and promoting EST transfer, I have recalled the opportunity (and the need) to subsidise FDI which includes EST transfer, both through export subsidies from industrialised countries and by means of tax measures in the country "importing" investments and related EST, possibly also with the aid of international organisations. Again, even if prima facie these measures might appear problematic *vis-à-vis* relevant GATT-WTO rules and principles, the motive of compliance with environmental needs and principles, as also foreseen in numerous MEAs, should compel an interpretation of such rules capable of permitting these instruments to be enforced.

This having been said, the catalogue of initiatives to improve EST transfer is far from being exhausted, especially within the linkage between technology transfer, on the one hand, and trade and investments, on the other. Other scholars have indicated further options, based on already existing experience or programmes: for instance, the strengthening of information clearing-houses to direct developing countries in choosing the most suitable EST available for their needs; but also the establishment of public-private ventures for creating intermediary international organisations, whose role is that of developing and adapting technologies in view of their commercial exploitation for environmental purposes, or for funding large projects aimed at developing environmental technologies for their subsequent distribution.[66] But the list, in fact, could be even longer.

One thing, however, should not be forgotten. As already pointed out, for the development, dissemination and worldwide use of EST it is paramount that developing countries—and hence their population and their firms—be placed in the position of being aware of the existence of such technology, and of the need to use it.

This requires a general effort by industrialized countries and international institutions to sponsor, fund and assist programmes in developing countries aimed at improving the level of education and eradicating poverty and consequent population growth.[67] From this point of view, the more international cooperation, assistance and integration between industrialised and developing countries is achieved, the more technology transfer and related environmental policy is possible. These ambitious goals may not necessarily be achieved on a wide international plane; in many ways, regional programmes may be more functional and yield better results, because of the their ability to focus on fewer countries, study their specific needs, and sponsor assistance, cooperation and integration programmes more efficiently in view of the limited numbers of actors involved. In the European scenario, I would refer, for instance, to the Mediterranean area and to the programmes of integration and development of its southern side, or to the prospective enlargement of the EU towards the East. These events should be exploited as an opportunity to address many of the questions I have summarised *supra*.

[66] See Verhoosel, *supra* n. 2, at pp. 70 and 75.

[67] While questions remain as to the magnitude of consequences arising out of the growth of population, it is certain that population growth *is* a great concern for the protection of the environment (see, implicitly but clearly, Sen, "Fertility and Coercion", (1996) 63 *U. Chicago L. Rev*. 1035).

8

A Perspective on Trade and Labour Rights

CHRISTOPHER McCRUDDEN and ANNE DAVIES*

I. INTRODUCTION

WHAT IS THE appropriate relationship between the liberalisation of the global economy and other national and international values? Environmental concerns, health issues and human rights are but some of the values which may come into conflict with the opening up of trade and investment opportunities. In this chapter, we consider several issues posed in the relationship between international economic law and international labour rights. In doing so, we will concentrate on recent debates about the role of the International Labour Organisation (ILO), the World Trade Organisation (WTO), and the respective international standards for which these bodies are primarily responsible. We aim to provide a comprehensible map of a complicated set of issues; we do not claim to resolve them, nor to be comprehensive.

II. A BRIEF HISTORY

Questions as to the appropriate relationship between free trade and labour rights are not, of course, new.[1] The current debates may be better appreciated if we place them, briefly, in their historical context. Following the First World War, the Treaty of Versailles in 1919 established a framework for a new world order. Part of the package that emerged was a set of treaty provisions setting up the ILO under the League of Nations.[2] It was established with a unique membership. It was an intergovernmental organisation, but with a tripartite structure: in addition to governmental representatives, labour organisations and

* An earlier version of this chapter was presented to a University of Michigan International Law Workshop. It also benefited from discussion by student participants in the Fall 1999 seminar on "The WTO and International Human Rights" at the University of Michigan Law School.

[1] See, generally, S. Charnovitz, "The Influence of International Labour Standards on the World Trading Regime: A Historical Overview", (1987) 126 *International Labour Review* 565.

[2] See generally H. Bartolomei de la Cruz, G. von Potobsky and L. Swepston, *The International Labor Organization: the International Standards System and Basic Human Rights* (1996).

employer organisations were full members. The ILO was given a broad mandate: to establish international labour standards in the form of Conventions, to persuade states to join these Conventions, and to resolve disputes concerning their implementation. In a break from international tradition, mechanisms were established to ensure that states conformed to international labour standards. Although the League of Nations perished in the inter-war years, the ILO continued in existence, surviving the Second World War and the creation of the United Nations, of which it became a part.

By the end of the Second World War, there was a further attempt to construct a new global institutional architecture. Of particular relevance for the purposes of the issues discussed in this chapter, new world financial and trade institutions were proposed: an International Monetary Fund (IMF), an International Trade Organization, and a World Bank.[3] Under the then prevailing economic orthodoxy, trade, financial and social issues were seen as part of a harmonious package that would underpin a new world at peace. Under the Philadelphia Declaration of 1944,[4] the ILO was given the task of ensuring that labour standards would be incorporated in the work of the IMF and World Bank. The Havana Charter setting up the International Trade Organisation also specifically linked labour standards and trade.[5] Labour rights were given a further important boost when they were included in the Universal Declaration of Human Rights of 1948,[6] and they also looked set to become part of a new enforceable international Bill of Rights that the member states of the United Nations set out to draft.

Much of this apparent harmony was shattered by the onset of the Cold War, and a growing resistance to internationalisation in some countries. The International Trade Organisation failed to come into existence and, instead, the GATT was set up on a provisional basis to deal with world trade issues, stripped (largely)[7] of the labour linkages included in the Havana Charter. The ILO produced much worthy work and ever-increasing numbers of ratified Conventions. But it was riven with disputes between Eastern-bloc countries and Western-bloc countries—disputes which largely immobilised it, and prevented it from exercising a coherent role in ensuring that labour issues were integrated in the new international financial institutions, or even from monitoring its own

[3] See further, J. H. Jackson, *The World Trading System* (2nd edn., 1997), pp. 7–8.

[4] ILO, Declaration Concerning the Aims and Purposes of the International Labour Organisation, in International Labour Office, (1944) 26 *Official Bulletin* 1.

[5] Havana Charter for an International Trade Organisation, 24 March 1948, U.N. Doc. E/Conf. 2/78, Art. 7 (not in force).

[6] Universal Declaration of Human Rights 1948, GA Resn. 217 A (III), U.N. Doc A/810 at 71 (10 December 1948), Arts 22–25, available on the website of the UN High Commissioner for Human Rights (http://www.unhchr.ch/html/intlinst.htm).

[7] Paragraph 1 of the Preamble to the General Agreement on Tariffs and Trade, 30 October 1947, 55 *UNTS 194*, requires trade and economic relations to be conducted with a view to raising "standards of living". See further, Friedl Weiss, "Internationally Recognised Labour Standards and Trade", in Friedl Weiss, Erik Denters and Paul de Waart (eds), *International Economic Law with a Human Face* (1998), pp. 79, 95.

Conventions effectively. The international Bill of Rights project stalled, and did not come to fruition until 1966. Even then, not one but two Covenants on human rights were finally agreed, one on social, economic and cultural rights (with the support of the Eastern bloc), and one on civil and political rights (with the support of the West).[8] Whilst the former included extensive references to labour rights (summarising several of the most important ILO Conventions),[9] the latter was thinner on such issues, largely confining itself to freedom of association rights.[10]

A further set of developments of particular significance to the topic of this chapter occurred during the 1980s. Of perhaps most importance, Communism collapsed and Western liberal democracy triumphed. Free-market ideology became dominant throughout most of the Western states and with it the pressure for domestic deregulation. At the same time, the trade union movement declined dramatically in many industrialised nations. Technological changes affected many aspects of the workplace, and increased exponentially our ability to know what was happening in other parts of the world. The liberalisation of trade and investment came to be seen by many as the key to world economic development.

But there were other developments too. As groups on the "left" of the political spectrum reinvented themselves in various countries, they adopted human rights as their predominant ideological rhetoric. Non-governmental organisations (NGOs) became significant political players in many Western states and on the world scene, helped in part by their willingness to embrace the new technologies of fax, e-mail, and the Internet. In part because of their influence, many issues were articulated as matters of international concern: the protection of the environment and women's rights, for example. Developing countries, no longer squeezed between the two "super-powers", began to develop a separate identity, with perceived differences of interest from the developed world, particularly on the subject of sustainable development.

The early 1990s set the scene for a series of attempts at establishing a new rapprochement between social development, economic liberalisation, human rights, and world trade. Several major world conferences during the early 1990s, held under the auspices of the United Nations, sought to establish linkages between progress on human rights (often including labour rights) and global economic liberalisation.[11]

[8] International Covenant on Economic, Social, and Cultural Rights, (1966) 993 *UNTS* 3, and International Covenant on Civil and Political Rights, (1966) 999 *UNTS* 171, respectively. Both are available on the website of the UN High Commissioner for Human Rights, *supra* n. 6.

[9] International Covenant on Economic, Social and Cultural Rights, *supra* n. 8, Arts 7, 8, 10, 11, 12.

[10] International Covenant on Civil and Political Rights, *supra* n, 8, Arts 8, 22.

[11] Notably the 1995 World Summit for Social Development in Copenhagen, and also conferences on environment and development (Rio 1992), population and development (Cairo 1994), and women (Beijing 1995).

This question of linkage between trade and labour issues came to a head in the final stages of the negotiations leading to the establishment of the World Trade Organisation (replacing the GATT).[12] In particular, several Western countries (the USA and France were both prominent) sought explicitly to build labour rights into the new architecture of world trade, partly at least to lessen concerns at home that globalisation could undercut social standards in the developed world. This led to a stand-off with some important states in the developing world. The latter perceived attempts to link further liberalisation of free trade to adherence to certain labour standards as protectionist or neo-colonial in their motivation. At Marrakesh, all that was agreed was that the issue would be kept under review until the Ministerial meeting following the conclusion of the Uruguay Round.[13]

At this meeting, in Singapore in 1996, the issue was discussed again. Starkly divergent opinions were expressed, and tension between those countries that supported further work on the issue within the WTO, and those that opposed it, increased significantly.[14] An invitation to the head of the ILO to address the Ministerial meeting was withdrawn at the last moment, due to pressure from several developing countries. Finally, a compromise statement was issued saying that, although those who were present all agreed that core labour standards should be upheld, the WTO was not the place to deal with them. The ILO was, and should remain, the body with responsibility.[15]

Attention then shifted to the ILO. The Director-General appeared to embrace the role identified for the ILO in Singapore with enthusiasm. He proposed two strategies to increase the effective enforcement of labour standards.[16] First, he proposed that the ILO should identify a set of core labour rights to which members of the ILO should be regarded as being committed simply by virtue of their membership of the organisation. A second strategy involved a scheme for increasing the effectiveness of consumer choice by labeling goods as having been produced in conditions that conformed to these core labour standards. The ILO would monitor the operation of this scheme.

After considerable debate within the ILO, the core labour rights approach was accepted, leading to the important Declaration on the issue in 1998.[17] This

[12] For an account, see Weiss, *supra* n. 7, pp. 81–3.

[13] See para. 8(c)(iii) of the Decision on the Establishment of the Preparatory Committee for the WTO, (1994) 33 *International Legal Materials* 1270, at 1272.

[14] For an account, see Robert Howse, "The World Trade Organization and the Protection of Workers' Rights", (1999) 3 *Journal of Small and Emerging Business Law* 131, at 166.

[15] WTO, Singapore Ministerial Declaration (13 December 1996), WT/MIN(96)/DEC, (1997) 36 *International Legal Materials* 218, para. 4.

[16] ILO, *The ILO, Standard Setting and Globalization: Report of the Director-General* (1997), International Labour Conference, 85th Session, available on the ILO website at http://www.ilo.org/public/english/10ilc/ilc85/dg-rep.htm.

[17] ILO, Declaration on Fundamental Principles and Rights at Work (1998), International Labour Conference, 86th Session, available on the ILO website at http://www.ilo.org/public/english/10ilc/ilc86/com-dtxt.htm. See also H. Kellerson, "The ILO Declaration of 1998 on Fundamental Principles and Rights: a Challenge for the Future", (1998) 137 *International Labour Review* 223.

identified the issues of child labour and forced labour, the establishment of freedom of association and collective bargaining, and freedom from discrimination, as the core of international labour rights. However, the attempt to link these to a labelling scheme was not accepted by the main decision-making body of the ILO, in large part because of the opposition of developing countries, the same countries which had been so adamant that the ILO was the place to deal with these issues.

Although the ILO continues to develop its new strategies, attention has never wholly shifted away from the WTO. The derailing of proposals within the OECD for an agreement on multilateral investment in 1998[18] increased the attention of NGOs on the Ministerial meeting in Seattle at the end of November 1999. This was expected, but failed, to agree an agenda for a new round of trade liberalisation negotiations. In preparation for the meeting, labour rights groups urged that the WTO should take this opportunity to tackle the issue in a more sustained way than it had done previously. Both the United States and the European Union proposed greater co-operation between the ILO and the WTO.[19] In addition, the United States called for a WTO working party to examine possible links between trade and labour rights issues.[20] The United States, indeed, made labour rights a highly visible part of its negotiating position, in public at least. President Cliton devoted a significant part of a speech in Seattle to the issue. He appeared to go beyond the then United States position by suggesting that core labour rights should be incorporated into trade agreements with sanctions to enforce them.[21] Trade unions were a highly visible presence on the streets of Seattle during the Ministerial meeting.[22] However, developing countries strongly opposed all these proposals, and concern was voiced too by the Secretary-General of the United Nations who argued that trade was seldom an appropriate way to tackle concerns about labour issues.[23] In the light of these developments, how should we think about the question of linkage between labour rights and trade? What are the current issues?

III. HOW FAR IS THERE A CONFLICT BETWEEN TRADE LIBERALISATION AND LABOUR RIGHTS?

So far in this chapter, we have assumed a conflict between trade liberalisation and labour rights. Is this in fact the case? The importance of the question should

[18] See generally L. Compa, 'The Multilateral Agreement on Investment and International Labor Rights: A Failed Connection', (1998) 31 *Cornell International Law Journal* 683.

[19] See, respectively, Guy de Jonquières, 'WTO Set for Showdown on Labour Rights', *Financial Times* (1 November 1999), and European Commission, 'The EU and the Millennium Round: More Trade Based on Better Rules' (26 October 1999), available on the Commission website at http://europa.eu.int/comm/dg01/mren.pdf.

[20] See the article by Lawrence Summers (US Treasury Secretary), 'A Trade Round That Works for People', *Financial Times* (29 November 1999).

[21] 'Clinton's Demands Threaten Turmoil at WTO Summit', *Financial Times* (2 December 1999).

[22] *Ibid.*

[23] 'Clinton Acknowledges Concerns', *Financial Times* (1 December 1999).

be obvious. If there is no tension or if the conflict is unimportant, then we can have both. If there are positive synergies between trade liberalisation and labour rights, no sacrifice is necessary. We can identify three different ways of viewing the issue. Is there a conflict between trade liberalisation and labour rights at the *theoretical* level? Is there a clash between them at the *empirical* level? Is there a problem at the *legal* level?

Empirical issues

Of these, the most attention has probably been devoted to the second, empirical, question. Some argue that there is no conflict because everyone benefits from trade liberalisation. The economic cake will get bigger, standards of living will improve.[24] But whilst the economic cake does seem to have increased, there is no reason to think that an acceptable distribution of that cake within countries will take place without further action, particularly in states which are not themselves democratic.

The argument that many have attempted to test empirically is whether national governments may be tempted to lessen social protection measures in order to be competitive in a global trading and investment economy. Will trade-dependent countries seek to gain a comparative advantage by lowering labour costs, even if that involves subverting their own laws or customs? Will that, in turn, lead to other countries lowering their labour costs to compete with the first country, and so on—a "race to the bottom"? To what extent are labour costs actually determinative in influencing multinationals to change countries?

The answer is that there is much evidence, but it is far from definitive.[25] There is clearly a perception in several developing countries that there is a problem. On only one major issue does a fairly clear consensus seem to have emerged in the literature. Trade liberalisation has led to a decline in real wages in *developed* countries in certain sectors of the economy, among some workers, but not more generally. (Even here, uncertainty remains as to whether trade adjustment assistance (such as in the USA) can assist those workers who do lose out as a result of trade.)[26] There seems to be considerable uncertainty as to the impact of trade and investment liberalisation on *developing* countries.

[24] See, for example, J. Sachs, "International Economics: Unlocking the Mysteries of Globalization", (1998) 110 *Foreign Policy* 97.

[25] For reviews of the evidence, see H. Grossman and G. Koopmann, "Social Standards in International Trade: a New Protectionist Wave?" in H. Sander and A. Inotai (eds), *World Trade After the Uruguay Round* (1996); E. Lee, "Globalization and Employment: Is Anxiety Justified?", (1996) 135 *International Labour Review* 485; M. J. Slaughter and P. Swagel, "Does Globalization Lower Wages and Export Jobs?", IMF, *Economic Issues* No. 11 (1997).

[26] For history and critique of trade adjustment assistance in the USA, see E. Kapstein, "Trade Liberalization and the Politics of Trade Adjustment Assistance", (1998) 137 *International Labour Review* 501.

Theoretical issues

The absence of clear empirical evidence raises the interesting question of whether, on a theoretical level, the ideologies of free trade are necessarily antagonistic to the ideology of labour (or indeed human) rights. Certainly the assumption behind the original post-Second World War deal was that they were not: the Bretton Woods package assumed that open international markets would go hand in hand with, indeed be embedded in, a structure of interventionist domestic policies of social protection.[27] Some few have attempted to address the issue of whether there is currently a theoretical dispute but without resolving the problem satisfactorily.[28] In part, the difficulty of addressing the issue lies in identifying a clear theoretical underpinning of labour rights. We need at this point to step back a little from the trade issues, and examine in particular the different labour rights we may be concerned with, and their different effects. Do some give rise to greater conflict than others?

Some have suggested, for example, that we should distinguish between "worker rights" and "labour standards".[29] For Blackwell, "[w]orker rights are human rights norms that govern the way in which labour is treated internationally, regardless of a country's level of development. They include individual rights like freedom of opinion, and freedom of expression, as well as collective rights like freedom of association, and freedom to organise." (We might also include rights such as freedom from forced labour and freedom from certain forms of discrimination.) On the other hand, he says, there are labour standards, such as rules for minimum wages or maximum hours, which "vary with a country's level of development". (We might also include standards relating to holidays with pay, the availability of occupational pensions, and some workplace health standards.) He argues that "worker rights are deontological and normatively more compelling than labour standards".

If we eliminate the more costly, developed country-specific labour standards from the debate, and focus on worker rights, it may also be possible to claim that there are positive economic benefits to be derived from the observance of these rights. Individual firms may gain from compliance with labour rights: "there is an argument that respect for human rights leads to more productivity and better quality products."[30] More generally, rights may promote economic

[27] Jeffrey L. Dunoff, "Does Globalisation Advance Human Rights?", (1999) 25 *Brooklyn Journal of International Law* 125, at 129–32.

[28] See, for example, Dunoff, *supra* n. 27; F. J. Garcia, "The Global Market and Human Rights: Trading Away the Human Rights Principle", (1999) 25 *Brooklyn Journal of International Law* 51; B. A. Langille, "Eight Ways to Think About International Labour Standards", (1997) 31 *Journal of World Trade* 27.

[29] R. Blackwell, in Human Rights Program, Harvard Law School, *Business and Human Rights: an Interdisciplinary Discussion held at Harvard Law School in December 1997* (1999), p. 15. Other writers have drawn a similar distinction: see, for example, R. Freeman, "A Hard-Headed Look at Labour Standards", in W. Sengenberger and D. Campbell (eds), *International Labour Standards and Economic Interdependence* (1994).

[30] R. Blackwell, *supra* n. 29, p. 21.

development over the longer term, even if they do not help individual firms in the short term: it might be argued that they "will spur development by improving education, health, and realisation of human capacity."[31]

The positive synergy argument can also be made from the trade perspective: that increased trade will promote rights. The values pursued by liberalisation may coincide with, and reinforce, human rights values such as openness, transparency, good governance and the rule of law. Some argue that "rights will grow out of economic development, as a developing middle class seeks guarantees and political voice."[32] So too, some argue that "the rule of law will grow as business demands more security and stability, and it will spill over into the protection of human rights."[33] This is a particularly complex issue. It is based in part on a belief that economic integration is neutral, whereas there is a stronger perception in developing countries that it is about the spread of American economic and political hegemony. To the extent that this is the perception, there may be a clear attempt to stop economic liberalisation leading to, as it is viewed, "Western" democratic ideology following in its wake. So we may have a free market, even one with the rule of law governing economic relations, but still have problems. As Raz argues, the rule of law can coexist with gross violations of human rights.[34] So, too, greater majoritarian democracy can coexist with violations of human rights, particularly against minority groups.

Claims that there is a positive synergy between trade and rights are, at best, unproven. But this leaves the more modest argument that some fundamental workers' rights can be pursued without harming trade. To gain widespread acceptance, such rights must have a reasonable claim to universality,[35] and must be free from the taint of protectionism. One option would be to argue that a country should be free to defend its own values from erosion, but should not be allowed to enforce those values on other countries. More subtly, Western governments might address the concerns of developing countries by acknowledging that labour rights are not simply for "export" to such countries.[36] Should we attack only child labour? Or should we attack the abuse of migrant workers in Germany and the existence of sweatshops in New York as well? The rights advocated need not focus solely on the problems faced by workers in developing countries.

All of these issues come together in the attempt to develop a set of "core" labour rights. What criteria should we use? Should the choice be based on the lowest common denominator? Or should some other criteria be adopted? The ILO's 1998 Declaration includes freedom of association, freedom from discrim-

[31] *Ibid*. p. 20.

[32] *Ibid*.

[33] R. Blackwell, *supra* n. 25, p.20.

[34] J. Raz, "The Rule of Law and Its Virtue", (1997) 93 *Law Quarterly Review* 195.

[35] For a discussion of the issue, see Ozay Mehmet, Errol Mendes and Robert Sinding, *Towards a Fair Global Labour Market: Avoiding a New Slave Trade* (1999), pp. 170–93.

[36] See J. Bhagwati, "The Agenda of the WTO", in P. van Dijck and G. Faber (eds), *Challenges to the New World Trade Organization* (1996).

ination, freedom from forced labour, and freedom from child labour.[37] There is a clear attempt to lessen the accusation of protectionism and the erosion of comparative advantage in the choice of these "core" rights. None of the rights identified touch directly, for example, on the appropriate wage that should be paid, nor even on the need for minimum wage-setting procedures. Perhaps more significantly, these rights may be seen as rights to a process, not rights to a particular outcome (however difficult that distinction is to draw in practice). They are linked, particularly, by an attempt to protect freedom of choice. Confining our list of labour rights to those that serve to increase freedom of choice, and freedom of contract, means that such labour rights would seem not only theoretically consistent with the ideology of free trade, but also required by it. If we select our labour rights carefully, it may thus be possible to avoid a theoretical conflict with trade liberalisation.[38]

Legal issues

Even if the theoretical conflict between labour rights and trade can be minimised or eliminated, approaches designed to link trade to the observance of rights may fall foul of WTO rules. First, some have argued that purely domestic laws may conflict with WTO rules: for example, some regulatory measures may have the effect of making it more difficult for market penetration to take place.[39] At the moment, this threat is more theoretical than immediate, but with the increasing number of complaints to the WTO, and the greater extent to which internal regulatory measures are being challenged, it is not at all unreasonable to expect that, in time, challenges to national labour laws may increase.

More clearly, WTO rules may stop national governments using trade measures in order to enforce domestic social preferences transnationally. There are at least two different kinds of measures that might be adversely affected. First, certain domestic sanctions provisions might be unlawful under WTO rules. For example, section 301 of the United States Trade Act of 1974 permits trade sanctions against states that fail to observe workers' rights, and section 307 of the Tariff Act of 1930 prevents the importation of goods produced by convicts or by forced labour. Both are arguably unlawful under the GATT.[40] Secondly, certain

[37] ILO, *supra* n. 17.

[38] The ILO's definition of the "core", while probably the most significant for the purposes of this chapter, is only one possibility. Other definitions of the "core" (by other international organizations and company codes of conduct, for example) are reviewed in L. Compa, "The Multilateral Agreement on Investment and International Labor Rights: a Failed Connection", (1998) 31 *Cornell International Law Journal* 683.

[39] In particular, they may violate GATT, Agreement on Technical Barriers to Trade (1994) (http://www.wto.org/wto/legal/finalact.htm).

[40] See M. J. Trebilcock and R. Howse, *The Regulation of International Trade* (2nd edn., 1995), at pp. 458–9. The key issue is whether sanctions could be justified under Article XX of GATT. For discussion, see S. Charnovitz, "The Moral Exception in Trade Policy", (1998) 38 *Virginia Journal of International Law* 689; C. T. Feddersen, "Focusing on Substantive Law in International

national government procurement rules, for example, the recent Massachusetts law relating to Burma, have been challenged under the Government Procurement Agreement.[41]

IV. WHERE THERE IS A CONFLICT, HOW SHOULD WE RESPOND?

There appears to be potential for conflict between trade liberalisation and labour rights on all three levels: empirical (in the absence of clear evidence), theoretical (depending on how the rights are defined) and legal. Where there is a conflict, several different positions are possible. We could argue that labour rights should not be subject to trade-offs and should be promoted regardless of the implications for world economic growth. We could argue that trade liberalisation should not be pursued because it is harmful in other ways (an argument which is especially popular among trade unions and some "social" NGOs). We could object to further trade liberalisation as pursuing an elitist agenda, driven by global capitalism and fundamentally anti-democratic, and claim that there is no evidence that it will lead to increased standards of living.

Alternatively, we could seek to argue that labour rights may be counterproductive (especially popular among some trade economists), for example, alleging that so-called "rights violations" are useful, perhaps even necessary, to enable developing countries to progress economically. We could seek to paint our opponents as operating in bad faith, as closet protectionists. Are efforts by union leaders in developed countries to enforce labour rights in developing countries motivated in fact by their desire to protect standards in their own (developed) countries? Are they seeking merely to advance their own narrow sectional interests?

Both these positions entail a simple (and, we would suggest, simple-minded) solution: there is no "real" intellectual or policy conflict; the task is to persuade as many people as possible of the rightness of one or other cause. We are hardly alone in thinking, surely, that things are more complicated than this, and that both sides have a point: that trade liberalisation is a good, but that it needs to be combined with social protection? This approach would accept that both trade liberalisation and social protection are in the public interest. But how should we respond when these values come into conflict? At the moment, the picture is mixed. Four models seem to exist in an uneasy relationship with each other.

Economic Relations: the Public Morals of GATT's Article XX(a) and "Conventional" Rules of Interpretation", (1998) 7 *Minnesota Journal of Global Trade* 75; A. Mattoo and P. C. Mavroidis, "Trade, Environment and the WTO: the Dispute Settlement Practice Relating to Article XX of GATT", in E.-U. Petersmann, *International Trade Law and the GATT/WTO Dispute Settlement System* (1997).

[41] C. McCrudden, "International Economic Law and the Pursuit of Human Rights: A Framework for Discussion of the Legality of "Selective Purchasing" Laws under the WTO Government Procurement Agreement", (1999) 2 *Journal of International Economic Law* 3.

Unilateral model

In what we might call the "unilateral model", the tension may be "resolved" (though that is hardly the right word) by unilateral action by one state. States might attempt to act unilaterally in at least three different ways, all increasingly common in the USA. Domestic norms may be exported through the extraterritorial application of domestic law. For example, US anti-discrimination law has been applied to the foreign operations of US companies.[42] Some states may provide a domestic forum for the adjudication of disputes involving the application of customary international law abroad (as in the US Alien Tort Act).[43] We also see further examples of this unilateral model in the (somewhat different) use of the Generalised System of Preferences (GSP) to favour certain countries over others on the basis of their conformity to labour rights, by both the USA and the EU.[44]

Of the four models discussed here, the unilateral model is perhaps the easiest to put into practice: it can simply be implemented by the government concerned, without the need for cooperation from other actors. But this very fact raises questions about its efficacy and legitimacy. For example, the use of a GSP incentive by one state may have little impact on the target state unless it believes that it will benefit significantly from improved access to the granting state's markets. More fundamentally, unilateral action is prone to allegations that it is selective and protectionist, governed more by domestic concerns than by "altruistic" motives. Affected countries may have little opportunity to put their side of the case.

NGO model

Recent years have seen an explosion of activity by non-governmental groups, such as consumers, shareholders, trade unions, and single-issue human rights and environmental pressure groups in several Western countries. Traditionally, activity by NGOs was in the form of support for governmental or international regulation of private sector actors. Increasingly, however, such groups now seek additional (alternative?) means of putting pressure on states because of the perceived ineffectiveness of much traditional regulation. With this scepticism over governments' ability or willingness to regulate effectively has come the development of tactics by citizen groups to put pressure on companies directly through

[42] Under the Civil Rights Act of 1991, the definition of "employee" in Title VII was amended to include a US citizen employed in a foreign country (§ 2000e(f)(a)), and the foreign operations of a foreign employer were rendered subject to Title VII where that employer is controlled by a US employer (§ 2000e-1(c)(1)).

[43] 28 USC §1350.

[44] US Trade Act of 1974, Title V, and Council Regulation 3281/94 of 19 December 1994, OJ L348/1, 31 December 1997, as amended, respectively. See M. J. Trebilcock and R. Howse, *The Regulation of International Trade* (2nd edn., 1995), pp. 458–60.

their own actions. These tactics include shareholder resolutions and other "ethical investment" activities, designing codes of practice or "social labelling" schemes in which firms may participate, and consumer boycotts.[45]

The feasibility of implementing the NGO model depends on at least two related factors: the degree of public interest, and the extent to which firms are willing to bow to public pressure. There are signs of greater interest among both groups. Although ethical consumption ideas are far from mainstream, they do appear to be playing an increasing role among some sectors of the population in developed countries. In turn, this has prompted a recognition by some businesses that their profits may suffer if labour rights issues are ignored. To retain the loyalty of consumers, the cooperation of workers, or simply to avoid disruption at shareholder meetings, they need to (at least appear to) be taking such concerns seriously. A firm may respond to this pressure in various ways, for example, by drafting its own code of practice, or participating in one of the NGO schemes described above.

But the NGO model has its limitations. It is most likely to be effective where a targeted firm produces consumer goods: here, the firm is likely to be particularly protective of its brand's reputation.[46] In other sectors, the efficacy of the approach depends on getting firms to recognise that they still have an interest in labour rights. For example, we noted above that respect for labour rights might increase workers' productivity and thus a firm's profitability. But this link to profit is less clear-cut, and firms may not be so willing to acknowledge it in the absence of conclusive evidence. Moreover, a firm that adopts socially responsible policies risks exposure to competition from firms which do not follow such policies. It is arguable that "enlightened companies need support from public authorities at some level in order to protect themselves from the free-riders".[47]

The NGO model also raises legitimacy issues. From the perspective of the targeted firm or country, it may be a very blunt instrument. For example, consumer pressure might prompt a company to cease trading with suppliers that use child labour. But unless alternative income is provided for the children, they may be plunged into worse poverty, or into more harmful forms of labour.[48] More fundamentally, we might take the view that some values are not appropriately regulated through markets. Should consumers really be allowed to choose how far

[45] See, for example, L. A. Compa and T. Hinchliffe Darricarrère, "Private Labor Rights Enforcement Through Corporate Codes of Conduct", in L. A. Compa and S. F. Diamond, (eds), *Human Rights, Labor Rights and International Trade* (1996); J. Diller, "A Social Conscience in the Global Marketplace? Labour Dimensions of Codes of Conduct, Social Labelling and Investor Initiatives", (1999) 138 *International Labour Review* 99; C. McCrudden, "Human Rights Codes for Transnational Corporations: What Can the Sullivan and MacBride Principles Tell Us?", (1999) 19 *Oxford Journal of Legal Studies* 167; J. Murray, "Corporate Codes of Conduct and Labour Standards", in R. Kyloh (ed.), *Mastering the Challenge of Globalization: Towards a Trade Union Agenda* (1998).

[46] Note that the US firms described by Compa and Hinchliffe Darricarrère, *supra* n. 45, as leading the way on voluntary codes are producers of consumer goods: Levi Strauss & Company, and Reebok Corporation.

[47] R. Blackwell, *supra* n. 29, p. 49.

[48] This issue, and other concerns about market-based initiatives to combat child labour, are explored in J. Hilowitz, "Social Labelling to Combat Child Labour: Some Considerations", (1997) 136 *International Labour Review* 215.

they disapprove of slave labour? Or do we expect the state to act on issues of this nature, for example by banning imports made by slave labour?

Regional model

A third model currently in operation is what we shall term the "regional model". By this we mean attempts to resolve the tension between trade and labour rights at a regional level rather than at either the national or the international levels of government. The European Union is, no doubt, the most obvious example of this. Within the EU, it is now clear that increased economic liberalisation, especially since the mid-1980s, was seen as crucially linked to the development of measures of social protection to cushion the blow for those who lost out in this process.[49] This is reflected, for example, in the relatively strong mix of economic and social issues in the Treaty of Amsterdam.[50] In a considerably weaker form, we can also identify the North American Free Trade Agreement (NAFTA), and in particular the labour side agreement,[51] as reflecting a similar attempt at developing a regional model.

The regional model's efficacy depends heavily on its design: critics of NAFTA's labour side agreement have blamed its limited effectiveness on weak dispute resolution mechanisms and a failure to set minimum standards applicable to the three member states.[52] Regional approaches may appear attractive to states, because reaching agreement with a smaller group of states may be much easier than achieving worldwide consensus. But there is a danger that regional approaches may fragment the global trading system by grouping nations into trading blocs.

Multilateral model

Our fourth model, the multilateral model, has the potential to address one of the most significant problems confronting nation states and regional blocs as they

[49] See Miguel Poiares Maduro, "Striking the Elusive Balance Between Economic Freedom and Social Rights in the EU", in Philip Alston (ed.), *The EU and Human Rights* (1999), p. 449

[50] The Treaty of Amsterdam was signed on 2 October 1997 and is incorporated in the Treaty on European Union, OJ C340/145 10 November 1997, and the Treaty establishing the European Community, OJ C340/173 10 November 1997. For a good example of the mix of economic and social issues, see particularly Art. 2 TEU (objectives of the Union). Whilst the EU's economic integration agenda was significantly carried forward, extensive additional measures were introduced in the areas of social protection and labour rights (see, in particular Arts 125–130 on employment, and Arts 136–145 on social policy).

[51] North American Agreement on Labor Cooperation, 13 September 1993, Canada-Mexico-USA, (1993) 32 *International Legal Materials* 1499.

[52] For discussion, see R. J. Adams and P. Singh, "Early Experience with NAFTA's Labour Side Accord", (1997) 18 *Comparative Labor Law Journal* 161; K. van Wezel Stone, "Labour in the Global Economy: Four Approaches to Transnational Labour Regulation", in W. Bratton, J. McCahery, S. Picciotto and C. Scott (eds), *International Regulatory Competition and Co-Ordination* (1996).

grapple with the issue of globalisation. This problem has been termed the "paradox of globalisation".[53] On the one hand, the dangers globalisation poses for some in both developed and developing economies, such as increased job insecurity, seem to lead to an increased demand for social protection measures, including labour rights. On the other hand, globalisation may constrain the ability of governments to respond effectively to that demand. This dilemma has contributed to pressure for the issue to be tackled at the international level. Yet, of the four existing models, the multilateral model is currently the weakest.

The current strategy (which emerged from the Singapore Ministerial meeting, as we have seen) is to address labour rights through the ILO, keeping the issue out of the WTO.[54] The approach has its attractions. By internationalizing the labour rights agenda, it should reduce the risk of labour rights being used for protectionist purposes by developed countries. It simplifies the task of the WTO, and allows an expert body, the ILO, to address labour issues with participation from all affected countries, and on a tripartite basis.

But the key difficulty here is the issue of effectiveness. The WTO has an elaborate system of adjudication and sanctions in order to enforce trade norms. The ILO relies, largely, on moral suasion and diplomatic pressure. The recent involvement of the ILO in the substantial problem of forced labour in Burma presents a mixed picture of the organisation's effectiveness.[55] The new initiatives on child labour have also yet to prove themselves.[56]The ILO has yet, under its new leadership and equipped with its enhanced, post-Singapore mandate, to prove itself any more effective than it has been in the past.[57] It therefore seems likely that pressure for WTO involvement in labour issues will continue, simply because of the greater power which the WTO has *vis-à-vis* recalcitrant national states. It might be claimed that the ILO's moral suasion would have greater impact if it were underpinned by credible threats of trade sanctions, enforced by the WTO. Some of the controversy surrounding this possible institutional link is explored in the next section.

[53] See E. Lee, Globalization and Employment: Is the Anxiety Justified?, (1996) 135 *International Labour Review* 485, at 496. See also, Dani Rodrik, "Sense and Nonsense in the Globalization Debate", *Foreign Policy* (Summer 1997), 19 at 26.

[54] See *supra* n. 15.

[55] ILO, Resolution on the Widespread Use of Forced Labour in Myanmar (June 1999), International Labour Conference, 87th Session, available on the ILO website at http://www.ilo.org/public/english/10ilc/ilc87/com-myan.htm, and see F. Williams, "ILO Bars Burma over Forced Labour", *Financial Times*, 18 June 1999.

[56] ILO Convention 182, Convention concerning the Prohibition and Immediate Action for the Elimination of the Worst Forms of Child Labour (1999) (http://www.ilo.org/public/english/10ilc/ilc87/com-chic.htm); ILO Recommendation 190, Recommendation concerning the Prohibition and Immediate Action for the Elimination of the Worst Forms of Child Labour (1999) (http://www.ilo.org/public/english/10ilc/ilc87/com-chir.htm).

[57] On the effectiveness of the ILO, see V. A. Leary, "The Paradox of Workers' Rights as Human Rights", in L. A. Compa and S. F. Diamond (eds), *Human Rights, Labor Rights, and International Trade* (1996); F. Maupain, "The Settlement of Disputes within the International Labour Office", (1999) 2 *Journal of International Economic Law* 273. For a comparison of the ILO and the WTO, see O. Mehmet, E. Mendes and R. Sinding, *Towards a Fair Global Labour Market: Avoiding a New Slave Trade* (1999), pp. 17–82.

V. ALTERNATIVES TO THE CURRENT APPROACHES

We mentioned earlier that there is an uneasy relationship between the four current models. Most obviously, it is questionable whether four layers of regulation will be able to coexist without significant conflicts. If there are conflicts, it is unclear which level of regulation will trump the others. But in the longer term, the key question will be whether this eclectic mix of regulatory techniques is sufficient to reassure concerned governments and NGOs that the issue of labour standards is being addressed in a principled and coherent way. We recognise, and stress, that attempting to address this question leads us into areas where speculation replaces analysis. But if dissatisfaction with the current models grows, two possible alternatives suggest themselves. We will label them "involuntary multilateralism" and "voluntary multilateralism".

Involuntary multilateralism

One option for states seeking to integrate labour standards and trade more fully is to make greater use of unilateral or regional approaches. Trading blocs might emerge, replacing the ideological blocs of the Cold War. They offer the possibility of making a trade/labour link, but without the need to obtain worldwide agreement on the mechanism for doing so. In this scenario, there would be an increased likelihood of trade disputes over labour and other human rights issues, as powerful states or blocs attempted to impose their preferences on weaker trading partners. Our suggestion is that the WTO would inevitably become embroiled in these disputes, hence the "involuntary multilateralism" option.

Some of the opposition to a trade/labour linkage appears to be based on the assumption that it is possible for the WTO to avoid dealing with labour issues. As we have seen, the WTO itself has been adamant in resisting linkage, and others have supported this position, including the Secretary-General of the United Nations.[58] But is this assumption plausible? If states take action on labour rights, either unilaterally or in bilateral agreements, WTO adjudicatory institutions are likely to be called on to determine whether their actions are in compliance with trade disciplines. In such cases, the issue will be the appropriate amount of legal space which states will be given to pursue such non-economic goals (centring on the flexibility of the exceptions contained in Article XX of the GATT)[59] and the WTO may not be able to avoid giving an answer. The dream which some seem to have of a WTO innocent of involvement with non-trade issues has already been

[58] Kofi Annan, "Secretary-General Proposes Global Compact on Human Rights, Labour, Environment, in Address to World Economic Forum in Davos", 1 February 1999, UN Press Release SG/SM/6881, available at http://www.un.org/News/Press/.

[59] See the references at *supra* n. 40.

shattered in the context of environmental norms, and it may only be a matter of time before the same occurs in the context of labour rights.

The "involuntary multilateralism" model raises interesting questions about the role of the WTO Appellate Body. How would it handle a case involving labour rights? The recent *Shrimp/Turtles* case[60] appears to show the need for a much more pragmatic case-by-case approach to the trade-environment issue, compared to earlier panel decisions such as the *Tuna/Dolphin* cases.[61] Whether such an approach would be taken in trade/labour issues remains to be seen. More fundamentally, is the Appellate Body the appropriate forum to resolve such cases?[62] Some see the Appellate Body as a court in evolution, making policy trade-offs in the way that other courts regularly do, confident in its legitimacy to interpret the text of the GATT. Others would reject this approach, claiming that it fails to understand the institutional fragility of the dispute settlement process, and would urge caution, regarding the need for trade-offs as centrally a role for the political actors.

Voluntary multilateralism

This brings us to the "voluntary multilateralism" approach, in which states would agree to give the WTO a more clearly articulated role in addressing labour issues. This might occur either as a result of dissatisfaction with other approaches to the link (including "involuntary multilateralism"), or simply as a result of the increasing interpenetration of world trade and domestic policies, as states become more interdependent in the global marketplace.

In this scenario, requiring the WTO to address the labour agenda itself as a principal actor would not seem so extraordinary. For example, membership of the organisation could be made conditional on a country's willingness to conform to minimum labour standards. Or we could go further, requiring labour and human rights standards to be promoted through "social clauses" in international trade and investment agreements.[63] Such social clauses would involve the parties promising to comply with particular labour or human rights standards, or risk trade sanctions being imposed.[64] In this case, trade law would

[60] *United States—Import Prohibition of Certain Shrimp and Shrimp Products*: *Report of the Appellate Body* (1999) 38 *International Legal Materials* 118.

[61] *United States—Restrictions on Imports of Tuna* (1991) 30 *International Legal Materials* 1594; *United States—Restrictions on Imports of Tuna* (1994) 33 *International Legal Materials* 936.

[62] S. P. Croley and J. H. Jackson, "WTO Dispute Procedures, Standard of Review, and Deference to National Governments", (1996) 90 *American Journal of International Law* 193 contains an interesting discussion of the appropriate role of an international dispute settlement body.

[63] Some of the precedents for this are reviewed in P. Waer, "Social Clauses in International Trade: the Debate in the European Union", (1996) 30 *Journal of World Trade* 25, at 27–8.

[64] The precise institutional mechanism for this merits careful consideration. For discussion, see P. Stirling, "The Use of Trade Sanctions as an Enforcement Mechanism for Basic Human Rights: a Proposal for Addition to the World Trade Organization", (1996) 11 *American University Journal of*

become the mechanism of better labour standards. It is important to note that it is only at this point that the immensely complex debate about the social clause becomes relevant. The arguments on both sides of the debate have been well-rehearsed, and we can only touch on a few of them here.

Many different arguments have been advanced in favour of incorporating labour standards into an amended GATT.[65] Such a link would defend the social achievements of developed countries from erosion, and facilitate further trade liberalization by reassuring voters in those countries. Externalities, such as the sense of outrage in many countries about the treatment of some workers abroad, would justify regulatory intervention, just as much as pollution crossing borders justifies regulation by the receiving country.[66] Promoting better labour standards would be an act of solidarity with the disadvantaged in the developing world. Other methods of ensuring such protection, such as through the ILO, are inadequate. Labour standards would have positive spillovers: support for trade unions might contribute to democratisation, as did support for Solidarity in Poland. An effective international regulatory structure would constrain the unilateral use of trade sanctions, and thus reduce the risk of covert protectionism.

It would be naive to think that there is not considerable opposition to any linkage between international trade and other non-economic issues such as environmental protection or human rights, particularly from developing countries. Again, many arguments have been advanced against an explicit linkage between the WTO regime and labour rights.[67] Differences in labour rights between countries are a legitimate source of comparative advantage. Current high-standard countries had much lower labour standards when they were developing and it is therefore unfair that developing countries should be denied the same opportunities. In any event, standards rise with *per capita* income and liberal trade promotes higher growth. Trade adjustment measures are better than trade restrictions to help those who lose out in globalisation. The labour rights agenda risks being captured by protectionist elements.[68] A link to core labour

International Law and Policy 1; E. de Wet, "Labor Standards in the Globalised Economy: the Inclusion of a Social Clause in the General Agreement on Tariff and Trade/World Trade Organization", (1995) 17 *Human Rights Quarterly* 443; and P. Waer, *supra* n. 63.

[65] See, for example, R. Kyloh, "The Governance of Globalization: ILO's Contribution", in R. Kyloh (ed.), *Mastering the Challenge of Globalization: Towards a Trade Union Agenda* (1998); E. de Wet, *supra* n. 60.

[66] This issue (and the analogy between environment and labour concerns more generally) is explored in H. Ward, "Common but Differentiated Debates: Environment, Labour and the World Trade Organization", (1996) 45 *International and Comparative Law Quarterly* 592.

[67] See, for example, J. Bhagwati, "The Agenda of the WTO", and T. N. Srinivasan, "International Trade and Labour Standards from an Economic Perspective", both in P. van Dijck and G. Faber (eds), *Challenges to the New World Trade Organization* (1996); H. Grossmann and G. Koopmann, "Social Standards in International Trade: a New Protectionist Wave?", in H. Sander and A. Inotai (eds), *World Trade After the Uruguay Round* (1996); M. A. A. Warner, "Globalization and Human Rights: an Economic Model", (1999) 25 *Brooklyn Journal of International Law* 99.

[68] For interesting empirical evidence on this point, see A. B. Krueger, "Observations on International Labor Standards and Trade", National Bureau of Economic Research Working Paper 5632 (1996).

rights would simply lead to demands for links to more and more labour standards. Stressing labour standards increases North-South tensions because of the sensitivity in developing countries over the issue of national sovereignty. Incorporating labour rights into the WTO would increase the number and difficulty of trade disputes; the WTO must be protected as an institution. If it is not, the global trading system might be undermined. Finally, it would be inappropriate for a body with primary expertise in trade to have to interpret labour rights standards. Trade law, in short, should not be used as a sword to enforce labour rights.

VI. SOME CONCLUDING THOUGHTS

The debate, in truth, has only just begun in earnest on these medium-term issues. At the very least, it seems appropriate that the major institutional actors involved (the ILO and the WTO) should each be considering how it could contribute to resolving the tensions we have identified. It seems increasingly anomalous, in particular, that the WTO should not even have a committee considering these issues and trying to assess more systematically than has yet been attempted the parameters of the problem, in the way that trade-evironment issues are now regularly considered within the WTO.

But we need, finally, to consider an extremely delicate issue in how this debate will be conducted in the future: who exactly will speak for whom? This issue arises in at least three different ways. First, when governments of countries purport to speak for their populations, what weight should we give to these statements? Under traditional international law, of course, the answer was relatively simple: governments represented states. Now, however, we are in the era of human rights and democratisation. How far should we accept that when a government opposes the linkage of trade and labour issues because of the adverse impact it believes it will have on that country, it is representing the interests of the country as a whole or the interests of a small elite within the country? Perhaps even more controversially, how far should other states place credibility on the positions of the governments of developed countries that seem to be beholden to the groups that make the largest contribution to their election campaigns? These are arguments regularly heard among labour and human rights groups.

But, equally, how far are the labour unions representative of "workers' interests"? This is a particular concern in the context of giving the ILO greater responsibility on the trade/labour issue. For ILO insiders, one of its greatest strengths is its tripartite composition. But is this now a strength or a weakness? The narrowness of the labour interests represented, often consisting of what is sometimes described as a "labour aristocracy", may limit the ILO's apparent legitimacy. Will the interests of those most likely to be adversely affected by globalisation (the poor, the unorganised, minority groups, women) have a place at the table? Some NGOs will claim that they represent these interests. But do they? When an NGO in New York speaks for women workers in Guatemala what weight should we give its views? How, in short, can we institutionalise the participation of those who have the most to lose from the success of globalisation in the new global architecture of international trade?

Any international institution that comes to have a significant impact on the daily lives of ordinary people is bound to face this problem of participation. The ongoing debate within the EU about the "democratic deficit" in its institutional structure is evidence of this. We acknowledge that the problem is highly complex and difficult to resolve. But the WTO should at least begin to identify the interested parties and engage them in debate on the various questions we have mapped out. In an area plagued with uncertainty, the one prediction that can be made with some confidence is that ignoring the issue of labour rights in the trade context will not cause it to disappear.

9

Human Rights Sanctions and the World Trade Organisation

SARAH H. CLEVELAND*

I. INTRODUCTION

IN OCTOBER 1978, the USA imposed sweeping unilateral trade sanctions on General Idi Amin's regime in Uganda. The legislation barred all imports and exports between Uganda and the USA until the President certified that Uganda was "no longer committing a consistent pattern of gross violations of human rights."[1] The embargo was adopted in response to gross human rights atrocities under Amin's brutal seven-year reign, including the state-sponsored murder of 100,000 to 300,000 civilians, and the expulsion of Asians from Uganda. Uganda was considered to be particularly vulnerable to US trade sanctions due to its substantial dependence on coffee exports to the US market.[2] The sanctions deprived Amin's regime of foreign currency from coffee exports and spare parts for US manufactured goods, and restricted the country's access to foreign oil. Within a few months of the sanctions' imposition, the Amin regime toppled to a military invasion by Tanzania. And while Tanzania's intervention was critical, most commentators who have examined the issue have concluded that the US sanctions played an important role in ending the Amin regime.[3]

* I am grateful for the advice and support of Francesco Francioni, for the comments of Hans Baade, Carl Baudenbacher, Patricia Hansen, Douglas Laycock, Christopher McCrudden, Neil Netanel, Steven Ratner, and Jay Westbrook, for the library assistance of Jonathan Pratter, and for the research assistance of Bradley Smith and Suzan Norton. Prior versions of this chapter have been presented at the University of Siena and Oxford University. Comments may be submitted to the author at scleveland@mail.law.utexas.edu.

[1] An Act to Amend the Bretton Woods Agreement Act, Pub. L. No. 95–435, § 5(c), 92 Stat. 1051, 1052 (1978), *repealed by* Pub. L. No. 96–67, § 2(a), 93 Stat. 415 (1979).

[2] Coffee exports provided 90 per cent of Ugandan government revenues and accounted for half of the country's gross national product. The USA was Uganda's largest trading partner and provided one-third of Uganda's coffee market. See Lillich and Hannum, *International Human Rights, Problems of Law, Policy, and Practice* (3rd edn., 1995), pp. 74–5. See also Hufbauer and Schott, *Economic Sanctions Reconsidered* (Washington, DC, 1985), pp. 455–60.

[3] See, e.g., Hufbauer and Schott, *supra*, n. 2, p. 459; Miller, "When Sanctions Worked", (1980) 39 *Foreign Pol.* (Summer) 118, 125–6; Comment, "U.S. Trade Sanctions Against Uganda: Legality Under International Law", (1979) 11 *Law & Pol. Int'l Bus.* 1149; Note, "The Legitimacy of the United States Embargo of Uganda", (1979) 13 *J. Int'l L. & Econ.* 651; "Recent Developments, International Trade: Uganda Trade Embargo", (1979) 20 *Harv. Int'l L. J.* 206.

States have long used trade sanctions to promote a range of foreign policy goals, and for at least the past 100 years, states have employed trade restrictions to promote improved human rights conditions abroad. In the last century, states adopted trade restrictions through treaty and statute to abolish slavery and the slave trade,[4] and Great Britain adopted aggressive measures to establish and enforce the international slaving ban.[5] The USA has restricted imports made with convict labour since the 1800s, and began barring imports made with other forms of forced labour in the early 1900s. Since the 1970s, the USA has adopted a wide range of laws conditioning trade benefits on foreign states' compliance with fundamental human and labour rights. Trade restrictions for such purposes may take the form of import or export bans, quotas, licensing requirements, tariffs, financing assistance, or conditions on government procurement. Nor is the USA alone in this practice. In the international community's now decade-long struggle to improve human rights conditions in Burma (Myanmar), for example, Canada and the European Union (EU) have joined the USA in suspending GSP (generalised system of preferences) benefits for Burmese imports.[6] Trade sanctions have been used against states that practice widespread genocide or torture, to dismantle apartheid regimes, and to promote the restoration of democracy. As the Ugandan example demonstrates, such sanctions may play an important role in discouraging rogue behaviour and bringing non-compliant states into conformity with fundamental norms of the international community.

The absence of effective international remedies for human rights atrocities has given sub-global action an increasingly important place in the modern human rights system.[7] "Unilateral" trade sanctions—or sanctions imposed without

[4] See, e.g., Declaration of the Eight Courts relative to the Universal Abolition of the Slave Trade, 8 February 1815 (Annex XV of the Treaty of Vienna), 63 Consol. T. S. 473, 474; Additional Convention between Great Britain and Portugal for the Prevention of the Slave Trade, 28 July 1817, arts. III, IV, 67 Consol. T.S. 373, 398 (barring importation of slaves into the Brazils other than by Portuguese-flagged ships with royal passports); General Act for the Repression of the African Slave Trade, 2 July 1890, arts. LXII, VIII, IX, 27 Stat. 886, 894–5, 912 (prohibiting the importation of slaves and barring the sale of firearms to sub-Saharan Africa due to the role of weapons in the slave trade and their destabilizing effect on local tribes). For further discussion, see Nadelmann, "Global Prohibition Regimes: the Evolution of Norms in International Society", (1990) 44 *Int'l Org.* 479, 491, 497 *et seq.*

[5] Thomas, *The Slave Trade* (New York, 1997), p. 573 *et seq.*; Jennings and Watts (eds.), *Oppenheim's International Law* (9th edn., 1992) vol. 1, pts. 2–4, § 429, pp. 979–80.

[6] The USA responded to the Burmese military's suppression of democracy and use of forced labour by indefinitely suspending Burma's GSP status in 1989: 103 Stat. 3010, 3011–13 (1989). Following Burma's refusal to allow an EU investigation into its forced labour practices, in December 1996 the EU Commission for the first time exercised the human rights clause of the European Generalised System of Preferences (GSP) programme to terminate Burma's GSP trade benefits on industrial exports to the EU. The Commission indicated that the restriction would remain in place until the use of forced labour was abolished. In 1997, the EU suspended GSP benefits for Burmese agricultural products, and Canada also withdrew General Preferential Tariff benefits from Burma: *Human Rights Watch World Report* 1998, "Burma", pp. 161–62; available at http://www.hrw.org (visited 20 July 2000).

[7] See Cleveland, "Norm Internalization and U.S. Economic Sanctions", (Winter 2001) 26 *Yale J. Int'l L.* 1, 3–5.

express regional or multilateral authorisation[8]—form one subset of a range non-coercive enforcement mechanisms available to individual states. Other such measures include withholding of recognition and diplomatic relations, denial of airplane landing rights, and economic measures such as restrictions on foreign assistance and investment and freezing of assets. Unilateral measures by states in turn form part of a broader concerted, but decentralised, effort on the part of the international community to encourage human rights compliance. Multilateral sanctions imposed by the UN Security Council, development projects of international financial institutions such as the International Monetary Fund and the World Bank, regional efforts by the European Union and under the North American Free Trade Agreement (NAFTA), lobbying and oversight by non-governmental organisations, transnational litigation, consumer boycotts, and voluntary corporate codes of conduct all form part of the multifaceted enforcement fabric of the international human rights regime. Thus, unilateral trade sanctions constitute one element in the dialogue that states engage in to encourage other states to internalise basic human rights norms into their domestic legal systems and to act consistently with the fundamental values of the global community.[9]

If trade sanctions traditionally have been one of the instruments used to promote international rights compliance, however, that normative function may now be threatened by recent developments in global trade liberalisation policy. President Carter expressed concern that the US sanctions against Uganda would violate GATT,[10] and recent WTO decisions threaten to eliminate many forms of trade sanctions as an option for promoting human rights compliance. The WTO has not, to date, considered the GATT-consistency of any human or labour rights measures, but WTO dispute proceedings consistently have invalidated analogous environmental measures as conflicting with GATT requirements.

Amendment of the GATT/WTO system to accommodate expressly human and labour rights considerations appears unlikely in the near future. WTO members from the developing world have refused even to discuss any linkage between human or labour rights and trade relations. At the Uruguay Round of trade negotiations, the USA and France proposed that consideration of the relationship between labour standards, social justice, and trade concerns should be

[8] For the purposes of this chapter, the term "unilateral" refers to action by individual states which is not taken pursuant to the mandate of a regional or global organisation. The term does not preclude the possibility that other states may also act unilaterally to support the same goals, as in the case of sanctions against Burma. "Regional" action refers to actions taken by states pursuant to the authorisation of regional entities such as the Organisation of American States, the European Union, ASEAN, or NATO. "Multilateral" sanctions refer to sanctions that are authorised by the United Nations, such as the former sanctions against Rhodesia and South Africa.

[9] See Cleveland, "Norm Internalization", *supra* n. 7, pp. 6–7.

[10] General Agreements on Tariffs and Trade, opened for signature 30 October 1947, 61 Stat. A3, TIAS No. 1700, 55 *UNTS* 187.

[11] The US implementing statute for the Uruguay Round called for the establishment of a working group within the WTO "to examine the relationship of internationally recognised worker rights

included on the WTO agenda.[11] And in 1994 the USA brokered a tentative agreement to consider labour rights issues in the next WTO negotiations.[12] These and subsequent efforts, however, have been thwarted by developing countries. Linkage was strenuously opposed at the 1996 Singapore Ministerial Conference of the WTO by India and other developing nations, despite support for the initiative from Canada, the EU, Norway, and the USA.[13] The recent WTO talks in Seattle brought unprecedented attention to the relationship between WTO trade issues and other social concerns, but the talks failed to make any progress toward accommodating these considerations in the trade liberalisation principles of GATT. Western states' desire to promote fundamental international rights through trade measures thus appears to be at loggerheads with developing countries and free trade advocates, who view such restrictions as disguised protectionist and imperialist measures that undermine the comparative advantage of low wage countries. As the USA lifts its longstanding annual review of China's human rights practices to make way for China's entry into the WTO, it is necessary to ask whether GATT has eliminated unilateral trade sanctions as a mechanism to enforce global human rights.

Some commentators, and several contributors to this book, have argued that certain targeted restrictions on trade, such as bars on imports of goods made with exploitative child labour, should be consistent with GATT requirements.[14] Few, if any, commentators, however, have considered the broader implications of the WTO decisions for the traditional state practice of using trade to sanction fundamental human rights violations—as in the case of Uganda—where the targeted violations are not themselves trade-related. In other words, the free trade system presents a broader question whether trade can and should be used to promote legitimate, non-trade values of the international community, such as the protection of human rights.

This chapter examines the use of unilateral trade sanctions to promote human and labour rights abroad, and considers the extent to which such sanctions can, or should, be consistent with GATT/WTO trade liberalisation mandates. Because there is little likelihood that GATT will be amended to accommodate labour and human rights concerns in the near future, the

. . . to the articles, objectives, and related instruments of the [GATT and WTO]": Uruguay Round Agreements Act, § 131, 19 U.S.C.A. § 3551 (1994).

[12] See Bergsman, "Kantor Announces U.S. Has Secured GATT Deal to Discuss Labor Rights", *Inside U.S. Trade*, 8 April 1994, p. S1.

[13] See "WTO: Ministers Agree to Do Nothing on Labour Standards", *Eur. Rep.*, 14 December 1996, available in LEXIS, News Library, CURNWS file. The 1996 Singapore Declaration committed WTO member states to "renew [their] commitment to the observance of internationally recognised core labour standards", but concluded that labour rights oversight should remain the exclusive purview of the ILO: WTO, Singapore Ministerial Declaration, 13 December 1996, WT/MIN(96)/DEC, (1997) 36 *ILM* 218, 221.

[14] See Francioni, *supra* Chapter 1, Lenzerini, *infra* Chapter 11, and McCrudden and Davies, *infra* Chapter 8. See also Howse, "The World Trade Organization and the Protection of Workers' Rights", (1999) 3 *J. Small & Emerging Bus. L.* 131.

chapter focuses on the extent to which GATT may be interpreted to be compatible with the fundamental values of the human rights system.[15] Part II briefly considers the international human rights regime, identifying the core substantive norms of the human rights system and examining the traditional authority of states under customary international law to use unilateral trade measures to promote human rights. Because the USA has made the most active use of unilateral human rights sanctions, Part III examines the major US laws conditioning trade privileges on human and labour rights compliance. Part IV sets forth the basic principles of the GATT free trade system, and considers the implications of the GATT text and recent WTO decisions for human rights measures. The section concludes that certain tailored restrictions on trade, such as restrictions on goods whose use or production violates human rights, may be consistent with present GATT analysis. But more general restrictions for human rights, which form the bulk of human rights trade measures, likely would fail. Part V offers alternative interpretive approaches that would reconcile sanctions for *jus cogens* violations with the textual requirements of GATT. In sum, the chapter considers the question whether unilateral trade sanctions remain a legally available option for the enforcement of international human rights, and whether the GATT system can be rendered consistent with the normative values of the international human rights regime. I conclude that while the WTO's present approach significantly limits the ability of states to use unilateral economic sanctions to promote basic human rights, if the GATT is interpreted consistently with other established norms of international law, as GATT rules mandate, a number of legitimate human rights measures may be accommodated within the current GATT/WTO structure.

II. DEFINING INTERNATIONAL HUMAN AND LABOUR RIGHTS

Before discussing the relationship of GATT to the human rights system, it is important to lay out the basic structure of the human rights regime and the existing authority of states, absent the GATT, to use economic measures to enforce human rights principles.

[15] The article considers only unilateral sanctions. Multilateral trade sanctions authorized by the UN Security Council, such as those imposed in the 1970s and 1980s against South Africa, fall within the GATT exception for actions taken pursuant to UN obligations. See Art. XXI(c) GATT (excepting actions taken "in pursuance of [member] obligations under the United Nations Charter for the maintenance of international peace and security"). Regional sanctions, authorised by regional entities such as the Organisation of American States (OAS), may pose GATT difficulties similar to unilateral sanctions, but are not examined here. This chapter also does not purport to address the policy question of the effectiveness and appropriateness of sanctions in any particular circumstance.

The international human rights regime

The international human rights regime is annunciated through a loose network of general instruments such as Universal Declaration of Human Rights,[16] the International Covenant on Civil and Political Rights (ICCPR),[17] and the International Covenant on Economic, Social, and Cultural Rights (ICESCR);[18] and rights-specific conventions addressing the prohibitions against genocide,[19] torture,[20] war crimes,[21] and racial discrimination,[22] labour rights,[23] and the rights of women[24] and children.[25] The rights and prohibitions set forth in these core conventions are incorporated into a number of regional regimes, such as the European Convention on Human Rights,[26] the American Convention on Human Rights,[27] the American Declaration of the Rights and Duties of Man,[28] and the African Charter on Human and People's Rights.[29] The human rights protections set forth in these instruments have been further refined and elaborated both by pronouncements of international and regional bodies constituted to monitor compliance with the conventions, such as the UN Human Rights

[16] Universal Declaration of Human Rights, G.A. Res. 217(AIII), U.N. GAOR, 3rd Sess., pt. 1, at 71, U.N. Doc. A/810 (1948) (hereinafter Universal Declaration). The Declaration was adopted as a General Assembly resolution in the immediate aftermath of the Second World War.

[17] International Covenant on Civil and Political Rights, adopted 16 December 1966, 999 *UNTS* 171, (1967) 6 *ILM* 368 (entered into force 23 March 1976).

[18] International Covenant on Economic, Social, and Cultural Rights, adopted 16 December 1966, 993 *UNTS* 3, (1967) 6 *ILM* 360 (entered into force 3 January 1976).

[19] Convention on the Prevention and Punishment of the Crime of Genocide, adopted 9 December 1948, 78 *UNTS* 277, G.A. Res. 2670 (entered into force 12 January 1951) (hereinafter Genocide Convention).

[20] Convention Against Torture and other Cruel, Inhuman, or Degrading Treatment or Punishment, approved by the General Assembly for consensus 10 December 1984, 1465 *UNTS* 85, (1985) 23 *ILM* 1027, as modified, (1985) 24 *ILM* 535 (entered into force 26 June 1987) (hereinafter Torture Convention).

[21] See especially Geneva Convention Relative to the Protection of Civilian Persons in Time of War, 12 August 1949, 75 *UNTS* 287 (hereinafter Geneva Convention).

[22] International Convention on the Elimination of All Forms of Racial Discrimination, done 7 March 1966, 660 *UNTS* 195, (1966) 5 *ILM* 350 (entered into force 4 January 1969) (hereinafter Racial Discrimination Convention).

[23] See discussion *infra*.

[24] Convention on the Elimination of All Forms of Discrimination Against Women, opened for signature 18 December 1979, 1249 *UNTS* 13, (1980) 19 *ILM* 33 (entered into force 3 September 1981) (hereinafter CEDAW).

[25] Convention of the Rights of the Child, adopted 20 November 1989, 1577 *UNTS* 3, (1989) 28 *ILM* 1448 (entered into force 2 September 1990).

[26] European Convention for the Protection of Human Rights and Fundamental Freedoms, opened for signature 4 November 1950, 213 *UNTS* 221, E.T.S. 5, as amended by Protocol No. 3, E.T.S. 45, Protocol No. 5, E.T.S. 55, and Protocol No. 8, E.T.S. 118, Protocol No. 11, E.T.S. 155 (hereinafter European Convention).

[27] American Convention on Human Rights, opened for signature 22 November 1969, 1144 *UNTS* 123, (1970) 9 *ILM* 673 (entered into force 18 July 1978).

[28] American Declaration of the Rights and Duties of Man, OAS Res. XXX, OAS Doc. OEA/Ser. L/V/I.4 Rev.XX (adopted by the Ninth Conference of American States (1948)).

[29] African Charter on Human and People's Rights, adopted 27 June 1981, 1520 *UNTS* 217, (1981) 21 *ILM* 59 (entered into force 21 October 1986).

Commission and Committee, the torture, genocide and race discrimination committees, and the Inter-American Human Rights Commission, and by international, regional, and domestic courts.

In addition to the rights detailed in the formal instruments of the human rights regime, certain rights are generally considered to be universally accepted and binding on all sovereign states as either *jus cogens* or *erga omnes* principles of customary international law. *Jus cogens* norms, such as the prohibitions against genocide, slavery, and torture, constitute a small subset of recognized international human rights principles which are universally binding on all states and which cannot be superseded.[30] Unlike other customary international law principles, states may not persistently object to avoid obligations under these norms, which prevail over all competing principles of treaty and customary international law.[31] On the other hand, certain human rights obligations that have achieved the status of customary international law, but are not yet peremptory norms, nevertheless enjoy status as obligations *erga omnes*, or obligations owing by and to all. These obligations, as the ICJ has explained, constitute "obligations of a State toward the international community as a whole" and include the "basic rights of the human person".[32] The International Law Institute has recognised the

[30] There is no universal agreement regarding the customary international norms that have attained the status of *jus cogens*, though general agreement has coalesced around the prohibitions against genocide, piracy, slavery and the slave trade. See *Oppenheim's International Law*, *supra* n. 5, § 2 p. 8. Forced labour and slave-like practices, and crimes against humanity and war crimes, are also broadly recognized as principles that no state officially claims the right to violate, which may be included among the *jus cogens* norms of customary international law. See Rome Statute of the International Criminal Court (17 July 1998), UN Doc. A/CONF.183/9 (1998), available at <http://www.un.org/icc> (hereinafter Rome Statute); see Geneva Convention, *supra* n. 21; Charter of the International Military Tribunal, 8 August 1945, 59 Stat. 1546, 82 *UNTS* 279; *Kadic* v. *Karadzic*, 70 F.3d 232, 241–243 (2d Cir. 1995) (recognizing that war crimes and crimes against humanity, as well as genocide, violated customary international law). The *Restatement (Third) of the Foreign Relations Law of the United States* also considers *jus cogens* rights to include torture or other cruel, inhuman, or degrading treatment or punishment; summary execution or causing the disappearance of individuals; prolonged arbitrary detention; systematic racial discrimination; and a consistent pattern or gross violations of internationally recognised human rights. See *Restatement (Third) of the Foreign Relations Law of the United States* (1987) § 702 (hereinafter *Restatement*).

[31] Vienna Convention on the Law of Treaties, concluded 23 May 1969, 1155 *UNTS* 331 (hereinafter Vienna Convention), Art. 53 (defining *jus cogens* norms as principles "accepted and recognised by the international community of states as a whole as a norm from which no derogation is permitted and which can be modified only by a subsequent norm of general international law having the same character"); see also *ibid*. Art. 64 (newly emergent *jus cogens* norms supersede existing treaties).

[32] *The Case Concerning Barcelona Traction, Light and Power Company, Ltd.* (*Belgium* v. *Spain*) [1970], ICJ 3, ¶ 32. See also *Case Concerning Application of the Convention on the Prevention and Punishment of the Crime of Genocide* (*Bosnia and Herzegovina* v. *Yugoslovia (Serbia and Montenegro)*) [1993] 325, ¶ 86 (Further Requests for the Indication of Provisional Measures of September 13) (separate opinion of Judge Elihu Lauterpacht) ("The duty to 'prevent' genocide is a duty that rests upon all parties and is a duty owed by each party to every other"); *Legal Consequences for States of the Continued Presence of South Africa in Namibia (South West Africa)* [1971] ICJ 16, ¶ 126 (21 June) (discussing *erga omnes* obligation of states to respect illegality of South African presence in Namibia).

international obligation to respect human rights as an obligation *erga omnes*, binding on all states.[33] Unlike other obligations under international law, such human rights obligations are considered owed to all members of the international community. All bound parties have a general interest in ensuring their observance and may take action to secure their enforcement.[34]

For our purposes, it appears that these *erga omnes* norms include the prohibition against forced and bonded labour, including exploitative child labour, and other slave-like practices.[35] Other emergent *erga omnes* obligations may include freedom of religion, the prohibition against gender discrimination and discrimination in fundamental human rights, the prohibition against the execution of juveniles (from which the USA is a notable dissenter), the right to a fair trial, the right to property, the right to freedom of association, and the prohibition against employment discrimination.[36] And while customary international law does not clearly prefer democracy over other forms of government, there is an emergent international law prohibition against the overthrow or thwarting of democratic institutions that are already in place.[37]

[33] "The Protection of Human Rights and the Principle of Non-Intervention in Internal Affairs of States", (1989) 63 *Institut De Droit International Annuaire* 338. See also *Oppenheim's International Law*, *supra* n. 5, § 1 pp. 4–5.

[34] See *Oppenheim's International Law*, *supra* n. 5, § 150, p. 515. But compare *South West Africa (Ethiopia and Liberia* v. *South Africa)* (Second Phase) [1966] ICJ 6 ¶ 88 (18 July) (holding that "an 'actio popularis', or right resident in any member of a community to take legal action in vindication of a public interest . . . . is not known to international law as it stands at present").

[35] See discussion of labour rights, *infra*.

[36] Both the UN Human Rights Committee and the International Law Association have suggested that these and a number of additional rights have attained the status of customary international law. See UN Human Rights Committee, General Comment 24 (52), General Comment on issues relating to reservations made upon ratification or accession to the Covenant or the Optional Protocols thereto, or in relation to declarations under article 41 of the Covenant, U.N. Doc. CCPR/C/21/Rev.1/Add.6 (1994) ¶ 8, available at <http://www.umn.edu/humanrts/gencomm/hrcom24.htm> (visited 26 September 2000) (hereinafter General Comment 24). International Law Association, Committee on the Enforcement of Human Rights Law, Final Report on the Status of the Universal Declaration of Human Rights in National and International Law, ILA, Report of the 66th Conference, 525, 544–9 (Buenos Aires, 1994), reprinted in Lillich and Hannum, *International Human Rights*, *supra* n. 2, pp. 166–71.

[37] See generally Fox and Roth (eds.), *Democratic Governance and International Law* (Cambridge, 2000); Franck, "The Emerging Right to Democratic Governance", (1992) 86 *Am. J. Int'l L.* 46. The United Nations General Assembly, and regional entities such as the OAS and the Organisation for Security and Cooperation in Europe (OSCE) have condemned the overthrow of democracies and established various response mechanisms. See, e.g., G.A. Res. 52/137, ¶ 8, U.N. GAOR, 52nd Sess., Supp. No. 49, at 292, 294, U.N. Doc. A/52/49 (1997) (urging restoration of democratic governance in Myanmar); G.A. Res. 52/144, ¶ 3(d), U.N. GAOR, 52nd Sess., Supp. No. 49, at 303, 304, U.N. Doc. A/52/49 (1997) (Nigeria). See also OAS Res. AG/RES. 1080, OAS Gen. Ass., 21st Sess., Proceedings, Vol. I, at 4, OAS Doc. OEA/Ser.P/XX1.0.2 (1991) (establishing processes to respond to "sudden or irregular disruption of the democratic political institution process"); Conference on Security and Co-operation in Europe: Document of the Moscow Meeting on the Human Dimension, 3 October 1991, (1991) 30 *ILM* 1670, 1677 ("condemn[ing] unreservedly" efforts to overthrow a representative government and promising vigorous support for governments subject to such overthrow). See also Ratner, "New Democracies, Old Atrocities: An Inquiry in International Law", (1999) 87 *Geo. L. J.* 707, 708–9.

International labour rights have received special attention in the WTO free trade debate, and merit brief additional attention here. The ILO has promulgated over 180 conventions relating to a wide range of labour rights, and has recognized a core set of these protections as "fundamental human rights". These include the rights to freedom of association and to form and join trade unions, and the prohibitions against discrimination in employment, exploitative child labour, forced labour, slavery and servitude.[38] With the exception of the conventions on child labour,[39] the ILO conventions supporting these core principles have been formally ratified by at least 124 nations.[40] The 1998 ILO Declaration on Fundamental Principles and Rights at Work established these core labour principles as binding on all ILO members, regardless whether the member state has ratified the applicable conventions.[41] These core labour rights principles

[38] ILO Declaration on Fundamental Principles and Rights at Work, International Labour Conference, 86th Session, Geneva, June 1998, art. 2, available at <http://www.ilo.org/public/english/standards/relm/ilc/ilc86/com-dtxt.htm> (visited 25 September 2000) (hereinafter ILO Declaration). The Declaration immediately received wide approval from all but about 25 of the ILO's approximately 175 members, with the rest abstaining. See also International Labour Organisation, Fundamental ILO Conventions <http://www.ilo.org/public/english/standards/norm/whatare/fundam/index.htm> (visited 25 September 2000) (hereinafter Fundamental ILO Conventions). The labour rights identified by the ILO Declaration also have been designated as fundamental by the OECD and the Copenhagen Summit for Social Development. See Organisation for Economic Co-operation and Development, *Trade, Employment, and Labour Standards* (Paris, 1996), pp. 26–7 (identifying "freedom of association, prohibition of forced labour, elimination of child labour exploitation and the principle of non-discrimination [as] well-established elements of international jurisprudence concerning human rights") (hereinafter OECD Report); *Report of the World Summit for Social Development*, Copenhagen, 6–12 March 1995, U.N. Doc. A/Conf.166/9 (1996), p. 12, Commitment 3(i).

[39] The prohibition against child labour remains controversial. The ILO's 1973 Child Labour Convention has been ratified by only 105 states, and in response to international disagreement regarding an appropriate minimum age for child labour, the ILO in 1999 drafted a new convention prohibiting the worst forms of child labour. See Convention Concerning the Prohibition and Immediate Action for the Elimination of the Worst Forms of Child Labour (No. 182), adopted 17 June 1999 (hereinafter Worst Forms of Child Labour Convention). The Convention has not yet come into force, and has received 66 ratifications, including the USA. See Fundamental ILO Conventions. The new Convention obligates party states to take steps to eliminate all forms of bonded, forced, and slave labour, child prostitution and pornography, the use of children in drug trafficking, and work "likely to harm the health, safety, or morals of children": Art. 3.

[40] See Fundamental ILO Conventions, *supra* n. 38. The USA is a notable exception, having ratified only ILO Convention No. 105 regarding the abolition of forced labour and No. 182 regarding the worst forms of child labour. The USA also is party to the 1926 and 1957 Slavery Conventions: Convention to Suppress the Slave Trade and Slavery, signed 25 September 1926, 46 Stat. 2183, 2191, 60 *LNTS* 253, 263; Supplementary Convention on the Abolition of Slavery, the Slave Trade, and Institutions and Practices Similar to Slavery, adopted 7 September 1956, 18 *UST* 3201, 266 *UNTS* 3 (hereinafter 1957 Supplementary Slavery Convention). The USA has not ratified ICESCR, CEDAW, or the Convention on the Rights of the Child.

[41] The ILO Declaration notes that in joining the ILO, all members endorsed the principles set out in the ILO Constitution and undertook to promote the overall objectives of the Organisation. Accordingly, "all Members, even if they have not ratified the Conventions in question, have an obligation arising from the very fact of membership in the Organisation, to respect, to promote, and to realise . . . the fundamental rights which are the subject of those Conventions": ILO Declaration, *supra* n. 38, ¶ 2.

also are recognised in foundational human rights instruments such as the Universal Declaration,[42] the ICCPR[43] and ICESCR,[44] CEDAW[45] and the Convention on the Rights of the Child.[46] Thus, this set of labour rights may be included among the core principles of the international human rights regime.

The use of economic coercion to promote human rights

Trade remedies under customary international law

Nothing in customary international law prohibits states from using trade measures to promote human rights compliance by a foreign state. As discussed below, although international law traditionally has protected the right of states to be free from interference by other states in the conduct of their sovereign domestic affairs, this principle of non-intervention does not clearly apply to the use of non-forcible, economic measures to promote international human rights. Even if human rights measures do violate the non-intervention norm, moreover, they may constitute an acceptable use of non-forcible countermeasures to retaliate against violations of international human rights.

(a) *The non-intervention norm.* Customary international law traditionally has allowed states to use economic coercion for a wide range of purposes.[47] Although non-aligned and developing countries have contended that Article 2(7) of the UN Charter[48] prohibits economic interference by one state into the domestic affairs of another, this provision is limited to action by the United Nations, not by its member states, and no international consensus has emerged to support a broader interpretation. In particular, the relatively frequent use of economic sanctions by the USA and other developed nations since the Second World War makes it difficult to conclude that a customary international norm exists against the practice. The compatibility of economic coercion with international law was confirmed by the International Court of Justice (ICJ) in the

[42] See Universal Declaration, Art. 4 (prohibition against slavery and servitude); Art. 20 (freedom of association); Art. 23(2) and (4) (rights to equal pay and to form and join trade unions).

[43] ICCPR, Art. 8 (prohibition against slavery, servitude and forced labour); Art. 22 (freedom of association and to form and join trade unions); Art. 26 (non-discrimination).

[44] ICESCR, Art. 7(a)(1) (equal pay); Art. 8 (freedom of association, right to form and join trade unions and to strike).

[45] CEDAW, Art. 11 (gender discrimination in employment).

[46] Convention on the Rights of the Child, Art. 19 (obligating states "to protect the child from all forms of physical or mental violence, injury or abuse, neglect or negligent treatment, maltreatment or exploitation, including sexual abuse").

[47] See Vattel in Chitty (ed.), *The Law of Nations* (1866), Bk. I, ch. VIII, § 94 ("every nation has a right to choose whether she will or will not trade with another, and on what conditions she is willing to do it, if one nation has for a time permitted another to come and trade in the country, she is at liberty, whenever she thinks proper, to prohibit that commerce—to restrain it—to subject it to certain regulations; and the people who before carried it on cannot complain of injustice") (citation omitted).

[48] See UN Charter, Art. 2(7) (barring intervention by the United Nations into the domestic affairs of states).

Nicaragua case, in which Nicaragua challenged both US military support for the contras and US economic coercion (in the form of terminated foreign aid, the reduction of Nicaragua's sugar import quota, and a trade embargo). The ICJ found that US military support for the contras was unjustifiable, but concluded with respect to the US economic measures that it was "unable to regard such action on the economic plane . . . as a breach of the customary-law principle of non-intervention".[49] Nothing in customary international law, therefore, appears to bar the use of economic coersion.

This is particularly true where economic measures are used to promote human rights, which are not strictly matters of domestic sovereignty, but matters of international concern which justify intervention by the international community.[50] As the *Barcelona Traction* Court wrote, "[i]n view of the importance of the rights involved, all States can be held to have a legal interest in their protection".[51] International law recognises a number of exceptions to state sovereignty to promote state compliance and enforcement of human rights. The Vienna Convention on the Law of Treaties, for example, provides that states may neither terminate their own obligations nor suspend performance due to a material breach by another party with respect to "provisions relating to the protection of the human person contained in treaties of a humanitarian character".[52] In 1994, the UN Human Rights Committee confirmed this principle by ruling that signatories to the ICCPR could not validly enter reservations to provisions that reflected *jus cogens* and *erga omnes* obligations of international law.[53] Core international human rights principles also have been recognized as exceptions to head of state immunity,[54] and to the US act of state doctrine.[56] Finally, principles of universal jurisdiction give states authority to punish *jus cogens* violations such as genocide, torture, war crimes, and the slave trade, regardless whether the state otherwise would enjoy jurisdiction. This unusual authority results from the global community's universal condemnation of those activities and collective interest in suppressing them.[57]

[49] See *Military and Paramilitary Activities (Nicaragua* v. *US)*, [1986] ICJ 14 (June 27) ¶ 245.

[50] See, e.g., Damrosch, "Politics Across Borders: Nonintervention and Nonforcible Influence over Domestic Affairs", (1989) 83 *Am. J. Int'l L.* 1, 39, 42 (arguing that economic intervention in foreign states for human rights purposes does not violate the non-intervention norm).

[51] *Barcelona Traction, supra* n. 32, ¶ 33.

[52] Vienna Convention, Art. 60(5).

[53] General Comment 24, *supra* n. 36, ¶ 8 ("Although treaties that are mere exchanges of obligations between States allow them to reserve *inter se* application of rules of general international law, it is otherwise with human rights treaties, which are for the benefit of persons within their jurisdiction. Accordingly, provisions in the Covenant [ICCPR] that represent customary international law (and *a fortiori* when they have the character of peremptory norms) may not be the subject of reservations").

[54] See, e.g. Genocide Convention, Art. IV (recognising liability for rulers and public officials); *Regina* v. *Bow Street Metropolitan Stipendiary Magistrate and Others, Ex Parte* Pinochet Ugarte (No. 3) [2000], (1999) 1 A. C. 147 (holding that former head of state lacked immunity following ratification of Torture Convention).

[56] See *Restatement, supra* n. 30, § 443, comment c.

[57] See, e.g., *United States* v. *Smith*, 18 U.S. (5 Wheat.) 153, 161–62, 5 L.Ed. 57, 59 (1820); *Filártiga* v. *Peña-Irala*, 630 F.2d 876, 890 (2d Cir. 1980) ("for purposes of civil liability, the torturer has become like the pirate and the slave trader before him—*hostis humanis generis*, an enemy of all

(b) *Non-forcible countermeasures.* Even if trade sanctions for human rights purposes did violate the non-intervention norm, the principle of non-forcible countermeasures would allow the application of such measures in retaliation for another state's breach of its international obligations to protect human rights.[58] Customary international law generally provides that a state that has violated an international obligation to another state, or an obligation to all states (*erga omnes*), is subject to peaceful retaliatory measures that would otherwise be illegal. The measures adopted, however, must be necessary to terminate the violation or prevent future violations and proportional to the violation or injury suffered.[59] Some commentators have argued that the reporting and oversight committees established by the various human rights conventions, such as the ICCPR Human Rights Committee or the ILO complaint procedures, preclude the use of unilateral coercive measures.[60] The treaties do not expressly address such measures, however, and the better view is that these formal international monitoring procedures—which lack enforcement mechanisms—were intended to complement the existing decentralised mechanisms that are available to states under customary international law. As discussed in the previous section, the widespread use of economic sanctions by Western states since the Second World War supports this interpretation. Thus, whether human rights sanctions fall beyond the reach of the non-intervention norm or are justifiable as non-forcible countermeasures, they are allowed under international law as an appropriate response to human rights violations.

Trade remedies under human rights treaties

While customary international law authorises the use of trade measures for human rights purposes, human rights treaties do not require the use of trade sanctions to promote human rights. Unlike various environmental treaties,

mankind"); *Demjanjuk* v. *Petrovsky*, 776 F.2d 571, 582 (6th Cir.1985), *cert. denied*, 457 U.S. 1016 (1986), *vacated on other grounds*, 10 F.3d 338 (6th Cir. 1993) ("the 'universality principle' is based on the assumption that some crimes are so universally condemned that the perpetrators are the enemies of all people"). The Statute of the International Criminal Court acknowledges that "it is the duty of every state to exercise its criminal jurisdiction over those responsible for international crimes". Rome Statute, *supra* n. 30, preamble ¶ 6. See also Ratner and Abrams, *Accountability for Human Rights Atrocities in International Law* (Oxford, 1997), p. 141; Orentlicher, "Settling Accounts: The Duty to Prosecute Human Rights Violations of a Prior Regime", (1991) 100 *Yale L. J.* 2537; *Restatement*, *supra* n. 30, § 404 comment a.

58 See generally Elagab, *The Legality of Non-Forcible Counter-Measures in International Law* (Oxford, 1988); Gerber, "Beyond Balancing: International Law Restraints on the Reach of National Laws", (1984) 10 *Yale J. Int'l L.* 185; Lillich (ed.), *Economic Coercion and the New International Economic Order* (1976); Farer, "Political and Economic Coercion in Contemporary International Law", (1985) 79 *Am. J. Int'l L.* 405. See *Restatement*, *supra* n. 30, § 905 and comments a, c.

59 The broad US sanctions against Iran imposed following the seizure of US consular personnel for example, were upheld by the ICJ as appropriate under the circumstances. See *United States Diplomatic and Consular Staff in Tehran (US* v. *Iran)* [1980] ICJ 3, 17. See also *Siderman de Blake* v. *Republic of Argentina*, 965 F.2d 699, 715 (9th Cir. 1992).

60 See, e.g., Weisburd, "The Effect of Treaties and other Formal International Acts on the Customary Law of Human Rights", (1995/96) 25 *Ga. J. Int'l & Comp. L.* 99, 115–16.

many of which expressly allow trade restrictions,[61] none of the major human rights treaties expressly authorises the imposition of unilateral trade restrictions to advance their goals. Nevertheless, many human rights treaties affirmatively obligate states to promote compliance with human rights. The UN Charter obligates member states "to take joint and separate action in cooperation with the Organisation for the achievement of [human rights and fundamental freedoms]",[62] though it is uncertain whether unilateral trade measures to promote human rights would be considered actions "in cooperation with the Organisation". Clearer support for unilateral measures can be found in the 1957 Slavery Convention, which broadly obligates states parties "to take all practicable and necessary legislative and other measures to bring about . . . the complete abolition" of forced labour and all other slave-like practices,[63] and the Apartheid Convention, which requires states "to adopt any legislative or other measures necessary to suppress as well as to prevent any encouragement of the crime of apartheid", without jurisdictional limitation.[64] The imposition of trade measures easily would fall within the broad mandates of these conventions.

Other treaty-mandated enforcement measures are limited to persons within the country's territorial jurisdiction, and thus provide little independent support for trade remedies targeting practices abroad. Article 2 of the ICCPR, for example, requires states parties to provide effective domestic remedies for all individuals within their territory.[65] The ILO Forced Labour Convention requires state parties "to suppress the use of forced or compulsory labour in all its forms"[66] in territories subject to their sovereignty.[67] Other international

[61] The Montreal Protocol on Substances that Deplete the Ozone Layer bans trade in chlorofluorocarbons with non-parties to the Protocol: United Nations, Protocol on Substances that Deplete the Ozone Layer, 16 September 1987, (1987) 26 *ILM* 1541 Art. 4. The Basel Convention on the Control of Transboundary Movements of Hazardous Wastes prohibits most trade in hazardous waste materials with non-party states. United Nations Environment Programme Conference of Plenipotentiaries on the Global Convention on the Control of Transboundary Movements of Hazardous Wastes: Final Act and Text of Basel Convention, 22 March 1989, (1989) 28 *ILM* 649, Art. 4, ¶ 5. The Endangered Species Convention also prohibits or allows the regulation of trade respecting a wide range of endangered species: Convention on International Trade in Endangered Species of Wild Fauna and Flora (CITES), 3 March 1973, (1976) 27 *UST* 1087, preamble, Art. III, ¶ 3(a)–(c); Art. IV, ¶ 2(a).

[62] UN Charter, Art. 56.

[63] 1957 Supplementary Slavery Convention, Art.1.

[64] International Convention on the Suppression and Punishment of the Crime of Apartheid, adopted 30 November 1973, Arts. IV and V, 1015 *UNTS* 243, 246.

[65] See ICCPR, Art. 2.

[66] See ILO Convention Concerning Forced Labour (No. 29), adopted 28 June 1930, 39 *UNTS* 55, Art. 1(1) (hereinafter 1930 Forced Labour Convention). Accord ILO Convention Concerning the Abolition of Forced Labour (No. 105), adopted 25 June 1957, 320 *UNTS* 291, Art. 2 (undertaking "to take effective measures to secure the immediate and complete abolition of forced or compulsory labour") (hereinafter 1957 Forced Labour Convention).

[67] 1930 Forced Labour Convention, Art. 26.

instruments, such as the Genocide,[68] Torture,[69] and 1949 Geneva Conventions,[70] obligate states to enforce human rights norms by imposing criminal responsibility on individuals.[71] Of these, only the Genocide Convention expressly recognises remedies against other states.[72]

In sum, the international legal system carves out a protected place for human rights norms, giving *jus cogens* and *erga omnes* obligations an elevated status under international law, and obligating all states to respect these values. Unlike ordinary customary international law principles, at least the core *jus cogens* norms of the human rights regime cannot be overridden by treaty; states cannot persistently object or enter reservations to their obligations, and principles such as territorial jurisdiction and foreign sovereign immunity, which ordinarily protect state practices from scrutiny by other states, may not apply. Under customary international law, states clearly are authorised to adopt trade sanctions to promote human rights values. On the other hand, neither the human rights treaties nor customary international law clearly establishes a right of states to impose human rights trade measures that cannot be overridden by treaty.

This absence of clear treaty-based authorisation for human rights trade measures presents some interpretive difficulties for reconciling the human rights regime with GATT. GATT could be interpreted as simply overriding international human rights law without creating a direct conflict between GATT and any human rights treaty provisions.[73] On the other hand, certain forms of trade clearly would be inconsistent with both the human rights treaties and *jus cogens* norms. The prohibitions against genocide and torture, for example, bar acts that aid and abet the commission of these crimes.[74] A trade agreement that promised to provide a state with military technology for the purpose of committing genocide would violate this norm. *Jus cogens* principles accordingly bar GATT from requiring trade in some human rights

[68] The Genocide Convention obligates member states "to prevent and to punish" genocide, and "to provide effective penalties" for genocidal acts committed on their soil. See Genocide Convention, Arts. I, V.

[69] The Torture Convention requires a state party to "take effective [legal] measures to prevent acts of torture in any territory under its jurisdiction". See Torture Convention, Art. 2(1).

[70] Geneva Convention, Art. 146; Protocol Additional to the Geneva Conventions of 12 August 1949, and Relating to the Protection of Victims of International Armed Conflicts, 8 June 1977, 1125 *UNTS* 3.

[71] For further discussion of individual accountability under international law, see Ratner and Abrams, *supra* n. 57; Ratner, *supra* n. 37.

[72] Genocide Convention, Art. IX (authorising submission of disputes over state responsibility for genocide to the ICJ).

[73] Vienna Convention, Art. 30(3) ("When all the parties to the earlier treaty are parties also to the later treaty . . . the earlier treaty applies only to the extent that its provisions are compatible with those of the later treaty").

[74] The Genocide Convention obligates states to prevent and punish genocide in all its forms, including conspiracy, public incitement, complicity, or attempts to commit genocide. See Genocide Convention, Art. III. The Torture Convention obligates states to criminalise both torture and attempts and conspiracies to commit torture on their soil. See Torture Convention, Art. 4.

circumstances. For the bulk of human rights sanctions, however, treaties and *jus cogens* principles provide no clear trump card, and identifying the correct balance between the global trade and human rights systems requires a more searching inquiry into the goals and values of each regime. The following two sections address how sanctions have been used by the USA to promote human rights compliance abroad, and the consistency of those measures with the GATT trade system.

III. US TRADE SANCTIONS AND PRACTICE

Human rights sanctions are employed by countries for a variety of purposes. They may be used to punish a foreign state's human rights practices, to deprive a rogue state of needed goods or foreign currency, to express the international community's outrage at human rights atrocities, to prevent a state's own markets from contributing to human rights violations, to morally distance a state from human rights violators, and to generate pressure for the adoption of multilateral action.

To facilitate analysis of the wide range of trade measures employed for human rights pruposes, I will argue that these measures may be viewed as falling into three categories: *tailored*, *semi-tailored*, and *general* sanctions. These categories span a continuum according to the degree of nexus between the trade measure employed and the human rights violation. *Tailored* sanctions maintain the closest relationship between the sanctioned good and the violation; *general* sanctions have the least close. The USA maintains sanctions of all three types, and all three forms of sanctions raise different concerns for the international trading system.

Tailored sanctions

Tailored sanctions target human rights violations that arise either from the *production* or *use* of the sanctioned goods. Such measures seek to prevent a state's domestic market from contributing to human rights violations abroad by barring trade in goods that are directly linked to human rights abuse.

Production, or *process-based*, tailored sanctions create a direct link between access to a state's domestic markets and respect for human rights in product manufacture. Bans on goods produced through the use of exploitative child labour or by a country that practices systematic racial discrimination in employment, for example, would constitute tailored sanctions based on human rights violations that occurred in production.

The most notable process-based US measure is section 307 of the US Tariff Act, which bars the importation of goods produced with convict, forced, or indentured labour, including "forced or indentured child labour".[75] During the 1990s, section 307 was invoked to exclude the importation of certain Mexican and Chinese products.[76] Government procurement laws, which condition government purchases of goods and services, also may take the form of tailored sanctions. In 1999, for example, President Clinton issued a selective purchasing order prohibiting federal agencies from purchasing any products made with forced or indentured child labour.[77]

The second type of tailored sanctions, *use-based* sanctions, bar exports of particular goods that may be used to commit human rights violations abroad. These typically limit the sale of military technology to repressive regimes. As with process-based measures, these provisions are motivated by a perceived direct linkage between the sanctioned product and a particular human rights violation. The measures seek to prevent domestic markets from contributing to foreign human rights atrocities by withholding the means through which violations are committed. And, although weapons restrictions are the most common form of use-based sanction, such measures are not limited to military technology. A hypothetical ban on exports to the USA of chemicals used for lethal injection, on the grounds that US capital punishment practices violate the customary international law prohibition against the execution of juveniles, would constitute a use-based, tailored sanction. Such a restriction would be much more closely linked to the human rights value at stake than would, for example, a ban on wine exports imposed for the same reason.

US law imposes a range of use-based restrictions. The Arms Export Control Act establishes an elaborate licensing scheme for the export of US weapons by private US manufacturers, and also requires US approval for the resale of certain US military technology by foreign states.[78] The Act has been used to bar weapons exports to Angola for human rights concerns. US export licensing requirements also have been used to bar the export of thumb cuffs to non-NATO countries. In 1996, Congress passed the Leahy Amendment, which prohibited US foreign assistance to foreign security units—including the sale of military technology—"if the Secretary of State has credible evidence to believe such unit has committed gross violations

[75] 19 U.S.C. § 1307 (1994), amended by Trade and Development Act of 2000, Pub. L. No. 106–200, § 411, 114 Stat. 251 (2000). See also 19 C.F.R. § 12.42–.45 (1993). The provision has been in force since 1930.

[76] 19 C.F.R. § 12.42(h) (2000). Pursuant to the China-United States Memorandum of Understanding on Prohibiting Import and Export Trade in Prison Labor Products, (1992) 31 *ILM* 1071, the USA barred specified leather imports from China following a determination by the US Customs service that goods produced at the Qinghai Hide and Garment Factory were produced with convict labour: 58 Fed. Reg. 32,746 (1993). In April 1996, the Customs Service again acted under § 307 to bar importation of certain iron pipe fittings from the Tianjin Malleable Iron Factory in China, based on a determination that the goods were being produced with prison labour: 61 Fed. Reg. 17,956 (1996).

[77] Exec. Order No. 13,126, 64 Fed. Reg. 32,383 (1999). The order prohibits a narrower range of child labour practices than those barred by the ILO Convention on the Worst Forms of Child Labour, and exempts goods from countries that are NAFTA members or parties to the WTO Agreement on Government Procurement.

[78] Arms Export Control Act, 22 U.S.C. § 2751 et seq. (1994).

of human rights".[79] The law was designed to direct trade sanctions precisely toward governmental units engaging in human rights abuse, while allowing trade and foreign assistance to other governmental departments. In 1998, the State Department acted under the Leahy Amendment to block government assistance for the sale of US attack helicopters to Turkey unless Turkey's human rights record significantly improved.[80] In the spring of 2000, Congress considered refusing to allow the sale of attack helicopters to the Columbian army due to its record of human rights atrocities, but ultimately approved the sale.[81]

Process- and use-based tailored sanctions are useful for targeting labour rights violations that occur in the production of goods made for export, and for banning sales of goods used directly to commit human rights atrocities. They are not useful for targeting labour rights violations that occur either in the production of goods for domestic consumption, or in non-trade sectors, such as the Burmese military's use of forced labour for government infrastructure projects. Tailored sanctions also cannot target other human rights violations that are not directly trade-related, such as torture, genocide, or the overthrow of democracy. And from a policy perspective, tailored sanctions may not be the most effective means for redressing even labour violations that occur in production. Bans on imports of goods made with child labour, for example, may simply divert child employment into more exploitative forums, such as the sex trades.[82] In some contexts, semi-tailored or general sanctions may be more appropriate for addressing these concerns.

Semi-tailored sanctions

Semi-tailored sanctions retain a nexus between the restricted goods or services and the targeted human rights violation, but are less directly linked than tailored measures. Semi-tailored sanctions commonly seek to deprive a government or entity committing human rights abuse of a critical source of capital, or to punish states for human rights violations by withholding goods that directly impact the government itself, rather than the general economy. Because revenues from diamond sales sustain the rebel movements in Angola and Sierra Leone, for example, bans on diamond imports from those states retain a link with the goal of preventing the rebels' human rights atrocities. Because the Burmese government supplies its military substantially with revenues from foreign petroleum sales, a ban on oil

[79] Pub. L. No. 104-208, 110 Stat. 3009-133 (1996). A 1998 amendment extended the law to apply to all Defense Department military training activities. Amendment No. 3406, S94621 (July 30, 1998).

[80] Priest, "New Human Rights Law Triggers Policy Debate", *Washington Post*, 31 December 1998, A34.

[81] Congress approved the aid package to Columbia conditioned on the Columbian military's compliance with certain human rights requirements. President Clinton, however, waived the human rights conditions in authorising the aid's release.

[82] See Cleveland, "Global Labor Rights and the Alien Tort Claims Act", (1998) 76 *Tex. L. Rev.* 1533, 1557–8.

purchases from Burma would constitute a semi-tailored sanction. (Sanctions may also have multiple functions. An embargo on Burmese oil could constitute a tailored sanction to the extent that the sanction was imposed in response to Burma's use of forced labour in the construction of the Yadana pipeline).

Most recent US examples of semi-tailored sanctions relate to weapons sales. In May 1994, President Clinton banned weapons and munitions imports from China in response to China's failure to make adequate progress on a bilateral agreement regarding human rights issues.[83] The sanction may be considered semi-tailored because it did not directly reduce China's ability to suppress human rights (the way a ban on exports of military goods to China might), but did target government products and reduce government revenues in retaliation for the government's human rights abuses. In November 1994, in response to Nigeria's hanging of nine environmental activists, the USA expanded existing sanctions against Nigeria to ban exports of military goods.[84]

Section 301(b) of the 1974 Trade Act may be used to impose either tailored or semi-tailored sanctions. The Act allows the President to withhold or deny trade preferences to US trading partners that engage in "unreasonable" or unfair trade practices, including a "persistent pattern of conduct" of violating internationally recognised worker rights.[85] This provision may be viewed as semi-tailored because the Act does not expressly require that a retaliatory sanction target the specific product being made through non-compliant labour practices. It does require that the labour violations be reasonably linked to trade with the USA, since retaliation is warranted only if the "unreasonable" conduct burdens or restricts US commerce. Thus, section 301 could not properly be used to impose retaliatory trade sanctions on a country which violated international labour standards in a sector that did not impact US trade. To date, however, section 301 has never been applied to promote labour rights abroad.[86]

The most controversial recent semi-tailored US measure is the 1996 "Helms-Burton" Act[87] which was advocated by its sponsors to both vindicate the human rights of US nationals whose property was expropriated by the Castro regime, and to promote human rights and democracy in Cuba.[88] The Act

[83] 22 C.F.R. § 126.1 (1994); 27 C.F.R. § 47.52 (1994).

[84] 60 Fed. Reg. 66,334 (1995). The sale of defence goods to Nigeria was generally prohibited in June 1993, 58 Fed. Reg. 40,845 (1993).

[85] Omnibus Trade and Competitiveness Act of 1988, 19 U.S.C. §§ 2411 (b), 2411 (d)(3)(B)(iii) (2000). The Statute defines internationally recognised worker rights as those set forth in the GSP: 19 U.S.C. § 2467 (4) (2000). See Hansen, "Note, Defining Unreasonableness in International Trade: Section 301 of the Trade Act of 1974", (1987) 96 *Yale L. J.* 1122.

[86] See Sykes, "Constructive Unilateral Threats in International Commercial Relations: The Limited Case for Section 301", (1992) 23 *L. & Pol. Int'l Bus.* 263.

[87] The Cuban Liberty and Democratic Solidarity (LIBERTAD) Act of 1996, Pub. L. No. 104-114, 110 Stat. 785 (1996), 22 U.S.C. §§ 6021 *et seq.* (Supp. III 1997).

[88] In support of the Act, Congress found that "[t]he United States has shown a deep commitment, and considers it a moral obligation, to promote and protect human rights" *ibid.* § 2(9). The Act provides that the sanctions in place as of 1 March 1996, "shall remain in effect" until the President finds that Cuba has become a "democratically elected government" *ibid.* §§ 102, 204.

codified and extended existing US trade and foreign assistance sanctions against Cuba, and purported to create remedies for Cuban expropriations. Title III accordingly authorises US nationals whose property was expropriated by the Cuban government to sue individuals who "traffic" in such property, including engaging in various forms of trade with Cuba.[89] Title IV of the Act denies US entry visas to any foreign national who has trafficked in such confiscated property. The Act thus employs non-trade measures to try to compel the international community to cooperate with the US trade embargo against Cuba.

The provisions of Title III and IV are not trade sanctions, per se, and it therefore is unclear whether they fall within the prohibitions of GATT. However, the Act's secondary boycott reach to third party states and companies provoked substantial international outcry. In response to Helms-Burton, Canada, Mexico, and the EU adopted retaliatory legislation,[90] Canada and Mexico pursued dispute resolution mechanisms under NAFTA,[91] and the European Community[92] formally initiated dispute resolution proceedings in the WTO.[93] The OAS Inter-American Juridical Committee also unanimously condemned Helms-Burton as an international law violation.[94] In response to the international opposition, President Clinton has continuously barred the Title III private right of action provision from taking effect, although the Title IV visa provisions remain operative.[95] Interestingly, the Helms-Burton dispute, which emerged soon after the creation of the WTO, raised concerns about the political limits of the WTO's authority. Some observers feared that a ruling against the USA would simply be ignored, given the strength of the USA's political commitment to the Cuban embargo, and thus would undermine the authority of the

[89] *Ibid.* § 4(13).

[90] Canada, Mexico and the EU adopted "blocking" and "clawback" legislation, barring their companies from complying with Helms-Burton, prohibiting the enforcement of judgments entered under the Act, and authorising companies to countersue for any damages resulting from the US sanctions measure. See Act to Protect Trade and Investment from Foreign Norms that Contravene International Law, 23 October 1996, (1997) 36 *ILM* 133 (Mexico); Foreign Extraterritorial Measures Act Incorporating the Amendments Countering the U.S. Helms-Burton Act, 9 October 1996, (1997) 36 *ILM* 111 (Canada); Council Regulation 2271/96 of 22 November 1996 Protecting against the effects of the extra-territorial application of legislation adopted by a third country, and actions based thereon or resulting therefrom, OJ 1996 L309. The EU measure also applied to the Cuban Democracy Act of 1992, 22 U.S.C. § 6001–6010 (1994). Council Regulation 2271/96, OJ 1996 L309, Annex, at 5–6.

[91] Oyer, "The Extraterritorial Effects of U.S. Unilateral Trade Sanctions and their Impact on U.S. Obligations under NAFTA" (1997) 11 *Fla. J. Int'l L.* 429, 456.

[92] The EC is the official World Trade Organisation member for its represented European states.

[93] *United States—The Cuban Liberty and Democracy Solidarity Act*, WTO Doc. WT/DS38/2 (1996).

[94] See Opinion of the Inter-American Juridical Committee on Resolution AG/DOC.3375/96, "Freedom of Trade and Investment in the Hemisphere", (1996) 35 *ILM* 1329, 1334 ("the exercise of jurisdiction by a State over acts of 'trafficking' by aliens abroad, under circumstances whereby neither the alien nor the conduct in question has any connection with its territory and there is no apparent connection between such acts and the protection of its essential sovereign interests, does not conform with international law").

[95] See Sanger, "Clinton Grants, Then Suspends, Right to Sue Foreigners on Cuba", *New York Times*, 17 July 1996, A1.

newly created trade organisation. A crisis of authority in the WTO may have been averted when the EU suspended its WTO challenge in exchange for US assurances that it would withhold enforcement of the Helms-Burton provisions and avoid extraterritorial sanctions measures in the future.[96]

General sanctions

General sanctions, which are the most common form of human rights trade measures, have no direct link between the targeted product or service and the human rights violation. Indeed, they often address human rights violations that have no direct connection to trade or the international economy. The overthrow of democracy in Haiti, the genocides in Rwanda, Kosovo, and Uganda, the use of forced labour in government infrastructure projects in Burma, the violation of due process in criminal proceedings in China—all of these constitute egregious human rights violations that have no direct relationship to international trade. Trade measures accordingly cannot be used directly to target the human rights conduct. General sanctions instead often target products that are most likely to have an economic impact on the sanctioned state. Or they may target goods that are least likely to hurt the economy of the sanctioning state. A US embargo against sugar imports from a major sugar exporting country would fulfil both of these considerations, since it would target a major export sector of the sanctioned state, and the USA could readily substitute sugar imports from other sugar producers. General sanctions may also, of course, be imposed as disguised protectionist measures, and thus raise particular concerns for the international trade system.

The USA has employed a number of general sanctions for human rights purposes. Import preference systems, the trade embargos against Uganda and Cuba, and the ban on agricultural sales to the Soviet Union following the invasion of Afghanistan all fall into the category of general sanctions.

Import preferences

Two longstanding US regimes—the Most Favoured Nation (MFN) system and the Generalised System of Preferences (GSP)—link import preferences to human or labour rights concerns. These measures technically do not constitute trade restrictions or "sanctions" for purposes of GATT, since GATT requires states

[96] In a meeting between the USA and the EU on 18 May 1998, the parties agreed that in the future they "will not seek or propose, and will resist, the passage of new economic sanctions legislation based on foreign policy grounds which is designed to make economic operators of the other behave in a manner similar to that required of its own economic operators": *Transatlantic Partnership on Political Co-operation* (London, 1998), ¶ 2(h).1 (unofficial text), cited in Smis and Van der Borght, "The E.U.-U.S. Compromise on the Helms-Burton and D'Amato Acts", (1999) 93 *Am. J. Int'l L.* 227, 231–2.

to bestow preferential MFN treatment on all other WTO members, and GSP tariff preferences to developing countries are authorised by GATT.[97] Nevertheless, when conditioned on human rights compliance, such measures have the same effect as sanctions on the receiving country, since they deprive countries engaging in human rights violations of trading privileges that are enjoyed by other trade partners.

(a) *Most favoured nation benefits.* The MFN system,[98] which was recently redesignated as "normal trade relations",[99] bestows "non-discriminatory" trade benefits on communist countries with acceptable human rights records. Notable historic uses of MFN sanctions for human rights purposes include President Reagan's withdrawal of MFN status from Poland in 1982 following the suppression of the Solidarity labour union movement.[100] Romania's MFN status was jeopardised in the 1980s due to its human rights practices, and Romania withdrew from the MFN system in 1988 as a result of its unwillingness to comply with US human rights demands.[101] Concern over the use of convict labour in China played a prominent role in the 1992 debates regarding China's MFN status, and the USA and China reached an agreement regarding the use of prison labour in 1992 which conditioned MFN renewal in part on China's improved compliance.[102] President Clinton granted only conditional MFN treatment to China in 1993, due in part to continued concern over China's suppression of the 1989 democracy demonstrations in Tiananmen Square, and in part to China's ongoing human rights record.[103] The Clinton administration subsequently decided to de-link trade with China from human rights concerns, although Congress continued its annual review of China's human rights practices under the MFN statute until China was granted permanent normal trade status in the spring of 2000.[104] The end of the Cold War has resulted in the extension of MFN benefits to most former Communist

[97] See discussion *infra* Part IV, p. 229.

[98] The Jackson-Vanik Amendment of the Trade Act of 1974, 19 U.S.C. § 2432 (1994), withholds "most-favoured-nation" (MFN) trade benefits from Communist governments which deny their citizens the freedom to emigrate, in order "to assure the continued dedication of the United States to fundamental human rights", *ibid* § 2432(a).

[99] Pub. L. No. 105–206, § 5003(b)(2), 112 Stat. 685, 789 (1998).

[100] 47 Fed. Reg. 49,005 (1982) (providing that the Polish Government "has taken steps further to increase its repression of the Polish people by outlawing the independent trade union Solidarity, leaving the United States without any reason to continue withholding action on its trade complaints against Poland"). Poland's MFN status was restored in 1987: 52 Fed. Reg. 5425 (1987).

[101] Romania's MFN status was renewed in 1993 and GSP status was granted in 1994: 58 Fed. Reg. 60,226 (1993); 59 Fed. Reg. 8115 (1994).

[102] Jackson, *Legal Problems of International Economic Relations*, 3rd edn., (St. Paul, 1995), p. 1008.

[103] See 58 Fed. Reg. 31,327 (1993). The MFN conditions included the granting of exit visas, compliance with the USA-China agreement on prison labour, progress in complying with the Universal Declaration of Human Rights, release of political prisoners, humane treatment of prisoners, protection for Tibetan religion and culture, and allowing international radio and television broadcasts into China.

[104] People's Republic of China—Trade Relations, Pub. L. No. 106-286, 114 Stat. 880 (2000).

countries, though the USA continues to withhold normal trade relations from Afghanistan, Cuba, Laos, North Korea, Vietnam, and Yugoslavia (Serbia and Montenegro).[105]

(b) *The Generalised System of Preferences (GSP).* In the past fifteen years, a number of US statutes have conditioned import preferences for less developed countries on compliance with "internationally recognised worker rights". These programmes include the GSP regime,[106] and specialised regimes for the countries of the Caribbean Basin,[107] and the Andean Region.[108] The GSP system has been the primary US trade measure utilised to promote labour rights. In the past twelve years, a wide range of countries have been removed or suspended from GSP treatment as a result of substandard labour practices.[109] The USA also continues to adopt such measures. The Trade and Development Act of 2000 conditioned import benefits for Sub-Saharan Africa on compliance with internationally-recognised human and worker rights.[110]

National security measures

Two major statutes—the International Emergency Economic Powers Act (IEEPA)[111] and the Export Administration Act of 1979 (EAA)[112]—have given

[105] See Harmonized Tariff Schedule for the United States (2000)—Supplement 1, General Note 3(b), available at <www.customs.gov/impoexpo/impoexpo.htm> (visited 15 October 2000).

[106] The GSP provides trade benefits to less developed countries by exempting certain products from US import tariffs. Since 1984, the GSP statute has required the President to condition GSP trading privileges to developing countries on consideration whether the country "has taken or is taking steps to afford workers in that country . . . internationally recognized worker rights": 19 U.S.C. § 2462 (c)(7) (2000).

[107] Caribbean Basin Economic Recovery Act, 19 U.S.C. § 2702(c)(8) (1994) (also known as the Caribbean Basin Initiative or CBI). CBI is a regional trade agreement that seeks to promote regional stability and economic development by allowing duty-free imports from 27 Caribbean nations. The Act originally required consideration of whether workers have "reasonable workplace conditions and enjoy the right to organise and bargain collectively" in granting duty free status, and thus was less specific than the GSP and section 301 labour protections. The programme was amended in 2000 to condition benefits on compliance with the GSP worker rights and elimination of the worst forms of child labour: 19 U.S.C. § 2703(b)(5)(B)(iii) and (iv) (2000).

[108] The Andean Trade Preference Act applies the GSP labour rights provisions to Bolivia, Columbia, Ecuador, and Peru: 19 U.S.C. §§ 3202(c)(7), (d)(8) (2000).

[109] Romania (removed 1987, restored 1994); Nicaragua (removed 1987); Paraguay (suspended 1987, restored 1991); Chile (suspended 1987, restored 1991); Burma (suspended 1989); the Central African Republic (suspended 1989, restored 1991); Liberia (suspended 1990); Yugoslavia (suspended 1991); Sudan (suspended 1991); Syria (suspended 1992); Mauritania (suspended 1993); the Maldives (suspended 1995); Pakistan (partially suspended 1996). Pre–1993 sanctions remain in effect against North Korea for labour rights violations. In 1993, the USA also placed El Salvador, Guatemala, Indonesia, Thailand, Malawi, and Oman on "six-month continuing review status" to determine whether the countries made "substantial concrete progress" toward addressing worker rights.

[110] Trade and Development Act of 2000, Pub. L. No. 106–200, 114 Stat. 251 (2000).

[111] 50 U.S.C. §§ 1701 *et seq.* (1994). If the President determines that "any unusual and extraordinary threat [exists], which has its source in whole or substantial part outside the United States, to the [U.S.] national security, foreign policy, or economy", the President may declare a national emergency under the National Emergencies Act, 50 U.S.C. §§ 1601, *et seq.* (1994).

[112] 50 U.S.C.A. App. §§ 2401–2420 (1994).

the President broad powers to impose trade restrictions for foreign policy and national security reasons. IEEPA was intended to be more restrictive than its predecessor statute, the Trading with the Enemy Act (TWEA), under which Cold War economic sanctions were imposed against countries such as Cambodia, Vietnam, North Korea, and Cuba.

IEEPA generally is invoked to address broad national security or international relations concerns, such as the 1979 Iranian hostage crisis, which provoked President Carter's imposition of sweeping sanctions against Iran.[113] The statute also has been used to address human rights concerns. President Reagan employed IEEPA to impose sanctions on South Africa during the 1980s,[114] and in 1990, the USA imposed trade and other sanctions on Iraq, motivated in part by Iraqi human rights violations in the Persian Gulf region.[115] The statute also has been invoked to impose sanctions on Panama, Haiti, the Angolan rebel force UNITA, Burma, Sudan, Serbia and Montenegro, and the Federal Republic of Yugoslavia.[116] In the spring of 2000, President Clinton lifted certain import restrictions on luxury goods from Iran, in an effort to reward Iran for the recent election of a reform government and to encourage future democratic reforms.[117]

IEEPA measures traditionally have been adopted in conjunction with sanctions under the Export Administration Act,[118] which imposed licensing requirements on the export of certain commodities to designated countries.[119] Export restrictions were imposed on Iran during the Iranian hostage crisis, on agricultural exports to the Soviet Union following the invasion of Afghanistan, and on Poland after the government's declaration of martial law.[120] Existing export measures prohibit all exports to North Korea and Cuba.[121] Other general sanctions provisions prohibit the USA from reaching agricultural trade agreements with countries that engage in a consistent pattern of gross human rights violations.[122]

The USA increasingly has recognised human rights violations abroad as presenting national security concerns. In imposing sanctions against Burma in 1997, for example, President Clinton certified, for the purposes of the federal

[113] See *Dames & Moore* v. *Regan*, 453 U.S. 654 (1981). On IEEPA sanctions generally, see Marks and Grabow, "The President's Foreign Economic Powers After Dames & Moore v. Regan: Legislation by Acquiescence", (1982) 68 *Cornell L. Rev*. 68.

[114] In 1985, President Reagan imposed limited sanctions on South Africa by executive order under IEEPA, in an unsuccessful effort to avert broader sanctions legislation that was pending in Congress: Exec. Order No. 12,532, 50 Fed. Reg. 36,861 (1985); Exec. Order No. 12,535, 50 Fed. Reg. 40,325 (1985) (forbidding imports of South African krugerrands).

[115] Pub. L. 101–513, §§ 586–586J, 104 Stat. 2047 (1990), codified at 50 U.S.C. § 1701 note (1994).

[116] See notes following 50 U.S.C. § 1701 for executive orders under IEEPA.

[117] Stout, "U.S. to Drop Longtime Ban on Luxuries from Iran", *New York Times*, 15 March 2000, A8.

[118] 50 U.S.C. §§ 2404(a), 2405(a), 2406(a). The EAA authorised the President to restrict US exports for reasons of foreign policy, national security, or short supply.

[119] The EAA has lapsed since 1994, and the President currently sustains EAA restrictions through his authority under IEEPA: Executive Order No. 12,924, 59 Fed. Reg. 43,437 (1994).

[120] See generally, Moyer and Mabry, "Export Controls as Instruments of Foreign Policy: The History, Legal Issues and Policy Lessons of Three Recent Cases", (1983) 15 *Law & Pol. Int'l Bus*. 1.

[121] 15 C.F.R. § 785.1 (1994); 22 C.F.R. § 126.1 (2000).

[122] 7 U.S.C. § 1733(j)(1) (1994).

Burma law, that Burma had "committed large-scale repression of the democratic opposition in Burma" and found that the Burmese Government's actions constituted "an unusual and extraordinary threat to the national security and foreign policy of the United States".[123]

Country-specific measures

A number of general sanctions have been adopted to target human rights abuses in a specific country. In the 1980s, for example, Congress barred the importation of sugar and other sweeteners from Panama until the President certified that "freedom of the press and other constitutional guarantees, including due process of law, have been restored to the Panamanian people".[124] The longstanding US embargo against Cuba is probably the most notorious and heavily criticised country specific sanctions measure. Although the embargo was originally imposed as a national security measure in response to the 1959 Communist revolution in Cuba, in the 1990s the USA has attempted to give the embargo a human rights justification. The Cuban Democracy Act of 1992[125] extended the embargo to include the foreign subsidiaries of US companies and denied US portage rights to ships that had visited a Cuban port in the previous six months.[126] Like its successor, Helms-Burton, the Act conditioned relaxation of the sanctions on movement toward democratisation and respect for human rights.[127]

Sub-national measures

A number of US states also have adopted government procurement laws targeting human rights violations abroad. In the 1980s, nearly half of US states and eighty cities adopted anti-apartheid sanctions against South Africa,[128] and approximately thirty state and local governments presently maintain human-rights based sanctions against Burma, Indonesia, Nigeria, Cuba, and countries engaging in religious persecution.[129] The best known sub-national measure was

[123] Executive Order No. 13,047, 3 C.F.R. 202, § 1 (1997 Comp.).

[124] Pub. L. No. 100–202, § 562, 101 Stat. 1329–175 (1987); see also Pub. L. No. 101–167, § 562(a), 103 Stat. 1241 (1989) (both codified at 7 U.S.C. § 3602 note (1994)).

[125] Pub. L. No. 102–484, 106 Stat. 2575 (1992), codified at 22 U.S.C. §§ 6001–6010 (Supp. V 1993).

[126] *Ibid*. §§ 1706(a) and 1706(b)(1).

[127] *Ibid*. at §§ 1703(6) and (8).

[128] See, e.g., *Board of Trustees* v. *Mayor of Baltimore*, 562 A.2d 720 (Md. 1989) (upholding Baltimore, Maryland ordinance withdrawing the city's investments in South Africa). The anti-apartheid sanctions eventually were repealed with the transition to majority rule in South Africa. For the history of prior sub-national sanctions efforts, see Bilder, "East-West Trade Boycotts: A Study in Private, Labor Union, State, and Local Interference with Foreign Policy", (1970) 118 *U. Pa. L. Rev*. 841; Fenton, "State and Local Anti-Apartheid Laws: Misplaced Response to a Flawed National Policy on South Africa", (1987) 19 *N.Y.U. J. Int'l L. & Pol*. 883; Spiro, "Note: State and Local Anti-South Africa Action as an Intrusion upon the Federal Power in Foreign Affairs", (1986) 72 *Va. L. Rev*. 813.

[129] The Organisation for International Investment, a business group which lobbies against trade sanctions, maintains a website cataloguing current local selective purchasing measures. See Organisation for International Investment, *State and Municipal Sanctions Report*, <http://www.ofii.org/issues/sanction.asp> (visited 2 October 2000).

the controversial Massachusetts selective purchasing law against Burma, which prohibited state and local government agencies from entering procurement contracts with entities doing business with Burma.[130] As with the Helms-Burton statute, the allegedly secondary boycott character of the Massachusetts statute prompted significant international opposition. Europe, Japan, and Thailand condemned the sanctions as violating WTO rules on governmental procurement,[131] and the EC and Japan initiated WTO dispute settlement proceedings.[132] When discussions with the USA failed to resolve the issue, Japan and the EC requested a WTO dispute panel, which was established in October 1998 over US objections.[133] The WTO controversy was defused when the United States Supreme Court recently invalidated the Massachusetts law on domestic law grounds.[134] That decision does not bar state and local selective purchasing measures that are not preempted by federal statute, however, nor does it address the validity of any similar government procurement rules that might be adopted by the national government. The validity of human rights restrictions on government procurement under international trade rules therefore is likely to remain a live issue.

The above discussion demonstrates that tailored, semi-tailored, and general human rights sanctions differ in their degree of nexus between the product or service being sanctioned and the targeted human rights violation. However, many of these measures share three characteristics that distinguish them from most trade restrictions.

First, the measures are primarily *externally-focused*. Many forms of trade sanctions are inwardly-focused, in that they are designed to protect a state's domestic markets from unfair trade practices, such as dumping, or to protect its populace and territory from harmful external influences, such as environmentally hazardous products. This is particularly true of import restrictions,

[130] 1996 Mass. Acts 239, ch. 130 (codified at Mass. Gen. Laws Ann. ch. 7, § 22 H(a), J(a) (West 2000) (barring state agencies from procuring goods or services from persons "doing business with Burma (Myanmar)").

[131] WTO Agreement on Government Procurement, Art. IV (1) ("A Party shall not apply rules of origin to products or services imported or supplied for purposes of government procurement covered by this Agreement from other Parties, which are different from the rules of origin applied in the normal course of trade and at the time of the transaction in question to imports or supplies of the same product or services from the same Parties"), available at <http://www.wto.org/english/docs_e/legal_e/final_e.htm> (hereinafter GPA). See, e.g., "Massachusetts Law on Burma Riles EU", *Chicago Tribune*, 19 December 1997, A34; "A State's Foreign Policy: The Mass that Roared", *Economist*, 8 February 1997, p. 32; Crampton, "Thailand May Take US to WTO", *Asia Times*, 24 December 1996.

[132] See *United States—Measure Affecting Government Procurement; Request for Consultations by the European Communities*, WTO Doc. WT/DS88/1; GPA/D2/1, 26 June 1997; *United States—Measure Affecting Government Procurement; Request for Consultations by Japan*, WTO Doc. WT/DS95/1; GPA/D3/1, 21 July 1997; World Trade Org., *Overview of the State-of-Play of WTO Disputes*, <http://www.wto.org/wto/dispute/bulletin.htm> (last visited 8 August 2000).

[133] See McCrudden, "International Economic Law and the Pursuit of Human Rights: A Framework for Discussion of the Legality of 'Selective Purchasing' Laws under the WTO Government Procurement Agreement", (1999) *J. Int'l Econ. L.* 3, 24–5.

[134] *Crosby* v. *National Foreign Trade Council*, 530 U.S. 363 (2000).

although export restrictions may also be designed to protect internal markets by depriving foreign countries of scarce goods and technology. Human rights measures, on the other hand, are primarily externally directed. On their face, they primarily seek to condemn and alter the behaviour of a foreign entity or state. Human rights measures have an internal component, in that they seek to prevent a state's own market activities from contributing to human rights violations abroad. They also have been criticised as serving to protect a state's own domestic workers and markets.[135] But, aside from foreign concerns about disguised protectionism, their object is primarily external, targeting practices of international concern.

Secondly, many human rights sanctions target conduct that is *non-trade-related*. Only tailored sanctions retain a direct link between the sanctioned product and the human rights violation. Semi-tailored sanctions have a logical, though looser relationship between the trade measure and the violation. And general sanctions, such as the Ugandan embargo, often target fundamental human rights violations that are not directly related to any commercial activity. Like intellectual property rights,[136] some environmental concerns, and many of the other topics considered in this book, therefore, general human rights sanctions raise a fundamental question under GATT regarding the propriety of using trade measures to promote non-trade values.[137]

Finally, and as elaborated more fully in the following section, the *effectiveness* of human rights sanctions can be extremely difficult to demonstrate. Trade sanctions play very diffuse roles in articulating and enforcing human rights norms, punishing rogue behaviour, and creating pressure for multilateral responses to human rights atrocities. Obtaining overt changes in the foreign state's behaviour is only one purpose of sanctions, and it is extremely difficult—indeed, inappropriate—to try to demonstrate that human rights sanctions will be "effective" in that narrow sense. As with all forms of trade sanctions, human rights measures may simply isolate and entrench the foreign state, or force it to seek other economic allies and markets.

Even the certainty that the sanction will actually impact the targeted human rights practice diminishes as the relationship between the sanctioned good and the targeted conduct becomes less direct. Tailored sanctions may be sufficiently linked to the processes and uses of products that effectiveness may be less of a concern. A ban on weapons sales to a rogue state will prevent at least those weapons from contributing to human rights abuse, while a ban on goods made with exploitative child labour (absent difficulties in monitoring) is likely to

[135] This argument is raised most frequently with respect to measures promoting international labour rights. See Bilahari Kausikan, "Asia's Different Standard", *Foreign Policy*, 22 September 1993, at 24 (arguing that concerns about economic competitiveness drive the AFL-CIO's critique of labour conditions in Malaysia and elsewhere).

[136] See Spence, *infra* Chapter 10.

[137] Regional trade agreements, such as NAFTA, also restrict members' use of trade measures to promote non-commercial interests. See, e.g., Hansen, *infra* Chapter 12.

reduce the use of child labour in that product sector.[138] Semi-tailored and general sanctions are less certain to impact the targeted conduct, due to the more indirect relationship between the sanctioned product and the human rights violation. On the other hand, by targeting an economic sector important to the foreign state, they may be much more effective than tailored measures. And as noted above, many forms of human rights violations cannot be reached other than through general sanctions, since they have no direct relationship to any commercial sector. While it may be difficult to demonstrate that sanctions will be "effective" in the narrow sense of altering state behaviour, therefore, it is equally difficult to demonstrate that sanctions will be ineffective in any given circumstance.

All three of these considerations raise important questions regarding the compatibility of human rights sanctions with the international free trade system. The main tenets of that trading system, and their implications for the various forms of human rights sanctions, are considered in the following section.

IV. THE GATT/WTO SYSTEM

The GATT trade system advances the fundamental goal of eliminating unilateral trade barriers that undermine free trade, including disguised protectionism. This purpose finds principal expression in the non-discrimination provisions of Articles I and III GATT, and in Article XI, which prohibits non-tariff barriers to trade. Articles XX and XXI GATT, in turn, create exceptions to the GATT free trade requirements to address certain non-trade values, such as human life, public morals, prison labour, and national security. Thus, the first question to be considered in addressing the GATT-compatibility of human rights measures is whether the measures violate the trade provisions of GATT. If so, the inquiry then turns to whether the measures nevertheless fall within a recognised GATT exception. The WTO dispute bodies have not interpreted any of the GATT provisions in the human rights context.[139] Thus, the following examination of the likely scope of the GATT free trade principles and possible "human rights" exceptions analogises from WTO national security disputes under Article XXI and environmental disputes involving Article XX (b) and (g).

In analysing the GATT structure, it is important to keep in mind that GATT is not a "hermetically sealed system", but is to be interpreted consistently with other international law principles. Under the principles of interpretation established by the Vienna Convention on the Law of Treaties, interpretation

[138] Depending on the definition of effectiveness, even tailored, *process-based* sanctions such as child labour measures may yield unintended consequences, such as disruption of rural developing economies or the shifting of child labour to other, less easily targeted forms of employment. Betten: *International Labour Law* (Boston, 1993), p. 316. Nevertheless, tailored sanctions at least directly target the violative conduct.

[139] Neither the Art. XX public morals nor the prison labour provision has been interpreted by the WTO to date, and Art. XX(b) has not been interpreted with respect to human rights measures.

of GATT, like any other treaty, should take into account "any relevant rules of international law applicable in the relations between the parties",[140] and cannot override peremptory, *jus cogens* norms of the international system.[141] This interpretive rule would require interpreting GATT in light of both international jurisdictional principles, and substantive principles established by human rights treaties and customary international law regarding *jus cogens* and *erga omnes* human rights obligations. The WTO Dispute Settlement Understanding recognises this rule by stating that WTO provisions may be "clarif[ied] . . . in accordance with customary rules of interpretation of public international law".[142] Recent WTO decisions also have recognised the role of international law in GATT interpretation, at least in principle. In the first dispute decided by the WTO, the Appellate Body ruled that GATT "is not to be read in clinical isolation from public international law".[143] The GATT text further acknowledges some relationship between trade and promoting the quality of human life, both in the WTO Preamble's recognition that trade policy should be conducted with the goal of improved "standards of living",[144] and in Article XX's exceptions for human life, public morals, and prison labour. The question to be explored *infra* is to what extent these principles allow or require accommodation of human rights measures within the structure of the international trade system.

The GATT free trade provisions

Article XI GATT bars states from imposing non-tariff barriers to trade, such as import and export quotas, licensing restrictions, and embargos.[145] The Article seeks to promote transparency in the international trading system by reducing the likelihood that non-tariff regulatory measures will be used to create disguised barriers to trade. Article XI on its face invalidates most US human rights sanctions, since few sanctions employ tariffs to promote human rights abroad. Other than the GSP and MFN provisions, most US measures discussed in the previous section rely on non-tariff import and export barriers and licensing requirements.

[140] Vienna Convention, Art. 31(3)(c).

[141] *Ibid*. Art. 53.

[142] Understanding on Rules and Procedures Governing the Settlement of Disputes, 15 April 1994, Marrakesh Agreement Establishing the World Trade Organisation, Annex 2, (1994) 33 *ILM* 1226 Art. 3(2) (hereinafter DSU).

[143] WTO Appellate Body, *Report of the Appellate Body in United States—Standards for Reformulated and Conventional Gasoline Treatment of Imported Gasoline and Like Products of National Origin*, 20 May 1996, (1996) 35 *ILM* 603, 620 (hereinafter *Reformulated Gasoline*).

[144] Marrakesh Agreement Establishing the World Trade Organisation, (1994) 33 *ILM* 1144, preamble.

[145] "No prohibitions or restrictions other than duties, taxes, or other charges whether made effective through quotas, import or export licenses or other measures, shall be instituted or maintained by any contracting party on the importation of any product of the territory of any other contracting party or on the exportation or sale for export of any product destined for the territory of any other contracting party". Art. XI GATT, ¶ 1.

The Article I and III non-discrimination provisions impose most-favoured-nation[146] and national treatment[147] requirements on trade policy. These provisions respectively require parties to give equal market access to "like" products from all other GATT members, and bar discrimination between a party's own products and "like" products of another state.

As a purely textual matter, not all human rights sanctions obviously violate these anti-discrimination provisions. Tailored, process-based sanctions, such as bars on imports made with child labour, arguably do not discriminate between "like" products, since goods made with or without child labour can be distinguished based on objective criteria recognised by international law. However, the WTO has interpreted the reference to "like" products in the anti-discrimination provisions as requiring equal treatment for all products sharing the same physical characteristics, and as barring distinctions relating to the "process", or production methods, through which products are made.[148] For example, in the *Tuna/Dolphin I* decision, the Panel held that US requirements that tuna be harvested with dolphin-safe nets discriminated between "like" tuna products, since the harvesting methods "could not possibly affect tuna as a product".[149] Under this approach, differential treatment of shoes and paint would not discriminate between "like" products, but differential treatment of shoes made with, or without, child labour would constitute such discrimination. The WTO arbitrators view this distinction as necessary to prevent states from imposing arbitrary distinctions between similar goods as barriers to free trade.

The product/process distinction is relevant to some human rights sanctions because few, if any, human rights measures discriminate based on the physical characteristics of the product. (A ban on trade in human organs and the ban on the slave trade might constitute sanctions where the "product" itself raises human rights concerns, but such examples are rare.) Indeed, only tailored, process-based sanctions (such as a ban on imports made with forced labour)

[146] "[A]ny advantage, favour, privilege or immunity granted by any contracting party to any product originating in or destined for any other country shall be accorded immediately and unconditionally to the *like* product originating in or destined for the territories of all other contracting parties": Art. I GATT (emphasis added).

[147] "The products of the territory of any contracting party imported into the territory of any other contracting party shall be accorded treatment no less favourable than that accorded to *like* products of national origin in respect of all laws, regulations and requirements affecting their internal sale, offering for sale, purchase, transportation, distribution, or use". Art. III GATT, ¶ 2 (emphasis added).

[148] GATT dispute panels have defined "like" products as those which are directly competitive, based on the product's uses, consumer tastes, "and the product's properties, nature and quality": GATT Dispute Panel Report, *Japan—Customs Duties, Taxes and Labeling Practices on Imported Wines and Alcoholic Beverages*, 10 November 1987, GATT B.I.S.D. (34th Supp.) 83, 93 (1988).

[149] GATT Dispute Panel Report, United States—Restrictions on Imports of Tuna, ¶ 5.15 (3 September 1991), DS21/R–39S/155 available at 1991 WL 771248. The Panel decision was not adopted by the GATT Council.

even distinguish products based on production methods. Use-based tailored, semi-tailored, and general sanctions (such as a ban on trade with a genocidal state), for example, discriminate against the products of a state for reasons entirely unrelated to the product's particular characteristics or the manufacturing processes involved. Thus, although loosening the GATT's product/process distinction would eliminate GATT anti-discrimination concerns for tailored, process-based sanctions,[150] this change would impact only human rights violations occurring in export processing sectors. It would not affect non-export related labour rights or general human rights abuses that are unrelated to international trade.

As a result of the above requirements, practically all human rights trade measures will initially violate either the anti-discrimination requirements of Articles I and III and/or the Article XI prohibition against non-tariff barriers. Thus, the critical question for human rights provisions is whether they fall into one of several exceptions to GATT.

Import preferences: GSP and MFN

GATT requirements regarding import preferences such as the GSP and MFN systems are fairly straightforward. Article I GATT requires bestowal of "unconditional" most-favoured-nation treatment on all GATT members. Thus MFN import preferences are a legal entitlement held by GATT members that can be denied only for reasons set out in the GATT Agreement (or possibly as lawful reprisals for the *illegal* conduct of another GATT member). They cannot otherwise be conditioned on a member state's compliance with human or labour rights practices. As a result, the USA's withdrawal of MFN treatment from Poland in 1982 likely would have been found to violate GATT, had Poland objected to the action. Similarly, China's admission into the WTO will eliminate the USA's historic practice of conditioning MFN status on scrutiny of China's human rights compliance.

By contrast, GSP import preferences are allowed. GATT creates an exception for the bestowal of import preferences on developing countries, such as the GSP and similar tariff systems.[151] This authority is discretionary, providing that member states "may" bestow such benefits, and the GSP exception is controversial. Nevertheless, at present, member states may condition import prefer-

[150] Professor Francioni argues compellingly in this volume that the distinction between process and product may be neither as clear nor as meaningful as current WTO rulings suggest, and that restrictions targeting goods made through *processes* that violate human rights, such as through exploitative child labour, should not violate GATT: Francioni, *supra* Chapter 1.

[151] In 1971, the GATT members adopted a 10-year waiver that permitted (but did not require), GATT countries to give more preferential treatment to less-developed countries. In 1979 the members adopted a decision on differential and more favourable treatment for developing countries that eliminated the need for extension of the GSP exception. See Jackson, *supra* n. 102, pp. 1132–35.

ences to developing countries on human and labour rights compliance. The utility of GSP measures for promoting international human rights compliance, however, is limited. A growing number of states have graduated from GSP status, and countries that are not classified as "developing" for GSP purposes may also be human rights violators.

Article XXI: the national security exception

One possible location for human rights measures within the GATT structure is the Article XXI exception for certain measures "necessary for the protection of [a member's] essential security interests".[152] States have invoked this exception to justify a range of trade measures. In 1945, the USA invoked Article XXI to justify a range of export restrictions against Czechoslovakia.[153] In 1975, Sweden attempted to justify a bar on imported shoes on national security grounds, and in 1961, Ghana grounded trade restrictions against Portugal on Article XXI.[154] In 1985, President Reagan prohibited all trade with Nicaragua on grounds of national security.[155] The EU in 1991 invoked the exception to justify trade restrictions against the warring states of the former Yugoslavia,[156] and the USA recently invoked the national security exception as justification for the Helms-Burton Act.

The national security exception is a potentially attractive *locus* for human rights sanctions for a number of reasons. Measures adopted for national security purposes are not subject to the necessity, proportionality, and other requirements imposed on measures adopted under Article XX (see discussion *infra*). Furthermore, the language of Article XXI suggests that national determinations regarding security interests will be entitled to greater deference than the WTO has given to state measures under Article XX.

Article XXI(b) imposes two requirements on measures falling within its purview. First, the measure must be one which "it [the sanctioning state]

[152] Art. XXI GATT, entitled "Security Exceptions", provides in relevant part that: "Nothing in this Agreement shall be construed . . . (b) to prevent any contracting party from taking any action which it considers necessary for the protection of its essential security interests (i) relating to fissionable materials . . . ; (ii) relating to the traffic in arms, ammunition and the implements of war and to such traffic in other goods and materials as is carried on directly or indirectly for the purpose of supplying a military establishment; (iii) taken in time of war or other emergency in international relations".

[153] See Schloemann and Ohlhoff, "'Constitutionalization' and Dispute Settlement in the WTO: National Security as an Issue of Competence", (1999) 93 *Am. J. Int'l L.* 424, 432; see also Decision of June 8, 1949, GATT B.I.S.D. 28 (1952).

[154] See Whitt, "The Politics of Procedure: An Examination of the GATT Dispute Settlement Panel and the Article XXI Defense in the Context of the U.S. Embargo of Nicaragua", (1987) 19 *Law & Pol'y Int'l Bus.* 603, 618–19.

[155] Exec. Order No. 12,513, 50 Fed. Reg. 18,629 (1985) (finding that the Government of Nicaragua posed an "unusual and extraordinary threat to the national security and foreign policy of the United States and declar[ing] a national emergency to deal with the threat").

[156] Schloemann and Ohlhoff, *supra* n. 153, p. 436.

considers necessary for the protection of its essential security interests".[157] Secondly, the "action" or measure taken must "relat[e] to" either (i) nuclear materials, (ii) military technology, or (iii) be taken in time of war or other international emergency. The first prong of this test appears to bestow broad discretion on a member state to determine what "it considers necessary" to protect "its essential security interests". Unlike the Article XX necessity requirement, this language appears to leave both the determination of what is "necessary" to protect essential security interests and the definition of those interests to individual states, not to the WTO. This prong may allow for some WTO review of the *sincerity* of a state's national security claim. But it appears to preclude the WTO from second-guessing a country's substantive determination of its own essential security concerns.

The second prong of the Article XXI requirement provides greater basis for WTO oversight. The Article on its face limits the "actions" which fall within the exception to trade in fissionable materials and military technology, and measures taken in time of war or international emergency. The WTO obviously is entitled to determine whether a state's measures "relate to" these specific categories. Otherwise, states would be free to designate almost any measure as necessary to their own essential security interests.

Determining compliance with Article XX(b)(i) and (ii) should be fairly straightforward. With a few exceptions for products that may have both military and non-military uses, the question of what relates to fissionable materials and military technology appears relatively clear. The difficult interpretive question is presented by the (b)(iii) provision for measures taken in time of war or international emergency. This is the provision upon which most states invoking Article XXI have relied. The concept of "war", while elusive on occasion, is familiar to international law, and both domestic and international courts have routinely applied it. The term nevertheless presents some interpretive difficulties. Does the provision require that the state imposing sanctions be a party to the war, or can sanctions be imposed against warring states nearby that are destabilising the region and threatening the sanctioning state's security interests (as the USA alleged in the *Nicaragua* case)? If the state must be a party to the war, does covert military activity such as that which the USA pursued in Central America in the 1980s constitute a 'war' authorising the imposition of trade restrictions?

The definition of "international emergency" is even more elusive. International emergency is not an international law term of art, and neither the GATT negotiating history nor GATT/WTO decisions provide substantial guidance on its meaning. What constitutes an international emergency? Must the emergency directly threaten the territory or populace of the sanctioning state? Is the concept limited, for example, to circumstances that would justify resort to the use of force in self-defence under Article 51 of the UN Charter? Or are

[157] Art. XXI(b) GATT.

sanctions warranted when a situation such as Rwanda poses a fundamental threat to the international community without directly threatening the security interests of many distant states? The text of Article XXI suggests that an international emergency includes circumstances that fall short of both war and threats to international peace and security within the meaning of the UN Charter, since Article XXI(c) creates a separate exception for trade measures adopted pursuant to Security Council authorisation. But the concept of international emergency also likely is intended to be narrower than the concept of national security in US domestic law. US law gives the President broad discretion to define and declare national emergencies and to impose trade sanctions pursuant to them.[158] The long-standing trade embargos against Cuba and North Korea were adopted on grounds of national security, and an international emergency doubtless existed with North Korea at the end of the Korean War and with Cuba at the time of the Bay of Pigs and the Cuban Missile Crisis. Nearly a half-century later, however, the original justifications for those measures have largely dissipated, and current relations with those states could hardly be portrayed as international *emergencies*, although the declared US national emergencies remain in place.

As troublesome as the definition of an international emergency is the question of who should decide whether such an emergency exists? The sanctioning state? The WTO? There are reasonably objective standards for the WTO to apply in determining whether an action relates to nuclear or military technology or even whether the measure is taken pursuant to war. But the question whether an international emergency exists to some degree turns on a state's own assessment of its security interests—a question which Article XX(b) gives individual states the power to determine. Thus, greater self-judging by states might be allowed in this area.[159]

GATT/WTO dispute proceedings have not clarified these interpretive difficulties. Only four disputes raising the national security exception have proceeded to formal dispute settlement, and none of these cases addressed Article XXI on the merits.[160] In the *Nicaragua* dispute, which gave the most extensive examination to Article XXI, Nicaragua contended that the international emergency exception "should be interpreted in the light of the basic principles of international law . . . and should therefore be regarded as merely providing contracting parties subjected to an aggression with a right to self-defence".[161] The USA, on the other hand, contended that mere invocation of the Article

[158] See, e.g., discussion of the IEEPA and the Export Administration Act, *supra* Part III.

[159] See Perez, "The WTO and U.N. Law: Institutional Comity in National Security", (1998) 23 *Yale J. Int'l L.* 301 (discussing literature on "self-judging" approaches to the security exception).

[160] See Schloemann and Ohlhoff, *supra* n. 153, pp. 432–8.

[161] Report of the Panel, *United States—Trade Measures Affecting Nicaragua*, 13 October 1986 (unadopted), GATT Doc. L/6053, ¶ 5.2 (hereinafter *Nicaragua*).

XXI(b)(iii) national security exception ousted the jurisdiction of WTO,[162] and consented to the establishment of a dispute panel only on the condition that the panel not examine the validity of the USA's Article XXI justification.[163] The GATT panel thus concluded that it lacked jurisdiction to consider the issue, while observing that the US embargo was "counter to the basic aims of the GATT".[164]

Whatever the resolution of the Article XXI (b)(iii) question, certain human rights measures could be accommodated under a reasonable interpretation of the GATT national security exception. Trade restrictions on weapons and military technology could be justified under Article XXI(b)(i) and (ii), regardless whether they were "tailored" to prevent abuse by a rogue state or simply imposed as punishment for other human rights conduct. Thus, a country could refuse, on national security grounds, to export uranium to a state that was threatening to develop nuclear weapons for use against its neighbour. Presumably, a country also could refuse to sell non-lethal compounds to a country believed to be using them to produce chemical weapons of mass destruction. A ban on weapons sales to a foreign country for violations of democracy or forced labour would not clearly be necessary to the essential security interests of the sanctioning state. Nevertheless, if WTO scrutiny under Article XXI(b)(i) and (ii) is limited to determining whether the measure relates to nuclear or military technology, Article XXI would allow any restriction on trade in such technologies, so long as the state contended that the measure was necessary to its essential security interests. Thus, Article XXI potentially would support laws barring weapons sales to China, Rwanda, Kosovo, and the security forces in Turkey or Columbia for human rights violations, if the sanctioning state claimed a national security justification.

The range of sanctions that may be justified under Article XXI(b)(iii) remains unclear, and will turn on the interpretation which the WTO gives to international emergencies and the latitude given to states to make this determination. Certain general sanctions are likely to be allowed even under a reasonably strict interpretation of international emergencies. The 1991 military coup in Haiti, for example, caused severe political violence within that country, produced thousands of Haitian refugees seeking asylum in the USA and elsewhere, and threatened political stability in the Caribbean region. The US sanctions on Haiti were imposed on national security grounds and to punish the overthrow of democracy. No war was present, but the incident reasonably constituted an international emergency that directly threatened US security interests. It is not clear, however, that the international emergencies exception would justify either the US sanctions against

[162] *Ibid.* ¶ 1.2 (reporting US position that "A panel could . . . not address the validity of, nor the motivation for, the United States' invocation of Article XXI: (b)(iii)"). The USA reasserted this position in the Helms-Burton dispute, though its position did not receive wide support in the international community.

[163] *Ibid.* ¶ 1.3.

[164] *Ibid.* ¶¶ 5.3, 5.16.

Nicaragua in the 1980s or the 1990s sanctions against Cuba. Nor is it clear that the exception could support the imposition of general sanctions against states engaging in forced labour or torture, or even in situations such as Uganda or Rwanda. Even genocide in such states, while posing a fundamental threat to the international human rights order, does not directly threaten the essential security interests of the USA or other Western states. The national security provision, therefore, may be an awkward basis for supporting many sanctions for human rights purposes. But the GATT/WTO's deferential approach to this clause will continue to make it a potentially attractive *locus* for human rights measures.

The Article XX exceptions

The other possible basis for human rights sanctions under GATT is Article XX, which creates general exceptions to the GATT trade requirements for a range of public policy goals.[165] The Article XX exceptions that most plausibly allow for human rights protections include the exception for measures "necessary to protect public morals" (Article XX(a)); the exception for measures "necessary" to protect "human life" (Article XX(b)), and the exception for measures "relating to the products of prison labour" (Article XX(e)). Two critical questions are raised by the Article XX exceptions for human rights purposes: *First*, what *normative values* legitimately can be promoted under the exceptions? Do they include promotion of human rights? In particular, do the protections for human life and public morals contemplate the promotion of these values extraterritorially, or are they limited to protection of a state's own population? *Secondly*, what *types of trade measures* can be used under Article XX to promote these values? Do the exceptions contemplate the use of semi-tailored and general sanctions? Although Article XX facially appears to contain the GATT exceptions most closely related to human rights concerns, the WTO's restrictive approach to these provisions may render them the least hospitable to human rights measures.

Normative values

(a) *Extraterritoriality*. The first and foremost question regarding the application of Article XX to human rights sanctions is *whose* human life and public morals may be protected. International law recognises that states have only

[165] Article XX, entitled "General Exceptions", provides in relevant part as follows:

"Subject to the requirement that such measures are not applied in a manner which would constitute a means of arbitrary or unjustifiable discrimination between countries where the same conditions prevail, or a disguised restriction on international trade, nothing in this Agreement shall be construed to prevent the adoption or enforcement by any contracting party of measures:

(a) necessary to protect public morals;
(b) necessary to protect human, animal or plant life or health; . . .
(e) relating to the products of prison labour; . . .
(g) relating to the conservation of exhaustible natural resources if such measures are made effective in conjunction with restrictions on domestic production or consumption".

limited jurisdiction to interfere legally in the operations of another sovereign state,[166] though developments of the past fifty years have established human rights as matters of international, rather than domestic, concern.[167] The two most prominent—and unresolved—WTO challenges to human rights measures have involved the allegedly extraterritorial provisions of the Helms-Burton and Massachusetts Burma laws. And while the validity of so-called secondary boycott measures is beyond the scope of this chapter, the WTO's approach to extraterritoriality generally has broad implications for human rights sanctions. As noted previously, human rights trade measures are externally focused, designed to criticise, target, and alter a foreign state's human rights practices. If the human life and public morals exceptions of GATT are limited to protecting human life and public morals within a state's own territory, therefore, they will provide no haven for human rights measures.

The GATT does not expressly address extraterritoriality, and the support for the extraterritorial application of these provisions is mixed. On the one hand, the prison labour provision of Article XX clearly recognises some "extraterritorial" scope for the Article XX exceptions, since it expressly allows states to impose trade barriers for conduct occurring in a foreign state.[168] The public morals provision also was adopted against a backdrop of trade agreements which recognised a moral exception to trade policy for international and "extraterritorial" concerns such as the slave and opium trades, trade in firearms, and foreign forced or compulsory labour.[169] On the other hand, the Agreement on the Application of Sanitary and Phytosanitary Measures (SPS Agreement), which was promulgated to interpret Article XX(b),[170] applies only to measures for the protection of human, plant, or animal life which have effects within a state's own jurisdiction. If the SPS Agreement constitutes a complete interpretation of Article XX(b), then the human life provision is not available for the protection of human rights values abroad.

[166] States have jurisdiction to regulate conduct affecting the interests of their nationals, persons and things present in their territory, and conduct which either occurs or has "substantial effects" on their territory: *Restatement*, *supra* n. 30, § 402. States also have limited universal jurisdiction to regulate and punish conduct such as genocide which is recognized by the international community as violating matters of universal concern: *ibid.* § 404.

[167] See discussion in *supra* Part II.

[168] Under classical jurisdictional analysis, of course, there is nothing truly "extraterritorial" about such measures. Trade with a foreign state by definition has a territorial nexus with the sanctioning state, and can be regulated by it. Nothing in customary international law bars a state from conditioning access to its own markets in this manner.

[169] Charnovitz, "The Moral Exception in Trade Policy", (1998) 38 *Va. J. Int'l L.* 689, 705–16.

[170] Agreement on the Application of Sanitary and Phytosanitary Measures, *Legal Texts of the Uruguay Round* 69 (WTO 1994), Art. 2(4) ("Sanitary or phytosanitary measures which conform to the relevant provisions of this Agreement shall be presumed to be in accordance with the obligations of the Members under the provisions of GATT 1994 which relate to the use of sanitary or phytosanitary measures, in particular the provisions of Article XX(b)"); available at <http://www.wto.org/english/docs_e/legal_e/final_e.htm> (visited 14 October 2000). See also *ibid.* Preamble (describing purpose of agreement as "to elaborate rules for the application of the provisions of GATT 1994 which relate to the use of sanitary or phytosanitary measures, in particular the provisions of Article XX(b)").

GATT's own approach to extraterritoriality under Article XX has evolved over time. In *Tuna/Dolphin I*, the Panel narrowly limited the environmental provisions of Articles XX(b) and (g) to a state's domestic jurisdiction. The Panel rejected the USA's effort to bar tuna harvested from countries using methods that were not dolphin-safe, holding that "Article XX(g) was intended to permit contracting parties to take trade measures primarily aimed at rendering effective restrictions on production or consumption *within their jurisdiction*".[171] In the *Tuna/Dolphin II* decision, involving the EC's challenge to the US policy, the Panel receded from this territorial restriction somewhat, finding that GATT did not absolutely proscribe "measures that related to things or actions outside the territorial jurisdiction of the party taking the measure".[172] The Panel acknowledged that the Article XX(e) prison labour exception contemplated measures targeting conduct in a foreign state, and that measures for the protection of the environment could be adopted when consistent with customary international rules regarding extraterritorial jurisdiction. The Panel nevertheless ruled that Article XX did not allow parties to compel other member states to alter practices within their own jurisdiction, since such practices would undermine the global free trade system.[173] Neither of the *Tuna/Dolphin* Panel Reports was adopted by the GATT Council,[174] which leaves their precedential value on this and other points somewhat uncertain.

In the subsequent *Shrimp/Turtle* decision, the WTO Appellate Body recognised a broader authority of states to target extraterritorial conduct. The *Shrimp/Turtle* complaint was filed by countries harvesting shrimp in the Indian ocean, and there was little likelihood that all the turtles affected would enter US waters.[175] The US measure thus required foreign states to protect their *own* turtles when harvesting shrimp destined for the USA. The Appellate Body nevertheless concluded that turtles were an internationally recognised endangered

[171] *Tuna/Dolphin I*, *supra* n. 149, ¶ 5.31 (emphasis added). The Panel reasoned that measures targeting foreign environmental practices could not be allowed absent agreement among the parties regarding "limits on the range of policy differences justifying such responses" and the development of "criteria so as to prevent abuse": *ibid.* ¶ 6.3. The Panel indicated that such concerns should be advanced through an amendment of GATT, not through interpretation of Article XX.

[172] GATT Dispute Panel Report, *United States—Restrictions on Imports of Tuna*, ¶ 5.16 (16 June 1994), DS29/R available at 1994 WL 907620.

[173] *Ibid.* ¶ 5.26 ("If . . . Article XX were interpreted to permit contracting parties to take trade measures so as to force other contracting parties to change their policies within their jurisdiction, including their conservation policies, the balance of rights and obligations among contracting parties, in particular the right of access to markets, would be seriously impaired").

[174] Prior to the establishment of the WTO in 1994, rulings of GATT dispute panels required adoption by the GATT membership in order to be effective. The WTO altered this procedure by providing for review of panel decisions by the Appllate Body. Such decisions are presumed effective unless their adoption is rejected by the GATT membership.

[175] WTO Appellate Body Report, *United States—Import Prohibition of Certain Shrimp and Shrimp Products*, WTO Doc. WT/DS58/AB/R, p. 51, ¶¶ 131 (12 October 1998), available at <http://www. wto.org/english/tratop_e/dispu_e/distab_e.htm> (visited 14 October 2000) ("The sea turtle species here at stake, . . . are all known to occur in waters over which the United States exercises jurisdiction. Of course, it is not claimed that *all* populations of these species migrate to, or traverse, at one time or another, waters subject to United States jurisdiction.") (footnote omitted).

species, and that the USA had a legitimate interest in using trade measures to protect a common global resource. The Appellate Body held in principle that Article XX allows states to affect foreign practices that impact valid international concerns:

> "It is not necessary to assume that requiring from exporting countries compliance with, or adoption of, certain policies . . . prescribed by the importing country, renders a measure *a priori* incapable of justification under Article XX. Such an interpretation renders most, if not all, of the specific exceptions of Article XX inutile, a result abhorrent to the principles of interpretation we are bound to apply".[176]

The Appellate Body qualified this approach by noting that the migratory nature of sea turtles created "a sufficient nexus between the migratory and endangered marine populations involved and the United States for purposes of Article XX(g)".[177] This approach might suggest that the Appellate Body was adopting an "effects" test, upholding jurisdiction over foreign activity that has effects within the sanctioning state's territory. It is unclear, however, how much weight the Appellate Body ultimately placed on the turtles' migratory nature. The Appellate Body did not require that the USA regulate *only* conduct affecting turtles that were likely to enter US waters, and expressly stated that it was not addressing "the question of whether there is an implied jurisdictional limitation in Article XX(g), and if so, the nature or extent of that limitation".[178]

The *Shrimp/Turtle* decision suggests that at least the public morals provision, and possibly the human life provision, could be interpreted to have extraterritorial reach. The Appellate Body's reliance on the migratory nature of turtles, however, also could limit the usefulness of the ruling for human rights measures. Strict reliance on migration to create a territorial nexus likely would preclude most human rights sanctions, except possibly those relating to refugee movements. Even genocide in a distant third country often does not have the same potential for creating a territorial effect as turtles that habitually wander upon a nation's shores. (Indeed, this is the difficulty that is addressed by universal jurisdiction.)

Interpreting GATT to be consistent with international law supports an extraterritorial interpretation of Articles XX(a) and (b) in the human rights context. As discussed in Part II, *supra*, customary international law allows for use of unilateral economic measures to promote the human rights system, and recognises an exception to ordinary jurisdictional rules for fundamental international crimes such as genocide, slavery, torture, and apartheid, which authorise universal jurisdiction over individuals. States are recognised as having an interest in prohibiting such conduct without any territorial nexus. Moreover, the *erga omnes* status of human rights norms establishes that all states have an interest in compelling compliance with human rights by other states, regardless

[176] Shrimp/*Turtle* supra n.175, p. 45, ¶ 121.
[177] *Ibid*. p. 51, ¶ 133.
[178] *Ibid*.

whether the violating state's conduct directly impacts other states' interests in the traditional sense. Nothing in the GATT text purports to override these international law principles. Thus, even if the GATT imposes territorial restrictions in other contexts, a strong case can be made that enforcement of human rights protections abroad should be consistent with GATT. Other than possibly secondary boycotts, trade measures motivated by fundamental human rights concerns do not improperly interfere with the territorial sovereignty of the sanctioned state. The WTO's position on extraterritoriality remains in flux, but the WTO appears to be moving in a direction that would interpret the GATT's unwritten "extraterritoriality" requirements consistently with these customary international law rules.

(b) *Incorporation of human rights values.* Assuming that the public morals and/or human life provisions can be interpreted to contemplate extraterritorial measures, the question remains what, if any, human rights values are included in these exceptions. Here again, the GATT text offers little assistance. The context in which the public morals provision arose suggests that the exception originally was conceived to accommodate some limited human rights concerns,[179] while the negotiating history of the human life clause suggests a narrow focus on sanitary and phytosanitary measures. Treaty text, however, takes precedence over negotiating history.[180] Moreover, in interpreting the Article XX(g) natural resources provision in *Shrimp/Turtle* the WTO Appellate Body adopted an "evolutionary" approach, holding that Article XX(g) "must be read by a treaty interpreter in the light of contemporary concerns of the community of nations about the protection and conservation of the environment".[181] The Appellate Body looked to international treaties for guidance on the question whether "exhaustible natural resources" was an evolutionary concept, and concluded that "the generic term 'natural resources' in Article XX(g) is not 'static' " and that its "interpretation cannot remain unaffected by the subsequent development of law".[182] Accordingly, Article XX exceptions which are "by definition evolutionary"[183] are to be construed in light of contemporary international values. This approach to Article XX is consistent with the requirement that GATT provisions be interpreted in light of applicable provisions of international law.

An application of the *Shrimp/Turtle* evolutionary approach would suggest that the Article XX public morals, human life, and prison labour provisions are evolving concepts that should take into account contemporary developments in the international law of human rights. In order to render the GATT exceptions consistent with human rights treaties and customary international law principles, the human life and public morals exceptions should be understood to encompass

[179] See Charnovitz, *supra* n. 169.

[180] Vienna Convention, Art. 32.

[181] *Shrimp/Turtle*, *supra* n. 175, p. 48, ¶ 129.

[182] *Ibid*. p. 48, ¶ 130 & n. 109, citing *Namibia (Legal Consequences) Advisory Opinion* [1971] ICJ Rep. 31.

[183] *Shrimp/Turtle*, *supra* n. 175, 48, ¶ 130.

the core *jus cogens, erga omnes*, and mutual treaty obligations of the human rights regime. The prison labour provision also supports an evolutionary approach to human rights concerns. GATT was drafted in 1947, at a time when coerced labour was the only widely-prohibited international human rights norm.[184] By including an express prohibition against prison labour, GATT thus arguably was incorporating the prevailing human rights norms of the day.[185] An evolutionary approach to the Article XX exceptions accordingly is consistent with the GATT text and WTO interpretations, and would keep GATT apace of developments in human rights law:

(1) *Human life*. Under this approach, the human life exception potentially could be understood to embrace values such as the prohibitions against genocide, summary execution, disappearance, crimes against humanity, and the execution of juveniles. Because of slavery's denial of personhood, the prohibition against slavery, the slave trade, and forced labour might also fall within the human life exception. Subject to the principles of necessity and proportionality discussed *infra*, protection of human life thus could justify sanctions ranging from tailored restrictions on weapons sales to general trade embargos against countries engaging in atrocities against human life. Sanctions against Amin's Uganda, Milosevic's Yugoslavia, and the genocidal regime in Rwanda all reasonably might fall within this exception.
(2) *Public morals*. An evolutionary approach to the public morals exception could include a number of fundamental human rights norms—such as the prohibition against systematic racial discrimination, the prohibition against slavery, forced labour, and exploitative child labour (if not encompassed by the human life exception), freedom of association, and possibly evolving norms *erga omnes* such as the right to property and the prohibitions against gender, religious discrimination and the overthrow of democracy. At the very least, the values that legitimately may be promoted under the public morals exception should embrace *jus cogens* norms and other human rights norms that are mutually binding on states by treaty.
(3) *Prison labour*. The prison labour exception on its face is less susceptible to broad interpretation than the public morals and human life provisions. Textually, "prison labour" is difficult to construe more broadly than traditional forms of penal servitude. At a minimum, however, an evolutionary approach to this exception should construe it to be consistent with current conventions regarding convict labour. And to the extent that the provision reflects a general concern about coerced labour, the provision plausibly

[184] See 1926 Slavery Convention; 1930 Forced Labour Convention; see also *Oppenheim's International Law*, *supra* n. 5, § 141 n. 1.

[185] It is unclear whether the prison labour exception was intended simply to prevent unfair trade practices and market distortions, or whether it was motivated by broader human rights concerns. See Armstrong, "American Import Controls and Morality in International Trade: An Analysis of Section 307 of the Tariff Act of 1930", (1975) 8 *NYU J. Int'l L. & Pol.* 19 (discussing the negotiating history of Art. XX(e)).

might be interpreted to allow restrictions on goods made under prison-like conditions, such as certain forms of forced or bonded labour, including certain forms of exploitative child labour.[186] Does the prison labour provision, for example, allow the prohibition of imports made with slave labour? If slave labour cannot be encompassed by either the prison labour, public morals, or human life exceptions, Article XX would yield the anomalous result that prison labour could be targeted under GATT, while the more egregious violation of slave labour could not.

Concerns may be raised regarding the breadth of the human rights values that legitimately might be promoted under Article XX. The concept of "public morals", in particular, is potentially quite broad. The evolutionary approach, however, would allow the GATT trade regime to accommodate core human rights norms while preventing abuse of the Article XX exceptions. The Article XX provisions necessarily must be limited to values which are either mutually binding on the sanctioning and target states by treaty, or which are core *jus cogens* and *erga omnes* obligations of the international community. Accordingly, the Article XX exceptions would not justify sanctions targeting a foreign state's abortion practices or death penalty practices not involving juveniles or pregnant women, where no treaty imposed mutual obligations on the sanctioning and target states. Trade measures to promote democratic political reforms likewise would be problematic in the absence of a mutually binding treaty, although measures retaliating against the overthrow of democracy might fall within a binding customary international law norm.[187] Furthermore, human rights norms such as torture and exploitative child and forced labour are extensively defined, both through international instruments and through the decisions of domestic regional courts and official international interpretive bodies. The WTO could look to both treaties and authoritative advisory bodies to determine whether a claimed human rights concern represented a legitimate value of the international community, in the same way that the Appellate Body looked to environmental treaties to determine whether protection of sea turtles constituted legitimate protection of an "exhaustible natural resource" in *Shrimp/Turtle*.

Acknowledging that the core human rights norms reflect legitimate interests that can be encompassed by the substantive concepts of human life, public morals, and prison labour does not complete the Article XX inquiry. The question still remains what trade measures may be validly employed to promote these goals under the Article XX necessity and reasonableness requirements and the *chapeau*.

[186] For further discussion, see Francioni, *supra* Chapter 1, Lenzerini, *infra* Chapter 11, and McCrudden and Davies, *infra* Chapter 8.

[187] Thus, the US sanctions against Cuba could not be justified on grounds of promoting democracy, because the present Cuban Government did not overthrow a democracy but replaced an existing authoritarian regime. By contrast, the sanctions imposed following the coup against Haiti's democratically-elected President, and following the Burmese Government's invalidation of the 1990 election, served a distinct and more widely accepted principle under international law.

Acceptable trade measures

(a) *The necessity requirement for public morals and human life.* Articles XX(a) and (b) create an exception for measures "necessary" to promote public morals and human life, and WTO decisions have narrowly construed the concept of necessity to foreclose many types of trade measures. In essence, the concept of necessity has been read to require that a measure be the *least trade restrictive measure* effective to promote the state's valid interest. In the *Reformulated Gasoline* case, for example, the WTO held that a US effort to regulate smog-causing contaminants in domestic and imported gasoline was not "necessary" under Article XX(b) because less trade-restrictive alternative measures were reasonably available and had not been pursued by the USA.[188] Other GATT proceedings routinely have found that measures were not sufficiently tailored to satisfy the necessity requirement.[189] As a result, Article XX(b) has been rendered of limited value to environmentalists, who have concentrated instead on the Article XX(g) exception for measures "relating to" exhaustible natural resources.[190]

The WTO's approach to necessity is not mandated by GATT, and creates a number of interpretive difficulties. Necessity on its face is susceptible to many interpretations, as the USA's approach to the constitutional concept of "necessary and proper" suggests.[191] The language of Article XX indicates that some distinction should be drawn between measures deemed "necessary" to achieve a particular goal, and those which merely "relate to" that goal. But there is no rational justification for interpreting necessity as imposing a least restrictive trade requirement on measures for the protection of *human life*, while measures merely need to "relate to" gold and silver or prison labour.[192] The WTO's approach produces the equally anomalous result that environmental measures must be the least trade restrictive measures available to protect animal life under Article XX(b), but need merely relate to the preservation of exhaustible natural

[188] GATT Dispute Panel Report, *United States—Standards for Reformulated and Conventional Gasoline*, WTO Doc. WT/DS2/R, at ¶ 6.28 (29 January 1996), as modified by Appellate Body Report, *United States—Standards for Reformulated and Conventional Gasoline* (20 May 1996), available at <http://www.wto.org/english/tratop_e/dispu_e/distab_e.htm> (visited 14 October 2000).

[189] See, e.g., *Tuna/Dolphin I*, *supra* n. 149, ¶ 5.28 (holding, under Article XX(b), that the USA had not "exhausted all options reasonably available to it to pursue its dolphin protection objectives through measures consistent with the General Agreement, in particular through the negotiation of international cooperative agreements"); GATT Dispute Panel Report, *Thailand—Restrictions on Importation of and Internal Taxes on Cigarettes*, 7 November 1990, GATT B.I.S.D. (37th Supp.) pp. 200, 223 (1991) (Thai ban on cigarette imports "could be considered to be 'necessary' in terms of Article XX(b) only if there were no [less trade-restrictive] alternative" available to achieve Thailand's goal of protecting human life).

[190] Neuling, "The Shrimp-Turtle Case: Implications for Article XX of GATT and the Trade and Environment Debate", (1999) 22 *Loyola Int'l & Comp. L. Rev.* 1, 19.

[191] See US Constitution, Art. I, § 8.

[192] Art. XX(c) and (e) GATT.

resources under Article XX(g). Moreover, as Thomas Schoenbaum has noted, the WTO's restrictive approach to the necessity requirement violates principles of treaty interpretation by rendering unnecessary and redundant the *chapeau*'s requirement that Article XX measures also not unjustifiably or arbitrarily discriminate. The approach also fails to give adequate deference to the non-protectionist policy determinations of GATT member states.[193]

A rule that human rights trade measures must be the least trade-restrictive measure available likely would eliminate the use of human rights sanctions under the Article XX human life and public morals exceptions. It is extremely difficult to demonstrate that trade sanctions are the least trade restrictive mechanism available to promote a legitimate human rights interest. As noted in the introduction, trade sanctions are generally one of many possible mechanisms that can be used against a deviant state. States may also isolate regimes through diplomatic measures, withholding of foreign assistance, and so forth. While it might be possible to demonstrate that *tailored* sanctions satisfy the necessity test, even these narrowly drawn sanctions are vulnerable under the WTO's approach. Is a ban on imports made with exploitative child labour the least trade restrictive means of promoting this public moral value? Is an embargo on weapons the least trade restrictive means of protecting human life in a state such as Rwanda? The analysis becomes even more difficult with semi-tailored and general sanctions. Is a bar on sugar imports necessary to promote democracy in Panama? A ban on Polish imports necessary to protect the Solidarity movement? Was the embargo on Uganda necessary to protect human rights in that state? The necessity requirement, as presently interpreted, thus constitutes one of the primary obstacles to reconciling human rights sanctions and GATT trade requirements.

(b) *Reasonableness and prison labour.* The prison labour exception is not conditioned on a necessity requirement, but applies to measures "relating to the products of prison labour". The "relating to" language, however, imposes a reasonableness requirement on such measures. The WTO has interpreted the term "relating to" in Article XX(g) as requiring a "reasonable" or "substantial" relationship between a trade restriction and the valid state interest it promotes. In *Reformulated Gasoline*, for example, the Appellate Body found that US rules regarding the smog-producing chemicals in gasoline had a "substantial relationship" to the goal of resource conservation, and were not "merely incidentally or inadvertently aimed" at this purpose.[194] The Appellate Body rejected the Panel's conclusion that the "relating to" language imposed a least restrictive means test equivalent to the necessity requirement.[195] In *Shrimp/Turtle*, the Appellate Body likewise found that the USA's semi-tailored ban on the

[193] Schoenbaum, "International Trade and Protection of the Environment: The Continuing Search for Reconciliation", (1997) 91 *Am. J. Int'l L.* 268, 277.

[194] *Reformulated Gasoline*, *supra* n. 188, Appellate Body, p. 19.

[195] *Ibid.* at 16.

importation of shrimp from countries not requiring turtle-safe nets was "reasonably related to" the goal of protecting sea turtles, an endangered species:

> "[The US restriction was] not disproportionately wide in its scope and reach in relation to the policy objective of protection and conservation of sea turtle species. The means [were], in principle, reasonably related to the ends".[196]

In other words, the ends-means relationship between the measure and the legitimate policy being advanced was "observably a close and real one".[197]

The WTO has not established the outer limits of what measures it considers reasonable, but *tailored* sanctions, such as a bar on imports made with prison labour, should satisfy this requirement. Such restrictions apply to the specific product from which the human rights violation arises and are narrowly tailored to bar only goods made through these harmful processes. The *Shrimp/Turtle* decision suggests that *semi-tailored* measures should also satisfy the reasonableness test. The US measure in that dispute was not limited to shrimp that had been harvested with non-turtle-safe methods, but barred all shrimp imports from countries that had not officially mandated turtle-safe methods, regardless whether the relevant harvesting fleet used such methods or not. By analogy, a measure that banned all imports of a certain product from countries where a high percentage of the product was produced with prison labour should satisfy the reasonableness test (though it might encounter difficulties with the proportionality requirement, discussed *infra*). More general trade sanctions targeting prison labour, however, such as the US embargo on imports of military goods from China following China's failure to comply with the 1992 US-China Agreement on Prison Labour, might not be considered reasonably to relate to the products of prison labour. Whatever substantive rights the prison labour exception may protect, then, the reasonableness requirement will to some degree constrain the range of trade measures that may be employed to promote this value.

(c) *The chapeau*. In addition to the necessity or reasonableness requirements of the individual Article XX exceptions, to be valid under Article XX, a trade measure must also satisfy the requirements of the Article XX preamble or "*chapeau*". The *chapeau* states that measures adopted under the Article XX exceptions must not constitute "arbitrary or unjustifiable discrimination . . . or a disguised restriction on international trade".[198] The WTO has held that "the nature and quality of this discrimination is different from the discrimination in the treatment of products" set forth in Articles I, III, and XI.[199] In other words, while the Article XX exceptions allow some forms of discrimination that are barred by Articles I and III, they do not exempt discrimination that is "arbitrary or unjustifiable". This approach to the *chapeau* is intended "to prevent abuse of

[196] *Shrimp/Turtle, supra* n. 175, p. 53, ¶ 141.

[197] *Ibid*. For further discussion of the Article XX(g) "reasonableness" requirement, see Hansen, "Transparency, Standards of Review, and the Use of Trade Measures to Protect the Global Environment", (1999) 39 *Va. J. Int'l L.* 1017, 1048–57.

[198] See Art. XX GATT.

[199] *Shrimp/Turtle, supra* n. 175, p. 57, ¶ 150.

the exceptions" set forth in Article XX and to ensure that the exceptions "should not be so applied as to frustrate or defeat the [GATT] legal obligations".[200] The WTO has applied stringent principles of proportionality, transparency, and a preference for multilateralism under the *chapeau* to invalidate a number of trade restrictions that were otherwise valid under Article XX, including the *Reformulated Gasoline*, *Tuna/Dolphin II*, and *Shrimp/Turtle* measures. Thus, in *Shrimp/Turtle*, the Appellate Body concluded that although the US measure served a legitimate Article XX purpose, by dictating the specific turtle-protective methods that foreign states must adopt, by banning all shrimp imports from uncertified states, by failing to pursue multilateral measures, and by employing non-transparent evaluation methods, the measure violated the *chapeau*.[201]

(i) *Proportionality*. The WTO has interpreted the arbitrary/unjustifiable discrimination requirement of the *chapeau* as requiring that a trade-restrictive measure be reasonably necessary to achieve the state's valid non-commercial purpose. In determining a measure's reasonableness, the WTO appears to have adopted a balancing approach which weighs the legitimate, non-trade interest being advanced against the competing free trade interests of other states. The measure "must be applied reasonably, with due regard both to the legal duties of the party claiming the exception and the legal rights of the other parties concerned".[202] "[T]hus, a balance must be struck between the *right* of a Member to invoke an exception under Article XX and the *duty* of that same member to respect the treaty rights of the other Members."[203]

This approach could be described as imposing a proportionality requirement on Article XX measures. Under this approach, the burden on international trade must be *proportional* to the legitimate interest at stake and the likely benefit to result from the measure. The greater the legitimate non-commercial *interest* at stake, the more *effective* the measure will be in advancing that purpose, and the lower the measure's impact on international *trade*, the more likely the measure is to satisfy the proportionality requirement. Stated in equation form, a proportionality test would allow a trade measure that satisfied the following:

$$\text{Policy Interest} + \text{Effectiveness of Measure} > \text{Burden on International Trade}$$

On its face, this balancing approach appears to take properly into consideration the relevant competing interests presented by the use of trade measures to promote non-trade policy values. In applying the *chapeau*, however, the WTO has focused exclusively on the presence of discrimination to restrict sharply the use of unilateral trade measures. In *Shrimp/Turtle*, for example, the Appellate Body concluded that while the USA had a legitimate interest in promoting the protection of an endangered species, the USA had "unjustifiably discriminated" against other states by narrowly dictating the precise technological means by

[200] *Reformulated Gasoline*, *supra* n. 188, p. 22.
[201] *Shrimp/Turtle*, *supra* n. 175, pp. 63–75, ¶¶ 161–84.
[202] *Ibid*. p. 57, ¶ 151, quoting *Reformulated Gasoline*, *supra* n. 188, p. 23.
[203] *Shrimp/Turtle*, *supra* n. 175, p. 60, ¶ 156.

which states could comply with that goal. By imposing a "single, rigid and unbending" standard which failed to take into consideration either other policies an exporting country may have adopted to protect sea turtles, or the differing conditions in other states, the measure unjustifiably and arbitrarily discriminated.[204]

The Appellate Body also found that the semi-tailored nature of the measure violated the *chapeau*. In the *Shrimp/Turtle* dispute, the US law at issue barred all imports from countries that were not certified as using turtle-safe methods, even if the specific imports from those countries had been harvested according to the US requirements. For example, a French fleet fishing in *uncertified* Mexican waters was not able to export its catch to the USA, even if France required turtle-safe methods, and the French fleet had used such methods in harvesting the catch. Thus, the measure barred imports of some products that had not contributed to environmental degradation.[205] The WTO concluded that such tailoring unjustifiably discriminated against foreign imports. The Appellate Body reasoned that by barring all imports from an uncertified country, the USA was more interested in dictating the precise policies that foreign states should adopt, than in simply preventing environmental degradation.[206]

Much of the Appellate Body's proportionality analysis remains in flux at this time. It is unclear, for example, whether the *Shrimp/Turtle* measure was considered overbroad simply because it dictated the means of compliance, or if it violated the *chapeau* because it targeted environmental practices beyond those directly effecting US bilateral trade. In *Shrimp/Turtle* the WTO appears to have raised only the former objection. On the other hand, if the WTO concluded that the USA had no legitimate *interest* in requiring other states to promote international environmental values with respect to goods sold domestically or to third countries, such a decision would have far-reaching implications for human rights sanctions. In essence, this approach would reimpose a rigid territoriality requirement on the use of trade measures to alter foreign conduct. *Tailored* sanctions would probably satisfy this requirement, since they precisely target the contribution of the sanctioning country's markets to the human rights abuse. A restriction on the importation of carpets made with exploitative child labour would not affect the target state's ability to use exploitative child labour in the production of domestic goods, or in carpets exported to other states. Even slightly broader *semi-tailored* measures would be invalid, however. A ban on all carpets imported from a country where child labour was prevalent in the industry would be overbroad. Perhaps the WTO would accept such a measure if a

[204] *Shrimp/Turtle, supra* n. 175, pp. 72–3, ¶ 177; see also *ibid.* pp. 64–5, ¶¶ 163–5.

[205] The measures in *Tuna/Dolphin II* also prohibited tuna imports from countries that themselves "imported tuna from countries maintaining tuna harvesting practices and policies not comparable to those of the USA", even if the country importing to the United States required that its own tuna be harvested with dolphin-safe methods, and the country required such methods: *Tuna/Dolphin II supra* n. 172, ¶ 5.23. The GATT panel found this provision invalid under both Art. XX(g) and the necessity provision of Art. XX(b): *ibid.* ¶¶ 5.39, 5.27.

[206] *Shrimp/Turtle, supra* n. 175, p. 65, ¶ 165.

state could demonstrate that, due to enforcement difficulties, only a prophylactic rule such as a blanket ban on carpet imports would be effective in promoting the legitimate state interest.[207] The WTO's approach to administrative difficulties in the *Reformulated Gasoline* case, however, suggests that the burden on the state invoking this justification would be high.

Furthermore, a strict approach to proportionality likely would bar other *semi-tailored* and *general* sanctions, since these sanctions use restrictions on trade in one sector in order to compel changes in other aspects of a state's behaviour. Targeting a state's primary source of foreign exchange (such as trade in oil or diamonds) is a classical means of sanctioning a rogue state. But it is not clear that the WTO would conclude that the relationship between such a trade restriction and the state's human rights interest was sufficiently direct and effective to satisfy the proportionality test. This difficulty increases with general sanctions, such as bars to trade in goods and services with countries committing genocide or apartheid. General sanctions are problematic from a proportionality perspective because they impose the greatest restrictions on trade and have the least direct relationship between the sanction and the human rights values being advanced. Was the embargo on trade with Uganda sufficiently proportional to the goal of ending the human rights atrocities in that state?

For both semi-tailored and general sanctions, the benefit or *effectiveness* prong of a proportionality test may be particularly problematic. Sanctions are blunt instruments that operate slowly over long periods of time. Their utility cannot effectively be measured by demanding a direct relationship between the sanction and the realisation of a particular policy outcome.[208] In particular, their important role in defining human rights norms, creating pressure for action on the international level, and pressuring a foreign state to internalise the resulting international values, may be too nebulous to be "balanced" effectively. The cause and effect relationship between trade sanctions and advancing a particular human rights value is sufficiently tangential that this requirement of proportionality, narrowly construed, is unlikely to be satisfied.

Thus, a narrow understanding of effectiveness, and a holding that states may not use trade sanctions to advance broader policy goals than those directly related to the products being traded, would effectively bar all general and semi-tailored sanctions. It would eliminate the policy option of using trade measures to target goods that provide critical foreign exchange to human rights violators, as well as preclude the use of trade to condemn non-trade related human rights violations such as genocide, torture, and the overthrow of democracy.

[207] See, e.g., Thomas, "Drive to Ban Child Labour Makes India's Poor Poorer", *The Times* 3 February 1996 (describing the difficulty in monitoring a cottage industry in which carpet production is carried out in thousands of mud houses across northern India), available in LEXIS, NEWS Library, NON-US NEWS File.

[208] Malloy, *Economic Sanctions and U.S. Trade* (Boston, 1990), p. 636. See also Parker, "The Problem with Scorecards: How (And How Not) to Measure the Cost-Effectiveness of Economic Sanctions", (2000) 21 *Mich. J. Int'l L.*, 235.

The Appellate Body's analysis in *Shrimp/Turtle* does not clearly raise these concerns, since the Appellate Body simply pointed to the measure's breadth as evidence that the US goal was imposing a specific policy solution on foreign states. The *Shrimp/Turtle* approach therefore is promising from a human rights perspective. Moreover, the Appellate Body has qualified its proportionality approach in ways. In *Shrimp/Turtle*, the Appellate Body contended that application of the *chapeau* was case-specific, and that:

> "[w]hen applied in a particular case, the actual contours and contents of these standards will vary as the kind of measure under examination varies . . . The standard of 'arbitrary discrimination', for example, under the chapeau may be different for a measure that purports to be necessary to protect public morals than for one relating to the products of prison labour".[209]

Thus, there may be room for future positive development of the proportionality principle in the human rights area.

(ii) *Preference for multilateral measures*. In evaluating whether a measure satisfies the *chapeau*, the WTO also has required states to explore multilateral options before pursuing unilateral trade measures. In both the *Reformulated Gasoline* and *Shrimp/Turtle* cases, the Appellate Body found the measures to be reasonable under Article XX(g), but nevertheless invalidated them under the *chapeau* due, inter alia, to the USA's failure to negotiate international agreements.[210] In *Shrimp/Turtle*, the USA had negotiated an inter-American convention for the protection of sea turtles, but had not pursued such an agreement with the complaining Asian states. The Appellate Body noted that international environmental instruments strongly preferred multilateral conservation efforts, and found that the inter-American agreement demonstrated "that an alternative [multilateral] course of action was reasonably open to the United States".[211] Accordingly, by failing to engage in "serious, across-the-board" negotiations with all states that would be targeted by the US measure, the USA unjustifiably discriminated.[212] The Appellate Body also criticized the USA for failing to pursue cooperative efforts at sea turtle protection through existing international mechanisms. The USA had made no effort, for example, to raise the issue of sea turtle protection before the CITES Standing Committee as a subject requiring concerted action. The USA also had failed to sign or ratify various environmental conventions relevant to sea turtle protection.[213]

[209] *Shrimp/Turtle*, *supra* n. 175, p. 44, ¶ 120.

[210] *Reformulated Gasoline*, *supra* n. 188, pp. 27–8 (holding that US environmental standards for domestic and imported gasoline fell within the Art. XX(g) exhaustible natural resources exception to promote clean air, but nevertheless failed under the *chapeau* arbitrary/unjustifiable test, since the USA had not, *inter alia*, pursued cooperative agreements with the complaining states).

[211] *Shrimp/Turtle*, *supra* n. 175, p. 70, ¶ 171. The Body found that the USA had negotiated with some members more seriously than others, and that this conduct was discriminatory.

[212] *Ibid*. pp. 65–6, ¶ 166.

[213] *Ibid*. p. 70, ¶ 171 and n. 174.

The Appellate Body has offered little guidance regarding the lengths to which a state must go to obtain international agreement before unilateral action will be warranted, and the extent to which the WTO will second-guess a state's multilateral efforts. However, the WTO's preference for multilateral action, if properly applied, would be a reasonable constraint on human rights measures. Requiring some resort to multilateral avenues seems consistent with the general goal of improving multilateral cooperation in the international system. As the WTO has recognized, unilateral measures may undermine the effectiveness of international institutions if nations prefer unilateral action to available international remedies, or purport to enforce international law obligations on other states that they themselves do not respect. The USA, in particular, has been notorious for preferring unilateral action in ways that are destructive to the international system.[214] The WTO's multilateral "exhaustion" requirement would discourage such abuse of unilateral measures.

On the other hand, depending on its application, the WTO's preference for multilateral action could unreasonably obstruct human rights measures. Unilateral measures often are adopted because meaningful multilateral intervention is not available for a variety of reasons. Articles 39 and 41 of the UN Charter, for example, authorise the Security Council to recommend multilateral economic sanctions only when human rights conditions threaten international peace and security. Even when this requirement is satisfied, members of the Security Council may be unwilling or unable for domestic political reasons to act collectively despite agreement on the underlying human rights atrocities, as recent cases such as Bosnia and Rwanda demonstrate.[215] The multilateral sanctions against South Africa, which were repeatedly opposed in the Security Council by the USA and Great Britain,[216] are further testament to the difficulty of achieving universal consensus. Moreover, multilateral measures take time. The 1994 genocide in Rwanda killed 800,000 people in one hundred days, and international mechanisms proved incapable of responding in a timely manner, despite several months of advance warning that the genocide was likely to occur. Requiring states to pursue years of lobbying at the international level

[214] In particular, the USA historically has been criticized for failing to ratify many of the core ILO conventions that it purports to enforce against other states through the GSP system. The USA has ratified only two conventions relating to the core ILO labour rights — the Convention (No. 105) on the Abolition of Forced Labor, and the recent Convention (No. 182) on the Worst Forms of Child Labor. The US track record in this area has improved somewhat of late, however. The ICCPR commits the USA to respect various labour rights, including the right to freedom of association and to form trade unions and the prohibitions against slavery, servitude, and forced labour, and the 1998 ILO Declaration obligates the USA to adhere to the remaining core labour rights. The USA's failure to ratify the Convention on the Rights of the Child and CEDAW, its failure to fully implement the Genocide Convention, and its extensive reservations to the ICCPR would remain substantial obstacles to the use of US sanctions to promote human rights abroad.

[215] See, e.g., Shawcross, *Deliver Us From Evil: Peacekeepers, Warlords, and a World of Endless Conflict* (New York, 2000); cf. Luck, *Mixed Messages: American Politics and International Organization, 1919–1999* (Washington, DC, 1999).

[216] See, e.g., UN Doc. S/PV.2738 at 67 (1987).

before adopting unilateral measures under such circumstances would render the unilateral option moot. Human rights abuses by permanent members of the Security Council also are insulated from multilateral sanctions. Atrocities by China in Tibet or Russia in Chechnya, for example, would be protected from Security Council sanctions by the state's own veto.

For human rights violations that do not rise to the level of violations of international peace and security, few effective multilateral remedies exist. States may file petitions with the ILO, with various UN human rights bodies, and with regional entities such as the Inter-American Human Rights Commission, all of which are authorised to investigate and report on state practices. None of these bodies, however, exerts any economic or other coercive authority over non-compliant states. The ILO, for example, lacks formal and effective mechanisms for either the resolution of disputes or their enforcement.[217] Multilateral and regional monitoring may not, therefore, constitute a reasonable substitute for more coercive unilateral economic remedies. The negotiation of bilateral agreements, which the WTO has promoted, also takes time, and may be futile in some circumstances. Bilateral agreements pose the additional risk that the WTO will find that differences between the negotiated agreements constitute arbitrary discrimination.

Finally, unilateral measures themselves often play a critical role in pressuring the international community to adopt multilateral remedies. Years of unilateral measures and complaints before the ILO were pursued regarding Burma's forced labour practices, for example, before the ILO finally expelled Burma from its proceedings in 1998. Thus, requiring pursuit of multilateral remedies before unilateral measures can be adopted in some circumstances may be putting the cart before the horse. In short, a rule mandating *prior exhaustion* of multilateral mechanisms in many circumstances would not effectively promote the legitimate human rights value at stake.

These concerns may well be premature however. While the *Reformulated Gasoline* decision appeared to impose a fairly high threshold for multilateral exhaustion, the *Shrimp/Turtle* decision merely criticised the USA for failing to pursue *any* international remedies or multilateral negotiations with the complaining states. It did not suggest that completion of international agreements or exhaustion of multilateral mechanisms was required. Instead, the Appellate Body acknowledged that Article XX appears to anticipate the adoption of unilateral measures by WTO members.[218]

[217] Member states are required to submit periodic reports on compliance with ILO conventions to the ILO Committee of Experts, which examines and reports on member compliance. Complaints regarding the compliance of another member state may be lodged with the ILO for referral to a commission of inquiry. See ILO Constitution, Art. 26, available at <http://www.ilo.org/public/english/about/iloconst.htm> (visited 14 October 2000). For further discussion, see Cox, "The International Labour Organisation and Fundamental Rights at Work", (1999) 5 *Eur. Human Rts. L. Rev.* 451.

[218] *Shrimp/Turtle*, *supra* n. 175, p. 45, ¶ 121 ("conditioning access to a Member's domestic market on whether exporting Members comply with, or adopt, a policy or policies unilaterally prescribed by the importing Member may, to some degree, be a common aspect of measures falling

(iii) *Transparency*. The WTO finally has interpreted the "arbitrariness" prong of the *chapeau* as requiring the creation of transparent decision-making mechanisms for unilateral trade measures which satisfy due process. In *Shrimp/Turtle*, the USA was condemned for employing unilateral, "ex parte inquiry or verification" processes for determining whether US trading partners were employing turtle-safe methods. The Appellate Body held that by failing to afford applicant countries notice and a formal opportunity to be heard, written findings of the US determination, and a right to appeal, the USA had employed an arbitrary procedure that denied other members basic due process.[219]

The transparency requirement will place additional procedural burdens on US human rights measures, since most US human rights sanctions are imposed either by the President or by the President and Congress, based on the USA's unilateral assessment of a foreign state's human rights record. Although a foreign state may submit information for consideration in this process, few US sanctions regimes afford the measures of due process required by *Shrimp/Turtle*. The GSP review process, for example, (which is exempt from GATT requirements) is triggered either independently by the US Trade Representative or by a petition submitted by any interested party that challenges a country's continued beneficiary status. The GSP Subcommittee, which is composed of representatives of relevant US agencies, may decline the petition for further monitoring, or accept it for formal review. Petitions that are accepted undergo a thorough one-year examination of the country's labour legislation and practices, including extensive communication with the state whose practices are in question. The Subcommittee ultimately may recommend that benefits be terminated or suspended, or that the review be extended for an additional period.[220] This process involves some of the more elaborate procedural mechanisms of US sanctions provisions, but still probably falls short of those required by *Shrimp/Turtle*.

The transparency requirement does not appear to burden human rights sanctions more than other forms of trade restrictions. The combination of Article XX's necessity, proportionality, multilateral exhaustion, and transparency requirements, however, imposes substantial transaction costs on all unilateral measures. Under the WTO exhaustion requirements, a state must make a good faith effort to pursue international agreements before imposing unilateral measures. If such efforts fail, the transparency principle requires the state to allow a foreign state to participate in its review and certification process, with full rights of notice and appeal, in determining whether the country is engaging in a prohibited practice. And once it is determined that a state is engaging in the prohibited practice, a sanctioning state may not establish an across-the-board rule. A state still must tailor its enforcement measures

within the scope of one or another of the exceptions (a) to (j) of Article XX"). See also Art. XX GATT ("nothing in this Agreement shall be construed to prevent the adoption or enforcement by *any contracting party* of [the designated] measures") (emphasis added).

[219] *Shrimp/Turtle*, *supra* n. 175, pp. 73–4, ¶ 180.

[220] OECD Report, *supra* n. 38, p. 184.

both to take individual country conditions into account and to avoid differential treatment of similarly-situated states in crafting a non-discriminatory measure. Finally, any trade measures adopted must satisfy the reasonableness or necessity requirements of Article XX. In combination, these requirements place tremendous administrative costs on states seeking to adopt unilateral measures under Article XX. These restrictions are likely to make Article XX a very unattractive *locus* for human rights measures. It is unclear what member states' response will be to the obstacles raised by Article XX. They may abandon use of unilateral trade sanctions for human rights purposes in favour of GATT compliance. They may instead seek to locate such measures in the national security provisions of Article XXI. Or they may flout the GATT requirements and adopt sanctions despite the risk of retaliation by WTO members.

The impact of WTO approaches on human rights sanctions

What, given the above, is the likely impact of the GATT on existing unilateral human rights sanctions practices?

First, import preferences for developing countries (such as the Caribbean Basin, Andean Region, Sub-Saharan Africa, and general GSP regimes) can be conditioned on human and labour rights compliance without GATT conflict. The GATT exception for GSP measures is controversial, however, and if the exception were lifted, the GSP provisions likely would constitute general trade measures that discriminated between states in violation of the GATT. And as noted previously, GSP measures are of limited utility in promoting international human rights compliance, because developing states do not hold a monopoly on human rights violations.

Secondly, measures relating to trade in nuclear and military technology are allowed under the national security exception of Article XXI(b), as are measures adopted in response to war or international emergency. Depending on the definition and scrutiny given to the concept of international emergencies, Article XXI(b)(iii) could cover a wide range of measures or be narrowly limited to sanctions adopted in self-defence to armed attack.

Thirdly, government procurement measures, such as the Clinton child labour executive order and the Massachusetts Burma statute, are not governed by GATT but by the accompanying WTO Agreement on Government Procurement (GPA). The GPA imposes requirements related to those of GATT, and the viability of such measures will be determined by future WTO interpretation of that instrument.[221] Nevertheless, because the GPA presently has only a limited number of

[221] See *supra* n. 131. The GPA provides that government contracts may not impose requirements that are not essential to ensure the ability of the supplier to perform the contract, Art. VIII(b), but also allows exceptions for contracts below a specified value, and for measures necessary for reasons of public order. These provisions and others may allow room for certain human rights conditions

signatories, government procurement measures conditioned on human rights compliance currently may be directed against a significantly larger number of states than other trade sanctions that are not GATT-compliant.

Fourthly, *tailored* sanctions (both use- and process-based) that advance legitimate human rights interests can reasonably be embraced by the Article XX exceptions and are likely to satisfy the necessity and *chapeau* tests. Tailored measures relating to prison labour are expressly covered by Article XX(e), and other tailored provisions redressing core human rights violations would reasonably fall within the exceptions for public morals or human life. Tailored measures, however, are of limited utility in the human rights context. Process-based measures are limited to protection of labour abuses that occur in export manufacture, while use-based measures tend to be limited to the use of military technology. Tailored measures cannot be used to target other human rights abuses.

Finally, unilateral measures still may be pursued without GATT restriction against the shrinking group of states that are not WTO members. These states presently include Algeria, Cambodia, China, Ethiopia, Russia, Saudi Arabia, Sudan, Vietnam, and Yemen.[222]

In short, a somewhat chaotic patchwork of sanctions measures may be sustained under current GATT/WTO approaches. On the other hand, a wide range of measures appear precluded by current GATT interpretations. Conditional MFN treatment, for example, is prohibited by GATT, and secondary boycotts may violate GATT jurisdictional requirements. More importantly, most *semi-tailored* and *general* sanctions would fail under the WTO's current approach to necessity and proportionality under Article XX. Barring resort to the Article XXI international emergencies exception, the WTO's approach would invalidate semi-tailored sanctions such as unilateral bans on imports of diamonds or oil that fund a rogue state. The approach also would preclude general sanctions against states that commit fundamental international violations such as genocide or torture, impose racial apartheid or use forced labour. In other words, it would bar the imposition of unilateral human rights sanctions in situations such as Uganda, Rwanda, and South Africa.

The normative question that follows is whether this result is beneficial to the international community. In a world where concerted international responses even to situations such as Bosnia and Rwanda are unavailing, and where other forms of unilateral remedies are limited, is it advantageous to eliminate the possibility of general, unilateral trade measures to sanction the most egregious human rights violations? Is this result in the interest of the international community? With China's pending entry into the WTO, and as an ever greater part of the global community is encompassed in the GATT trade system, is the

in government procurement agreements. For a thoughtful argument that the GPA does not bar selective purchasing laws such as the Massachusetts Act, see McCrudden, *supra* n. 133.

[222] See World Trade Organization membership list, <http://www.wto.org/english/thewto_e/whatis_e/tif_e/org6_e.htm> (visited 14 October 2000).

WTO to become a shelter to protect human rights violators? Indeed, does GATT *require* states to trade with genocidal states and other countries committing gross human rights atrocities?

V. RECONCILING FREE TRADE WITH THE HUMAN RIGHTS REGIME

Reduction of international trade barriers is a goal of the international trading system, and devout free traders will argue that all trade barriers, including those adopted for fundamental human rights purposes, are inconsistent with the goal of trade liberalisation. Yet it is clear that GATT tolerates many exceptions to the free trade system for non-trade values, including measures to protect intellectual property and national historic treasures, and involving the importation of gold and silver.[223] The critical question for the GATT system thus is not whether *any* trade-restrictive measures will be allowed, but whether human rights measures should be included among the social values that may be advanced through trade policy.

Once it is recognised that the GATT does not advance a pure free-trade agenda at the expense of all non-trade values, it is very difficult to argue that international human rights should not be among the GATT-protected values. Is it logical and in the international community's interest, for example, for the trade system to allow trade barriers to protect intellectual property rights but not to protect against bonded child labour, genocide, and torture? Moreover, GATT's present relationship to human rights values is haphazard and sporadic, with certain types of human rights norms and certain types of trade sanctions tolerated, while other measures which may promote more fundamental human rights values, are not.

Nothing in either the text of GATT or the underlying purposes of the free trade system compels this result. Indeed, as discussed below, GATT could accommodate general sanctions for core human rights violations, either under Article XX, through modification of the necessity and proportionality requirements, or through an interpretation of the Article XXI international emergency provision that takes into consideration the *jus cogens* concerns of the human rights regime. Either of these approaches would help to rationalise the haphazard human rights/free trade relationship and would promote GATT's reconciliation with other international law values.

Article XX: necessity and proportionality

Assuming that the WTO continues to recognize the possibility of promoting extraterritorial measures under Article XX and does not impose an overly

[223] See Art. XX(c), (f) GATT; and Agreement on Trade-Related Aspects of Intellectual Property Rights (TRIPS) 14 Apr. 1994, Marrakesh Agreement Establishing the World Trade Organisation, Annex 1C, Legal Instruments—Results of the Uruguay Round, vol. 31, (1994) 33 *ILM* 81.

restrictive approach to exhaustion of multilateral options, these considerations, together with transparency and reasonableness, should not pose insurmountable barriers to human rights measures. The primary obstacles to the adoption of general sanctions for *jus cogens* violations under Article XX are the proportionality requirement of the *chapeau*, and the Article XX(a) and (b) necessity requirement.

Proportionality

The basic premise of the proportionality test is that the burden on international trade should be balanced against the importance of the legitimate, non-commercial interest at stake, and the measure's benefit or effectiveness in promoting that interest. This requirement, however, says little about the way in which the proportionality balancing test is to be conducted, or about the standard of review to be applied to state practices. A reasonable construction of both the "interest" and "effectiveness" prongs of the proportionality balancing test would accommodate general sanctions for fundamental *jus cogens* human rights violations.

Interest: Properly applied, the outcome of any balancing test turns on the relative weight of the elements being balanced. In the GATT context, the extent of the tolerable "burden on trade" accordingly should increase with the importance of the legitimate non-trade interest being advanced. The *Shrimp/Turtle* Appellate Body acknowledged this relationship, stating that the "equilibrium" between the interests of the sanctioning party and other members "is not fixed and unchanging; the line moves as the kind and the shape of the measures at stake vary and as the facts making up specific cases differ".[224]

Applied to human rights measures, this should mean that the greater the significance of the human rights violation, the greater the burden on trade that should be tolerated. Violations of fundamental *jus cogens* human rights norms such as genocide, torture, and slavery should weigh more in this balance, and thus justify broader trade restrictions, than lesser treaty-based rights. *Jus cogens* principles are peremptory norms, which override conflicting rules of treaty and customary international law, which are universally binding on all states, and which are generally subject to universal jurisdiction for criminal enforcement. International law accords them unique weight, and it is appropriate that they likewise should enjoy greater weight in the free trade calculus. The systematic nature and scope of the atrocities also should be considered in the balancing process. Thus, a rule that allowed semi-tailored and general sanctions for widespread violations of *jus cogens* norms would be fully consistent with the interest balancing that undergirds the proportionality test.

Effectiveness: The effectiveness prong of the proportionality balancing test also should be framed to accommodate the nature of human rights sanctions. A

[224] *Shrimp/Turtle*, *supra* n. 175, p. 62, ¶ 159.

requirement that states demonstrate *prospectively* that a human rights measure will be effective in terms of altering a state's behaviour would be either cynical or naive, since human rights sanctions operate in intangible ways. Given the fundamental nature of the rights at stake and the role of sanctions in articulating human rights values, the difficulty of establishing that trade sanctions will accomplish a particular desired end should not preclude the use of human rights measures. The fact that a rogue regime such as the government of Libya, Burma, or the former South Africa may have substantial protected assets that will be impervious to sanctions may influence the *policy* decision regarding whether and what sanctions should be employed. But it should not render *GATT-illegal* trade measures that are imposed to retaliate for gross human rights atrocities.

Instead, once it is established that a measure is imposed to promote a legitimate *jus cogens* value, a presumption in favour of the measure's effectiveness should be applied in the proportionality balancing test. In other words, general sanctions imposed for legitimate human rights grounds should be presumed to be effective, broadly defined, absent some compelling evidence to the contrary. At the very least, human rights sanctions should not be presumed *ineffective* if a state is unable prospectively to demonstrate their effectiveness. This approach to effectiveness would allow the burden on trade to vary with the importance and scope of the human rights interest at stake.

There is WTO precedent for such an approach. In the *Hormones* case, the WTO Appellate Body held that states should not be required to meet a threshold of scientific justification for the regulation of biohazards that was so high as to frustrate a state's responsibility to its populace. In other words, the demonstration of a measure's reasonableness should take into account realities of scientific uncertainty and the limits of objective proof.[225] The new Biosafety Protocol (BSP)[226] goes even further in this direction by establishing a precautionary principle in favour of state efforts to protect their territory from biohazards. The BSP creates a favourable presumption for state restrictions on imports of certain living modified organisms, and in particular, eliminates any requirement that states demonstrate the measure's effectiveness to a scientific certainty:

> "Lack of scientific certainty due to insufficient relevant scientific information and knowledge regarding the extent of the potential adverse effects of a living modified organism on the conservation and sustainable use of biological diversity in the Party of import, taking also into account risks to human health, shall not prevent that Party from taking a decision, as appropriate, with regard to the import of that living

[225] GATT Appellate Body Report, *EC—Measures Concerning Meat and Meat Products (Hormones)*, WT/DS26/AB/R (January 16, 1998), ¶ 194 ("By itself, [scientific uncertainty] does not necessarily signal the absence of a reasonable relationship between the SPS measure and the risk assessment, especially where the risk involved is life-threatening in character and is perceived to constitute a clear and imminent threat to public health and safety. Determination of the presence or absence of that relationship can only be done on a case-to-case basis, after account is taken of all considerations rationally bearing upon the issue of potential adverse health effects").

[226] See Cartegena Biosafety Protocol, p. 32.

> modified organism intended for direct use as food or feed, or for processing in order to avoid or minimize such potential adverse effects".[227]

In other words, the Protocol recognises that scientific uncertainty exists regarding the possible hazards posed by many living modified organisms, and that this uncertainty should not preclude states from acting to protect their interests. (The standard contrasts with that in the SPS Agreement which requires a state to demonstrate scientific justification for restrictive measures.)[228] A presumption similar to the precautionary principle for *jus cogens* norms would presume that sanctions imposed for that purpose will advance that goal.

The above approach to the proportionality requirement would preserve general trade sanctions for *jus cogens* human rights violations while narrowing the circumstances under which states legitimately could impose broad trade sanctions for human rights purposes, and thus reduce the opportunity for abuse. General sanctions would not be allowed under the balancing test for emergent values of the international community, such as the promotion of democracy (though restrictions on military sales for such purposes would remain available). The rule also makes logical and normative sense. It does not seem unreasonable to say that committing genocide should suspend a state's entitlement to the protection of the international trade regime.

Necessity

The necessity requirement currently poses the greatest obstacle to trade measures under the Article XX human life and public morals provisions. As noted above, however, nothing in the necessity requirement compels the stringent "least trade restrictive measure" standard that has been adopted by the WTO. The necessity requirement could be modified in a number of ways to allow for greater accommodation of *jus cogens* human rights measures.

GATT's fundamental purpose is the promotion of free trade, and a preference for non-trade sanctions is thus reasonable under the GATT system. Indeed, states traditionally employ other measures, such as diplomatic overtures and restrictions on foreign assistance, before resorting to trade sanctions for human rights purposes. Yet, a requirement that states demonstrate that other non-trade remedies are not reasonably available should be sensitive to the concept of effectiveness in the human rights context, as discussed *supra*, and accordingly to the comparative *appropriateness* of the non-trade measures. This approach would allow states to demonstrate that non-trade measures, such as restrictions on foreign aid or GSP benefits, were not adequate alternatives to trade sanctions. There may be circumstances where resort to non-trade measures, such as limits on foreign assistance, will harm the

[227] *Ibid*. Art. 11(8).

[228] See discussion in Schoenbaum, *supra* Chapter 2.

populace rather than advance a human rights value. Burma, for example, is a country with a severely impoverished populace, an underdeveloped economy, and a military government which obtains most of its foreign exchange from trade in illicit drugs, gems, and foreign oil transactions. Limiting foreign assistance in the form of basic medical and humanitarian aid to the country could simply further impoverish the populace while having little negative impact on the governing junta. Trade sanctions targeting gem and oil imports, by contrast, would more directly and negatively impact the government, while causing less harm to the general population. An approach to effectiveness which accommodated for such considerations would create greater flexibility for human rights measures.

Thus, if GATT is to be interpreted to be consistent with other international values, it would be appropriate to require that states pursuing unilateral trade measures to make a good faith effort first to pursue other *appropriate* non-trade measures, such as diplomatic overtures or foreign assistance, and that they *simultaneously* pursue any available international remedies. This may include pursuing multilateral remedies before the ILO or the UN Human Rights Committee, and pressing for Security Council action, where appropriate. It may also involve diplomatic overtures to encourage other states to join in the unilateral effort, such as those mandated by the *Shrimp/Turtle* statute and by the present US sanctions statute against Burma.[229] Such an approach to less trade restrictive measures would allow unilateral measures to retain their legitimate role of promoting the interests of the international system without unnecessarily burdening trade or undermining multilateral mechanisms.

Finally, the restrictiveness of the necessity requirement also depends in large part on the standard of review which the WTO applies to this question. At this point, it is unclear what standard of review the WTO is applying to determine whether a measure is the least trade-restrictive measure available, and in particular, whether the WTO will defer to a state's own determination that less trade-restrictive measures are not reasonably available or effective to promote the legitimate state interest. Greater deference to state determinations that are made through transparent processes and for legitimate non-protectionist purposes would improve the ability of the necessity requirement to accommodate human rights measures. Indeed, the very availability of Articles XX(a) and (b) for human rights concerns is likely to turn on these considerations.

[229] See 1997 Omnibus Consolidated Appropriations Act, Pub. L. No. 104–208, 110 Stat. 3009–166 (1996), § 507(c) (directing the President to work to develop "a comprehensive, multilateral strategy to bring democracy to and improve human rights practices . . . in Burma").

Article XXI international emergencies

Alternatively, the Article XXI(b)(iii) international emergencies provision also could be construed to accommodate general sanctions to promote *jus cogens* human rights norms. A restrictive construction of the clause that limited "international emergencies" to situations directly threatening a particular state's territory and populace would ignore the extent to which human rights violations are now recognised as the concern of all states. It would also impose a geographically arbitrary limit on use of the national security clause to redress human rights violations in third world countries. Human rights atrocities in a country that closely borders the world's major economic powers, such as the conflict in Kosovo, legitimately could be characterised as an emergency threatening the essential security interests of those powers. Atrocities occurring in farther flung reaches of the globe, such as Africa and Asia, could not arguably be characterised as threatening the security interests of the major economic powers, however, and thus the countries most capable of wielding economic clout to promote political change would be barred from intervening. This approach is illogical from a normative, human rights enforcement perspective. It also is inconsistent with evolving concepts of international security. The international community increasingly has been willing to recognise *jus cogens* human rights atrocities as matters which threaten international security and warrant economic, humanitarian, and even military intervention, in places as varied as Rhodesia, South Africa, Somalia, Rwanda, Bosnia, Haiti, and Kosovo. In Somalia, for example, the United Nations found that the "magnitude of human tragedy" constituted a threat to international peace and security warranting armed intervention.[230] The United Nations also has recognised a number of human rights conflicts resulting in transnational refugee flows as threats to international peace and security[231]—a determination which some commentators have interpreted as a pretence for intervening in situations involving gross violations of human rights.[232] And Tanzania's invasion of Uganda in the 1970s is by no means the only example of regional or unilateral intervention by states motivated at least partially by human rights and refugee concerns.[233]

230 See Cassidy, "Sovereignty Versus the Chimera of Armed Humanitarian Intervention", (1997) 21 *Fletcher Forum of World Affairs*, 47, 59.

231 UN Security Council Resolution 688 authorised military assistance to Kurdish refugees in northern Iraq as a result of the threat of refugee flows to international peace and security. See Martin, "Strategies for a Resistant World: Human Rights Initiatives and the Need for Alternatives to Refugee Interdiction", (1993) 26 *Cornell Int'l L. J.* 753, 766–68. The Security Council also found that refugee flows in Bosnia contributed to the threat to international peace and security. See Riley, Note, "Neither Free Nor Fair: The 1996 Bosnian Elections and the Failure of the U.N. Election-Monitoring Mission", (1997) 30 *Vand. J. Transnat'l L.* 1173, 1202–03.

232 See Auth, "Protecting Minorities: Lessons of International Peacekeeping", (1977) 91 *Am. Soc. Int'l L. Proc.* 429, 438; Piczak, "The Helms-Burton Act: U.S. Foreign Policy Toward Cuba, The National Security Exception to the GATT and the Political Question Doctrine", (1999) 61 *U. Pitt. L. Rev.* 287, 315.

233 In 1990, the Economic Community of West African States (ECOWAS) relied on refugee flows

These developments in international practice relating to *jus cogens* norms suggest that a twenty-first century definition of international emergencies should include systematic violations of *jus cogens* norms, wherever they occur. Such violations *are* threats to international security, and tear fundamentally at the fabric of the international community. An interpretation of the national security clause that allowed the general imposition of such sanctions would be consistent with developments in human rights law, and would eliminate the normative anomaly that GATT could *compel* states to do business with states that violate the most sacred values of the international community.

Institutional competence

I have argued that GATT may be understood, as an interpretive matter, to accommodate a range of trade sanctions for human rights violations, including general sanctions for violations of *jus cogens* norms. A difficult question remains whether the WTO is institutionally competent to oversee and adjudicate trade measures applied for human rights purposes. The WTO's expertise and mandate is in the promotion of free trade, not the interpretation of human rights instruments, and any balancing of trade and human rights concerns that is conducted by that body is likely to undervalue human rights norms. Delegating this responsibility to the WTO thus is unlikely to produce interpretations of international human rights law that conform to the values of the human rights system.

The WTO Dispute Settlement Understanding (DSU), however, establishes various mechanisms for educating the WTO and soliciting expert advice.[234] The Appellate Body has recently recognised that the DSU authorises WTO panels to accept and consider *amicus* briefs from NGOs and other entities with expertise in a particular field.[235] More importantly, Article 13 of the DSU establishes a mechanism by which dispute panels may seek expert advice on international principles beyond WTO expertise,[236] "leav[ing] to the sound discretion of a panel the determination of whether the establishment of an expert review group

to justify regional enforcement of Security Council resolutions against Liberia. See Ofodile, "The Legality of ECOWAS Intervention in Liberia", (1994) 32 *Colum. J. Transnat'l. L.* 381, 410.

[234] DSU, *supra* n. 142, p. 353.

[235] *Shrimp/Turtle*, *supra* n. 175, p. 38, ¶ 108.

[236] DSU, *supra* n. 142, Art. 13 ("1. Each panel shall have the right to seek information and technical advice from any individual or body which it deems appropriate . . . 2. Panels may seek information from any relevant source and may consult experts to obtain their opinion on certain aspects of the matter. With respect to a factual issue concerning a scientific or other technical matter raised by a party to a dispute, a panel may request an advisory report in writing from an expert review group"). See also *ibid.*, Appendix 4 (setting forth procedures for establishment of an expert review group).

is necessary or appropriate".[237] Article 12(1) also allows panels to alter the DSU working procedures as necessary. As a result, "the DSU accords to a panel . . . ample and extensive authority to undertake and to control the process by which it informs itself both of the relevant facts of the dispute and of the legal norms and principles applicable to such facts".[238] The WTO Agreement further provides that "[t]he General Council shall make appropriate arrangements for effective cooperation with other intergovernmental organisations that have responsibilities related to those of the WTO" and may "consult . . . and cooperat[e] with non-governmental organisations concerned with matters relating to those of the WTO".[239]

The WTO has employed the expert review mechanism in disputes implicating intellectual property questions and scientific evidence.[240] This mechanism likewise would allow the WTO to seek advisory opinions from authoritative human rights bodies such as the UN Human Rights Commission and Committee, the UN Sub-Commission on the Promotion and Protection of Human Rights (which focuses specifically on the relationship between human rights and trade), or the ILO, regarding the legitimacy and nature of a human rights norm, and the validity of its application to a specific set of circumstances. Such advice could assist the WTO in determining whether an asserted human rights value should be recognised as legitimate under Articles XX or XXI. The human rights body could also advise the WTO regarding the relative importance and severity of the human rights violation, to assist the WTO in the proportionality balancing test. This option does not entirely resolve the problem of institutional expertise, since there are a number of international bodies with competing authority to interpret international human rights norms.[241] Nevertheless, the approach would serve the valuable goal of providing the WTO with specialised guidance regarding questions of human rights law, while

[237] *Shrimp/Turtle*, *supra* n. 175, p. 37, ¶ 103, quoting *Argentina—Measures Affecting Imports of Footwear, Textiles, Apparel and Other Items*, 22 April 1998, WT/SD56/AB/R ¶¶ 84–6.

[238] *Shrimp/Turtle*, *supra* n. 175, p. 38, ¶ 106.

[239] Marrakesh Agreement, *supra* n. 144, Art. V.

[240] In the recent dispute over § 110(5) of the US Copyright Act, for example, the WTO panel requested and received advice on the application of the Berne Convention from the International Bureau of the World Intellectual Property Organisation (WIPO). See WTO Dispute Panel Report, *United States—Section 110(5) of the US Copyright Act*, 15 June 2000, WT/DS160/R, 2000 WL 816081, Attachment 4. There is a WTO/WIPO agreement providing for cooperation and consultation between the two bodies, though the agreement does not mandate consultation with WIPO in WTO intellectual property disputes. See also Christoforou, "Settlement of Science-Based Trade Disputes in the WTO: A Critical Review of the Developing Case Law in the Face of Scientific Uncertainty, " (2000) 8 *NYU Environmental L. J.* 622.

[241] For example, the UN Human Rights Commission has general authority over the principles of the Universal Declaration; the Human Rights Committee has specific oversight responsibility over the ICCPR, and a separate Committee is responsible for interpretation and oversight of the Race Discrimination Convention. The authority of all three entities includes interpretation of international rules regarding race discrimination. Likewise, the Human Rights Committee and the Committee Against Torture are both responsible for defining and overseeing compliance with the international prohibition against torture, and authority over core labour rights provisions such as forced labour and freedom of association is shared by the Human Rights Committee and the ILO.

relieving the WTO of the burdens of developing internal expertise in this area. It would also promote cooperation among international bodies, thus reducing the isolation of the GATT system and encouraging its greater integration into the international community.

VI. CONCLUSION

National practice currently appears to be moving away from the use of unilateral trade measures in favour of non-trade options. This trend no doubt is in part a response to GATT requirements, and is beneficial to the extent that unilateralism can be replaced with effective non-trade or multilateral responses to human rights abuse. It is possible that developments in international co-operation regarding the enforcement of human rights norms may some day render the need for unilateral action obsolete. That day is a significant distance away, though, and in order for plurilateral and multilateral options to develop, it is critical that the option of unilateral responses to core human rights atrocities should be preserved.

The relationship between international trade and human rights, however, poses a fundamental dilemma for the international community. Either the goal of free trade eliminates trade sanctions as a mechanism for horizontal enforcement of the most fundamental human rights, or present interpretations of GATT must be modified to accommodate the legitimate values of the human rights regime. In particular, the use of general trade sanctions to target *jus cogens* human rights abuse—a core traditional use of human rights sanctions—is directly threatened by current WTO approaches.

GATT's preclusion of such human rights measures is not necessary as an interpretive matter; nor is it clear that the option of eliminating such human rights sanctions is realistic. In the absence of effective global remedies for core human rights abuses, the WTO's resistance to the use of trade sanctions for this purpose may simply result in other abuses. States may also force general human rights sanctions into the WTO national security exception and argue that the measures are insulated from WTO scrutiny. States may also flout the WTO's authority altogether, or simply seek other, less palatable unilateral means for asserting such interests.

Failure to reconcile the WTO system with the human rights regime also may ultimately undermine the promulgation of human rights norms. In the absence of international oversight, states are largely left to define for themselves what they consider to be "human rights" concerns worthy of unilateral measures. International oversight of unilateral sanctions, preferably through a form of WTO/ILO/Human Rights Commission cooperation, would allow even unilateral human rights concerns to be addressed in a principled and coherent manner. International oversight would help ensure that sanctions are not merely imposed as protectionist measures or to promote unilateral policy interests, that they comport with reasonable interpretations of international law, and that they are proportional to valid international law purposes. Accommodating GATT to the human rights regime accordingly could promote rationality, coherence, and increased respect for international standards in the use of unilateral human rights measures.

10

Which Intellectual Property Rights are Trade-Related?

MICHAEL SPENCE

I. INTRODUCTION

IT MIGHT BE hoped that the TRIPS[1] negotiators could have clearly explained both why some types of intangible ought to be the subject of intellectual property rights and why some types of intellectual property ought to be enforced as part of the world trade system. After all, it is acknowledged in the Preamble to the agreement that a failure to identify which types of intellectual property regimes ought appropriately to be included in TRIPS has high costs for a system of free trade.[2] Some such regimes might constitute no more than non-tariff barriers to trade, unjustifiable state-enforced monopolies over the supply of particular products. The TRIPS negotiators should have had some way of distinguishing those intellectual property rights that were properly the subject of the agreement from those that were not.

Indeed, the need for a method of distinguishing between such rights arguably still exists. First, calls for the expansion of the agreement have already begun. For example, at the 1999 Ministerial Conference in Seattle, Bolivia, Colombia, Ecuador, Nicaragua and Peru argued that a new regime for the protection of the traditional knowledge of local and indigenous communities ought to be introduced.[3] At the 1999 Ministerial Conference, Kenya, on behalf of the African group,[4] and Turkey[5] argued that protection for geographical indications ought to be extended to cover new types of product "recognisable by their geographical origins (handicrafts, agro-food products)".[6] It is the experience of lawyers in the European Union that the very process of harmonisation exacerbates the demand for both new property regimes and for existing regimes to be strengthened. Second, the WTO panels will need to interpret the existing regimes as parties seek to expand their coverage in new ways. For example, Article 27

[1] Agreement on Trade-Related Aspects of Intellectual Property Rights 1994.
[2] TRIPS Agreement, Preamble, Recital 1.
[3] WT/GC/W/362, 12 October 1999.
[4] WT/GC/W/302, 6 August 1999.
[5] WT/GC/W/249, 13 July 1999.
[6] WT/GC/W/302, 6 August 1999.

provides that patents shall be available "for any inventions . . . in all fields of technology". It might be questioned whether this provision requires the patentability of, for example, business methods, which are currently patentable in some jurisdictions[7] but not others.[8] Assuming that the TRIPS Agreement should develop in a coherent and justifiable way, TRIPS negotiators and WTO panels will need a principle or set of principles for the identification of the intellectual property rights that might appropriately be enforced through the world trade system.

However, not surprisingly, this task of identifying principles to determine which intellectual property rights might properly be included in the Agreement was largely, but not completely, avoided by the TRIPS negotiators. Nation states have recognised intellectual property rights for a complex variety of economic, cultural and ethical reasons. The TRIPS negotiators could avoid assessing the merits of those reasons, and thereby explaining why a particular intellectual property right ought to be included in the Agreement, by relying upon the existing international intellectual property conventions. Particular intellectual property rights have been so widely endorsed as part of those conventions for so long that their recognition seems almost axiomatic.

In that the TRIPS negotiators did give some indication of which intellectual property rights ought to be included in the Agreement, they did so in Article 7. While the Preamble to the agreement alludes vaguely to "the need to promote effective and adequate protection of intellectual property rights", Article 7 sets out a far more precise objective for the Agreement. Article 7 might also be read as a guide to the type of intellectual property rights that should be included in TRIPS: that is, we might assume that only such intellectual property rights should be included as further the Article 7 objectives.[9]

Article 7, the current text of which was proposed by a group of developing countries at the 1990 Brussels Ministerial Conference,[10] reads:

> "*Objectives*
> The protection and enforcement of intellectual property rights should contribute to the promotion of technological innovation and to the transfer and dissemination of technology, to the mutual advantage of producers and users of technological knowledge and in a manner conducive to social and economic welfare, and to a balance of rights and obligations".

From the outset, two features of Article 7 should be emphasised.

First, the Article is different to the statements of the objectives of TRIPS

[7] For example, in the USA after *State Street Bank & Trust Co.* v. *Signature Financial Group, Inc.*149 F.3d 1368 (1st Cir. 1998) *cert. denied* 119 S. Ct 851 (1999).

[8] For example, under Art. 52(2)(c) of the European Patent Convention.

[9] Thus Gervais writes: "[The use of this provision], notably in dispute settlement procedures, is likely to be frequent, as it could be invoked to limit an obligation to protect or enforce a given intellectual property right where no promotion of intellectual innovation and/or transfer or technology can be proven": D. Gervais, *The TRIPS Agreement: Drafting History and Analysis* (London, Sweet & Maxwell, 1998), p. 64.

[10] For the two versions of the Article see Gervais, *ibid.* at 64.

contained in earlier drafts of the Agreement and in at least one important decision of the Appellate Body since the adoption of the current text. Thus, Article 1B of the draft contained in the Chairman's Report to the Group of Negotiation on Goods,[11] a seminal draft in the history of the agreement, was built upon the assumption that intellectual property rights are primarily granted "in acknowledgement of the contributions of inventors and creators". Similarly, in outlining the "object and purpose" of the TRIPS Agreement, the Report of the Appellate Body in *India-Patent Protection for Pharmaceutical and Agricultural Chemical Products*[12] does not even mention Article 7. Rather, it focuses upon the phrase in the Preamble to the Agreement acknowledging "the need to promote effective and adequate protection of intellectual property rights". Such statements obviously imply a far broader understanding of the purpose of the TRIPS Agreement, and therefore of the rights it might appropriately include, than the rather constrained language of Article 7.

Second, the constrained language of Article 7 has a particular purpose in that it reflects the objectives outlined in the recitals to the Agreement Establishing the WTO. Thus, like the first recital to the Agreement Establishing the WTO, it expresses a concern for increasing global welfare. Similarly, like the second recital to the Agreement Establishing the WTO, it demonstrates a particular concern for developing countries which might be assumed to benefit most from the transfer and dissemination of technology. Article 7 sets out to paint TRIPS as "less an exercise in international rent transfer away from the south and more of an inducement of research and development and an enhancement of global social welfare".[13]

However, it is the contention of this chapter that Article 7 is inadequate to identify which intellectual property rights ought appropriately to be included in the Agreement, indeed that it is unable to justify the inclusion of even many of those intellectual property rights that currently form part of TRIPS. As this becomes apparent and alternative justifications for the recognition of various types of intangible are articulated, TRIPS will raise far broader questions about the political and economic goals that might appropriately be pursued through the world trade system. The TRIPS Agreement may prove to have repercussions far beyond the field of intellectual property. This chapter first sets out the difficulties inherent in Article 7. It then briefly considers two other possible approaches to the identification of intellectual property rights for inclusion in TRIPS and some of the broader issues that they raise for the world trade system as a whole. Throughout the chapter, I will assume that countries with lower levels of effective intellectual property protection and enforcement are typically

[11] MTN.GNG/NG11/W/76, 23 July 1990.

[12] WT/DS50/AB/R, 19 December 1997.

[13] A. Subramanian, "Putting Some Numbers on the TRIPS Pharmaceutical Debate" (1995) 10 *Int J Technology Management* 252. This phrase is not taken from a discussion of Art. 7, but from a passage in which Subramanian suggests, rather doubtfully, that the dynamic benefits that a TRIPS Agreement could confer might modify his initial conclusions that, at least in the pharmaceutical industry, TRIPS is precisely such an exercise in rent transfer.

developing countries (including least developed countries) and that those with higher levels of effective intellectual property protection and enforcement are typically developed countries.

II. ARTICLE 7

The difficulty with Article 7 is that it consists of two highly contested claims about the function of intellectual property rights in the process of innovation and the dissemination of technology. As TRIPS is analysed and fought over in the coming years, the tenuity of those claims will arguably weaken the role that Article 7 can have in determining the inclusion or exclusion of particular rights. Article 7 may come to play a far less important role in shaping the future of TRIPS than might be expected of a provision setting out the objectives of the Agreement.

Intellectual property rights and technological innovation

The first claim made in Article 7 is that intellectual property rights contribute to the promotion of technological innovation. This claim has been fiercely contested, but it is particularly dubious in the context of many of the intellectual property rights included in the TRIPS Agreement.The notion that intellectual property rights contribute to innovation stems from the categorisation of innovation as a "public good". A typical exposition of this notion might be found in Gordon's work on copyright.[14] Gordon begins by asserting that "voluntary transfers between individuals will create a socially desirable pattern of resource allocation"[15]—that they will "result in the maximisation of value"[16]—as long as a market is characterized by particular competitive conditions. She claims that the market for copyright works is not marked by those competitive conditions because such works are "public goods" in the sense that they are "virtually inexhaustible once produced", and that "persons who have not paid for access cannot readily be prevented from using them".[17] Therefore works "will be under-produced if left to the private market".[18] Copyright law cures this "market failure"[19] by providing a means of excluding non-purchasers and so allows a market for works to function. Alternative methods of solving the "public goods" problem, such as taxation and centralised purchasing, are rejected because a "democratic society demands decentralised and diverse creation in the

[14] W. Gordon, "Fair Use as Market Failure: A Structural and Economic Analysis of the *Betamax* Case and its Predecssors" (1982) 82 *Col. L. Rev.* 1600.

[15] *Ibid.* at 1605.

[16] *Ibid.* at 1606.

[17] *Ibid.* at 1611.

[18] *Ibid.* at 1611.

[19] *Ibid.* at 1610.

intellectual sphere; freedom from state control is essential lest freedom of expression be curtailed by fear of governmental reprisal".[20] This notion that intellectual property rights promote innovation gains added political force by its endorsement in the United States Constitution . Article I, section 8, clause 8 of the Constitution gives Congress power to make law "[t]o promote the Progress of Science and the useful Arts, by securing for limited Times to Authors and Inventors the exclusive Right to their respective Writings and Discoveries".

The first difficulty with the claim that the rights enshrined in the TRIPS Agreement promote innovation, and particularly technological innovation, is that it clearly does not cover all the rights to which the Agreement gives force. Thus no-one would claim that systems of protection for trade marks or geographical indications have the effect of promoting innovation and certainly not *technological* innovation. The primary economic justification for trade mark systems is that they reduce consumer search costs,[21] rather than that they provide an incentive for investment in marks.[22] Further, even if it might be argued that copyright provides incentives for innovation in the arts, it can hardly be said (at least outside the field of computer software protection) to promote *technological* innovation.[23] Yet it would have been unthinkable that TRIPS should have been finalised without the inclusion of, for example, protection for motion pictures. The motion picture industry has been central to the intellectual property foreign policy of the USA.[24]

The second difficulty with the claim that the rights enshrined in TRIPS promote innovation is that assessing whether a particular right does, in fact, promote innovation is an enormously difficult task when undertaken even in relation to purely national economic welfare. Such assessments may prove almost impossible if global economic welfare is the negotiators' goal. There are, no doubt, contexts in which the claim that intellectual property rights promote innovation is perfectly justified. But it is by no means true that stronger intellectual property rights lead, as a general rule, to greater innovation. Intellectual property rights are monopolies that can just as easily stifle innovation as promote it. Whether or not an intellectual property right promotes innovation is dependent upon a host of factors, three of which are important to emphasise here.

[20] *Ibid.* at 1612.

[21] For a summary of the economic arguments see W. M. Landes and R. A. Posner, "The Economics of Trademark Law" (1988) 78 *TMR* 267.

[22] "This analysis suggests that we do not need trademark protection just to be sure of having enough words, though we may need patent protection to be sure of having enough inventions, or copyright protection to be sure of having enough books, movies and musical compositions": *ibid* at 275.

[23] The only sense in which copyright in material such as musical, literary, dramatic and artistic works and films might be said to promote *technological* innovation would be by sustaining industries that encourage investment in associated technologies (for example, better printing presses or machines to create special effects). However, these innovations might themselves by protected by patent.

[24] See, for example, W. P. Alford, "Making the World Safe for What? Intellectual Property Rights, Human Rights and Foreign Economic Policy in the Post-European Cold War World" (1997) *N.Y.U. J. Int'l L. & Pol.* 135 at 150–1.

First, whether an intellectual property right promotes innovation will depend upon the particular product that it protects and the available market for that product. In relation to some types of product in some types of market, the intellectual property incentive may be unnecessary. Alternative incentives might flow from the competitive advantage implicit in innovation itself. Intellectual property is more likely to be important in contexts in which research and development costs are high in comparison to a competitor's imitation costs and there is a ready and affluent market for the new product. In relation to other types of product and other types of market, even strong intellectual property incentives may prove inadequate to promote innovation and therefore not justify their monopoly costs. This is an important consideration in the context of TRIPS. Pharmaceutical companies have been trying to persuade developing countries that more effective systems of intellectual property protection will lead to both local and foreign investment in drugs to fight diseases that are specific to the developing world.[25] But it remains an open question how specific the pharmaceutical needs of the developing world actually are. Moreover, it is questionable whether potential returns from markets in developing countries will be sufficient to induce pharmaceutical companies in the developed world to divert resources into investigating cures to diseases that are specific to the developing world. It is also highly questionable whether many pharmaceutical companies in the developing world, at least in countries with small populations,[26] will have either the research and development capacity to produce such drugs or, even if they do, the prospect of sufficient returns to justify investment in locally relevant research. The often cited example of India, in which the impact of TRIPS has allegedly been a marked increase in local research and development,[27] may be misleading given that India has an extremely developed pharmaceutical industry built on low-cost imitations of foreign drugs.[28] India is also an important exporter of drugs and it remains to be seen how much of the new research and development is undertaken with the local market, rather than the more lucrative export market, in view.

Second, whether an intellectual property right promotes innovation will depend upon the extent of the protection that it offers. Endless economic arguments have been mounted about the precise scope of particular rights that are

[25] "In this age of emerging and re-emerging serious infectious diseases, particularly in tropical climates, the lack of intellectual property protection for pharmaceuticals is an example of national and regional *disarmament* against the invasion and destruction of such diseases": H. E. Bale (Senior Vice President, International Pharmaceutical Research and Manufacturers of America), "Patent Protection and Pharmaceutical Innovation" (1997) 29 *N.Y.U. J. Int'l L. & Pol.* 95 at 100. See also C. R. Frischtak, "Harmonization Versus Differentiation in International Property Rights Regimes" (1995) 10 *Int. J. Technology Management* 200 at 210–11.

[26] On the impact of TRIPS on pharmaceutical supply in small countries see Subramanian, *supra* n. 13, p. 252.

[27] See, for example, M. J. Adelman and S. Baldia, "Prospects and Limits of the Patent Provision in the TRIPS Agreement: The Case of India" (1996) 29 *Vand. J. Transnat'l L.* 507 at 529.

[28] *Ibid.* at 525–8.

necessary to promote innovation in relation to particular types of products.[29] In the TRIPS context, the question of the extent of protection necessary to promote innovation becomes whether protection in additional countries is necessary to increase global technological output. It may be that the intellectual property systems of the developed world are so organised that they provide strong incentives for research and development and that the addition of protection in further countries will not produce a sufficient increase in incentive to outweigh the potentially stifling effects of the larger monopoly, far less its social costs.[30] For example, assume the proposition advanced in the preceding paragraph that the advent of TRIPS is unlikely to lead to increased investment by the pharmaceutical companies in drugs that are specific to the needs of the developing world. In relation to drugs that are useful in both developing and developed countries, it may be argued that increased profits from protection in additional countries will lead to more investment by companies in the developed world and hence to more new drugs. However, it is likely that there is a diminshing return from increased investment in research and development and it may well be that pharmaceutical companies in the developed world already have a close to optimal level of incentive for investment in drugs that are useful in their own countries: provided, of course, that they can exclude the importation into their home markets of both low-cost imitations of drugs from the developing world and, perhaps, low-cost drugs that they themselves have manufactured or licensed in the developing world.[31] Profit from the addition of new markets may be little more than rent.

[29] See, for example, the following debates about ideal patent scope: R. Gilbert, and C. Shapiro, "Optimal Patent Length and Breadth" (1990) 21 *RAND J. Econ* 107; P. Klemperer, "How Broad Should the Scope of Patent Protection Be?" (1990) 21 *RAND J. Econ.* 113; R. P. Merges, and R. R. Nelson, "On the Complex Economics of Patent Scope" (1990) 90 *Colum. L. Rev.* 830; N. T. Gallini, "Patent Policy and Costly Imitation" (1992) 23 *RAND J. Econ.* 52; J. Lerner, "The Importance of Patent Scope: An Empirical Analysis" (1994) 25 *RAND J. Econ.* 319; C. Matutes, P. Regibeau, and K. Rockett, "Optimal Patent Design and the Diffusion of Innovations" (1996) 27 *RAND J. Econ* 60. Note also that fine tuning intellectual property systems so that they offer precisely the type of incentive required in a particular field may increase the legal costs associated with the intellectual property system, reducing its overall effectiveness in the promotion of innovation; see, for example, J. O. Lanjouw, "Economic Consequences of a Changing Litigation Environment: The Case of Patents", National Bureau of Economic Research Working Paper: 4835 (August 1994) and J. Lerner, "Patenting in the Shadow of Competitors" (1995) 38 *J. L. & Econ.* 463.

[30] See A. S. Oddi, "TRIPS—Natural Rights and a 'Polite Form of Economic Imperialism' " (1996) 29 *Vand. J. Transnat'l L.* 415 at 443–5.

[31] The countries of the developed world have been criticized for allowing intellectual property rights to be used to exclude the importation of goods marketed by the rights holder, or under her licence, from the developing world into the developed world. See, for example, Oddi, *supra* n. 30, pp. 455–6, where it is argued that allowing countries to prevent the importation of goods made with the consent of the rights holder is incompatible with the enhancement of free trade. However, allowing international price discrimination may be important to encouraging both investment in research and devleopment and technology transfer, by allowing the rights holder to maximise the return on her intellectual property rights in the developed world. Such an argument could certainly be made in relation to rights in patent, copyright and designs, although it is far less convincing in relation to rights in trade mark, the field in which much of the debate concerning the issue has been conducted (for a summary of the arguments in relation to trade mark see A. Ohly, "Trade Marks and Parallel Importation—Recent Developments in European Law" (1990) 30 *IIC* 512). Importantly, TRIPS left the issue of the exhaustion of rights untouched; see Art. 6 TRIPS.

Third, whether an intellectual property right promotes innovation will depend upon the maturity of the industry in which that intellectual property right is operative.[32] In the TRIPS context, the relative stage of development of different industries is a particularly important consideration. In the initial stages of a local industry's development, imitation may be essential in order to build up production and marketing capacity. An obvious example is again the Indian pharmaceutical industry in which a period of imitation arguably led to the development of an industry that is now able to invest in research and development.[33] Of course, in any given industry a period of imitation is not automatically followed by a period of innovation,[34] but it may sometimes be a necessary pre-condition to it. As Abbott points out, a country that permits industries in their infancies to imitate established technologies is only "replicating the economic development models followed to a varying extent by the United States, Japan, Korea and Taiwan".[35]

A consideration of even these three factors (and there are many more), underscores the difficulty in assessing whether a particular intellectual property right promotes innovation. If Article 7 were taken seriously as expressing the objective of the TRIPS Agreement and were used to determine which intellectual property rights it might appropriately include, the task of balancing these factors would have to be undertaken on a global scale. The benefits to innovation would have to be weighed against the very obvious monopoly costs associated with intellectual property rights. As Frischtak points out, these calculations become even more complicated if the welfare gains of developing countries are valued more highly than those of developed countries, as arguably they should be, in the assessment of global welfare.[36] On the one hand, inovation that benefits the developing world ought perhaps to be valued more highly than innovation that does not. On the other hand, the cost of an intellectual property system increases if its tendency to create rent transfer from the developing to the developed world is valued more highly than its general monopoly costs.

The difficulty of making such calculations raises real questions about the utility of the Article 7 criterion that an intellectual property right ought to be included in TRIPS if it promotes technological innovation. Of course, it could be argued that the difficulty of making such calculations does not, of itself, render the attempt to do so illegitimate. Policy-makers are regularly called upon to make difficult welfare calculations. However, there must come a point at which

[32] See, for example, J. Reichman, "From Free Riders to Fair Followers: Global Competition Under the TRIPS Agreement" (1997) 29 *N.Y.U. J. Int'l L. & Pol.*11.

[33] See J. Reichman, "Compliance with the TRIPS Agreement: Introduction to a Scholarly Debate" (1996) 29 *Vand. J. Transnation'l L.* 363 at 380–2.

[34] See, for example, F. M. Scherer, and S. Weisburst, "Economic Effects of Strengthening Pharmaceutical Patent Protection in Italy" (1995) 26 *IIC* 1009 at 1023–4.

[35] F. M. Abbott, "The Enduring Enigma of TRIPS: A Challenge for the World Economic System" (1998) 1 *Journal of International Economic Law* 497 at 505.

[36] C. R. Frischtak, "Harmonization Versus Differentiation in International Property Rights Regimes" (1995) 10 *Int. J. Technology Management* 200 at 210–11.

a particular welfare calculation is so complex that its utility as a basis for decision-making is limited and the calculations required by Article 7 are arguably close to that order of complexity. *National* intellectual property rights may be justified as incentives for innovation and appropriately shaped to constitute such incentives, but *international* intellectual property rights are far less obviously so.

Intellectual property rights and the transfer and dissemination of technology

Unfortunately, the utility of Article 7 can no more depend upon the second of its claims regarding the function of intellectual property rights than it can the first. The second claim made in Article 7 is that intellectual property rights promote the transfer and dissemination of technology.

Intellectual property is overwhelmingly the property of the developed world[37] and, at least in the short term, the developing world might be expected to lose most from the TRIPS Agreement.[38] Increasing intellectual property protection in the developing world is likely to increase the export of protected products into those markets.[39] As the final stages of the TRIPS negotiations were in progress, the Rural Advancement Fund International warned that royalty payments under the proposed agreement could "double or even triple the foreign exchange outflow caused by Third World annual debt repayments".[40] An even gloomier forecast might now be made in light of the increasing importance of intellectual property rights in the field of agricultural research and development.[41] Of course, prophecies of this kind are unrealistic in that the ability of companies in the developed world to extract such royalties is going to be limited and the developing world will have strategies for mitigating the full potential effect of TRIPS.[42] Nevertheless, the agreement will have at least the short term effect of increasing the flow of income from the developing to the developed world.

The second claim made in Article 7 is one of a number of similar claims intended to convince the developing world that the benefits of TRIPS outweigh its costs.[43] It is suggested that foreign companies which are reluctant either to license their technology or to invest directly in its local exploitation in countries

[37] See C. A. Primo Braga and C. Fink, "Reforming Intellectual Property Rights Regimes: Challenges for Developing Countries" (1998) *Journal of International Economic Law* 537 at 544–5.

[38] For a different long term forecast, at least in relation to newly industrialised countries, see Oddi, *supra* n. 30, pp. 455–60.

[39] See K. E. Maskus and M. Penubarti, "How Trade Related Are Intellectual Property Rights?" (1995) 39 *Journal of International Economics* 227.

[40] *RAFI Communiqué*, May-June 1989, at p. 8.

[41] See Primo Braga and Fink, *supra* n. 37, pp. at 539–40.

[42] See J. Reichman and D. Lange, "Bargaining Around the TRIPS Agreement: The Case for On-going Public-Private Initiatives to Facilitate Worldwide Intellectual Property Transactions" (1998) 9 *Duke J. Comp. & Int'l L.* 11.

[43] These range from the pragmatic argument discussed *infra* that implementing TRIPS might protect a country from American trade retaliation to the optimistic argument that the introduction of intellectual property rights has a positive effect on good governance. On this latter point see the arguments of Cottier discussed in Abbot, *supra* n. 35, p. 510 n.44.

offering only weak intellectual protection, will be keen to do so once standards of intellectual property protection have been raised. The developing world will thus benefit, not only from increased incentives to local innovation and to innovation in the developed world that is appropriate to meet developing world needs, but also from the transfer of technology from the developed world to the benefit of local industries. The use of this technology under licence, or its use by the owners of the rights themselves in local production, is seen as preferable to the use of the technology without permission, even assuming the technology is appropriable, because it will be associated with training, the transfer of associated "know-how" and, perhaps, the capital necessary to exploit the technology. In this context the establishment of a regime of trade secret protection under Article 39 TRIPS is seen as essential.

However, once again this claim is both highly contested and particularly dubious as regards many of the rights already in the TRIPS Agreement. It is an often noted irony that the intellectual property systems of the USA effectively denied protection to foreigners during the period of that country's development, presumably because to do so was thought to be good for the development of local industries.[44]

A first objection to the claim that the rights enshrined in TRIPS promote the transfer and dissemination of technology, is that many of those rights do not deal, either primarily or at all, with subject matter that might be important for technological development. Consider, for example, systems of protection for copyright,[45] trade marks and geographical indications. It is at least initially difficult to see how the payment of royalties to authors of fiction in the developed world, or the prevention of the manufacture of "Gucci" t-shirts or local "champagne", will encourage either the transfer of technology to, or foreign investment in the exploitation of technology in, the developing world. Two responses might be made to this objection. First, the protection of some types of subject matter which is not itself important for technological development might nevertheless lead to foreign direct investment in the local production of such subject matter with the incidental transfer of associated technology and "know-how". Encouraged by a strong system of copyright for motion pictures, the argument runs, a foreign studio might be persuaded to establish operations in a developing country. Second, companies who are seeking to license, or to exploit locally, subject matter that is directly important to technological development may also need to know that their marketing operations are adequately protected by strong intellectual property rights. A system which only protected intangibles directly relevant to technological development, for example patentable products and processes, may have difficulty acquiring licences and foreign direct investment because such products and processes may form part of a business that is dependent for its success upon the protection of other types of

[44] For a short summary of the disadvantaged position in which foreigners were placed see Alford, *supra* n. 24, pp. 146–7.

[45] At least outside the protection of computer programmes and educational works.

intangible as well. However, whether these arguments are convincing depends upon the assumption that the existence and strength of intellectual property rights are crucial to decisions about technology transfer. This very assumption is the focus of the second objection to the claim made in Article 7 that systems of intellectual property promote the dissemination and transfer of technology.

The second objection to the claim that the rights enshrined in TRIPS promote licensing and foreign direct investment is that the existence of intellectual property rights may be less important to decisions about technology transfer than has been assumed. A considerable amount of work has been done on the issue of whether the existence of intellectual property rights is an important criterion to companies making decisions about foreign direct investment. The results of these studies have been inconclusive. Some have suggested that the existence and strength of intellectual property protection is an important criterion in foreign direct investment decisions.[46] Many others have suggested that there is little empirical basis for the claim that strong intellectual property rights increase foreign direct investment, and some evidence that foreign direct investment, even in sectors traditionally dependent upon intellectual property such as pharmaceuticals, can be plentiful in their absence.[47] In short, intellectual property rights seem to be merely one of a host of factors that determine foreign direct investment. Their precise impact on the process of technology transfer and dissemination is arguably impossible to measure on a global scale. The impact of increased intellectual property protection in the developing world seems impossible to assess, not only in relation to its impact on innovation, but also in relation to its impact on technology transfer. The TRIPS negotiator who sought to argue for the extension of the TRIPS Agreement on the basis of the claims made in Article 7, or the WTO Panel which sought to understand the terms of the agreement on the same basis, would inevitably be attempting to make calculations of global welfare maximisation that have so far proved beyond the reach of economists.

If these two objections have any weight, then the second claim in Article 7 may be no more helpful than the first claim in establishing either an achievable objective for the TRIPS Agreement or an understanding of which intellectual property rights the Agreement might properly include. Both face the problem that they are inadequate to justify even the intellectual property rights that are currently included in the Agreement. Both face the problem that they are dependent upon

[46] See, for example, B. Seyoum, "The Impact of Intellectual Property Rights on Foreign Direct Investment" (1996) 31 *Columbia J. World Business* 50 and C. A. Primo Braga and C. Fink, "The Relationship Between Intellectual Property Rights and Foreign Direct Investment" (1998) 9 *Duke J. Comp. & Int'l L.* 163.

[47] See, for example: Transnational Corporations and Management Division, United Nations Department of Economics and Social Development, *Intellectual Property Rights and Foreign Direct Investment* U.N. Doc. ST/CTC/SER.A/24 (1993); A. Tankoano, "L'accord relatif aux aspects des droits de propriété intellectuelle liés aux commerce" (1994) 20 *Droit et pratique du commerce international* 428 at 467; C. M. Correa, "Intellectual Property Rights and Direct Investment" (1995) 10 *Int. J. Technology Management* 173 ; C. R. Frischtak, "Harmonization Versus Differentiation in International Property Rights Regimes" (1995) 10 *Int. J. Technology Management* 200 at 208.

calculations of global welfare of impossible complexity. Article 7 seems to offer little hope to those who would wish to find a basis for the coherent and principled development of the Agreement.

III. ALTERNATIVE JUSTIFICATIONS FOR THE INCLUSION OF RIGHTS IN TRIPS

If Article 7 proves unsatisfactory as a basis for the development of TRIPS, various alternative bases will begin to emerge as the Agreement continues to be fought over. Two possible alternatives are already identifiable in the TRIPS Agreement or in recent discussions of it. Neither of these alternatives are more satisfactory than Article 7, but they are interesting in the implications that they raise for the TRIPS Agreement. Each of them suggests that a far broader range of political and economic objectives might be pursued through the world trade system than those identified in Article 7. These alternative bases for the TRIPS Agreement, and the identification of the rights that it ought properly to include, are (1) the arguments from commutative justice and (2) the argument from human rights.

The arguments from commutative justice

There are five important arguments from commutative justice which seem, at least tacitly, to underpin much discussion of TRIPS in the developed world. Indeed, such arguments might explain why the first recital to TRIPS assumes that inadequate intellectual property protection constitutes a "distortion to trade". However, none of these arguments can provide a very satisfactory objective for the TRIPS Agreement or means of identifying those property rights that it ought appropriately to include.

The difficulty with all five of these arguments from commutative justice is two-fold. First, there is an inherent difficulty with each of these arguments in that they simply assume the answer to the question they purport to address. Each argument only works if a given intangible can be appropriately identified as the subject of a property right. Perhaps this can be assumed in relation to such rights as any given country already has an international treaty obligation to respect. But it cannot be assumed in relation to rights which a country does not have such an obligation to respect either because they are not a party to the relevant treaty, the relevant treaty does not oblige them to recognise the particular right, or the right is one of a new type that is sought to be included in the TRIPS Agreement. Second, were the developed world to advance any of these arguments from commutative justice, it would also have to face competing arguments of both commutative and distributive justice from the developing world. The five arguments from commutative justice and their inherent difficulties will first be described and then the competing justice claims of the developing world set out.

First, there is an argument about the need for the reciprocal recognition of the products or wealth of trading nations. Many commentators emphasise that the exports of the developed world consist primarily in intellectual property or intellectual property dependent products[48] and stress the importance of intellectual property rights to maintaining the competitive position of the developed world.[49] The implicit argument of much of this literature is that if the developed world is to open its markets and to buy the tangible products and commodities of the developing world, the developing world ought to open its markets and to buy the intangible products of the developed world. If one country invests heavily in making movies and another in growing corn, fair exchange might require that each treat the other's product as property, whether tangible or intangible. Similarly, if the wealth of one country consists in ideas, and the wealth of another country consists in commodities, fair exchange might require that each treat the products that constitute the other's wealth as property. As Reichman puts it:

> "The historical distinction between intellectual property and other forms of property becomes increasingly anachronistic the more that economies everywhere are driven by the need to innovate . . . All countries know what these rights are and why foreign intellectual goods retain their economic value once admitted into the national territory, even when those who govern the territory choose not to protect equivalent national creations . . . To pretend that aliens have no legal claims arising from wholesale unauthorised uses of their most valuable property while respecting law that protect less valuable property only because it is tangible rather than intangible is to exalt form over substance".[50]

However this first argument from commutative justice is flawed because there is no necessary nexus between investment and property or between wealth and property. There is much in which a country might invest or that might constitute a part of its wealth—for example the education of its people—that has nothing to do with trade. Whether something either in which there has been investment or that might be called wealth constitutes a tradeable commodity, depends upon whether it is properly the subject of a property right. And that is the very issue that the argument is seeking to determine.

The second argument from commutative justice focuses upon the need to ensure that all the partners in a trading system are operating under similar regulatory constraints. If firms operating in one country are required to respect intellectual property rights and to bear the cost of doing so, commutative justice might suggest that those with whom they trade ought also to bear such costs. Thus Liu claims that the function of the world trade system is to is "to level the playing field so that all participants may conduct their business on mutual

[48] See, for example, M. L. Doane, "TRIPS and International Intellectual Property Protection in an Age of Advancing Technology" (1994) 9 *Am. J. Int'l L. and Pol'y* 465; T. C. Bickham, "Protecting U.S. Intellectual Property Rights Abroad with Special 301" (1999) 23 *AIPLA Q. J.* 195 and B. A. Lehman, "Intellectual Property: America's Competitive Advantage in the 21st Century", (1996) 31 *Columbia J. World Business* 6.

[49] See, for example, Lehman, *supra* n. 48, p. 11.

[50] J. H. Reichman, "Intellectual Property in International Trade: Opportunities and Risks of a GATT Connection" (1989) 22 *Vand. J. Transnat'l L.* 747 at 806–7 and 810–11.

terms".[51] This type of thinking has often been used to justify the harmonisation of intellectual property regimes in the European Union.

However, this second argument from commutative justice is flawed because firms operating in different countries are inevitably operating in different regulatory environments that impose very different costs and commutative justice cannot require that all such differences be ironed out. To argue that it does, would be to argue that countries can only trade fairly if they operate with identical regulatory systems, systems which may have very different effects in different economic environments. The difficult question therefore remains as to why some regulatory systems ought to be harmonised as between different members of a trading system; the question as to which regulatory systems are "trade-related". And this, of course, is again the question at the heart of the debate as to which, if any, intellectual property systems ought to be enforced as a part of TRIPS.

The third argument from commutative justice focuses upon the claims of the creators of intellectual property to control over the use of that property as their just deserts. This is the argument implicit in the early drafts of what became Article 7 TRIPS when they assume that intellectual property rights are granted "in acknowledgement of the contributions of inventors and creators".[52] Arguments from desert might focus upon either the efforts of such creators in producing the relevant intellectual property or upon the contribution that they make to global cultural and economic life.[53]

This third argument from commutative justice is also unlikely to support many of the intellectual property rights already included in TRIPS. If the criterion for desert is contribution, then many countries might ask what contribution, for example, the US film industry makes to their shared cultural life. It is at least arguable that the influx of foreign copyright material into a country does more harm than good. It is such considerations that led, for example, to the French proposal for the exception of cultural products from the world trade system altogether.[54] But even if the criterion for desert is effort as well as contribution, and even if the contribution made by creators of all types is acknowledged, the question remains as to why some effort or contribution deserves recognition through a property regime when other types of effort or contribution in economic and cultural life are not thought to do so. Other types of reward for effort and contribution abound. The concepts of effort and contribution are no more capable of identifying the appropriate subject matter

[51] P. B. Liu, "U.S. Industry's Influence on Intellectual Property Negotiations and Special 301 Actions" (1994) 13 *UCLA Pac. Basin L.J.* 87 at 117.

[52] Chairman's Report to the Group of Negotiation on Goods, Draft Agreement, Article 1B, MTN.GNG/NG11/W/76, 23 July 1990.

[53] For a fuller discussion of the use of arguments from desert to support and identify intellectual property and the problems with such arguments see M. Spence, "Passing Off and the Misappropriation of Valuable Intangibles" (1996) 112 *L.Q.R.* 472 at 486–9.

[54] Compare T. Bishop, "France and the Need for Cultural Exception" (1997) 29 *N.Y.U. J. Int'l L. & Pol.* 187 and J. B. Prowda, "U.S. Dominance in the 'Marketplace of Culture' and the French 'Cultural Exception'" (1997) 29 *N.Y.U. J. Int'l L. & Pol.* 193.

of intellectual property rights than the concepts of investment and wealth. Further, even if some creative activity deserves recognition through the grant of a property right, there is the question of how much effort or contribution needs to be evinced before a property right is appropriately granted. The desert argument simply assumes that we can identify what should count as intellectual property and then goes on to make a weak claim for why it should be protected. But the question of what should count as intellectual property is the difficult question at issue.

The fourth argument from commutative justice focuses upon alleged harm to countries in the developed world by the unauthorised use of intellectual property in the developing world. This is the argument that is most popular with intellectual property owner groups. When such groups speak of the need to raise standards of intellectual property in the developing world they speak of their "losses" and estimate them to be in the range of billions of dollars.[55] In counting this loss, such groups generally count, not only revenue lost because of infringements of existing rights in foreign countries, but also the income that could be gained if types of intellectual property not currently recognized in particular countries were to be introduced there.[56]

However, the fourth argument from commutative justice is flawed because it cannot be counted as a harm to be denied profits flowing from a monopoly right to which a party has no legal entitlement. The only way in which an intellectual property owner in the developed world would be able to show that she had suffered harm would be if the unauthorised use of a particular intangible in the developing world has left her worse off than she would have been had that use not been made at all. However this will rarely be the case. First, the intellectual property owner will rarely be able to show harm to the intangible itself. Most intangibles are non-crowdable in the sense that use of the intangible by one person does not alter it such that it cannot be used, even simultaneously, by another.[57] Second, the intellectual property owner will rarely be able to show harm even in the much weaker sense of harm to existing rights in the developed world. After all, she will generally be able to rely upon her existing rights to prevent the importation of unauthorised goods which might undercut her home market. Indeed, it may well be that she can rely upon her intellectual property rights to prevent the importation of goods which she has either manufactured or licensed in the developing world herself.[58] Again the argument simply assumes the existence of the right in the foreign country whose recognition it is sought to justify.

[55] See, for example, the figures cited in T. C. Bickham, "Protecting U.S. Intellectual Property Rights Abroad with Special 301" (1995) 23 *A.I.P.L.A. Q. J.* 195 at 196; Lehman, *supra* n. 48, p. 15 and R. J. Pechman, "Seeking Multilateral Protection for Intellectual Property: The Untied States 'TRIPS' over Special 301" (1998) 7 *Minn. J. Global Trade* 179 at 204.

[56] For a fuller discussion of the use of arguments from harm to support and identify intellectual property and the problems with such arguments see M. Spence, "Passing Off and the Misappropriation of Valuable Intangibles" (1996) 112 *L.Q.R.* 472 at 483–6.

[57] But see *ibid.* at 485.

[58] See *supra* n.31.

The fifth argument from commutative justice focuses upon the potential "unjust enrichment" of countries with low levels of intellectual property protection, at the expense of countries in which particular types of intellectual property originate. As McGrath writes: "It would be unfair if a country, or indeed a company, were able to reap significant economic benefits from the innovations worked out by other entities without ever contributing to the admittedly huge expenses incurred in the relevant R&D".[59] This argument applies to the international context an argument for intellectual property rights generally that assumes it is presumptively wrong to "reap without sowing".[60]

The problem with the fifth argument flows from the fact that, as even one of the fiercest proponents of the unjust enrichment approach acknowledges, "in an interdependent world, we all reap without sowing".[61] To ban all reaping without sowing would be, amongst other things, to ban all imitation and imitation is both essential to competition and to the development of culture. How, other than by imitation, can competitors establish their products as acceptable substitutes for the products of another trader? How, other than by imitation, can the dialogue which fosters cultural development be carried on? Those who would rely upon the unjust enrichment argument to prevent the unauthorized use of intangibles must be able to identify which types of imitation constitute acceptable reaping without sowing and which do not. But, as McBride and McGrath point out in their work on general restitutionary theory, the only clear case of unjust enrichment is when one party has used the property of another.[62] And whether particular types of intangible ought to count as property, and particularly as property for the purposes of the world trade system, is precisely the question that the unjust enrichment theorists are seeking to answer. Once again, this argument from commutative justice seems simply to assume the answer to the question that it is seeking to address.

In addition to these inherent difficulties of the five arguments from commutative justice, the countries of the developed world, in arguing for the recognition of particular intellectual property rights, will also have to face competing commutative justice claims from many countries currently offering only low levels of protection. The developing world has very strong commutative justice claims of its own in relation to intellectual property rights.

First, the developing world may not have received what it was promised in return for the inclusion of intellectual property rights in the world trade system.[63] Thus the developing world might not find the developed world as eager to

[59] M. McGrath, "The Patent Provisions in TRIPs: Protecting Reasonable Remuneration for Services Rendered—or the Latest Development in Western Colonialism?" [1996] *EIPR* 398 at 399.

[60] For fuller exposition of the unjust enrichment arguments and the problems they face see Spence, *supra* n. 56, pp. 489–91.

[61] W. Gordon, "On Owning Information: Intellectual Property and the Restitutionary Impulse" (1992) 78 *Virginia L. Rev.* 149 at 199.

[62] N.J. McBride and P. McGrath, "The Nature of Restitution" (1995) 15 *OJLS* 33.

[63] See generally, F. M. Abbott, "Commentary: The International Intellectual Property Order Enters the 21st Century" (1996) 29 *Vand. J. Transnat'l L.* 471 at 472–3.

share technology as they were led to expect that it would be. The argument that licences and foreign direct investment do not necessarily follow the implementation of effective intellectual property rights has already been considered. Complaints were made at the Seattle Ministerial Conference that "no specific mechanisms have been implemented" to attain the Article 7 goal of technology transfer[64] and that no action has been taken under Article 66(2) to promote technology transfer specifically to the least developed countries.[65] On the contrary, antitrust law has been increasingly relaxed in the developed world to allow intellectual property firms to keep a tight control over technological knowledge, and this, "coupled with strong market power and high levels of transnational intellectual property protection, make[s] it harder for firms in developing countries to gain access to the most valuable new technologies".[66] Indeed, in TRIPS the developing world may not even have exchanged stronger intellectual property rights for protection from US unilateral trade action to promote intellectual property interests. Notwithstanding a challenge from the European Union,[67] the Trade Act of 1974[68] still provides the legal basis for unilateral action to be taken by the USA on the basis of the perceived inadequacy of a country's intellectual property system and, at the time at which the Uruguay Round was implemented, the President of the USA emphasised his country's readiness to take such action.[69] While the USA may be unlikely to take unilateral action against a WTO member for violation of the Agreement,[70] it is more open to question whether it would take unilateral action to promote the introduction of new intellectual property rights not included in TRIPS. Congress has specifically provided that unilateral action may be taken to protect intellectual property interests even against a WTO member which is fully TRIPS compliant.[71] It may well be that the developing world received what it was promised from the Uruguay Round as a whole, but it is difficult to argue that this was the case with TRIPS itself.

Second, the developed world is increasingly mounting a commutative justice claim in relation to the protection of traditional knowledge. Thus at the 1999

[64] See, for example, *Communication from Columbia*, Preparations for the 1999 Ministerial Conference WT/GC/W/316, 14 September 1999.

[65] See *Communication from Venezuela*, Preparations for the 1999 Ministerial Conference WT/GC/W/82, 26 July 1999 and *Communication from Kenya on behalf of the Africa Group*, Preparations for the 1999 Ministerial Conference WT/GC/W/302, 6 August 1999.

[66] Reichman, *supra* n. 33, p. 375. See also Reichman, *supra* n. 32, p. 20 n. 22.

[67] *United States—Sections 301–310 of the Trade Act of 1974*, WT/DS152/R, 22 December 1999.

[68] Trade Act of 1974 §301–310, 19 U.S.C. §2411–2420.

[69] Statement of Administrative Action, H.R. Doc No 103–316, 103d Cong., 2d Sess. at 1029 (1994). For a discussion of the likelihood and desirability of such action being taken, see N. Telecki, "The Role of Special 301 in the Development of International Protection of Intellectual Property Rights After the Uruguay Round" (1996) 14 *B.U. Int'l L. J.* 187 and Pechman, *supra* n. 55, p. 179.

[70] *United States—Sections 301–310 of the Trade Act of 1974*, WT/DS152/R, 22 December 1999, at 36–7.

[71] Trade Act of 1974, §301(d)(3)(B)(II), 19 U.S.C. §2411(d)(3)(B)(II). This section "clarif[ies] that a foreign country may be [the subject of unilateral action on the part of the United States] . . . notwithstanding that it may be in compliance with the specific obligations of the TRIPS Agreement": H.R. Rep. No 826, 103d Cong., 2d Sess. 133 (1994).

Ministerial Conference in Seattle, Bolivia, Colombia, Ecuador, Nicaragua and Peru called for the inclusion of traditional knowledge in the world trade system by asserting that "[t]he future development of intellectual property must be based on the *mutual recognition* of the creations and intangible goods generated by various sectors concerned in the different WTO Members".[72] This claim that TRIPS ought to be expanded to include traditional knowledge was framed in precisely the terms of the first argument from commutative justice. It was said: "The economic, commercial and cultural value of this traditional knowledge for its possessors warrants and justifies a legitimate interest that this knowledge be recognised as the subject matter of intellectual property".[73] The developed world is used to operating as a supplier of intellectual property. Its reluctance to become a consumer of intellectual property might be evinced by the failure of the USA even fully to implement TRIPS so as to give complete credit to the activities of foreign inventors.[74] Yet if an argument from commutative justice were to be developed to support TRIPS, it may be difficult logically to resist a call for the introduction of traditional knowledge rights.

But perhaps more interesting than either the inherent difficulties of the three arguments from commutative justice, or even the way in which the commutative justice claims of the developed and developing world might be at odds, is the way in which the commutative justice arguments open up questions about the purpose of the world trade system generally. If the commutative justice arguments were to be more clearly articulated, the developing nations might argue that they are weakened, not only by competing claims of commutative justice, but by strong claims of distributive justice. Even if the commutative justice claims of the developed world were accepted, requiring developing countries to expend resources on meeting those claims might be unjust in a context in which those resources are limited by distributive injustice. Such a claim cannot be fully explored in this chapter. It requires, for example, a notion of what it might mean for nations to have distributive justice claims against one another and a consideration of the complex interrelation of claims to commutative and distributive justice. But, what is interesting here is that the explicit articulation of the commutative justice claims might highlight issues of justice in a way that would lend weight to the current attempts to increase the development role of the WTO,[75] a role that is acknowledged in the second recital to the Agreement Establishing the WTO. Indeed, Reichman and Lange have argued that the developed nations are unlikely to have their expectations for increased international intellectual property protection met in the TRIPS Agreement unless they are prepared to take on board their responsibilities for improving access to technology in the

[72] WT/GC/W/362, 12 October 1999 (emphasis added).

[73] *Ibid.*

[74] H. C. Wegner, "TRIPS Boomerang-Obligations for Domestic Reform" (1996) 29 *Vand. J. Transnat'l L.*535.

[75] See, for example, the report of the Seattle Symposium on International Trade Issues in the First Decades of the Next Century, 29 November 1999, in (1999) 34 *Sustainable Developments* 1.

developing world and have started a private initiative to encourage technology transfer.[76] A commitment by the developed world, as a development issue, to improving global access to technology, seems a far more important corollary of the TRIPS project than might initially appear.

The arguments from human rights

Were Article 7 and the arguments from commutative justice to prove inadequate as a basis for TRIPS and the identification of the intellectual property rights it might properly include, the only remaining basis for TRIPS is as a document protecting human rights. Article 27 of the Universal Declaration of Human Rights recognises the right "to the protection of the moral and material interests resulting from any scientific, literary or artistic production of which [a person] is the author". Arguments about intellectual property protecting human rights have not been important so far in the context of TRIPS. However, this account of intellectual property rights has been particularly powerful in the development of copyright law (at least outside the USA) and it is conceivable that language about the human rights of creators could slip into TRIPS discourse.

The usual basis upon which intellectual property rights are said to be human rights is that the recognition of such rights is essential to the protection of the autonomy of the creator. Like the arguments from commutative justice, this argument is both fraught with difficulty and raises thorny questions about the goals that might appropriately be pursued through the world trade system.

The two most widely cited arguments that protection of intellectual property is essential to the protection of the creator's autonomy and that only such intellectual property ought to be recognized as is necessary to achieve that goal parallel the justifications for tangible property offered by Locke in his *Two Treatises of Government*[77] and by Hegel in his *Philosophy of Right*.[78] Locke argues that every person has a property in her own person and her labour; which property seems to amount to a conception of personal liberty.[79] When a person labours on something which is not owned by anyone else she joins that something with her own property, her labour, and thereby makes it hers. "For this labour being the unquestionable property of the labourer, no man can have a right to what that is once joined to, at least where there is enough, and as good left in common for others".[80] Thus if a labourer joins her labour with some type of intangible object, then the only way in which to give her property in her person and her labour (and thereby to preserve her liberty) may be to give her property in the intangible object.

[76] See Reichman and Lange, *supra* n. 42, p. 11.

[77] J. Locke, *Two Treatises of Government* (M. Goldie (ed.), London, Everyman, 1993).

[78] G. W. F. Hegel, *Philosophy of Right* (T.M. Knox (trans.), Oxford, Clarendon Press, 1967).

[79] See J. Waldron, *The Right to Private Property* (Oxford, Clarendon Press, 1988), p. 177; T. G. Palmer, "Are Patents and Copyrights Morally Justified? The Philosophy of Property Rights and Ideal Objects", (1990) 13 *Harv. J. L. & Pub. Pol'y* 775 at 833.

[80] Locke, *supra* n. 77, p. 128.

Hegel argues that ownership of property is essential to the development of autonomous persons. Waldron summarises his argument in this way:

> "Hegel argues that individuals need private property in order to sustain and develop the abilities and self-conceptions definitive of their status as persons . . . [T]hey need to be able to 'embody' the freedom of their personalities in external objects so that their conceptions of themselves as persons cease to be purely subjective and become concrete and recognisable to themselves and others in a public and external world".[81]

In other words, the appropriation of objects in the external world, helps individuals to develop as autonomous persons by: (1) forcing upon them the discipline of interacting with external objects in a way which makes concrete the "pure subjectivity of personality";[82] and (2) allowing the pure subjectivity of personality, once made concrete in an object, to be recognised by others.[83] While for these purposes Hegel argues that "[m]ental aptitudes, erudition, artistic skill, . . . inventions, and so forth"[84] do not themselves count as objects capable of appropriation, they may be embodied in "something external"[85] and thereby may be able to be appropriated. To the extent that intangible objects are somehow "embodied" they may appropriately be the subject of property rights.

Both of these approaches to the justification and identification of intellectual property rights have strong intuitive appeal. To value individual autonomy must involve granting an individual at least some control over those objects with which she is most intimately associated: to allow her to carve out an area of individual dominion. If an individual can show a close association with a particular intangible object, then respect for her autonomy may require that she be given at least some degree of control over its use.

However, at least three important difficulties arise with such arguments. The first difficulty is that Locke and Hegel are primarily concerned with the liberty or autonomy of *natural* persons. But claims to intellectual property rights are predominantly made by *legal* persons. The extent to which corporations might enjoy human rights, and particularly human rights built upon the protection of autonomy, is obviously a difficult issue.

The second difficulty is that an association between a particular individual and an intangible object strong enough to argue that a recognition of that association is essential to the recognition of her autonomy, may be hard to demonstrate. In particular, neither of the accounts of that association offered by Locke or Hegel will do the work required of them by the autonomy argument.

Locke's account of the association focuses on the difficult concept of mixing labour, and the problems with this account are at least threefold. First, Waldron demonstrates "mixing" to be a concept without substance in this context

[81] Waldron, *supra* n. 79, p. 353.

[82] Hegel, *supra* n. 78, p. 235.

[83] For an extended discussion of the moral importance of these two aspects of the appropriation of things in the external world, see Waldron, *supra* n. 79, p. 370.

[84] Hegel, *supra* n. 78, p. 40.

[85] *Ibid.* at 41.

because labour, as a series of actions, is not capable of being mixed with an object, even an intangible object, which could become the subject of a property right.[86] Second, even if labour is capable of being mixed with an object, it is frequently noted that mixing labour does not necessarily amount to an association with the labourer strong enough to justify his claim to the resulting product. As Nozick points out, if I mix my can of tomato juice with the sea I simply lose my tomato juice.[87] Third, Locke seems to assume that more than 999 of a thousand parts of a thing's value are the result of labour and that a close association between the labourer and his product may therefore be assumed.[88] This is often not the case with intangible products, the value of which might depend, for example, on the life they have acquired away from the creator's hands and as a part of a community's cultural life.[89] Locke's argument about mixing labour does not seem to provide an association between the intangible and the labourer strong enough to be useful in justifying intellectual property.

Hegel's account of this association focuses on a person's "putting his will into any and everything and thereby making it his".[90] The difficulty with this account is twofold. First, it is difficult to identify, in the context of intangibles, into what "thing", what "external" embodiment, the creator of such an intangible has put his will. For example, Hegel struggles with the question why it is possible to alienate a particular copy of an individual intellectual work, without also alienating the right to produce facsimiles of that work. This latter intangible he calls a "capital asset"[91] and seems to treat as property, but he fails to deal with the difficult question of what the external embodiment of that property is. It cannot be the copies of the intellectual work themselves, for they are the subject of a different property right. But what, then, is it? How can something intangible count as the external embodiment of a will? Second, even if an intangible can count as the external embodiment of a will, why does a person's putting her will into that intangible constitute a sufficient association with it to justify her having a right to continuing control over its use? In the context of tangible property, the answer to this question is explained by Waldron to be that a person's actions in relation to an object may change that object, "registering the effects of willing at one point of time and forcing an individual's willing to become consistent and stable over a period".[92] This effect would be lost if others were allowed to alter the object after the initial registering of the individual's will. Some type of continuing control over the object is therefore desirable for the development of the individual as an autonomous person. In relation to intangible objects, however this argument for some type of control over the use

[86] Waldron, *supra* n. 79, p. 184.

[87] R. Nozick, *Anarchy, State and Utopia* (Oxford, Basil Blackwell, 1974), p. 175.

[88] Locke, *supra* n. 77, p. 136.

[89] See, for example, R. C. Dreyfuss, "Expressive Genericity: Trademarks as Language in the Pepsi Generation" (1990) 65 *Notre Dame L. Rev*. 397.

[90] Hegel, *supra* n. 78, p. 41.

[91] *Ibid*. pp. 54–6.

[92] Waldron, *supra* n. 79, p. 373.

of the embodiment of a person's willing does not always work. In particular, it will not work whenever an intangible can be said to be non-crowdable. Just as with Locke, it would seem that Hegel is not necessarily able to provide an association between a creator and an intangible product strong enough to do the work required of that association by the autonomy argument.

A third difficulty with the autonomy approach to the justification and identification of intellectual property rights concerns the autonomy of the would-be user of an intangible object. Palmer points out that to grant the creator of an intangible object the right to control its use may be just as great a threat to the autonomy of a would-be user of that intangible as would denying the creator of the intangible be a threat to hers.[93] Waldron demonstrates that this point is tenable no matter what particular conception of autonomy is used.[94] It is therefore necessary to demonstrate that the autonomy restrictions for the creator of an intangible product in not granting her control over that intangible somehow outweigh the autonomy restrictions for the would-be user of a particular intangible involved in granting the creator that control.

This is a task that neither Locke nor Hegel undertakes, though at least Hegel considers the problem. Hegel acknowledges that given that "the purpose of a product of mind is that people other than its author should understand and make it the possession of their ideas",[95] it must sometimes be legitimate for others to take the ideas which underpin that valuable intangible and embody them in a different form. Indeed, so much might others take on those ideas that they might embody them in something external in a way that might give them as strong a claim to those ideas as has the original "creator".[96] In other words, preventing them from using an intangible will sometimes be an unjustified restraint on their autonomy. Hegel argues that a principled answer to the question of when preventing the use of an idea is justified is impossible[97] and problems with more recent attempts to break this deadlock may well suggest that he was right.[98]

But perhaps more important than these inherent difficulties with the human rights approach to intellectual property rights, are two implications of such an approach for the world trade system. First, the focus of the TRIPS Agreement has unwaveringly been on the economic rights of intellectual property owners. But the autonomy-based approach to the protection of at least copyright works is just as concerned with what have been called the "moral rights" of the creator: her right to be identified with a work and to prevent its being altered in any way even by the owner of copyright. These rights are clearly more central to the

[93] T. G. Palmer "Are Patents and Copyrights Morally Justified? The Philosophy of Property Rights and Ideal Objects" (1990) 13 *Harv, J. L. & Pub. Pol'y* 775 at 827.

[94] Waldron, *supra* n. 79, p. 868.

[95] Hegel, *supra* n. 78, p. 55.

[96] *Ibid*. pp. 55–6.

[97] *Ibid*. p. 56.

[98] For a full discussion of the autonomy arguments and their difficulties, see Spence, *supra* n. 56, pp. 491–6.

protection of the creator's autonomy than her right to control the reproduction of the work because they ensure her control over the way in which her work presents her to the world. For many intellectual property theorists, failure to include moral rights in TRIPS is a glaring lacuna.

Second, given all the difficulties with the autonomy argument, intellectual property rights, if they are human rights at all, must be human rights of only secondary importance. This point is obviously of considerable importance in the context of TRIPS. A constant theme in the development of the WTO has been the need to avoid the multilateral trade system becoming a mechanism for the enforcement of human rights. But if TRIPS is best justified as an agreement protecting human rights of only very secondary importance, then the argument that human rights ought to be enforced in other ways becomes rather weaker. Those who would want to avoid the enforcement of human rights through the world trade system, must resist talk about the human rights justification of TRIPS.

IV. CONCLUSION

It is not unreasonable then, to regard the TRIPS Agreement as something of an agreement in search of an objective. As the Agreement is increasingly debated and fought over, the weakness of Article 7 as an objective for the Agreement and means of identifying those rights that it might appropriately protect, will become increasingly apparent. Of course, in practice this may have little impact on the development of an agreement that might just be shaped by political and economic force. But, if the Agreement is to develop in a principled and coherent way, it will need to find some alternative to the Article 7 objectives. Five possible alternative arguments for the agreement based in commutative justice have begun to emerge. None of these is particularly convincing, but as a whole they are interesting as they raise real questions about the commutative and distributive justice claims of the developing world in the context of TRIPS. A final possible alternative argument is based on the notion that intellectual property rights are human rights. Again, this argument is highly contestable, but the introduction of human rights language into the defence and development of TRIPS could have major repercussions for the development of the world trade system as a whole.

11

International Trade and Child Labour Standards

FEDERICO LENZERINI

I. INTERNATIONAL TRADE AND HUMAN RIGHTS: WHAT KIND OF INTERACTION?

DURING THE "URUGUAY Round" (1986–1993) of the Multilateral Trade Negotiations, which led to the establishment of the World Trade Organisation (WTO),[1] various parties proposed the adoption of a "social clause". The introduction of this clause was aimed at conditioning the enjoyment of trade advantages by the respect of minimum international labour standards. However, as has so often happened in the past,[2] no appreciable result came

[1] Final Act Embodying the Results of the Uruguay Round of Multilateral Trade Negotiations, 15 April 1994, (1994) *ILM* 1. It includes the Final Act itself, the Agreement Establishing the World Trade Organization ((1994) *ILM* 1144) with its four Annexes and additional Ministerial declarations and decisions, as, inter alia, the Marrakesh Ministerial Declaration ((1994) *ILM* 1263). The first three Annexes of Agreement Establishing the WTO (hereinafter "WTO Agreement"), contain the Multilateral Trade Agreements, automatically binding on all WTO members. Annex 4, instead, binds only those members that have accepted the Agreements (Plurilateral Trade Agreements) contained therein. Annex 1, which contains, inter alia, GATT 1994 (composed of the original text of the Agreement (GATT 1947, (1950) 55 *UNTS* 194 as modified and amended to the date of entry into force of the WTO Agreement, plus several protocols and Understandings), the General Agreement on Trade in Services (GATS) and the Agreement on Trade-Related Aspects of Intellectual Property Rights (TRIPS), is particularly remarkable, like Annex 2, which consists of the Understanding on Rules and Procedures Governing the Settlement of Disputes in the WTO system. See Introductory Note by Porges, (1994) *ILM* 1; (1994) *ILM* 1125. In this chapter the term "GATT" will be used to indicate GATT 1994, except where otherwise specified.

[2] See Leary, "Workers' Rights and International Trade: the Social Clause (GATT, ILO, NAFTA, U.S. Laws)", in Bhagwati and Hudec (eds), *Fair, Trade and Harmonization*, vol.2: *Legal Analysis* (Cambridge/London, 1996), pp. 198–9. The author points out that one explicit provision stating that the need for state parties to guarantee fair labour standards was included in the 1948 draft Havana Charter (cf. Havana Charter for an International Trade Organisation, US Department of State Pub. No. 3117, Commercial Policy Series 113 (1948); Terril, *Havana Charter for an International Trade Organization*, March 24, 1948, Including a Guide to the study of the Charter, U.S. Department of State Pub. No. 3206, Commercial Policy Series 114 (1948)), which has never brought into force, that had the purpose to constitute the agreement establishing International Trade Organisation (ITO). Article 7 (part of chapter 2), in fact, said stated States parties had to recognise "that all countries have a common interest in the achievement and maintenance of fair labour standards related to productivity, and thus in the improvement of wages and working conditions as productivity may permit. The Members recognise that unfair labour conditions, particularly in production for export, create difficulties in international trade and, accordingly, each Member shall take whatever action may be appropriate and feasible to eliminate such conditions within its territory". In addition,

out of this proposal, mainly because of the opposition exercised by developing countries against the explicit acknowledgment of a link between trade and labour conditions as part of the global trading system.[3] Reference to the request of some government delegates relative to "an examination of the relationship between the trading system and international recognised labour standards",[4] included in the Concluding Remarks of the Chairman of the Trade Negotiations Committee, leaves only the hope for a possible future change of trend in the matter, without having any legal meaning. Even the 1996 Singapore Ministerial Declaration, although it proclaims (paragraph 4) the solemn commitment of the parties "to the observance of internationally recognised labour standards",[5] does not imply the possibility of suspending the GATT privileges for the protection of workers' rights. Indeed, the same paragraph contains a statement whose contents leave no doubt in this sense: "We reject the use of labour

the following attempts to insert a "social clause" in general agreements on international trade have failed, as happened to the USA in 1953 (the US Government suggested amending GATT 1947 with the following provision: "The Contracting Parties recognise (1) that all countries have a common interest in the achievement and maintenance of fair labor standards related to productivity, and thus the improvement of wages and working conditions as productivity may permit, and (2) that unfair labor conditions (i.e., the maintenance of labor conditions below those which the productivity of the industry and the economy at large would justify), particularly in production for export, may create difficulties in international trade which nullify or impair benefits under this Agreement. In matter relating to labor standards that may be referred to the Contracting Parties under Article XIII they shall consult with the International Labor Organisation"; see US Commission on Foreign Economic Policy, Staff Papers 437–8 (1954). See also Charnovitz, "The Influence of International Labour Standards on the World Trading Regime", (1985) *International Labour Review* 574–5); the same failure characterised the Nordic countries' similar attempt during the "Tokyo Round", because the developing countries successfully argued that the invocation of a social clause represents disguised protectionism; see Leary, cited *supra*, p. 199.

[3] See Leary, *supra* n. 2, p. 198–9. This strenuous resistance by the developing countries is mainly due to the fact that they often do not conform to the recognised minimum international labour standards and are afraid that the acknowledgment of a bond between the said standards and international trade may prevent them, for the above mentioned reason, being eligible for the enjoyment of advantages guaranteed by the GATT/WTO system, since conformation to such standards would bring about unsustainable working costs; according to such countries, the improvement of labour conditions could be achieved by guaranteeing them an adequate socio-economic development (i.e."trickle-down" theory). See Quaker Council for European Affairs, *Around Europe* (1994). For a reference to "Millenium Round" (Seattle, USA, 30 November–3 December 1999), see *infra* n. 125.

[4] Concluding Remarks of H.E. Sergio Abreu Bonilla, Chairman of the Trade Negotiations Committee, Multilateral Trade Negotiations of the Uruguay Round at Marrakesh, GATT Doc. MTN.TNC/MIN(94)/6, (15 April 1994); see Leary, *supra* n. 2, p. 199, who observes how the impact of such a reference, already not very effective, is all the more reduced by the fact that other aspects are included in the same declaration (amongst which, inter alia, immigration policies, financial and monetary area, reduction of poverty, political stability, regionalism and investments) for which eventual relations with trade must be examined; this obviously implies a wide generalisation, and the consequential loss of importance, of the contents of the declaration in question.

[5] Singapore Ministerial Declaration, adopted on 13 December 1996, during the WTO Ministerial Conference, Singapore, 9–13 December 1996; Doc. WT/MIN(96)/DEC of 18 December 1996. Paragraph 4 cited in the text also proclaims "[t]he International Labour Organisation (ILO) [as] the competent body to set and deal with [labour] standards" and affirms the WTO support for "its work in promoting [such standards]". The same paragraph continues by stating the conviction that "economic growth and development fostered by increased trade and further trade liberalisation, contribute to the promotion of these standards".

standards for protectionist purposes and agree that the comparative advantage of countries, particularly of low-wage developing countries, must in no way be put into question".[6]

The non-inclusion of a "social clause" in the instruments of regulation of interstate trade raises a delicate problem of coordination between different norms of international law, that is the need to verify what degree of protection may be assured in terms of human rights within the area of trade relations between states. In other words, it is necessary to verify if, and within what limits, the basic criteria provided for by trade law (namely the most favoured nation (MFN) clause,[7] the principle of national treatment of products imported from state parties,[8] and the prohibition of quantitative restrictions on imports from such countries)[9] can be derogated where members are responsible for the violation of human rights. This issue becomes relevant when the products subjected to international trade are manufactured by the use of iniquitous working conditions, including the exploitation of individuals employed in the production of such goods. These forms of exploitation can be characterized by an extremely heterogeneous degree of intensity, from the slight breaking of the obligations to guarantee adequate labour standards up to very serious violations of fundamental human rights, as is the case of particularly inhumane child labour (the so-called "worst forms").[10] Consequently, it is necessary to keep the different cases in point separate, because international law provides for a protection level against violations of human rights which varies according to the extent and gravity of the breach on the scale of values reflected in the legal conscience of the international community at a given time.

The aim of this chapter consists in attempting to verify the possible interactions between international trade norms and the principles laid down for the protection of children from working forms which, because of their intrinsic character or because of the particularly oppressive way in which they are carried out, are susceptible to cause serious damage on minors so as to jeopardise their psycho-social development, and to constitute serious violations of their internationally recognised fundamental rights. In an era of progressive globalisation of international trade the risk that such violations may actually occur increases.[11] States which are at an economic disadvantage can weaken their own mechanisms of control of the respect of human rights in the domestic working environment in such a way as to release producers from the responsibility to

[6] *Ibid.*

[7] Art. I GATT.

[8] Art. III GATT.

[9] Art. XI GATT.

[10] For a typology of the worst forms of child labour see, *infra* Part II, in particular text accompanying n. 22.

[11] For a comprehensive survey on the effects of the globalisation of commerce on labour, see ILO, *Human Resource Implications of Globalization and Restructuring in Commerce. Report for Discussion at the Tripartite Meeting on the Human Resource Implications of Globalization and Restructuring in Commerce* (Geneva, 1999).

adhere to minimum labour standards, in order to maintain their competitivity on a global market without barriers.

This hypothetical interaction would be particularly useful in those contexts where the worst forms of child labour take place; such forms constitute an absolutely unacceptable offence to children's dignity and, as we shall try to demonstrate in this chapter, they are inconsistent with emerging standards for the protection of children themselves.

II. CHILD LABOUR STANDARDS AND THEIR PLACE IN INTERNATIONAL LAW

Child labour standards have been developed by some extremely important ILO conventions, but the general condemnation of child labour can also be found in other fundamental international treaties. In this sense the main provision, without any doubt, is that of Article 32 of the 1989 International Convention on the Rights of the Child,[12] which reads as follows: "States parties recognise the right of the child to be protected from economic exploitation and from performing any work that is likely to be hazardous or to interfere with the child's education, or to be harmful to the child's health or physical, mental, spiritual, moral or social development". The provision then imposes upon parties to "take legislative, administrative, social and educational measures to ensure the implementation of the present article", providing for "a minimum age or minimum ages for admission to employment", "appropriate regulation for the hours and conditions of employment", and "appropriate penalties or other sanctions to ensure the effective enforcement of the present article".

At the international level the specification of these obligations is realized by the ILO conventional instruments on child labour, and principally by the 1973 Minimum Age Convention (No. 138).[13] This treaty obliges the parties "to pursue a national policy designed to ensure the effective abolition of child labour and to raise progressively the minimum age for admission to employment or work to a level consistent with the fullest physical and mental development of young persons".[14] The minimum age for employment is generally fixed at fifteen years, but is reduced to fourteen for the members "whose economy and educational facilities are insufficiently developed" (Article 2); Article 3 and Article 7 establish, respectively, the limit of eighteen years (reducible to sixteen under particular conditions) for hazardous labour and that of thirteen years for light work (the latter can be reduced to twelve in states lacking in adequate educational opportunities). Other ILO conventions institute rules for the employment of children in specific kinds of work, such as painting activities involving the use

[12] UN GA Res.44/25, 20 November 1989.

[13] (1973) LVI *ILO Official Bulletin*, No. 1, p. 21. This Convention was completed by the 1973 Minimum Age Recommendation (No. 146) ((1973) LVI *ILO Official Bulletin*, No. 1, p. 34), which specifies the lines of action to be put in place for the implementation of the Convention.

[14] Minimum Age Convention, Art.1.

of white lead,[15] night work in non-industrial[16] and industrial sectors[17] and work involving radioactive substances[18] or benzene;[19] at the same time young persons are subjected to particular attention with regard to the prevention of any consequences jeopardising their health and safety caused by labour activities.[20]

Despite this wide normative framework, child labour standards are still insufficiently implemented by the international community as an autonomous concept. To illustrate this reality, the Minimum Age Convention has been ratified by only seventy-eight states (although there are signs of an encouraging change of trend, as during the last three years twenty-nine countries, including China and Nepal, have adhered to this treaty).[21] For this reason the need to take urgent measures for the protection of children from those jobs which are likely to cause irreparable damage to their physical and psychological development is strongly felt in the ILO context. Thus, in 1999 the Worst Form of Child Labour Convention (No. 182)[22] was adopted; this qualifies such forms as being:

> "(a) all forms of slavery or practices similar to slavery, such as the sale and trafficking of children, debt bondage and serfdom and forced or compulsory labour, including forced or compulsory recruitment of children for use in armed conflict; (b) the use, procuring or offering of a child for prostitution, for the production of pornography or for pornographic performances; (c) the use, procuring or offering of a child for illicit activities, in particular for the production and trafficking of drugs as defined in the relevant international treaties; (d) work which, by its nature or the circumstances in which it is carried out, is likely to harm the health, safety or morals of children" (article 3).[23]

[15] See Art. 3 of White Lead (Painting) Convention, 1921 (No. 13), (1921) IV *ILO Official Bulletin*, Supplement, No.23 (7 December) p. 13.

[16] Night Work of the Young Persons (Non-Industrial Occupations) Convention, 1946 (No. 79), (1946) XXIX *ILO Official Bulletin*, No. 4 (15 November) p. 274.

[17] Night Work of Young Persons (Industry) Convention (Revised), 1948 (No. 90), (1948) XXXI *ILO Official Bulletin*, No. 1 (31 August) p. 24.

[18] See Arts 6 and 7 of the Radiation Convention Protection, 1960 (No. 115), (1960) XLIII *ILO Official Bulletin*, No. 2, p. 41.

[19] See Art. 11 of the Benzene Convention, 1971 (No. 136), (1971) LIV *ILO Official Bulletin*, No. 3, p. 246.

[20] See, e.g., Medical Examination of Young Persons (Sea) Convention, 1921 (No. 16), (1921) IV *ILO Official Bulletin*, Supplement, No. 23 (7 December) p. 24; Medical Examination of Young Persons (Industry) Convention, 1946 (No. 77), (1926) XXIX *ILO Official Bulletin*, No. 4 (15 November) p. 254; Medical Examination of Young Persons (Non-Industrial Occupations) Convention, 1946 (No. 78), (1946) XXIX *ILO Official Bulletin*, No. 4 (15 November) p. 261; Arts 1 and 7 of the Maximum Weight Convention, 1967 (No. 127), (1967) I *ILO Official Bulletin*, No. 3, Ser. I (July 1967), p. 1; Art. 38 of the Occupational Safety and Health (Dock Work) Convention, 1979 (No. 152), (1979) LXII *ILO Official Bulletin*, No. 2, Ser. A (1979), p. 70.

[21] See list of ratification to Convention 138, in the ILO website (http://ilolex.ilo.ch:1567/scripts/ratifce.pl?C138).

[22] Adopted 17 June 1999; see ILO website (http://ilolex.ilo.ch:1567/scripts/conv.de.pl?C182).

[23] The kinds of work referred to under Art. 3(d) must be specified, *ex* Art. 4 of the Convention, by national normative acts, taking into consideration the indications pointed out by paras 3 and 4 of the Worst Forms of Child Labour Recommendation, 1999 (No. 190), adopted on 17 June 1999 (see ILO website, http://ilolex.ilo.ch:1567/scrpts/convde.pl?R190).

At the time of writing the Worst Forms of Child Labour Convention is not yet in force, but, as underlined by the recent ILO Declaration on Fundamental Principles and Rights at Work,[24] virtually all states composing the international community are bound to suppress almost the entire list of the worst forms of child labour as part of the obligations undertaken by previous conventional instruments on fundamental human rights, as well as by international customary law.

First, international standards that regulate forced labour[25] clearly cover forced child labour too.[26] However, assuming that most of forms of concrete exploitation of child labour have a private character, the definition of forced labour as "all work or service which is exacted from any person under the menace of any penalty and for which the said person has not offered himself voluntarily",[27] includes only a small portion of the phenomenon at issue. Nevertheless, the use of forced child labour is far from being completely eradicated, as has been shown by the widespread resort to such a practice in Myanmar.[28]

Outside the area of forced labour, the forms of exploitation provided for by Article 3(a) and (b) of the Worst Form of Child Labour Convention are covered entirely by the customary and conventional norms on slavery[29] and sexual

[24] Enacted by the International Labour Conference during its 86th Session, Geneva, June 1998; see http://www.ilo.org/public/english/standards/relm/ilc/ilc86/com-dtxt.htm; this Declaration recalls "that in freely joining the ILO, all Members have endorsed the principles and rights set out in its Constitution and in the Declaration of Philadelphia, and have undertaken to work towards attaining the overall objectives of the Organisation" (No. 1(a)); it also declares "that all Members, *even if they have not ratified the Conventions in question* [emphasis added], have an obligation arising from the very fact of membership in the Organisation, to respect, to promote and to realise . . . the principles concerning the fundamental rights which are the subject of those Conventions, namely: . . . (c) the effective abolition of child labour" (No. 2).

[25] See, e.g., ILO Forced Labour Convention, 1930 (No. 29), 39 *UNTS* 55; ILO Convention Concerning the Abolition of Forced Labour, 1957 (No. 105), 320 *UNTS* 291; Art. 5 of the 1926 Slavery Convention, 212 *UNTS* 17; Art. 8(3) of the International Covenant on Civil an Political Rights (1966), GA Res.2200, UN GAOR, 21st Session, Supp. no. 16, UN Doc.A/6316 (1967); Art. 2(e) of the International Convention on the Suppression and Punishment of the Crime of Apartheid, 1015 *UNTS* 243; Arts 40 and 51 of the 1949 Geneva Convention Relative to the Protection of Civilian Persons in Time of War, (1950) *UNTS* 287; Art. 4(2) of the European Convention on Human Rights (Council of Europe, *ETS*, No. 5); Art. 6(2) of the American Convention on Human Rights (OAS, *Treaty Series*, No. 36).

[26] See Diller and Levy, "Child Labour, Trade and Investment: Toward the Harmonisation of International Law", (1997) *Am J Intl L* 663, at 670; Bartolomei De La Cruz, Von Potobsky and Swepston, *The International Labour Organization: The International Standard System and Basic Human Rights* (1996) p. 143 See also ILO, *Governing Body Report*, ILO Doc.GB.265/2, Geneva, 1996, para. 32.

[27] ILO Convention No. 29, Art. 2.

[28] See UN Docs E/CN.4/Sub.2/1995/28 and E/CN.4/Sub.2/1996/24; ILO, Governing Body, Doc.GB.286/15/1, Geneva, 1997; US Department of Labor, Bureau of International Labor Affairs, *Report on Labor Practices in Burma*, 25 September 1998 (http://www.dol.gov/dol/ilab/public/media/reports/ofr/burma/main.htm). For the practice of exploitation of forced labour Maynmar has also been suspended by the ILO; see ILO, Resolution on the Widespread Use of Forced Labour in Myanmar, 17 June 1999, in (1999) *ILM* 1215.

[29] See, e.g., Slavery Convention 1926; Supplementary Convention on the Abolition of Slavery, the Slave Trade and Institutions and Practices Similar to Slavery, 1956 (266 *UNTS* 3); Art. 8(1) of the

exploitation of children[30] which, with no reasonable doubts, may be considered as included in the broad concept of slavery itself.[31] Moreover, according to the most progressive views,[32] the involvement of children in certain illicit activities (provided for by Article 3(c)) also has to be considered as a contemporary form of slavery. The impact of such a determination in the context of this survey is extremely important, if we consider that the *jus cogens* character of the customary principle which prohibits slavery[33] makes such a prohibition absolutely

International Covenant on Civil and Political Rights; Art. 4(1) of the European Convention on Human Rights; Art. 61 of the American Convention on Human Rights; Art. 5 of the African Charter on Human and Peoples' Rights 1981 (OAU, Doc. CAB/LEG/ 67/ 3/Rev. 5). See also Art. 4 of the Universal Declaration on Human Rights (GA Res.217/A, UN Doc.A/810, 1948).

[30] See, e.g., Convention for the Suppression of the Traffic in Persons and of the exploitation of the Prostitution of Others, 1949 (96 *UNTS* 271); Art. 1(d) of the Supplementary Convention on Slavery; Art. 6 of the Convention on the Elimination of All Forms of Discrimination Against Women 1979 (UN, GA Res. 34/ 180; UN Doc. A/ 34/ 46 (1979)); Art. 34 of the Convention on the Rights of the Child 1989; Arts 27 and 29 of the African Charter on the Rights and Welfare of the Child 1990 (OAU, Doc. CAB/LEG/TSG/Rev.1).

[31] Slavery is defined, by Art. 1.1 of the 1926 Slavery Convention, as "the *status* or condition of a person over whom any or all of the powers attaching to the right of ownership are exercised"; considering the substantial nature of sexual exploitation of children, the lack of foundations of its inclusion in the concept of slavery cannot be reasonably sustained. Child victims of sexual exploitation are, as a matter of fact, abducted, compelled with threats or sold by parents, and then definitely subjugated by a rape; during their stay under the exploiters' control they are subjected to debt bondage (which is expressly included by Art. 1(a) of the Supplementary Convention on Slavery in institutions and practices similar to slavery) and to brutal violence; often they are kept in chains. Long-standing practice of states and international organisations confirms the legal characterisation of the sexual exploitation of children as a form of slavery. See Degani and De Stefani, "Note su schiavitù e diritti umani. L'attività del Gruppo di Lavoro delle Nazioni Unite sulle forme contemporanee di schiavitù", *Pace, Diritti dell'Uomo, Diritti dei Popoli*, 3/1993, 90; Fairclough, "Slaves to the Law", (1996) *Far Eastern Economic Review* (23 May) 65; Johnston, *Trafficking in Women in Asia and Pacific; A Regional Report, for Regional Meeting on Trafficking in Women, Forced Labour and Slavery-like Practices in Asia and Pacific* (Bangkok, 1997); Lan Cao, "Illegal Traffic in Women: a Civil RICO Proposal", (1987) *Yale Law Journal* 1297; Muntarbhorn, *Sexual Exploitation of Children* (United Nations Center for Human Rights, Geneva, 1996); Schmetzer, "Slave Trade Survives, Prospers Across Asia", *Chicago Tribune*, 17 November 1991, p. C1; Specter, "'Traffickers' New Cargo: Naive Slavic Women", *New York Times*, 11 January 1998; Waring, "The Exclusion of Women from Work and Opportunity", in Mahoney and Mahoney (eds), *Human Rights in the Twenty-first Century: a Global Challenge* (Dordrecht/London/Boston, 1993), pp. 109, 113; Yoon, *International Sexual Slavery* (1994), http://www.alternatives.com/crime/PART7.HTML; Lenzerini, "Sfruttamento sessuale dei minori e norme internazionali sulla schiavitù", *Comunità Intern*, 1999, 474. The fact that Art. 3 of the Worst Form of Child Labour Convention expressly distinguishes between forms of slavery and sexual exploitation of children cannot be considered a relevant argument to deny the coincidence between the two phenomena, because the intent of the Convention is clearly to cover all forms of labour prejudicial to the physical and psychological health of children, without taking any position on the legal qualification of these forms.

[32] This position is supported by UN organs competent on the matter of protection of human rights, particularly by the Working Group on Contemporary Forms of Slavery (see annual reports; the last is Doc. E/CN.4/Sub.2/1999/17). In the field of states' practice see the position of Italian Supreme Court of Cassation (see, in particular, Sec. V, 7 December 1989, No. 3909, *Repertorio generale della giurisprudenza italiana*, 1990, p. 2635; Sec. V, 9 February 1990, No. 4852, *Repertorio generale della giurisprudenza italiana*, 1991, p. 2547; Sec. V, 24 October 1995, No. 1470; *Cassazione Penale*, 1996, 2585.

[33] See Brownlie, *Principles of Public International Law* (1998), p. 514; Diller and Levy, *supra* n. 26, p. 669; Frowein, "Jus cogens", *Encyclopedia of Public International Law*, vol. 7, p. 327; Staker, "Public International Law and the *Lex Situs* Rule", (1987) *Brit Yrbk Intl L* 51; Trebilcock, "Slavery",

binding in the implementation of an international treaty.[34] GATT is no exception to this.

There is no doubt that the reference to slavery constitutes the main reference on which the obligation on states to suppress the worst forms of child labour can be based. Nevertheless, in some limited situations, such forms can be traced back also to torture and other cruel, inhuman or degrading treatment,[35] and racial discrimination (or *apartheid*).[36] When the exploitation of child labour reaches the level of such human rights violations, some scholars argue that there exists a violation of norms of a fundamental and peremptory character.[37]

Further, some important universal conventions on human rights either expressly or implicitly condemn child labour itself as an autonomous phenomenon. This is chiefly[38] the case of Article 32 of the Convention on the Rights of the Child.[39] In addition, Article 24 of the International Covenant on Civil and Political Rights,[40] which sets out the child's right to be protected "as a minor,

Encyclopedia of Public International Law, vol. 8, p. 484. See also (1966) II *Yearbook of International Law Commission* 247; UN Docs. A/CN.4/SER.A/1966/Add.1, E/CN.4/Sub.2/1993/30, E/CN.4/Sub.2/1994/33.

[34] See Art. 53 of the 1969 Vienna Convention on the Law of Treaties; (1155 *UNTS* 331; (1969) *ILM* 679).

[35] See Diller and Levy, *supra* n. 26, p. 673; Leary, *supra* n. 2, p. 221; Schachter, *International Law in Theory and Practice* (1991), p. 343. See also *Restatement (Third) of the Foreign Relations Law of the United States* (1987), para. 702.

[36] Article 2.1(d) of the 1966 International Convention on the Elimination of All Forms of Racial Discrimination (660 *UNTS* 211), stating that "Each State Party shall prohibit and bring to an end, by all appropriate means . . . racial discrimination *by any persons, group or organization*" (emphasis added), implicitly introduces the obligation to suppress racial discrimination in the workplace too. See Rogge, "Racial Discrimination and the Market Place", in Beadles and Drewry, Jr., *Money, the Market and the State* (Athens, 1968), p. 146; Findlay and Lundahl (eds), "Racial Discrimination, Dualistic Labor Markets and Foreign Investment", (1987) *Journal of Development Economics* 139; Diller and Levy, *supra* n. 14, p. 675.

[37] The *jus cogens* character of the international norm which prohibits torture is supported by a solid doctrine and jurisprudence; see, e.g., Diller and Levy, *supra* n. 26, p. 673; Kuhner, "Torture", *Encyclopedia of Public International Law*, vol. 8, p. 510; O'Boyle, "Torture and Emergency Powers Under the European Convention on Human Rights: Ireland v. The United Kingdom", (1977) *Am J Intl L* 674; *United States Diplomatic and Consular Staff in Tehran (U.S. v. Iran)*, [1980] ICJ Report 42; US Court of Appeal, *Filartiga* v. *Pena Irala*, 630 F.2d 876 (2nd Cir. 1980); Swiss Federal Supreme Court, 22 March 1983, (1983) 10 *Europaische Grundrechte Zeitschrift* 253. Regarding racial discrimination the question is more uncertain, but, according to the position expressed by the International Court of Justice in the *Barcelona Traction* case ([1970] ICJ Report 33) the repression of this phenomenon constitutes an obligation *erga omnes*; for some scholars the Court's reference to such a principle makes an implicit reference to the concept of *jus cogens* (see Frowein, *supra* n. 33, p. 328; Meron, *Human Rights and Humanitarian Norms as Customary Law* (Oxford, 1989), p. 81; Staker, *supra* n. 33, p. 51).

[38] There are many other conventional and *soft law* international instruments that implicitly stigmatize child labour; for an exhaustive survey of these instruments see Diller and Levy, *supra* n. 26, p. 673.

[39] The Convention on the Rights of the Child contains other provisions pertinent to child labour: see, in particular, Art. 19 (protection "from all forms of physical or mental violence, injury or abuse, neglect or negligent treatment, maltreatment or exploitation, including sexual abuse"), Art. 34 (protection from sexual exploitation), Art. 35 (prevention of "the abduction of, the sale of or traffic in children for any purpose or in any form") and Art. 39 (recovery and social reintegration of a child victim of any form of neglect, exploitation or abuse, torture or similar treatment, armed conflicts).

[40] See *supra* n. 25.

on the part of his family, society and the State", can be interpreted as a provision which protects the child against forms of labour that are prejudicial for his physical and psychological growth.[41]

This legal background highlights a context in which most of the worst forms of child labour are perceived by the international community as an intolerable violation of basic human rights which may amount to breach of *jus cogens*. In this regard, the most relevant issue is slavery, the prohibition of which constitutes a *jus cogens* principle,[42] as well as an *erga omnes* obligation.[43] This context is useful in order to explore the applicability of Article XX GATT exceptions (see *infra*) to products made by practices that entail the most extreme forms of child labour.

III. LEGAL CONSEQUENCES: CAN STATES PARTIES SUSPEND GATT TO PROTECT CHILDREN AGAINST THE WORST FORMS OF LABOUR?

Human rights conditionality in regional and national policies: EU and USA

Before trying to examine the possible legal links between international trade and child labour standards, it is useful to look at contemporary practice in the matter. Economic sanctions have been practised over many years at a regional level by the EC/EU and at a national level by the USA for the implementation of human rights (in which area child labour is included). These sanctions are also used in the relationship with GATT members.

Economic sanctions constitute the most powerful weapon for the enforcement of EU policies. In order to profit from them, the EU has developed a system of human rights clauses that have been inserted into external agreements.[44]

[41] According to the Human Rights Committee, "the rights provided for in article 24 are not the only ones that the Covenant recognises for children and . . ., as individuals, children benefit from all of the civil rights enunciated in the covenant . . . It is for each State to determine them in the light of the protection needs of children in its territory and within its jurisdiction . . . For example, every possible economic and social measure should be taken to . . . prevent [children] from being . . . exploited by means of forced labour or prostitution" (General comments adopted by the Human Rights Committee, No. 17, 1989, para. 1, in UN Doc.HRI/GEN/1/Rev.1, 1994); see Diller and Levy, *supra* n. 26, p. 675.

[42] See *supra* n. 33.

[43] See Ago, "Obligations Erga Omnes and the International Community", in Weiler, Cassese and Spinedi (eds), *International Crimes of State* (Berlin/New York, 1989), p. 237; Bianchi, "Globalization of Human Rights: the Role of Non-State Actors", in Teubner (ed.), *Global Law Without a State* (Aldershot/Brookfield U.S.A./Singapore/Sidney, 1997), p. 179; Bodansky, "Human Rights and Universal Jurisdiction", in Gibney (ed.), *World Justice? U.S. Courts and International Human Rights* (Boulder/San Francisco/Oxford, 1991), p. 1; Gaja, "Obligations *Erga Omnes*, International Crimes and *Jus Cogens*: a Tentative Analysis of Three Related Concepts", in Weiler/Cassese/Spinedi (eds), *International Crimes of State* (Berlin/New York, 1989), p. 151; Meron, *supra* n. 37, pp. 81 and 188; Trebilcock, *supra* n. 33, p. 484. See also *Barcelona Traction* case (see *supra* n. 37).

[44] For the legal bases of these clauses in the EC Treaty, see Riedel and Will, "Human Rights Clauses in External Agreements of EC", in Alston, *The EU and Human Rights* (Oxford, 1999), p. 732 In relation to the lawfulness of the clauses at issue in the light of general international law (the investigation of which constitutes the purpose of the present survey), see, in general, the present and the following section.

These clauses are part of a multifaceted strategy, aimed at the protection of human rights, which is also constituted by a Generalised System of Preferences (GSP),[45] that can be withdrawn in the case of violations, and a scheme of incentives, generally shaped by even lower tariffs, offered to countries that respect minimum labour standards.[46] In general, after having examined the best way for putting into practice their human rights' policies in the concrete situation, EU institutions retain full decisional power about the kinds of provision to be implemented for the fulfilment of their goals. Thus, sometimes, they prefer to provide for measures of relief to the advantage of economic partners which do not fully respect basic labour rights in the productive processes, rather than to use sanctions.[47]

The European system of "human right clauses" is applied with a variable degree of cogency. Thus, some treaties include a simple reference to the "respect for the democratic principles and human rights, which inspire the domestic and external policies of the Community and [the other contracting Party]".[48] Other treaties, particularly those concluded in most recent years, qualify respect for human rights as "an essential element of [the] agreement".[49] Such a formula confers on the clause at issue the character of an essential provision; thus, in the

[45] See Council Regulation 3281/94 of 19 December 1994, concerning the GSP for 1995–1998 for certain industrial products originating in developing countries, OJ 1994 L348/1; Council Regulation 1256/96 of 20 June 1996, in relation to the GSP from 1 July 1996 to 30 June 1999 for agricultural products. Art.9 of the GSP Regulation explicitly authorises the total or partial withdrawal of benefits for those countries found guilty of the exploitation of forced or prison labour (as defined by conventions on slavery and forced labour) in the course of production of goods exported. See Diller and Levy, *supra* n. 26, p. 690; Brandtner and Rosas, "Trade Preferences and Human Rights", in Alston (ed.), *The European Union and Human Rights* (Oxford, 1999), p. 713

[46] See Lester, "The Asian Newly Industrialized Countries to Graduate from Europe's GSP Tariffs", (1995) *Harvard Intl LJ* 220.

[47] Thus, for example on 24 March 1997, a Council Regulation (OJ 1997 L85/8) temporarily withdrew access to the GSP from Myanmar for the massive exploitation of forced labour perpetrated in that state. Just a year before, the EU had responded to a complaint made by the Trades Union Confederations against Pakistan, for the exploitation of child labour (see Parliament Resolution of 14 December 1995 (OJ 1996 C17/201), deciding to support the ILO's International Programme for the Eradication of Child Labour (IPEC) in relation to the Asian country (see Commission's Answers to Written Questions 1728/96 of 3 July 1996 (OJ 1996 C305/122); 2468/96 of 23 September 1996 (OJ 1997 C91/6); 3404/96 of 5 December 1996 (OJ 1997 C105/71)). For a complete examination of such a question see Brandtner and Rosas, *supra* n. 45, p. 713.

[48] This is the so-called clause of "Democratic Basis for Co-operation"; see, e.g., treaty with Argentina of 2 April 1990 (OJ 1990 L295/67).

[49] See, e.g., treaty with Albania of 1992 (OJ 1992 L343/2). These clauses usually make reference to international instruments that establish human rights standards to be implemented in the course of the fulfilment of the agreement, as the CSCE Helsinki Final Act of 1975 ((1975) *ILM* 1292), the Charter of Paris for a New Europe of 1990 ((1971) *ILM* 190) or the Universal Declaration on Human Rights. However, to date, the only time that the human rights clause has been invoked for the suspension of an EU agreement was in July 1998, when the Council requested consultations with Togo (on the basis of Art. 366a of the IV Lomè Convention, see (1990) *ILM* 783) for presumed irregularities in the presidential elections of 21 June; see Communication from the Commission to the Council on the issue, SEC(1998)1189 final. For a complete survey of European human rights clauses, see Riedel and Will, *supra* n. 44, p. 726; Cremona, "Human Rights and Democracy Clauses in the EC's Trade Agreement", in O'Keeffe, *The European Union and World Trade Law after the GATT Uruguay Round* (Chichester/New York/Brisbane/Toronto/Singapore, 1996), p. 62.

case of breach, parties are allowed to terminate or suspend the treaty, in conformity with general international law and with Article 60(3)(b) of the 1969 Vienna Convention on the Law of Treaties.[50]

The conditioning of trade concessions on respect for workers' rights, now implemented by the EU, has been part of the US Government's foreign policy from a long time. Indeed, back in 1930 a Tariff Act was enacted, which forbade the import into the USA of every "goods, wares, articles, and merchandise mined, produced or manufactured wholly or in part in any foreign country by convict labor or/and forced labor or/and indentured labor under penal sanctions".[51] With the 1997 amendment[52] the ban expressly includes products manufactured with resort to "forced or indentured child labor". In addition, in recent years, a policy of trade preferences and aid programmes, reserved to countries implementing labourers' rights in working places, was introduced into a number of legislative acts, as, e.g., the Omnibus Trade and Competitiveness Act,[53] the Generalised System of Preferences (GSP)[54] and the Caribbean Basin Economy Recovery Act.[55]

The above attitude, finally, was reiterated in some regional agreements to which the USA is party, especially in the NAFTA context; the principal example of such a practice is furnished by the North American Agreement on Labor Cooperation (NAALC), the main objective of which is constituted by the enforcement of "working conditions and living standards", by means of the strengthening of each party's pertinent laws.[56]

This practice shows that the conditioning and subsequent suspension of benefits under trade agreements as a function of workers' rights protection, does not constitute, in the light of contemporary international law, a futuristic or

[50] See *supra* n. 34.

[51] Tariff Act of 1930, 19 U.S.C. § 1307 (1994), s. 307. See Diller and Levy, *supra* n. 26, p. 687. The authors make it clear that the term "forced labor", "copied word for word" from the definition used in the ILO Convention No. 29 (see 1929 hearings on Tariff Act by Senator J. Blaine of Wisconsin, 71 Cong. Rec. 4488, 4491, 1929, quoted in Diller and Levy, *supra* n. 26, p. 687), includes forced child labour too. It is important to underline the fact that the term "penal sanctions" is also used in this Convention, and means not only sanctions inflicted by official authorities, but also the deprivation of a free choice of work (see General Survey of the Committee of Experts on the Reports Concerning the Forced Labour Convention, 1930 (No. 29) and the Abolition of Forced Labour Convention, 1957 (No. 105), IL Conf. 38th Sess, Report III, Pt. 4, 1968, para. 27, quoted in Diller and Levy, *supra* n. 26, p. 688).

[52] Amendment to s. 307 of Tariff Act, 19 U.S.C. § 1307 (1997).

[53] Omnibus Trade and Competitiveness Act of 1988, Pub. L No.98–573, § 503, 98 Stat.2948, 3019 (1988).

[54] Generalized System of Preferences (GSP), 19 U.S.C. § 2461 (1994).

[55] Caribbean Basin Economy Recovery Act (CBERA), 19 U.S.C. § 2701 (1994). See also the economic sanctions recently imposed by the US Government on Myanmar for the widespread use of forced labour perpetrated in that Country. See Foreign Operations, Export Financing, and Related Programs Appropriations Act, 1997, § 570, 110 Stat.3009–166 to 3009–167 (enacted by the Omnibus Consolidated Appropriations Act, 1997, Pub. L. No.104–208, § 101(c), 110 Stat.3009–121 to 3009–172 (1996)). For a complete examination of US resort to unilateral trade sanctions, see Cleveland, *supra* Chapter 9.

[56] North American Agreement on Labor Cooperation, Final Draft, 13 September 1993, (1993) *ILM* 1499, Art.1.

extravagant technique. Rather, it is a policy option practised by the two largest trading blocks in the World: the EU and the USA. That being so, what we now have to ascertain is whether international law provides a legal basis to support the lawfulness of such practice.

Suspension based on the GATT/WTO system

From a general point of view, it can be said that both GATT and the constitutive Agreement of the WTO contain certain regulations which can be regarded as being more or less relevant to the topic of human rights, and therefore, *potentially* appropriate for authorising the parties to derogate from the requirements of the above agreements with regard to those states which violate workers' rights. However, recourse to such norms for the purpose of trade restrictions is not only relatively rare, but has met with failure in the attempt to insert a "social clause" into GATT during the "Uruguay Round" (see *supra*).

Before proceeding to examine these provisions, it is appropriate to reflect for a moment upon an objection of a general character against the effective functioning, for the purposes of the present chapter, of such norms, that is, whether human rights can be considered as a "trade-related issue".[57] The presumed inconsistency of this kind of link was claimed during the "Uruguay Round", in which those states against the insertion of a social clause in GATT tried to negate the existence of a connection between the subject of protection of workers' rights and the system of international trade law. Despite this point of view, the above-mentioned correlation cannot be negated, especially if one considers that during the "Uruguay Round" general consensus had emerged that international trade is linked with many matters, such, e.g., intellectual property, services and environmental protection.[58] On the other hand, even from a logical point of view, it is extremely difficult to negate the existence of a close relationship between working conditions in industries which produce goods subjected to export and their trading conditions. This results clearly from the following examination of the relevant GATT/WTO provisions.

GATT Article VI

Some scholars argue that the "anti-dumping"[59] discipline provided for by Article VI of GATT has to be extended to so-called "social dumping".[60] According to this theory, such a norm obliges the parties to avoid allowing work

[57] See Leary, *supra* n. 2, p. 200.

[58] *Ibid*. pp. 200–1; see also *supra* n. 1.

[59] Art. VI GATT ("Anti-Dumping and Countervailing Duties"), see *supra* n. 1; this provision affirms the principle that the equilibrium of international trade should not be altered by exporting products at a lower price than that practised in the internal market or in a third country market.

[60] See Jackson, *World Trade and the Law of GATT* (1969), § 16.02.

to be done in iniquitous conditions in order to make products which can then be sold at lower price as compared to that which would be required by the observance of the minimum international labour standards.[61] But the applicability of Article VI exclusively to price "dumping" was expressly decided during the 1947 GATT negotiations, when the majority of states[62] successfully opposed[63] a proposal by the Cuban delegate, according to which every form of "dumping" should be considered as included in Article VI "whether practiced through the mechanism of price, freight rates, currency depreciation, *sweated labor*, or by any other means"[64] (emphasis added). Moreover, the examination of the documents produced during the "Uruguay Round" does not provide a basis to support the view that states harboured a different intention on this issue (nor does the laconic statement contained in paragraph 4 of the Singapore Ministerial Declaration).[65]

GATT Article XIX

Even the argument which makes reference to Article XIX GATT[66] is not easily sustainable. This allows a temporary suspension of the execution of obligations as provided for in the General Agreement in the case where the massive importation of certain consumer goods is liable to provoke unexpected damage to domestic production. In theory, this could allow for the suspension of the above obligations when the imported products are manufactured through recourse to iniquitous labour conditions. But, in order to put this suspension into practice a causal relationship between the damage to the national production and the recourse by the exporting state to the infringement of minimum labour standards as internationally provided for, during the manufacturing phase of the exported goods, must be ascertained. In other words, what must be demonstrated is both that the damage to the internal production derives from the purchase of goods manufactured by the unlawful exploitation of work of others,[67]

[61] See Diller and Levy, *supra* n. 26, p. 680. See also Lunati, "Liberalizzazione degli scambi internazionali e costo del lavoro: esiste il dumping sociale?", in Sacerdoti and Venturini (eds), *La liberalizzazione multilaterale dei servizi e i suoi riflessi per l'Italia* (Milano, 1997), p. 165.

[62] The opposite position was supported with particular strength by Canada and the USA; see Working Party on Technical Articles, GATT Doc. E/PC/T/WP.1/SR/8 (1947). See also Diller and Levy, *supra* n. 26, p. 681.

[63] The following drafts (see Working Party on Technical Articles, GATT Doc. E/PC/T/103, 1947; Draft Charter, Arts 16–23 and 37, GATT Doc.E/PC/T/142, 1947; GATT Doc.E/PC/T/180, 1947) contained no references to the wide concept of "dumping" previously pleaded by the Cuban delegation ; see Diller and Levy, *supra* n. 26, p. 681.

[64] Secretariat Note on Article 17 ("Anti-Dumping and Countervailing Duties"), GATT Doc. E/PC/T/W/97 (1947).

[65] See Diller and Levy, *supra*. n. 26, p. 681; according to their position, the will manifested in 1947 by states parties would be confirmed by the 1994 Agreement on Implementation of Article VI GATT (included in Annex 1A of WTO Agreement; see *supra* n. 1) and the 1994 Agreement on Subsidies and Countervailing Measures (also included in Annex 1A of WTO Agreement), in which is clearly found the exclusive reference to economic criteria.

[66] Art. XIX GATT ("Safeguards").

[67] See Diller and Levy, *supra* n. 26, p. 681.

and that this latter has determined the conditions of an excessive importation (for example allowing the exporting state to set prices which are particularly competitive). In this way it would be hypothetically possible, even if only indirectly, to deny preferential treatment as provided for by the GATT/WTO system to states which are responsible for the violation of workers' fundamental rights. But, again, what renders unlikely the procedure described *supra* is the fact that, in reality, it is extremely difficult to demonstrate the existence of the above-mentioned causal link between the prejudice caused to internal production and the exploitation of work under iniquitous conditions by the exporting state.

GATT Article XX

The norm which seems to be most suitable to coordinate the discipline of international trade law with the need to protect human rights (and, therefore, to protect children from the worst forms of labour) appears to be Article XX GATT.[68] This norm identifies some "general exceptions" to the application of the principles decreed by the General Agreement. It provides, in particular, that "nothing in this Agreement shall be construed to prevent the adoption or enforcement by any contracting party of measures: . . . (a) necessary to protect public morals; . . . (b) necessary to protect human, animal or plant life or health; . . . (e) relating to the products of prison labour; . . . (h) undertaken in pursuance of obligations under intergovernmental commodity agreements". When a factual situation can fit one of the above exceptions, each state party may suspend the application of the Agreement. However, the difficulty with this approach is that one must prove that the violation of international standards on child labour constitute a threat to one of the values recognized in Article XX.

Paragraph (a) of Article XX offers a first criterion which may permit the conditioning of enjoyment of trade advantages for the purpose of protecting children against the worst forms of work, since it is undoubted that the forms of child labour listed by Article 3(b) (use, procuring or offering of a child for prostitution, for the production of pornography or for pornographic performances) and (c) (use, procuring or offering of a child for illicit activities, in particular for the production and trafficking of drugs) of the ILO Convention No. 182[69] may entail an offence to public morals.[70]

As far as Article XX(b) is concerned, one can argue that the productive activities carried out where minimum standards concerning safety and working conditions are not guaranteed can put workers' lives in danger or be dangerous to human health. Such a risk is even greater in the case of particularly serious violations, such as those constituting the worst forms of child labour, which,

[68] Art. XX GATT ("General Exceptions").

[69] See *supra* n. 22.

[70] For the concept of "public morals", as provided for by Art. XX(a) GATT, see Francioni, *supra* Chapter 1, Part III.

arguably, are likely to seriously jeopardise the life and/or health of children. Support for this argument can be found in the 1994 panel on *Restrictions on Import of Tuna*,[71] according to which the clause under Article XX(b) can be applied without limits of jurisdiction. The panel reached this conclusion on the basis of a textual interpretation of Article XX[72] and on the basis of the negotiations for the conclusion of GATT and the Havana Charter[73] (which has never come into force).[74]

As for Article XX(e), one may reasonably sustain the extension of its scope to forms of work analogous to prison labour, such as forced labour or work carried out under conditions of slavery, and those forms of child labour which imply the substantial withdrawal of the victim's capacity of choice and self-determination. Such an extension is supported by numerous arguments: first, it is possible to note that the same logical base which authorises states to block the import of goods produced by prisoners' work[75] also supports the execution of the same measure when the manufacturing phase is performed in equally intolerable cases of exploitation, such as forced labour.[76] There seems to be a general consensus on this point, because it is extremely difficult to argue that states do not have the right to refuse goods produced under conditions of slavery.[77] Such a position is backed up by the practice of some countries, particularly the USA, which, at the moment of adhesion to the 1927 Convention for the Abolition of Import and Export Restrictions,[78] maintained that the exception relating to prison labour should be considered to include "goods the product of

[71] *United States—Restrictions on Imports of Tuna*, Report of the Panel, June 1994, para. 5.31, (1994) *ILM* 839.

[72] *Ibid*., para. 5.16. The panel has observed that other exceptions provided for by Art. XX, such as that relating to prison labour (art. XX(e)), refer to situations which necessarily take place beyond the territory of the importer's country; the same can be said for other dispositions of GATT. See Diller and Levy, *supra* n. 26, p. 682.

[73] According to the Panel, such negotiations do not allow interpretations which impose limits to be supported "with respect to the location of the living thing to be protected under Article XX(b)"; see *United States—Restrictions on Imports of Tuna*, *supra* n. 71, para. 5.33.

[74] See *supra* n. 2.

[75] It must be noted that the introduction into GATT 1947 of the exception relating to prison labour was not originally inspired by ethical reasons, but was inserted through the pressure of those states whose internal legislation had already provided for such a clause for quite some time: the national norms in question were based upon the need to protect internal production, since this was unable to maintain competitive prices in comparison with goods produced by manpower at "zero" cost (see Leary, *supra* n. 2, p. 22). However, there is no doubt that nowadays such an exception meets, above all, requirements of a moral character.

[76] See Leary, *supra* n. 2, p. 204; according to this writer the "general exceptions" contained in Art. XX could also be extended to goods produced breaking the main international fair labour standards, such as freedom of association.

[77] See the "Leutwiler Group" Report to the Director-General of GATT, quoted in Charnovitz, "Fair Labor Standards and International Trade", (1986) *Journal of World Trade Law* 61, at 68; see also (with reference to forced labour) Srinavasan, "International Labor Standards Once Again!", in *International Labor Standards and Global Economic Integration: Proceedings of a Symposium* (US Department of Labor, Bureau of International Labor Affairs, July 1994), p. 35; Charnovitz, "Promoting World Labor Rules", (1994) *Journal of Commerce* (19 April), p. 8A.

[78] International Convention for the Abolition of Import and Export Restrictions, 1927, League of Nations Doc. C.I.A.P. 1927; such a treaty can be considered a predecessor of GATT 1947.

forced or slave labor however employed".[79] Moreover, upon analysis of the draft GATT 1947, the US Government expressed its own official position according to which the exceptions as provided for by Article XX reflected pre-existing customary norms applicable to all "international commercial agreements".[80]

The execution of such a principle may, however, come into conflict with a practical difficulty which should not be ignored; where a country intends to suspend the obligations provided for by GATT in relation to goods produced by forced labour or in any way manufactured under conditions of slavery, therefore extending the area of application of Article XX(e), the existence of an interdependent relationship between slave labour and the product subjected to the restriction[81] must be demonstrated. This conforms with the interpretation of the same Article XX as given by the 1994 Panel on *Taxes on Automobiles*[82] and by the 1996 Appellate Body Report on *Standards for Reformulated and Conventional Gasoline*,[83] according to which the term "relating" implies the existence of an effective, and not "merely incidental", relationship between the goods subjected to restrictive measures and the phenomenon to be suppressed. The state which resorts to the application of the norm under examination for cases that are not expressly provided for by the text of Article XX may therefore incur a violation of GATT where the goods, the object of the restrictions, do not constitute the product of the activities which are targeted by the selected restrictive measures.[84]

Finally, also Article XX(h) implicitly authorises the parties to derogate from the GATT obligations for (inter alia) the protection of human rights, because states often agree upon the necessity to guarantee adequate working standards concerning the production of goods which are the object of the intergovernmental treaties.[85]

[79] Letter of Ratification from President Herbert Hoover to the League of Nations, 20 September 1929, quoted by Diller and Levy, *supra* n. 26, p. 684 (such letter is available on file with the United Nations Library, League of Nations Archives). It can be considered remarkable that, during the "Uruguay Round" the European Parliament has unsuccessfully tried to extend the text of Art. XX(e) to child labour; see Organisation for Economic Co-operation and Development, *Trade, Employment and Labour Standards (OECD): A Study of Core Workers' Rights and International Trade*, OECD Doc.COM/DEELSA/TD(96)8/FINAL, 1994, para. 288.

[80] U.S. Department of State, Pub. No. 2983, Analysis of the General Agreement on Tariffs and Trade, 1947.

[81] Such a condition must be satisfied because Art. XX(e) makes reference to measures *relating* to prison labour. See Diller and Levy, *supra* n. 26, p. 684.

[82] *United States—Taxes on automobiles*, 11 October 1994, (1994) *ILM* 1397, at 1456. The Panel notes that the fact that other more effective measures may be taken "d[oes] not imply that the measure could not be justified", there where it does not respond to the requirements provided for by the provision; it must be pointed out that the decision refers to Art. XX(g), but the conclusion of the same can easily be extended even to Art. XX(e), because both are introduced by the same term ("relating").

[83] *United States—Standards for Reformulated and Conventional Gasoline*, Appellate Body Report, 20 May 1996, (1996) *ILM* 603, at 621.

[84] See Diller and Levy, *supra* n. 26, p. 684. See also *United States—Restrictions on Imports of Tuna*, *supra* n. 71, para. 4.34; *United States—Standards for Reformulated and Conventional Gasoline*, *supra* n. 83, p. 621.

[85] It must be pointed out that regarding the possibility in practice to derogate from the basic principles of GATT "in pursuance of obligations under intergovernmental commodity agreements" (see Art. XX GATT) para. 7 of the Singapore Ministerial Declaration (see *supra* n. 5), seems to be

Notwithstanding its broad scope, Article XX must be applied consistently with its *chapeau*; that is, in a manner that does not "constitute a means of arbitrary or unjustifiable discrimination between countries where the same conditions prevail, or a disguised restriction on international trade".[86] This preamble, although absolutely justifiable and coherent with the functions pursued by GATT, risks raising a formidable obstacle to the adoption of trade-related human rights measures because of the undefined nature of the concept of "unjustifiable" and "arbitrary" discrimination.

According to the author's knowledge, no dispute has yet arisen before GATT/WTO from a party's decision to suspend another party's benefits for its violation of human rights in connection with the productive processes of goods subjected to international trade. This lack of precedent, however, does not constitute an insurmountable obstacle to the application of Article XX to child labour. On the contrary, we can analogically extend to child labour the interpretation given to Article XX by the WTO DSB in disputes regarding the protection of the environment. Someone could object that the principles developed for the environment cannot be extended to human rights, because such rights do not pertain to the products as such, but to the productive processes. But the idea, supported by the *Tuna* Panel decision,[87] that Article XX can be applied only in relation to products and not to productive processes, is to be rejected for several reasons,[88] as implied by the "evolutive interpretation" given by the Appellate Body in the *Shrimp* case.[89]

particularly relevant which reads as follows: "The expansion and extent of regional trade agreements make it important to analyse whether the system of WTO rights and obligations as it relates to regional trade agreements needs to be further clarified. We reaffirm the primacy of the multilateral trading system, which includes a framework for the development of regional trade agreements, and we renew our commitment to ensure that regional trade agreements are complementary to it and consistent with its rules".

[86] Article XX GATT.

[87] *United States—Restrictions on Imports of Tuna, supra* n. 71.

[88] For example, it should be rejected because it cannot be asserted that productive processes are outside of Article XX, because para. (e), referring to "prison labour", cannot be applied except in relation to productive processes. For a complete examination of the distinction between "product requirements" and "process or production methods", see Francioni, *supra* Chapter 1, Part III.

[89] *US—Import Prohibition of Certain Shrimp and Shrimp Products*, Appellate Body Report, WT/DS58/AB/R, 12 October 1998, (1999) *ILM* 118. The Appellate Body points out that, as required by Art. 3.2 of the Dispute Settlement Understanding (see *supra* n. 1), the interpretation of GATT has to be made applying the "customary rules of interpretation of public international law", which "call for an examination of the ordinary meaning of the words of a treaty, read in their context, and in the light of the object and purpose of the treaty involved" (para. 114). Thus, Article XX must be interpreted focusing on its purpose (that is, to protect public morals, human, animal or plant life or health, and the other values listed therein) "in the light of contemporary concerns of the community of nations" (para. 129). Since the need to protect fundamental human rights constitutes, just like the environmental protection, "a goal of national and international policy" (*ibid.*; see also paras 130 and 131), we may conclude that the general exceptions of Article XX have to be interpreted as being for the protection of such rights, because they are strictly linked with some of the values covered by Article XX itself (in particular by paras (a), (b) and (e)). This kind of interpretation, the so-called principle of "*evolutive interpretation*", sanctifies the applicability of Article XX relevant exceptions to the fundamental child labour standards, leaving aside any consideration relating to the distinction between products and productive processes. On the principle of evolutive interpretation see Francioni, *supra* Chapter 1.

In this case,[90] the Appellate Body pointed out that WTO members can lawfully adopt unilateral measures restricting trade for the protection of the values recognised by the Article XX general exceptions. As regards child labour, this conclusion is strengthened by the fact that the principle of evolutive interpretation used by the Appellate Body imposes, in the course of interpretation of GATT, the need to take account of the "acknowledgement by the international community"[91] of the fundamental value of *jus cogens* norms which prohibit the worst forms of child labour (see *supra*). But, according to the introductory clauses of Article XX, the unilateral measure must be implemented in a manner which do not constitute arbitrary or unjustifiable discrimination in the treatment of the parties to the Agreement or a disguised restriction on international trade,[92] or, which is the same, "an abuse or misuse of the provisional justification made available by Article XX".[93]

Such an interpretation is well-suited to satisfy fully the need to protect children's basic rights in the course of implementation of the multilateral trading system. Nevertheless, the above mentioned undefined nature of the concept of "unjustifiable" and "arbitrary" discrimination can bring the interpreter to weaken the concrete usefulness of Article XX. Thus, in the author's opinion, some of the reasons advanced by the Appellate Body in the *Shrimp* case to sustain the unjustifiable discriminatory character of the US restrictions on the importation of shrimps caught using fishing techniques liable to kill sea turtles, are not to be supported. In particular the Appellate Body held that (1) the USA, having became party to the 1996 Inter-American Convention for the Protection and Conservation of Sea Turtles,[94] and having failed "to engage the appellees, as well as other Members exporting shrimp to the United States, in serious, across-the-board negotiations . . . for the protection and conservation of sea turtles",[95] have thus "negotiated seriously with some, but not with other Members" for such a purpose;[96] (2) there have been "differences in the levels of effort made by the United States in transferring the required [by Section 609] TED [turtle excluder device] technology to specific countries".[97] This kind of reasoning seem to require, in the course of implementation of unilateral measures aimed to protect the values covered by Article XX, standards of diligence so high as to reduce greatly the usefulness in practice of such a provision.

[90] See *supra* n. 89, in particular para. 121; see also, e.g., Panel Report on *US Taxes on Petroleum and Certain Imported Substances*, BISD 34 S/136–166 (1987); *US—Taxes on Automobiles*, *supra* n. 82; *US—Standards for Reformulated and Conventional Gasoline*, *supra* n. 83.

[91] *US—Import Prohibition of Certain Shrimp and Shrimp Products*, *supra* n. 89; see, in particular, para. 130.

[92] *Ibid.* para. 160.

[93] *Ibid.* paras 160 and 116; see also *US—Standards for Reformulated and Conventional Gasoline*, *supra* n. 83, para. 22.

[94] See http://www.seaturtle.org/iac/convention.shtml.

[95] *US—Import Prohibition of Certain Shrimp and Shrimp Products*, *supra* n. 89, para.166.

[96] *Ibid.* para. 172.

[97] *Ibid.* para. 175.

However, Article XX offers the best way for the implementation of child labour standards in the multilateral trading context. It permits the adoption of unilateral measures restricting trade advantages, with only the limit of avoiding abuse of the general exceptions contained therein. To avoid such abuse, it seems sufficient to achieve a preventive comparative evaluation between the potential measure and the value of the good it aims to protect, in such a way that the first is proportional to the second.

GATT Article XXIII

A further provision, potentially functional for the protection of human rights, could be Article XXIII GATT, concerning the procedures to which every party may have recourse where it claims that it has suffered a nullification or an impairment of the advantages guaranteed it by GATT.[98] The USA has proposed an interpretation of this norm such as to characterize the maintaining by a state of iniquitous working standards as a form of nullification or impairment of benefits assured by GATT to the other parties. This characterisation, recently suggested also by an ILO paper,[99] would create the prerequisite for possible complaints based upon Article XXIII, or even unilateral measures.[100] However this remains a minority thesis, as demonstrated by the fact that all the attempts carried out to date for the insertion of a "social clause" in GATT have always failed.[101]

WTO Agreement Article XIII

The WTO Agreement contains a norm which could be used, at a negotiation level, as a strong form of pressure to persuade an aspirant new member of the WTO to improve the working conditions existing in its jurisdiction.[102] This is Article XIII,[103] and it allows a member of the WTO to refuse to apply the

[98] Art.XXIII GATT, "Nullification or Impairment".

[99] See *The Social Dimension of the Liberalization of World Trade*, ILO Doc.GB.261/WP/SLD/1, 1994, para. 25.

[100] See US Commission on Foreign Economic Policy, Staff Papers 438, *supra* n. 2; Perez and Lopez, "Conditioning Trade on Foreign Labor Law: the U.S. Approach", (1988) *Comparative Labor Law* 257; Diller and Levy, *supra* n. 26, p. 686. It must be emphasised that one of the main objectives pursued by the US delegation during the "Uruguay Round" was to introduce into the area of international trade law a provision which would assure respect of workers' rights; successively the USA has continued to follow this goal, restating it, once more without success, during the WTO Ministerial Conference held in Singapore in 1996 (see Diller and Levy, *supra* n. 26, p. 686; U.S. H.R. 5110, 103d Cong., 2nd Sess.1142, 1994).

[101] During the Singapore Ministerial Conference (see *supra* n. 5), members of the European Union found themselves in disagreement with relation to the eventual insertion of a social clause into GATT; see "WTO: Ministers Agree to Do Nothing on Labour Standards", *European Reporter*, 14 December 1996. See also Leary, *supra* n. 2, p. 202.

[102] See Diller and Levy, *supra* n. 26, p. 686.

[103] Article XIII WTO Agreement, "Non-Application of Multilateral Trade Agreements between Particular Members".

Agreement to another state by ad hoc declaration at the moment at which the latter makes a request to became a WTO party. This faculty would allow parties to weigh the degree of the target state's implementation of fundamental workers' rights and to condition acceptance of membership on such implementation. The limit to this approach is that unless the position of the declaring state is generally shared by the other members of the WTO, or at least by the majority of them, the effective value of such a declaration risks being extremely limited. It is obvious, in fact, that without a general consensus about such a measure, it is very difficult to create a coercive force strong enough to persuade the target state to improve the working conditions guaranteed in its own territory. In the real world, the likelihood of reaching a consensus across the board in relation to child labour standards seems to be rather remote. However, it is to be hoped that at least in the case of huge violations of the international standards protecting children, including the standards relating to the exclusion of the worst forms of labour, current practice may develop with the development of human rights norms.

Relationship Between the GATT/WTO System and Treaties on Child Labour

The evolutive interpretative analysis of Article XX GATT discussed in the last paragraph seems still stronger when one considers that all WTO member states are bound by several treaties on human rights that oblige them to render effective the protection of children from the worst forms of labour (see *supra*). In this regard, a fundamental provision is Article 31(3)(c) of the Vienna Convention on the Law of Treaties,[104] which states that every international treaty must be interpreted by taking into account "any relevant rules of international law applicable in the relations between the parties". GATT (and any agreement related to it), being an international treaty, does not escape this rule.[105] Thus, in the course of its implementation, parties have to take in consideration their conventional (and customary) duties to repress the worst forms of child labour.[106]

The next question concerns the "hierarchical relationship" between GATT/WTO and child labour conventional norms in the system of the sources

[104] See *supra* n. 34.

[105] See Francioni, "La Tutela dell'Ambiente e la Disciplina del Commercio Internazionale", in SIDI, *Diritto e Organizzazione del Commercio Internazionale dopo la Creazione della Organizzazione Mondiale del Commercio* (Napoli, 1998), p. 161. See also *The Social Dimension of the Liberalization of World Trade*, *supra* n. 99,where it is underlined that nearly all members of WTO are part of the ILO too, and that such a "membership of both organisations means that States concerned endeavour in good faith to take account in each of these organisations of the objectives and obligations they have undertaken in the other" (para. 25).

[106] As an example of the practical implementation of this principle, consider the duty of the members of the EU to execute all their international obligations pursuant to respect for human rights. Such a duty results by virtue of Arts 6 and 11 of the Treaty on European Union, which include amongst the fundamental principles of the Union itself, precisely that of the respect for human rights and fundamental freedoms.

of international law. If one leaves aside the fact that, as seen *supra*, implementation of GATT/WTO is fully compatible, with that of child labour standards, we must conclude that these standards prevail over the multilateral trading system since they are part of the principles covered by the UN Charter. By virtue of Article 103 of the Charter "in the event of a conflict between the obligations of the Members of the United Nations under the present Charter and their obligations under *any other international agreement*, their obligations under the present Charter shall prevail" (emphasis added). Such a provision sanctions the precedence of "universal respect for, and observance of, human rights and fundamental freedoms for all"[107] over GATT/WTO. Noone can deny that such rights and freedoms, as elaborated in the Universal Declarations of 1948 and in the 1966 UN Covenants,[108] are gravely infringed by the worst forms of child labour. This strengthens the idea that recourse to unilateral measures restricting trade, for the purpose of targeting these forms of labour, is to be considered absolutely lawful in conformity with contemporary international law.

Nevertheless, such measures certainly do not constitute the best way to be followed in pursuing a global system based on international relations and collaboration, in both the fields of human rights and of international trade. The necessity of finding lines of convergence between the opposite needs of these two fields has been perceived by various parties. The ILO itself has acknowledged that multiplication of unilateral actions would "generat[e] uncertainty and weaken . . . political support for liberalisation—leading to new protectionism".[109] A possible solution has been suggested by a coalition of international organisations representative of workers and trade unions. They have proposed the institution of a Joint Advisory Committee of the ILO and GATT/WTO with the role of identifying a basic group of minimum labour standards to be inserted in a social clause.[110]

[107] Art.55(c) of the UN Charter.

[108] The prevailing doctrine considers the 1948 Universal Declaration of Human Rights, the International Covenant on Civil and Political Rights and the 1966 International Covenant on Economic, Social and Cultural Rights (993 *UNTS* 3) as the authoritative elaboration of Art. 55(c) of the UN Charter; see, e.g., Buergenthal, "International Human Rights Norms and Institutions: Accomplishments and Prospects", (1998) *Washington Law Review* 1; Diller and Levy *supra* n. 26, p. 673; Pocar, "Codification of Human Rights Law by the United Nations", in Jasentuliyana (ed.), *Perspectives in International Law* (1995), p. 139; Schacter, "United Nations Law", (1994) *Am J Intl L* 3; Sloan, "General Assembly Resolutions Revised (Forty Years Later)", (1987) *Brit Yrbk Intl L* 39.

[109] See *International Trade and Labour Rights: ILO Director-General Calls for the Establishment of Universal Ground Rules*, 1997, Doc. ILO/97/10. Such a document suggests, as possible solutions, the development of social progress and the institution of a system of labels to be affixed to goods subject to international trade, which attests that such products are "child labour (or forced or bonded labour) free". The latter idea is also expressed by, inter alia, Diller and Levy, *supra* n. 26, p. 686. See also ILO Declaration on Fundamental Principles and Rights at Work, *supra* n. 24, which declares that "labour standards should not be used for protectionist trade purposes, and that nothing in this Declaration and its follow-up shall be invoked or otherwise used for such purposes; in addition, the comparative advantage of any country should in no way be called into question by this Declaration and its follow-up" (n. 5).

[110] See *The Social Dimension of International Trade*, Joint Statement by World and European Trade Union Confederations, ICFTU (International Confederation of Free Trade Unions), WCL (World Confederation of Labour) and ETUC (European Trade Union Confederations), 43/94 (2 February 1994).

A different approach, suggested by scholars for the protection of the environment, but analogically extensible to human rights and child labour, advocates the coordination and reconciliation of trade goals with competing objectives set out in non-commercial treaties.[111] According to such a doctrinal approach, if the treaty on human rights does not provide for its own dispute settlement mechanism, it would be up the WTO DSB to take the responsibility of settling disputes arising from trade-related human rights measures by way of evolutive interpretation of GATT.[112]

As we have seen, the problem analysed here is a very controversial one, and one that is undergoing rapid evolution. Unfortunately, on account of the strong opposition expressed by developing countries, the development of a common system to coordinate international trade goals with the protection of human rights, seems at the moment to be still remote. As a consequence, recourse to unilateral measures is, in most cases, the only way to protect children against the worst forms of labour in the multilateral trading context.

Jus Cogens Character of Fundamental Norms on Child Labour

The existing link between the worst forms of child labour and some particularly egregious violations of human rights covered by peremptory norms of customary law (see *supra*), attributes to those practices the character of grave breaches of norms of paramount importance in the hierarchy of the sources of international law. In this perspective it is our view that a functional connection exists between child labour itself and slavery, whose definition includes the extreme forms of child labour.

To support such an assertion, we can usefully look at the contemporary extension of the concept of slavery, which is internationally defined as "the *status* or condition of a person over whom any or all the powers attaching to the right of ownership are exercised".[113] This means, in other words, that according to this definition, when labour is forcibly imposed upon a child, without leaving him any possibility of freedom of choice and self-determination, we can reasonably assert that this child is subjected to slavery. Moreover, a huge number of children exploited in labour are subjected to debt bondage, which is expressly qualified as a practice similar to slavery by Article 1(a) of the 1956

[111] See Francioni, *supra* n. 105, p. 168; Francioni, *supra* Chapter 1. The coordination between instruments for settlement of disputes consequently implies the same operation among substantial provisions contained in the two agreements; see Francioni, *supra* n. 105, p. 169

[112] See Francioni, *supra* n. 105, p. 169.

[113] See Slavery Convention, Art. 1(1) (see also *supra* n. 31); Supplementary Convention on Slavery, Art. 7(a); the high rate of ratification of these two conventions, and the constant reference to such a definition by international and national authorities competent in the field of human rights, attribute customary value to it. See also Art. 7 of the constitutive agreement of the International Criminal Court, (1998) 37 *ILM* 999.

Supplementary Convention;[114] in Asia alone 25 million children are estimated to work under such a condition.[115] Finally, Article 1(d) of the same Convention qualifies as a form of slavery "any institution or practice whereby a child or young person under the age of 18 years is delivered . . . to another person, whether for reward or not, with a view to the exploitation of the child or young person *or of his labour*"[116] (emphasis added). All the foregoing norms, considered in their cumulative effect, go to define a broad concept of slavery, in which only a few of the worst forms of child labour are not included. It can therefore be stated that, according to long-standing states' practice, this wide concept of slavery today has customary value.[117] As a consequence, the worst forms of child labour are prohibited by an international customary norm of *jus cogens* (see *supra*), i.e. that which forbids slavery in all its forms.

According to Article 53 of the Vienna Convention of the Law of Treaties,[118] "[a] treaty is void if, at the time of conclusion, it conflicts with a peremptory norm of international law"; Article 64,[119] moreover, adds that "if a new peremptory norm of general international law emerges, any existing treaty which is in conflict with that norm becomes void and terminates". In the case of GATT, obviously, this does not mean that such an agreement has to be considered void; but, without any doubt, it has to be interpreted and applied in such a way as not to break the fundamental child labour standards, because it can easily be fully implemented in compliance with the requirement of the respect of such standards.[120]

Consequently, when goods, subject to international trade within the scope of GATT, are produced (or exported) perpetrating any of the worst forms of child labour, every party can lawfully suspend the Agreement and refuse to apply the trade advantages provided for therein in favour of the member responsible for the violation of minimum child labour standards. Economic sanctions are probably the most effective (lawful) measures to persuade a government to respect human rights.

[114] Art.1(a) reads as follows: "[d]ebt bondage, that is to say, the *status* or condition arising from a pledge by a debtor of his personal services or of those of a person under his control as security for a debt, if the value of those services as reasonably assessed is not applied towards the liquidation of the debt or the length or nature of those services are not respectively limited and defined".

[115] See "Slavery—By any other name", *The Economist*, 6 January 1990, p. 50; Working Group on Contemporary Forms of Slavery, Report of Jai Singh (North Indian Coordinator of SACCS), Geneva, 1996 (reprinted in synthesis in the UN Doc. E/CN.4/Sub.2/1996/24 of 19 July 1996); UN Doc. E/CN.4/Sub.2/1991/41 of 20 August 1991; UN Doc. E/CN.4/Sub.2/1994/33 of 23 June 1994.

[116] Supplementary Convention on Slavery, Art. 1(d). The practice of selling children for the exploitation of their work is very widespread in poor countries; see ILO, *Child Labour, Targeting the Intolerable* (Geneva, 1996), p. 15.

[117] For an analysis of such a practice, see Lenzerini, *supra* n. 31, p. 499.

[118] See *supra* n. 34.

[119] *Ibid.*

[120] On the interpretative function of *jus cogens* norms see also Conforti, *Diritto Internazionale*, (Napoli, 1997), p. 184.

No objection may be raised based on the fact that the alleged violation, being perpetrated against individuals of the state "agent",[121] does not directly affect any other country. The *erga omnes* character of the international norms which protect children against the worst forms of labour, authorises all states to act for the implementation of such norms.[122]

IV. CONCLUSIONS: THE SANCTITY OF THE PROTECTION OF CHILDREN AND THE NEED TO LIMIT STATES' UNILATERALISM

The search for some form of interaction between the GATT/WTO system and the protection of children from the worst forms of labour raises a serious problem of values. On the one hand, international trade constitutes the engine of the contemporary system of international relations. On the other, the life and dignity of the child are, without any doubt, mankind's most precious assets. Clearly, these two issues often come into conflict.

To say that such a problem could be resolved by guaranteeing poor countries adequate social development would be pure rhetoric, in the sense that while everyone agrees on this, it is also well known that the industrialised states will never freely accept this course of action. Thus, the gravity of the problem is magnified by the fact that the social growth of developing countries cannot afford to by-pass the potential of progress as this is supplied by international trade. Paradoxically, the possibility of development offered by the contemporary economic system to these countries actually resides in their lower wages and the lower levels of social protection provided for in them, and the unilateral imposition of international labour standards on such states would cancel their economic competitivity and remove them from international trade, thus excluding them from the opportunity of development. Moreover, any resort to "punitive" unilateral measures could lead to much uncertainty in trade relations and to a decentralisation of such measures; such a situation would constitute a sharp reversal within the sphere of a legal system which, in general, aims towards the

[121] The adjective "agent" is used not only to mean the state which directly perpetrates any of the worst forms of child labour, but also the state which does not prevent and repress the exploitation of such forms in all territories subject to its jurisdiction. The contemporary evolution of international law in the fields of human rights, indeed, indicates that states have the customary duty to guarantee the full enjoyment of basic human rights by their citizens. See Forde, "Non Governmental Interferences with Human Rights", (1985) *Brit Yrbk Intl L* 253; Meron, *supra* n. 37, pp. 138 and 160; Lenzerini, *supra* n. 31, p. 508 See also Human Rights Committee, Comm. No.16/1977, *Monguya Mbenge* v. *Zaire*, UN Doc. A/38/40 (1983), Comm. No.156/1983, *Solòrzano de Pena v Venezuela*, UN Doc. A/41/40 (1986); European Court of Human Rights, *Case of X and Y* v. *The Netherlands*, Eur. Ct HR, Ser.A, 1985, p. 11, and *Bozano* case, Eur. Ct HR, Ser.A, 1986, p.28; Inter-American Court of Human Rights, *Velasquez Rodriguez,* 29 July 1988, Inter-American Ct HR, Ser.C, Decisions and Judgments, no. 4, paras 41–5. Finally, see the decision of an Australian Tribunal in *Koowarta* v. *Bjelke—Petersen and others* (1982) [1985] *International Law Reports* 181.

[122] See, e.g., Ago, *supra* n. 43, p. 137; Bianchi, *supra* n. 43, p. 183; Charney, "Third State Remedies in International Law", (1989) *Michigan International Law Journal* 57; Gaja, *supra* n. 43, p. 152; Meron, *supra* n. 37, p. 81.

development of global common ground in which to centralise international relations.

The other side of this issue is that there is a minimum level of protection of human beings (especially of the child), ideally represented by a bottom line which there is an absolute prohibition of falling beneath. Neither must the need for economic development be taken by developing countries as a pretext to maintain artificially low levels of protection for workers, "as a commercial strategy".[123]

It is obvious that the ideal solution to such a conflict would reside in the introduction of a social clause (or in the coordination between commercial and humanitarian needs, especially at the level of dispute settlement)[124] in the GATT/WTO system; but this eventuality seems in practice to be "as welcome as a dog at a wedding" to most of the international community.[125] Probably, if developed countries would water down their aims, and agree to include in the hypothetical social clause only the most fundamental labour standards,[126] developing states could not refuse such a clause; it is extremely difficult for a government, in the international order, to stand out against a rule which has the aim of forbidding exploitation in slavery or slavery-like practices.

A system for placing side-by-side the globalisation of international trade and universalisation of the implementation of basic child labour standards could be brought into practice, and it depends on the will of Western countries to make such an implementation effective. The best way might be that of following, at a global level, a system of incentives already experimented with by the EU and the USA.[127] It needs not necessarily come into conflict with the GATT/WTO system, especially if it is structured as a scheme of incentives (or provision for the reduction of external debts), not directly linked with imported goods, in such a way as not to cause any arbitrary or unjustifiable discrimination. Provided this last condition is fully respected, it cannot be denied that a state is completely free to provide incentives to those countries which distinguish themselves for the protection of children rights, in the course of production of goods subject to international trade.

[123] See *International Trade and Labour Rights*, *supra* n. 109.

[124] See *supra*. For a comprehensive examination of the possible solutions to resolve the conflict between international trade and labour rights, see McCrudden and Davies, *supra* Chapter 8.

[125] See *supra*. This is confirmed by a briefing note prepared by the WTO for the works of the 3rd WTO Ministerial Conference ("Millenium Round"), held in Seattle from 30 November to 3 December 1999 (see briefing note, *Trade and Labour Standards, Subject of intense debate*, http://heva.wto-ministerial.org/english/about_e/18lab_e.htm) with no appreciable outcome (the new round had to be postponed to the next year). This note seems to be in objective terms, limiting itself to referring to the opposite positions of Western and developing countries. But, at the end, it betrays the attitude of the WTO underlining that "[a] recent World Bank study estimated that less than 5% of child workers in the developing world are involved in export related activities". Leaving aside doubts about the reliability of such a study, if we consider that child labourers in the world are numbered at around 250 million (most in developing countries; see ILO, *supra* n. 116, p.7; "Slavery—By any Other Name", *supra* n. 115), the problem involves 12.5 million children. Besides, since when has the protection of fundamental human rights been a question of numbers?

[126] On this position see also Leary, *supra* n. 2, p. 222.

[127] See *supra*.

In any event, whilst waiting for a treaty resolution of the problem in issue, when a basic right of a child is infringed, by means of exploitation of any worst form of labour in the course of the production of goods subject to international trade, the right of every party to GATT to suspend the Agreement in its relationship with the country responsible for the violation is quite clear. This kind of action is not only lawful, but also proper, because of the higher value of the norm protected than that sacrificed. However, it would be preferable if any measure was taken at a multilateral level, at least by a coalition of states, in such a way as to guarantee the proportionality between the measure itself and the violation, minimise the risk of protectionism and above all promote the process of international cooperation among the relevant actors in the international community.

12

The Interplay Between Trade and the Environment Within the NAFTA Framework

PATRICIA ISELA HANSEN

THE RECENT PROTESTS at the Seattle summit of the World Trade Organisation (WTO) revealed a deep rift in the international community concerning the impact of trade on environmental protection. An increasingly vocal coalition of environmental organisations asserts that increased international trade will undermine efforts to protect the environment, because businesses will be able to escape national environmental regulations merely by moving their production facilities to countries with lower environmental standards. Others are equally adamant in their belief that free trade helps to generate the economic resources that make it possible to address environmental problems, and that trade rules must prevent environmental law from becoming a disguised form of economic protection.[1] The conflict between these two views has not yet been resolved in the WTO, which has formed a committee to examine the interaction between trade and environmental protection.[2]

Environmental issues also played a prominent role in the negotiation of the North American Free Trade Agreement (NAFTA), which entered into force for

[1] For a sampling of the growing literature on the trade-environment conflict, see, e.g., D. Zaelke, P.Orbuch and R.F. Housman (eds.), *Trade and the Environment: Law, Economics & Policy* (Washington DC, Island Press, 1993); D. Esty, *Greening the GATT: Trade, Environment and the Future* (Washington DC, Institute for International Economics, 1994); W. Bradnee Chambers and G. Sampson (eds.), *Trade, Environment and the Millennium* (UNU/IAS,1999). For a critical view of international trade rules, see Earth Island Institute (ed.), *The Case Against Free Trade* (San Francisco, Earth Island Press, 1993).

[2] The WTO and the World Bank have recently issued reports on the trade-environment conflict. See, WTO Secretariat, *Special Studies 4, Trade & Environment* (<http://www.wto.org>, 1999); see also, Per G. Frederiksson (ed.), *Trade, Global Policy and the* Environment (World Bank Discussion Paper No. 402, 1999) For a critical view of the WTO report, see S. Charnovitz, "World Trade and the Environment: A Review of the New WTO Report", (2000) 12 *Geo. Int'l Env. L. Rev.* 523. See generally, P. I. Hansen, "Transparency, Standards of Review, and the Use of Trade Measures to Protect the Global Environment", (1999) 39 *Va. J. Int'l L.* 1017; J. P. Trachtman, "The Domain of WTO Dispute Resolution", (1999) 40 *Harv. Int'l L.J.* 333: R. Steinburg, "Trade-Environment Negotiations in the EU, NAFTA and WTO: Regional trajectories of Rule Development", (1997) 91 *Am. J. Int'l L.* 231; T. J. Schoenbaum, "Int'l Trade and Protection of the Environment: The Continuing Search for Reconciliation", 91 *Am. J. Int'l L.* 268.

the United States, Canada and Mexico in 1994.[3] The NAFTA was the first international trade agreement to include in its preamble an express reference to the principle of "sustainable development," and to recognise the objective of strengthening the "development and enforcement of environmental laws and regulations".[4] It also contains a number of other specific provisions addressing environmental concerns, including a unique "side agreement" dedicated entirely to environmental issues.

The NAFTA appears to have had some influence on developments in the WTO, which has now adopted a reference to sustainable development similar to the NAFTA's in its new preamble.[5] NAFTA's other provisions on environmental issues have also been suggested as models for other international trade agreements, including a proposed free trade agreement that would encompass nearly all of the countries in the Western Hemisphere,[6] and the now-dormant OECD proposal for a Multilateral Agreement on Investment (MAI).[7]

However, early experience under the NAFTA suggests that the agreement is still far from achieving a consistent approach for resolving regional disputes involving economic and environmental issues. As discussed in Part I, the NAFTA rules on regional trade have significantly weakened the ability of the NAFTA countries themselves to challenge environmental measures under international trade rules. At the same time, however, the NAFTA investment rules discussed in Part II have made it possible for private investors to bring their own claims for monetary damages resulting from environmental measures, even if their own governments do not support the claims. Part III discusses ways in which the NAFTA's environmental side agreement has succeeded in promoting public information and public participation in addressing regional environmental concerns. The side agreement's emphasis on public participation stands in

[3] North American Free Trade Agreement, 17 Dec. 1992, Can.-Mex. U.S., 32 ILM. 289 [hereinafter "NAFTA"]. For a discussion of environmental concerns related to the NAFTA, see P. Johnson and A. Beaulieu, *The Environment and NAFTA: Understanding and Implementing the New Continental Law* (Washington DC, Island Press, 1996) at 24–34. See also NAFTA, Environmental Issues: Hearings Before the Subcommittee on Rules of the House Committee on Rules, 102d Cong., 1st Sess. (1991).

[4] NAFTA, *supra* n. 3, preamble, 32 ILM at 289.

[5] Agreement Establishing the WTO, 15 Apr. 1994, (1995) 33 ILM 1144 [hereinafter "WTO Agreement"], preamble. See also, United States: Import Prohibition of Certain Shrimp and Shrimp Products, 12 Oct. 1998, (1998) 38 ILM 118 [hereinafter "Shrimp/Turtle Decision"] (noting the importance of the preamble in the context of environmental issues).

[6] The United States has sought to include trade-related environmental issues in ongoing negotiations aimed at establishing a hemispheric Free Trade Area of the Americas (FTAA). However, a number of countries have strongly opposed these efforts. See, "Latin Leaders Signal Desire to Build FTAA without Labor, Green Issues," *Americas Trade*, 4 Sept. 1997, at 11–13. Instead, negotiators agreed to create a committee to receive and consider the views of civil society, including environmental groups. See, Second Summit of the Americas, Declaration of Principles and Plan of Action, 19 Apr. 1998, (1998) 37 ILM 947.

[7] The MAI proposal, and the events leadings up to the current decision to suspend the MAI negotiations, are discussed in P. T. Muchlinski, "The Rise and Fall of the Multilateral Agreement on Investment: Where Now?", (2000) 34 *Int'l Law* 1033. For the negotiating text and commentary of the proposed agreement, see OECD, The Multilateral Agreement on Investment (last modified 14 Dec. 1998), *available at* the OECD Website, <http://www.oecd.org/daf/cmis/mai/negtext.htm>.

sharp contrast to the closed proceedings used to resolve environmental issues when they are raised in private investor claims.

The following discussion is divided into three parts, focusing separately on NAFTA's rules on regional trade rules, its rules on investment, and the side agreement on environmental cooperation. Since the NAFTA is still quite new and not yet well known or understood even in North America, I begin each section with a brief review of the relevant provisions. I then discuss the early results that have emerged as a result of these provisions, and the impact these provisions are likely to have on environmental and health regulation in the NAFTA countries. The conclusion sets forth some preliminary suggestions regarding changes that might help to reduce some of the tensions that have begun to arise in the NAFTA framework for resolving conflicts between economic and environmental interests.

I. THE RULES ON REGIONAL TRADE: BUILDING ON THE GATT MODEL

The NAFTA rules on regional trade are built on the GATT model. The NAFTA will completely eliminate tariffs on nearly all NAFTA-originating goods by 2009.[8] In addition, the NAFTA adopts a number of GATT provisions on non-tariff barriers to trade.[9] The agreement expressly incorporates the GATT's general prohibition on non-tariff barrier to trade,[10] as well as its requirement of National Treatment for imported goods,[11] and its General Exception for measures that relate to conservation of exhaustible natural resources or are "necessary" to protect public health.[12] As discussed below, however, the agreement

[8] NAFTA provides for elimination of most tariffs for trade in originating goods between Mexico and the United States within 10 years, although a few import-sensitive products will have a 15-year transition period. NAFTA, *supra* n. 3, 32 ILM at 299. Most US–Canada bilateral tariffs were phased out by January 1998, according to the schedule set out in their previous bilateral agreement. See, US–Canada Free Trade Agreement, 2 Jan.1988, US–Can., (1988) 27 ILM 281, art. 401(2). As of 1 Jan. 1996, due to the phase-in of the scheduled duty reductions, the average Mexican tariff on US products had fallen from 10% to 4.9%, and the average US tariff on Mexican products, from 4.0% to 2.3%. Office of the US Trade Representative, *1995 Annual Report—Regional Negotiations 1* (1996).

[9] The NAFTA also adopts a far more comprehensive approach to trade in services than the WTO. For a comparison of the two approaches, see H. G. Broadman, "International Trade and Investment in Services: A Comparative Analysis of the NAFTA", (1993) 27 *Int'l Law* 623 and B. Hoekman and M. Kostecki, *The Political Economy of the World Trading System: From GATT to WTO* (Oxford, Oxford University Press, 1995) 127–43.

[10] NAFTA, *supra* n. 3, art. 309 (prohibiting most import or export restrictions on regional trade unless the restriction is imposed in accordance with GATT Article XI).

[11] *Ibid.* art. 301 (requiring each party to treat goods of other parties in a manner "comparable" to the manner in which the party treats goods of domestic origin that are "directly competitive or substitutable"). Certain listed products are exempt from this requirement. *Id.*

[12] *Ibid.* art. 2101.1 (incorporating GATT art. XX with respect to trade in goods and technical barrier to trade. The agreement also creates a separate exception for its provisions regarding trade in services. *Ibid.* art. 2101.2 (creating exception for measures "necessary to secure compliance with

also contains a number of provisions that were expressly designed to ensure greater sensitivity to environmental concerns than had emerged under prior GATT rules.

Trade Measures Pursuant to International Environmental Agreements

A number of international environmental treaties, such as the Convention on International Trade in Endangered Species ("CITES"),[13] authorise restrictions on certain types of environmentally-harmful trade. As a number of commentators have explained, such trade restrictions may be inconsistent with the GATT rules governing non-tariff barriers to trade.[14] However, it is not clear whether the GATT rules supercede those set forth in the environmental agreements.

The NAFTA clarifies that its provisions generally prevail over inconsistent provisions in any other international agreement involving a NAFTA party.[15] However, it also expressly subordinates its provisions to the provisions of five specific environmental agreements.[16] In addition to CITES, these agreements include: the Montreal Protocol on Substances that Deplete the Ozone Layer (the "Montreal Protocol");[17] two bilateral environmental agreements involving NAFTA parties;[18] and, upon its entry into force for all three NAFTA countries, the Basel Convention on the Control of Transboundary Movements of Hazardous Wastes and Their Disposal (the "Basel Convention").[19] The NAFTA parties may agree to add other agreements to this list in the future.[20]

The obligations set out in the listed environmental agreements will generally prevail over any inconsistent provision in the NAFTA. However, the NAFTA parties are required to use the least restrictive means that is "reasonably available" and would be "equally effective" for achieving compliance with their

laws or regulations that are not inconsistent with" the agreement, provided that the measures are not applied in a manner that would constitute "a means of arbitrary or unjustifiable discrimination" or a "disguised restriction on trade").

[13] Convention on International Trade in Endangered Species of Wild Fauna and Flora, 3 Mar. 1973, 12 ILM 1085 [hereinafter "CITES"].

[14] For a discussion of the potential conflicts between international trade rules and multilateral environmental agreements, see R. G. Tarasofsky, "Ensuring Compatibility Between Multilateral Environmental Agreements and GATT/WTO", (1998) 7 *Y.B. Int'l Envtl. L.* 52; see also Hansen, *supra* n. 2.

[15] NAFTA, *supra* n. 3, art. 103.2.

[16] *Ibid.* art. 104.

[17] Montreal Protocol on Substances that Deplete the Ozone Layer, 16 Sept. 1987, 26 ILM 1550 [hereinafter "Montreal Protocol"].

[18] See Mexico–United States Agreement to Cooperate in the Solution of Environmental Problems in the Border Area, 14 Aug. 1983, 22 ILM 1025 [hereinafter the "La Paz Agreement"]; Canada–United States Agreement Covering Transboundary Movement of Hazardous Waste, 28 Oct. 1986, T.I.A.S. No. 11099.

[19] Basel Convention on the Control of Transboundary Movements of Hazardous Waste and Their Disposal, 22 Mar. 1989, 28 ILM 649 [hereinafter "Basel Convention"].

[20] NAFTA, *supra* n. 3, art. 104.2.

obligations under the listed agreements.[21] Thus, a measure taken pursuant to a listed environmental agreement may still be deemed inconsistent with NAFTA.

Regulatory Harmonisation

The NAFTA, like the WTO, encourages regulatory harmonisation. NAFTA countries must use the guidelines and recommendations adopted by international standardising organisations, such as the International Organisation for Standardisation (ISO) and the Codex Alimentarius Commission, as the "basis" for their product standards.[22] Moreover, the NAFTA countries may apply their product standards only to the extent "necessary" to achieve legitimate regulatory goals.[23] Food safety measures and other "sanitary and phytosanitary" measures must be based on a "risk assessment" and take into account "scientific evidence".[24] The NAFTA has also established a number of special committees, including representatives from each NAFTA country, to facilitate greater harmonisation of product standards in the NAFTA countries.[25]

However, the NAFTA also contains a number of provisions designed to prevent *downward* harmonisation of product standards. Specific NAFTA rules make it clear that harmonisation should not involve any reduction in the NAFTA countries' current levels of environmental and health protection.[26] Moreover, the standards adopted in NAFTA countries may not be presumed to be inconsistent with the NAFTA merely because they are more stringent than the standards recommended by international standardising bodies.[27] Finally, although committees may recommend the adoption of harmonised measures, each NAFTA country establishes its own product standards.[28]

Dispute Settlement

In general, NAFTA countries may pursue disputes that arise under both NAFTA and WTO rules in either forum.[29] A different rule applies, however, to

[21] *Ibid.* art. 104.1.

[22] *Ibid.* arts. 713.1 (referring to sanitary and phytosanitary measures) and 905.1 (other standards-related measures).

[23] *Ibid.* arts. 712.5 (sanitary and phytosanitary measures) and 904.4 (other standards-related measures).

[24] *Ibid.* arts. 712.3. Sanitary and phytosanitary measures are measures adopted to protect animal or plant life or health from risks involving food safety, pests or disease. *Ibid.* art. 724.

[25] See, e.g., *ibid.* arts. 722–23 and 913–14.

[26] *Ibid.* arts. 713.1, 714.1 and 906.2.

[27] *Ibid.* art. 713.2; see also arts. 723.6 and 914.4 (party challenging product standards has the burden of establishing inconsistency with the agreement).

[28] *See ibid.* arts. 712.2 and 904.2 (each NAFTA party sets its own "appropriate levels of protection").

[29] *Ibid.* art. 2005.1.

disputes involving environmental or health issues. A NAFTA country may require a dispute involving its environmental measures to be brought exclusively under NAFTA's dispute settlement provisions if it asserts that the measure is justified under one of the environmental agreements expressly recognised as superior to NAFTA.[30] A NAFTA country may also preclude recourse to the WTO in disputes involving product standards that were adopted to protect its own environment or public health, or that raise factual issues related to "the environment, health, safety or conservation".[31]

Like the WTO, the NAFTA permits member countries to submit disputes arising under the agreement to *ad hoc* panels of independent experts.[32] Private parties are not permitted to participate in NAFTA dispute settlement proceedings, which are closed to the public. However, NAFTA panels may seek "information and technical advice" from any expert person or body, and may request a written report of a scientific review board on environmental, health, safety and other scientific issues.[33]

The provision for exclusive NAFTA jurisdiction over most environmental issues was in part based on substantive differences between NAFTA and GATT rules on environmental measures. However, the substantive differences between the GATT and NAFTA have been significantly eroded by recent developments in the WTO. As discussed above, the WTO preamble now includes a reference to "sustainable development" similar to the NAFTA's.[34] The Appellate Body's decision in the *Shrimp/Turtle* case has adopted a new balancing test that may make it substantially more difficult to challenge treaty-based trade restrictions in the WTO.[35] The Appellate Body's decision in the *Hormones* case has also clarified that national standards may not be presumed to be inconsistent with WTO rules merely because they are more stringent than international standards.[36]

On the other hand, the NAFTA dispute settlement system remains significantly weaker than that of the WTO. NAFTA panels retain much closer ties to the disputing parties than panels in the WTO. WTO panelists are generally not nationals of either of the disputing parties.[37] Moreover, the decisions of WTO panels are subject to review by a permanent Appellate Body.[38] By contrast, most NAFTA panelists are nationals of the disputing parties themselves, and the decisions of NAFTA panels are not subject to review by any permanent appellate body or court. Under a process known as "reverse selection," each of

[30] NAFTA, *supra* n. 3, art. 2005.3.

[31] *Ibid.* art. 2005.4.

[32] See generally NAFTA, *supra* n. 3, ch. 20.

[33] *Ibid.*, arts. 2012.1(b), 2014–2015.

[34] *See supra* n. 5 and accompanying text.

[35] *See* Shrimp/Turtle Decision, *supra* n. 5. For a general discussion of the impact of this decision on environmental trade measures, see Hansen, *supra* n. 2.

[36] See Report of the WTO Appellate Body, EC Measures Concerning Meat and Meat Products (Hormones), WT/DS26/AB/R and WT/DS48/AB/R (16 Jan. 1998), at paras. 97–109.

[37] See Understanding on Rules and Procedures Governing the Settlement of Disputes, WTO Agreement, *supra* n. 5, Annex 2, art. 8.3, 33 ILM at 1226.

[38] *Ibid.* art. 17.

the disputing parties chooses two citizens of the other disputing party to act as panelists.[39] The panel chair is chosen by agreement of the parties *if* they can reach an agreement within fifteen days.[40] If no agreement is reached in time, a lottery is held to decide which disputing party may choose the panel chair. The panel chair may not be a citizen of the country that selects the chair.[41]

Moreover, the NAFTA does not expressly require the disputing parties to comply with panel decisions. Instead, the disputing parties are required to arrive at an agreement on the resolution of the dispute. The agreed solution should "normally" conform with the panel's decision and, "wherever possible," involve withdrawal of measures found to be inconsistent with NAFTA.[42] If a "mutually satisfactory" resolution is not reached within 30 days after the final panel report is issued, the prevailing party in the dispute may impose economic sanctions against the losing party.[43]

Not surprisingly, the NAFTA countries have tended to rely heavily on diplomacy to resolve their NAFTA disputes. In the more than seven years since NAFTA entered into force, only three decisions have been issued by a panel established under NAFTA's state-to-state dispute settlement mechanism.[44] None of these decisions involved environmental or health issues. However, a panel recently ruled that concerns about the safety of Mexican trucks were not sufficient to justify the United States' refusal to allow Mexican trucks to operate in its territory according to the express timetable set out in the agreement.[45] The United States has also lost the two other decisions issued by NAFTA panels. The first panel decision rejected the United States' claim that the NAFTA prohibited Canada from converting certain agricultural quotas into tariffs in accordance with the Uruguay Round agreement on agricultural trade.[46] A second panel decision found that the United States' temporary restrictions on imports of Mexican broom corn brooms were not justified under NAFTA rules permitting restriction of imports that cause "serious injury" to a domestic industry.[47]

[39] NAFTA, *supra* n. 3, art. 2011.1.
[40] *Ibid.* art. 2011.1(b).
[41] *Ibid.*
[42] *Ibid.* art. 2018.
[43] *Ibid.* art. 2019.
[44] For an overview of the early experience under NAFTA's dispute settlement provisions, including NAFTA's special dispute settlement provisions for antidumping and countervailing duty cases, see David A. Gantz, "Dispute Settlement Under the NAFTA and the WTO: Choice of Forum Opportunities and Risks for the NAFTA Parties", (1999) 14 *Am. U. Int'l L. Rev.* 1025.
[45] See Cross-Border Trucking Services and Investment, USA–98–2008–01, Report of the NAFTA Panel (6 Feb. 2001), available at the NAFTA Secretariat Website <http://www.nafta-sec-alena.org>.
[46] See Tariffs Applied by Canada to Certain US-Origin Agricultural Products, CDA–95–2008–01, Report of the NAFTA Panel (2 Dec. 1996), available at the NAFTA Secretariat Website, <http://www.nafta-sec-alena.org>.
[47] See US Safeguard Action Taken on Broom Corn Brooms from Mexico, USA-97-2008-01, Report of the NAFTA Panel (30 Jan. 1998), available at the NAFTA Secretariat Website, <http://www.nafta-sec-alena.org>. Like the WTO, NAFTA permits the imposition of temporary ("emergency") measures on imports that have been found to cause "serious injury" to a domestic industry. See NAFTA, *supra* n. 3, ch. 8.

Summary

The NAFTA rules on regional trade make it significantly more difficult for NAFTA countries to challenge each other's environmental measures. The NAFTA countries can effectively preclude disputes involving environmental and health issues from being brought in the WTO. Instead, such disputes will be resolved under NAFTA rules, which expressly permit limited measures pursuant to certain multilateral environment agreements, and expressly prohibit the "downward" harmonisation of product standards. Moreover, the decisions resolving these disputes will be issued by panelists that are nationals of the disputing parties themselves, are not legally binding, and are less likely to result in economic sanctions than decisions in the WTO. The NAFTA countries have submitted very few of their disputes to dispute settlement panels, and have not requested that a panel be established in any dispute involving environmental issues.

II. THE RULES ON INVESTMENT: CREATING PRIVATE REMEDIES FOR NAFTA INVESTORS

Although the NAFTA rules on regional trade have not yet produced any panel decisions on environmental or health issues, the agreement's rules on investment have produced a growing number of decisions with significant implications for environmental and health regulation in the NAFTA countries. This section reviews the principle NAFTA investment rules involved in these decisions, and the ways in which NAFTA investors are beginning to use these provisions to challenge environmental, health and other regulatory measures.

The Substantive Rules on Investment

The NAFTA goes far beyond the WTO in the field of investment. The NAFTA investment rules apply to any "investment" made by a citisen of a NAFTA country, or by an enterprise organised under the laws of a NAFTA country.[48] An "investment" is broadly defined to include not only enterprises and equity securities in enterprises, but also any interest in an enterprise "that entitles the owner to share in income or profits," any interest "arising from the commitment of capital or other resources" in the territory of a NAFTA country, and any "tangible or intangible" property acquired in the expectation of an economic benefit or used for a business purpose.[49]

[48] NAFTA, *supra* n. 3, art. 1139 (defining "investor of a [NAFTA] Party").
[49] *Ibid.* (defining "investment").

The NAFTA investment provisions grew out of the Bilateral Investment Treaty (BIT) Program, which the United States and several other developed countries launched in the 1970s to help promote direct investment abroad.[50] More than 1300 BITs currently exist, many containing provisions similar to those of NAFTA.[51] As Daniel Price has noted, however, the NAFTA is the first major agreement to attempt to extend BIT-based rules to investment between two developed countries.[52] Moreover, the gradual decline of traditional barriers to foreign investment has focused new attention on the potential impact of these disciplines on non-traditional investment barriers, such as environmental regulation. Attempts to use NAFTA's investment provisions as a model for a Multilateral Agreement on Investment (MAI) met with strong opposition from environmental and consumer groups, and were recently suspended.[53]

As discussed at greater length below, four NAFTA investment provisions have proved to be particularly important for environmental and health regulation. First, NAFTA governments may not treat investors from other NAFTA countries in a manner that is "less favourable" than the treatment they accord to their own investors "in like circumstances" (the "national treatment" obligation).[54] Secondly, NAFTA governments may not require investors from other NAFTA countries to satisfy specific "performance requirements" with respect to the level of goods that they export or import.[55] Thirdly, NAFTA governments must treat investors from other NAFTA countries "in accordance with international law, including fair and equitable treatment and full protection and security" (the "minimum standard" of treatment).[56] Finally, NAFTA governments must pay compensation equivalent to "fair market value" whenever they "directly or indirectly" nationalise or expropriate an investment owned by an

[50] See K.Vandevelde, "The Bilateral Investment Treaty Program of the United States", (1988) 21 *Cornell Int'l L.J.* 201; M. S. Bergman, "Bilateral Investment Protection Treaties: An Examination of the Evolution and Significance of the U.S. Prototype Treaty", (1983) 16 *N.Y.U.J. Int'l L. & Pol.* 1; "ICSID and the Rise of Bilateral Investment Treaties: Will ICSID be the Leading Arbitration Institution in the Early 21st Century?", (2000) 94 *Am Soc'y Int'l L. Proc.* 41. For discussion of the reasons that have led to the proliferation of BITs, see K. Vandevelde, "The Economics of Bilateral Investment Treaties", (2000) 41 *Harv. Int'l L.J.* 469; A. T. Guzman, Why LDCs Sign Treaties That Hurt Them: Explaining the Popularity of Bilateral Investment Treaties", (1998) 38 *Va. J. Int'l L.* 639.

[51] For a recent listing of these treaties, see United Nations Conference on Trade and Development, Bilateral Investment Treaties in the Mid-1990s, at 159–218, U.N. Doc. UNCTAD/ITE/11T/7, U.N. Sales No. 98.11.D.8 (1998).

[52] See D. M. Price, "Chapter 1—Private Party vs. Government, Investor–State Dispute Settlement: Frankenstein or Safety Valve?", (2000) 26 *Can.–U.S. L. J.* 107, 109.

[53] *See supra* n. 7 and accompanying text.

[54] NAFTA, *supra* n. 3, art. 1102. As discussed further below, the NAFTA rules apply to subnational as well as national governments. See *infra* nn. 97–9, 114–26 and accompanying text (discussing the *Metalclad* decision). State and provincial governments must accord investors from other NAFTA countries treatment no less than favourable than "the most favourable treatment" they accord in like circumstances to their own investors, or to investors from other states or provinces of their own country. *Ibid.* art. 1102.3.

[55] *Ibid.* art. 1106.

[56] *Ibid.* art. 1105.

investor from another NAFTA country, or take a measure "tantamount to" nationalisation or expropriation of such an investment.[57]

Provisions On Environmental Protection

The NAFTA expressly recognises the potential relationship between investment and environmental regulation. However, the NAFTA provisions addressing this conflict are both very vague and very limited. For example, NAFTA Article 1114 expressly states that its investment provisions should not be construed "to prevent a Party from adopting, maintaining or enforcing" a measures that "it considers appropriate" to ensure that investment activity in its territory is "undertaken in a manner sensitive to environmental concerns."[58] This express exception for measures that *the regulating state itself* considers appropriate could suggest a high degree of deference to each country's environmental measures. Indeed, many have argued that similar trade rules exempting measures that a signatory itself "considers necessary" to protect its essential security interests are essentially "self-judging" and beyond review.[59]

However, others have argued that treaty exceptions based on a signatory's own views permit review to determine whether the signatory has acted in "good faith."[60] In the case of Article 1114, the argument for deference is further weakened by a provision limiting the exception to measures that are "otherwise consistent with" the agreement's investment provisions.[61] Moreover, the exception does not apply to health, safety, or other non-environmental measures.

Article 1114 also recognises that it is "inappropriate" to encourage investment by relaxing domestic health, safety or environmental measures, and that parties "should not" waive or derogate from such measures in order to encourage foreign investment.[62] Unlike other investment provisions, however, this provision is purely hortatory. Allegations that a NAFTA party has inappropriately relaxed its environmental or health regulation may not be raised in any formal dispute settlement proceedings. The NAFTA countries need only "consult" with each other "with a view to avoiding any such encouragement."[63]

[57] NAFTA, *supra* n. 3. art. 1110.

[58] *Ibid*., art. 1114.1.

[59] See A. Perez, "WTO & UN Law: Institutional Comity in National Security", (1998) 23 *Yale J. Int'l L*. 301, 324–51.

[60] See, e.g., H. Schloemann and S. Ohlhoff, "'Constitutionalization' and Dispute Settlement in the WTO: National Security as an Issue of Competence", (1999) 93 *Am. J. Int'l L*. 424; M. J. Hahn, "Vital Interests and the Law of the GATT: An Analysis of GATT's Security Exception", (1991) 12 *Mich. J. Int'l L*. 558, 587–91; see also North American Free Trade Agreement Implementation Act of 1993, Statement of Administrative Action, H.R. Doc. No. 103–159, at ch. 21, 103d Cong., 1st Sess. (1993) (expressing US view that NAFTA's national security exception is "self-judging" but is expected to be applied in "good faith").

[61] NAFTA, *supra* n. 3, art. 1114.1.

[62] *Ibid*. art. 1114.2.

[63] *Ibid*.

Dispute Settlement

As in the case of the NAFTA rules on regional trade, the NAFTA countries themselves may resort to *ad hoc* panels to resolve disputes arising under NAFTA's investment rules.[64] However, the NAFTA also permits private NAFTA investors to initiate their own proceedings against NAFTA countries to recover any "loss or damage" they may have incurred as a result of a breach of NAFTA's investment provisions.[65] Any private party from a NAFTA country that "seeks to make, is making, or has made" an investment in another NAFTA country may seek redress from that country under international rules.[66] The private investor is no longer required to persuade its own governments to espouse its claim.[67]

The NAFTA's approach to private remedies is very different from that of the European Communities (EC). In the EC, private parties may assert claims under certain treaty provisions in national courts, which may request a ruling from the European Court of Justice on issues of treaty interpretation.[68] The United States has made it clear that such a remedy is not possible in US courts, which are expressly precluded from addressing claims under NAFTA by anyone other than the federal government.[69] Instead, NAFTA investors may submit their claims to *ad hoc* arbitral tribunals established under the rules of UNCITRAL or of the ICSID Additional Facility.[70] Under the applicable rules, the disputing

[64] *See ibid.* art. 1115 (preserving the right of NAFTA member states to pursue Chapter Twenty dispute settlement procedures).

[65] *Ibid.* art. 1116. Investor–state arbitration is also available for losses incurred as a result of a breach of certain NAFTA provisions involving state enterprises and monopolies, but does not apply to any other NAFTA provisions. *Ibid.*

[66] *Ibid.* art. 1139 (defining "investor of a Party").

[67] Historically, private parties have been required to obtain diplomatic protection in order to pursue claims against other governments under international law. A state that agreed to espouse a claim by one of its nationals could initiate international judicial proceedings on behalf of its national, by "asserting its own right . . . to ensure in the person of its nationals respect for the rule of international law." See *Panevezys-Saldutiskis Railway (Est.* v. *Lat.)*, 1939 P.C.I.J. (ser. A/B) No. 76 (28 Feb. 1939). See generally G. I. F. Leigh, "Nationality and Diplomatic Protection", (1971) 20 *Int'l & Comp. L. Q.* 453.

[68] For a discussion of the "direct effect" of EC law in national courts, see S. Weatherill and P. Beaumont, *EU Law* (3rd edn., London, Penguin, 1999) 392–432.

[69] See North American Free Trade Agreement Implementation Act of 1993, Pub. L. No. 103–1082, secs. 102 (a), 102(b)(2), 102(c), 107 Stat. 2057 (1993) (codified at 19 U.S.C. § 3312 (1994)) (no provision of NAFTA to have any effect except as specifically incorporated into U.S. law; noone other than the United States government may bring a legal action to declare a state law invalid on the grounds that it is inconsistent with NAFTA; noone other than the United States may assert any claim or defense based on NAFTA, or challenge any government action or inaction under the provisions of NAFTA). The United States has adopted similar provisions with respect to the WTO agreements. See Uruguay Round Agreements Act of 1994, Pub. L. No. 103–465, § 102, 108 Stat. 4809 (1994) (codified at 19 U.S.C. § 3512 (1994)). See also NAFTA, *supra* n. 3, art. 2021 (prohibiting the establishment of a private right of action under the domestic law of the NAFTA countries for violations of NAFTA by other member countries).

[70] NAFTA, *supra* n. 3, art. 1120. The agreement also permits a claim to be submitted under the ICSID Convention if both the disputing Party and the Party of the investor are ICSID parties; however, the United States is currently the only NAFTA party that is also a party to ICSID.

parties themselves select the three arbitrators that are to decide their dispute. One arbitrator is chosen by the investor, and another by the government involved in the dispute.[71] The third presiding arbitrator is chosen either by agreement of the disputing parties or by the ICSID Secretary-General.[72] The arbitration may not proceed unless the investor has waived any right it may have to "initiate or continue" any related proceedings in domestic tribunals arising under national law.[73]

If an investor succeeds in establishing its claim, the tribunal may award only compensatory damages (including any applicable interest) or restitution of property.[74] It may not award punitive damages or injunctive relief.[75] Arbitral awards are binding on the parties, and may be enforced in the national courts of each NAFTA country pursuant to the United Nations Convention on the Recognition and Enforcement of Foreign Arbitral Awards (the "New York Convention"), and the Inter-American Convention on Commercial Arbitration (the "Inter-American Convention").[76] However, arbitral decisions have no binding force "except between the disputing parties and in respect of the particular case".[77]

Investor-state arbitrations are highly secretive. Arbitral awards involving the United States or Canada may generally be made public with the consent of either party.[78] However, the consent of both parties may be required to disclose a final award in disputes involving Mexico.[79] Moreover, hearings must be held *in camera,* and materials submitted by the parties are treated as confidential, unless the parties otherwise agree.[80] Thus, although a number of arbitral awards have now

[71] NAFTA, *supra* n. 3. art. 1123.

[72] *Ibid.* art. 1124.

[73] *Ibid.* art. 1121. The waiver does not apply to proceedings for injunctive relief, declaratory relief, or other extraordinary relief not involving the payment of damages. If an investor brings a claim on behalf of an enterprise, or for loss or damage to its interest in an enterprise, a waiver must also be submitted on behalf of the enterprise. An investor may not raise any alleged Mexican violation of NAFTA's provisions on state monopolies or state enterprises that it has previously raised before a Mexican tribunal. *Ibid.* annex 1120.1.

[74] *Ibid.* art. 1135. NAFTA countries must be permitted to pay monetary damages in lieu of restitution. *Ibid.* The tribunal may also award costs, and order interim measures to "preserve the rights of a disputing party" or to ensure that its jurisdiction is made "fully effective." *Ibid.* art. 1134.

[75] *Ibid.* art. 1134–35. See also *Pope & Talbot* v. *Canada*, Award on Motion for Interim Measures (7 Jan. 2000) (no jurisdiction to enter injunctive relief), available at NAFTALaw.Org Website, <http://www.naftalaw.org>.

[76] *Ibid.* art. 1136.6 and 1136.7; see generally United Nations Convention on the Recognition and Enforcement of Foreign Arbitral Awards, 10 Jun. 1958, 330 U.N.T.S. 38 [hereinafter the "New York Convention"]; Inter-American Convention on International Commercial Arbitration, 30 Jan. 1975, (1975) 14 ILM 336 [hereinafter "Inter-American Convention"].

[77] *Ibid.* art. 1136.1 and 1136.2.

[78] *Ibid.* Annex 1137.4.

[79] *Ibid.*; see also UNCITRAL Arbitration Rules, (1976) 15 ILM 701 [hereinafter "UNCITRAL Arbitration Rules"], at Art. 32(5), and International Centre for the Settlement of Investment Disputes: Additional Facility Arbitration Rules, (1982) 21 ILM 1458 [hereinafter "ICSID Additional Facility Arbitration Rules"], at art. 14(2) (requiring arbitrator to keep all information obtained as a result of proceeding and content of awards confidential).

[80] See UNCITRAL Arbitration Rules, *supra* n. 79, art. 25(4); ICSID Additional Facility Arbitration Rules, *supra* n. 79, art. 39. See also NAFTA Chapter Eleven Arbitral Tribunal: *Ethyl Corp.* v. *Canada* (Procedural Order, 2 Jul. 1998), (1999) 38 ILM 736; *Pope & Talbot* v. *Canada*,

been published, it is quite difficult to locate all of the specific claims and defenses that are being made under NAFTA's investment provisions.[81]

The applicable rules make almost no provision for participation by parties other than the claimant and the government that is alleged to have breached its investment obligations. NAFTA countries that are not parties to a dispute may make submissions to the tribunal on questions of treaty interpretation.[82] Unless both disputing parties disapprove, tribunals may also appoint one or more experts to report on factual issues involving environmental, health, safety or other scientific matters.[83] An arbitral tribunal has recently ruled that it has the power to accept *amicus curiae* submissions from non-governmental organisations concerning a Canadian investor's claim for damages resulting from a California ban on the MTBE fuel additive.[84] The tribunal based its decision on a provision of the UNCITRAL Arbitration Rules that confers broad discretion on tribunals regarding the conduct of an arbitration.[85] However, it also ruled that the organisations could not become parties to the proceeding, and would not be able to attend hearings or have access to the submissions of the parties except with the consent of the disputing parties.[86]

Assessing the Early Experience

As discussed above, there have been few panel decisions concerning disputes among the NAFTA countries themselves. Moreover, none of the decisions issued in state-to-state dispute settlement proceedings have involved the agreement's investment rules. On the other hand, private investors have filed an increasing number of claims. In the past four years, private investors have filed at least sixteen separate claims under NAFTA's investment rules: seven involving Canadian measures, five involving Mexican measures, and four involving United States measures.[87] As discussed below, many of these claims have raised important environmental and public health issues.

Procedural Order No. 5 (17 Dec. 1999), available at NAFTALaw.Org Website, <http://www.naftalaw.org>; *Ibid.*, Procedural Order No. 1 (29 Oct. 1999); *Ibid.*, Award on Confidentiality (27 Sept. 2000) (ordering payment of $10,000 in costs for the attorney's disclosure to the media a letter inadvertently sent to it by the Canadian government).

[81] A Canadian attorney named T. Weiler has, however, made a number of documents available on his website. See NAFTALaw.Org Website, <http://www.naftalaw.org>.

[82] NAFTA, *supra* n. 3, art. 1128.

[83] *Ibid.* art. 1133.

[84] *Methanex Corp.* v. *United States*, Decision of the Tribunal on Petitions from Third Persons to Intervene as "Amici Curiae," 15 Jan. 2001, available at NAFTALaw.Org Website, <http://www.naftalaw.org>.

[85] *Ibid.*, ¶¶ 31, 48–52, citing UNCITRAL Arbitration Rules, *supra* n. 79, art. 15(1).

[86] *Ibid.*, ¶¶ 27, 47.

[87] A list of claims filed under NAFTA's investment rules, along with a number of related documents, is available at the NAFTALaw.Org Website <http://www.naftalaw.org>. As discussed above, investors may have filed additional claims that are not reported on this list.

In the first three years after the NAFTA entered into effect, its provisions for investor-state arbitration attracted little attention and few if any investor-state arbitration proceedings were initiated.[88] In September 1997, however, a US company known as the Ethyl Corporation filed a claim seeking $251 million in damages from Canada.[89] Ethyl alleged that a Canadian law restricting trade in a fuel additive known as MMT violated NAFTA's national treatment provision, was tantamount to expropriation, and constituted a prohibited performance requirement. Canada argued that the ban was justified by concerns about the environmental and health risks of MMT.[90] The dispute was ultimately settled in July 1998, after an adverse ruling was issued in a separate proceeding challenging the legislation under a Canadian inter-provincial agreement.[91] Under the settlement, the Canadian government agreed to withdraw the legislation, and to pay Ethyl $13 million in compensation.[92] Not surprisingly, the decision produced an outcry among various environmental and consumer groups.

Since the *Ethyl* case was settled, at least fifteen more investor-state arbitration proceedings have been initiated, many raising important environmental and health regulation issues. The following sections examine the rulings that have been issued in these proceedings, and the implications of these rulings for environmental and health regulation in the NAFTA countries.

No Exception for Environmental Measures

As discussed above, Article 1114 expressly states that the NAFTA investment rules should not be construed to prevent a NAFTA country from adopting measures "it considers appropriate" to ensure that investment is conducted in a manner that is "sensitive" to environmental concerns.[93] To date, however, arbitral tribunals have paid scant attention to this provision.

In *S.D. Myers* v. *Canada*, for example, the tribunal found that a US investor was entitled to monetary damages as a result of a temporary Canadian ban on exports of PCBs, even though the ban's stated purpose was to "prevent any possible significant danger to the environment or to human life or health" from

[88] For an account of several early threats by private investors concerning possible claims under NAFTA's investment rules, see G. N. Horlick and A. L. Marti, "NAFTA Chapter 11B: A Private Right of Action to Enforce Market Access Through Investments", (1997) 14 *Int'l Arb.* 43.

[89] See NAFTA Chapter Eleven Arbitral Tribunal: *Ethyl Corp.* v. *Canada* (Award on Jurisdiction, 24 Jun. 1998), (1999) 38 ILM 708, 722 [hereinafter "Ethyl Award on Jurisdiction"]; see also *ibid.* (Decision Regarding the Place of Arbitration, 28 Nov. 1997) (1999) 38 ILM 700; A. Swan, "*Ethyl Corp.* v. *Canada,* Award on Jurisdiction", (1999) 94 *Am. J Int'l L.* 159.

[90] The regulatory concerns raised by MMT are further discussed in J. A. Soloway, "Environmental Trade Barriers Under NAFTA: The MMT Fuel Additives Controversy", (1999) 8 *Minn. J. Global Trade* 55; see also J. J. Timoneda, "The Legal Dynamics of the Regulation of MMT: Air Quality Standards and the Salt Lake City Airshed", (1997) 17 *J. Land Resource & Envt'l L.* 283.

[91] See Ethyl Award on Jurisdiction, *supra* n. 89.

[92] *Ibid.*

[93] See *supra* nn. 58–63 and accompanying text.

these substances.[94] The majority opinion did not even address Article 1114. In a separate concurring opinion, a third arbitrator acknowledged that Article 1114 could be viewed as nothing more than "tautologies" and "empty rhetoric," since "whatever acknowledgement of environmental concerns" it stated was "tempered" by the requirement that measures must be "consistent with this Chapter".[95] The arbitrator concluded that Article 1114 was intended to "reconcile" the competing objectives of free trade and environmental protection, by permitting NAFTA countries to pursue "high" environmental standards *so long as* the standards do not constitute "unnecessary" obstacles to trade.[96]

In *Metalclad* v. *United Mexican States*, an arbitral tribunal ordered Mexico to pay $16.7 million in damages resulting from a municipality's refusal to grant a construction permit for a hazardous waste landfill, and a state Ecological Decree declaring the site to be part of a natural area for the protection of rare cactus.[97] The arbitrators found that Article 1114 was inapplicable because the *federal* government had indicated that the landfill satisfied *its* environmental concerns when it granted the investor a federal permit for the landfill.[98] Thus, whatever Article 1114 may mean, it may not be sufficient to justify measures based solely on the concerns of local governments.

No Exception for Trade Measures

As discussed above, a US company has succeeded in obtaining a $13 million settlement of a claim based on a Canadian ban on imports of an allegedly harmful fuel additive.[99] Since that time, two other tribunals have confirmed that private investors may seek damages for trade measures that adversely affect their investments, even though such measures are also subject to challenge under specific trade rules that do not authorise the pursuit of private claims. As discussed below, the tribunals' approach to investor claims involving environmental trade measures has closely resembled the approach adopted by dispute settlement panels with respect to the trade rules of the WTO. However, Canada recently initiated proceedings seeking to set aside one of these decisions in a Canadian court.[100]

[94] *S.D. Myers, Inc.* v. *Canada*, Partial Award (13 Nov. 2000), available at NAFTALaw.Org Website, <http://www.naftalaw.org> [hereinafter "S.D. Myers Partial Award"]. The actual amount of damages is to be determined in a second stage of the arbitration proceedings.

[95] *S.D. Myers, Inc.* v. *Canada*, Separate Opinion by Dr. B. Schwartz (12 Nov. 2000), ¶ 117, *available at* NAFTALaw.Org Website <http://www.naftalaw.org>.

[96] *Ibid.* at ¶ 118.

[97] *Metalclad Corp.* v. *United Mexican States*, ICSID Case No. ARB (AF)/97/1 (Award of the Tribunal, 30 Aug. 2000), *available at* the ICSID Website <http://www.worldbank.org/icsid/cases/award.htm> [hereinafter "Metalclad"].

[98] *Ibid.* at ¶ 98.

[99] See *supra* nn. 89–92 and accompanying text.

[100] See "Canada Appeals NAFTA Chapter Eleven Case, Arguing Panel Exceeded its Jurisdiction", (2001) 18(7) *Int'l Trade Rptr.* 273. The disputing parties may initiate proceedings to revise, set aside, or annul an arbitral award issued under the ICSID Additional Facility Rules or the UNCITRAL Arbitration rules in a court of the place of arbitration, so long as the action is filed within three months after the date the award is rendered. NAFTA, *supra* n. 3, art. 1136(b).

In *Pope & Talbot* v. *Canada*, the tribunal found that the U.S. owner of a Canadian lumber company could seek damages under NAFTA based on Canadian restrictions of the company's exports to the United States.[101] Canada had put the export restrictions in place in order to implement a US–Canada agreement regulating softwood lumber trade.[102] The tribunal agreed that the international agreement between the United States and Canada regarding trade in softwood lumber was not a "measure" of a NAFTA country, and therefore was not subject to challenge in investor-state arbitration.[103] Moreover, Canada's imposition of higher permit fees for exports above specified levels did not constitute a prohibited export "requirement," since Canada had not actually prohibited exports above any specific level. The investor could not obtain damages for a measure that merely "deters" exports.[104] However, the decision suggested that investors might be able to obtain damages for measures that require companies to reduce exports or imports of certain products to specified levels.

Subsequently, the *S.D. Myers* tribunal ruled that the US owner of a Canadian firm established to solicit Canadian customers for the owner's US waste remediation facility was entitled to damages incurred as a result of a temporary ban on Canadian exports of PCB wastes to the United States. The arbitrators found that the export ban had accorded "less favorable treatment" to the claimant because it had the "practical effect" of preventing the company from carrying out its business, and placed it at a "clear disadvantage" with respect to its Canadian competitors.[105]

The tribunal recognised that the mere fact that the ban had resulted in more favorable treatment of Canadian companies in the claimant's area of business was not dispositive, since NAFTA only requires equal treatment of investors in "like circumstances." Accordingly, Canada could legitimately favor domestic investors over their foreign competitors "in order to protect the public interest."[106]

However, the tribunal also found that there was "no legitimate environmental reason" for the Canadian export ban.[107] It rejected Canada's contention that the ban was justified by concerns about the US regulatory regime for PCB waste management. The Basel Convention prohibits Canada from exporting PCB wastes to countries (such as the United States) that are not parties to the agreement, unless it has adequate assurances about the importing country's waste management regime.[108] However, the tribunal concluded that the export

[101] *Pope & Talbot Inc.* v. *Canada*, Interim Award of 26 Jun. 2000, available at NAFTALaw.Org Website <http://www.naftalaw.org> [hereinafter "Pope & Talbot Interim Award"].

[102] See *Pope & Talbot Inc.* v. *Canada*, Award on Canada's Preliminary Motion to Dismiss, ¶¶ 16 and 26, 7 Jan. 2000, available at NAFTALaw.Org Website <http://www.naftalaw.org>.

[103] *Ibid.* at ¶ 37.

[104] Pope & Talbot Interim Award, *supra* n. 101, at ¶ 75.

[105] *S.D. Myers Partial Award,* supra n. 94, ¶ 193.

[106] *Ibid.* at. ¶ 250.

[107] *Ibid.* at. ¶ 195.

[108] *Ibid.* at. ¶ 106.

ban was in fact intended to protect the fledgling Canadian PCB waste remediation industry from foreign competition.[109]

The tribunal recognised that protection of domestic remediation providers might involve an "indirect" environmental objective, since a strong Canadian waste remediation industry would ensure Canada's continued capacity to process PCBs. Like the WTO, however, it concluded that the parties must adopt the least-restrictive means for pursuing such an objective.[110] Although Canada might seek to protect its PCB waste remediation industry by means of discriminatory government subsidies or preferential government procurement, it could not do so by means of a temporary export ban.[111] As mentioned above, Canada has initiated proceedings to set aside this ruling in a Canadian court.

Rules, Processes and the Principle of Transparency

The NAFTA investment rules have also been used to challenge non-trade measures, on the grounds that the processes that led to the measures violated the requirement of "fair and equitable treatment" in accordance with international law. This provision has been the subject of two recent decisions. The first decision, *Metalclad* v. *United Mexican States*,[112] addressed Mexican laws and processes for regulating hazardous waste sites. The second decision, *Loewen* v. *United States*,[113] addresses procedural rules in commercial litigation between a U.S. company and a Canadian competitor in a U.S. court.

Regulatory Processes and the Metalclad Decision

The claim in *Metalclad* was filed by the US owner of a Mexican firm, which had obtained federal permits to construct and operate a hazardous waste landfill near the city of Guadalcazar, in Mexico. The company began construction on the site after federal agencies assured it that no further permits were required. However, municipal authorities subsequently issued a stop work order based on the company's failure to obtain a municipal construction permit.[114] The investor applied for the construction permit, but was assured by federal officials that the application would be approved as a matter of course.[115] It subsequently resumed construction without waiting for its application to be approved.

[109] See *ibid.* at ¶ 162 (the lead minister's "protectionist intent" was reflected in every stage of decision making, and may have been directly responsible for the ban).

[110] *Ibid.* at ¶ 215, 221, 255; *see also ibid.* at ¶ 298 (noting that Canada's export ban would not satisfy the requirements of GATT Article XX, which is incorporated in the NAFTA).

[111] *Ibid.* at ¶¶ 195, 255 & n.33.

[112] *Metalclad*, *supra* n. 97.

[113] *R. Loewen and Loewen Corp.* v. *United States*, ICSID Case No. ARB (AF)/98/3 (Award on Jurisdiction, Jan. 5, 2001), *available at* NAFTALaw.Org Website <http://www.naftalaw.org> [hereinafter "Loewen").

[114] *Metalclad*, *supra* n. 97, at ¶ 67.

[115] *Ibid.* at ¶¶ 41, 88.

As construction neared completion, large public demonstrations prevented the company from opening the site.[116] In order to appease local opponents, the company entered into an agreement with the Mexican government requiring it to satisfy a number of new conditions, including correction of various deficiencies detected in an environmental audit, construction of a buffer zone, establishment of a citizen supervision committee, and provisions for economic and social benefits to local residents.[117] Despite the agreement, city authorities decided to deny the company's application for a construction permit. The decision was made thirteen months after the company had submitted its permit application, at a meeting held without any prior notice to or participation by the affected company.[118] The city based its decision on the extent of local opposition, ecological concerns, and the company's failure to seek a permit before construction was begun.[119] Three days before his term expired, the state governor issued an Ecological Decree declaring the landfill site to be part of a natural area for the protection of rare cactus.[120]

The *Metalclad* tribunal found that the municipality's insistence upon a construction permit, and its denial of the company's application for such a permit, violated the requirement of "fair and equitable treatment" in two separate respects. First, the tribunal noted that the municipality appeared to lack authority under Mexican law to deny permits for any reason unrelated to physical construction or defects.[121] Even if the city authorities did have such authority, the absence of any "clear rule" regarding the city's authority violated the principle of "transparency," which is recognised as one of NAFTA's central objectives.[122] In the tribunal's view, this principle required Mexico's central government to clarify "promptly" any "doubt or uncertainty" in federal and local law, so that investors could "proceed with all appropriate expedition in the confident belief that they are acting in accordance with all relevant law".[123] Finally, the tribunal found that city authorities had failed to establish an "orderly process" for handling permit applications, or to dispose of the company's application in a "timely" manner.[124]

Mexico has instituted an action seeking to set aside the *Metalclad* award in the Supreme Court of British Columbia, based in part on the tribunal's alleged failure to pay sufficient attention to the actual decisions of Mexican courts.[125]

[116] *Metalclad*, *supra* n. 97. at ¶¶ 45–46.
[117] *Ibid*. at ¶¶ 47–48.
[118] *Ibid*. at ¶ 91.
[119] *Ibid*. at ¶ 92.
[120] *Ibid*. at ¶¶ 59, 96.
[121] *Ibid*. at ¶ 81.
[122] *Ibid*. at ¶ 76, citing NAFTA, *supra* n. 3, at ¶ 102(1) (expressly referring to principle of transparency); see also preamble ¶ 6 (noting the importance of a "predictable commercial framework for business planning and investment"), and art. 1802.1 (requiring prompt publication of all laws, regulations and rulings of general application).
[123] *Ibid*. at ¶ 76.
[124] *Ibid*. at ¶ 99.
[125] Transcripts of the Canadian court proceedings are available at the NAFTALaw.Org Website <http://www.naftalaw.org> The permissibility of court proceedings to set aside a NAFTA award is discussed *supra* at n.100.

Judicial Processes and the Loewen Case

In *Loewen*, a Canadian company filed a claim for damages resulting from a $500 million judgment entered against it in a commercial lawsuit brought by a Mississippi competitor in a Mississippi court.[126] The lawsuit involved certain contracts related to the funeral home and funeral insurance business in Mississippi. Only $25 million of the award was based on compensatory damages. The remainder of the award was for emotional distress ($75 million) and punitive damages ($400 million).[127] The Canadian company alleged that the seven-week trial was tainted by a number of discriminatory comments by the plaintiff's witnesses and counsel, including anti-Canadian comments, and various racial and class-based comments.[128] When it sought to appeal the verdict, however, it was confronted by a Mississippi law requiring an appeal bond for 125 per cent of the judgment unless there is "good cause" for reducing or dispensing this requirement.[129] The Mississippi Supreme Court refused to reduce the appeal bond, and required the company to post bond for $625 million in order to pursue its appeal. The company chose instead to settle the dispute for $175 million.[130]

The Loewen company proceeded to file a NAFTA claim alleging that the trial court's failure to instruct the jury to disregard the "discriminatory" comments, together with the court's refusal to reduce the "excessive" verdict, and the Mississippi Supreme Court's "arbitrary" application of the bonding requirement, were inconsistent with the requirements of national treatment and "fair and equitable" treatment, and were tantamount to expropriation of its US investment.[131]

An arbitral tribunal has ruled that it has jurisdiction over the *Loewen* claim, even though the claim involves judicial decisions issued in a private commercial dispute. The tribunal rejected the US argument that such rulings were not "measures" subject to investor–state arbitration.[132] In the tribunal's view, the "text, context and purpose" of the NAFTA's investment provisions support a "liberal" interpretation of the word "measures" that would provide "protection and security for the foreign investor and its investment".[133] The arbitrators also supported the "modern view" that states are responsible for the decisions of their municipal courts under general principles of international law.[134]

[126] Loewen, *supra* n. 113, at ¶ 1. See also M. I. Krauss, "NAFTA Meets the American Torts Process: *O'Keefe* v. *Loewen*", (2000) 9 Geo. Mason L. Rev. 69.

[127] *Ibid.* at ¶ 2.

[128] *Ibid.*

[129] *Ibid.* at ¶ 3.

[130] *Ibid.* at ¶ 4–5.

[131] *Ibid.* at ¶ 30.

[132] *Ibid.* at ¶¶ 40, 58.

[133] *Ibid.* at ¶ 53, citing Ethyl Award on Jurisdiction, *supra* n. 89 at ¶ 83 (NAFTA's investment provisions are intended to create "effective procedures . . . for the resolution of disputes" and to "increase substantially investment opportunities").

[134] *Ibid.* at ¶ 70, citing International Law Commission, Draft Convention on State Responsibility, art. 4, (1976) 2 *Y.B. Int'l L. Comm'n* 91 ("conduct of an organ of the State shall be considered an act of the State under international law, where the organ be legislative, executive or judicial"), and

However, the tribunal has not yet decided whether the United States may be held liable for acts by *lower* courts that are not appealed to the court of last resort. Under customary international law, claimants are generally required to exhaust their local remedies before pursuing international arbitration.[135] However, the NAFTA does not expressly address this issue. Instead, it requires investors to waive their right to "initiate or continue" local remedies *after* arbitration is commenced.[136] An arbitral tribunal has ruled that this provision deprived it of jurisdiction over a claim submitted by an investor who had subsequently pursued related commercial litigation in Mexican courts.[137] More recently, the *Metalclad* tribunal found that the requirement of exhaustion was implicitly waived by the NAFTA rule prohibiting claimants from initiating or continuing any *further* proceedings under local law.[138] This prohibition on *subsequent* local remedies appears to imply that claimants need not exhaust local remedies *prior* to a NAFTA ruling. However, the *Loewen* tribunal has postponed resolution of the issue until after the hearing on the merits.[139]

Compensation for Measures "Tantamount To Expropriation"

As discussed above, the NAFTA investment rule also require compensation for any measure that "directly or indirectly" expropriates an investment owned by a NAFTA investor. This provision is not new to international law. Previous international tribunals have required compensation not only in cases of direct physical "takings" of foreign investments, but also for measures that have been deemed to constitute indirect (or "creeping") expropriation of an investment.[140]

E. Jimenez de Arechaga, "International Law in the Past Third of a Century", (1978) 159 *Recueil des Cours* 1.

[135] See C.F. Amerasinghe, *Local Remedies in International Law* (Cambridge, Grotius, 1990); A.A. Cancado Trindade, *The Application of the Rule of Exhaustion of Local Remedies in International Law: Its Rationale in the International Protection of Individual Rights* (Cambridge, Cambridge University Press, 1983); D. R. Mummery, "The Content of the Duty to Exhaust Local Judicial Remedies", (1964) 48 *Am. J. Intl L.* 389.

[136] See *supra* n. 73 and accompanying text.

[137] See *Waste Management, Inc.* v. *United Mexican States*, ICSID Case No. ARB (AF)/98/2, Award of the Tribunal (June 2, 2000), available at the ICSID Website, <http://www.worldbank.org/icsid/cases/award.htm>. A separate dissenting opinion in the case expressed the view that investors should not be required to abandon local remedies that were not themselves based on NAFTA, even though they had some bearing on NAFTA claims. *Ibid.* (Dissenting Opinion of Keith Highet).

[138] *Metalclad, supra* n. 97 at n. 4; see generally W. Dodge, "National Courts and International Arbitration: Exhaustion of Remedies and Res Judicata Under Chapter 11 of NAFTA", (2000) 23 *Hastings Int'l & Comp. L. Rev.* 357.

[139] Loewen, *supra* n. 113 at ¶ 74. The court invited the parties to discuss a number of specific issues related to this issue, including an advisory opinion issued by the International Court of Justice.

[140] See R. Dolzer, "Indirect Expropriation of Alien Property", (1986) 1 *ICSID For. Inv. L. J.* 41; G.C. Christie, "What Constitutes a Taking of Property Under International Law", (1962) 38 *Brit. Y.B. Int'l L.* 307; D. F. Vagts, "Coercion and Foreign Investment Rearrangements", (1978) 72 *Am. J. Int'l L.* 17; R. Higgins, "The Taking of Property by the State: Recent Developments in International Law", (1983) 176 *Recueil des Cours*, vol. III at 259; G. H. Aldrich, "What Constitutes a Compensable Taking of Property? The Decisions of the Iran–United States Claim Tribunal",

However, indirect expropriation has generally been found only in cases where government interference with a foreign investor's use or enjoyment is so substantial that it can reasonably be deemed to have the same effect as a physical taking of property. A measure short of a physical taking may be deemed to constitute expropriation if it is "confiscatory," if it "prevents, unreasonably interferes with, or unreasonably delays enjoyment of property,"[141] or if it justifies an inference that the owner "will not be able to use, enjoy or dispose of" its property.[142]

However, NAFTA also requires compensation for measures that are "tantamount to" an expropriation. Although some commentators have suggested that this new language may broaden the requirement of compensation to include measures that would not be subject to compensation under customary international law,[143] two arbitral tribunals have now expressly rejected this view. The tribunals in *Pope & Talbot* and *S.D. Myers* found that "tantamount" means nothing more than "equivalent."[144] This view is consistent with the French and Spanish translations of the agreement, which use the terms "équivalent" and "equivalente" in place of "tantamount."

That leaves the issue of exactly when a regulatory measure should be considered equivalent to expropriation under customary international law. The issue presents fairly new terrain, since there are very few decisions that directly address it. As discussed below, however, early NAFTA decisions suggest three conclusions. First, regulatory conduct by public authorities may be tantamount to expropriation, even if it is nondiscriminatory and within the state's legitimate police powers. Second, compensation is likely to be denied unless the regulatory measure imposes a "substantial" loss. Finally, tribunals may be reluctant to require compensation for an investment that a national court has found to be invalid under pre-existing national law.

No Exception for Regulatory Measures

Two arbitral tribunals have expressly rejected the notion of a blanket exception for nondiscriminatory regulatory measures. The *Pope & Talbot* tribunal stated that such an exception would create a "gaping loophole in international protections against expropriation".[145] However, it also cautioned that regulatory

(1994) 88 *Am. J. Int'l L.* 585; B. H. Weston, "'Constructive Takings' Under International Law: A Modest Foray into the Problem of 'Creeping Expropriation'", (1975–1976) 16 *Va. J. Int'l L.* 103. See generally M. Sornarajah, *The International Law on Foreign Investment* (Cambridge, Cambridge University Press, 1994); B. Wortley, *Expropriation in Public International Law* (Cambridge, Cambridge University Press, 1959).

[141] Restatement (Third) of the Foreign Relations Law of the United States § 712 comment g (1987) [hereinafter "U.S. Restatement"].

[142] Draft Convention on the International Responsibility of States for Injuries to Aliens, art. 10(3) (Harvard Law School 1961), reprinted in (1961) 55 *Am. J. Int'l L.* 545.

[143] See, e.g., A. Z. Hertz, "Shaping the Trident: Intellectual Property under NAFTA, Investment Protection Agreements and the World Trade Organization", (1997) 23 *Can.–U.S. L.J.* 261, 478.

[144] See Pope & Talbot Interim Award, *supra* n. 101, at ¶ 102–104; S.D. Myers Partial Award, *supra* n. 94, at 286.

[145] Pope & Talbot Interim Award, *supra* n. 101, at ¶ 99.

measures "must be analysed with special care".[146] The *S.D. Myers* tribunal found that it was "unlikely" that the regulatory conduct of public authorities could be the subject of "legitimate" complaint, but ruled that it must nevertheless examine the "real interests involved, and the purpose and effect" of Canada's ban on exports of PCB waste.[147]

The Extent and Nature of the Deprivation

As discussed above, regulatory measures must generally involve a "substantial" deprivation in order to be treated as an expropriation under customary international law (and thus, under the NAFTA). In *Pope & Talbot*, the tribunal ruled that export restrictions that merely reduced the profits of a NAFTA investment could not be deemed tantamount to an expropriation. There could be no expropriation when the investment continued to make "substantial" profits, and to enjoy a "substantial" volume of business.[148] Similarly, the *S.D. Myers* tribunal found that a temporary Canadian export ban that produced an eighteen-month "delay" in the claimant's business could not be deemed tantamount to an expropriation.[149] However, the tribunal also suggested that compensation might be required if the ban had produced a "direct benefit" to Canada, or a transfer of a benefit to another party.[150]

In *Metalclad,* however, the tribunal found that regulatory measures adopted by the state and local government were tantamount to expropriation, because they had "effectively and unlawfully prevented" the claimant from operating a landfill that it *reasonably expected* it would be allowed to operate.[151] The "totality of the circumstances" created by the Mexican government's representation that no municipal requirements applied, together with the municipality's subsequent stop work order, denial of the construction permit, and pursuit of legal remedies in federal court had an effect tantamount to expropriation.[152] Moreover, the state governor's issuance of an ecological decree was also tantamount to expropriation.[153] The tribunal dismissed arguments concerning the governments' "motivation or intent" as irrelevant to its analysis.[154] However, it did reduce the amount of damages awarded to the investor by the amount Mexico would be required to pay to remediate the site.[155]

A measure may be deemed tantamount to expropriation even if it interferes with only a single portion of a company's overall business. In *Pope & Talbot*, the tribunal suggested that the claimant might have been entitled to damages

[146] Pope & Talbot Interim Award, *supra* n. 101. at ¶ 99.
[147] S.D. Myers Partial Award, *supra* n. 94, at ¶¶ 285, 287.
[148] Pope & Talbot Interim Award, *supra* n. 101, at ¶¶ 101–102.
[149] S.D. Myers Partial Award, *supra* n. 94, at ¶ 287.
[150] *Ibid.*
[151] *Metalclad, supra* n. 97 at 89, 106–107.
[152] *Ibid.*
[153] *Ibid.* at ¶ 110.
[154] *Ibid.* at ¶ 111.
[155] Pope & Talbot Interim Award, *supra* n. 101. at ¶ 127.

incurred as a result of Canada's export restrictions on softwood lumber, if those restrictions had significantly impaired its exports to the United States—even if the rest of its operations remained profitable. The tribunal noted that NAFTA's expropriation provisions apply to any "investment," including "any property, tangible or intangible" acquired or used for business purposes.[156] Canada would be required to compensate the investor if its export ban "substantially" interfered with the company's exports to the United States, since these exports were a "very important part" of the company's business.[157] However, no compensation was required because the company continued to export "substantial quantities" of softwood lumber to the United States, and to make "substantial profits" on these exports.[158]

A measure may also be deemed tantamount to expropriation if it substantially impairs an "intangible" asset, such as a trademark or a company's "goodwill." The NAFTA definition of "investment" expressly includes intangible property. Although no tribunal has yet addressed a claim based on intangible property, cigarette companies have argued that anti-smoking proposals that would require cigarettes to be sold in plain paper packages might be deemed tantamount to expropriation of cigarette trademarks.[159] In addition, the *Ethyl* complaint asserted that public statements made by government officials regarding potentially harmful effects of the company's MMT fuel additive might be tantamount to expropriation of the company's "goodwill."[160]

Investments that Violate Pre-existing Laws

The first arbitral decision issued under NAFTA's investment provisions, *Azinian* v. *Mexico,* involved a decision by a municipal government to cancel a concession contract author ising a company owned by US investors to implement a solid waste collection system for the city.[161] The city had annulled the contract after a change in administration, on the basis of various contractual "irregularities," including alleged misrepresentations concerning the company's ability to carry out the contract. The company had challenged the annulment under Mexican law in a Mexican administrative tribunal and a Mexican federal court. Both of these tribunals found that the annulment was valid under Mexican law.

The *Azinian* tribunal found that a contractual breach by a NAFTA government could be treated as an expropriation if it was "confiscatory," destroyed contractual rights "as an asset," or was so "egregious" that it should be deemed a "repudiation" of the agreement.[162] However, a contract could not be

[156] *Ibid.* at ¶ 97.
[157] *Ibid.* at ¶ 98.
[158] *Ibid.* at ¶ 101.
[159] See Hertz, *supra* n. 143.
[160] See Ethyl, *supra* n. 89.
[161] International Center for the Settlement of Investment Disputes (ICSID) (Additional Facility): *Azinian* v. *United Mexican States* (Award, 1 Nov. 1999), (2000) 39 ILM 537 [hereinafter "Azinian"].
[162] *Ibid.* at ¶¶ 87–90.

expropriated if it was invalid under Mexico's own laws, unless the applicable law itself constituted a violation of NAFTA.[163] The claimants did not contend that the applicable Mexican legal standards themselves breached any specific NAFTA provision. However, they contended that the contract was in fact valid under Mexican law.

The arbitral tribunal found that it was required to accept the decision of Mexico's courts regarding the validity of the contract under Mexican law unless the decision involved a "denial of justice" or a "pretence of form to achieve an internationally unlawful end."[164] The tribunal found no denial of justice, since the claimants had not alleged that the Mexican court had refused to entertain its suit, had subjected it to "undue delay," or had administered justice in a "seriously inadequate way."[165] And there could be no "pretence of form," since the judicial decisions were neither "arbitrary" nor "malicious," and did not involve "a fundamental departure from established principles of Mexican law."[166] Evidence indicating that the claimants had in fact misled city authorities about the contract was sufficient to "dispel any shadow" over the *bona fides* of the Mexican judgment.[167]

Summary

Although it is still too early to draw definitive conclusions about NAFTA's investment rules, a few tentative generalisations can be made. First, NAFTA tribunals have paid little attention to the agreement's exception for measures that the NAFTA parties themselves deem necessary for environmental reasons. Some arbitrators appear to have viewed the exception as having little or no meaning. One arbitrator has viewed the exception as justifying only those measures that are the least restrictive means for pursuing an environmental objective. A third decision suggests that the exception may not be invoked on the basis of the policy concerns of state and local governments.

Secondly, it appears that the NAFTA investment provisions have created a new avenue for private investors to challenge trade restrictions that adversely affect their investments in NAFTA countries. If the trade measure causes economic harm to a NAFTA investor, it may be challenged under rules quite similar to those that apply in traditional trade disputes involving member states. However, private investors can seek damages even if their own governments are unwilling to support their claims.

Thirdly, the NAFTA investment rules have created a new mechanism for private challenges to the regulatory and judicial processes established in the

[163] International Center for the Settlement of Investment Disputes (ICSID) (Additional Facility): *Azinian* v. *United Mexican States* (Award, 1 Nov. 1999), (2000) 39 ILM 537 [hereinafter "Azinian"]. at ¶¶ 96,100.

[164] *Ibid*. at ¶¶ 96–97, 99.

[165] *Ibid*. at ¶ 102.

[166] *Ibid*. at ¶¶ 103, 120.

[167] *Ibid*. The tribunal found that the claimant's failure to make certain disclosures to city authorities was "unconscionable." *Ibid*. at ¶ 110.

NAFTA countries. In order to resolve such claims, NAFTA tribunals have been required to resolve important issues of domestic law involving the proper allocation of power between different levels of government. They have also been required to apply broad general principles of customary international law, such as the principle of transparency and the principle of "fair and equitable" treatment.

Fourthly, NAFTA countries may be required to compensate investors when regulatory measures result in "substantial" loss to any part of an investor's business or property, or to the investor's reasonable expectations under pre-existing laws. Compensation may not be required if a national court has determined that the investment was invalid under pre-existing national laws. However, tribunals have been less willing to defer to legal determinations made by national regulatory authorities under pre-existing environmental statutes. It is not yet clear how the NAFTA rules on expropriation will apply in cases involving intangible property.

Finally, arbitral tribunals have not required investors to exhaust local remedies with respect to regulatory decisions by administrative authorities. However, it is not yet clear whether investors will be required to appeal to a NAFTA country's court of last resort before seeking a NAFTA remedy for decisions issued by a lower court.

III. THE ENVIRONMENTAL SIDE AGREEMENT: THE PROBLEM OF EFFECTIVE ENFORCEMENT

After the NAFTA negotiations were completed, a number of critics argued that the agreement would result in a "race to the bottom," by increasing the incentive for signatories to lower their environmental protection in order to attract investment from other countries. Critics noted that the NAFTA itself contained no provision requiring the signatories to adopt adequate measures for dealing with the environmental consequences of increased trade and investment.[168] Moreover, although NAFTA provides that signatories "should not" waive their environmental, health or safety measures in order to encourage investment, this "soft" obligation gives rise to nothing more than a right to insist on ministerial consultations "with a view to avoiding any such encouragement."[169]

The perceived imbalance between the agreement's protection of economic interests and its protection of environmental interests became a critical issue during the 1992 US presidential elections, which took place after the NAFTA

[168] This concern was famously captured by presidential candidate Ross Perot, who argued that NAFTA would produce a "giant sucking sound" as US companies and job moved across the border to Mexico in order to enjoy the benefits of lower wages and more lenient environmental enforcement. See, e.g., R. Perot, "Save Your Job, Save Our Country: Why NAFTA Must Be Stopped—Now!" (New York, Hyperion, 1993).

[169] See *supra* nn. 62–63 and accompanying text.

countries had signed the original agreement, but before any of them had ratified it. In the campaign leading up to those elections, Bill Clinton stated that he would not support ratification of NAFTA unless an additional agreement was negotiated concerning both environmental and labor protection. Clinton subsequently won the election and, despite initial protests from Canada and Mexico, was able to secure a new environmental "side" agreement shortly before he submitted NAFTA to the US Congress for ratification.[170] The side agreement marks the first time that environmental obligations have been negotiated as part of an international trade agreement.[171]

Unlike the current EC agreements, the environmental side agreement does not require its signatories to comply with any specific regional environmental norms or standards. Instead, the side agreement expressly recognises the "right" of each signatory to establish its own levels of domestic environmental protection.[172] This apparent flexibility is belied, however, by the fact that all three NAFTA countries had already established substantially similar environmental laws before entering NAFTA.[173] As a result of this *de facto* harmonisation of environmental law in the NAFTA countries, the NAFTA debate over environmental protection focused primarily on the level of enforcement of national environmental laws. Concerns about environmental enforcement were particularly acute with respect to Mexico and the US-Mexico border area.[174]

[170] See North American Agreement on Environmental Cooperation, 17 Dec. 1993, Can.–Mex.–U.S., (1993) 32 ILM 1480 [hereinafter "NAAEC"]. The NAFTA parties also negotiated side agreements on labour cooperation and protection against import surges. See North American Agreement on Labour Cooperation, 14 Sept. 1993, Can.–Mex.–US, (1993) 32 ILM 1499; Understanding Between the Parties to the North American Free Trade Agreement Concerning Chapter Eight—Emergency Action, 14 Sept. 1993, Can.–Mex.–US, (1993) 32 ILM 1519. In the United States, ratification of the NAFTA was expressly conditioned on approval of the environmental and labor side agreements. See North American Free Trade Agreement Implementation Act, Pub. L. 103–182, § 101(b)(2), 107 Stat. 2060 (1993) (codified at 19 U.S.C. § 3311).

[171] For general discussion of the environmental side agreement, see, e.g., J. Garvey, "Trade Law and Quality of Life—Dispute Resolution Under the NAFTA Side Accords on Labor and the Environment", (1995) 8 *Am. J. Int'l L.* 439; R. Steinberg, "Trade—Environment Negotiations in the EU, NAFTA and WTO: Regional Trajectories of Rule Development", (1997) 91 *Am. J. Int'l L.* 231.

[172] NAAEC, *supra* n. 170, art. 3.

[173] Mexico's 1988 environmental law was largely modelled on US law. See L. Van Pelt, "Countervailing Environmental Subsidies: A Solution to the Environmental Inequities of the North American Free Trade Agreement", (1994) 29 *Tex. Int'l L.J.* 123, 133; M. E. Kelly et al., *Mexico–US Free Trade Negotiations and the Environment: Exploring the Issues* (Texas Center for Policy Studies 1991) at 18. For a detailed comparison of US and Mexican environmental laws, see Office of the US General Counsel, "Evaluation of Mexico's Environmental Laws, Regulations and Standards" (5 Nov. 1993), reprinted in D. Magraw (ed.), *NAFTA & the Environment* (Washington DC, ABA Publications, 1995) at 583.

[174] See Office of the U.S. Trade Representative, "The NAFTA: Report on Environmental Issues" (4 Nov. 1993), reprinted in D. Magraw (ed.), *NAFTA & the Environment* (Washington DC, ABA Publications, 1995) at 393; Office of the U.S. Trade Representative, "Review of U.S. Mexico Environmental Issues" (25 Feb. 1992), reprinted in D. Magraw (ed.), *NAFTA & the Environment* (Washington DC, ABA Publications, 1995) at 205.

The Legal Framework

The environmental side agreement creates an institutional framework for addressing these concerns, known as the Commission for Environmental Cooperation (CEC).[175] The CEC Council, which includes the senior environmental ministers of each NAFTA country, is charged with strengthening regional cooperation in environmental matters and developing recommendations to further this objective.[176] The Council is supported by an independent Secretariat, which is located in Montreal.[177] It receives advice from a Joint Public Advisory Committee (JPAC) composed of five citizens from each country.[178]

The CEC Council is also charged with ensuring that each NAFTA country "effectively" enforces its own environmental laws.[179] This obligation is not clearly defined in the agreement, which states only that the parties should not be deemed to have enforced their laws ineffectively if its authorities have exercised their discretion in a "reasonable" manner, or made "bona fide" decisions to allocate resources to enforcement "in respect of other environmental matters determined to have higher priorities".[180] Moreover, the side agreement does not apply to several important areas of environmental law. For example, although most environmental legislation in Canada falls within the jurisdiction of its provinces, the agreement applies only to provinces that have expressly agreed to participate in the agreement.[181] To date, only three Canadian provinces have agreed to do so.[182] Moreover, the enforcement provisions do not apply to laws that are "primarily aimed at" managing the harvesting or commercial exploitation of natural resources.[183]

175 NAAEC, *supra* n. 170, art. 8.

176 *Ibid.* arts. 9–10.

177 *Ibid.* arts. 11–13.

178 *Ibid.* art. 16–18.

179 *Ibid.* art. 7. Signatories also agree to provide private access to remedies, and to ensure that their administrative, quasi-judicial, and judicial proceedings are "fair, open, and equitable." *Ibid.* art. 6.

180 *Ibid.* art. 45.1.

181 *Ibid.*, Annex 41. Canada may not invoke the agreement's dispute settlement provisions concerning "persistent pattern of ineffective enforcement" unless provinces representing 55% of its GDP agree to be bound, and these provinces account for 55% of Canadian production in the sector or industry involved. *Ibid.*

182 The provinces of Alberta, Quebec and Manitoba have all entered into a special agreement with the Canadian government concerning implementation of the environmental side agreement. See Canadian Intergovernmental Agreement Regarding the North American Agreement on Environmental Cooperation, available at the Environment Canada Website <http://www.naaec.gc.ca>.

183 NAAEC, *supra* n. 170, art. 45; see also CEC Secretariat, Determination Under Articles 14(1) and 14(2) Concerning SEM–98–002 (*Hector Gregorio Ortiz Martinez* v. *United Mexican States*) (18 Mar. 1999), available at North American Commission for Environmental Cooperation (CEC) Website <http://www.cec.org> (rejecting petition involving commercial forestry dispute).

Dispute Settlement

As critics are quick to point out, the mechanisms established to enforce the obligations created by the side agreement fall far short of the mechanisms established in the NAFTA agreement itself. The side agreement authorises an international arbitral panel[184] to impose monetary fines on a country that is found to have engaged in a (i) "persistent pattern" of ineffective enforcement of its environmental law that (ii) is related to products or services that are the subject of regional trade or competition.[185] However, a panel may not be convened unless it is requested by a NAFTA country, and approved by a two-thirds vote of the CEC Council.[186] Moreover, imposition of sanctions involves a cumbersome process that requires a minimum of 775 days to complete, compared to only 240 days required to resolve disputes initiated under NAFTA Chapter 20.[187]

The agreement also permits any person that resides or is established in a NAFTA country to submit a petition to the CEC Secretariat concerning a NAFTA country's alleged failure effectively to enforce its own environmental laws.[188] The petitioner need not allege that the ineffective enforcement has produced any unfair trade advantage. In fact, only a few petitions have raised unfair trade issues.[189] Most side agreement petitions have been submitted by non-governmental organisations.

[184] The panel is to be comprised of five members chosen from a rosters of independent experts. Each disputing party selects two panelists who are citizens of the other parties. If the disputing parties cannot agree on the chair, a disputing party chosen by lot must choose a chair who is not one of its citizens. NAAEC, *supra* n. 170, art. 25–27.

[185] *Ibid.* art. 24.1, 34. A "persistent pattern" is defined as a "sustained or recurring course of action or inaction beginning after the date of entry into force of this Agreement." *Ibid.* art. 45.1. The monetary fine cannot exceed .007% of the total trade in goods between the parties during the most recent year for which data is available, and should be expended to improve environmental conditions in the sanctioned country. *Ibid.* Annex 34. Canada has agreed that fines assessed against it will be enforceable in Canadian courts. *Ibid.* Annex 36A. The United States and Mexico pay be subject to trade sanctions if they fail to pay fines assessed against them. *Ibid.* art. 36.

[186] *Ibid.* art. 24.

[187] *Ibid.* art. 22–35; see also S. Charnovitz, "The NAFTA Environmental Side Agreement: Implications for Environmental Cooperation, Trade Policy, and American Treatymaking", in S. Rubin and D. Alexander, (eds.), *NAFTA and the environment* (Boston, Kluwer Law International, 1996) at 37 (noting minimum time required to complete dispute resolution under two mechanisms).

[188] NAAEC, *supra* n. 170, art. 14.

[189] See *British Columbia Aboriginal Fisheries Commission et al.* v. *Canada*, SEM–97–001 (filed 2 April 1997), available at North American Commission for Environmental Cooperation (CEC) Website <http://www.cec.org> (alleging that Canada's failure to enforce its fisheries laws gave British Columbia's hydro-electric company an unfair competitive advantage over US hydropower producers); see also *David Suzuki Foundation, et al.* v. *Canada,* SEM–20–004 (filed 15 Mar. 2000), *available at* North American Commission for Environmental Cooperation (CEC) Website <http://www.cec.org> (alleging that Canada's enforcement policies with respect to logging activities in British Columbia were motivated by the need to persuade foreign buyers that Canadian forest products are "sustainable and environmentally friendly").

If the Secretariat determines that the petition meets certain threshold criteria, it may request a response from the party concerned.[190] The decision to request a response is based on a number of specific factors, including whether the submission alleges harm to the petitioner, whether private remedies have been pursued, and whether further study of the issues raised would advance the goals of the agreement.[191] After reviewing a response, the Secretariat may determine that the submission warrants preparation of an objective "factual record".[192] However, the Secretariat may only initiate an investigation if it obtains the prior approval of two-thirds of the ministerial Council. Council approval is also required before the factual report can be published.[193] Finally, the report may only set forth factual findings, and cannot include any legal conclusions or policy recommendations.

The side agreement author ises the CEC Council to assist in consultation involving allegations that a NAFTA country is derogating from its environmental law to encourage investment, in a manner that is inconsistent with the agreement's investment provisions.[194] However, the agreement provides no other mechanism for the CEC to participate in any proceedings involving environmental measures brought under NAFTA's trade or investment rules.

Assessing the Early Experience

Facilitating Regional Cooperation

The CEC has been quite successful in collecting and disseminating information on regional environmental issues. For example, the CEC has published an inventory of releases of specific pollutants by specific industries in each country.[195] It has also published a number of scientific studies and investigations into specific environmental issues,[196] and has completed an analytical framework for identifying and assessing the effects of NAFTA on the environment.[197] A great

[190] Among other requirements, the submission must appear to be aimed at promoting enforcement rather than at harassing industry; must clearly identify the submitters; and must indicate that written notice of the matter has been provided to the Party alleged to have ineffectively enforced its environmental laws. NAAEC, *supra* n. 170, art. 14.1.

[191] *Ibid.* art. 14.2.

[192] *Ibid.* art. 15.

[193] *Ibid.*, art. 15.2 and 15.7.

[194] *Ibid.*, art. 10.6(b).

[195] See North American Commission for Environmental Cooperation, *Taking Stock: North American Pollutant Releases and Transfers, 1997* (May 2000)

[196] See, e.g. North American Commission for Environmental Cooperation, *Silva Reservoir: An Example of Regional Environmental Cooperation in North America* (June 1999); *North American Commission for Environmental Cooperation, Ribbon of Life: An Agenda for Preserving Migratory Bird Habitat on the Upper San Pedro River* (June 1999).

[197] See North American Commission for Environmental Cooperation, *Environment and Trade Series 6—Assessing Environmental Effects of the North American Free Trade Agreement (NAFTA): An Analytic Framework (Phase II) and Issue Studies* (March 1999). See generally North American Commission for Environmental Cooperation, *2000–2002 North American Agenda for Action: A Three-Year Program Plan for the Commission for Environmental Cooperation* (2000).

deal of this information is available at the CEC's website.[198] In addition, the CEC has been instrumental in bringing together interested persons from the public and private sectors in all three NAFTA countries.[199]

The CEC has had more limited success in producing concrete solutions to regional environmental issues. It has developed a number of regional action plans to reduce or eliminate the use of specific toxic chemicals within the NAFTA region,[200] and has initiated negotiations aimed at creating a new Transboundary Environmental Impact Assessment Agreement.[201] It has also created a special fund for small community based projects.[202]

Effective Enforcement

Not surprisingly, the NAFTA countries themselves have not yet convened a single arbitral panel under the side agreement provisions concerning "persistent patterns" of ineffective enforcement. However, the provisions allowing private petitions to request independent investigations of cases involving allegedly ineffective enforcement have produced more significant results. As of 1 March 2001, twenty-nine petitions had been filed, and factual records had been prepared and published in two separate cases involving alleged enforcement failures in Mexico and in Canada.[203] The Secretariat has also initiated a third investigation with respect to Mexico's alleged failure to enforce its hazardous waste laws at an abandoned lead smelter near the US-Mexico border.[204]

[198] See North American Commission for Environmental Cooperation (CEC) Website <http://www.cec.org>[hereinafter "CEC Website"].

[199] The CEC has held a number of workshops and symposia for law enforcement officials and environmental groups. For a list of currently scheduled events, see the CEC website, *supra* n. 198.

[200] See North American Commission for Environmental Cooperation, *Sound Management of Chemicals Project, PCB Regional Action Plan* (Dec. 1996); North American Commission for Environmental Cooperation, *North American Regional Action Plan on DDT* (June 1997); North American Commission for Environmental Cooperation, *North American Regional Action Plan on Chlordane* (June 1997); see generally North American Commission for Environmental Cooperation, *North American Cooperation for the Sound Management of Chemicals* (June 1998).

[201] See North American Commission for Environmental Cooperation, Council Resolution No. 97–03 (12 Jun. 1997), available at CEC Website, *supra* n. 198.

[202] See North American Commission for Environmental Cooperation, Council Resolution No. 95–09 (13 Oct. 1995), available at North American Commission for Environmental Cooperation (CEC) Website <http://www.cec.org>. The United States and Mexico negotiated a separate agreement establishing an institutional framework for bilateral funding of environmental infrastructure projects in the US–Mexico border area. See Agreement Concerning the Establishment of a Border Environment Cooperation Commission and a North American Development Bank, 16 and 18 Nov. 1993, Mex.–US, (1993) 32 ILM 1545 [hereinafter "NADBank/BECC Agreement"]. However, this agreement serves primarily as a supplemental source of financing for these projects. For more information on the BECC and NADBank, see the NADBank Website <http://www.nadbank.org>.

[203] A registry of citizen submissions, including a summary of the current status of submissions and numerous documents filed during the petition process, is available at the CEC Website, *supra* n. 198. Twelve of the petitions filed have involved Mexico; nine involve Canada; and eight involve the United States. *Ibid.*

[204] *Environmental Health Coalition et al.* v. *United Mexican States*, SEM–98–007 (filed 23 Oct. 1998), available at CEC Website, *supra* n. 198.

The Council has not shied away from exercising its power to stop independent investigations of matters raised in private petitions. In May, 2000, the Council refused to approve a proposed investigation of certain allegedly harmful practices on hog farms in the Canadian province of Quebec.[205] It also voted to defer another proposed investigation, pending the conclusion of related proceedings in Canadian court.[206] Although the Commission has proposed two additional investigations in the past seven months (involving Mexico's alleged failure to prosecute a shrimp farm accused of various environmental offenses, and a US policy that allegedly exempts logging operations from a statute requiring a permit for the killing of migratory birds), the Council has yet to vote on either recommendation.[207]

The Secretariat has also exercised significant restraint in responding to private petitions. For example, the Secretariat has determined that the petition process cannot be used to challenge enforcement failures that are specifically mandated by a legislative act. Accordingly, it did not investigate complaints about a US statute that eliminated funding for a program mandated by the Endangered Species Act,[208] and another statute that expressly suspended enforcement of US environmental laws with respect to certain logging programs.[209] The Secretariat has also refused to process petitions regarding a country's alleged failure to implement international environmental treaties that have not been incorporated into domestic law,[210] and enforcement failures that were either over,[211] or had not yet occurred, when the petition was reviewed by the Secretariat.[212]

[205] North American Commission for Environmental Cooperation, Council Resolution No. 00–001 Concerning SEM–97–003 (16 May 2000), available at CEC Website, *supra* n. 198.

[206] North American Commission for Environmental Cooperation, Council Resolution No. 00–002 Concerning SEM–97–006 (16 May 2000), available at CEC Website, *supra* n. 198.

[207] See North American Commission for Environmental Cooperation, *Citizen Submissions on Enforcement Matters: Submission Status*, available at CEC Website, *supra* n.198.

[208] See CEC Secretariat, Determination Under Article 14(2) Concerning SEM–95–001 (*Biodiversity Legal Foundation et al.* v. *United States*) (21 Sept. 1995), available at CEC Website, *supra* n. 198.

[209] See CEC Secretariat, Determination Under Articles 14(1) and 14(2) Concerning SEM–95–002 (*Sierra Club et al.* v. *United States*) (8 Dec. 1995), available at CEC Website, *supra* n. 198.

[210] See CEC Secretariat, Determination Under Article 14(1) Concerning SEM–97–005 (*Animal Alliance of Canada et al.* v. *Canada*) (26 May 1998), available at CEC Website, *supra* n. 198 (rejecting petition alleging that Canada was failing to implement the Biodiversity Convention, because the treaty had not been implemented by way of statute or regulation and was therefore not part of Canada's domestic law). Treaties may also be unenforceable in U.S. courts, unless they are found to be "self-executing." See generally C. Vazquez, "The Four Doctrines of Self-Executing Treaties",(1995) 89 *Am. J. Int'l L.* 695. The status of treaties in Mexican law has not yet been addressed by Mexican courts. See "International Treaties and Constitutional Systems of the United States, Mexico and Canada: Proceedings of the Seminar", (1998) 22 *Md. J. Int'l L. & Trade* 221, 246–59.

[211] See CEC Secretariat, Determination Under Article 14(1) Concerning SEM–97–004 (*Canadian Environmental Defense Fund* v. *Canada*) (25 Aug. 1997), available at CEC Website, *supra* n. 198 (rejecting challenge to decision that had been "completely acted upon" three years earlier under a law that was no longer in force); CEC Secretariat, Determination Under Article 14(1) Concerning SEM–98–001 (*Instituto de Derecho Ambiental et al.* v. *United Mexican States*) (11 Jan. 2000), available at CEC Website, supra n. 198 (rejecting challenge to a 1994 order staying prosecution of nine

Although petitioners are not required to exhaust local remedies before filing a petition,[213] the Secretariat has also refused to prepare a factual record where pending judicial proceedings "closely resemble," or are likely to have a direct impact on, the issues raised in the petition.[214] Most recently, the Secretary refused to conduct an investigation into a petition challenging a California ban on a fuel additive known as MTBE, on the grounds that the matter was the subject of a pending arbitration proceeding under NAFTA's investment provision.[215] The petitioner (a Canadian company that produced MTBE's principal component) had previously filed a claim for damages under the NAFTA investment rules, on the grounds that the ban was discriminatory, had denied it "fair and equitable treatment" and was tantamount to expropriation of its investment in California.[216] California has argued that the ban is justified by concerns about potentially harmful effects of MTBE, which has been detected in high levels in state groundwater supplies. The company responded by filing a petition in the CEC Secretariat asserting that California should have adopted a more "effective" means of addressing its regulatory concerns, without actually banning the fuel additive.[217] The Secretariat did not, however, pursue this issue.

The two reports that the Secretariat has managed to prepare and publish have produced mixed results. The first factual report revealed a number of significant irregularities in Mexico's permitting process for a proposed pier that allegedly endangered a protected coral reef near the island of Cozumel.[218] As critics have

individuals charged with a 1992 explosion in Guadalajara, because the order did not prevent current prosecutions of other individuals).

[212] See also CEC Secretariat, Determination Under Article 14(1) Concerning SEM–20–003 (Hudson River Audubon Soc. of Westchester, Inc. Save Our Sanctuary Committee) (12 Apr. 2000), available at CEC Website, *supra* n.198 (rejecting challenge to proposed project that had not yet been finally approved).

[213] In determining whether to request a response from a NAFTA party, the Secretariat must consider whether the petitioners have "pursued" private remedies, NAAEC, *supra* n. 170, at. 14.2.

[214] See CEC Secretariat, Determination Under Article 14(2) Concerning SEM–96–002 (28 May 1996), available at CEC Website, *supra* n. 198 (rejecting petition because pending judicial proceeding in Canadian courts involved the "same facts" and was "likely to impact directly on the issues raised in the submission"); see also CEC Secretariat, Article 15(1) Determination Concerning SEM–96–003 (*Friends of the Oldman River* v. *Canada*) (2 Apr. 1997), SEM–96–003 (filed 7 Jul. 1996), available at CEC Website, *supra* n. 198 (rejecting petition because pending judicial proceedings in Canadian courts involved similar issues); but see CEC Secretariat, Notification to Council Under Article 15(1) Concerning SEM–97–006 (19 Jul. 1999), available at CEC Website, *supra* n. 198 (Secretariat recommended preparation of factual record despite judicial proceeding in Canadian court that "touched on" the case but raised distinct legal issues) and Council Resolution 00–02 Concerning SEM–97–006 (deferring consideration of petition pending completion of judicial proceedings).

[215] *Methanex Corp.* v. *Canada*, SEM–99–001 (filed 18 Oct. 1999), available at CEC Website, *supra* n. 198 [hereinafter "Methanex CEC Petition"]. The Secretariat consolidated the petition with a related petition by another Canadian company. See *Neste Canada Inc.* v. *Canada*, SEM–20–002 (filed 21 Jan. 2000), available at CEC Website, *supra* n. 198.

[216] See *Methanex Corp.*v. *Canada*, Draft Amended Claim, 12 Feb. 2001, available at NAFTALaw.Org Website (visited March 1, 2001), <http://www.naftalaw.org>.

[217] See Methanex CEC Petition, *supra* n. 215.

[218] See North American Commission for Environmental Cooperation, *Final Factual Record of the Cruise Ship Pier Project in Cozumel, Quintana Roo* (1997).

pointed out, the report did not result in the imposition of any penalties on Mexico, or prevent the construction of the pier.[219] On the other hand, the report appears to have played a significant role in securing subsequent improvements in Mexico's laws for the protection of coral reefs, in the establishment of a new comprehensive environmental plan for Cozumel, and in strengthening the position of non-governmental organisations in the regulatory process.[220] The second published report, involving allegations that Canada was failing to enforce its laws to protect fish in British Columbia's rivers from the ongoing effects of hydro-electric dams,[221] was strongly critic ised by all three countries on the grounds that several of the statements in the report resembled conclusions and recommendations.[222]

Summary

The NAFTA side agreement on environmental cooperation focuses primarily on facilitating environmental cooperation and achieving more effective environmental enforcement in the NAFTA countries. It has been quite successful in disseminating public information on regional environmental issues, and thereby made it easier for citizens to understand the specific environmental problems in their own communities. The information disseminated by the CEC has also helped to generate pressures for improved environmental practices in specific sectors and industries, and facilitated public participation in environmental decision making.

Although the agreement's provision for imposing monetary fines on countries that engage in a "persistent" pattern of ineffective environmental enforcement has so far proved to have little real effect, the mechanism for investigating and reporting on specific environmental issues raised in private petitions appears to have helped the NAFTA countries identify a number of important environmental issues. However, the effectiveness of the petition process has been weakened by the agreement's failure to address important areas of Canadian environmental law and natural resource laws; by the Secretariat's dependence on the very countries it is asked to investigate; by the ability of member states to block proposed investigations and reports; by the Secretariat's inability to include any conclusions or recommendations in its report; and by the absence of

[219] See, e.g., A. Da Silva, "NAFTA and the Environmental Side Agreement: Dispute Resolution in the Cozumel Port Terminal Controversy",(1998) 21 *Environs Env. L. & Pol'y J.*

[220] See S. Kass and J. McCarroll, "NAFTA's CEC: First Lessons for the Americas" (1999) *N.Y.L.J.* 3 (22 Oct.); B. Feagans, "Free Trade and the Environment", *The News*, 20 Mar. 1997; see also "Mexican Legislators Ask Carabias Others to Address CEC Investigation on Cozumel", *BNA Int'l Env. Daily*, 20 Nov. 1997.

[221] Factual Record for Submission SEM–97–001 (11 Jun. 2000), available at CEC Website, *supra* n. 198.

[222] See Comments from the Parties concerning SEM–97–001 (8 and 11 May 2000) available at CEC Website, *supra* n. 198.

any express role for the Secretariat in proceedings involving complaints about environmental and health measures raised by private investors under the NAFTA rules on regional trade and investment.

IV. CONCLUSIONS

The NAFTA and its environmental side agreement include a number of provisions aimed at reducing the conflict between regional integration and environmental protection. The agreement itself permits NAFTA countries somewhat wider latitude than the GATT in imposing trade measures pursuant to certain international environmental agreements, and contains provisions aimed at preventing the "downward" harmonisation of regulatory standards. In addition, the side agreement has significantly enhanced public awareness of environmental concerns in each of the NAFTA countries, and created a new forum in which environmental organisations and other members of civil society can come together and deliberate on issues that raise common environmental concerns.

At the same time, however, the NAFTA has also created a new avenue for a potentially vast number of private challenges to environmental trade measures, and made it possible for private investors to challenge non-trade measures that are perceived to have resulted from unfair regulatory and legal processes, or to have had a "substantial" effect on an investment owned by an investor from another NAFTA country. A number of private claims have raised important issues regarding environmental and health laws in the NAFTA countries, their judicial and regulatory processes, and the allocation of power between central and state authorities within each NAFTA country.

Under NAFTA, these issues may be resolved by *ad hoc* arbitral tribunals chosen by the disputing parties themselves, in closed proceedings that allow little or none of the public input and public participation encouraged by the environmental side agreement. If investors are not required to exhaust local remedies, there may also be little opportunity for the national courts and legal institutions of the NAFTA countries to address domestic legal issues raised by private investor claims.

One possible solution might be for the NAFTA countries to adopt a statement of interpretation[223] clarifying that regulatory measures may not be deemed tantamount to expropriation if they are applied in a non-discriminatory manner for a legitimate regulatory purpose.[224] As recent arbitral tribunals have pointed out,

[223] *See* NAFTA, *supra* n. 3, art. 1131.2 (arbitral tribunals must decide investment disputes in accordance with interpretations issued by the NAFTA Free Trade Commission, a body comprised of cabinet-level representatives from the NAFTA countries or their designees). Canada has already proposed that the Commission develop such a statement. See N. Sherif, "Canadian Memo Identifies Options for Changing NAFTA Investment Rules", *Inside U.S. Trade,* 12 Feb. 1999, 1, 20–23.

[224] See, e.g., H. Mann and K. von Moltke, "NAFTA's Chapter 11 and the Environment: Addressing the Impacts of the Investor–State Process on the Environment" (1999), available at the International Institute for Sustainable Development (IISD) Website, <http://iisdl.iisd.ca/trade investment_regime.htm>.

however, such an exception could create a potentially "gaping" loophole to the NAFTA protections for regional investment, and make it overly easy for governments to discriminate against investors from other NAFTA countries by adopting facially non-discriminatory regulatory measures.

On the other hand, the possibility of large damage awards may also have an undesirable chilling effect on domestic regulatory authorities. This consideration suggests a need for greater public input regarding public law issues raised in private investor claims. The recent decision by an arbitral tribunal to permit *amicus* briefs by non-governmental organisations is an important step in the direction of greater public participation. However, the NAFTA countries should also consider other ways to improve the transparency of investor-state arbitration, including provisions for publication of materials submitted by the disputing parties. In addition, the NAFTA countries should seek to create an advisory role for the CEC, and to increase the role of national courts in investor-state disputes. Even if the parties are not required to exhaust local remedies, it may be possible to permit arbitrators to refer important issues of local law to national courts.

Finally, the NAFTA countries might consider measures to narrow the current discretion of arbitral tribunals, and to strengthen the institutions created under the environmental side agreement. For example, the NAFTA countries could adopt an interpretation clarifying whether and when a measure that harms only part of a business, or that harms intangible property, can be considered tantamount to expropriation. In addition, the NAFTA countries might adopt an interpretation to clarify the application of the principle of transparency for relatively new rules affecting relatively small and unsophisticated local governments. The NAFTA countries might also consider creating a role for the CEC Secretariat in investment disputes raising issues of environmental concern, and allowing the Secretariat (or some other body) greater independence in reviewing citisen petitions under the environmental side agreement. In short, the NAFTA countries have taken important steps toward reconciling the goals of regional economic integration and environmental protection, but a long road remains ahead.

Index

Please note that references to footnotes are denoted by the page number, followed by 'n' and then number of note.

Ad Hoc Intergovernmental Task Force on Foods, Codex Alimentarius Commission, 76–7
African Charter on Human and People's Rights (1981), 204
Agenda 21, 79, 107–8, 110, 158
Agreement on Reduction of Dolphin Mortality in Eastern Pacific Ocean (1992), 114
Agriculture Committee, WTO, 40, 84
AIA (Advance Informed Agreement), 32–3, 34–5, 37, 58, 59–60
American Convention on Human Rights (1970), 204
American Declaration on Rights and Duties of Man (1963), 204
Amin, General Idi, 199, 238
Amsterdam Treaty (1997), 191
ANZFA (Australia-New Zealand Food Authority), 55
Anzilotti, Dionisio, 137
Apartheid Convention (1973), 211
Appellate Body, WTO *see* WTO (World Trade Organisation): Appellate Body
Argentina, GMOs in, 45
Article XX, GATT exceptions *see* GATT (General Agreement on Tariffs and Trade): Article XX exceptions
Australia:
  GMOs in, 55
  salmon, import prohibition, 31, 124–5
  Symposium on sea turtle conservation (1999), 115
Australia-New Zealand Food Authority (ANZFA), 55

Bamako Convention on the Ban of Import into Africa (1991), 79
Barboza, Julio, 137
Basel Convention on Hazardous Waste (1989), 8, 21, 114, 159, 318
beef, import ban, 28, 30
Beijing Conference on Women (1995), 181
Belgium, chicken-dioxin problem (1999), 28
Benefit-sharing concept, 44
Bin Cheng, 138
Biodiversity Convention (1992), 115
Biodiversity protection, biotechnology risk, 43, 44
Biopiracy, 88
Biosafety concept:
  defined, 57n44, 87
  EPO, paradigm of trade/environment disputes, 89–99
  'genetic pollution', 89
  and intellectual property rights, 87–9
  ordre public notion, 93, 96, 99–102
  see also Biotechnology
Biosafety Protocol *see* Cartagena Protocol on Biosafety (2000)
Biotechnology:
  definitions, 171
  developing countries, 82–3
  opportunities, 40, 41–3
  risks, 44–5
  and TRIPS, 172
  WTO Working Party on, 57, 78
  see also Biosafety concept; GMOs (genetically modified organisms), international trade in; LMOs (living modified organisms, international trade in); Patentability
Bovine spongiform encephalopathy, 28
Bretton Woods Conference (1944), 4, 184
British beef, import ban, 28, 30
Brundtland Report, 158
Brussels Ministerial Conference (1990), 264
BSP (Cartagena Protocol on Biosafety) *see* Cartagena Protocol on Biosafety
Burma, sanctions against, 187, 200, 223, 248, 251

Cairo Conference on Population and Development (1994), 181
Canada:
  GMOs in, 45, 55, 66, 74–5, 80
  necessity principle, 148
  trade sanctions by, 200, 317–9
Cartagena Biosafety Protocol (2000):
  on AIA procedure, 32–3
  Clearing-House, 32, 35, 60
  on FFP-LMOs, 33–4, 61
  on GMOs, 21, 40, 65–73
  on LMOs, 32–4, 60
  on multilateral environmental agreements, 115
  negotiating groups, 58–9
  on precautionary principle, 79, 115–16

CBA (cost-benefit analysis), 24, 89, 96–7, 102
CBD (Convention on Biological Diversity):
and biosafety, 87–8
and BSP, 34
and EST, 159, 172, 173
and export restrictions, 21
and GMOs, 41, 44, 57–8, 83
and ITL, 130
and precautionary principle, 79
CBERA (Caribbean Basin Economy Recovery Act) 1994, 220, 297
CDM (Clean Development Mechanism), 131
CEC (Council of Environmental Cooperation), 321, 323
CEDAW (Convention on the Elimination of All Forms of Discrimination Against Women), 208
CEE (Central and Eastern European bloc of countries), 59
Child labour standards, 287–312
dumping, 298–9
GATT, suspension of, 295–310
Article VI, 298–9
Article XIX, 299–300
Article XX, 300–5
Article XXIII, 305
regional and national policies, 295–8
treaties on child labour, 306–8
International Convention on the Rights of the Child (1989), 208, 290, 294
international law, place in, 290–5
international trade and human rights, interaction, 287–90
Jus Cogens character of fundamental norms on child labour, 308–10
legal consequences, 295–310
and pornography, 11, 300
treaties on, 306–8
unilateralism, need to limit, 310–2
Worst Form of Child Labour Convention (1999), 6n22, 291, 292
WTO Agreement:
Article XIII, 305–6
and treaties on child labour, 306–8
see also Human rights protection; Labour rights
China, human rights concerns, 202, 219–20, 229, 242, 252
CITES (Convention on Trade in Endangered Species), 1973:
conformity principle, 22
import licenses, 114
and NAFTA, 315
nature protection, 15
precautionary principle, 79
sea turtles, protection of, 117, 119, 247
trade restrictions, 8
Clean Development Mechanism (CDM), 131
Climate Change Convention (1992), 15, 79, 91, 159, 174
Codex Alimentarius Commission, 41, 68–9, 76–7, 78, 126
Colombia, precautionary principle, 80
Commission, European *see* European Commission
Commission on Sustainable Development (CSD), 107–8
Committee on Science and Technology Policy (CSTP), 78n78
Commutative justice, 274–81
Compromise Group (GMO negotiations), 58, 59
Convention for Abolition of Import and Export Restrictions (1927), 301–2
Convention Against Torture and Degrading Treatment (1984), 6n19
Convention on Biological Diversity (CBD) *see* CBD (Convention on Biological Diversity)
Convention on Desertification (1994), 15
Convention on the Elimination of All Forms of Discrimination Against Women (CEDAW), 208
Convention on the Protection and Use of Transboundary Watercourses (1992), 79
Convention on the Rights of the Child (1989), 208, 290, 294
Convention on Trade in Endangered Species, 1973 *see* CITES (Convention on Trade in Endangered Species, 1973)
Copenhagen, World Summit for Social Development (1995), 181
COPS (Cost Per Unit Service), 108
Cost-benefit analysis (CBA), 24, 89, 96–7, 102
Council of Environmental Cooperation (CEC), 321, 323
Council of Grocery Distributors, Canada, 55
Council of Ministers, 49
CSD (Commission on Sustainable Development), 107–8
CSTP (Committee on Science and Technology Policy), 78n78
CTE (WTO Committee on Trade and Environment):
Cartagena Protocol, 62
creation, 107
ITL,
creation of CTE, 107
dispute settlement mechanisms, 129
future challenges, 130–1
information-gathering, co-ordination, 111, 112

Declaration on Fundamental Principles and Rights at Work, ILO (1998), 6, 182–3, 186

Definitions:
biosafety, 57n44, 87
biotechnology, 171
GMOs, 40
human rights regime, 204–8
international emergency, 231
investment, 317
LMOs, 27, 57
necessity principle, 24
proportionality test, 25
slavery, 293
sui generis systems, 72n67
technology, 162
unilateralism, 201n8
Desertification Convention (1994), 15
Developing countries, biotechnology, 41, 82–3, 85
Discriminatory import restrictions, 11
Dispute settlement principles, 22–5
evolutive interpretation, 23–4
presumption of conformity, 22–3
WTO *see* WTO (World Trade Organisation): Appellate Body; WTO-DSU (WTO Dispute Settlement Understanding)
see also Necessity principle; Proportionality principle
DPGs (domestically prohibited goods), 130
DSU (Dispute Settlement Understanding), 128–30
dumping legislation, 298–9
Dworkin, Ronald, 137

EAA (Export Administration Act), 1979, 221
EC *see* European Community (EC)
ECHR (European Convention on Human Rights), 101, 204
Energy Charter Treaty (1994), 159
Environment, protection of:
challenges to government actions, 319–20
import bans, 317–19
dispute settlement principles, 22–5
export restrictions, 20–2
free trade, 4–7, 135
human rights issues, 20–2
imports, unilateral measures affecting, 7–20
lowering of standards to attract foreign investment, 320–1
NAFTA framework, 313–24
side agreement, environmental, 313, 321–4
technology transfer, 157–77
tobacco legislation, Thailand, 143–5
see also EST (environmentally sound technology); ITL, impact on environmental law and process; Nature protection, GATT/WTO practice; PPM (process/production methods)
Environmental Risk Management Authority, New Zealand, 55
Environmentally sound technology *see* EST (environmentally sound technology)
EPC (European Patent Convention), 92, 101
EPO (European Patent Office), jurisprudence of, 90–9
Erga omnes doctrine, human rights:
biosafety, international public policy, 100, 102
international human rights regime, 205, 206
normative values, 237, 238, 239
trade remedies, 209, 212
EST (environmentally sound technology):
export incentives for investments carrying, 175–7
lack of demand for, 173–5
problems in promoting at international level, 161–4
propositions of international law, implementation, 158–60
protection of environment, 157
sponsored supply, replacing with, 173–5
ultimate beneficiaries of, 163–4
EU (European Union):
British beef, import ban, 28, 30
Consultative Forum on the Environment and Sustainable Development, establishment, 109
GMOs,
legislation on, 47–51
negotiating group, 58
precautionary principle, invoking of, 66
GSP programme, amendment, 7n26
harmonisation of environmental standards, 126–7
institutional structure, 'democratic deficit' in, 197
soybeans, American exports to, 46
trade sanctions by, 200
European Commission, 48, 50, 81
European Community (EC), 47–51
European Convention on Human Rights (ECHR), 101, 204
European Court of Human Rights, 101
European Parliament, 48
European Patent Convention (EPC), 92, 101
European Patent Office (EPO), 90–9
European Union *see* EU (European Union)
Evolutive interpretation principle, 23–4
Exhaustible resources concept, 20, 148, 237, 240
Export incentives, 175–7
Export restrictions, 20–2
Extraterritorality principle, 234–7

FAO (Food and Agriculture Organisation), 41, 77–8, 83, 86, 126, 167
FCCC (Framework Convention on Climate Change), 1992, 15, 79, 91, 159, 174

FDA (US Food and Drug Administration), 52–3, 54
FDI (foreign direct investment), 164, 173–7
FFP-LMOs (Food, feed and process living modified organisms), 33–5, 61
Fish, protection of *see* Nature protection, GATT/WTO practice: *Shrimp/Turtle* dispute; *Tuna Dolphin* case
Food and Agriculture Organisation (FAO), 41, 77–8, 83, 86, 126, 167
Foreign direct investment (FDI), 164, 173–7
Framework Convention on Climate Change (FCCC) 1992, 15, 79, 91, 159, 174
Free trade:
  human rights regime, reconciliation with, 252–60
    GATT provisions, 227–8
  international labour rights, 207
  limits of, 4–7, 135
  trade sanctions, 201
  see also NAFTA (North American Free Trade Agreement)

GATS (General Agreement on Trade in Services), 131, 287n1
GATT (General Agreement on Tariffs and Trade):
  acceptable trade measures (human rights),
    chapeau, 12, 18, 117–20, 134, 143, 243–50, 251
    child labour, 295
    multilateralism, 246–9
    necessity requirement, public morals and human life, 240–1
    prison labour, 241–2
    proportionality, 243–6
    reasonableness concept, 241–2
    transparency, 249–50
  Article I ('external' parity/non-discriminatory treatment), 8–9, 11, 225
  Article II (customs tariff, limiting), 9
  Article III ('internal' parity), 9–13, 17, 70, 125, 141, 225
  Article VI, 298–9
  Article XI (non-tariff restrictions, elimination), 9, 11, 13, 70, 141, 225, 227
  Article XIX, 299–300
  Article XX exceptions,
    acceptable trade measures, 240–50
    application of, 148–50
    case law, 11–13
    chapeau, 12, 18, 117–20, 134, 143, 243–50, 251
    CITES, 8
    and domestically prohibited goods and technology, 167
    exhaustible resources, 20, 148, 237, 240
    export restrictions, 20
    GMOs, 71–2
    human rights, 4, 17–20, 233–50, 253–7, 300–5
    labour rights, 193
    'line of equilibrium', 119
    MEAs, validation of, 133, 134
    multilateralism, labour rights, 193
    nature protection, 14–15
    necessity principle, 142–50, 255–7
    normative values, 234–40
    proportionality principle, 25, 253–5
    public morals, 11, 13, 18–20, 24, 238–9, 240–1
    SPM agreement, 16–17
    TBT agreement, 16–17
    unilateral measures, ITL, 116–22
  Article XXI exceptions (national security), 225, 229–33, 257–8
  Article XXIII, 305
  environmental protection *see* Nature protection, GATT/WTO practice
  establishment, 180
  extraterritorality, 234–7
  GMOs, implications for international trade in, 65, 70–2, 84, 86
  'greening' the, 5
  human rights, 225–50
    acceptable trade measures, 240–50
    amendment of policies, 201–2
    Article XX exceptions, 4, 17–20, 233–50, 253–7, 300–5
    Article XXI exceptions, 225, 229–33, 257–8
    child labour standards, 295–310
    free trade provisions, 227–8
    import preference, 228–9
    interpretation principles, 226
    national security exception, 225, 229–33
    normative values, 234–40
    reconciliation of regime, 212
  imports, unilateral measures affecting, 8–9, 14–15
  ITL, scope of unilateral measures, 116–22
  national security exception, human rights, 225, 229–33
  nature protection *see* Nature protection, GATT/WTO practice
  necessity principle, 141–50, 255–7
  preamble (1947), 4, 5
  presumption of conformity principle, 22, 23
  sovereignty principle, recognition of, 10
  subsidy rules, investments carrying, 175–7
  suspension of, child labour standards, 295–310
    Article VI, 298–9
    Article XIX, 299–300

Article XX, 300–5
Article XXIII, 305
regional and national policies, 295–8
transparency issue, 112–13
unilateral measures (ITL), scope of, 116–22
see also nature protection, GATT/WTO practice; WTO (World Trade Organisation)
General Agreement on Trade in Services (GATS), 131, 287n1
General trade sanctions, 218–25, 245–6, 251
Generalised System of Preferences (GSP) *see* GSP (Generalised System of Preferences)
Genetic pollution, 89
Genetically modified (GM) foods, 28, 42, 50, 53
Genetically modified organisms *see* GMOs (genetically modified organisms), international trade in
Geneva Conventions (1949), 212
Genocide Convention, 212
Genocide, Rwanda (1994), 248
German Association for Technical Co-operation (GTZ), 110n20
Germany, Republic of, precautionary principle, 80
Global Industry Coalition, 59
GM (genetically modified) foods, 28, 42, 50, 53
GMOs (genetically modified organisms), international trade in, 39–86
Australia, 55
benefits of GMOs, 42
biotechnology, risks and opportunities, 41–5
Cartagena Protocol on Biosafety, 57–64
Codex Alimentarius Commission, 41, 68–9, 76–8, 86
definitions, 40
EC/EU, 47–51
Food and Agriculture Organisation, 76–8
Japan, 51–2
Korean Republic, 56
labelling,
EU Directives, 50–1
Japan, 51–2
USA, 54
like products concept, 9, 68, 69, 74, 227, 228
'live GMOs', 47
market for, 45–6
Mexico, 56
multilateral solutions, 56–79
New Zealand, 55
OECD, 78–9
precautionary principle, 66, 79–82
regulatory framework, 47–56
Seattle Conference (Third WTO Ministerial Conference), 1999, 1, 73–6
Sri Lanka, 56
standards and regulations, 39
substantial equivalence test, 68–9, 74
Switzerland, 55–6
Thailand, 56
US, 45–6, 52–4
WTO agreements, implications for, 65–73, 75
see also LMOs (living modified organisms), international trade in
GPA (WTO Agreement on Government Procurement), 251
Greenhouse gas emissions, restriction of, 15
Grotius, Hugo, 136
GSP (Generalised System of Preferences):
import preferences, 228–9, 250
and labour rights 7n26, 189
trade restrictions, 200, 220, 250, 296
transparency requirement, 249
GTZ (German Association for Technical Co-operation), 110n20
Guidelines on Trade and Environment (1993), 109

Hague Convention (1954), 3n6
Haiti, overthrow of democracy in, 218, 233
Havana Charter for an International Trade Organisation (1948), 5, 180, 287n1
Hegel, G.W.F., 281, 282, 283, 284
Helsinki Convention (1992), 159
Horizontal legislation, EU, 47, 49
Human life, protection of, 43, 233, 238, 240–1
Human rights protection:
definitions of international human and labour rights, 203–13
economic coercion to promote,
customary international law, trade remedies under, 208–10
human rights treaties, trade remedies under, 211–13
non-forcible countermeasures, 210
non-intervention norm, 208–10
export restrictions, 20–2
free trade, relationship with, 4–7, 201, 207, 252–60
GATT *see* GATT (General Agreement on Tariffs and Trade): human rights
institutional competence, 258–60
intellectual property rights, 281–5
international regime, 204–8
normative values (GATT, Article XX application),
extraterritoriality, 234–7
human life, 238, 240–1
incorporation of human rights values, 237–40
prison labour, 11, 13, 239, 241–2
public morals, 11, 13, 18–20, 24, 238–9, 240–1, 300
PPM, 17–20

Human rights protection (*cont.*):
- prison labour, 11, 13, 239, 241–2
- trade remedies,
  - under customary international law, 208–10
  - under treaties, 211–13
- US trade sanctions,
  - country-specific measures, 222
  - general, 218–25, 245–6
  - import preferences, 219–20
  - national security measures, 221–2
  - semi-tailored, 215–18, 242, 251
  - sub-national measures, 222–5
  - tailored, 213–15
  - *see also* Trade sanctions, imposition of
- WTO, 250–2
- *see also* Child labour standards

ICCPR (International Covenant on Civil and Political Rights), 6, 181, 204, 208, 210, 211, 294, 307
ICESCR (International Covenant on Economic, Social and Cultural Rights), 6, 181, 204, 208, 307
ICJ (International Court of Justice), 136, 138, 140, 141, 205, 208–9
ICSID (International Centre for the Settlement of International Disputes), 2n4, 320
IEEPA (International Emergency Economic Powers Act) 1994, 221
ILC (International Law Commission), 139, 140, 141
ILO (International Labour Organisation):
- Child Labour Convention (1973), 207n39
- Declaration on Fundamental Principles and Rights at Work (1998), 6, 182–3, 186, 207
- Forced Labour Convention (1930), 211–12
- free trade debate, 207
- and global civil society, 2
- history of labour rights, 179–83
- institutional structure, 5
- multilateral approach to labour rights, 192, 248
- unionism, 196

IMF (International Monetary Fund), 1, 5, 180, 201
Import bans, 71, 317–19
Import Licensing Procedures, Agreement on, 113
Import preferences, 219–20, 228–9
Imports, unilateral measures affecting, 7–20
- GATT, 8–9, 14–15
- nature protection, GATT/WTO practice, 14–15
- PPM, 13–20
- processes/production methods, 15
- product requirements, 9–13
- SPS, 16–17
- TBT, 16–17
- *see also* Trade sanctions, imposition of

India, Agreement on Conservation of Marine Turtles (2000), 115
Innovation, technological, 266–71
Intellectual property rights (IPRs) *see* IPRs (intellectual property rights)
Inter-American Convention for Protection of Sea Turtles (1996), 304
Inter-American Human Rights Commission, 205, 248
International Centre for the Settlement of International Disputes (ICSID), 2n4, 320
International Convention on Elimination of All Forms of Racial Discrimination (1965), 6n18
International Convention on the Rights of the Child (1989), 208, 290, 294
International Court of Justice (ICJ), 136, 138, 140, 141, 205, 208–9
International Covenant on Civil and Political Rights (ICCPR), 6, 181, 204, 208, 210, 211, 294, 307
International Covenant on Economic, Social and Cultural Rights (ICECR), 6, 181, 204, 208, 307
International Electrotechnical Commission, 126
International emergency, 230–1
International Labour Organisation (ILO) *see* ILO (International Labour Organisation)
International Law Commission (ILC), 139, 140, 141
International Law Institute, 205
International Monetary Fund (IMF), 1, 5, 180, 201
International Office of Epizootics, 126
International Plant Protection Convention, 126
International Rubber Study Group (IRSG), 110n20
International Standardisation Organisation (ISO), 126, 127, 128
International Trade Centre (ITC), 110n20
International trade law *see* ITL (international trade law), impact on environmental law and process
International Trade Organisation, 5, 180
International Union for the Protection of New Varieties of Plants (UPOV), 72–3
Inventions, patentability of *see* Patentability
Investment rules, NAFTA, 316–21
- challenges to government actions in environmental arena, 319–20
- definitions, 317
- lower environmental standards as means of attracting foreign investment, 320–1
- provisions concerning trade in goods and services, 314–16

IPRs (intellectual property rights), 263–85
  and biosafety, 87–90
  copyright law, 266
  and environmental security, 90
  GMOs, 72–3
  technology transfer, 266–85
  see also TRIPS (Trade-Related Aspects of Intellectual Property Rights Agreement)
Iraq, trade sanctions against, 221
IRSG (International Rubber Study Group), 110n20
ISO (International Standardisation Organisation), 126, 127, 128
ITC (International Trade Centre), 110n20
ITL (international trade law), impact on environmental law and process, 105–34
  capacity to accommodate environmental concerns, 131–4
  case law on marine life, 114–22, 146–8
  coherence clauses, 112
  communication processes among international bodies, strengthening of, 110–12
  CTE, 130–1
  on domestic regulation, 2
  GATT law, 116–22
  'greening' of, 110
  marine life, case law, 114–22, 146–8
  market-based mechanisms, 125–8
  multilateral environmental agreements, adoption of, 114–16
  on national public policy, 2
  national regulations, enhanced transparency of, 112–14
  and necessity principle, 137–8
  new institutional arrangements, spurring creation of, 107–10
  notification requirements, 112–14
  product standards and PPM, harmonisation of, 125–8
  regulations, 125–8
  savings clauses, 112
  and SPS, 122–5
  and TBT, 122–5
  trade in services, 130–1
  unilateral measures, scope of, 116–22
  WTO-DSU, enforcement, 128–30
IUCN (World Conservation Union), 109–10

Japan:
  GMOs, 51–2, 67, 75
  SPS measures, 123–4
Joint Working Party on Trade and Environment (1991), 109
JPAC (Joint Public Advisory Committee), 321
Jus cogens doctrine, human rights:
  biosafety, international public policy, 100, 102
  child labour, 304, 308–10
  and free trade, 253–5
  international regime, 205
  normative values, 238, 239
  slavery, 293
  trade remedies, 209, 212, 213

Korean Republic, GMOs, 56
Kosovo, genocide in, 218
Kyoto Protocol (1998), 131, 174

labelling requirements:
  FFP-LMOs, 35
  GMO produce,
    EU Directives, 50–1
    Japan, 51–2
    US, 54
  ITL, 127
  social labelling schemes, 189
  TBT, 67–8
Labour rights, 179–97
  'core', 186–7
  history, 179–83
  international, defined, 203–13
  multilateralism,
    involuntary, 193–4
    voluntary, 194–6
  standards of labour, 185
  trade liberalisation, conflict with,
    empirical issues, 183–4
    legal issues, 187
    response to, 188–92
    theoretical issues, 184–7
  'worker rights', 185
  see also Child labour standards; Human rights protection; Non-discrimination principle
League of Nations, 179
  demise of, 5, 180
Leahy Amendment (1996), 215
Least-trade restrictiveness test, 97, 154, 255
Lex generalis/specialis, 63
licensing, compulsory, 169–71
Like products concept, 9, 13, 17, 68, 69, 74, 227–8
Like-Minded Group (GMO negotiations), 58, 59
Liu, P.B., 275–6
LMOs (living modified organisms), international trade in, 27–38
  benefits of LMOs, 28
  Cartagena Biosafety Protocol, 32–4, 60
  contained use, 60
  definitions, 27, 57
  direct use, 61
  FFP-LMOs, 33–5, 61
  intentional introduction into environment, 62

LMOs (*cont.*):
  precautionary principle, 35–6
  SPS Agreement, 29–32, 61, 62
  United States, 27
  see also GMOs (genetically modified organisms), international trade in
local working requirements, 169–71
Locke, J., 281, 282, 283, 284
Locus standi, 7

McGrath, M., 278
MAFF (Ministry of Agriculture, Forestry and Fishery), 51, 52
Marine Environment Conventions (1992), 79–80
Marine life, protection of *see* Nature protection, GATT/WTO practice: *Shrimp/Turtle* dispute; *Tuna Dolphin* case
Marrakesh Ministerial Declaration (1994), 1, 4–5, 22, 25–6, 182, 287
MEAs (Multilateral Environmental Agreements):
  CTE, 107
  EST, 160
  GATT, amendment of Article XX, 133, 134
  'immunisation' of, 134
  information-gathering, co-ordination of, 111
  ITL, scope of unilateral measures, 118
  WTO-DSU, 128–30
Mexico:
  death of water birds, 323
  GMOs, 56
MFN (Most Favoured Nation):
  GATS, 131
  import preferences, 219–20, 228–9
  national standards, 122
  social clauses, 289
Miami Group, 58, 59, 115
Minimum Age Convention (1973), 290–1
Ministry of Agriculture, Forestry and Fishery (MAFF), 51, 52
MMT (fuel additive), import bans, 317, 318, 319
Monarch Butterfly Research Symposium (1999), 28n4
Montreal Protocol on Ozone Layer (1987), 8, 23, 79, 114, 159, 315
morals, public, 11, 13, 18–20, 24, 238–9, 240–1, 300
Most Favoured Nation *see* MFN (Most Favoured Nation)
Multilateral Environmental Agreements (MEAs) *see* MEAs (Multilateral Environmental Agreements)
Multilateralism:
  acceptable trade measures (GATT *chapeau*), 246–9
  GMOs, 56–79
    Cartagena Protocol, 57–64
    Codex Alimentarius Commission initiatives, 41, 68–9, 76–8, 86
    Food and Agriculture Organisation initiatives, 76–8
    OECD, 78–9
    precautionary principle, 79–82
    Third WTO Ministerial Conference, 73–6
    WTO Agreements, 65–73, 75
  involuntary multilateralism, 193–4
  ITL as catalyst for adoption of agreements, 114–16
  labour rights,
    involuntary multilateralism, 193–4
    response to conflict, 191–2
    social clauses, 194, 289, 298, 305
    voluntary multilateralism, 194–6
  trade sanctions, 201
  voluntary multilateralism, 194–6
  see also MEAs (Multilateral Environmental Agreements)

NAAEC (North American Agreement on Environmental Cooperation), 108, 321–4
NAALC (North American Agreement on Labor Cooperation), 297
NAFTA (North American Free Trade Agreement):
  interplay between trade and environment, 313–24
  investment rules, 316–21
    government actions, challenges to, 319–20
    import bans, 317–19
    lower environmental standards to attract foreign investment, 320–1
  and NAAEC, 108, 321–4
  regional model, labour rights, 191
  side agreement, environmental, 313, 321–4
  trade sanctions by, 201
  see also Free trade
National treatment (NT) clauses, 9, 70, 122, 141, 318
Nature protection, GATT/WTO practice:
  Gasoline case,
    human rights, acceptable trade measures, 240, 242, 243, 249
    necessity principle (Article XX exception), 146, 149, 151, 153
    unilateralism, 118
  generally, 14–15
  objectives, 4
  Shrimp/Turtle dispute,
    child labour, 303, 304
    'effects' test, 236
    evolutive interpretation principle, 23

extraterritorality, human rights, 236–7, 238, 244
human rights, 236–7, 238, 242, 243, 246, 249, 256
multilateral agreements, 114–15, 193–4, 246, 249
necessity principle (Article XX exception), 147, 149, 153
PPM import restrictions, 14
unilateralism, 117, 118, 120–1
Tuna Dolphin case,
child labour, 303
human rights, 227, 235, 243
multilateral agreements, 114, 194
necessity principle (Article XX exception), 146, 148
PPM import restrictions, 14
unilateralism, 116, 118, 121
Necessity principle:
CBA, 97
defined, 24
GATT, in, 141–50, 240–1, 255–7
as general principle of international law, 137–8
human rights, acceptable trade measures, 240–1
as instrument of balance, 135–55
least-trade restrictiveness test, 97, 154, 255
legal principles, 137, 138
reasonableness test, 154
SPS Agreements, 150–3
state of necessity, public international law, 139–41
TBT agreements, 150–3
trade and environmental protection, balancing of, 135–6, 153–5
WTO, 251
see also Proportionality principle
New Zealand:
fisheries sector, elimination of subsidies, 130
GMOs, 55
NGOs (non-governmental organisations):
and global civil society, 2
import restrictions, 7
international trade law, new institutional arrangements, 106, 109–10
labour rights, 181, 189–90, 196
NIEO (New International Economic Order) 1974, 161
Non-discrimination principle, 8, 9, 10, 125–6, 141
Normative values (GATT, Article XX application):
extraterritoriality, 234–7
human life, 238, 240–1
incorporation of human rights values, 237–40
prison labour, 11, 13, 239, 241–2
public morals, 11, 13, 18–20, 24, 238–9, 240–1, 300
North American Agreement on Environmental Cooperation (NAAEC), 108, 321–4
North American Agreement on Labor Cooperation (NAALC), 297
North American Free Trade Agreement (NAFTA), 313–24
Novel Foods Regulation, 49, 50
Nozick, R., 283
NT (national treatment) clauses, 9, 70, 122, 141, 318

OAS (Organisation of American States), 203n15, 217
OECD (Organisation for Economic Co-operation and Development):
GMOs, initiatives taken on 55n36, 78–9
international trade law, new institutional arrangements, 109–10
'Polluter Pays Principle', 10
Ordre public clause, 93, 96, 99–102
Organic products, 51, 52, 54
Organisation for Economic Co-operation and Development *see* OECD (Organisation for Economic Co-operation and Development)
Ozone layer, protection of, 8, 15, 23, 79, 114, 159

Paris Convention (1883), 170
Patentability:
and biological diversity, 171–3
case law, 91, 94
CBA, 96–7
and international environmental law, 90–3
litigation, 90–3
neutral instruments, patents as, 92
ordre public clause, 93, 96, 99–102
preclusion when risks outweigh benefits of invention, 96–9
and public policy, 92, 93
scientific evidence tests, 93–6, 102
sufficient substantiation test, 96
technical conception of, 92, 93
see also Biosafety; Biotechnology
PCBs, import bans, 317–19
PIC (prior informed consent), 167
Plant Breeders' Rights, UPOV system of, 72–3
'Polluter Pays Principle' (PPP), 10
Pornography, 11, 300
PPM (process/production methods):
environmental product standards, harmonisation with, 125–8
genetic modification, 69
and human rights protection, 17–20
GATT free trade provisions, 227, 228
import restrictions based on, 13–20
PPP ('Polluter Pays Principle'), 10

Precautionary principle:
GMOs, 40–1, 66, 67, 79–82
international environmental law, patent litigation, 91
LMOs, 35–6
Presumption of conformity principle, 22–3
Principles of dispute settlement *see* Dispute settlement principles
Prior informed consent (PIC), 167
Prison labour, 11, 13, 17, 239, 241–2
Probatio diabolica, 153
Process/production methods *see* PPM (process/production methods)
Product requirements, import restrictions based on, 9–13
Proportionality principle:
defined, 25
effectiveness, 254
GMOs, 68
human rights sanctions, 243–6, 253–5
interest, 253–4
and necessity principle, 140, 154, 155
patentability, preclusion of, 97
Protests, anti-globalisation, 1
Public morals (GATT exception), 11, 13, 18–20, 24, 238–9, 240–1, 300
Public policy, international, 99–103

Quantitative restrictions, prohibition of (GATT, Article XI), 9

Ratione materiae, 122
Reichman, J.H., 275, 280–1
Rio Declaration on Environment and Development (1992), 4, 21, 114, 158, 181
risk assessment:
biotechnology, 31, 35, 41–5
necessity principle, 152
SPS Agreement, 17
Romania, MFN status, 219
Rotterdam Convention of Prior Informed Consent for Certain Hazardous Chemicals (1998), 21
Rumania, death of Tibiscus river in, 157
Rwanda, genocide in (1994), 218, 238, 248

Sanitary and Phytosanitary Agreement (SPS) *see* SPS (Sanitary and Phytosanitary Agreement)
Sanitary and Phytosanitary Measures (SPM), 16–17
Committee on, 40
savings clauses, 112
Scientific evidence tests, 93–6, 102, 123–4
Seattle Conference (Third Ministerial Conference of World Trade Organisation, 1999), 1, 73–6, 81–2, 183, 263, 279–80, 313
Semi-tailored trade sanctions, 215–18, 242, 245, 251
Singapore Ministerial Conference (1996), 107, 192, 202, 288, 299
Slavery, 200, 211, 292–4, 301
Slavery Convention (1926), 293
Slavery Convention (1957), 211
Smoking restrictions legislation, 143–5
Social clauses, 194, 289, 298, 305
Sovereignty principle, 10
SPM (Sanitary and Phytosanitary Measures), 16–17
SPS (Sanitary and Phytosanitary Agreement):
BSP (Cartagena Protocol), 35, 61
GMOs, implications for international trade in, 65–7, 83, 84, 86
Hormones case (1998), 17, 30–1, 35–6, 66–7, 123, 124
human rights, normative values, 234–5
import restrictions, 11
LMOs, 29–32, 61, 62
NAFTA, 314
national measures, limits on, 122–5
necessity principle, 150–3
standards and regulations, 39
trade/environment disputes, 94
transparency clause, 113
Sri Lanka, GMOs in, 56
Stockholm Declaration, UN Conference on Human Environment (1972), 4, 21, 157, 158
Substantial equivalence test, 68–9, 74
Sufficient substantiation test, 96
Sui generis systems, 72
Sustainable development, promotion of, 107–9
Switzerland, GMOs, 55–6

Tailored trade sanctions, 213–15, 232, 241, 251
Tanzania, invasion of Uganda (1978), 199
Task Force for the Safety of Novel Foods and Feeds, OECD, 78
TBT (Technical Barriers to Trade Agreement):
Cartagena Protocol, 63
Committee, 40
GMOs, implications for international trade in, 65, 67–9, 83
import restrictions, 16–7
labelling issues, 67–8
like products concept, 68
NAFTA, 314
national measures, limits on, 122–5
necessity principle, 150–3
notifications of environment-related measures, 113
proportionality test, 68
standards and regulations, 39
transparency clause, 113

Technical Barriers to Trade Agreement *see* TBT (Technical Barriers to Trade Agreement)
Technological innovation, 266–71
Technology transfer:
  acquisition of technology as social process, 162–3
  actual owners and recipients of technology, applicable rules, 161–2
  biological diversity, patenting of, 171–3
  definition of technology, 162
  'dynamic' concept of technology, 163
  environmentally sensitive sectors, hazardous technology and foreign investments,
    domestically prohibited goods/technology, 167
    products allowed in home country subject to adoption of precautions and standards, 167–8
    pseudo-voluntary means to achieve compliance with home country standards, 168–9
  environmentally sensitive sectors, hazardous technology and foreign investments in, 164–9
  EST:
    lack of demand for, 173–5
    problems in promoting at international level, 161–4
    propositions of international law, implementation, 158–60
    and sponsored supply replacement, 173–5
    ultimate beneficiaries of, 163–4
  intellectual property rights, 271–4
    technological innovation, 266–71
  licensing, compulsory, 169–71
  local working requirements, 169–71
  property rights, allocation between poor and rich countries, 171–3
  as 'side-effect' of public-sponsored FDI, 'export incentives', 175–7
    sponsored supply, 173–5
  states, applicable rules, 161–2
  subjective framework, 161–2
  supply and demand of technology, 162–3
technology-inherent risks, 44
technology-transcending risks, 44
TEDs (Turtle Exclusion Devices), 14, 120, 304
Thailand:
  GMOs, 56
  tobacco legislation, 10, 143–5
Tiananmen Square demonstrations (1989), 219
TNCs (transnational corporations):
  and EST, promotion at international level, 161, 162
  hazardous technology, transfer of, 165, 166, 168
  local working requirements, 169
  and patents, 160, 171, 172, 173
Torture Convention (1984), 6, 212
Trade and Environment, Committee on, 40, 83–4
Trade and Environment, Guidelines on (1993), 109
Trade and Environment, Joint Working Party on, 109
Trade liberalisation, conflict with labour rights:
  empirical issues, 183–4
  ethical investment activities, 189
  legal issues, 187
  response to conflict,
    multilateral model, 191–2
    NGO model, 189–90
    regional model, 190–1
    unilateral model, 188–9
  shareholder resolutions, 189
  social labelling schemes, 189
  theoretical issues, 184–7
Trade Related Environmental Measures (TREMS), 169
Trade sanctions, imposition of, 199–261
  'blocking' legislation, 217n90
  Burma, against, 187, 200, 223, 248, 251
  by Canada, 200
  'clawback' legislation, 217n90
  country-specific measures, 222
  effectiveness, 224–5
  by EU, 200
  externally-focused, 224
  general, 218–25, 245–6, 251
  Helms-Burton Act (1996), 216–18
  import bans, 317–19
  import preferences, 219–20
  MFN benefits, 219–20
  multilateralism, 201
  by NAFTA, 201
  national security measures, 221–2
  process-based, 213–14, 215, 225n138
  semi-tailored, 215–18, 242, 245, 251
  sub-national measures, 222–5
  tailored, 213–15, 232, 241, 251
  Uganda, against, 199, 201, 218
  unilateralism, 200–1
  by United States, 200, 213–25
  use-based, 214, 215
  see also Human rights protection; Imports, unilateral measures affecting
Trade-Related Aspects of Intellectual Property Rights Agreement *see* TRIPS (Trade-Related Aspects of Intellectual Property Rights Agreement)
Transcending risks, 44–5
Transgenic crops, 42, 45
Transnational corporations (TNCs) *see* TNCs (transnational corporations)

Transparency principle, 112–14, 249–50
Travaux préparatoires, 116
Treaty of Amsterdam (1997), 191
Treaty of Versailles (1919), 179
TREMS (Trade Related Environmental Measures), 169
TRIPS (Trade-Related Aspects of Intellectual Property Rights Agreement):
  alternative justifications for inclusion of rights,
    commutative justice, 274–81
    human rights, 281–5
  Article 7, and, 264–74, 285
  benefit-sharing, not addressed in, 44
  biosafety, 88
  EST, 160, 171
  GMOs, implications for international trade in, 65, 72–3
  identification of IPRs, 263–4
  ITL, 130
  and licensing, compulsory, 170
  ordre public clause, 101
Turtle Exclusion Devices (TEDs), 14, 120, 304

Uganda, trade sanctions, 199, 201, 218, 238
UN *see* United Nations
UNCED (United Nations Conference on Environment and Development), 79, 107–8, 159
UNCLOS (United Nations Convention on the Law of the Sea), 158
UNCTAD (United Nations Conference on Trade and Development), 109–10, 161
UNEP (United Nations Environmental Programme):
  domestically prohibited goods and technology, 167
  Guidelines on Banned or Severely Restricted Chemicals (1987), 21
  international trade law, new institutional arrangements, 109
  and Stockholm Declaration (1972), 4
UNESCO Convention (1970), 3n6
UNIDROIT Convention (1995), 3n6
Unilateralism:
  child protection, 310–12
  defined, 201n8
  import restrictions,
    GATT, 8–9, 14–15
    nature protection, 14–15
    PPM, 13–20
    product requirements, 9–13
    SPS, 11, 16–17
    TBT, 16–17
  ITL, impact on environmental law and process, 116–22
  labour rights, response to conflict, 188–9
  trade sanctions, 200–1
United Nations:
  Climate Change Convention (1992), 15, 79, 91, 159, 174
  Conference on Environment and Development (UNCED), 79, 107–8, 159
  Conference on Human Environment (1972), 4, 157, 158
  Conference on Trade and Development (UNCTAD), 109–10, 161
  Convention on the Law of the Sea (UNCLOS), 158
  Environmental Programme *see* UNEP (United Nations Environmental Programme)
  Human Rights Convention/Committee, 204–5, 206, 259
  ICCPR, 6, 181, 204, 208, 210, 211, 294, 307
  ICESCR, 6, 181, 204, 208
  Universal Declaration of Human Rights (1948), 5
United States (US):
  Agricultural Department (USDA), 53, 63
  American Convention on Human Rights (1970), 204
  American Declaration on Rights and Duties of Man (1963), 204
  anti-discrimination law, 188–9
  Corn Growers Association, 46
  Environmental Protection Agency (USEPA), 12, 53
  FDA, 52–3, 54
  GMOs, 45–6, 52–4
  Inter-American Convention for Protection of Sea Turtles (1996), 304
  Inter-American Human Rights Commission, 205, 248
  labour rights issues, 201–2
  LMOs, 27
  OAS (Organisation of American States), 203n15, 217
  Panel Report on Taxes on Automobiles (1994), 10
  sea turtles, legislation on protection of, 114–15, 117, 120
  Seattle Conference (Third Ministerial Conference of World Trade Organisation, 1999), 1, 73–6, 81–2, 183, 263, 279–80, 313
  trade sanctions, human rights,
    Burma, against, 187, 200, 223, 248, 251
    country-specific measures, 222
    effectiveness, 224–5
    externally-focused measures, 224
    general, 218–25, 245–6
    Helms-Burton Act (1996), 216–18
    historical developments, 200
    import preferences, 219–20
    MFN benefits, 219–20

national security measures, 221–2
process-based, 213–14, 215, 225n138
semi-tailored, 215–18, 242, 245
sub-national measures, 222–5
tailored, 213–15
use-based, 214–15
USTR, 249
Worldwatch Institute, 46
Universal Declaration of Human Rights (1948), 5, 180, 204, 208, 307
UPOV (International Union for the Protection of New Varieties of Plants), 72–3
Uruguay round (1986–1993):
GMOs, 56–7, 82, 85
labour standards, 201, 287, 298
LMOs, 29
presumption of conformity principle, 22
role of international trade 1, 2n4
WTO, establishment of, 287
USA *see* United States (US)
USDA (US Agricultural Department), 53, 63
USEPA (United States Environmental Protection Agency), 12, 53
USTR (US Trade Representative), 249

Versailles Treaty (1919), 179
Vertical legislation, EU, 49
Vienna Convention on Law of Treaties (1969), 23, 36, 99, 205, 226, 297, 309
Vienna Convention for the Protection of the Ozone Layer (1985), 79, 158

War, concept of, 230–1
WHO (World Health Organisation), 86
'Worker rights', 185
Working Group for the Harmonisation of Regulatory Oversight in Technology (OECD), 78
World Bank, 1, 5, 180, 201
World Bank Convention (1965), 2n4
World Conservation Union (IUCN), 109–10
World Health Organisation (WHO), 86
World Summit for Social Development, Copenhagen (1995), 181
World Trade Organisation *see* WTO (World Trade Organisation)
Worldwatch Institute, 46
Worst Form of Child Labour Convention (1999), 6n22, 291, 292
WTO (World Trade Organisation):
Appellate Body,
and Biosafety Protocol, 63
child labour, 304
and evolutive interpretation principle, 23
Hormones case, 30, 35, 36, 66, 123–5, 152, 154, 254, 316
and human rights, 226
on import prohibitions, 31, 32
on marine life protection, 14, 114–15, 118–21, 134, 147, 236, 244–7
on 'natural resources, 64n52
on necessity principle, 134, 147, 149–50, 153–5
see also Dispute settlement: WTO
and biotechnology products, trade in, 40–1
and child labour standards, 305–8
creation (1994), impact of, 1, 4–5, 22, 25–6, 182, 287
CTE *see* CTE (WTO Committee on Trade and Environment)
and GMOs, 65–73
and human rights protection, 250–2
on labour rights, legal issues, 187
and presumption of conformity principle, 22–3
and subsidy rules, investments carrying, 175–7
Trade Policy Reviews carried out by, 114
and trade-restrictive environmental regulations, 94–6
Working Party on Biotechnology, 57, 78, 115
see also GATT (General Agreement on Tariffs and Trade); GPA (WTO Agreement on Government Procurement); Nature protection, GATT/WTO practice; Seattle Conference (Third Ministerial Conference of World Trade Organisation), 1999; SPS (Sanitary and Phytosanitary Agreement); TBT (Technical Barriers to Trade Agreement)
WTO-DSU (WTO Dispute Settlement Understanding), 63, 90, 114–15, 128–30, 226, 258–9, 303